THE ELITE PRESS

THE ELITE PRESS

Great Newspapers of the World

JOHN C. MERRILL
SCHOOL OF JOURNALISM
UNIVERSITY OF MISSOURI

Pitman Publishing Corporation
NEW YORK TORONTO LONDON

Library of Congress Catalog Card Number: 68-18784
Manufactured in the United States of America
Typography and binding by Tere LoPrete
1.987654321

To my own elite editions:

CHUCK
JUDI
JON
LINDA

Contents

40 Newspaper Profiles

(In Order of Appearance)

ABC *(Spain)*
Aftenposten *(Norway)*
Dagens Nyheter *(Sweden)*
Le Figaro *(France)*
The Scotsman *(Scotland)*
La Stampa *(Italy)*
Svenska Dagbladet *(Sweden)*
The Yorkshire Post *(England)*
Borba *(Yugoslavia)*
Ha'aretz *(Israel)*
Helsingin Sanomat *(Finland)*
Izvestia *(U.S.S.R.)*
Pravda *(U.S.S.R.)*
Die Presse *(Austria)*
The (Baltimore) Sun *(United States)*
The Christian Science Monitor *(United States)*
St. Louis Post-Dispatch *(United States)*
The Globe and Mail *(Canada)*
Winnipeg Free Press *(Canada)*
O Estado de S. Paulo *(Brazil)*
The Age *(Australia)*
Al Ahram *(Egypt)*
Die Burger *(South Africa)*
The Hindu *(India)*

Foreword

I feel that all journalists, politicians, and certainly also historians will join with me in welcoming this scholarly work presenting a clear picture of the growing influence in our time of the press the world over, even to the extent of giving life portraits of typical individual contemporary newspapers from many nations.

The press is, as we all ought to have realized by now, the only existing means of publishing topical information that can be both read and reread, and even analyzed and discussed at leisure. This, of course, is the *sine qua non* of the thriving of any modern society, and it therefore seems to me of the greatest importance that this work should be published just in these fateful years of trying to realize the old humane ideas. Moreover, this book carries the hallmark of independent modern university research with its dedication to the freedom of information and teaching.

Also it seems to me most fitting that the first edition of this work should be written in the language used in the world's first official declaration of human rights and that it is presented in the first really United States where the necessity of safeguarding the freedom of information has become a cornerstone for the federal government and a living force in Congress. This is not simply a book about specific "great" newspapers; it is also a discourse on quality journalism itself and its impact on contemporary societies.

Characteristics which make newspapers great are very largely the same ones which make men great, and Dr. Merrill has turned the spotlight of analysis on these. And he has gone beyond this: He has advanced the thesis that the elite press of the world, regardless of its diverse membership, is really a mighty force ever working to infuse dignity and civility into international communication. Those of us familiar with the great newspapers of the world are likely to agree that there is a strain of supranational "greatness" running through the elite press that offers hope for a troubled world.

DR. VINCENT NAESER

Copenhagen, Denmark

Preface

This book represents what is possibly the first attempt to discuss the *elite press* in general and to present sketches or "profiles" of a representative sample of elite newspapers. The forty dailies included as separate sketches are believed to be especially important in shaping world opinion and improving world journalism. Many readers will object to the inclusion of certain newspapers published in "closed" societies both on the Left and on the Right. These newspapers, however, are felt to best represent the serious, informed, and influential journalism of their respective nations and their omission would have left substantial gaps in such a book as this.

At least it can be said that such papers as Spain's *ABC* and the Soviet Union's *Pravda* fall into the category of the *elite press* if one is willing to accept the definition of such a press given in the first five chapters which follow. Those not willing to accept such a definition are welcome to formulate their own definitions and exclude from their range of interest any papers they wish. This, however, might prove unfortunate and intellectually restricting. It is believed that considering all important newspapers of the world among the *elite* is the rational approach, however much it might tend to go against the grain of our national and ideological loyalties. And, by omitting certain papers from this book and concentrating only on "our kind" of quality paper, we would in effect be retreating into a peaceful, but antirational, harbor where our world consciousness shrinks while our provincialism grows.

It should be pointed out, however, that the author agrees (and has stressed this belief in various parts of the book) that the newspapers published in what we in the West think of as "free" or "pluralistic" societies offer the highest type journalism and go farthest in creating a world community of reason. This belief has led to a greatly overbalanced representation of libertarian or "free" (from the Western viewpoint) newspapers on the following pages.

This book should be of interest to students in several disciplines, to scholars interested in international journalism, to journalists in many countries, and to librarians who desire a handy reference book—not available before—on the best-known newspapers of the world. The first five chapters of Part I give a background for the profiles of elite papers which follow. Various surveys are reported on, listing elite newspapers and giving "determinants" or evaluative criteria. The whole matter of context in quality journalism is explored in some depth, and considerable commentary on quality newspapers has been collected from a number of worthy spokesmen.

Innumerable persons in many parts of the world have contributed to this book. It is as impossible to name all of them as it is to forget their help. Most, connected in some way with journalism or with university teaching and research, are named in the "Notes" at the end of the book. A few, deserving special thanks because of "extra" contributions and encouragement, should be mentioned here: Dr. Fred Luchsinger, *Neue Zürcher Zeitung*; Dr. Erich Welter, *Frankfurter Allgemeine*; Dr. Vincent Naeser, *Berlingske Tidende*; Dr. Paolo Bonaiuti and Alfio Colussi, *Corriere della Sera*; W. Joachim Freyburg, *Die Welt*; Heinz-Dietrich Fischer of the University of Münster; Einar Ostgaard of Haslum, Norway; Sir William Haley, *The Times* (London), and Michael Perceval, "Radio Liberty" correspondent in Madrid.

For translation help, the author is indebted to: his son, Charles Jefferson Merrill (Spanish and German); Robert Chang of Taipeh, Formosa (Chinese); Dr. Yong Chang of Seoul, South Korea (Japanese and German); Yoshihide Yada and Kensei Yoshida of Tokyo, graduate students at Missouri, 1966–1967 (Japanese), Christo Cameris of Nicosia, Cyprus, graduate student at Missouri, 1965–1966 (French and Arabic), and Loik Le Floch, graduate student at Missouri, 1967–1968 (French). For special insights into the Indian press, the author is grateful to Sauripada Bhattacharya of Calcutta, a Ph.D. student in political science and journalism at Missouri from 1965–1967. To Dr. Marvin Alisky of Arizona State University and Dr. Bruce Underwood of Temple University goes the author's appreciation for valuable information and suggestions on Latin American newspapers. And, finally, the author thanks his wife, Dorothy, for her patience, suggestions, and help in untangling confused sentences.

J. C. M.
University of Missouri, 1968

PART I

The Community and Its Members

1

The Promise of Improved Journalism

Before plunging into a survey of the rather bleak and disheartening aspects of the world's press today, it should be made clear at once that this is an optimistic book. It sees hope on the horizon of international journalism in the form of a small, but growing, number of serious, responsible newspapers which in an atmosphere of freedom are striving to allay world misunderstanding and to bring mankind into a community of reason. Although this group of serious and responsible newspapers is not large at present, it is a very important nucleus around which a more refined and cosmopolitan world press can be built. And there are signs that more and more editors and publishers in many parts of the world are desirous of improving their products, of shattering bonds of provincialism and nationalism, and of joining the elite press.

This optimistic approach will be scoffed at by many critics of the press who see bad publications tending to drive out good ones by a kind of journalistic Gresham's Law. And these critics can point to numerous cases where, indeed, poor newspapers have lived on where good ones have died. Regardless of these cases, however, increasing quality of the press can be noted around the world: at least during the twentieth century more dailies (and weeklies to a lesser degree) have taken their places as serious, intellectually oriented journals with cosmopolitan outlooks. It appears to this writer that increasing numbers of publishers are finding it can be quite profitable, and much more satisfying, to deal with serious discussion, to value truth and balance, and to present news interpreted in a responsible way. As the international newspaper readers become better educated, raise their level of taste, and seek a higher standard of press performance, there will be a wide assortment of quality newspapers ready to take them on as readers.

Without a doubt these elite papers are among us, getting better all the while, and expanding their numbers with every passing year. It is unfortunate that so many Americans feel that beyond a few United States journals such as *The New York Times*, *St. Louis Post-Dispatch*, and *The Christian Science Monitor* there is only journalistic mediocrity throughout the world. Little do they realize that newspapers of just as high standards, serious purpose, and international significance exist in many nations, and that daily journals such as West Germany's *Die Welt*, Britain's *Guardian*, France's *Le Monde*, Switzerland's *Neue Zürcher Zeitung*, Japan's *Asahi Shimbun*, and Mexico's *Excélsior* take a journalistic back seat to no paper in the United States. It is ignorance, provincialism, or blind nationalism that keeps more of the American people from recognizing the tremendous and notable strides that have taken place in recent years throughout the world. It is cause for hope, for optimism, that such journals exist and, even more, that they appear to be getting better and their number is increasing.

From this optimistic position which sets the tone of the book, let us note briefly the more discouraging aspect of the world press situation—the aspect that is the loudest, the gaudiest, the biggest; the aspect that tends to overshadow the encouraging dimension to such an extent that many citizens tend to lose all hope for the press playing a significant part in cementing international fellowship and in stimulating a rational society.

The pessimistic picture that the average person gets of the world press does not stem from a deficiency in the amount of journalism crossing national borders. Certainly, the person exposing himself to the printed media of communication recognizes that he has no shortage of information. Quantitatively, the world press is far advanced. But, in spite of the fact that the mass media are pouring out a glut of material over vast audiences, distrust and misunderstanding among peoples everywhere reach alarming proportions. This situation may well result from the fact that this verbal glut is still largely tenuous and superficial and not very helpful in overcoming international frustration, animosity, and irrationality.

Alan Simpson, president in 1962 of Britain's Institute of Journalists, has echoed a growing chorus of concerned journalists throughout the world in commenting that "we are living in difficult and dangerous days" and that "it is vital that the public be provided with the fullest and most objective coverage of the news."[1] Certainly the world's press has the potential to provide this full and objective news coverage, to help ease tensions and erase unrealistic stereotypes that exist; but in the main it is not living up to this potential. Instead, it either lulls its readers into an unthinking and dangerous complacency or frenetically stretches international animosities and worsens the world's psychic crisis.

An informed public opinion must be forthcoming throughout the world if judicious decisions are to be made; a free-flowing and intelligent supply of news and views must nourish this public opinion. Irrational acts by national groups or nations can have dire consequences in our close-knit world, where, as Barbara Ward has said, "We are all neighbors, sitting on each other's doorsteps."[2]

Writing in 1960, Lester Markel, then Sunday editor of *The New York Times*, stressed that we "cannot have understanding—and thus peace—among the peoples of the world unless they come to know one another better, unless they have better, truer, information about one another."[3] And he said that the main avenue for this information is the newspaper. Unfortunately, however, there are far too few newspapers like the one for which Markel works; in general the world's press is a heterogeneous hodgepodge of triviality, too busy entertaining and flashing atypical and distorted images before its readers to pay much attention to presenting a sane, dignified, and balanced world view. With few exceptions, the world's press is more concerned with the "gamelike" aspect of its operation, of helping the reader to forget the deadly seriousness of national and international affairs and to enjoy himself in the "play" of newsreading.[4]

In other words, the vast majority of the world's newspapers are entertainment/play-oriented and cater in varying degrees to the superficial whims of "mass" audiences. Perhaps this press orientation is psychologically refreshing to the readers who would like to escape from the efforts of thinking and concern, but it does seem sad that so many newspapers fill their columns with shallow, often inconsequential and incoherent stories when world conditions call for a more thoughtful world citizenry and more responsible journalism. Even if news (the accounts of world happenings) is simply a playful exercise at which the multitudes enjoy themselves, it is discomforting that the real events behind the verbal images are pragmatically significant and need to be confronted and dealt with realistically and intelligently.

A mere chronicling of negative aspects of reality, a steady diet of sensation (war, crime, sex, rioting, etc.) may satiate the mass appetite for vicarious and effortless "adventure," but it does little to create a homogeneity of thought or thoughtful people. "We have no right," says James Reston, "to twist the mass of facts into forms which are exciting but misleading; to take out of it that portion that conforms to our prejudices, to preserve the shocking or amusing, and to leave out the dreary but important qualifications which are necessary to essential truth."[5] Most editors and publishers, no doubt, would agree with Reston's premise, but unfortunately few of them manage to follow it on the pages of their newspapers.

The popular press—the "hodgepodge press"—calls the people of the world to play. It does not call them to think, to assess, to become concerned, involved, or empathic. Its journalism is splashy, superficial, thoughtless, and tenuous. It is complacent journalism that appeals to self and to *status quo*, to mere verbal frolicking about the surface of vital issues. It is "supermarket" journalism—a little of everything for everybody. It shows no thoughtful selection, assessment of editorial matter, meaning or interpretation. It is vulgar in the truest sense of the word—speaking to the masses of semiliterates who feel they need to read something called a "newspaper" but who have no desire to understand the vital issues of the day, and even less desire to concern themselves with these issues.

In a lecture at the University of Minnesota School of Journalism, Reinhold Niebuhr dealt with many of these shortcomings and pointed out the need for depth, for interpretation, for a dissatisfaction with mere facts:

> The problem is that our nation, like every other nation, needs not so much isolated facts to inform its mind as the understanding of facts in their setting. This means the interpretation of facts. Facts without interpretation may more easily lead to erroneous conclusions than interpreted facts. This is particularly true in the reporting of foreign affairs, of which the reader does not possess the background of general knowledge to put isolated facts into a proper setting.[6]

When one glances about at the reading fare offered by the world's press generally and at the disjointed manner in which it is presented, he can understand why astute press critics indict newspapers for being mainly inane sheets of gossip or instruments of national propaganda seeking to create barriers to understanding by presenting without interpretation "unreal" and "alarmist" news without a context of meaning and often without follow-up. Many see the press as perpetuating psychological war among nations and peoples, or as purveying images of personalities which would imply that eccentric and dangerous persons are the only significant newsmakers.

"The malignant germs of misunderstanding and misinformation are at work in the minds of men twenty-four hours every day," said President Eisenhower in 1954, speaking to the American Newspaper Publisher's Association. "Every newspaper . . . has the mission of bringing home to all our people and to as many other people of the world as we can reach, the facts of existence today."[7] Eisenhower felt strongly about the international benefits of an intelligent press for he added: "Facts must be related one to the other in truthful perspective. Only within such framework shall we reach . . . a peaceful world."

Envy, resentment, suspicion, and hatred are leaving their marks everywhere and one wonders if there is a chance for humanity to survive intact and in a civilized way. The press generally gives little help.

Instead of being conveyors of enlightenment, the national press systems tend too often to be press agents for individual nations or special groups. This nationalistic and conflict-oriented tone is very evident in most of the world's press. In this regard, George V. Ferguson, editor of the *Montreal Star*, has said:

> . . . while fair reporting now dominates the writing of domestic news, the same standard of reporting has not spread as yet anything like so fully into the field of international affairs. The basic reason for this is, I think, the almost unconscious operation of nationalism. We interpret news in terms of conflict; and this is, of course, particularly easy to do under the pressure of the cold war when almost the whole world, with one or two notable exceptions, is lined up with the United States or with the Soviet Union. . . .[8]

The serious observer of the world press, like Mr. Ferguson, sees contradictions in the news columns, discrepancies in reporting among world news agencies, slantings, exaggerations and exclusions, and opinion in news columns that is shallow and uninformed. Is it any wonder that the world press is doing so little to supplant ignorance with knowledge, bewilderment with understanding, and irrationalism with reason?

But now we should get back to the original thesis: In spite of the dismal picture just painted, there is hope. For there is, in the midst of this desert of journalistic anonymity and mediocrity that is the popular and middle-level press, a small group of newspapers in many nations striving constantly to rise above the hodgepodge journalistic formula. These are the serious newspapers whose standards of editorial practice are conditioned more by an intellectual orientation and an idealistic vision than by a desire for mammoth circulation or impressive profits. Although they are serious in tone and lacking in flippancy so common in journalism, they are the really optimistic papers. They offer the invitation to consider ideas hopefully and critically, to dissect issues, to solve problems. If they were not basically optimistic, they would not take serious things so seriously. These papers say to the reader in effect: Let us reason together; let us not shout and call names and wave flags and brandish weapons; let us be calm and rational.

These few notable newspapers found in some fifteen to twenty of the world's nations, often struggling against great odds, comprise the cream of the *elite press* of the world. They are the concerned papers, the knowl edgeable papers, the serious papers. And they are the papers which serious people and opinion leaders in all countries take seriously. They are interested in international undercurrents of similarity, not differences; they appeal to thought and logic, not to prejudices and emotion. They are interested in solidifying the world, not in further splintering it. They are interested in ideas and issues, not in mere facts. They are all relatives of one another, regardless of place of publication or language. They have the same concerns, and they are stubborn and outspoken—no matter what their circulations may be.

They are all striving together, wherever they may be, for a world community of seriousness and dignity.

While it is true to a degree that "the press rightly holds up a mirror to society," as a noted British journalist has remarked,[9] a quality or elite paper must do more. It must judge events and not simply report them, and have definite opinions and express them courageously. The elite paper, even if it believed it could do so, would not be satisfied to merely "reflect" society; its mission is far greater than that. It sees itself as a leader, an interpreter, a pioneer into the frontiers of human and international relations. More than attempting simply to reflect society in all of its imperfections, the elite newspaper hopes to present such news and views as to reform society, or portions of it. The aim of the elite press, then, is directing in a reasonable way instead of reflecting in a fragmented and distorted way.

The elite papers continually sort and coordinate the endless stream of news reports, attempting to arrange them so as to give meaning to the news, for these papers realize that news items out of context are only confusing to the reader. As the editors of Switzerland's first-rate *Neue Zürcher Zeitung* have put it, a newspaper should offer "a picture of events, not a blurred mosaic, and to the extent that a newspaper is able to make events clearer and easier to understand, to that extent does it fulfill its mission."[10] *The New York Times'* James Reston echoes this important point when he says that "the news we have to report and explain these days . . . is more intricate and many-sided." He continues, "It does not fit easily into the short news story with the punch lead. It often defies accurate definition in very short space. Very often it rebels against our passion for what is bright and brief."[11]

Looking a little further at the elite press, still rather generally, we will note that this small group of dailies (and some few weeklies) will not appeal to the typical reader looking over a wide assortment of journals at a newsstand. First of all, the makeup or physical appearance of these elite papers will not attract him. For example, the *Neue Zürcher Zeitung*, without a doubt one of the two or three best papers in the world, has a rather dull, ultraserious tone to its page makeup. Headlines are small, pictures are few, and there are no comics, no entertainment (or very little), no crossword puzzles, no women's page. Another top-ranking elite daily, *Le Monde* of Paris, also is in staid typographical dress and is "top-heavy with analytical writing at the expense of the 'All-we-want-is-the-facts-Ma'am' school."[12]

Not all elite papers are as typographically and editorially conservative in tone as these two tabloids of Switzerland and France; the few quality dailies of Scandinavia (*Berlingske Tidende* of Copenhagen, for instance) are much more sprightly, both in dress and in editorial character. It can definitely be said, however, that there is little in any of the elite papers of the general levity, splash, crackle, and pop that characterizes the general press of the world. The elite press actually attempts to do what the Commission on Freedom of the Press said the press should do for society in its 1947 report—"to present a truthful, comprehensive, and intelligent account of the day's events in a context which gives them meaning."[13] With intelligent realism, editors of the elite papers realize, however, that the most difficult standard to meet is that of "comprehensiveness." The realities of publishing—time, space, money, staff—predicate against comprehensive coverage by any one newspaper, even the massive *New York Times*. But the elite paper, through intelligent editing, tries to compensate for this intrinsic shortcoming.

The underlying thesis of this book is that the best of this elite press of the world is actually a community of serious dialogue and that as other newspapers strive to meet the high standards of the elite, the potential for world understanding increases and mankind is led toward a world of rationality and peace.

Many readers will smile condescendingly at this idealistic and optimistic thesis, and will argue that the small core of thoughtful and intellectual figures and journals through the years has done little or nothing to raise the hopes and exalt the reason of the masses. These critics would be hard put to prove that these isolated figures and journals have not propelled the world toward reason, but we will grant the general validity of their objection.[14]

However, it should be stressed at this point that prior to this century the serious voices speaking to mass audiences were virtually nonexistent. Isolated intellectual spoke to isolated intellectual usually in an intranational or intracultural context. No truly international newspapers were to be found, and when excellent ones did exist within countries, there was slight chance of their being read abroad except in a few academic centers.

Today, on the other hand, a larger slice of the world's population is literate, even well-educated. And of this educated group more and more persons are able to read foreign languages or have access to serious journals—like *Atlas* of the United States—which give them a rich diet of informed world news and views in translation. In addition, each year more general magazines and newspapers quote in part or in whole from foreign journals. In other words, serious journalism is crossing national borders in an ever-increasing flow and more and more people are being exposed to it directly, through translation, or through opinion leaders in their respective countries. One elite paper quotes another, and a "quality journalism" spreads across nations and across languages and develops a common denominator, not of popular *event/reportorial* journalism, but of *idea/interpretation* journalism that is a catalyst to world reason.

This cooperation of the press of the world in an effort to achieve understanding and international stability should not be simply idealistic theorizing; it should be expected of more and more newspapers as literacy increases and education expands, and as editors and publishers see the good that quality journalism can do. Clarence K. Streit, an American journalist with an outstanding career, has asked if it is too much to expect for the press to help in giving publicity to "reasonable men" who are trying to avoid "the twin dangers of war and endless tension . . . by appeal to sober common sense"?[15] From the elite newspapers of the world would come a resounding "No, it is not too much to expect!"

In the following chapters of this book the attempt is made to discuss the characteristics of the elite press in a general way, to present several surveys which have been made to try to isolate and rank these serious newspapers, and to provide case studies of a few of the most notable of the elite papers of several nations. Part I attempts to define the "elite" newspapers, to discuss their potential, and to give an idea of which papers around the world belong to this proud journalistic group and which ones are aspiring to membership. Part II is devoted to fourteen individual newspapers which are outstanding representatives of the elite press.

The book is designed to show something of the nature of an elite press—what makes it great, how it has developed, and its present-day journalistic philosophy. It aspires to serve not only as an introduction to the world's elite press but as an encouragement to those who would like to see the press a powerful agent for social stability and progressive leadership, and to be an inspiration to those publishers and editors who would like to raise their sights, their standards, their quality, and join the elite-press group.

2

The "Elite Press"— A Matter of Context

Throughout the world there has grown up an institution which may be called the "elite" press, read by the elite of the country where it exists as well as by the elite in other countries and expressing a significant segment of international elite opinion. This press is aimed at a rather cohesive audience, and in general its readers are better educated and have a greater interest in public affairs than the average readers of the mass (or popular) press. It is aimed at the educated citizen who is aware of, and concerned about, the central issues of his time, and undoubtedly it is read by more opinion leaders than are other types of newspapers.

In one of its forms, this press has built a reputation for being well informed and expressing serious, well-seasoned opinion of the nation concerned. In a less commendable sense (from a Western viewpoint) it is considered the voice or one of the principal voices of the particular government that permits it to exist. In any sense, it is this press that people who desire to be informed, or indoctrinated with the "line," will want to read regularly.

Through the elite press is disseminated either the thoughtful, pluralistic, and sophisticated dialogue of a free society, or the necessary social and political guidance of the closed society. The free man reads the elite press (the name it is given in this book) heuristically; the person in an authoritarian society reads it pragmatically. In the first case, the elite paper offers ideas which the reader wants to consider; in the other, it gives the reader what he *must* know to be a well-integrated member of his society. In one case, the reader of the elite newspaper is stimulated to free individual thought and action; in the other, he is indoctrinated for concerted activity. In one case, the paper is a catalyst to democratic self-determination; in the other it is an instrument with which to control the social system.

In one case, pride in the principles of free journalism and in the particular newspaper motivates staff members to high standards; in the other, journalism has become a deadly serious business in which mistakes—typographical or otherwise—are not tolerated. In other words, on the one hand the high standards and serious tone are maintained freely from within; and on the other they are enforced from without. For example, Yugoslavia's *Borba* and *Politika* are elite in the sense of being serious, influential, typographically immaculate, and carefully written. So are Czechoslovakia's *Rude Pravo*, Rumania's *Scinteia*, and any of the other Communist Party organs that set the tone, policy, and standards for the newspaper press of the Communist societies. So, also, are well-edited and literate journals like Egypt's *Al Ahram*, or Spain's *ABC*, or Nationalist China's *Central Daily News*. These are all serious, carefully edited papers with considerable prestige in certain circles, but they lack one important ingredient—freedom.

It is this absence of freedom, perhaps as much as any other thing, that places a large group of the world's influential papers in a separate category of eliteness—and a lower, less desired one, from the Western democratic viewpoint. In a very real sense, then, there are actually two main classes of elite papers: (1) the free paper of the open society, and (2) the restricted or managed paper of the closed society.

Across the spectrum of serious world journalism are many elite papers juxtapositioned in extremely paradoxical ways, illustrating the validity of placing such papers into the two main classes just mentioned: a Cuban *Granma* and a Brazilian *O Estado de S. Paulo*; a Spanish *La Vanguardia Española* and an Italian *Corriere della Sera*; a Japanese *Mainichi* and a Chinese *Jen-min Jih-pao*; a West German *Frankfurter Allgemeine* and an East German *Neues Deutschland*.

In every major country one newspaper, and often two or three, stands out as a journal of elite opinion, catering to the intelligentsia and the opinion leaders, however variously defined. Well informed on government matters, they achieve a reputation for reliability, for expert knowledge, and even for presenting the most accurate image of governmental thinking. Although their circulations are seldom larger than 300,000, their influence is tremendous, for they are read regularly by public officials, scholars, journalists, theologians, lawyers and judges, and business leaders. And what is more, they are read in other countries by those persons whose business it is to keep up with world affairs. Even papers like *Pravda* and *Izvestia* are read seriously by persons in the free world who consider these journals as accurately reflecting official viewpoints of the Soviet Union. And, no doubt, Soviet officials, regardless of their feelings about Western journalistic bias and capitalistic exploitation of the press, peruse *The New York Times* and the London *Times* regularly for their picture of the United States and Britain.

As is true with so many really important institutions and concepts, the elite press is difficult to define. Its nature is rather tenuous, ephemeral, temporary and, most of all, relative. Part of it speaks coldly, with detached scientific precision; another part involves itself with the reader in a warm and personal manner. While one part snarls, another purrs. One part, trying for quantity as well as quality, submerges the reader in a flood of facts; another carefully sifts through the news and thoughtfully offers the reader a coherent and rich diet of significance. But regardless of the differences among the elite newspapers, they are all serious, concerned, intelligent, and articulate. One writer has said that "although these newspapers differ among themselves, they are a distinct species" and that "the pattern of the prestige paper is sufficiently uniform for us to describe it as an institution."[1]

However true it may be that these papers "are a distinct species," it is quite obvious that there are types or natures of quality and of prestige among the world's papers, and these distinctions make categorizing and defining extremely difficult. Some papers, quite qualitative in one sense, are so vastly different from other papers (also qualitative) that it is difficult to talk of them in the same context, or to judge them against the same set of criteria. First of all, elite papers fall into the two main types or contexts already mentioned: (1) libertarian, or those published in a free or open society, and (2) authoritarian, or those published in a restricted or closed society. Certainly it is unwise, or at least disconcerting, to try to compare meaningfully the elite paper of Context 1 with the elite paper of Context 2.

Then, in each of these two basic contexts there are other (or "sub") contexts into which elite papers might fall, and one paper is found in more than one context at one time: (3) daily, (4) weekly, (5) specialized, and (6) general. Of course, there are other contexts, for example, a semiweekly in a quasi-authoritarian country; but these six contexts are quite useful in talking about elite newspapers.

Obviously a daily and a weekly newspaper would be of different quality types, even if their basic context (Nos. 1 or 2) was the same. This might be due to differing directions in editorial emphasis or ideological orientation, or simply to the differentiating factor of daily and weekly deadlines. For instance, in the United States it is difficult to compare the *National Observer* (weekly) and *The Washington Post* (daily), both elite papers. Although they have many characteristics and a certain tone in common, they are different. One of the most interesting differences, but certainly not the most important one, is that the weekly has a conservative orientation, while the daily has a liberal one. Of quite different natures also are the influential weeklies *Jeune Afrique* of Tunis (which is socially and politically oriented and speaks for the new

African nationalism) and *Christ und Welt* of Stuttgart (religiously oriented). And certainly, Britain's weekly *Observer* is as different from the daily *Guardian* as West Germany's weekly *Zeit* is from the daily *Welt.*

Two elite daily papers, moreover, may be of very distinct natures, perhaps with Contexts 5 and 6 different, or perhaps, 1 and 2. For example, the daily *The Wall Street Journal* and the daily Baltimore *Sun* little resemble one another because one is a specialized, and the other is a general, journal. Nor would the *Berlingske Tidende* of Denmark (published for the serious general reader in an open society) be of the same nature as the very prestigious *Komsomolskaya Pravda* of Russia (published for the Young Communists in a closed society). Wilbur Schramm of Stanford University has even pointed out that great differences exist among free society elite papers and gives the examples of (1) the "analytical" types such as *Le Monde* and the *Frankfurter Allgemeine*, and (2) the "news-oriented" types such as *The New York Times.*[2]

All sorts of combination games could be played by shuffling papers around in the major and minor contexts for comparative purposes. Consider the specialized (Context 5), daily (Context 3), semifree (Contexts 1, 2) *Osservatore Romano* of Vatican City; actually it is difficult to consider it in the same class with either Red China's *People's Daily* (Contexts 2, 3, 6) or with England's *Times* (Contexts 1, 3, 6). One should recognize, of course, that the *Osservatore Romano* is different from *The Times* for reasons other than the fact that it is published in a more closed society, has a more restricted editorial policy, or is the reflection of a quite different kind of institution. These differences, however, are significant and many press observers would feel that the Church paper is closer to the *People's Daily* than to *The Times*. This, too, is quite misleading and unfair, for beyond the fact that both the Chinese and the Vatican paper lack the libertarian publishing context, considerable and important differences exist between them. They are both restricted, it is true, but we must always be aware of the fact that Restricted Paper "A" can be, and often is, quite different from Restricted Paper "B." Without belaboring this point, we should add that considering only one of these contexts for comparative purposes is not enough. The distinctiveness of *Osservatore Romano* comes more from other factors, such as its specialized religious orientation and its failure to present much factual news, than from the *freedom* (or lack of it) with which it is published.

In comparing elite papers it is obviously advantageous (really indispensable) to use the context method. Correlation of several contexts places newspapers of relative similitude before us. For example, if we are considering general daily papers of a conservative leaning we must include in the list *Svenska Dagbladet* of Stockholm, the *Chicago Tribune*, *The Times* of London, *The Scotsman* of Edinburgh, the *Corriere della Sera* of Milan, and the *Frankfurter Allgemeine* of Frankfurt am Main. Their free-world counterparts among the liberal dailies would include *The Guardian* of Manchester and London, *Dagens Nyheter* of Stockholm, the *Post-Dispatch* of St. Louis, *Le Monde* of Paris, *Neue Zürcher Zeitung* of Zurich, and *Süddeutsche Zeitung* of Munich.

A list of general discussion weekly elite papers would include *Die Zeit* of Hamburg, *Weltwoche* of Zurich, *Sunday Times* of London, *National Observer* of Washington, D.C., and *France Observateur* of Paris. Of course, in order to compare the great variety of quality newspapers intelligently, one must have at hand certain basic data about these publications. In addition, he must read the papers with some regularity or keep up with appraisals of them presented by knowledgeable press observers.[3]

The word "prestige" is likely to be used synonymously with "quality" when referring to an admired newspaper,[4] and there is perhaps no reason to quibble with this. However, it might be helpful to make a distinction between a quality and a prestige paper for the sake of discussion. A very simple distinction might be this:

> QUALITY: a good, influential, *free* newspaper.
> PRESTIGE: a good, influential, *restricted* newspaper.

Prestige papers, in the above sense, would include official government organs such as *Pravda* in the U.S.S.R. or *El Nacional* in Mexico, or perhaps *Osservatore Romano* of Vatican City. These are good papers, to be sure, but they are "kept" organs operating in the strict confines of some official policy. They are influential, but their appeal to the intellectual elite is a narrow, specialized, ideological appeal. Their basic nature is quite different from that of a free elite journal (or quality paper) such as Switzerland's *Neue Zürcher Zeitung*, Sweden's *Dagens Nyheter*, or West Germany's *Die Welt*. It seems that some confusion could be removed if one would talk of the free elite as the quality paper and the authoritarian elite as the prestige paper.

This book largely deals with quality papers (*e.g.*, *Le Monde*) which have prestige, not prestige papers (*e.g.*, *Pravda*) which have quality. In other words, the emphasis here is with the elite press in the Westernized, libertarian sense. It might be well to reiterate this distinction between what we are calling the quality paper and the prestige paper:

> QUALITY PAPER: a courageous, independent, news-views-oriented journal, published in an open society.
>
> PRESTIGE PAPER: a serious journal of some power elite, concerned with dogma or policy dissemination, spokesman or propagandist for some person or group, and published in a closed society.

A prestige paper, then, is well known primarily (or solely) because it is the voice of some authoritarian institution and as such wields influence among the audience submissive to that institution. It is more concerned with being a "bulletin board" for the power elite than with reporting and discussing current events. In spite of its influence, it is closed to but one viewpoint—usually the government's—and is wary of those persons or groups with deviant ideologies. These papers, without a doubt, are tremendously important today as instruments of agitation, indoctrination, and social control.

But it is chiefly with the quality or free-press elite newspapers that this book concerns itself in the following chapters. These are the papers that open minds and stimulate discussion and intelligent reflection. These are the papers—whether they be dailies or weeklies, specialized or general, large or small—that offer hope to the world. They are the reasonable journals, freely and courageously speaking out calmly above the din of party politics and nationalistic drum-beating. They are urging peoples to work together for the good of all, to consider all sides of complex issues, to refrain from emotional decisions, to cherish that which has proved good and discard that which has been detrimental, to consider seriously the basic issues and problems that confront mankind.

Whether they are called "conservative" or "liberal" in their own societies is of no consequence. These labels have little or nothing to do with quality journalism or with the elite press; they are simply tags, having some vague meaning within their societal fabric but little or none elsewhere. The quality of the liberal *Guardian* is no better than the quality of the conservative *Times*, and both the conservative *Frankfurter Allgemeine* and the more liberal *Welt* of West Germany are quality dailies. Many persons in the United States equate all quality papers and all intellectuals with liberalism. This is unfortunate and quite erroneous and simply shows an illiberalism of thought. This sort of thing is unheard of in Europe where liberalism is more along classic lines, closely connected with an open mind and a progressive spirit and a sense of tolerance than with one's purported position on a Left-Right continuum.

Without a doubt, the ideological position which a press critic sees himself as taking affects his evaluation of a particular newspaper. This is a quite human tendency, although it evidences considerable lack of sophistication. Liberals should read quality newspapers of all ideological persuasions if they are to be truly liberal, and conservatives should do the same thing if they are to be truly conservative. With persons, as with newspapers, the tag that one carries should have little or nothing to do with his quality or with the sincerity with which he seeks the truth.

Dr. Robert Desmond of the University of California has pointed out that newspapers can be no better than the persons who read them. It is unfortunate, he says, that "if a newspaper honestly supports, editorially, either a liberal or a conservative outlook, those holding the contrary view abuse it unmercifully, and rarely even credit it with sincerity."[5] Perhaps Dr. Desmond has exaggerated the seriousness of this problem, for if what he says is true, the effectiveness of the quality press is limited by the closed minds of serious readers who are unwilling to break through the curtain of labels and seek enlightenment from all sources.

If one characteristic of an enlightened and quality newspaper is its seeking the truth wherever it may be found, it is not unreasonable to expect the same of an enlightened intellectual. The quality papers fight mental and emotional rigidity; they try to break down prejudices and to open minds. This is why they are great. And this is why, in short, they are the papers that comprise, or at least represent, a world community of reason.

3

Marks of the "Free" Elite

Although the effort was made in the last chapter to explain the distinctions among the various types of press "elite," it should be re-emphasized that this book is primarily concerned with the elite of the libertarian nations—the "free" elite—which, as has been pointed out, may be distinguished rather easily from the elite of the authoritarian nations by considering their political and social setting. These free elite will be referred to as "quality" (rather than "prestige") papers. However, most writers do not make such a distinction and it is quite common to find the leading serious papers of the world (regardless of where they are) referred to by an assortment of terms used interchangeably.

The British call these papers quality or class papers, distinguishing them from popular or mass papers. The French often refer to them as *journaux de prestige*, while Germans frequently allude to them as *Weltblätter*, stressing their international reputation.[1] In the United States there seems to be no standard name—serious, quality, and prestige being adjectives usually applied to them. Here and there they are also referred to as great, intellectual, international, and elite.

Quite obviously these terms can reasonably be used synonymously to talk about this type of newspaper, but it would seem useful to differentiate, at least, among those of a free and of an authoritarian society. This is the reason an elite paper in Spain or in the Soviet Union is called a prestige paper, while one in a country like Britain, Japan or the United States is referred to as a quality paper. Both types can be considered as part of the elite press although they are certainly of distinct natures.

Even though the prestige papers of the closed society are quite different from the quality papers of the open society, they would still appear to have a considerable amount of reasonableness and national and international concern; for this reason a paper like *Pravda*, appealing to opinion leaders with a serious turn of mind, can be accommodated under the label "elite" as well as can a paper like *The Times* of London. (See the "Elite Press Pyramid" at end of Chap. 4.) Many persons will, if they are of the Western world, disagree with this premise, saying that *Pravda* and its ilk, because of their doctrinaire orientation and attachment to one party, cannot contribute to reason. From a nonauthoritarian perspective, this is quite true, but a Communist might just as well say that since the Western capitalistic newspaper is tied to the vested interests of "big business," it is not really free and cannot present news and views without considerable bias, subjectivity, prejudice, and selfish motivation.

Both viewpoints are to some degree valid and invalid. At any rate, there is no cause for rejecting the premise that within the serious, influential press of any political system there is a certain respect and concern with seriousness, humanity, and social progress. And this is the basic premise of this book. Of course, the emphasis here is on the free elite press, since the writer is convinced that these papers are the ones which offer the greatest hope for personal, national, and international discourse and liberalizing "mind-opening." Nevertheless, however superior we may think the libertarian elite to be, this seems little justification for dismissing the entire government-controlled press of the world as no more than propaganda and unreasonable journalism.

While this chapter is concerned with the free elite newspaper, it recognizes the importance, leadership, seriousness, and considerable reasonableness of the authoritarian elite. The purpose here is to highlight the free elite and to discuss the characteristics or criteria by which it is judged. Marks of the authoritarian elite, touched on lightly in the preceding chapter, will receive little further attention. These prestige papers of the closed societies are intentionally de-emphasized for two main reasons: (1) they are not felt to be as intellectually potent as the free elite and thus not as significant in creating a world community of reason, and (2) very little of a reliable nature is known about these papers, much of their operations and policies being wrapped in secrecy.

Therefore, let us proceed with a discussion of the free elite of the world and attempt to determine the characteristics which define them. These papers will generally be referred to as quality papers except where they are given some alternate name by other writers.

Even though it is obvious that quality newspapers have many natures, there is a certain character which they all have in common. The overall tone and style, plus the interest and emphasis which the quality papers share with one another, make them a recognizable segment of the total press system.

If a reader looks through several copies of a few of the quality papers, he will find an obvious emphasis on idea-oriented news—stories that bear a significance beyond the straight facts (or bits of information) which they carry. They are stories which present the news "as a piece," relating the varying stories in a subtle (not always immediately recognizable) fashion. The economic stories relate to the political, the political to the cultural and social, and so on. Even the so-called human interest item (when it appears) puts the spotlight briefly on an important social (in a broad sense) point of contention, and taken together with the edition's total editorial focus, helps set the tone of the national and international events.

A quality paper's popularity is not built on voyeurism, sensationalism, or prurience. It offers its readers facts (in a meaningful context), ideas, interpretation; in short, it presents a continuing education. It gives its reader the feeling that he is getting a synthesized look at the most significant happenings and thinking of the day. The reader of the quality paper, unlike the reader of many of the popular and general "middle-area" papers (see "Elite Press Pyramid" at end of Chap. 4), does not feel like a news-scrap collector; rather he has at hand carefully selected and written stories that mean something, that present background and point out trends, that give insights into personalities who run the world or who might step into such positions tomorrow.

The respected publisher of Buenos Aires' *La Prensa*, Dr. Gainza Paz, in a speech in New York in 1965, had the following comments to make about a quality paper's relation to its readers:

> We know the responsibility of all good editors: to stimulate reader interest in the progress and development of their country. We also know that we ought to find ways of awakening that interest, despite the fact that sometimes uninformed readers appear to be indifferent.
>
> We also know that newspapers should interpret the news without bias, and without fear of giving conflicting viewpoints. And most importantly . . . a paper should express its own view clearly and without concern for the consequences.
>
> But even beyond its duty to inform, beyond its editorial policy, no matter how courageous that may be, the true journalist must somehow create a bond of confidence between the readers and the newspaper. Only then can he expect to have their support in defense of a press freedom that guarantees the people's right to know.[2]

Although the quality paper reflects a serious and intellectual orientation, its editors and chief writers seek a minimum of specialized jargon and strive always for clarity of expression. The editors realize, however (unlike their counterparts on many mass papers), that technical, specialized, and scientific words are often better than lay terms, and if they are to educate, they must use these more difficult (but more precise) expressions.

The late French writer and journalist, Albert Camus, perhaps has given as clear a view of the philosophy of quality journalism as has been given. With several others he founded in Paris the newspaper *Combat* in 1944, and made it in many ways the prototype of what he meant by an elite or quality journal. He attacked most newspapers as being too popularized, commercial, insincere, unconcerned, and careless with the truth. The press generally, he believed, was seeking to please rather than to enlighten.

Camus defined a good journalist in this way: "One who, first of all, is supposed to have ideas. Next, his task is to inform the public on events which have just taken place. He is a sort of day-to-day historian whose prime concern is the truth." He elaborated on this, however, by saying that the "first news" is not always the best news and that "it is better to come in second and report the truth than to be first and false."[3] He reprimanded the popular papers for their gaudy makeup and sensational content, saying that they are overly concerned with colorful details and eye-catching layout. Taking issue with those who said that this is the kind of journalism the public wants, he said: "No, this is what the public has been taught to want over a period of twenty years, which isn't at all the same thing. . . . But if a score of newspapers spew forth the same mediocrity and distortion every day, the public will breathe in this poisoned air and be unable to get along without it."[4]

Camus recommended that serious and responsible newspapers make some sacrifices in profits and in readership in order to provide daily reflection and the scrupulous reporting necessary to keep high-level journalistic standards. What he advocated, he illustrated in *Combat*—makeup and content which were serious but not academic, dignified but lively. Virtue, to Camus, was by no means boring, and he demanded conciseness of expression, a feeling for form, a nonrigidity in style, incisive interpretation, and a piercing wit. He had several little catchwords to illustrate his journalistic principles. To define an editorial, he would say, "One idea, two examples, three pages," and to report a news item, "Facts, local color, juxtapositions."[5]

In 1955, long after the *Combat* period, Camus renewed his ties with journalism by writing regularly for the weekly serious paper of Paris, *L'Express* (now a magazine). What Camus left behind him for the world of quality journalism is a legacy of values which, in a way, might serve to guide the free elite papers of the world. Jean Daniel, writing about Camus in 1964, noted that his main contribution was critical reporting, which Daniel defined in this way: "A passionately dedicated effort to eliminate passion from reporting; in other words, complete candor as to the limitations of the observer in his understanding of the phenomenon observed. It is an attitude of respect toward those to whom one is responsible for communicating the journalistic fact, once that fact has been defined."[6]

One of the chief concerns of the free elite—and Camus would have considered it so—is the editorial page or section. Editorials, essays, cartoons, columns, and letters to the editor are not bland "stay-out-of-trouble" types; rather they are strong, vital, outspoken, knowledgeable, thoughtful, and thought-provoking. They are often critical of government, regardless of what government or party is in power. The free elite takes very seriously its place as critic of government and of excesses in other institutions of society. It also offers what Roy E. Larsen has called "a platform for debate, a forum for the expression of people's viewpoints and ideas."[7]

Elite newspapers, of all the many types, seem most concerned about the future, about the implications of current events in days to come. They are insightful and predictive because of their concern and knowledge. Andrew Sharf, in a book written in 1964 analyzing the behavior of the British press during the rise of Hitler, repeatedly praised the three quality papers—*The Times*, *The Guardian*, and *The Daily Telegraph*—for their general coverage of the news from Germany during the 1930's. Although he singled out *The Guardian* as the most astute and the only one which consistently saw clearly what was happening in Germany and pointed to the direct connection between antisemitism and the Nazis' other policies, Sharf noted that the accuracy and completeness of German coverage was outstanding in all three papers.[8]

The elite paper's philosophy might be capsuled in a comment made about the *St. Louis Post-Dispatch* several years ago:

> Its general philosophy is that its readers . . . deserve and are capable of understanding important news from any part of the world, on any subject, and of any nature. It looks on its readers as changing and sees the frontiers of news as expanding.[9]

In one sense, the elite press serves as the true conscience of a nation, and even, to a large degree, as the conscience of the world. Even many papers which are not very well known internationally like to consider themselves part of their national conscience. This concern is important and indicates that such papers are progressing up the elite pyramid, or they are at least contemplating the invigorating climb. Undoubtedly key staff members, especially policy-making editors (such as John W. Dafoe of the *Winnipeg Free Press* in Canada, 1901–1944) largely forge the quality of a paper and see to it that there is a continuity of editorial policy and hire men who can be counted on to contribute further to the paper's prestige.

Continuity of policy and serious purpose is thus an important characteristic of a free elite paper. And this, of course, filters down from the managerial top. The Mexican columnist, Gena Pastor, writing in

Mexico City's *Excélsior* in 1964, stressed this point of the importance of continuity. Commenting on *Excélsior*'s being named by American journalism professors as one of the world's twenty best newspapers, Pastor wrote that all the characteristics or criteria used for the determination of a quality paper would not have been sufficient without another thing: continuity.[10] He made the point that in too many enterprises, and especially in bureaucratic offices, the chief executive, in order to preserve his sense of importance, does not delegate responsibility. Too often, wrote Pastor, subordinates are relegated by *el jefe* to a secondary category "in order that he may maintain his prestige and superiority," with the result that when he leaves, the organization tends to fall to pieces.

Pastor commended *Excélsior*'s director (Rodrigo de Llano) for not taking such an attitude. Consequently, when the outstanding director died in 1963, the paper's staff was fully capable of perpetuating its quality journalism and another director was ready to step in to continue "on a firm foundation, a newspaper still superior."[11]

What exactly is meant by "editorial policy"? Although it is broad and complex, there are certain things which can be said about it which might be helpful to an understanding of it. It has to do with consistency in outlook and in publishing practices; it is the course a newspaper chooses to follow as it answers the two all-important questions: What shall we print? How shall we print it? Editorial policy is composed of the practices, rules, and principles which the paper sets as a guide and standard for itself. As such, it really governs every phase of the newspaper from the type of staff sought, the kind of news dealt with, the ideological orientation embraced, and even the size of type used in printing.

Seldom are the most important phases of a paper's editorial policy expressed in writing; they are simply understood. The staff member (as does the reader) comes to know through experience the editorial policy of the paper. Usually the policy of a paper is established when the paper is founded; there is a certain permanence and stability about it, although it would be wrong to think that it does not change over the years. So far as a quality paper is concerned, an inflexible editorial policy is no sign of excellence. (Even the traditional *Times* of London cleared its front page of advertising for news in the spring of 1966.)

In countries which have several or many national dailies, one would expect to find a larger quality press—at least in the sense of dealing largely with national and international topics. In Britain, for example, the national serious dailies have almost completely taken over the job of informing the public on major topics, leaving most of the provincial press with the responsibility of dealing with provincial matters. In the United States, on the other hand, where there is really no national press, every paper (with the exception of many grass-roots weeklies) feels it must be something to everybody. Consequently, most general

American dailies are unfocused, undisciplined in basic journalistic philosophy, offering up all types of disorganized bits and snippets of entertainment, comics, puzzles, fiction, columns, and sensational or conflict-oriented news, and fair portions of undigested (and usually bland) local editorial opinion or comment.

In fairness, it must be said that most of these middle-area general United States dailies provide more news about world affairs than most of their counterparts in other nations; but it is so scattered among all the other assorted journalistic goodies that its importance and impact is lost on the average American reader.

Canadian editors of middle-area dailies, on the other hand, although greatly influenced by American journalism, tend to feel that the lack of a national press in Canada imposes a special obligation on them to present to their readers a comprehensive picture of the world. This may result, as some critics of the Canadian press have suggested, in masses of gray and dull type, but at least the Canadian reader of the average daily, in the opinion of the editor of the *Montreal Star*, gets a more thorough world picture than does his opposite number south of the border.[12] Canada's dailies, then, might be called provincial (in the same sense as U.S. dailies) but with a more cosmopolitan orientation.

The international elite paper must evidence a *cosmopolitanism* quite alien to mass papers and only occasionally approached in middle-area general appeal papers. Concern for news and views of other countries is a definite characteristic of the elite paper; thus the emphasis on international trade, political relations, cross-cultural economic, social, scientific, and educational affairs. The elite paper not only takes its serious national affairs seriously, but also deems it important to inform its readers of the salient international affairs and the concerns of other nations. The elite paper is able to see the world as a piece, not simply as a hodgepodge of nationalistic states isolated and unimportant to one another. It, unlike the popular paper, would not cause the kind of reaction that stimulated Reinhold Niebuhr to indict a segment of the press in a 1950 lecture:

> Nothing is more disconcerting to an American visitor in Britain than to find that the afternoon press in that country has no other news from this country than little snippets of sensational items which cannot possibly give the reader a balanced view of our nation. I would not claim that our papers of similar stripe do any better for Britain or for any other continental nation.[13]

The elite press would not have affected Dr. Niebuhr as did the popular British afternoon papers. The elite papers would have given him a heavy diet of news and views of four main types: (1) politics/international relations, (2) business/economics, (3) education/science/

culture, and (4) the humanities with emphasis on the fine arts, literature, philosophy, and religion. Dr. Niebuhr or any other reader of the elite paper would have received much more, however, than serious facts and opinion. He could have actually come to better know people of other nations and cultures; he could have, as Quincy Howe has said, learned how people live in other nations, how they "think, feel and express themselves" in moments of great concern and seriousness.[14]

An aura of dignity and stability is a characteristic of the elite paper. This manifests itself not only in a conservative, soft-sell makeup but also in a rather heavy, semiacademic writing style that approaches the type one finds in such journals as London's *Economist* or *The Reporter* of the United States. In the elite paper there is an overriding tone of seriousness, of respect for the reader's intelligence and store of knowledge; there is an absence of sensation or hysteria that tends to dominate the general newspaper press of the world. The elite paper has a clearer conception of what is really significant and vital than do other types of papers. It has a serious-minded and moral approach to news that keeps it digging and interested in the news at any cost. All of this, of course, makes the quality press *reliable*.

The elite paper is courageous. The mere fact that it has foregone the temptation to popularize, to sensationalize, to build up a large readership shows that it has courage. It dares to give the readers a serious and heavy portion of news and views; it constantly attempts to lead, not follow, public opinion. This, in itself, takes courage. It has a reputation for speaking out on issues when it is not popular to do so; is forward-looking, progressive, and eager to change when the change is in accord with society's best interests, regardless of whether it is considered (or considers itself) liberal or conservative (or something else).

The elite paper is *responsible*: responsible to its readers. In a free society, of course, this makes it also responsible to its government and to people everywhere. Its main job is, as *The New York Times'* James Reston has said, "to get all the facts the people need to reach correct judgments."[15] (Authoritarian prestige papers like *Pravda* or *Jen-min Jih-pao* are also responsible, but their responsibility is of a different nature, being directed toward the system and emphasizing the solidarity of the state rather than considering the individual citizen as the object of its responsibility. In a sense, the authoritarian elite paper's responsibility is one of Party-Government-People consensus, a sort of responsibility for conformity and harmony, not a responsibility which enthrones honesty and pluralistic discourse.)

If Reston is right, then the free elite press should be reliable; the readers should be able to trust it. It must be adequate to a free people's needs. Often indictments are made of a nation's press and these would evidently, in their generalized form, include the quality or elite papers, for it must be remembered that they are available to a nation's readers.

One wonders, for example, how much blame is shared by the quality press of the United States for a situation which Felix Greene (a British journalist) discusses relative to the American public's information about Mao's China. Here are some of Greene's rather strong words about the American reader, his press, and the type of journalism he is getting:

> The evidence . . . has shown, at least as far as reporting about China is concerned, that the unusual freedom granted the press has not resulted in better news. The sad but irrefutable fact is that the American people today are less informed and more misinformed about China than the people of any other Western nation. . . .
>
> As a result of this inquiry into America's information on China I have reached the conclusion that the American people have not received the minimum of necessary information on supremely important developments. . . . Unless the people are assured of news that they can trust, a democratic government cannot successfully be administered.[16]

Another indictment of the United States press came more recently from an American, the late Dr. Bernard B. Fall of Howard University, who was a part-time journalist and considered one of the top American authorities on Vietnam. (Dr. Fall was killed in Vietnam in 1967.) In April, 1966, Dr. Fall said that United States newspaper coverage of the Vietnam situation "lacks depth and breadth" and that "most newsmen settle for reporting the battles, the blood and thunder, instead of the economic, social, and political problems created by the war."[17] The only American paper he excepted from his indictment was *The New York Times.*

Regardless of the validity or error of Greene's or Fall's analyses, one thing remains certain: the free elite papers of the United States and elsewhere try to provide their readers with adequate and trustworthy information. When a quality paper fails in some such basic responsibility referred to by Greene and Fall, the probability is great that the reason is without, not within, the newspaper. The problem, in other words, is most often external to the quality newspaper and has developed in spite of the determination of the paper that it not develop.

Before surveying some specific studies of criteria of the quality press, it should be re-emphasized that elite papers are written and edited for the discerning reader, the inquisitive reader, the knowledgeable reader, the thoughtful reader, the issue-oriented (not the fact-oriented) reader. The quality paper, in short, is designed for the person who takes serious things seriously and is conscientiously seeking the truth.

Many persons, most, in fact, do not take serious things seriously, and they have their press. The person who reads the London *Daily Mirror* or the Sunday *News of the World* may want or need these trivial forays into a crazy-quilt world of gaudiness and news anarchy. Thus, the popular press has its place, serves its purpose, but it should be recognized for what it is. Admittedly, the reader of the *Daily Mirror* may also be a reader of an elite paper in his more serious moments, but the point is that he knows the difference. His journalistic habits are consciously schizophrenic. But he probably is not a typical newspaper reader, for there is reason to believe that serious persons, opinion leaders, intellectuals would not be comfortable reading the *Daily Mirror*. However, if a single person does read both types of papers, he knows they are of quite different characters, speak different languages, have different goals, and address different audiences, or at least appeal to the different tastes or sensibilities of an individual.

Let us turn now to several studies and discussions (since 1959) which have dealt with the marks of the free elite. Many other articles and books have approached quality journalism and its characteristics from a variety of perspectives during this same period, and even before, but the four studies which follow reflect the thinking of scholars and practicing journalists of many nations relative to the marks or characteristics of the quality, or free elite, newspapers.

In 1959 Wilbur Schramm, of Stanford University's Institute for Communications Research,[18] wrote that a prestige or quality newspaper (in a democratic nation) is privately owned, but that "it may or may not speak for a political party"; he pointed out that *Dagens Nyheter* of Sweden, for example, usually follows the Liberal Party line. In addition, such a quality paper may or may not have an official quality (the London *Times*, for instance, is often considered the unofficial voice of the British Government, although it is completely independent). But Schramm believes one thing is certain: In a democracy the quality newspaper speaks for its owner and publisher.[19] Schramm emphasizes that neither size nor circulation nor great financial prosperity determine a prestige paper. He says that the main distinguishing characteristics (aside from the type of readers) are content and the newspaper's relation to its public.[20]

The great newspapers of the world, writes Schramm, tend to focus on the big events of the day—news of national and international scope at the expense of local news, human interest items, sensational content; and they try to treat these larger events at greater length than do other papers. The quality papers also tend to deal with the news more seriously, to stress political and economic affairs, the serious side of social problems, and scientific developments. Schramm says that the quality papers attract influential readers by the breadth and depth of their coverage, and tend to be independent and often critical of government. No central authority controls their policy, and they serve as observers and critics of their governments rather than as representatives.[21]

In 1961 the United States magazine, *Saturday Review*, undertook a mail-questionnaire survey of all deans, full professors, and associate professors in the 46 schools accredited by the American Council on Education for Journalism.[22] Object: to discover which of the 119 American dailies with circulations of 100,000 or more were most highly regarded by these journalism educators and what criteria were used in rating a daily paper. Selecting from the responses of the 125 respondents, here are the 10 main criteria used to adjudge an American daily as superior:

1. Completeness of coverage in foreign and international affairs, business, the arts, science, and education.
2. Concern with interpretive pieces, backgrounding articles, and depth news articles.
3. Typographical and general editorial dignity.
4. Lack of sensationalism.
5. Depth and analytical perception of stories.
6. Absence of hysteria and cultural tone.
7. Thorough and impartial news coverage and serious-minded, moral approach to news.
8. Imagination, decency, interest in democratic problems and humanity.
9. Excellent editorial page.
10. Orientation that rises above provincialism and sensationalism.

In the summer of 1964 a survey of a panel of 26 professors of international communication in the United States was conducted to help determine criteria used, in this case, to rate a newspaper in the top twenty quality papers of the world.[23] In addition, names of newspapers so considered were solicited. The newspapers actually listed by this panel of specialists are named in the next chapter, but it is appropriate here to give the most significant criteria for judging a quality paper in an international context. These are given below in the order corresponding to the panel's opinion of their importance.

The most important criterion in the panel's view was an emphasis on political, economic, and cultural news and views. A long tradition of freedom and editorial courage was considered second most important. This, of course, would eliminate highly controlled newspapers of the authoritarian nations from a roster of quality papers. The third criterion of political and economic independence was closely related to the second.

A strong editorial page and/or section given over to opinion and interpretive essays was named as fourth most important for a quality paper, followed by staff enterprise in obtaining and writing news and commentary.

Other criteria thought by the panel very important for determining a quality paper:

Large proportion of space given to world affairs; lack of provincialism; consistently good writing in all sections of the paper; high regard by opinion leaders and by other serious publications; large, well-educated staff; typographical and printing excellence and general makeup dignity; de-emphasis of sensational news and pictures; high overall quality of coverage on world, national, and local levels; active integrity; consistent opposition to intolerance and unfairness; active community leadership, and comprehensive news coverage in its pre-empted area, and influence with the decision-makers and policy-makers at home and in other countries.

It is rather obvious from the above criteria that this American panel of journalism professors, at least, thinks about an international quality daily in a rather special or restricted way. First, the panelists see it as a general newspaper, not as one which specializes in a certain type of material (*e.g.*, *The Wall Street Journal*, as good as it may be) nor as one which represents some organization or institution and largely is concerned with policy-dissemination (*e.g.*, the Vatican's *Osservatore Romano*), however qualitative and prestigious it may be in a limited context. Secondly, they mainly see the international quality newspaper as a free (libertarian) journal, unattached to, and uncensored by, government. This would, of course, eliminate such papers as *Pravda* of the U.S.S.R. and *ABC* of Spain, however prestigious the first may be in the Communist system or however qualitative in a certain literary-cultural sense the latter may be in a Rightist totalitarian regime.

Thirdly, the panel's criteria indicate that its members felt a quality paper must stress politics, economics, and culture, and that this emphasis must extend to the international scene and not simply to the country where it is published. Cosmopolitanism, then, was considered to be very important, along with editorial courage and an impact on the opinion leaders of its own nation and of other nations. A dignity of page makeup as well as a large, enterprising, well-educated staff rounds out the basic image of a quality paper as seen by the 1964 American panel. Underlying implications here are that the quality paper must be supranational in circulation and scope, literate, courageous, forceful, free, knowledgeable, stimulating, credible, serious, socially concerned, world-conscious, and dignified. It is little wonder that the group of international quality newspapers is small.

One other survey should be mentioned. The author, in late 1965, sent a brief questionnaire to 185 editors in the United States, Britain, West Germany, Denmark, Switzerland, Italy, Japan, Mexico, Australia, and India.[24] The purpose of this survey was to follow up the author's 1964 survey and to get some comment from an international panel relative to the world's leading elite newspapers—this time from newspaper editors instead of journalism professors. Questionnaires were sent to editors of newspapers (with more than 50,000 circulation) chosen at random from the 1965 *Editor & Publisher International Yearbook*. Ninety-two were returned (a very high response) and after an additional group of forms was mailed to other editors and the total return numbered exactly one hundred, the seeking of completed questionnaires stopped, although response from Indian and Australian editors was disproportionately small.

The returns from various countries follow:

United States (18); West Germany (14); Britain (12); Japan (12); Switzerland (11); Italy (10); Mexico (9); Denmark (8); Australia (4), and India (2).

Admittedly, this is a small sample, but the intent was not to take a statistically reliable survey (and claim any scientific validity for it), but to elicit some comments (hopefully representative) from respondents in ten free-world countries. This, it is felt, was accomplished with some comments more incisive and more frank than had been anticipated.

The questionnaires had only two brief parts: (1) the editors were asked to name five dailies of the world (no more than one from a single country) which they considered good examples of leading quality, influential, or elite newspapers, and (2) they were asked to give at least five main determinants or characteristics which they used in deciding on the five dailies.

Instead of summarizing in detail the criteria deemed important in classifying a quality newspaper by the international panel of editors, it will suffice here to say that their standards of evaluation included all those mentioned by Schramm (1959), the *Saturday Review* survey (1961), and the Merrill survey of United States professors teaching international communications (1964). This, of course, did not come as a surprise, but did reinforce the previous surveys, or said another way, it extended or projected these criteria into an international context. It showed that newsmen in diverse countries (nonauthoritarian) tend to have a common set of standards which they use in determining the leading newspapers of the world.

It should be noted at this point that many of these editors stated their evaluative criteria in various terms, but it was quite clear that the basic values were the same and the variously worded responses could quite easily be structured as to common or standard themes.

What were these main themes or criteria considered most important by the international panel for determining a leading quality paper? They have been grouped in five rather large categories, and although they reiterate in large part what has already been said, their presentation should serve well to summarize and conclude this chapter. Marks of the free elite are these:

(1) Independence; financial stability; integrity; social concern; good writing and editing.

(2) Strong opinion and interpretive emphasis; world consciousness; nonsensationalism in articles and makeup.

(3) Emphasis on politics, international relations, economics, social welfare, cultural endeavors, education, and science.
(4) Concern with getting, developing, and keeping a large, intelligent, well-educated, articulate, and technically proficient staff.
(5) Determination to serve and help expand a well-educated, intellectual readership at home and abroad; desire to appeal to, and influence, opinion leaders everywhere.

4

The Elite: Names and Rank

After reading the last chapter, one may wonder if any newspaper in the world really qualifies for membership in the elite international press. The answer to such a question is that, if all the characteristics and standards are not applied too stringently to a newspaper at all times, most certainly there are journals which would qualify for membership. Of course, the whole matter is one of "degree" of achievement, concern, independence, cosmopolitanism, rationality, social responsibility, seriousness, and the like. One must attune himself to "continuum thinking" (thinking in gradations or degrees, not "black-white" thinking) and not to compartmentalized and undynamic thinking when considering the subject of quality journalism. However, if a person takes continuum thinking too far and falls under the spell of extreme relativity, he cannot adjudge or criticize newspapers for fear of making unwarranted evaluations.

Journalists, educators, and interested laymen should not shirk from making judgments and from trying to determine for themselves excellence among newspapers, even to the establishing of a "hierarchy," however difficult and subjective this enterprise may be. Granted the complexity of such a venture, it should be remembered that historians (and many others) classify statesmen, military leaders, universities, philosophers, writers, and even nations as great, second-rate, mediocre, and so forth. There appears equal justification in classifying newspapers. At any rate, it is done every day by an assortment of people, many of whom, unfortunately, do offer their judgments out of an empty chamber of ignorance.

Persons in any country who study the press of the world and seriously attempt to compare newspapers, analyze their contents, and criticize them should be encouraged, not discouraged. Perspectives may be different among students of the press, values and standards may vary somewhat (although not substantially, as was seen in the last chapter), but they make their opinions known out of a concern, an interest, and a constantly growing fund of knowledge. Usually, the statements and appraisals coming from press critics bring no real surprises, but occasionally a writer will overturn rather well-established beliefs and challenge prevalent conceptions with his opinions. For example, how many persons would consider Latin American papers serious competitors in quality with comparable papers in the United States? Not very many, probably.

Yet in 1962, D. H. Radler, a student of Latin America, wrote a book[1] in which he declared that in the United States there are "few papers to compare in quality with *Excélsior* of Mexico, except *The New York Times*."[2] He even said that Latin America's press was superior to that of the United States and noted that his view was seconded by Professor Ronald Hilton, then director of Latin American studies at Stanford University.[3] "We have little besides *The Times*," he wrote, "to compare with either *Excélsior* or the leading papers of Brazil, Argentina, or Chile." He even went further to assert that even smaller papers "such as Costa Rica's *La Nación*, Honduras's *El Día*, and Guatemala's *Imparcial* are head and shoulders above the press of comparable size in the United States in range, completeness, and accuracy of coverage, to say nothing of acumen and courage."[4]

Serious journalistic iconoclasts like Radler perhaps are rather irritating in the certainty of their statements and the bluntness of their rhetoric. And their appraisals may seem oversimplified and unsubstantiated to the more demanding scholar; but they do serve a useful purpose by causing us to break the bonds of traditional and conventional stereotypes and look more closely at our longtime assumptions. They raise the possibility that perhaps we accept many things uncritically, and that we may be wrong.

Critics who are interested in the world press, who attempt constantly to keep up with it, who read numerous newspapers in the native language or in translation, or who receive impressions about them from respected persons who do: these people would seem to be as well qualified as any to criticize, rank, and pass judgment on newspapers. Those who belittle such critics and such labors as senseless and valueless because of the subjectivity involved only evidence an ignorance of the serious critic and of the whole realm of criticism and evaluation in every area. Certainly a critic such as John Tebbel is qualified to appraise the press as he does in this case:

> There are more 'serious' newspapers in the United Kingdom, in the manner of *The New York Times*. The quality of the daily London *Times, The Daily Telegraph,* the Manchester *Guardian*, and the *Financial Times*, and the Sunday edition of *The Telegraph*, along with the *Sunday Times* and *The Observer* (to name some of the best), is matched in America only by *The New York Times, The Wall Street Journal,* and *The Christian Science Monitor*. In some respects, notably political analysis and critical writing, these 'serious' British papers are in general better than most of ours, and more comprehensive in their coverage than all save the Gray Lady of Forty-third Street.[5]

The serious student of the international press may be exemplified by Dr. Robert W. Desmond of the University of California, who since the early 1930's when he wrote his doctoral dissertation at the London School of Economics on the world press, has been conscientiously studying and evaluating the world press and who wrote a pioneering book in English called *The Press and World Affairs* (1937). In a letter to the author in 1964, Dr. Desmond wrote:

> You and I think we know something about the papers (foreign papers), and we do . . . we are at the mercy of others for most of what we know. We have to talk with persons who do know the papers, who do read them, who do have the language, who do themselves also (preferably) know the best of the U.S. press (and the worst, too, perhaps) so that they have a standard of comparison and judgment. I know I always ask people in other countries and from other countries, persons whose judgment and opinion I respect, to comment—and I try to keep up to date that way, also, on changes such as do occur now and then, where a paper that once didn't rate may now have advanced (or another declined in quality) so the order is different. This sort of ranking is subjective, but when you get enough witnesses and enough evidence it becomes pretty satisfactory, I would say. So our judgments—that is, what we say —may have to be second or third hand, but they are not without validity, even so.[6]

In spite of the fact that there will always be some who will not grant any validity or value to classification or ranking surveys, and will consider arguments such as Dr. Desmond's as inadequate, there is good reason to believe that international press scholarship, and the tremendous growth in journalism literature since World War II, has given a sound foundation on which to build a valid set of standards for judging newspaper quality and for naming certain papers to the elite fraternity.

Since the 1930's, at least, there has been a growing concern with establishing the names (and ranking) of newspapers of the world belonging to the exclusive fraternity of the elite. Journalists and academicians in many nations have concerned themselves in various ways with evaluating and analyzing newspapers which tend to go beyond purely serving as local or national organs and make an impact on international policy and thinking. Outstanding German press scholars like Walter Hagemann, Otto Groth, Heinz Gollwitzer, Emil Dovifat, Karl d'Ester, Karl Böhmer, H. J. Prakke, and Winfried B. Lerg have done outstanding work in the area of international quality journalism.

In Britain, the influence and character of the class press has interested many persons, notable among them Francis Williams, Harold Herd, William H. Mills, Linton Andrews, and Stanley Morison. France's leading scholar in recent years, concerned with this aspect of journalism, was undoubtedly the late Jacques Kayser; other Frenchmen making significant contributions have been P. N. Devolder, Jean Stoetzel, Abel Chatelain, and Noël Jacquemart. Other Europeans interested in elite journalism include Maarten Schneider, Maarten Rooij, and D. H. Couvée (Holland); Troels Fink, Franz de Jessen, K. B. Anderson, and Vincent Naeser (Denmark); Bertrandus Janssens and Marcel Stijns (Belgium); Ignazio Weiss (Italy); Karl Weber (Switzerland), and Juan Beneyto and Nicolás Gonzáles Ruíz (Spain).

Among India's chief students of the quality press have been the late H. P. Ghosh (the "dean of Indian journalism"), Amitabha Chaudhury, Chanchal Sarkar, and Chapalakanta Bhattacharya. Japanese making important contributions have been many, among them Elizo Koyama, Ichiro Iguchi, Kanesada Hanazono, Hideo Ono, and Akira Tsujimura. And representing Latin America these might be named: Danton Jobim of Brazil; Jacinto Duarte of Uruguay; Oscar Beltrán of Argentina, and Salvador Borrego of Mexico.

In the United States, university professors who pioneered in the study of international journalism were Walter Williams and Frank Luther Mott (Missouri); Ralph Nafziger (Wisconsin); Raymond Nixon (Minnesota); Robert Desmond (California), and Kenneth Olson (Northwestern University). Most of the younger journalism professors currently engaged in international press studies[7] owe much of their interest to one or more of the above.

Although there will be skeptics who cannot see any value in surveys, polls, and rankings, let us proceed to consider some surveys which have been made to determine members of the elite press and their places in this select group.

In 1951 the late Jacques Kayser, who enjoyed an international reputation as a press researcher, in a study for UNESCO,[8] selected seventeen dailies as major dailies for a comparative analysis. The following list indicates that Kayser was thinking of major papers, not necessarily of the elite papers, and he was also considering those which fall in many spots along an authoritarian-libertarian continuum:

> *Borba* (Belgrade), *Times of India* (Bombay), *La Nación* (Buenos Aires), *Al Misri* (Cairo), *Hürriyet* (Istanbul), *Rand Daily Mail* (Johannesburg), *Daily Express* (London), *La Prensa* (Mexico City), *Corriere della Sera* (Milan), *Pravda* (Moscow), *Daily News* (New York), *Le Parisien Libéré* (Paris), *Rudé Právo* (Prague), *O Estado de São Paulo* (Brazil), *Ta Kung Pao* (Shanghai), *Dagens Nyheter* (Stockholm), and the *Daily Telegraph* (Sydney).

Noteworthy is the fact that when compared with more recent lists of quality papers only six of Dr. Kayser's dailies would be considered as members of the elite club: *Times of India, La Nación, Corriere della Sera, Pravda, O Estado de São Paulo,* and *Dagens Nyheter.* Kayser's list, however, was not intended to include only quality papers, but others which he felt would be representative of various segments of the press of the nations of various political orientations. These ranged from the rather flamboyant *Borba* of Belgrade and *Ta Kung Pao* of Shanghai, representing varieties of Communist journalism, to New York's tabloid *Daily News* and London's standard-format *Daily Express*, representing varieties of rather nationalistic journalism with a sensational flavor.

Then, in 1959, Wilbur Schramm did another comparative study (of one day during the 1956 Suez Crisis)[9] in which he chose important dailies which he felt were representative of world journalism. It is interesting that three of the five Communist papers on Schramm's list were also on Kayser's. Here are Schramm's dailies, with the Communist papers listed first; Schramm refers to all of them as great papers and says that they fall into the class which is usually called the prestige papers:

> *Pravda, Trybuna Ludu* (Warsaw), *Rudé Právo* (Prague), *Borba, Jen-min Jih-pao* (Peking); *Le Monde* (Paris), *Frankfurter Allgemeine Zeitung* (Frankfurt am Main), *Dagens Nyheter, Al Ahram* (Cairo), *Asahi Shimbun* (Tokyo), *La Prensa* (Buenos Aires), *Times of India, The Times* (London), and *The New York Times.*

Schramm's list appears to be much more in line with informed thinking than Kayser's as to what is an elite paper. For example, Schramm's papers include the London *Times*, *The New York Times*, *La Prensa* of Buenos Aires, *Jen-min Jih-pao* of Peking, the *Frankfurter Allgemeine Zeitung*, and *Le Monde*, all omitted from Kayser's 1951 study. And Schramm dropped completely these mass appeal papers (which Kayser studied): Britain's *Daily Express*, the United States' *Daily News*, and France's *Le Parisien Libéré*.

The inclusion by Schramm of such dailies as *Jen-min Jih-pao* (the leading Party organ of Red China), *La Prensa* (long the outstanding paper of Argentina), *The Times* of London (always in the top three or four in a roster of quality papers), *Asahi* (without a doubt the best paper in Asia), *Le Monde* (probably one of the two best dailies in continental Europe), and *The New York Times* (certainly the most complete serious paper in the world) indicates that he was choosing papers of a higher international prestige level than had Kayser.

In 1961, Edward L. Bernays (New York public relations counsel) conducted a national poll of 1,596 U.S. daily newspaper publishers on their ranking of the top ten foreign (non-U.S.) papers.[10] He also asked for their ranking of the top ten domestic newspapers. The fact that only 7.2 per cent ranked foreign papers as to 17.2 per cent ranking United States papers indicates perhaps, among other possibilities, the low degree of familiarity American publishers have with the foreign press. What were the foreign papers thought most important by the American publishers who responded? They follow in order of the percentage of publishers listing them:

> *The Guardian* (England), *The Times* (England), *La Prensa* (Argentina), *Toronto Daily Star* (Canada), *The Daily Telegraph* (England), *Le Monde* (France)/*Mainichi* (Japan), *Le Figaro* (France), *The Observer* (Britain)/*France-Soir* (France), *Asahi Shimbun* (Japan), and the *Montreal Star* (Canada).

This listing by United States publishers is quite interesting. First of all, it indicates that English-language papers were considered most prominently in the ten, probably because the publishers read, or felt they read, them. It is unusual that two Canadian dailies made the list. And it is strange indeed that Britain's ultraserious weekly *Observer* (the only weekly in the list) and France's outstanding mass or popular (sensational) *France-Soir* tied for eighth place. It should be noted, however, that with the exception of *France-Soir*, all the papers named are usually considered as serious quality or elite journals. Unlike Kayser and Schramm, the American publishers omitted completely any Communist paper from their list. The reason obviously lies in the fact that the Bernays' Poll set forth as the basis for the publishers' judgment the following statements by Joseph Pulitzer in 1883, by Adolph Ochs in 1896, and by Thomas Gibson in 1860:

* JOSEPH PULITZER, *New York World*, May 10, 1883

> An institution that should always fight for progress and reform, never tolerate injustice and corruption, always fight demagogues of all parties, never belong to any party, always

oppose privileged classes and public plunderers, never lack sympathy with the poor, always remain devoted to the public welfare, never be satisfied with merely printing news, always be drastically independent, never be afraid to attack wrong, whether by predatory plutocracy or predatory poverty.

* ADOLPH S. OCHS, *The New York Times*, August 18, 1896

It will be my earnest aim that *The New York Times* give the news, all the news, in concise and attractive form, in language that is permissible in good society, and give it early, if not earlier, than it can be learned through any other medium. To give the news impartially, without fear or favor, regardless of party, sect, or interest involved; to make the columns of *The New York Times* a forum for the consideration of all public questions of public importance, and to that end, to invite intelligent discussion from all shades of opinion.

* THOMAS GIBSON, *Rocky Mountain Herald* (Denver), May 1, 1860

A newspaper untrammeled by sinister influence from any quarter—the advocate of the right and the denouncer of the wrong—an independent vehicle for the free expression of opinions of all candid, honest and intelligent minds—a medium of free discussion, moral, religious, social, and scientific.

According to the Bernays' poll, runner-up newspapers receiving at least three percent of the votes, were these: *Dagens Nyheter*, Paris *Herald-Tribune* (in a sense not a foreign newspaper), *Berliner Morgenpost*, *The Times of India*, *El Mercurio* (Santiago, Chile), *Frankfurter Allgemeine*, *Neue Zürcher Zeitung*, *Aftenposten* (Oslo), *El Tiempo* (Bogotá, Colombia), *Il Messaggero* (Rome), *La Nación* (Buenos Aires), and *The Scotsman* (Edinburgh).

In the Bernays' Poll, the top ten United States papers listed in order of frequency of publishers' mention, and using the same judgmental standard as for the foreign papers, were:

The New York Times, St. Louis Post-Dispatch, The Christian Science Monitor, Milwaukee Journal, Louisville Courier-Journal, New York *Herald Tribune, The Washington Post, Los Angeles Times, Chicago Tribune*, and *Kansas City Star.*

Notice how the above correspond with the top ten of the *Saturday Review* poll the same year (1961):

The New York Times, The Christian Science Monitor, The Wall Street Journal, St. Louis Post-Dispatch, Milwaukee Journal, The Washington Post, New York *Herald Tribune, Louisville Courier-Journal, Chicago Tribune*, and *The* (Baltimore) *Sun.*[11]

The criteria for judgment most often cited in the *Saturday Review* survey were these: complete and comprehensive news treatment; unbiased, objective treatment of news; judgment in selection of news; layout-typography; good writing style, and accuracy.

In 1962 this writer, in a chapter for a new journalism textbook,[12] presented a list of daily papers which appeared to him at the time to be gravitating toward the top of the elite pyramid. This list was composed of both libertarian and authoritarian elite, and was limited to non-United States papers. Dailies appearing in this 1962 list follow:

> *Neue Zürcher Zeitung, The Guardian, The Times, Le Monde, Pravda, Scotsman, Izvestia, Asahi Shimbun, Le Figaro, El Tiempo, Frankfurter Allgemeine, La Nación, Journal de Genève, The Hindu, Corriere della Sera, Süddeutsche Zeitung, Nieuwe Rotterdamse Courant, Berlingske Tidende, Die Welt, Excélsior, The Globe and Mail,* and *Jen-min Jih-pao (People's Daily)*.

Some of these dailies had not appeared in any of the lists already mentioned, but were thought to be extremely qualitative and prestigious journals. For example, it seemed to the writer at the time that such dailies as *The Hindu* of Madras, *Süddeutsche Zeitung* of Munich, *Nieuwe Rotterdamse Courant* of Rotterdam, *Berlingske Tidende* of Copenhagen, *Die Welt* of Hamburg, and *Izvestia* of the Soviet Union must definitely be considered among the truly great papers of the world. This opinion has not changed to date. These papers were listed in rough order of their influence and prestige at the time (in the writer's opinion) and if such a list were compiled today, the same papers would appear, but the order would not be the same.

In 1963 the faculty of the School of Journalism, Syracuse University (New York), determined a list of the ten leading dailies of the world, using stylistic quality, journalistic courage, editorial independence, and decency as principal evaluative criteria.[13] The Syracuse University list presented the newspapers in the following order:

> *Neue Zürcher Zeitung, Frankfurter Allgemeine Zeitung, The New York Times, The Christian Science Monitor, The Guardian* (London/Manchester), *Le Monde, Asahi Shimbun, La Prensa* (Buenos Aires), *The Times* (London), and *Dagens Nyheter* (Stockholm).

In the summer of 1964 a survey was made in the United States by the writer and was intended to elicit a ranking of elite dailies of the world from twenty-six professors of international communications from as many schools of journalism throughout the country.[14] The criteria of evaluation used by respondents were given in the last chapter, and only the names of the papers and their ranking will be given here. The top ten:

1. *The New York Times* (United States)
2. *The Times* (London)
3. *The Christian Science Monitor* (United States)
4. *The Guardian* (Britain)
5. *Le Monde* (France)
6. *Neue Zürcher Zeitung* (Switzerland)
7. *The Washington Post* (United States)
8. *La Prensa* (Argentina)
9. *Asahi Shimbun* (Japan)
10. *Frankfurter Allgemeine* (West Germany)

In addition to the first ten, the United States faculty panel named the following among the world's best dailies:

> *Dagens Nyheter* (Stockholm), *Corriere della Sera* (Milan), *Berlingske Tidende* (Copenhagen), *La Nación* (Buenos Aires), *Times of India* (Bombay), *Die Welt* (Hamburg), *Excélsior* (Mexico City), *Journal de Genève, The Scotsman* (Edinburgh), *Nieuwe Rotterdamse Courant* (Rotterdam), *The Sun* (Baltimore), *Süddeutsche Zeitung* (Munich), *Aftenposten* (Oslo), *O Estado de São Paulo* (Brazil), *Svenska Dagbladet* (Stockholm), *Die Presse* (Vienna), *Izvestia* (Moscow), *Los Angeles Times* (United States), *El Tiempo* (Bogotá), *Pravda* (Moscow), *Courier-Journal* (Louisville), *Milwaukee Journal* (United States), New York *Herald Tribune* (United States), *Minneapolis Morning Tribune* (United States), *Winnipeg Free Press* (Canada), *The Globe and Mail* (Toronto), *The Daily Telegraph* (London), *The Age* (Melbourne), *La Stampa* (Turin), and *Helsingin Sanomat* (Helsinki).

The writer in late 1965 followed up this survey of American journalism professors with an international survey of newspaper editors.[15] As was pointed out in the last chapter, questionnaires were received from one hundred editors in ten countries (including the United States)[16] on which this international panel ranked what they considered were the top five quality dailies of the world, naming no more than one from any one country. Asking for no more than one daily from any country may have distorted the survey somewhat, but it forced the respondents to think of top newspapers in at least five nations and tended to disperse the papers to a degree not found in some of the other surveys.

So far as is known, this survey was the largest such poll conducted through 1965 and tended to reinforce opinions made by independent students and smaller samples of respondents. No real surprises came from the 1965 survey, although it is interesting to note that United

States papers tended to be a little lower in the list than in several previous studies. Two factors could account for this: (1) this was an international survey, whereas most of the others were conducted among Americans, and (2) the request that no more than one paper from any one country be listed may have eliminated the naming of additional American papers by respondents.

At any rate, here are the ten dailies of the world which received the most mentions by the international panel of editors, presented in the order of frequency of mention:

1. *The New York Times* (United States)
2. *Neue Zürcher Zeitung* (Switzerland)
3. *The Guardian* (Britain)
4. *Le Monde* (France)
5. *The Times* (Britain)
6. *Asahi Shimbun* (Japan)
7. *Dagens Nyheter* (Sweden)
8. *Excélsior* (Mexico)
9. *Corriere della Sera* (Milan)
10. *Frankfurter Allgemeine Zeitung* (West Germany)

The second ten dailies getting the most mentions by the international panel are these:

> *O Estado de São Paulo* (Brazil), *St. Louis Post-Dispatch* (United States), *Die Welt* (West Germany), *The Christian Science Monitor* (United States), *Times of India, Globe and Mail* (Canada), *The Washington Post* (United States), *The Daily Telegraph* (Britain), *Berlingske Tidende* (Denmark), and *La Prensa* (Argentina).

A book was written in 1965 by Danish writers Steen Albrectsen and Niels Holst which included a list of leading non-Danish dailies considered by the authors to be most important. This list showed a significant overlapping with the list obtained through the Merrill international survey just mentioned. The Albrectsen-Holst list follows:[17]

> *La Prensa* (Argentina); *Le Soir* and *Het Laatste Nieuws* (Belgium); *The Times, The Guardian,* and *The Telegraph* (Britain); *Helsingin Sanomat* and *Uusi Suomi* (Finland); *Combat, Le Figaro,* and *Le Monde* (France); *Algemeen Handelsblad, de Telegraaf* and *Nieuwe Rotterdamse Courant* (Holland); *Corriere della Sera* and *Il Messaggero* (Italy); *Asahi Shimbun* and *Mainichi* (Japan); *Borba* (Yugoslavia); *People's Daily* (China); *Aftenposten, Arbeiderbladet,* and *Dagbladet* (Norway); *The Christian Science Monitor, The* (Baltimore) *Sun,* New York *Herald Tribune, The New York Times, St. Louis Post-Dispatch, The Washington Post,* and *Chicago Tribune*

(United States); *Osservatore Romano* (Vatican City); *Frankfurter Allgemeine, Süddeutsche Zeitung,* and *Die Welt* (West Germany); *Neues Deutschland* (East Germany), and *Die Presse* (Austria).

One other list of great newspapers should be mentioned, and it is certainly one of the latest: the dailies included in Heinz-Dietrich Fischer's 1966 book, *Die grossen Zeitungen.* In this attractive paperback published in Munich, Fischer (of the Institut für Publizistik at the University of Münster) gives brief "portraits" of thirteen leading or great newspapers of the world but makes no attempt to rank them. Fischer's newspapers include representatives from the Communist world as well as from the non-Communist world, and it is interesting that all of them appear in one or more of the lists already given in this chapter. Without a doubt, they are all in the very top levels of the world's elite press. Fischer quite logically includes the Communist world's two most prestigious dailies—Russia's *Pravda* and Red China's *Jen-min Jih-pao* (People's Daily). *The New York Times* represents North America, and *La Prensa* of Buenos Aires represents South America. All the rest of Fischer's papers are from Europe—*Berlingske Tidende* (Denmark), *Neue Zürcher Zeitung* (Switzerland), *The Times* (Britain), *Die Presse* (Austria), *Corriere della Sera* (Italy), *Svenska Dagbladet* (Sweden), *Le Monde* (France), and *Die Welt* and *Frankfurter Allgemeine* (Germany).

Perhaps the heavy weighting of these outstanding newspapers toward Europe is natural considering Fischer's nationality and the tendency of European intellectuals to have an affinity for European serious journalism. Although from an American perspective, the Fischer book seems too European, there is absolutely no cause to argue with the papers which he selected for discussion. It should be noted that seven of the eleven free-world papers in Fischer's list were in the top papers of the 1965 Merrill survey of editors in ten countries.

Although this chapter indicates that there is some disharmony or variation in the newspapers various persons or groups would place in the elite category, and rankings are not correlated perfectly, it should appear obvious (and rather surprising) that such a high degree of consistency and agreement exists in regard to which newspapers should have places in the world's elite press. Even the same newspapers, although their rank order presents some variation, tend to consistently appear again and again in about the same position on a scale of quality. For something as subjective as evaluating journalistic greatness or eliteness, this would lead one to grant some validity or meaning to such listings and rankings by individual writers and survey panels.

Out of a study of surveys of others and considering his own serious endeavors to determine the world's leading dailies, the writer has attempted to develop a structure which will categorize the papers into levels of eliteness. An "Elite Press Pyramid" has been constructed largely on the basis of the recurrence of certain names in the lists and surveys which have been presented in this chapter. In this press pyramid (found at the end of the chapter), it will be noted that the various papers are placed in four levels, with the most qualitative or prestigious at the apex. Obviously such a press pyramid is subjective and crude, but as a result of considerable study and from longtime sampling of opinions of knowledgeable persons from all over the world, it appears to be quite realistic.

The pyramid of the elite papers rests on a large and very solid block of what are called "middle-area" newspapers which comprise about 99 per cent of all the world's dailies. These middle-area papers are, quite naturally, of many types and levels, but they are all general appeal papers with something for all types of readers. While many of them, gravitating upward toward the bottom of the pyramid, have many features of the elite, as a group they are more parochial than the elite, oriented toward local and national affairs and tending to use many entertainment features, bland editorials, and noninterpretative news. Below the middle-area newspapers is a rather small group of popular or mass (sensational-appeal) papers which are primarily entertainment-oriented with little or no appeal to the reader seeking serious information or interpretation.[18]

Out of all the world's dailies, there are probably no more than one hundred which belong in the elite fraternity and the pyramid is structured accordingly, with ten members in the *primary* level, twenty in the *secondary*, thirty in the *tertiary*, and forty in the *near-elite* category (which is considered part of the pyramid). So as we proceed to the next chapter which will present some basic patterns in the development of the world's elite, it will be useful to think about the press pyramid which follows and recognize that a diversity of elite types fall into each of the pyramid's levels.

THE MERRILL ELITE PRESS PYRAMID*

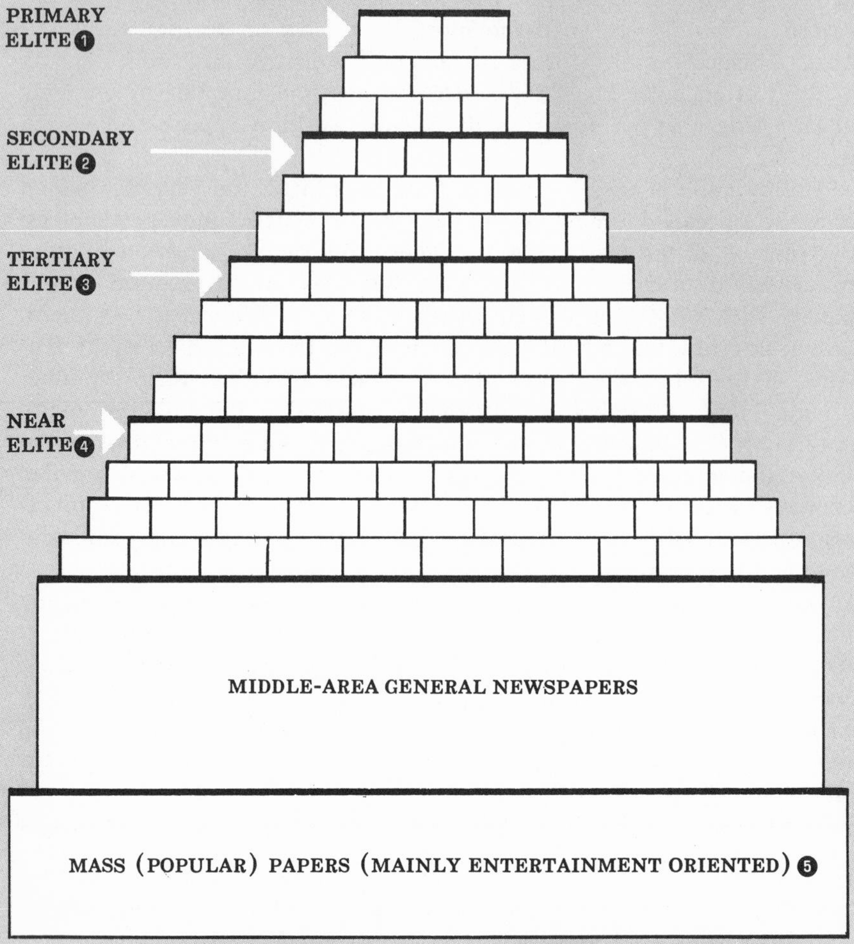

EXAMPLES:

❶ The New York Times • Le Monde • Pravda • ABC

❷ Washington Post • Die Welt • Asahi Shimbun

❸ The Scotsman • Svenska Dagbladet • Los Angeles Times Rand Daily Mail • The Age

❹ Novedades • Die Burger • Houston Post • O Globo

❺ Daily News • Daily Express • Bild Zeitung • France Soir

*NOTE: Certainly nobody should think that the papers listed in the "primary elite" group are all better than the ones in the "secondary elite" group; papers like *Pravda* and *Osservatore Romano* were admitted to the top group so that extremely prestigious dailies of a nonlibertarian nature would have proper representation. "Free press" advocates will not like this, of course, but this type of elite paper cannot be ignored.

Membership Structure of the "MERRILL ELITE PRESS PYRAMID"

PRIMARY ELITE (10): *The New York Times, Neue Zürcher Zeitung* (Zurich), *Le Monde* (Paris), *The Guardian* (London/Manchester), *The Times* (London), *Pravda* (Moscow), *Jen-min Jih-pao* (Peking), *Borba* (Belgrade), *Osservatore Romano* (Vatican City), *ABC* (Madrid).

SECONDARY ELITE (20): *Asahi Shimbun* (Tokyo), *Berlingske Tidende* (Copenhagen), *The Christian Science Monitor* (Boston), *Corriere della Sera* (Milan), *Dagens Nyheter* (Stockholm), *The Daily Telegraph* (London), *Die Presse* (Vienna), *Die Welt* (Hamburg), *Excélsior* (Mexico City), *Frankfurter Allgemeine* (Frankfurt), *The Globe and Mail* (Toronto), *Izvestia* (Moscow), *La Prensa* (Buenos Aires), *La Vanguardia Española* (Barcelona), *Le Figaro* (Paris), *O Estado de São Paulo* (Brazil), *The Statesman* (Calcutta), *St. Louis Post-Dispatch, The Washington Post, Yorkshire Post* (Leeds).

TERTIARY ELITE (30): *The Age* (Melbourne), *Aftenposten* (Oslo), *The* (Baltimore) *Sun, El Universal* (Mexico City), *Ha'aretz* (Tel Aviv), *Het Vrije Volk* (Amsterdam), *The Hindu* (Madras), *Il Messaggero* (Rome), *Johannesburg Star, Journal de Genève, Komsomolskaya Pravda* (Moscow), *La Nación* (Buenos Aires), *Los Angeles Times, Louisville Courier-Journal, Le Soir* (Brussels), *Ma'ariv* (Tel Aviv), *Mainichi* (Tokyo), *Miami Herald, Nieuwe Rotterdamse Courant, Nihon Keizei Shimbun* (Tokyo), *Novedades* (Mexico City), *Politika* (Belgrade), *Rand Daily Mail* (Johannesburg), *The Scotsman* (Edinburgh), *Süddeutsche Zeitung* (Munich), *Svenska Dagbladet* (Stockholm), *Times of India* (Bombay), *Voix du Nord* (Lille), *The Wall Street Journal* (New York), *Winnipeg Free Press* (Canada).

NEAR-ELITE (40): *Al Ahram* (Cairo), *Algemeen Handelsblad* (Amsterdam), *Atlanta Constitution, Cape Times* (Cape Town), *Chicago Tribune, Cleveland Plain Dealer, Cumhuriyet* (Istanbul), *Dallas Morning News, Denver Post, De Volksrant* (Amsterdam), *Diario de Noticias* (Lisbon), *Die Burger* (Cape Town), *El Comercio* (Lima), *El Mercurio* (Santiago), *El Tiempo* (Bogotá), *Globe-Democrat* (St. Louis), *Het Laatste Nieuws* (Brussels), *Helsingin Sanomat* (Helsinki), *Houston Post, Information* (Copenhagen), *Kansas City Star, Kathimerini* (Athens), *Kölnische Rundschau* (Cologne), *La Stampa* (Turin), *La Presse* (Montreal), *Le Progrès de Lyon, Milwaukee Journal, Manila Times, Minneapolis Tribune, Montreal Star, O Globo* (Rio), *Ouest-France* (Rennes), *Philadelphia Inquirer, Portland Oregonian, Rheinische Post* (Düsseldorf), *Ta Kung Pao* (Peking), *Tagesspiegel* (Berlin), *Times-Picayune* (New Orleans), *Toronto Daily Star, Westdeutsche Allgemeine* (Essen).

5

Patterns and Trends

Although the elite press of the world has been referred to as a "community," it is clearly an uneven, multifaceted one. A seriousness of tone and purpose and a high readership among influential persons are about the only common denominators of the elite press. The membership of the elite, because of differences in language, economic stability, freedom from government control, and basic philosophy, is splintered and fragmented and suffers from too little rapport and theoretical consensus. Thus, the world's elite press is heterogeneous and pluralistic in spite of its commonalities of seriousness, general civility, and influence. Struggling against great obstacles everywhere but with renewed hope and vigor, it is developing unevenly throughout the world. It falls roughly into at least three major patterns.

The first pattern is primarily *political or ideological.* Elite papers tend toward separation from government or they tend toward integration with government. While the free elite see themselves as independent agents, standing aloof from, and unaffected by, government, the authoritarian elite envision themselves as partners in government, cooperative agents of their government bent on carrying forth the sociopolitical system of their people.

Both groups of elite papers are dedicated to their philosophies and take their responsibilities, as they see them, quite seriously. It should be noted, however, that such a binary classification of the world's elite is too simple in reality and that all papers everywhere are free to varying degrees and restricted to varying degrees, although the character of the freedom and the restraint may differ significantly.

Many students of the press place considerable emphasis on social responsibility in determining the elite status of a newspaper. To what degree is the paper socially responsible? The answer to this question, to many, will largely determine the quality or eliteness of a newspaper. In the United States and other Western democracies social responsibility is thought of generally in terms of nonauthoritarianism or freedom from government control. In other words, social responsibility is the press utopia into which only libertarian-oriented papers may pass. This, however, seems much too simple a theory and is unsatisfactory in the modern world of fragmented and pluralistic serious journalism.

It is this writer's contention that all conscientious and serious newspapers, regardless of what nation or political ideology they may represent, are socially responsible. This idea was put forth in a paper in early 1965 and met with considerable objection from some quarters; however, it was also embraced by large numbers of persons who had previously failed to challenge the concept of press social responsibility being connected only to a libertarian press.[1] Why cannot the authoritarian press or the Communistic press claim to be socially responsible also? In fact, in certain respects, a newspaper would be more "responsible" if some type of governmental supervision existed; indeed, reporters could be kept from nosing about in critical areas during critical times. And, as the Russians are quick to point out, the amount of sensational material could be controlled in the press, or eliminated altogether. Government activities could always be supported and public policy could be pushed on all occasions. The press could be more educational in the sense that more news of art exhibits, concerts, national progress, and the like could be stressed. In short, the press would eliminate the negative and stress the positive. Then, with one voice the press of the nation would be responsible to its society; and the definition of responsible would be functional—defined and carried out in the context of the existing government and social structure.

So it seems realistic to believe that all newspapers (of any political system) which reflect the philosophy of their governmental system and try to present serious, educational reading fare are not only responsible to their society but are members of the elite press, or they are climbing into that select fraternity.

Assuming that a nation's sociopolitical philosophy determines its press system, and undoubtedly it does, then it follows that the nation's leading and most prestigious papers are socially responsible and form the elite. For example, the Marxist or Communist press system considers itself socially responsible, and certainly it is responsible to its own social system. A capitalistic press, operating in a pluralistic context, would be socially irresponsible if suddenly transplanted into the Communist country.

The same thing might be said of the so-called authoritarian press system, exemplified in Spain. A critical press such as found in the United States, a press which by its pluralistic nature would tend to undermine national policy and disrupt national harmony, would be anathema in a nation like Spain. It would be considered anything but responsible in that context. Newspapers of Spain, such as the most serious *ABC* and *Ya* of Madrid and *La Vanguardia Española* of Barcelona, are exceptionally responsible to the Spanish society; and, it should be added, they supply a surprising diversity of orientations and viewpoints *within the confines of the national policy.*[2] In other words, the elite press of a nation, even one under considerable governmental control, will still prove its eliteness through its subtleties, skillful restraint, and capacity to make the most of the situation in which it finds itself. In many ways, of course, it takes much more journalistic ability and acumen, as well as courage, to be an elite newspaper in a country such as Spain than in a country like Britain or Sweden.

A second important pattern among the world's elite, and one that is even more ragged than the political one just mentioned, is that of *economic diversity.*

This pattern, of course, is related to the political context, but actually it is quite different. For example, one elite paper in a libertarian nation can run into dire financial difficulties while another in the same country prospers and grows. An elite paper is not determined by how much property it owns or the profit it makes. Elite papers throughout the world exemplify a wide range of economic development and prosperity, but their overriding concern with serious news and views manifests itself quite apart from such differences in economic health.

Naturally, there is a point below which an elite paper (or any paper) may not fall and keep up its desired level of quality. Certainly, it must have the facilities to do good printing. It must be able to pay enough to get conscientious, well-educated staff members. It must be able to receive a variety of services from news agencies, as well as to collect much national and world news with its own correspondents. It must, therefore, either have a rather sizable circulation, or it must develop a special elite readership which will offset a small circulation. Although some elite papers like *Asahi Shimbun* of Japan and *Pravda* of the Soviet Union have tremendous circulations, most of the world's elite have only modest ones.[3] The elite newspaper (especially in a libertarian nation) runs the risk of lowering its quality when it makes a bid for larger readership, at least unless it does it very slowly. For it is the popular or mass press that is after the big circulations; the elite press is after readers of discernment and seriousness. Unfortunately for international rationality, the public, as Leo Rosten has said, "chooses the frivolous as against the serious, the lurid as against the tragic, the trivial as against fact, the diverting as against the significant." Rosten points out that very few people in any society "have reasonably good taste or care deeply about ideas" and that even fewer appear to be "equipped—by temperament and capacity, rather than education—to handle ideas with both skill and pleasure."[4] The elite press is unwilling to sacrifice its high purpose for a larger circulation which it might obtain by being more lively and readable in the sense of the popular press. Elite newspapers recognize that their readership will probably be small, but they know that it is unusually potent, sapient, and prestigious. It should be mentioned, however, that there are some few elite papers—in nations such as Sweden where the whole public is literate and uncommonly serious—which manage to be rational and serious and at the same time furnish all types of reading material.

The third pattern of the elite press is *geographical.* And this, of course, is closely related to national development. Most of the elite are published in developed or modern countries, although there are a few that represent the developing (modernizing) or transitional nations. A close look at the "Press Pyramid" at the end of the last chapter will show that Europe and North America are the principal homes of the elite newspapers. This is not surprising since these two continents are the most industrialized, the most technological, and the most literate of all the continents. As the economic bases become stabilized and literate and well-educated populations of other continents grow, the evenness of dispersion of the elite press throughout the world should improve significantly. Presently, however, elite newspapers are scattered about the earth in a very uneven fashion. This pattern of clusters and vast gaps greatly hinders the total impact of serious, concerned journalism in the world as a whole. It might be well to look more closely at this geographical pattern of the world's elite press.

Asia, with the exception of China, Japan, and India, is virtually without an elite press. Of the three, Japan stands out for its great progress in quality journalism, and popular journalism too, for that matter. *Asahi Shimbun* (see Chap. 18) is without a doubt the best quality daily in Japan and shows that an elite paper can, with editorial flexibility and sagacity, develop a large circulation within a free-market press. *Pravda* and its counterpart in Peking, *Jen-min Jih-pao*, of course, have fewer problems building circulation since Communist Party members and many others find that they need to have these daily journals of guidance and news. In India, the problems of the elite papers are much more acute than in either the U.S.S.R., China, or Japan. There are many reasons for this, but the chief one is probably the problem of too many languages. At present the major elite papers of India are published in English, understood only by the educated found mainly in a few of the large cities. And, even within the English-reading public, the circulation of the English elite is segmented since there are three very important elite dailies in the country—*The Statesman* of Calcutta, *The Hindu* of Madras, and the *Times of India* of Bombay. The vernacular languages of India, of which Hindi is the official one, have not caught on as press languages. Although there are a few well-written and edited papers in some of these dialects, they have little or no national or international prestige. To the language problem facing the development of the Indian elite press must be added these (generally applicable throughout Southeast Asia): low literacy rate, underdeveloped educational system, scarcity of training facilities and trained journalists, and old and inadequate printing equipment.

In Africa, with the exception of Egypt in the extreme northeast and the Republic of South Africa in the far south, there is no significant elite press;[5] and even in these two republics considerable governmental sensitivity has hindered development of a truly quality press. Egypt, with its nationalized newspapers, would, from a Western viewpoint, have to take second place to South Africa as a libertarian press nation with elite papers of a pluralistic nature. In South Africa, for example, in spite of government sensitivity to what it feels are press "excesses," the papers, especially those in English, show clearly that "the searchlights of inquiry and criticism are still able to shine, only slightly filtered, and to concentrate on those dark areas where a regime is most sensitive."[6] Without a doubt, South Africa has the freest newspapers on the continent, and within the English-language press are papers which are the equal in quality and tone to the elite of most nations of the world.

Johannesburg's morning *Rand Daily Mail* is a good example. It has consistently presented facts and opinion which has irritated the government, and has given its readers healthy portions of national and foreign news. Although most Afrikaans-language papers present a rather narrow progovernment picture, an important exception is *Die Burger* of Cape Town, committed generally to the policies of the Nationalist Party but often refreshingly independent and unconventional.[7] It is also interesting that in South Africa the freest papers, generally the English-language papers, have the largest circulations. For instance, the Johannesburg *Star* (about 170,000), has a circulation of almost double the combined circulations of the city's two Afrikaans papers, the *Transvaler* and the *Vaderland*.

The Egyptian press (which might better be considered part of the Middle Eastern press), has slowly but increasingly become a government-controlled press. In 1956 came the biggest blow to press freedom: President Nasser transferred the ownership of all papers to the National Union (the Government party) in order to assure popular support for his regime. And in 1960 the Egyptian papers were placed in groups or units, each having an administrative council appointed by the government. Nasser claims this is not nationalization; rather he sees it as giving the ownership to "the people." In spite of this nationalization (or "people's press") of the newspapers with accompanying restrictions, a few of the highly regarded old dailies of Cairo still provide their Arab readership with substantial amounts of serious journalism. For example, *Al Ahram* gives a good selection of news and features, and uses UPI and Reuters and other foreign agencies (and many interpretive articles on international affairs) to keep its cosmopolitan tone. Probably the most influential papers of the Arab world are still found in Egypt in spite of the fact that free, vigorous, and critical journalism has shifted from Cairo to Beirut, Lebanon.[8]

In the neighboring Middle East the press systems are mainly transitional, caught between the severe problems of many parts of Asia on one side and of Africa on the other. One hindrance to elite press development in this area is that these nations cannot decide whether to have their press systems (and governments) veer toward libertarianism or toward authoritarianism. Governments through the region are generally suspicious of the press and sensitive to its criticism. The press of Israel is probably improving faster than any other in the Middle East, and has been called the most "internationally minded in the world."[9] For instance, *Ma'ariv* of Tel Aviv, with a circulation of only about 100,000, subscribes to Reuters, UPI, AP, and the London *Daily Telegraph* services and has several correspondents and their families in foreign capitals.[10] And this paper, although the country's largest, is not as serious as others such as the staid *Ha'aretz* (discussed in Chap. 7).

Latin America, in spite of awesome economic and literacy problems, has somehow managed to develop a rather sizable group of elite newspapers. Without a doubt, this region of the world has a far more advanced press in all respects than is generally found in Asia and Africa. One obvious explanation for this is the fact that Spanish is the almost common language of the press in Latin America,[11] whereas in both Asia and Africa the polyglot of languages and dialects makes the development of newspapers of substantial influence and circulation extremely difficult, if not impossible.

Many Latin American dailies meet the demands of serious readers for percipient journalism; most every major nation south of the United States has at least one journal which is in, or aspires to, the elite press. Argentina has its *La Nación* and *La Prensa*, Chile its *Mercurio*, Peru its *Comercio*, Colombia its *Tiempo*, and Mexico its outstanding trio—*Excélsior*, *Novedades*, and *El Universal*. These and many other serious dailies of Latin America do an outstanding job of providing large proportions of scientific and humanistic news and views, with much emphasis on foreign affairs. Perhaps the Latin American serious press, like its ancestral press of Iberia, places undue stress on philosophical, theological, and literary discussion; but this is simply an intellectual Latin proclivity and the elite press does well to serve it.

In Oceania, Australia alone has a press which includes newspapers of the elite type. Barriers to press growth in this sprawling island region are mainly (1) small populations, (2) technological underdevelopment, (3) scarcity of trained journalists, and (4) geographical isolation from the mainstream of international concerns. In Australia several papers might be included among the elite and several others are aspirants. *The Age* of Melbourne is usually considered the most serious and influential with the country's power elite. Even a paper like the same city's *Herald*, which is an afternoon journal which does not avoid some appeal to all classes, furnishes some 500,000 readers a day a substantial diet of serious material. Its economic coverage and its weekly book page are especially laudable. Its international emphasis is reflected by the fact that in 1966 it had 24 foreign correspondents stationed in 17 cities. *The Australian*, begun in 1964, has become an excellent national daily with its offices in several cities.

In North America (above the Mexican border) the elite press thrives. Whereas Canadian elite tend to cluster in that country's South, especially in Toronto and Montreal, the elite of the United States are rather well dispersed throughout the country. *The Globe and Mail* of Toronto, with a circulation of 230,000, is Canada's only truly national daily. The same city's *Daily Star* is the country's largest (about 340,000) and contains much serious material, although it displays it in a rather sensational manner. Canadian newspaper makeup is much closer to that typically found in the United States than it is to that of Britain. Montreal's evening *La Presse*, a comprehensive afternoon daily with an exceptionally fine weekend edition, is the largest French-language daily in the Western Hemisphere. In Winnipeg, Manitoba, the *Free Press* provides excellent international coverage and national coverage of the central and western portions of Canada.

Although there are elite and near-elite papers in every major section of the United States, most of them are concentrated along the East Coast and in the Middle West and around the fringes of the South. In the East are such sophisticated dailies as *The New York Times, The Washington Post, The Christian Science Monitor, The* (Baltimore) *Sun,* and *The Miami Herald*. In the Middle West a few of the leaders among the elite are the *St. Louis Post-Dispatch*, the *Minneapolis Tribune, The Des Moines Register,* and *The Kansas City Star*. In Kentucky, there is *The Courier-Journal* of Louisville; in Georgia, *The Atlanta Constitution*; in Louisiana, the New Orleans *Times-Picayune*; in Texas, *The Dallas Morning News* and the *Houston Post*. Quality papers of national and international prestige tend to fade out in the plains and mountain area of the West, with *The Denver Post* ruling a vast empire from its strategic position. Along the West Coast, there are several good dailies but the *Los Angeles Times* and *The Oregonian* of Portland are probably the best.

If the press of North America is well developed and the elite papers numerous, the press of Europe (western Europe) might be said to be overdeveloped and the elite papers very numerous. From Scandinavia to Spain, and from Britain to Russia, elite dailies (and weeklies) spread their serious journalism into every corner of the continent and, increasingly, into distant lands. The elite dailies of Europe are probably the most erudite and knowledgeable in the world, providing insights which Quincy Howe (first editor of the United States' *Atlas*) has said are available nowhere else.[12] European papers, says Howe, "speak with authority" and it is not only a matter "of Germans reporting on Germany, French on France and British on Britain," but also "of Germans writing about the French, the French writing about the British, the British writing about the Germans."[13]

And delving further into the reasons behind the European press sagacity and cosmopolitanism, Howe says that it is important to remember that

> the British have had long experience in India and China; the French in North Africa and Southeast Asia, and the Germans in Latin America, the Middle East and Southwest Africa. And the Italians and Swiss have travelled, worked, and settled everywhere. Their newspapers and the people who write for them—even the people who read them—reflect this interest and experience.

All types of quality papers are to be found in Europe. There are the free elite of most of western Europe, led by the superserious *Neue Zürcher Zeitung* of Switzerland, *Le Monde* of France, *The Times* and *The Guardian* of Britain, and *Frankfurter Allgemeine* of West Germany. There are the authoritarian elite of Spain such as *ABC* and *La Vanguardia Española*, and the Communist elite such as *Pravda* and *Izvestia* of Russia and *Borba* and *Politika* of Yugoslavia. There are the dailies of Scandinavia such as Oslo's *Aftenposten*, Copenhagen's *Berlingske Tidende*, and Stockholm's *Dagens Nyheter* that combine a rather flashy typographical dress with a heavy diet of serious news and views. There are also such dailies as *Die Welt* of Hamburg and *Corriere della Sera* of Milan which are able to combine a modern demeanor with a solid seriousness. And, of course, there is the stolid drabness of ultraseriousness to be found in the daily of Vatican City, *Osservatore Romano*. The European elite press offers the reader a wide selection of packaging and political orientation; there is a paper whose journalistic style and philosophy, as well as size, layout, and typographical tone, appeal to any kind of serious newspaper reader.

In addition to the elite daily papers with which this book deals, it should be remembered that many excellent elite weekly papers exist in a number of countries (most of them in Europe) which reinforce the international concern and reasonableness of the elite dailies. No one should minimize the extremely high-type journalism of such papers as the London *Observer* and *Sunday Times*, the *National Observer* of the United States, *Weltwoche* of Zurich, *Embros* of Athens, *Le Canard Enchaîné* of Paris, *Die Zeit* of Hamburg, *Christ und Welt* of Stuttgart, *Rheinische Merkur* of Cologne, *Jeune Afrique* of Tunis, and *The Nation* of Rangoon.

And, of course, adding to reasonable and serious international journalism, though probably not as substantially as the elite newspapers, are the well-edited weekly news magazines of the *Time-Newsweek-U.S. News & World Report* variety sprinkled around the world—notably *Der Spiegel* of West Germany, *L'Express* of France, *Tiempo* of Mexico, *Link* of India, *Veritas* of Argentina, *Reporter* of Kenya, *Akis* of Turkey, and *Shukan Asahi* of Japan.

It is interesting to note that in the areas of the world where daily journalism is most advanced and there are many elite newspapers, there are also the largest numbers of journalism schools, press institutes, and training programs of one type or another. This concern with, or emphasis on, journalism education is coupled with a high development of education generally. In the underdeveloped nations, such as are common in Asia and Africa, the little emphasis on journalistic training which has been begun is still concerned chiefly with the technical aspects of journalism: typesetting, printing, newsprint acquisition, and the overcoming of basic economic handicaps. On the other hand, in the more advanced nations where the elite press is strongest, these elemental problems are secondary in journalism education and a concern with editorial quality, ethical standards, and social responsibility come in for more consideration. This nontechnical and noneconomic emphasis or approach inevitably results in a higher quality journalism.

So far in this book very little has been said about the natures of individual elite or near-elite papers except in the general way of noting common denominators of emphasis and characteristics of makeup and content. Many of the elite papers, with representatives from the four levels of the "Elite Press Pyramid" (Chap. 4), will be discussed, albeit briefly, in the next four chapters. And in Part II of the book, a few of the elite will be examined in more detail.

The purpose of the four chapters which follow, and for that matter of Part II which looks more closely at some of the elite papers, is not to present exhaustive histories or analyses of the elite; rather, the aim is to offer a brief view of typical elite papers in an attempt to highlight their common and differentiating characteristics. An underlying purpose, and perhaps the most important one, is to show that among the thousands of daily papers of the world, there are conscientious and intelligent journals dedicated to serious discourse and bound together by invisible cords into a fraternity of prestige and excellence.

6

Profiles: Western Europe

Europe is well supplied with elite newspapers of many varieties, typifying the entire spectrum of distinguished journalism from controlled prestige journals to independent quality organs. It is safe to say that the serious newspaper reader of Europe, the one who desires intellectual stimulation and interpretation as well as entertainment and information, has around him the world's widest selection of daily papers to satisfy his demand. Also, the reader who desires to have access to daily journals which provide him with reliable guidance of a social, political, or religious nature will have them in profusion in Europe.

While it is true that Europe exemplifies popular or mass-appeal (entertainment-oriented) journalism on a grand scale with such dailies as the *Daily Mirror*, *Bild-Zeitung*, and *France-Soir* commanding huge readerships, it is also true that no other comparable geographical segment of the world has so many elite newspapers which are taken so seriously by so many people.

Profiles of eight daily newspapers from Western Europe appear in this chapter, representing Great Britain, Sweden, Norway, Spain, France, and Italy. Certainly these (and others presented in Part II) are not all of the elite papers of Western Europe, but the number selected as well as the particular ones selected should give an indication of the proportion of great dailies in this region as well as an insight to their characteristics and heritage.

The profiles of this chapter (and of the three which follow) are presented in alphabetical order. They are brief profiles, presenting what is felt to be significant historical data combined with something of the current status of the journals. It is hoped that they will provide a useful introduction to these outstanding newspapers and will serve as a stimulus to those readers who would like to delve deeper into them.

Newspapers discussed in this chapter are these: *ABC*, Spain; *Aftenposten*, Norway; *Dagens Nyheter*, Sweden; *Le Figaro*, France; *The Scotsman*, Scotland; *La Stampa*, Italy; *Svenska Dagbladet*, Sweden, and *The Yorkshire Post*, England.

ABC
(SPAIN)

Serrano 61 in Madrid is the headquarters of Spain's most prestigious daily, with a daily circulation very close to 200,000 and a Sunday edition passing the 240,000 mark.[1] An edition of the paper is also published in Seville (begun in 1929), circulating some 70,000 copies.[2] *ABC*, a small tabloid openly advocating Spain's return to the Monarchy, might be considered a combination picture paper and general news-feature paper. Although the first pages comprise a picture magazine section in rotogravure, its inside pages provide very thorough (for Spain) news coverage neatly compartmentalized.

ABC was founded as a weekly in 1903 by Torcuato Luca de Tena y Alvárez-Ossorio. On June 1, 1905, it was converted to a daily in a three-column tabloid format with solid news on the front page. The first daily issue stated that "*ABC* is a newspaper of general information" but indicated that pictures would be stressed.[3] It has always had a political and literary emphasis and the quality of its writing (especially in many of its frequent contributed pieces) is considered throughout Spain as the country's best. Many of Spain's foremost intellectuals and literary figures have written for *ABC*. Its founder, without a doubt, ranks in Spanish journalism history as one of the two or three greatest journalists.

The newspaper began the use of photoengravings in the Spanish daily press; it has pioneered in many other areas also. For example, it was the first Spanish tabloid, the first to have so many pages, and the first to use rotogravure printing. Its language has always been intense and precise, and it has set the tone of all Spanish journalistic writing. Its vigorous journalistic style which to a large extent has been accepted as a sort of "formula" in Spanish journalism was largely established by José Cuartero (1869–1946). Cuartero never wasted a word, and his articles were forceful and expressive—especially his political editorials.[4]

DIARIO EDITADO POR PRENSA ESPAÑOLA, SOCIEDAD ANONIMA MADRID

ABC

REDACCION, ADMINISTRACION Y TALLERES: SERRANO, 61

FUNDADO EN 1905 POR DON TORCUATO LUCA DE TENA

SALESIANISMO

CON este nombre designo el gran movimiento educador de la juventud obrera promovido en nuestros días por San Juan Bosco, que vivió de 1815 a 1888.

La vida y la obra de San Juan Bosco es una de las que más tangiblemente se señalan como asistidas de la Providencia divina. Nacido Juan Bosco en la aldea de Bechi, a cinco leguas de Turín, en una familia humildísima y una casita que he tenido el gusto de visitar, se mostró desde sus primeros años dotado de prendas religiosas, morales e intelectuales muy relevantes, pero que, dada la penuria de medios de su familia parecían abocadas a la esterilidad. Con la ayuda de unos y de otros, sin embargo, Juan Bosco fue aprendiendo las primeras letras en la escuela de Castelnuovo, la segunda enseñanza en el Liceo de Chieri e iniciándose al sacerdocio en el Seminario de Turín, donde se ordenó.

La peculiaridad de su apostolado se revela desde sus primeros días. Aficionado desde chico a los juegos de acrobacia, prestidigitación y similares, pronto se vio rodeado de "birichini", o sea, de golfillos abandonados a los que recogió para enseñarles el catecismo y las oraciones, a la par que les adiestraba en juegos y oficios y les moralizaba en sus costumbres. La turba alborotada de aquellos centenares de muchachos no fue muy del agrado del ambiente ciudadano, incluso de las autoridades, que trataron primero de frenar al promotor de todo aquello, y luego de imposibilitar su labor echándoles de las calles, de los patios y hasta de las iglesias a que se acogían. La hostilidad a Don Bosco llegó hasta la agresión personal.

Contra viento y marea, Don Bosco se impuso creando el Oratorio festivo, inspirado en los Oratorios de San Felipe Neri, y poco a poco fue cobrando el favor del pueblo, de los poderosos y de los príncipes, y hasta del Sumo Pontífice, que aprobó su labor. Esta cuajó finalmente en una institución permanente, la de la Congregación Salesiana, masculina y femenina, que hoy cuenta ya en el mundo con más de 20.000 miembros varones y un número prodigioso de centros de enseñanza. Sólo en España tiene ya siete provincias, cada una de las cuales alberga numerosos Institutos.

La particularidad de la enseñanza salesiana es la llamada profesional. Cada día más el trabajo humano se va especializando, o sea, aplicándose la tarea en las que se aborda la fabricación de un artículo determinado o la producción de un artefacto de la gran industria, que integrado con otros nos brinda la maravilla técnica actual. El salesianismo se caracteriza por la creación de centros donde cultivan los trabajadores labores de oficialía y de maestría que les permiten ejecutar tareas cada vez más difíciles y minuciosas y de dirección de los que las ejecutan. Recientemente se ha creado en Rentería una Ciudad Laboral con más de mil alumnos que se inician a varias importantes modalidades de la industria en talleres espléndidamente dotados, gracias a la generosidad de la Caja de Ahorros de Guipúzcoa. Y en Urnieta, otro pueblo de esta laboriosa provincia, se está terminando un gran Instituto de Maestros de Taller, dotado de los últimos adelantos en la materia.

Pero con esta labor de enseñanza profesional no ha echado en olvido el salesianismo la de la escuela primaria (y aun la secundaria), en la que, junto a la función docente, gratuitamente dada, se reúnen los chicos el domingo en el Oratorio festivo, con toda clase de diversiones que les entretienen y mantienen adictos a sus deberes religiosos y prácticas de piedad.

Esta conjunción del aprendizaje con el juego es otra de las características del salesianismo, la que más popular le hace donde quiera que actúa; sus antiguos alumnos no lo olvidan y frecuentan sus casas durante toda su vida.

San Juan Bosco no fue solamente un formidable hombre de acción, sino también de pensamiento. Predicó, escribió en periódicos, publicó libros en los que se traduce toda su pedagogía. La pedagogía de San Juan Bosco se señala ante todo como asociación de la tarea escolar con el juego, que ha pasado mucho tiempo por ser un desahogo vital pero inútil para la vida, pero que actualmente es considerado como el mejor orientador vocacional del niño y del adolescente y el mejor entrenador de su formación. A esto se agrega en él la pretensión de ganarse al alumno por la persuasión y la enseñanza y por el ejemplo y modelo de quien se la da en su vida. Lo menos posible de castigos y nunca corporales ni denigrantes por su publicidad. Por todos estos conceptos la pedagogía de San Juan Bosco se halla en la vanguardia de la pedagogía moderna. La ciencia pedagógica es cultivada por los salesianos en su prestigioso Colegio Superior de Roma.

Pero destaca el salesianismo sobre todo por su espléndida labor en el dominio de la enseñanza profesional. Esta enseñanza aventaja a la general en que, aplicándose a una tarea muy circunscrita de la industria, le hace al alumno en ella un maestro capaz de una mayor perfección en su labor que si se dedicara a formas variadas de ella. Tiene ello, sin embargo, un inconveniente, y es el mutilar la formación del alumno en cuestión en orden al complejo de la formación humana. Los especialistas salen muy peritos en los oficios de montador, de tornero, de tipógrafo, de electricista y de otros por el estilo—y lo mismo podríamos decir de las profesiones intelectuales de abogacía, de ingeniería o de medicina—, pero olvidados de su condición de hombres. El salesianismo, a la par que forma sus especialistas, no descuida el abrirles a los problemas y soluciones fundamentales de la vida humana, intelectual, moral y religiosa.

Digna de admiración, y sobre todo de protección, es la labor de la Congregación Salesiana en sus dos ramas, masculina y femenina. No se da esta labor sólo en el ambiente de la Europa y América, ya ganadas al cristianismo, sino también en las Misiones que sostienen en otros continentes y que no podemos detallar aquí. Baste lo dicho para darnos una sucinta idea de cuanto se encierra en la palabra que rotula este artículo.

Juan ZARAGUETA

Others of *ABC*'s staff, like Alfonso Rodríquez Santa Maria who is considered the most forceful and versatile writer in Spain in recent years, have carried on the newspaper's concern for quality writing.

Today *ABC* is thought of as a Spanish institution. Its readership extends beyond Spain, and its modern airmail edition which was launched in 1950 has constantly grown in popularity.[5] *ABC*, existing as it does today in an authoritarian regime, has learned to temper its onetime fiery political pieces and has tried to keep its quality up in noncontroversial areas. Its cultural features of many types and its literary critiques are extremely good and much of its photography is outstanding in the context of the newspaper press. While its quality of printing and the layout of its pages are not up to the standard of most elite dailies, its many and varied news features and its emphasis on literature, music, and philosophy give it an aura of intellectualism and quality that compensates to a large degree for its deficiencies in "hard news" and general technical matters.[6]

The newspaper today has fifty-one writers and editors, forty-three regular collaborators (contributors), sixty correspondents throughout Spain, and nine foreign correspondents. A large proportion of *ABC*'s editorial space is given over to foreign reportage; most of this material comes from the nine correspondents abroad in Bonn, Buenos Aires, Lisbon, London, Paris, Rome, Saigon, Tangiers, and Washington. Other material, of course, comes from the Spanish news agency "Efe" and agencies with which it has exchange agreements.[7]

ABC's top asset probably is its large group of famous contributors who write for its pages stimulating pieces on a wide variety of subjects. Its group of critical writers are the best in Spanish journalism—Melchor F. Almagro (books), A. Marquerie (theater), M. P. Ferrero (movies), Camón Aznar (art), F. Cid (music), and D. Cañabate (bullfighting). Then there are several talented, versatile collaborators such as Cézar González Ruano who is able to write on almost any subject with power and charm.[8]

The paper's founder directed its activities until 1929 when he died.[9] His son, Ignacio, directed the paper until 1939. From that date until 1947 the director was José Losada de la Torre. He was succeeded by Ramón Pastor y Medívil, who quit as director in 1952 in favor of the founder's grandson, Torcuato Luca de Tena y Brunet, who remained at the helm for two years. Luis Calvo Andaluz took over the directorship in 1954 and remained in that position until 1962 when Luca de Tena y Brunet returned to head the paper. He holds the position today.[10]

ABC's history has not been without vicissitudes. For speaking out strongly in favor of the Monarchy, it was taken over by the Republican Government in May, 1931. The paper, even while watched closely by the Government, proved to be a maverick and in August, 1932, it was suspended for nearly four months for urging less censorship by the Republican Government. Then again in June, 1936, the Government stepped in, this time actually taking over the building of "Prensa Española, S.A." (the publishing company that printed *ABC* and other publications).[11] The entire editorial and printing organization of *ABC* was held under tight control of the Republicans until Madrid was "liberated" by Franco's forces in March, 1939.[12]

Since the advent of Franco's Government, *ABC* has suffered like the rest of the Spanish newspapers from stringent press laws but it has continued its advocacy of a return of the Monarchy and has tried to offset its inability to have pungent and critical political articles by improving the quality of its nonpolitical pieces and pictures in noncontroversial areas. In the context of Spain and all authoritarian press systems of the present century, *ABC* would have to be considered an "elite" newspaper in that it contains some of the best prose in Spain and is taken seriously by all elements of Spanish society. Within the bounds permitted (and these bounds are expanding all the time), *ABC* exercises considerable courage and skill in making its voice heard—even with sly critical undertones—in important places in Spain.

Aftenposten

(NORWAY)

The most prestigious daily of Norway, and certainly one of the four or five best in all Scandinavia, is Oslo's *Aftenposten* (Evening Post). It is also the country's largest circulation daily with a morning circulation of some 185,000 and an evening circulation of about 150,000. No Sunday edition is published, in keeping with the general Norwegian practice, but the big weekend edition on Saturday circulates some 200,000 copies.[1]

Like most Norwegian newspapers, *Aftenposten* has no formal party affiliation, but does favor the Conservative Party. Its main ideological competitor is Norway's second largest paper, *Dagbladet* of Oslo, a liberal afternoon paper with a circulation of about 90,000.[2] If any Norwegian daily might be considered a national paper it is *Aftenposten*. At least 60,000 copies circulate outside Oslo on weekdays and perhaps as many as 80,000 on Saturdays.

A standard-format, eight-column paper founded in 1860, *Aftenposten* averages thirty pages for its morning issues and twelve for its evening editions. Advertising accounts for some 55 per cent of the morning editions and about 45 per cent of the evening issues. The paper uses four colors in advertisements quite often, and places some advertising on its front page, relegating it to the bottom portion. Its makeup is neat and

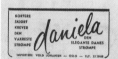

Aftenposten

Aftennummer 80 øre. Fredag 15. september 1967. 108. årgang. Nr. 426.

Særpensjon til de eldste 1968

Barnefamilienes økonomi styrket siden 1965

Sosialdepartementet regner med i løpet av 1968 å ha løst spørsmålet om en inntektsøkning for de grupper av trygdede som efter folketrygdloven ikke får tilleggspensjon, opplyste statssekretær Kåre Kristiansen i et foredrag i Rakkestad igår kveld. Økningen vil gjelde dem som er født før 1898, og vil bli gitt enten som en hevning av grunnpensjonen, eller en form for tilleggspensjon. Det arbeides for tiden sterkt med saken i Sosialdepartementet, sa statssekretæren. En tre-barnsfamilie har under samarbeidsregjeringen fått en reell forbedring i sin nettoinntekt på 6,9 prosent,

Fortsatt side 2 (2)

Godværet holder i helgen, men så mere usikkert

Det går mot slutten av den fine godværsperioden vi har hatt nu. Høytrykksryggen svekkes og går østover. Likevel kan

Fortsatt side 2 (1)

Med Oslo rådhus og enda litt til på dekket

Rådhuset servert ytterst på et brett, — det er virkningen fotograf Rolf Chr. Ulrichsen har oppnådd. «Brettet» er i dette tilfelle helikopter-dekket på boreskipet «Drillship» — ex «Thorshøvdi» — som nu ligger ved Nylands Verksted. Ombyggingen av hvalkokeriet til verdens største boreskip har vært omfattet med stor interesse i olje- og skipsbyggerkretser. Det eies av Drill Ship Ltd., London, er chartret av Drill Sea Associates, Texas, hvor A/S Akers Drilling Company Ltd. er medeier. «Drillship» skal bore for Amoco-Noco i den norske sektor i Nordsjøen. Tradisjonsrike «Thorshøvdi» hadde 17 sesonger bak seg i Antarktis. I sitt nye «liv» i oljeleternes tjeneste, er fartøyet blitt en av de mest moderne boreenheter i verden.

Tariffoppgjøret for varehandel inn i kritisk fase

Sannsynlig at det kommer til brudd på lønnskravet i løpet av dagen

Forhandlingene mellom Handelens Arbeidsgiverforening og Norges Handels- og Kontorfunksjonærers Forbund om ny landsoverenskomst for ansatte i varehandelen, går idag inn i en avgjørende fase.

Efter flere dagers forhandlinger er man nu kommet frem til selve hovedspørsmålet — lønnstillegget. Et engere utvalg fra begge sider kom sammen kl. 9

Fortsatt side 2 (4)

Roma trues av konkurs, kassen tom

Roma, 15. sept.

(AP) Hvis bystyret i Roma ikke klarer å skaffe til veie 150 millioner kroner før 1. oktober, vil byen gå konkurs for første gang i historien.

I et desperat brev til Italias finansminister Emilio Colombo, offentliggjort idag, ber borgermester Americo Petrucci om øyeblikkelig hjelp slik at Roma kan reddes fra økonomisk katastrofe.

Hvis ikke borgermesterens bønn blir oppfylt, vil romerne måtte klare seg uten busser, politikonstabler, renovasjonsarbeidere og andre ansatte i kommunen — hvis disse ikke går med på å arbeide gratis, selvfølgelig.

Innen 1. oktober må Roma betale lønningen til 40 000 ansatte.

„Lederne i Sovjet lavtstående lus"

Ny salve mot Kreml i kinesisk avis

Tokyo, 15. september.

(AP) — Folkets Dagblad innrømmet igår at kineserne liker krig og beskrev de sovjetiske lederne som «en bande lavtstående lus» fordi de ikke går inn for væpnede konflikter.

I en artikkel av Chung Hsian i Hang i formann Mao Tse-tungs hovedorgan het det videre at «alle revisjonister i historien har uten unntagelse fart med løst snakk om revolusjon, men har alltid gått imot revolusjonære tendenser».

Chung gikk hardt i rette med organet for den sovjetiske hær, Røde stjerne, for at dette har bragt en artikkel hvor betydningen av krig under revolusjon ble bagatellisert.

— Politisk makt gror ut av en kanon-munning, skrev Chung som dermed siterte en av Maos læresetninger. — Det faktum at den sovjetiske revisjonist-klikken har utviklet en læresetning som går imot bruk av våpen, beviser hvor lavt moralen har sunket i Sovjet-Samveldet. Du usle feiging som Røde stjerne har skrevet at kineserne liker krig, du har faktisk rett på dette punkt. Vi liker kriger som utkjempes av de revolusjonære masser. Dette viser at vi trofast holder oss til marxist-leninismens prinsipper.

Barnetrygd også til ett-barnsfamiliene?

Venstre tar for seg familienes stilling

Det er tydelig at den generelle stønads- og skattepolitikk ikke har tatt tilstrekkelig hensyn til den ekstra økonomiske belastning som hviler på større familier, heter det i en innstilling fra Venstres utvalg for familiepolitiske spørsmål. Utvalget, som fremla sin utredning på en pressekonferanse i middags, har påvist at familier med barn har en meget lavere levestandard enn familier uten barn og enslige. For å rette på disse forhold, har utvalget vurdert en rekke tiltak og påpeker bl. a. at det bør overveies om familier med ett barn skal ha barnetrygd og at barnetrygden bør utbetales til barna er fylt 18 år.

Fortsatt side 2 (3)

Farlig etsende væske solgt som amerikansk olje

En mann som onsdag eftermiddag kjøpte en flaske amerikansk olje på Fredriksvern Apotek i Stavern, oppdaget like efter at flasken istedet inneholdt vannstoffhyperoksyd i konsentrert form. Han skulle akkurat til å svelge den munnfull han hadde tatt, da det plutselig begynte å etse i munnen. Han fikk spyttet ut væsken. Mannen går nå til legebehandling.

Fra lensmannskontoret i Stavern er det sendt ut en advarsel gjennom kringkastingen til alle sommergjester som var i distriktet, og handlet amerikansk olje på apote-

Fortsatt side 2 (5)

Norge sett med satellittens „øye"

Slik ser Norge ut fra himmelrommet, fra 140 mils høyde. Bildet er tatt fra værsatellitten «ESSA 4» i mai måned, mens sneen i fjelltraktene ennu gav god kontrastvirkning til de mørke havområder utenfor vår kystlinje. Man ser tydelig Sognefjorden og Hardangerfjorden som er avmerket slik at man bedre skal få «landkjenning». Hvis rotasjonspressen farer vel med bildet skulle man kunne bestemme en lang rekke andre fjorder i bildet, fordi de avtegner seg som mørke forgreninger mot de lysere partier. Bildet er hentet fra Meteorologisk Institutt, hvor man hittil har fått værfotos fra satellittene formidlet fra Danmark. Til høsten skal forbindelsene fra satellittene tas direkte inn på Blindern.

USA betrakter Hanois fredsinteresse med tvil

Hanoi har hittil ikke gitt offisielle antydninger om forandret holdning

Washington, 15. september.

(New York Times) En melding fra Hanoi om at den nord-vietnamesiske regjering skal ha slått av på sine betingelser for fred i Vietnam, er foreløbig blitt møtt med skepsis på offisielt hold i den amerikanske hovedstaden. Det franske telegrambyrået AFP har meldt at pålitelige kilder i Hanoi sier at forhandlinger mellom amerikanere og nord-vietnamesere kunne komme i gang tre eller fire uker efter at bombingen av Nord-Vietnam opphører.

Meldingen fra Hanoi sitere bl. a. en uttalelse av Nord-Vietnams statsminister Pham Van Dong den 30. august, hvor det het: — Dersom

Fortsatt side 2 (8)

Plan om å sjøsette Nelsons „Victory"

Skipet har siden 1922 ligget i tørrdokk

Fra Aftenpostens London-kontor
London, 15. september

(Nils Morten Udgaard) Skal admiral Nelsons flaggskip «HMS Victory» på ny stikke til sjøs og pløye bølgene i Kanalen under sine 4800 brusende kvadratmeter av hvite seil? For «Victory»s kaptein idag, kommandørkaptein Dick Whittington, har dette lenge vært en stor og hemmelig drøm.

Nu har han erklært at hans høyeste ønske er å se den 2162 tonn store «Victory» på sjøen igjen. — Tanken har opptatt meg i svært lang tid. Jeg er sikker på at det vil

Fortsatt side 2 (7)

Underslag av ialt 165 000 kr. ved el-verk i Vestfold

Fra Aftenpostens korrespondent,
Tønsberg, 15. september.

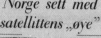

Foreløbige undersøkelser viser at et tidligere omtalt underslag foretatt av en kvinnelig kasserer, 21 år, ved Hofs El-verk i Vestfold beløper seg til ca. 165 000 kroner, fremgikk det av kommunerevisors melding, som ble referert i Hof herredsstyres møte igår. Beløpet fordeler seg med ca. 51 000 kroner på regnskapsåret 1966 og 114 000 kroner på inneværende år.

Av fylkesrevisors rapport om sa-

Fortsatt side 2 (9)

Hellas-spørsmålet inn for menneskerettskonvensjonen

Regjeringen ga i statsråd idag samtykke til at spørsmålet om hvorvidt den greske regjering har overtrådt bestemmelsene i den europeiske konvensjon om beskyttelse av menneskerettigheter og de grunnleggende friheter, skal innbringes for den europeiske menneskerettskommisjon.

Samtidig fikk Utenriksdepartementet fullmakt til å oppnevne en agent til å representere Norge ved behandlingen av saken for den europeiske menneskerettskommisjon.

Skal alle kvinner bli „fru"

Venstres utvalg for familiepolitiske spørsmål — som avgav sin innstilling imiddags — beskjeftiger seg bl. a. med de enslige og ufullstendige familier og hevder i den forbindelse at det ikke lenger er grunnlag for å

Fortsatt side 2 (6)

attractive and three colors are often used on its front pages—generally yellow, blue, and red. Like many Scandinavian papers, *Aftenposten* seems to combine the best of German-style makeup with the best of the United States-style and comes up with a very pleasing result. Like other Scandinavian papers, its pages are agglutinated at the fold.

Reflecting a general pattern in Swedish papers, *Aftenposten* is strong on art, music, literary, and other cultural material. This material is presented on well-made-up pages giving the immediate impression of seriousness and responsibility. In respect to foreign news, *Aftenposten* is the largest Norwegian paper as regards the number of sources, amount of copy printed, and the amount of wordage received. From *Norsk Telegrambyra*, the Norwegian national news agency which subscribes to *Reuters* and *Agence France-Press* and a few other agencies, it receives some 25,000 words a day; from *The New York Times* news service the paper gets about 25,000 additional words daily. *Aftenposten* is the only Norwegian paper which gets this copy which includes columnists like James Reston.[3]

From the Associated Press it gets 10,000 words; from the United Press International, about 8,000. About 10 per cent of *The New York Times* copy is used, and about the same amount of the United Press International copy. It is difficult to tell about the other sources, but a breakdown of foreign copy printed during the first four months of 1966 shows that *The New York Times* was the source for 21.5 per cent of its foreign news, United Press International 11.5 per cent, and all others (including *Norsk Telegrambyra*, the national agency) 57 per cent. *Aftenposten* has its own correspondents of full-time status in Bonn, London, Paris, and Washington. Other foreign reporters, of a part-time or "pool" type, serve the paper from Rome, Copenhagen, Stockholm, Moscow, and a few other important world centers.[4]

The editorial staff comprises three chief editors and seven subordinate editors. Three staffers serve the business page, three the family page, six the arts and culture page, two the automotive page, seven the political page, and forty are general reporters. Seven are on the sports desk, nine on the foreign desk, and fifteen on what is called the central desk in the main editorial office. Counting the full-time foreign correspondents, there are close to 125 full-time editorial workers on *Aftenposten*. Morale of staff members is very high. In addition to the pride felt in working for so influential a paper, the *Aftenposten* employee can expect many fringe benefits, some of which are quite unusual—such as the fact that the paper continues to pay wages to its employees who are ill, regardless of how many months or years the sickness lasts.[5]

Although *Aftenposten* favors the Conservative Party of Norway, it does not evidence an inflexible attitude and its party partiality is not as strong as that of some of the other papers. Perhaps the most anti-Communistic of the major Norwegian papers, *Aftenposten* also tends to take a more uncritical attitude toward the United States than do other major

Scandinavian dailies. Its political and foreign news coverage is extremely good, and its economic pages are considered superior. Especially noteworthy is the paper's coverage of educational problems, science, and medical news; it also gives outstanding coverage to local news of the Oslo area.

In the cultural field, however, the paper is sometimes criticized for what is considered inadequate coverage considering the paper's size and wealth. For example, recently a critic stated that *Aftenposten* did not have any full-time paid people to cover literature. This, however, is a criticism which might be hurled at most dailies. *Aftenposten*, in fact, does hire many fine book reviewers by the article, and is beginning to improve its general book pages.[6]

Aftenposten, like its fellow Norwegian dailies, enjoys one of the freest presses in the world. Press freedom is guarded carefully and any Government encroachment, however insignificant it may seem, is promptly denounced and tends to fade away quickly. An exceptional period in Norway's tradition of press freedom, however, can be found during the Nazi domination of the country in World War II. *Aftenposten*, which had patriotically warned the people of the dangers of German expansionism just prior to the occupation, suddenly found its freedom gone in April, 1940, when the Germans took over its plant.[7] During the war, *Aftenposten* and the rest of Norway's newspapers filled their columns with Nazi propaganda. By 1941 *Aftenposten* was a dull and monotonous voice of Hitler's "new order" and was really quite similar to Quisling's mouthpiece, *Fritt Folk*, in its regular parroting of German propaganda.[8] The paper lost little time, however, regaining its former status and vigorous voice once the Nazi armies were ousted from Norwegian soil at the end of the war.

Today *Aftenposten* seeks to avoid sensational presentation and as is true of other large-circulation Scandinavian papers, has never catered to the mass taste for crime, sex, and other lurid material. It must be remembered that in Norway and all of Scandinavia the quality papers, unlike those of Britain and certain other nations, are usually also the very large papers. In spite of the sober appearance of *Aftenposten*'s pages, the paper does give rather thorough coverage to crime news. Like other Scandinavian papers, *Aftenposten* is careful not to probe into private affairs in reporting crime news. When it does report on an important trial of a sensational nature, it often does not give the names of defendants, even though radio and other papers might be doing so. While all Norwegian papers very seldom report suicides or attempted suicides, *Aftenposten* never does.

The attitude of the paper was expressed in a June 7, 1966, editorial when it said that radio should broadcast only "what ordinary people find appropriate."[9] *Aftenposten* certainly follows this dictum itself. It tries to please its readers; at least it does not try to displease or disturb large numbers of them. In a controversial issue, the paper often stands in the middle, except in politics when it usually sides with the Conservatives against Labor. It presents the minority view, or opposing view, very often in its news columns or in its debate columns. On some issues the paper keeps silent, often in the area of morals. Recently it did not review a book by a well-known author, although it was reviewed by most other papers. Reason: the editors felt it had too much sex in it, and that its literary merits did not offset this catering to the prurient interests of the reader. The "liberals" in Norway—those of the Left Wing who demonstrate against the bomb and the United States' Dean Rusk—often complain of *Aftenposten*'s biased coverage and lack of courage.[10]

Aftenposten considers one of its prime purposes the educating of the people. While not neglecting human interest and general entertainment features, the paper presents a steady diet of serious information features and news stories. One of the characteristic serious articles found in *Aftenposten* (and other Norwegian papers) is the *kronikk* (chronicle), which is spread across the bottom of the editorial page. It is usually an essay of high order, usually serious and dealing with some national or international problem. The editorial page resembles one in the United States with certain modifications (*e.g.*, the tone is more informal, usually there is only one editorial, and the columns used are locally written and not syndicated).

This elite paper, in short, seems to embody the main characteristics of the quality paper (freedom) and the prestige paper (influence in high places). In addition, it presents a wholesome, well-rounded diet for the entire Norwegian family. It is serious and intellectually oriented, yet not exclusively so. As one press observer has put it, *Aftenposten* is "a unique paper read by top people throughout the country."[11] And, if Norwegian were an international language, there is no doubt but that this paper would make a significant impact on the thinking of the world as a whole.

Dagens Nyheter
(SWEDEN)

A top quality newspaper, with Sweden's largest circulation (about 380,000), *Dagens Nyheter* combines readability, range, and reliability with another important journalistic ingredient—reasonableness. Since its founding in 1864 by Rudolf Wall, it has progressively grown more readable and lively in makeup as it has penetrated new areas of readership; but it has not forsaken its serious and rational tone. In Sweden, as in many other small nations, the potential reading public is not large enough to permit newspapers to aim at separate sectors of the community as in Britain where there is a clear distinction between "mass" and "class" papers. Swedish papers, even the most serious of them, must offer something for everybody. *Dagens Nyheter* (Daily News) has been especially successful in doing this while at the same time satisfying the needs of that small and sophisticated group of readers which demands an intellectually oriented newspaper.

In Sweden there is a deep interest in current history, international politics, theology, economics, music, art, literature, and philosophy. *Dagens Nyheter* is careful to supply material to satisfy this interest. Because there is little outlet for writers of quality in the weekly magazines, the cultural position of the newspaper (and a few others of its type) is especially high. Much that passes for news in other countries is automatically absent from *Dagens Nyheter*. For example, stories of crime, trials, divorce, and suicide are considered personal matters and of no interest to, or business of, the public.[1]

Dagens Nyheter has always followed a liberal line, and has usually supported liberal parties. However, the paper has never been joined to any party, and its spirit is liberal in a nonpartisan sense. Its editorial columns offer a free forum for discussion. Actually, the paper can most fairly be described as "independent," and often its writers criticize the Liberal Party and in many cases lean toward the Social Democrats.[2]

All long articles in *Dagens Nyheter* carry by-lines. This is believed to encourage reliability. Copyreading (or subediting) is kept to a minimum and the writer's individual style is encouraged. This makes for some unevenness among the contents and it is obvious that certain weaknesses and outright errors could be caught if an editor were to check over the stories. In spite of this, however, the policy leads to what Wilbur Schramm has called an imaginative, lively, and interesting paper whose chief characteristic is vivid reportage.[3] The interest value of *Dagens Nyheter* is helped by a lively makeup and skillful use of pictures —two tone and color. Pages are "open" (plenty of white space) and the makeup is modern and horizontal.

Dagens Nyheter has permanent correspondents in London, Paris, Bonn, Rome, Copenhagen, Oslo, Helsinki, and New York. It also gets foreign news from the Associated Press, United Press International, Agence France-Presse, Deutsche Presse Agentur, and Reuters. In addition, it dispatches a special correspondent to any place in the world where a big story breaks. Most good newspapers, of course, do this, but what distinguishes *Dagens Nyheter* is the thorough way it backgrounds and interprets in feature stories and editorials the main problems and issues of the day. Writers such as Herbert Tingsten (who was editor until 1960), Olof Lagercrantz (cultural editor for many years and now editor), and Ulf Brandell have filled the paper's columns with erudite historical, literary, sociological, and political analyses which are more often found in scholarly magazines than in newspapers.[4]

Some forty-five staff members concentrate on music, literature, and

VÄDRET IDAG

DAGENS NYHETER.

DEL 1

Onsdagen den 27 September 1967

TELEFON 22 40 00
RIKSSAMTAL 08/22 40 20
TELEFONANNONSER 22 40 90
PRENUMERATIONER 22 40 60
VARDAGAR 50 öre
SÖNDAGAR 75 öre
• • • Nr 262

Ändrat system för pensioner krävs av staten

Ett förslag om helt nytt pensionssystem för de 300 000 statstjänstemännen håller, enligt vad Dagens Nyheter erfar, på att arbetas fram av avtalsverket. Arbetsgivarsidan vill slopa det nuvarande statliga pensionssystemet, som är bundet till tjänsterna, och i stället gå över till en tilläggspension efter samma modell som används inom industrin, den s k ITP-planen. Samtidigt väntas avtalsverket föreslå höjda pensionsåldrar för stora grupper av statstjänstemännen. Även här vill man ha en anpassning till den privata sidan, där tjänstemännens pensionsålder i dag är 62 år för kvinnor och 65 för män.

För närvarande är statstjänstemännens pensioner inte reglerade i kollektivavtal. Det skall de dock vara enligt den förhandlingsrätt som trädde i kraft i fjol.

De förhandlingar som skall leda fram till ett kollektivavtal om pensionerna beräknas komma i gång om en månad mellan avtalsverket och statstjänstemännens organisationer, Statstjänarkartellen, TCO-S, SACO och Statstjänstemännens riksförbund.

ITP-planen, som alltså står modell för avtalsverkets utspel, innebär en tilläggspension till ATP.

Se sidan tjugotvå, spalt fem

Facklig kritik mot JO

Vill begränsa strejkrätten

Uttalandet från JO Alfred Bexelius med anledning av förra höstens skolkonflikt kritiseras skarpt av representanter för arbetstagarna. SACO-direktören Bertil Östergren anser att det skulle vara en uppenbar nackdel om regeringen skulle besluta om stridsåtgärder för statens räkning. TCO:s 1:e ombudsman John Östlund säger kort och kärnfullt att regeringen inte har med detta att göra.

Gustaf Kolare, förbundsordförande i Statstjänarkartellen, anser att JO visar en anmärkningsvärd inställning till förhållandena på arbetsmarknaden. Han betraktar det som olyckligt om arbetsgivarfunktionen i en förhandling skulle delas upp på två händer.

Regeringen, och inte som nu avtalsverket, skall ha rätt att besluta om lockout i en avtalskonflikt med statliga anställda. Det behövs också en beredskapslagstiftning för svåra avtalskonflikter på det statliga området. Detta är de resultat som justitieombudsmannen Alfred Bexelius kommit fram till sedan han studerat förra höstens lärarkonflikt, då avtalsverket lockoutade Saco-lärarna och därigenom enligt JO gjorde det omöjligt för en statlig myndighet att fullgöra sina lagstadgade skyldigheter.

Se sidan tjugotre, spalt åtta

Rättegången mot Jules Régis Debray inleddes på tisdagen

Armé följde Régis Debray till krigsrätt

Med bajonetterna påskruvade kantade ett massuppbåd av militärer och poliser den sex kvarter långa väg Jules Régis Debray och hans fem medanklagade på tisdagen äntligen fick vandra efter fem månaders väntan, från den bolivianska staden Camiris fängelse till oljearbetarförbundets bibliotek, där regeringens krigsdomstol installerat sig. Den 26-årige franske filosofen-journalisten står anklagad för mord, stöld och väpnat uppror i samband med gerillarörelsens aktioner.

Fotografer och TV-män från många länder fick tio minuter på sig att göra sitt jobb innan de första förberedande förhandlingarna inleddes mot Debray, Castros nära vän och vid sidan av Ernesto Ché Guevara, Latinamerikas främste revolutionsteoretiker.

En av försvarsadvokaterna förklarade att han skickat in en inlaga som starkt ifrågasätter krigsrådets behörighet och kompetens att döma Debray och den argentinske konstnären Ciro Roberto Bustos. Han sade att ingen lag får användas retroaktivt vilket president Barrientos ämnar göra sedan han förklarat att det område där Debray greps är en krigszon.

Se sidan sex, spalt fem

BYGGARLARM:

Stadshuset gör oss rättslösa

Stadsplanen har upphört att vara ett rättsinstrument i Stockholm. Stadshuset agerar godtyckligt från fall till fall. Denna uppfattning råder bland byggherrar, fastighetsägare och konsulter, deklarerar Svenska byggnadsentreprenörföreningen i en från skrivelse till fastighetskontoret. Detta som svar på en remiss om stadsplaneexperternas krav att införa smalare bostadshus med särskilda entrévåningar i Stockholms innerstad.

"Tillämpning av långvariga byggförbud, som hindrar genomförande av bebyggelser enligt gällande plan, i kombination med av planorganen upprättade interna normer har medfört, att stadsplanemässig byggnadsrätt ersatts av någon form av tillståndsgivning från fall till fall. Detta kan icke vara en godtagbar lösning", heter det. Vice direktören Lars Ranheim i Byggnadsentreprenörföreningen har skrivit under remissvaret.

Att använda entrévåningar för tvättstugor är en föråldrad tanke, nu när nästan alla hushåll har egna moderna tvättmaskiner, påpekar byggentreprenörerna.

Om stadshuset ändå vill genomföra förslaget, må man göra det som experiment på de tomter som staden själv äger. Byggentreprenörerna vill inte vara med om det på sina privata tomter i innerstan. Först får staden visa att ett sådant experiment verkligen lyckas.

Man tror ej heller på stadsbyggnadskontorets nya, smala hus. Det blir svårt att placera framtidens bad- och våtutrymmen i de smala huskropparna. Badrummen blir med säkerhet betydligt större än i dag.

Men mest ilskna är byggentreprenörerna över stadshusets sätt att bolla med stadsplaner. De långvariga byggförbuden protesterar man också mot.

Strid i Enköping om brandalarmet

ADVOKAT
SÖREN FALKMAN
BRANDCHEF
SVEN ANDERSSON:
JO, DÅ VAR JAG DÄR,
MINNS JAG, FÖR DÅ BLEV
JAG BJUDEN PÅ KAFFE
mas

Brandlarmet i Enköping går först till polisstationen. Därifrån larmar man brandkåren genom ett signalsystem som emellertid inte ger något besked om var det brinner. De utryckningsklara brandmännen måste först ringa poliskontoret för att få besked om vart de skall åka. Detta avslöjande om larmsystemet i Enköping gjordes vid rättegången på tisdagen mot stadens brandchef, Sven Andersson, som åtalats för försummelse när det gällt att utföra brandsyn och att föra protokoll över sådana. Rättegången var epilogen till branddramat i Enköpingsskolan den 30 januari, som krävde fem liv. Brandchefen bestred bestämt anklagelserna. Dom meddelas den 10 oktober.

Se sidan sexton, spalt ett

Uteslutning av fribytare partihot (s)

Vattenbatalj "öppen strid"

Från Dagens Nyheters medarbetare

VARBERG, tisdag

Öppen och oförsonlig strid med sina forna partivänner levererar nu de socialdemokratiska fribytarna i Varberg. Slaget står kring en en konkret kommunalpolitisk fråga. Kampen inleddes med en interpellation vid tisdagens stadsfullmäktigesammanträde. Fribytargruppen, som har en stark ställning med nio mandat och vice ordförandeposten i fullmäktige, anser sig kunna bespara staden en onödig utgift på 15 miljoner kronor genom sitt alternativ till lösning av Varbergs framtida vattenförsörjning.

Bataljen kring vattenfrågan blir den stora offentliga uppgörelsen inför ögonen på alla intresserade Varbergsbor, dvs praktiskt taget hela stadens befolkning.

Internt slåss man redan i det socialdemokratiska lägret så hårt som gärna tänkas kan. "Gammalmossarna" har tagit till storsläggan och begär att fribytarna skall uteslutas ur partiet. En uteslutningsdelegation från partistyrelsen i Stockholm kommer till staden på lördag. Den får brett om dromen.

Fribytarna med John Höög i spetsen känner sin styrka. Med sin parallellista i fjolårets kommunalval lyckades de i ett enda svep klyva partiet mitt itu. Fribytarna rakade till sig nio av de arton socialdemokratiska mandaten och satte in John Höög som stadsfullmäktiges vice ordförande.

I den positionen behöver fribytarna inte kämpa ett defensivkrig.

Forts. sidan sexton, spalt fyra

England ger inte Sverige hjälp i EEC

Från DN:s utsände medarbetare Bo A Ericsson

STRASBOURG, tisdag

Den brittiska Europaministern lord Chalfont avböjde i Europarådet på tisdagen att ge några löften om att England — om det blir medlem av EEC — skall verka och jämna vägen för det neutrala Sveriges inträde. — Vi har fullt upp med våra egna problem, sade Chalfont i sitt tal i Strasbourg och vi kan inte också ta upp några andra länders problem med de sex.

Beskedet om att Sverige och de övriga Eftaländerna inte kan räkna med någon speciell brittisk hjälp vid EEC-förhandlingar gav Chalfont som svar på en fråga från riksdagsman Stig Alemyr (s), en av de svenska delegaterna i rådsförsamlingen, och senare vid en presskonferens.

Frågan om det neutrala Sveriges ansökan till EEC betecknades av Chalfont som "svår".

Forts. sidan sju, spalt ett.

Wedén ger motbud om höjda skatter

Folkpartiet gjorde på tisdagen ett utspel i skattefrågan. Partiledaren Sven Wedén framhöll i ett anförande inför partiets riksdagsgrupp att den föreslagna omläggningen av barnbidragen bara kan accepteras om den kombineras med skatteomläggningar som minskar marginalskatten i särskilda inkomstgrupper. Av en förberedande diskussion i försvarsfrågan framgick vidare att partiet tills vidare ställer sig avvaktande till regeringens krav på skattehöjningar som villkor för höjda försvarsanslag.

ÖB presenterar sina svar på partiernas olika utredningsalternativ på onsdagen, men innehållet är i själva verket redan känt inom partierna. Den allmänna uppfattningen inom folkpartiets riksdagsgrupp synes ha varit att det socialdemokratiska alternativet innebär en så väldig omstöpning av försvaret att en helt ny strategi måste tillgripas. Konsekvenserna av mittpartiernas räkneexempel betraktades som något förmånligare.

Se sidan tjugofyra, spalt ett

Sluta röka minskar ej risken för lungcancer

Risken för lungcancer minskar inte om en cigarrettrökare slutar röka. Denna medicinska sensation lades fram av den engelske cancerexperten dr Richard Doll vid det internationella forskarmötet om cancer och åldrande som Thule på tisdagen startade i Stockholm. Och den teorin strider mot alla tidigare gjorda undersökningar. Dr Doll stöder sig emellertid på ett omfattande material — cirka 34 000 rökande engelska läkare, som han följt sedan mitten av 1950-talet.

Svenska cancerexperter betecknar resultatet som mycket intressant och menar att det finns all anledning sätta tilltro till dr Dolls undersökning.

Se sidan trettifyra, spalt fyra

Den engelske cancerexperten dr Richard Doll (längst t v), som presenterade en teori om cancer och rökning, som går emot alla tidigare undersökningar, med professor emeritus Folke Henschen och den ryske professorn N N Kipshidze.

Pilsnerflaska i papperskvarn

Från DN:s Örebroredaktion

ÖREBRO, tisdag

En flaska pilsner, klass II, har i tre år snurrat runt i det närkingska rättsmaskineriet. Flaskans ägare, en 37-årig finländare, har sökts av polisen i Fjugesta och centralkriminalen i Helsingfors, men förgäves. Nu har Västernärkes domsaga i Örebro fått en redogörelse för fallet från en åklagare som vill att flaskan skall förklaras förverkad.

Flaskan togs i beslag när finländaren greps för fylleri 1964. När han släpptes fick han inte ta med sig pilsnern.

Sedan började det med att man sökte finländaren med en fylleristämning. Han var försvunnen och brottet preskriberades. Eftersom mannen aldrig blev dömd fick myndigheterna inte handskas hur som helst med pilsnerflaskan, den skulle återställas. Finländska polisen fick börja spana efter 37-åringen igen.

"För bekväm" kriminalvård Fast hierarki

Om kriminalvården en dag fick de resurser som man ständigt ropar på skulle det uppstå en stor förlägenhet inom hela fångvården — man skulle helt enkelt inte veta vad man skulle göra med resurserna, säger dr Gustav Jonsson på Skå apropå tisdagens TV-program om Välfärds-Sverige. Det finns många friska idéer som skulle kunna prövas utan stora kostnader, och det finns personal och intagna som är mer än villiga att få pröva dem, men i hela kriminalvården har man låst fast sig i en stor bekvämlighet, en fast hierarki och gammal behandlingsslentrian som ingen orkar rucka på.

Se sidan nitton, spalt fem

INSIDORNA

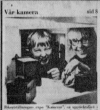

art; about thirty-five on the humanities, law, and politics, and about twenty-five on medicine and science. The cultural pages maintain a very high standard, and the emergence of Sweden in world politics has created a large and well-informed group of international correspondents and analysts.

A typical issue of *Dagens Nyheter* contains forty pages. Along with the serious fare will be found household hints, human interest stories, and advice columns for people with personal problems. Almost two-thirds of the paper's total space is given over to advertising, a rather high proportion for an elite paper. Foreign news normally takes up a page and a half, political commentaries about four pages, and cultural material of various types about six pages. Entertaining features, including comic strips, account for about a page, and athletic events get about the same emphasis.

Dagens Nyheter has a staff of some 165 full-time journalists, many of them holding higher university degrees. In order to attract the best writers, *Dagens Nyheter* has the best salaries in Swedish journalism. Along with *Svenska Dagbladet*, its conservative counterpart in Stockholm, the paper is able to attract many superior staff members because of its prestige and tradition of rationality and courage.

Throughout its history, the paper has wielded great political influence; however, it probably reached its zenith of influence and respect during the editorship of Otto von Zweigbergk (1898–1921). Although it was quick to point out the dangers of the rise of German, Spanish, and Italian authoritarianism in the late twenties, its criticism of Hitler's Germany during World War II was not very sharp.[5] The reason: it supported the neutrality policy of the Swedish coalition government and did not want to cause unnecessary trouble for the country.[6]

Herbert Tingsten, one of the truly great editors of Europe, was instrumental in giving *Dagens Nyheter* added respect among the continent's intellectuals during his editorship from 1946 until 1960. He steered the paper away from a policy of neutrality in international politics and urged that Sweden join the Western defense community. His successors, Olof Lagercrantz and Sven-Erik Larsson, have retreated into a more neutralist attitude and in recent years the paper has been more critical of the West than was true under Tingsten.[7]

Although *Dagens Nyheter* and its few Swedish elite fellow dailies are excellent in most respects, some critics have pointed to a certain deterioration in recent years which should be mentioned. As television has spread throughout Sweden, domestic news has tended to become more trivial. This indictment has been brought by Ian Rodger of Britain's *Guardian*.[8] Rodger contends that the cheapness and availability of newsprint "encourages prolixity and makes a high overall standard hard to maintain." Concentration upon trivia at home is hurting the quality of the overall Swedish press, a press which, maintains Rodger, "a few years ago could have been cited as a model for the world."[9]

In spite of such criticisms reflecting on one aspect of the paper's coverage, Sweden is undoubtedly fortunate to have a journal which exerts so much effort and money to provide news and views about important issues in a lively and readable, yet reliable and rational, manner.

Le Figaro
(FRANCE)

At 14 Rond-Point on the Champs-Elysées stands the sturdy buildings which houses Paris' oldest daily newspaper, and the one which is usually considered the best written. *Le Figaro*, with a daily circulation of nearly 400,000 and the most stable economic position in the French press,[1] has come a long way from the tiny satirical sheet begun by Maurice Allhoy in January, 1826. The original *Figaro*, as its name might imply,[2] filled its columns with the artistic life of Paris—feminine fashions, theatrical activities, and gossip. The paper still retains these features to some degree, but has added many serious dimensions never imagined in early nineteenth-century Paris.

Le Figaro in its infancy admirably filled a journalistic gap left by the influential papers of Paris, presenting witty commentary on literature, politics, manners, and morals.[3] However, in those early days, it apparently went along with the common French practice of staff members taking sizable bribes for favorable reviews.[4] It was Henri de Villemessant who brought popularity to the paper when, in the 1850's, he started hiring talented writers such as Léo Lespès, Rochefort, Alexandre Dumas, and Baudelaire.[5] In 1856 the paper became a biweekly and began a letters column which precipitated some of the most vigorous political dialogue in France. Villemessant would usually reply to letters with one-line retorts which exemplified his talent for biting satire.[6] *Le Figaro* became a daily in 1866. Villemessant was one of the first editors to departmentalize the news, and compared a newspaper to a department store in which the buyer must know where to locate the various merchandise.[7]

After Villemessant, *Le Figaro* passed through a number of editorships: Francis Magnard, Fernand de Rodays, Antonin Périvier, Gaston Calmette, Alfred Capus, and Robert de Flers. In 1922 the paper fell victim to François Coty's venture into journalism. A millionaire cosmetics manufacturer, Coty bought the paper and used it to support him in his political adventures.[8] Until after his death in 1934 the paper declined; however, his ex-wife (Mme. Yvonne Cotnareanu) took over and gave the editorship to Pierre Brisson, Lucien Romier, and Pierre Lafitte who were capable journalists and who built the paper into one of the best in pre-World War II France. A critique of the European press by an American scholar in 1937 referred to *Le Figaro* as "particularly well written, giving much attention to literary and theatrical affairs."[9]

Shortly before Hitler's armies swept through France in 1939, *Le Figaro* was established as the leading morning paper of the country and while its circulation was not a record one, it had prestige and an impressive array of by-lines.[10] In 1940 when Paris fell to the Germans, Pierre Brisson, who was then the top editor, moved the paper to Lyons in the unoccupied zone and continued publication under the Petain regime. He had decided to stop circulation of *Le Figaro* as early as November, 1942, rather than be forced by the Vichy Government and the German censorship to express opinions that he knew would be hostile to the majority of his readers. Even while the German garrison and the Gestapo were still active in Paris in August, 1944, *Le Figaro* resumed publication.[11] The paper has published continuously ever since, and its prestige and circulation have consistently risen until presently it is considered one of the best dailies of Europe and circulates close to a half-million copies to leading Frenchmen in every part of France and in many parts of the world.

The period 1945 through 1950 was one of the high-water marks in the paper's history; its circulation reached almost 450,000. It was also during this period that *Le Figaro* began a campaign against the rapid growth of Communism in France. François Mauriac, *Le Figaro* columnist and outstanding novelist, launched a daily attack on *L'Humanité*, Communist organ and a leading Paris paper at the time.[12] *Figaro* also was backing a movement to bring General de Gaulle back into power. In 1946 it was called the "favorite paper of the Frenchman who believes himself to be an enlightened liberal." By 1947, however, it was being called "conservative."[13] Since then *Le Figaro* has generally been considered conservative and the chief representative of the French bourgeoisie. It has usually been pro-United States, except at certain times when de Gaulle has veered antagonistically away from American policies.

Writing in 1950, Theodore H. White said that *Le Figaro* "combines the widest coverage of world news with elegantly written prose and distinguished by-lines."[14] In 1958 it was called "the bible of France's upper-middle class" and was praised for its foreign news, music, literary, and theater coverage.[15] In 1964 John Hohenberg of Columbia University praised its foreign coverage, calling it "thoughtful and well-ordered,"[16] and in 1966 Kenneth Olson also lauded its "excellent foreign coverage and backgrounding" and called it the "most influential" of the French dailies, particularly with the upper-middle class.[17] *Le Figaro* was France's only daily to cover the Jack Ruby trial in Texas and the only one to send a reporter on President Johnson's trip to Southeast Asia in November, 1966.

Among *Le Figaro*'s contributors in recent years have been some of the most famous literary figures of the country, such as François

Pages 4, 5, 5 A et 5 B : **LES CANTONALES ET LES RÉSULTATS PAR DÉPARTEMENT**

0,40 F

LE FIGARO

ÉDITION DE PARIS

141e ANNÉE — N° 7.153 — depuis la Libération

« Sans la liberté de blâmer, il n'est pas d'éloge flatteur. » BEAUMARCHAIS.

LUNDI 2 OCTOBRE 1967 — 275e JOUR DE L'ANNÉE

Le Gaulois

Directeur : Pierre BRISSON (1934-1964)

ÉLECTION, MERCREDI

des présidents des Conseils généraux renouvelés

• HIER ENCORE : ENVIRON 40 % D'ABSTENTIONS

AU SECOND TOUR DES CANTONALES

Cet après-midi, à l'Assemblée et au Sénat : **OUVERTURE DE LA SESSION PARLEMENTAIRE D'AUTOMNE qui prendra fin le 20 décembre**

— PAGES 4 et 5 : L'ENSEMBLE DE NOS INFORMATIONS
— PAGES 5 A et 5 B : les résultats par département

Double polarisation

C[illegible]

Michel Bassi.

(Suite page 4.)

AUJOURD'HUI

Manifestations paysannes dans la plupart des régions

RASSEMBLEMENTS PLUS HOULEUX ATTENDUS DANS L'OUEST

PAGE 6 : NOTRE INFORMATION

A l'occasion du XVIIIe anniversaire de la Chine populaire

MAO S'EST MONTRÉ AUX GARDES ROUGES mais il n'a pas parlé

Le numéro 2, Lin Piao, critique, dans son discours, le « révisionnisme soviétique » :

Les diplomates de l'U.R.S.S. et de six pays communistes quittent la tribune officielle

PAGE 7 : NOTRE INFORMATION

HIER A LA T.V.

COCKTAIL d'émissions COULEUR pour la 1re journée

Une victoire due principalement à la technique

PAGE 25 : l'article d'André BRINCOURT et nos informations

Aujourd'hui dans

LE FIGARO LITTÉRAIRE

MALRAUX PARLE

Une interview exclusive de l'auteur des Antimémoires par **MICHEL DROIT**

En dernière page : la suite du sommaire

LA « ROUE D'OR » A ENCORE ÉTÉ CELLE D'ANQUETIL...

[illegible] (P. 21 : les commentaires de **Louis VINCENT**.)

Pour la première fois

Liaison Ajaccio-Saint-Raphaël en hélicoptère

Un Super-Frelon avec 8 hommes à bord

[illegible]

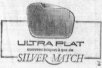

LONDRES : **P. BERTRAND**

Troisième homme de l'affaire Burgess-Maclean

JOHN PHILBY as des services secrets britanniques TRAVAILLAIT POUR L'U.R.S.S. DEPUIS 1933

PAGE 6 : notre dépêche

WASHINGTON : J.-JACQUET-FRANCILLON

MALGRÉ TOUTES SES AMBIGUITÉS

Le discours de Johnson : un pas important vers la conciliation ?

• Le président U.S. ne lie plus l'arrêt des bombardements du Nord-Vietnam à un « acte de réciprocité »

[illegible]

Jacques Jacquet-Francillon.

(Suite page 7, col. 1, 2.)

INCIDENT EN MARGE DU PROCÈS DEBRAY

L'ENVOYÉ SPÉCIAL DE L'A.F.P. EXPULSÉ

PAGE 3 : la dépêche de **Philippe NOURRY** (Camiri)

CAVALIER SEUL

Bonne traversée !

O[illegible]

André Frossard.

(Dessin de Piem.)

— Il y aurait comme une dominante rouge.

CHRONIQUE

PLEIN LA VUE

par **JAMES DE COQUET**

SUR la place de la Concorde, la circulation s'était soudain figée. Rien n'avançait plus, dans aucune direction. [illegible]

— C'est pas beau à voir...

[illegible]

JAMES DE COQUET.

Mauriac, Paul Claudel, and Georges Duhamel. Leading economists such as André Siegfried and Raymond Aron typify the specialists who write for the paper in certain fields. Its special weekly literary edition, *Le Figaro Littéraire*, is generally considered the finest such paper in Europe.

In order to indicate the usual composition of *Le Figaro*, let us look at a randomly chosen issue (May 3, 1966). This is a typical issue of thirty-two pages with the standard format of eight columns. Page 1 is about half filled with headlines, mainly referring the reader to inside stories; also there are several short articles a column, a couple of pictures, and an editorial cartoon. On page 2 are advertisements and a few national stories. Foreign articles appear on pages 3, 4, and 5. Page 6 is given over to political and social issues. Pages 7, 8, and 9 are financial pages. Deaths, police news, accidents, and an assortment of local and national miscellaneous items are on pages 10 and 11. Pages 12 and 13 contain articles related to high culture and education.

An indication of the prosperity of the paper is the fact that pages 14 through 19 contain classified advertisements or *petites annonces* (12 columns per page). Pages 20 and 21 carry depth or interpretative features on economic matters. Page 22 is filled with cartoons, page 23 with stories and pictures about television and films. Display advertising fills page 24. Page 25 carries medical stories. Page 26 is a literary page, and page 27 is given over to weather and tourism. The sports stories, pictures, and features are found on pages 28 and 29, and pages 30 and 31 are filled with material relative to movies and other entertainment. The last page (page 32) is filled with items pertaining to agriculture and miscellaneous events.

A look at the contents of *Le Figaro* indicates that, although it is known in France as an "information" paper, it gives considerable emphasis to political affairs. It stresses foreign affairs, economics, music, art, and literature. Its many features are of a hybrid nature—a cross between editorials, commentaries, essays, and literary criticism and factual news accounts. In tone the paper is very serious, although its rather haphazard use of headlines detracts somewhat from its dignified character. Without a doubt, *Le Figaro* is one of the best-informed and best-edited dailies of Europe; and it is fair to say that much of its current reputation is owed to its great post-World War II director, Pierre Brisson.

On December 31, 1964, Brisson died, leaving *Le Figaro* in the hands of a board of editors and under the directorship of Louis Gabriel-Robinet.[18] Brisson's son, Jean-François, became the new editor-in-chief, replacing Gabriel-Robinet. Today *Le Figaro* is continuing in the tradition of Pierre Brisson and is giving the French reader a solid diet of serious news and views written by a distinguished staff and by outside contributors representing the best minds of France.

The Scotsman
(SCOTLAND)

It is not strange that Edinburgh's stately *Scotsman* has often been referred to as the "London *Times* of Scotland." For this daily, founded in 1817, combines all the progressive spirit, dignity, prestige, and conservative political orientation which have characterized its fellow journal in London. Like *The Times, The Scotsman* represents stability, responsibility, and reliability. And it, too, is a national institution.

In 1963 the University of Missouri School of Journalism bestowed on *The Scotsman* an Honor Medal (given to very few foreign newspapers), citing it for its "editorial independence, good writing, and usually acute judgment of events, men, and situations." The citation, presented to the paper's editor, Alastair Dunnett, further acknowledged its "leadership in technological advances . . . prestige that has led Sir Winston Churchill to refer to it as a 'national institution' . . . its advances in the last decade under the perceptive ownership of Roy Thomson and the outstanding editorship of Alastair MacTavish Dunnett."[1] This citation summarizes well the qualities which make this Edinburgh morning daily one of the world's elite.

The Scotsman has its main office in Edinburgh with branch offices in London and Aberdeen, and publishes four daily editions totaling more than 75,000 copies. Readership is mainly composed of lawyers, doctors, teachers, big businessmen, and intellectuals. The separate editions go to the Highlands, borders, and East and West Scotland, thereby assuring each district its own local news as well as national and world coverage.

In order to publish these four editions *The Scotsman* calls upon its main office staff of twenty reporters, twenty subeditors, four full-time photographers in Edinburgh (a total of twenty photographers in their three combined offices). In addition to these, the paper hires hundreds of freelance correspondents who are paid a few cents per line used.[2]

Besides using the Press Association and Reuters for foreign news, *The Scotsman* also makes use of the foreign news service of *The Observer*, a London quality Sunday paper which has highly paid first-class journalists in all capitals of the world.[3] If any of these men sends back a story on Tuesday, the news (obviously no news to a Sunday paper) is sent to a number of papers that pay *The Observer* a retaining fee of three hundred dollars per year for use of these midweek stories. These papers get the use of all midweek stories except those received on Friday or Saturday, which are kept for exclusive use by *The Observer*. Papers paying the fee to *The Observer* usually by-line their stories "by our own correspondent."[4]

The Scotsman is conservative (opposed to socialism) in its policies, but has often attacked the Conservative Party and the Conservative Government if its editors thought they were wrong. The paper treats the news seriously and "spikes" as worthless news items such as those which record that a film actress has been divorced for the third time. Parliament is reported thoroughly and seriously on its pages and occasionally one or two entire pages are devoted to important debates. The paper supports the idea of more self-government, but does not advocate a complete, or even partial, separation from England.

The Scotsman, from the earliest days, has attracted many notable contributors, and its informed and well-written special articles are highly regarded. Sir Linton Andrews, former editor of the *Yorkshire Post* and vice-chairman of the Press Council, had this to say about *The Scotsman*:

> As one of its constant readers for half the century, I appreciate the scholarly care and integrity in its editing, the soundness of its reporting, and the weight of its influence. Nor can I, as a journalist, fail to acknowledge its outstanding technical enterprise, especially in leading the way to more delicate reproduction of scenic pictures and in the fast and full transmission and setting of London Exchange dealings. . . . The public spirit we need for the best working of democracy has its champions. While papers of national standing and influence like *The Scotsman* keep to their historic character we need not dispair of our method of government. It is a fine thing for the Highlands and Lowlands alike that this great paper keeps their just interests to the forefront in Britain's political agenda. . . .[5]

The history of *The Scotsman*, founded as a weekly in 1817, sparkles with notable personalities and an unerring philosophy of responsible journalism that helps explain its current prestige and influence. In its earliest days as a weekly, the paper had pledged itself to impartiality, firmness, and independence and it fulfilled its pledge with such determination and responsibility that its voice came to be listened to eagerly by friends of progress all over the country.[6]

The Scotsman went daily in 1825, the first issue being a small sheet roughly tabloid size and costing only a penny. At first the newspaper used a four-cylinder Hoe press capable of producing from 7,000 to 8,000 copies an hour, printed only on one side. This sufficed for a while, but in 1863 a six-cylinder Hoe was added. As circulation grew rapidly, especially in the country, a Walter press capable of printing 12,000 eight-page sheets both sides from a continuous web in one hour was installed in *The Scotsman* plant on Coburn Street. This was the first rotary press to be used in Scotland.[7]

In the early days of telegraphy, *The Scotsman* pioneered again by leasing a special wire between London and Edinburgh for the paper's

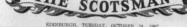

MUSICALLY MINDED PEOPLE are aware of the Comprehensive Stocks of RECORDS and MUSIC at RAE, MACINTOSH & CO. LTD. 39 GEORGE STREET, EDINBURGH

THE SCOTSMAN

a man's drink... BANANA JAMAICA RUM

No. 38,817 EDINBURGH, TUESDAY, OCTOBER 24, 1967 PRICE 5d.

£400,000 EXTRA AID PLANNED FOR AREAS SHORT OF TEACHERS

Selective recruitment

BY OUR POLITICAL CORRESPONDENT

Mr William Ross, the Secretary of State for Scotland, is proposing a two-pronged plan to help areas, mainly in the West of Scotland, hard hit by the teacher shortage. It embodies £400,000 worth of extra inducement to 4000 teachers to work in Ayrshire, Dunbartonshire, Glasgow, Lanarkshire and Renfrewshire and proposals to reintroduce arrangements for restraint on the recruitment of teachers for better staffed areas.

The plan was revealed in a Commons written reply yesterday and further details were given in a letter from the Scottish Education Department to local authority associations.

It is intended that the payments should take effect from April 1 next year as part of the revision of salaries due then. They would be made to all teachers at schools designated as short of teachers.

The proposals for cash inducements are an adaption of the main recommendation of the Roberts Committee on the distribution of teachers in Scotland ...

Commons hint of action on fee-paying Scots schools

By Our Political Correspondent

Some of Scotland's best-known fee-paying schools may lose their ...

DIVIDED IDEAS ABOUT SINGING

Caught by the camera at the opening ceremony at St Margaret's Primary School, Galashiels, yesterday, these youngsters appear to have divided ideas about how to sing the opening hymn. The new £90,000 school, adjacent to Galashiels Academy, was opened by the Very Rev. Gordon J. Gray, Archbishop of St Andrews and Edinburgh.

Lords drop opposition to Abortion Bill

By Our Political Staff

AGREEMENT LIKELY IN NEWSPAPER DISPUTE

France states two key conditions for U.K. entry

BANDA ORDERS BAN ON 'WITNESSES'

IMPS MAY CUT COST OF COUPON CIGARETTES

Counter to proposed gift schemes ban

BY OUR OWN REPORTER

The Imperial Tobacco Company plan to reduce the price of their cigarette brands which carry coupons if the Government's proposed ban on coupon gift schemes becomes law.

The company, which hold 43 per cent of the coupon market with their Embassy and Players No. 6 cigarettes, intend to cut the price by the value of the coupons, between 2d and 2½d, an estimated annual saving to the 11 million smokers of coupon brands of some £32 million.

The proposed legislation, which is aimed at combating the increase in lung cancer, was announced in the Commons yesterday by the Minister of Health, Mr Kenneth Robinson. The decision by the Government follows the failure of protracted negotiations with the tobacco industry to limit sales promotion.

... no further progress is possible by voluntary agreement," Mr Robinson told the Commons.

As cigarette smoking was "a serious danger to health and a major cause of preventable deaths," the Government had decided to introduce legislation in due course to take powers to ban coupon gift schemes, to control or ban other promotional schemes, to forbid or limit certain forms ...

Redundancy feared

A spokesman for British Rail said in York last night that some of the 14 men employed at the fourth goods depot in Newcastle, which handles the gifts from the Embassy cigarettes coupons, may be made redundant because of the legislation announced yesterday.

He said the yard, which was closed when the new Tyneside freight depot was opened at Gateshead and reopened at the request of Wills and two other companies, handles about 1300 gift packages a day.

The Imperial Tobacco Company claim that the proposed ban could lead to 10,000 people being put out of work, apart from those directly involved with coupons inside the tobacco industry itself. At present 350 firms supply about £30 million worth of goods a year for coupon schemes.

DAYAN'S WARNING OVER DESTROYER

Hint of retaliation

TEL-AVIV, Monday. — General Moshe Dayan, Israel's Defence Minister, said tonight that the ...

"We, too, will know how to move step after step as we did then," he said.

"It is not difficult to violate the cease-fire and to fire," he added. "The (Suez) Canal is only 150 yards wide, but we have accepted the cease-fire and lived according to its rules."—Reuter.

Pressure for retaliation—Page 7

LATEST NEWS

FRENCH H-BOMB

Paris, Monday. — The Armed Forces Minister, M. Pierre Messmer, said tonight France hoped to explode first hydrogen bomb in the Pacific next summer on schedule.—Reuter.

POSTAGE

£30,000 JEWELS STOLEN

London office ambush

Edinburgh's busmen demand talks on pay

BODIES FOUND IN ANGUS COTTAGE

Gunshot wounds

SIX QUESTIONS

Where does sculpture come into hair culture?

How do computers help the fashion industry?

Which shipping lines are best for investors?

How can you insure against twins — or quads?

What are the advantages of the franchise business?

Why are they fighting in Fraserburgh?

Answers to these and many other questions can be found in tomorrow's issue of "The Financial Scotsman."

THE FINANCIAL SCOTSMAN

ON OTHER PAGES

Financial	2-4	Women	9
Scottish	5	Agriculture	17
Letters	6	Weather	13
Foreign	7	Sport	13-14
Parliament	8	Crossword	14

TV and radio—Page 13

exclusive use. The London staff was enlarged, and in 1868 *The Scotsman* became the first provincial daily to set up offices on Fleet Street. And when the telegraph system was taken over by the Post Office in 1873, a second special wire was leased to *The Scotsman.* The paper was also the first British (or European) journal to operate a machine which sent photographs by wire.[8]

On the editorial side many developments also took place. The paper established the institution of a regular "London Letter," based on factual information rather than gossip; this brought to the paper's readers the opinions of many of the nation's leading personalities. *The Scotsman* also pioneered in treating book reviews as news, giving notice of books very soon after publication, something that was not common in Britain. Greater emphasis was given to foreign news, and *The Scotsman* instituted depth discursive features on international problems which gave the paper an unusual tone for a provincial paper. By 1877 the daily circulation of *The Scotsman* was 50,000, nearly equal to *The Times* of London.[9] The paper grew slowly but constantly and its prestige both in Britain and abroad was built ever more solidly. By World War I it was the leading intellectual voice of Scotland, and it proceeded its dignified, cautious way through World War II and into the early 1950's without much noticeable change. In 1953, Roy Thomson, probably the most powerful newspaper owner in the world, entered British journalism by purchasing *The Scotsman.*

Thomson, who was soon to become Lord Thomson of Fleet, kept *The Scotsman*'s policies and staff very much the same as they had been. In 1956 he hired Alastair Dunnett from a Kemsley paper in Glasgow to edit *The Scotsman.*[10] Since Thomson became publisher the paper has changed, but mainly in a technical way. For example, Thomson dispensed with front page advertising in 1957, replacing it with news. He also made certain typographical reforms.[11] But in spite of a few changes of this sort, the paper has retained its serious, intellectual tone, and under Dunnett's editorship has prospered and grown. For example, in 1953 the circulation was 55,000; today it is nearly 80,000.

La Stampa
(ITALY)

The quality press of Italy (which is not large) is typified by *La Stampa* of Turin which has managed quite effectively to combine a strong provincial orientation with authority and prestige all over the country. Along with nearby Milan's *Corriere della Sera* (see Chap. 15), *La Stampa*

Anno 101 · Numero 217

LA STAMPA

Giovedì 14 Settembre 1967

REDAZIONE, AMMINISTRAZIONE, TIPOGRAFIA: 10100 TORINO, VIA ROMA 80. Centralino telefonico autom. 57.78 - Telex 21.121

La visita del Capo dello Stato in Canada

Saragat all'«Expo» di Montreal accolto da migliaia di italiani

Il commissario generale dell'Esposizione, Pierre Dupuy (ex ambasciatore a Roma) saluta il Presidente in italiano - Poi dichiara commosso: « L'Italia è il seme della terra. Noi l'accogliamo con rispetto infinito ed infinita riconoscenza, perché ci rende fieri della nostra dignità di uomini » - E aggiunge: « Io non vi ho più lasciato né col pensiero né col cuore » - Un caldo elogio ai modelli d'auto di Torino « che non si contano più in tutti i continenti » - La risposta di Saragat spesso interrotta dagli applausi scroscianti della folla

(Dal nostro inviato speciale)

Montreal, 13 settembre.

Il presidente Saragat ed il suo seguito hanno trascorso praticamente l'intera giornata all'« Expo 67 » ed il tempo continua ad essere una meraviglia: un cielo azzurro come a Capri, una brezza fresca come a Cortina d'Ampezzo. Alle 11 in punto Saragat è arrivato ...

Il presidente Saragat, alla cui destra è il ministro Fanfani, visita il padiglione italiano a Montreal (Tel. A.P.)

... aveva visitato i padiglioni allestiti dal Canada e dalle sue province: l'edificio principale è una piramide rovesciata, alta 33 metri ed è costata una dozzina di miliardi di lire. E' stato battezzato Katimavik, una parola esquimese che significa luogo d'incontro.

Nicola Adelfi

Truppe egiziane sparano su una pattuglia d'Israele

Sul Canale; nessuna vittima

Gerusalemme, 13 settembre.

Nelle prime ore di stamane gli egiziani hanno aperto il fuoco contro una pattuglia israeliana di otto uomini che stava perlustrando il terreno otto chilometri a nord di El Qantara. La sparatoria è durata cinque minuti e non ha provocato vittime. (A.P.)

Consulto medico per Paolo VI Forse sarà operato in novembre

Un comunicato, a firma dei professori Valdoni, Arduini e Fontana, dice che si ricorrerà ad un intervento chirurgico se la terapia in corso non sarà sufficiente - Probabile un'ipertrofia prostatica e in Vaticano si dà per certa l'operazione tra un paio di mesi - Per il Papa « impedito » non è prevista nessuna supplenza - Per il Codice Canonico egli è Vicario di Cristo sino alla morte, a meno che sia infermo di mente o si renda responsabile di eresia

(Nostro servizio particolare)

Città del Vaticano, 13 sett.

Paolo VI quasi certamente dovrà essere operato. Le cure antibiotiche non bastano a rimuovere le cause più gravi che hanno determinato, come già in passato, la cistopielite acuta di cui il Papa soffre da lunedì 4 settembre. Un anormale ingrossamento della prostata ...

... Perciò ha nominato i tre cardinali delegati a presiedere il Sinodo; e lo decise poche ore prima di abbandonare Castel Gandolfo in gran fretta sotto la minaccia dell'infezione.

Lamberto Furno

Alcuni romani leggono sull'«Osservatore» le notizie sulle condizioni di salute di Paolo VI (Telef. Ansa)

La malattia del Papa

Quella responsabilità primitiva della prostata, che ogni medico, data l'età inoltrata del paziente, aveva intuita alla base della diagnosi ufficialmente emessa giorni fa dall'archiatra pontificio, si è andata confermando chiaramente nelle ultime notizie sull'andamento del morbo del Santo Padre. ...

... Va da sé che stando così le cose l'intervento chirurgico trova chiara indicazione; ma è pure logico, se altri fatti clinici non accelerino l'urgenza, che l'atto operatorio, necessario ad evitare il rinnovarsi di episodi drammatici come l'attuale, sia aggiornato a quando il fattore infettivo attuale sarà pienamente debellato e nello stesso tempo la funzionalità renale, nonché lo stato generale del Paziente forniranno migliori garanzie di riuscita.

Angelo Viziano

Chiusa l'istruttoria per il caso Bazan Arrestato a Torino il filatelico Bolaffi

Un sottufficiale dei carabinieri si è recato ieri sera nella sede della ditta del dott. Bolaffi e gli ha notificato l'ordine di cattura ricevuto per telegrafo da Palermo - Si ritiene che saranno eseguiti altri arresti - Il giudice istruttore ha consegnato a tarda ora la sentenza di rinvio a giudizio alla cancelleria del Tribunale di Palermo - Il documento sarà reso noto oggi

(Dal nostro corrispondente)

Palermo, 13 settembre.

... sicilana. f. d.

(Vedere a pag. 2 altre notizie sull'arresto di Giulio Bolaffi).

Il bilancio statale per il '68 al Senato entro il 12 ottobre

Roma, 13 settembre.

Il bilancio dello Stato per il 1968 dovrebbe essere sottoposto all'esame dell'assemblea di Palazzo Madama subito dopo la prima decade di ottobre. In una riunione dei rappresentanti dei gruppi parlamentari svoltasi oggi a Palazzo Madama si è stabilito di cominciare e concludere nella settimana prossima (da mercoledì a venerdì) l'esame degli stati di previsione dei dicasteri finanziari.

Il bilancio potrà quindi essere approvato entro il 12 ottobre. (Ag. Italia)

(The Press) stands at the pinnacle of Italian serious journalism and exemplifies in its progressive outlook and intellectual tone the best in world journalism.

Since he took over as editor of the paper in 1948, Dr. Giulio de Benedetti has established for himself a special niche in Italian journalism; while retaining the basic traditions of *La Stampa*, he has managed to imprint his image vividly on the character of the paper. He has insisted on clear, precise writing and the newspaper's once bleak page makeup is now atractive and well ordered. In Italy this is significant, for most papers still retain wordy and often pompous prose displayed on old-fashioned and tightly printed pages.

Although *La Stampa*, with a daily circulation of some 330,000,[1] is owned by the Fiat automobile company, De Benedetti is his own boss and his own political and journalistic philosophy is clearly manifest in the newspaper's pages. Like Alfio Russo, editor of Milan's *Corriere della Sera*, De Benedetti prides himself on being an editor who not only directs the editorial functions of the paper but actually concerns himself personally with the technical and routine aspects of getting out the paper. Even though in his seventies, he is in his office every day and remains until 3 or 4 A.M., often literally standing over the chases in the composing room supervising page makeup and helping with details. Without a doubt, Dr. De Benedetti is the authority at *La Stampa*, both in editorial policy and in practical matters of craftsmanship.[2]

La Stampa can trace its history back to the *Gazetta Piedmontese* founded in 1867 and its great prestige to two outstanding editors, Luigi Roux and Alfredo Frassati, who bought the old *Gazetta* in 1895 and changed its name to *La Stampa*. From 1901 on, Frassati edited the paper alone and later bought it and continued improving it in all departments. It was considered one of the main liberal voices of the country.[3]

When Mussolini and his Fascists came to power in 1925, Frassati refused to sign a Fascist card and realized that his days with *La Stampa* were over.[4] He sold the paper in 1926; it reopened with a Fascist staff. After World War II the newspaper was re-established in its present form. Dr. De Benedetti has been editor since 1948, and along with Frassati has done most to make *La Stampa* the quality journal it is today.[5]

In the city of Turin *La Stampa* has no serious rival; its circulation saturates the city and its environs. It is published every day but Monday and has an evening edition called *Stampa Sera* (Evening Press) which comes out on Monday (but not Sunday) and carries more sports news and pictures than any other general newspaper of Italy. Turin's citizens are very proud of the paper and insist that it is the best in the entire country. (It certainly ranks with Milan's *Corriere* and Rome's *Messaggero* in the "Big Three" of Italian elite dailies.) Much of *La Stampa*'s reputation has come from its concern with Italian social problems. Probably no other paper in the country gives as much emphasis to economic and social changes—and need for change. One reason for its concern with economic matters, of course, is that Turin is in the industrial and bustling north Italian Piedmont region and, along with Milan to the east, has the most cosmopolitan outlook of the country.[6] Foreign news is stressed, too, and its local coverage is as thorough as any other Italian paper. Other than that of Milan's *Corriere della Sera*, its "third page"[7] stands without a peer in Italian journalism where this cultural-literary page is a national institution.

Its daily letters from readers' section (an unusual feature in Italy) adds to the paper's popular following. Letters of all types appear—from those about people in difficulty requesting help to those from well-educated people discussing serious philosophical questions. Although letters to the editor are quite common in most quality papers of the world, *La Stampa* can be said to have pioneered in this area of Italian journalism and it is typical of the paper's progressive, flexible policies which have placed it among the elite dailies of Italy and of the world.[8]

What about the paper's politics? They are rather clear-cut. Its reporters and commentators give support to the center-left Government's program of introducing internal reforms "called for by a country in a state of radical social transformation."[9] Oftentimes the paper's stand on social issues are in agreement with that of Italy's Socialist Party. It should be noted, however, that *La Stampa*'s general attitude fits into the liberal orientation found throughout the paper's history. *La Stampa* is definitely anti-Fascist; at the same time it is vigorously anti-Communist. In short, it is "liberal" in the old European, and perhaps the truest, sense of the term. It is its own master and plays each policy decision in a way which it thinks is called for at the time under the special circumstances which prevail. It is not a slave to doctrinaire politics.

Svenska Dagbladet
(SWEDEN)

In spite of the fact that it is not printed in one of the "international languages," Stockholm's *Svenska Dagbladet* has achieved a prominence in Europe that has caused it to be called *The Times* of Sweden. Founded December 18, 1884, it has served as the main organ of Swedish conservatism and is closely associated with the Conservative Party, although it has no financial dependence on it. Until 1897, the *Svenska Dagbladet* (Swedish Daily Sheet) was in one economic crisis after another. When a new regime took over in this year, the paper as it is today came into being. It was during the next two decades that it established itself as the journal for the educated classes, and especially contributed a new

SVENSKA DAGBLADET

LÖRDAGEN DEN 16 SEPTEMBER 1967

Blodtest för kolos på 120 poliser

En vanlig personbil ger ifrån sig lika mycket koloxid som 50 diesellastbilar. Varje år släpps det ut en miljon ton koloxid i Sverige, och varje år förekommer det dödsfall på grund av koloxidförgiftning. Detta framhölls vid FOA-konferensen på torsdagen i Stockholm. Över 120 patrullerande Stockholmspoliser gick på torsdagen direkt efter sin tjänst som trafikdirigerande poliser till Karolinska sjukhusets yrkesmedicinska klinik för bl. a. blodprovstagning. Först om en vecka vet man på Arbetsmedicinska institutet i Stockholm hur farligt det är att dirigera trafiken i Stockholm.

Se sidan 11 7

LBJ-regeringen attackeras åter "USA vilseleds"

Kritiken mot Johnsonregeringen för att medvetet försöka föra det amerikanska folket bakom ljuset beträffande Vietnamkriget har tagit ny fart efter den senaste upptrappningen av bombningarna mot Nordvietnam. Dessa har också breddat spekulationerna om en åsiktsbrytning mellan presidenten och försvarsminister Mc Namara. Den sistnämnde förklarade så sent som den 25 augusti att bombning av de nu angripna hamnstäderna inte effektivt skulle hindra infiltrationen av materiel till Sydvietnam och därtill medföra risker som "jag för närvarande anser alltför stora för att ta".

USA har alltjämt världens största krigsmakt med sina 3.4 miljoner man under fanorna jämfört med Sovjets 3.22 miljoner och Kinas 2.7 miljoner. Även på kärnvapenområdet ligger USA före men förhållandet mellan USA:s och Sovjets kärnvapenarsenaler håller på att förskjutas i rysk fördel. Ett nytt ryskt vapen bestående av ett knippe vätebomber vilka avfyras med samma raket och sedan träffar flera mål samtidigt hotar att helt eliminera det amerikanska försprånget, framgår det av den årliga rapporten från det brittiska institutet för strategiska studier.

I SYDVIETNAM har sex av de besegrade civila presidentkandidaterna meddelat att de har bildat en "kampfront för demokratin" mot generalerna Nguyen Van Thieu och Nguyen Cao Ky. — Vi brännmärker högtidligt denna regims förtryckande och korrumperade maktutövning, förklarade kandidaterna. Fronten leds av "tvåan" i valet nyligen, Saigonadvokaten Truong Dinh Dzu. Samtidigt meddelades det att de amerikanska förlusterna steg kraftigt under den gångna veckan till följd av häftig stridsaktivitet i norra Sydvietnam.

Utlandsnytt se sid. 8

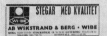

Ny SvD-serie: *Höstens bostäder*

Hyrorna släpps fria 1969 Ny lag ger besittningsskydd

Radiotekniker Roland Waax och hans fru Marianne tillhör dem som fått lägenhet i Orminge-området i Saltsjö-Boo. På fredagen var de ute och tjuvtittade på sin fyra i nybyggarsamhället.

På lördagen börjar inflyttningen i Familjebostäders bostadskomplex vid Orminge i Saltsjö-Boo. Bolaget bygger där totalt 1 100 lägenheter . . . Aldrig förr har bostadsproduktionen gått på så högt varv som just nu, säger experterna. SvD har undersökt var de nya lägenheterna uppförs — och vad de kostar. Serien börjar med en titt på bostadsbyggandet i de sydöstra förorterna.

Se sidan 11

Myndighet kan pröva höjning

Om två år — 1 oktober 1969 — blir det premiär för den friare hyressättningen i Sverige. Regeringen har nämligen beslutat proposition till riksdagen om en ny hyreslagstiftning. Nu gällande hyresreglering avskaffas för hela landet vid utgången av år 1968, och den nya hyreslagen träder i kraft 1 januari 1969. Den hyra, som gäller vid utgången av 1968, skall dock tillämpas under den löpande hyresperioden, vilket i regel innebär tiden fram till 1 oktober 1969. Huvudregeln blir att hyresregleringen ersätts med avtalsfrihet mellan hyresvärd och hyresgäst inom ramen för den permanenta hyreslagens bestämmelser.

— Vilka hyreshöjningar, som kan bli en följd av den nya ordningen, är det omöjligt att i dag ge något svar på. En mängd faktorer spelar in. I vissa hyreshus blir det kanske endast fråga om smärre justeringar — i andra om mera betydande höjningar.

Till saken hör att hyresgästen får direkt besittningsskydd. Det innebär, att hyresgästen får rätt till förlängt hyresavtal, när hyrestiden går ut, om inte någon viss i lagen angiven situation föreligger. Och detta besittningsskydd skall inte kunna sättas ur spel genom obilliga hyreskrav. Om hyresvärden sätter höjd hyra, som villkor för att han skall gå med på att förlänga hyreskontraktet, skall den begärda hyrans skälighet kunna prövas av myndighet.

Särskilda övergångsregler föreslås för bostadslägenheter i bristorterna. De innebär att hyrorna får successivt anpassas till hyresläget för likvärdiga lägenheter under en övergångstid. För de tre storstadsregionerna skall denna tid omfatta fyra år, alltså till utgången av år 1972.

För övriga bristorter blir övergångstiden 2-årig och gäller således till utgången av år 1970.

I orter med mera påtaglig bostadsbrist skall den s. k. förstagångshyran — d. v. s. i princip den

Forts. sid. 14, sp. 1 HYROR . . .

Måste vi vänja oss vid buller?

Är flygbullerstörningar någonting som nutidsmänniskan får lov att vänja sig vid i hela samhällets intresse? Eller är jetplansljudet en stressfaktor, som man visserligen inte vet så mycket om i dag men som man ändå måste försöka bekämpa på alla fronter? Frågan är högaktuell, inte minst mot bakgrund av den strid om jetplanens eventuella återinsläppande på Bromma flygplats, som kan förutses blossa upp i höst.

Det första exemplaret av DC 9 (ett lånat sådant i väntan på leverans av den riktiga versionen) kom till Arlanda på torsdagen. SAS skall nu pröva maskinen under en tid. I oktober skall DC 9 användas för bullermätningar på Bromma för kontroll av de teoretiska bullervärdena för planet, som inom kort lämnas till Luftfartsverket från en konsultfirma i Göteborg.

Fjärde artikeln i SvD:s bullerserie återfinns på sista sid.

Världsbanken vill ta upp lån i Sverige för hjälp åt u-länder

Världsbanken har hos svenska riksbanken begärt att få placera ett stort obligationslån, uppger Sveriges radio. Om riksbanken går med på denna begäran blir det första gången världsbanken lånar pengar i Sverige. Ett beslut kan väntas om ett par dagar. Det har aldrig tidigare hänt att världsbanken emitterat ett lån på den svenska marknaden. För fyra år sedan gav visserligen riksbanken tillstånd till en sådan emission, men det blev inget av det hela, i huvudsak beroende på det höga svenska ränteläget.

Storleken på det lån som världsbanken nu begärt att få emittera är inte känd men det tippas att det kommer att röra sig om 50 eller 100 milj. kr., eller avsevärt mer än vad som är vanligt på den svenska lånemarknaden.

Världsbanken, som upprättades 1947, har till uppgift att finansiera kreditvärdiga utvecklingsprojekt i företrädesvis u-länderna. Kommer det svenska lånet till stånd kan det alltså ses som en utvidgning av den svenska u-hjälpen.

Tidigare har världsbanken i huvudsak emitterat sina lån på den amerikanska marknaden men på senare år har banken även byggt upp en marknad i Europa. Lån har bl.a. placerats i Nederländerna, Belgien, Italien och Västtyskland. Under en tid hade banken svårigheter att placera lån på grund av kapitalbristen ute i världen men situationen har nu förändrats.

Sjuk baby i ilfärd 23 mil

GÖTEBORG/ Ett nyfött barn med gulsot fördes på torsdagskvällen i ilfart med ambulans de 23 milen mellan Eksjö och Göteborg. Ambulansen kom strax före kl. 21 fram till barnsjukhuset i Göteborg, där man under natten skulle förse den sjuka babyn med nytt friskt blod.

Sjuktransporten startade från Eksjö kl. 18.45. I alla större tätorter hade polisen förvarnats så att man kunde hålla genomfartsvägarna fria. I Borås var t. ex. hela centrum avstängt medan sju polisfordon eskorterade ambulansen genom staden. En mil från Göteborg fick ambulansen punktering, men efter däckbyte i rekordfart lotsade en polispatrull fram den till målet.

Att babyn fördes till Göteborg förklarades av att barnsjukhuset där är blodbytescentral för hela Västsverige, däribland Eksjö.

Ännu en förfalskad 1 000-lapp

Ytterligare en falsk 1 000-kronorssedel, den elfte i ordningen, har nu inrapporterats till kriminalpolisens bedrägerirotel i Stockholm.

Sedeln växlades in på ett postkontor på Kungsholmen i Stockholm. Detta tros ha skett redan i måndags, men först på torsdagskvällen upptäcktes det att sedeln var oäkta. Man kontaktade då kriminalen som nu skall höra postpersonalen om händelsen.

Man tror emellertid att det kan bli mycket svårt att få något signalement på den person som gjort transaktionen då det gått för lång tid och personalen kan ha svårt att minnas episoden.

Den 22-årige man, som anhållits i sin frånvaro i samband med utprångling av falska tusenlappar, hade ännu på fredagen inte kunnat gripas.

Billigare tågresor mitt i veckan på lågtrafiklinjer

JÖNKÖPING (SvD:s utsände medarbetare) I början av oktober blir det billigare att åka tåg på vissa sträckor och om resan påbörjas en tisdag, onsdag eller torsdag. SJ skall pröva ett nytt rabattsystem som ger andraklassresenärerna upp till 30 procents nedsättning på tur och returbiljetten på flera sträckor inom landet. Försöken skall pågå hela vintern fram till slutet på februari.

— Vi vänder oss i första hand till de resenärer som själva får betala sin biljett, alltså folk som mest reser andra klass, berättade direktör Anders Ekelund vid SJ:s kommersiella avdelning inför Svenska Turisttrafikförbundets turistriksdag i Jönköping på torsdagen. Mitt i veckan har vi en lägre resandefrekvens än kring veckoslutet. Hittills har flertalet föredragit att ta bilen på sträckor ända upp till 300 km.

Rabattbiljetterna gäller en månad och skall finnas på en rad sträckor. Från Stockholm kan man köpa rabattbiljetter till exempelvis Sundsvall, Härnösand, Umeå och Örebro. Däremot inte till Göteborg och Malmö av den enkla anledningen att där är beläggningen konstant mycket god särskilt efter högertrafikomläggningen. Några prisexempel: Göteborg—Kalmar kommer med rabattbiljett att kosta 70 kr. Tok Stockholm—Sundsvall 75 kr., Stockholm—Umeå 115 kr., Stockholm—Örebro 50 kr.

Turistexplosionen har drabbat oss så snabbt och överraskande att många fortfarande yrvaket och misstroget betraktar denna företeelse, framhöll fil. dr Sven Rydenfelt, Lund, i ett anförande under rubriken "Turismen erövrar världen", att trots att turismen i dag är vår

Forts. sid. 14, sp. 5 SJ . . .

Professorerna Hannes Alfvén och Karl Birger Blomdahl i Tekniska högskolans datacentral — assisterade av professor Alfvéns dotter Inger.

Unik triangelförbrödring bakom opera

Operan, Tekniska högskolan och Sveriges radio ingår en unik triangelförbrödring för att gemensamt kunna realisera ett svenskt operaprojekt som tillika är en världsnyhet. Det gäller Karl Birger Blomdahls kommande tredje opera som bygger på pseudonymen Olof Johanessons — alias atomprofessor Hannes Alfvén — hösten 1966 utkomna bok "Sagan om den stora datamaskinen". Operan beräknas bli färdig säsongen 1969/70. Uruppförandet blir på Stockholmsoperan med operachefen Göran Gentele som regissör. Det är säkerligen första gången en opera skrivs där temat är förankrat i nutida teknologiska problemställningar som berör hela mänskligheten. Likaså är det etablerade samarbetet mellan teknik och konst unikt i operakonstens historia. Halva föreställningen skall innehålla levande musik, halva elektronisk musik utarbetad på Sveriges radios elektronstudio. Vid något tillfälle skall den kosmiska strålningen direkt styra bandspelaren med varierande föreställningsresultat från kväll till kväll som följd.

Se sidan 13

Olika uppfattningar om TV-frågor

Sveriges industriförbund och TV:s Åke Ortmark har olika uppfattning om formuleringen av några enkätfrågor, som TV-reportrarna Ortmark och Mats Fagerström för närvarande låter ingå över industrimän i Sverige inför ett kommande program. Det gäller EEC och neutraliteten. Industriförbundet anser att frågorna är felaktigt ställda samt ledande. Ortmark finner att Industriförbundet citerar frågorna fel . . .

Se sidan 9

Toppvinster till städer

Högsta vinsten i fredagens dragning i penninglotteriet gick till Örebro, dit även en 50 000-kronorsvinst gick. Göteborg kammade hem både 200 000 och 100 000. Den fullständiga dragningslistan återfinnes på sid. 14

Förgubbning hotar skogen

I Skåne har hundra man inlett operation "Sågverk 70" — en finansieringskampanj som går ut på att skaffa 15 milj. kr till ett modernt sågverk. Det anses att den skånska skogen hotas av "förgubbning" om inte snara åtgärder vidtas för att öka avsättningen.

Se sidan 20

Omväxlande morgonsamling

Morgonsamlingarna får ett mer meningsfyllt innehåll och kristendomsläraren avlastas mycket arbete med planläggningen sedan skolöverstyrelsens nya anvisningar nu kommit ut. 150 färdiga program för omväxlande och berikande samlingar i grundskolan har utarbetats.

Se sidan 10

H-trafikkurs

Alla kan bli medarbetare i en studiekurs som hjälper till att kartlägga högertrafiken, meddelade HTK på torsdagen när man presenterade den första delen av den nya kursen.

Se sidan 10

Domaren bröt dimhöljd allsvensk match

En tät dimma tvingade på torsdagskvällen fotbollsdomaren Sune Modigh, Örebro, att avbryta matchen mellan IFK Norrköping och GAIS. Dimman var så tjock att spelarna på planen inte kunde ses från läktaren. Matchavbrottet kom i matchens 70:e minut, men efter ett uppehåll på 20 minuter kunde man fortsätta. Norrköping vann med 1—0.

På torsdagskvällen ökade Malmö FF ytterligare på sitt försprång sedan man slagit Örgryte på bortaplan med 1—0 och Djurgården hemma förlorat med 1—5 mot Elfsborg. Malmö leder nu med 6 poäng.

Se Idrotten!

Simon Wiesenthal:

Nazitidens mördare finns mitt ibland oss

Simon Wiesenthal, jagar nazitidens mördare över hela världen.

Med få undantag lever alla mördare från nazitiden, några är dödförklarade och t. o. m. omgifta med sina änkor. Många av dem finns mitt ibland oss. Detta hävdade österrikaren Simon Wiesenthal, mannen som jagar nazistiska krigsförbrytare och har ett arkiv i Wien med 22 500 namn på efterlysta, under en konferens i Stockholm på onsdagen. Han är övertygad om att Martin Bormann lever, liksom många andra framstående nazister, någonstans i Latinamerika, skyddad av anonymitet, pengar och speciella organisationer. Även i östländer finns gamla nazister, speciellt i Östtyskland.

Se sidan 7

Studenter lär per TV hösten -68

Redan nästa år får kanske 6 000 studenter vid universitet och högskolor lära algebra i intern TV. Samtidigt startar interna TV-program för studerande i företagsekonomi och nästa år blir det också TV-program i studieteknik, i yrkesvägledning och radiokurs i tillämpad matematik. Det planerar kommittén för TV och radio i utbildningen, som begär drygt 13 miljoner för sin verksamhet nästa år.

Se sidan 11

Tårgasrån mot bank Byte 37 000

GÖTEBORG. (SvD:s Göteborgsred.) **Vid ett rån i Svenska handelsbankens lokalkontor på Första Långgatan i Göteborg på torsdagen kom en ung tysk över cirka 37 000 kronor, sedan han med en sprayflaska sprutat tårgas mot personalen. Två timmar efter rånet greps han medan hans kompan, som väntade i en bil utanför banken, försvann.**

Rånet inträffade strax före kl. 15. Tysken gick in bakom disken i bankkontoret och började spruta tårgas ur sprayflaskan. Samtidigt gav de han en rush lånes kassorna och

Forts. sid. 14, sp. 4 RÅN . . .

dimension to Swedish journalism by giving emphasis to the arts and sciences.[1]

Outstanding intellectuals, such as the author Verner von Heidenstam, contributed articles to the paper and it soon was known throughout Scandinavia as a journal of concern and reasonableness, appealing to the opinion leaders of the country. One of its primary characteristics right up until today has been its devotion to cultural matters.

Now that *The Times* of London has eliminated its front-page advertisements, *Svenska Dagbladet* is probably the most important daily left which carries advertising on its front page. Its third page is its main-news page, although the reader can find substantial quantities of news throughout the paper. While the makeup of the pages is more lively than is usually found in elite papers, the news and interpretation is handled in a serious and dignified manner. Its circulation of about 170,000 (four editions a day) is small, but considering the fact that the paper appears in a country of under eight million people, its readership is considered quite good for a paper of its type.

Although it is generally conservative, *Svenska Dagbladet* is not inflexible or reactionary, for it has pioneered in many areas of Swedish journalism and in cultural and artistic life of the country in general. It was the first paper to devote much space to cultural affairs and to provide the major outlet for articles on education, science, art, literature, and theology.

Ambivalent politically during its first thirty years, it has held to a firm conservative line since World War I and has been the leading journal of this orientation in the country. Its ties with the Conservative Party, if any, are purely informal and nonfinancial. In fact, there are instances of *Svenska Dagbladet* deviating drastically at times from the policy of the Party.

Its system of ownership has attracted international interest because of its stability and effectiveness in protecting it from economic transactions which might endanger its freedom. It is owned by a foundation, formed in 1940; soon the foundation took over privately owned shares and after a few years all private shares were eliminated. All profits go back into the paper for all types of improvements. The beautiful and functional new 14-story plant in central Stockholm (at Marieburg) completed in 1962 illustrates one use for the profits.[2] Making up the foundation are representatives of various segments of Swedish society —industry, the Church, the armed forces, and educational and cultural institutions. Members appoint a board, which appoints the editor of the newspaper. The editor alone decides what will go in the paper as long as he does not deviate too far from the main lines established when the foundation was formed. A lawsuit may be brought against him by the board if he is thought to have failed in his responsibilities as an editor.[3]

Under Allan Hernelius, who succeeded Ivar Anderson as editor in 1955, *Svenska Dagbladet* retains its position as the leading journal of what is often called progressive conservatism. Although it consistently upholds conservative ideals, strongly favors defense and the State Church, and wages a running war against oversocialization or against the people's creeping tendency toward total dependence on government, it is devoted to democracy as it demonstrated in World War II when it took a leading part in opposing the Nazis.[4]

Its readership reflects its informed, progressive, and flexible character; in addition to reaching high government officials, intellectuals, and industrial and financial leaders, *Svenska Dagbladet* is read by the politically influential in all parties. Its chief editor, Allan Hernelius, believes it influences Swedish public opinion "to a considerable extent."[5] The paper is the main critic of the powerful Social Democratic Party, which has governed Sweden since 1932, and its literate, informed, and sophisticated criticism in the area of politics is considered by friend and foe to be one of the most significant forces in Swedish politics.[6]

Svenska Dagbladet's main and long-standing editorial policy is to present good international coverage, both in news and commentary. And this is perhaps its strongest area. It receives the London *Times* news service as well as that of *The New York Times*. In addition, it has co-operative news-exchange agreements with Copenhagen's *Berlingske Tidende* (see Part II) and Oslo's *Aftenposten*; its Scandinavian coverage is thus greatly enhanced, supplementing its excellent world coverage. It has twelve foreign correspondents stationed in Bonn, Paris, London, Brussels, Helsinki, Oslo, Copenhagen, Rome, Moscow, New York, Vienna, and The Hague.[7] The paper's writing and editing staff in Stockholm numbers about a hundred, at least half of whom have university degrees.[8] They produce a newspaper, the typical edition of which runs from twenty to twenty-four pages, presenting to the Swedish reader a high-quality product that can hold its own in comprehensiveness and enlightenment with the best papers of Scandinavia and all of Europe.

The Yorkshire Post
(ENGLAND)

In the North of England, in the city of Leeds in Yorkshire, is published a daily paper which began in the summer of 1754. It has made its influence felt throughout Britain as a worthy representative of a quality newspaper which has always determined to be an excellent regional organ. A counterpart to the liberal *Guardian* of Manchester in politics, *The Yorkshire Post* has been satisfied to serve its locality well, to be read by serious opinion leaders outside its own county, and to have a substantial number of influential readers in London.

The Yorkshire Post was founded by Griffith Wright as *The Leeds Intelligencer*, a modest weekly paper in four-page folio containing four columns to the page.[1] (It took its present name in 1866.) Like most early provincial papers its pages were filled largely with news from the London journals, and with advertisements. From the start, although mildly at first, the paper was a Tory paper, and its local competition with the *Mercury*, a paper of vigor in its own right, forced the *Intelligencer* constantly to improve. From the first the paper was never a mere parochial newssheet, and it very soon gained a reputation as a paper interested in the events and problems of surrounding counties and of London. Under the title of *The Intelligencer*, the paper became well written and energetic, flourishing through the years of swift scientific progress and economic development. In 1866 the paper became a daily and its name was changed to *The Yorkshire Post*, indicating an appeal to a wider area but bringing no change in its long-established literary and political traditions. The title change made no break in continuity of thought and purpose, and it is quite common to think of the paper, despite its change of name on becoming a daily, as having been founded in 1754.[2]

Following the example set by *The Times*, the makeup of the new daily was austere and made use of every inch of space. On some days the front page was given over to advertisements and public announcements, but often three or four of its columns contained some news—often dispatches from the foreign correspondents of *The Times* or *The Daily Telegraph* of London. In the Saturday issue was a supplement of literary articles, book reviews, and dramatic and music criticism, all packed neatly into only four pages.[3]

One of the paper's most outstanding early editors was Charles Pebody, who took over the paper in 1882 and led *The Post* to seek a wider circle of readers by expanding the range of the paper's contents. For the next twenty years this was the objective of the journal: "To reflect the genius of the people among whom it circulated, and to represent and identify itself with what was distinctive in the Yorkshire character."[4] Under Pebody *The Post* prospered in every way and an evening edition, *The Yorkshire Evening Post*, was begun. Pebody died in 1890, whereupon Henry John Palmer, who had been an editor in Birmingham, became editor.

Palmer had little use for the new journalism of the cheaply sensational kind which was becoming popular in England; he believed in the dignity of the press in all of its manifestations. Palmer thought of his paper as a moral force and always determined "to write nothing and say nothing that was not for the good of his fellowmen."[5] He improved *The Post*'s makeup; its page was enlarged to eight columns, and by the

The Yorkshire Post

ESTAB. 1754 No. 37,440 LEEDS THURSDAY OCTOBER 12 1967 PRICE 4d. TEL. LEEDS 32701

Australia and Britain: ways 'now parting'

THERE WERE unhappy signs of change in the close relationship between Britain and Australia, Sir Alexander Downer, High Commissioner for Australia, said yesterday.

The old trade was declining—" not in absolute terms but in percentages." This was partly due to the desire " to revolutionise Britain's economy by joining the European Economic Community."

" Australians, among other Commonwealth countries, being threatened with the loss of their free entry, or preferences, in the United Kingdom market, have deliberately taken out insurance policies, as it were, by developing alternate markets in Asia, North America, and elsewhere.

SIR ALEXANDER DOWNER "Paths diverging."

" In return," Sir Alexander continued, " we must naturally buy from our new customers, and so the British manufacturer suffers.

'Trade at peril'

" There is still a sizable proportion of Australian trade with Britain at peril should this country become part of Europe, and it is idle to pretend that we will be other than severely injured by the loss of the present preferential trade arrangements.

" No Australian Government, of course, would presume to dictate to Great Britain what see ought to do. That would be most impertinent.

" I hope you will agree, however, that we are entitled to point out the consequences for our producers at home as well as for British exporters here should they, in turn, lose their own highly valuable preferences in Australia as a result of Britain joining the European Community."

Disappointment

The paths of the two countries were diverging in other aspects of the overall Commonwealth relationship, said Sir Alexander, who was addressing the Royal Commonwealth Society at Bath.

" We would not be human if we were not disappointed by the British Government's decision, last July, to abandon what is colloquially-termed the East of Suez defence policy.

" This remarkable land of our ancestors, unique in so many respects, is going to count for less and less in world affairs in proportion to her retreat from global responsibilities.

" If the ultimate destination of Britain is merely to become one of a group of European States, a member of a European economic and political confederation, then her diplomatic influence will be confined chiefly to Europe."

Canada, Australia, New Zealand, and the smaller partners in the " Old Commonwealth " would have to redesign their foreign, defence, and commercial policies, and proceed independently of Britain.

The sufferer

" This, I must tell you, is what Australia is now being compelled to do."

Sir Alexander said that if restrictions on British investment in Australia and other sterling area countries, imposed by the Treasury in 1966, remained for more than a temporary period, " in the long run the sufferer will not be us but you."

18-mile oil slick off Yorks. coast

Yorkshire Post Correspondents

AN OIL SLICK located by an RAF Shackleton on patrol off the Yorkshire coast was last night 18 miles long and 15 miles south-east of Flamborough Head. It was coming from a ship moving south-south-east from Flamborough at 12 knots.

The slick had been reported earlier to be six miles off Flamborough Head easterly and to be six miles long. The Shackleton aircraft was diverted to investigate and the Ministry of Defence said last night that the RAF would take whatever action was desired.

Coastguards said the weather forecast was for strong south-westerly winds so there was little chance of the oil coming ashore. All local authorities on the Yorkshire coast have been notified so that they could take precautions if necessary.

International law

A Board of Trade spokesman said last night that an International Convention for the Prevention of the Pollution of the Sea by Oil had been drawn up in the 1950s by the Inter-Governmental Maritime Consultative Organisation.

This was signed by most countries, including Britain.

The procedure is that evidence of pollution is obtained usually by an aircraft, or coastguard. If the offending ship is British her owners can be prosecuted in British Courts.

If foreign, the evidence is sent to the Government with which she is registered, and they prosecute. There have in fact been many cases of prosecutions by foreign governments.

Among defences that might be accepted by Court are that oil was discharged accidentally or, if, for example, a ship was in danger of sinking, to safeguard both her and her crew.

The spokesman could not say if a Royal Navy vessel would be sent out to intercept an offending ship in territorial waters.

In a recent case a civil airline pilot had reported a ship discharging oil in the Channel. An RAF aircraft was sent to identify her and the Board of Trade then traced her to Liverpool where one of their officials went aboard and told the captain he would be reported.

TODAY'S WEATHER

LANCASHIRE, WESTMORLAND, CUMBERLAND: Scattered showers rather heavy at times with risk of thunder in a few places. Sunny intervals. Winds south-westerly moderate becoming fresh and strong in a few places. Max. 13C (55F).

NORTHUMBERLAND, DURHAM, YORKSHIRE, LINCOLNSHIRE: Sunny periods, dry at first, isolated showers in afternoon. Wind southwesterly moderate to fresh in a few places. Max. 13C (55F).

LONDON AREA: Cloudy with scattered showers and some bright intervals. Max. 15C (59F).

OUTLOOK: Showers heavy at times and sunny intervals. Temperatures near or rather below normal.

* * Sunshine and other details.— * P. 9.

ON OTHER PAGES

MAO WARNS PEASANTS — P. 8.

Mr. Marsh rejects higher oil surcharge

THE MINISTRY of Power has told the oil companies that Mr. Richard Marsh does not consider any further increase in the temporary surcharge on oil prices is necessary at present, the Ministry stated last night.

"The position will be reviewed from time to time," the Ministry added. "The existing 2d. a gallon surcharge (allowed on June 30) on the prices of all petroleum products will continue."

A spokesman for Shell-Mex and BP said last night: "We have nothing to say."

'We never asked'

A spokesman for Esso Petroleum Company commented: "Esso never asked for a further surcharge on oil products.

"Our recommendation to the Ministry was that the situation should remain unchanged. We are neither surprised nor disappointed at the Ministry's decision."

Regent Oil Company stated: "We have duly noticed the views expressed by the Minister."

Meeting today on beer prices

The National Federation of Licensed Victuallers is to meet the Brewers' Society in London today to decide whether to approach the Minister of Agriculture over beer prices, which have been "frozen" for the last 18 months.

Overheads of many licensees have risen by more than 10 per cent.: over the last two years.

Bank hours plan goes to union

PLANS FOR new banking hours proposed by the 11 clearing banks are being considered by the National Union of Bank Employees.

Mr. Alfred Brooks, general secretary of the union, was given details of the plans when he met officials of Barclays Bank, one of the banks which officially recognise the union, in London yesterday. But he would not disclose them when he arrived in Manchester later to address a meeting.

He told reporters: "All I can say about it is that certain proposals have been made to the union by the banks regarding banking hours of a rather complicated nature. They fell far short of the union's policies."

Mr. Brooks said the union's policy was for a five-day working week with no Saturday working. The proposals by the banks were more comprehensive than anything he had imagined and more comprehensive than anything that had been published.

The union was expected to give some reply early next month.

'Wrong figures' argument after professor reports

STEAM IS TAKEN OUT OF RAIL GUARDS' DISPUTE

By RONALD KERSHAW, Yorkshire Post Industrial Correspondent

FINDINGS of a Court of Inquiry into railway guards' pay published yesterday, took the steam out of the dispute that led to the National Union of Railwaymen imposing a ban on guards doing second man duties.

The findings showed that there was insufficient money coming from proposed increased productivity to meet the 4s. 9d. a day rise demanded by the union.

The inquiry, ordered by Mr. Gunter, Minister of Labour, and conducted by Prof. D. J. Robertson, of Glasgow, also revealed that the Railways Board had made "faulty" assumptions so that savings calculated to be made under a 1965 "single manning" agreement affecting drivers did not materialise. In fact they made a loss and this did not look like turning into a gain until 1971.

The reaction of Mr. Sidney Greene, NUR General Secretary, was "there is no point in trying to burgle a house twice if the money has already gone." He is expected to recommend to his executive today that the ban on second man duties be removed and negotiations for increases start all over again.

The report ruled that the amount of extra work carried out by guards on single-manned trains was minimal. Under the circumstances the Board's offer of 2s. 4½d. a day was reasonable and even generous.

The report recommends that such a productivity bonus should be confined to guards who actually do second man duties and should not be given all round. Shunters engaged in extra duties should receive a bonus of 2s. a day.

Prof. Robertson says he cannot support the NUR's claim for treatment comparable to that of drivers and second men under the 1965 single manning agreement.

'Do two wrongs make a right?'

He indicates that because of the Board's faulty assumptions, the Board were wrong to grant productivity increases to the drivers. He says: "This raises the question in simple, colloquial terms of whether two wrongs make a right."

The report makes an alternative suggestion that a flat rate productivity bonus be negotiated.

Mr. Gunter met both sides last night and commended to them the recommendations in the report.

He drew particular attention to Prof. Robertson's suggestions for flat-rate productivity payments for all guards and the board's proposals for improvements in efficiency which could make substantial sums of money available for this purpose.

Union urged to lift ban

A Ministry statement said: "He suggested negotiations on these proposals should be pursued urgently through the pay and efficiency talks under his chairmanship, on which the board have undertaken to begin pay negotiations for railway staff generally by the end of the year."

The Minister urged the NUR representatives in the light of the report to lift their current ban on guards carrying out "second man" duties which could now only lead to further loss of work from the industry, to enable these negotiations for further improvements in pay to be pressed ahead without distractions.

The Minister urged the board to press ahead with their study of possibilities for increasing the productivity of guards and other grades, "in order that progress might be made as rapidly as possible in the pay and efficiency talks."

The report, said Mr. Greene, had

(Continued on P. 9)

Sacked union man back in car talks

Yorkshire Post Reporters

A UNION official dismissed on Monday from his post as area organiser will lead the Luton and Dunstable Vauxhall Motors delegation at today's peace talks between unions and management at Harrogate.

The National Executive of the National Union of Vehicle Builders dismissed Mr. Arthur Leary because of an alleged "scurrilous attack" on the union. Mr. Leary was barred from the Harrogate conference table.

Union officials of the Luton and Dunstable factories met two local Labour MPs, Mr. Robert Maxwell and Mr. Will Howie, and drew up the plan to reinstate him behind locked doors.

One district delegate resigned from the team and Mr. Leary as an ordinary NUVB member took his place. Then Mr. Jim Watts resigned as district secretary. Mr. Leary was elected as his successor and as will be the union's "spearhead" for the wage talks.

Boycott threat

Since the sacking fears grew concerning the pay and productivity talks which effect 25,000 hourly paid workers, the Luton District Committee of the union decided on Tuesday to boycott talks unless Mr. Leary was there to represent them.

The meeting, at the Majestic Hotel, Harrogate, is due to start at 11 a.m. Harrogate was chosen because it was convenient for union delegates who are attending a conference at York.

Mr. Alf Roberts, general secretary of the NUVB, said in York last night that there was no division between the Executive and the Luton District Committee, which had been handling negotiations.

Mr. Roberts said that £20 per week for Vauxhall workers could not be accepted while Rootes, at Coventry, paid £30 a week and, it was understood, £27 a week was being negotiated by other firms.

New atom power chief appointed

AT HIS OWN REQUEST Lord Penney, who assisted with the design and building of the first atomic bomb, is to be replaced as chairman of the United Kingdom Atomic Energy Authority, it was announced last night.

The Ministry of Technology said his successor is Dr. John M. Hill, a production member with the Authority since 1964.

Lord Penney, 58, who witnessed the atom bombing of Nagasaki and directed Britain's development of the atomic bomb, retires from the chairmanship on October 15 to take up the rectorship of Imperial College.

Dr. Hill was a lecturer at London University when he joined the Authority in 1950. He was appointed to the board in 1964, with direct responsibility for the Authority's production group.

Girl's body found on railway

The body of a girl aged 19 was last night found on railway lines at Colne Bridge, Huddersfield. She had been struck by a train.

A police spokesman said: "We believe we know the identity of the girl but we are waiting for positive identification."

S. Africa ban ends

Liverpool City Council, Conservative-controlled since May, decided last night to lift its ban on the purchase of goods from South Africa because of her Apartheid policy.

Mr. Thomson to meet Rhodesia Governor

Yorkshire Post Political Staff

MR. GEORGE THOMSON, Commonwealth Secretary, has decided to accept an invitation from the Rhodesian Governor, Sir Humphrey Gibbs, to visit Salisbury during his tour of African capitals.

An official announcement is expected any day now. The tour arrangements have now been pencilled in and the dates and time will be released as soon as confirmation has been received of all the details.

Sir Humphrey has been anxious to meet Mr. Thomson for some time and the new Commonwealth Secretary will also want to make an on-the-spot assessment of the working of the sanctions policy.

It is understood that the rebel Rhodesian regime has made it known that Mr. Thomson would be given safe conduct if he did wish to visit Salisbury but it was still uncertain last night whether he will meet Mr. Smith.

The exchange of letters that has been going on since Lord Alport's visit has yielded small hope that meaningful negotiations could be resumed.

Now that the governing parties in both London and Salisbury have had their party conferences, it may be timely to reassess the chances of further peace moves. The emotion and exaggerations which party conferences are apt to throw up were not considered conducive to a settlement.

In Lusaka Mr. Kamanga, Zambian Foreign Minister, said yesterday that Zambia felt the coming visit to Rhodesia by Mr. Thomson could mean a complete sell-out over Rhodesia, Reuter reports.

He said he had told Mr. Thomson in discussions in London it was "very ridiculous" for him to be going to what Britain described as her colony while South African forces were there.

Vice - Admiral Sir Norman Denning, who has been appointed Secretary of the Services, Press and Broadcasting committee.— Details—P. 9.

Six 'oui' or 'non'

PARIS, Wednesday.—The French Government will define its position on Britain's application to join the European Common Market at next Wednesday's weekly Cabinet meeting, M. Georges Gorse, Information Minister said today.—Reuter.

* * French use delaying tactics— * P. 9.

Mrs. Kennedy

Norfolk, Virginia, Wednesday.—Lord Harlech has declined to comment on a report he will marry Mrs. Jacqueline Kennedy. Nancy Tuckerman, Mrs. Kennedy's secretary, has denied the report and said Mrs. Kennedy was not about to announce her engagement to anyone.—A.P.

Finland devalues

HELSINKI, Thursday. — The Finnish Government today announced the devaluation of the Finnish mark by 31¼ per cent. The devaluation is effective immediately.—U.P.I.

THE £12,500,000 TYNE TUNNEL, which the Queen will open a week today, nears completion. Work on the tunnel, which links the north and south banks of the Tyne, began in November, 1961. Breakdowns in the tunnel will be spotted immediately by closed-circuit TV, but motorists unlucky enough to be stranded will have to pay £5 to be towed out by a rescue truck.

Five prisoners at large

POLICE last night were looking for five prisoners who had absconded from different gaols. One serving seven years failed to return from a shopping trip, said the Home Office.

He was Edward Jeffreys, 32, serving his sentence for burglary and larceny at Winson Green, Birmingham, under the hostel scheme.

Matthew Ingram, 49, serving 12 years for wounding and attempted suicide failed to return from home leave to Wakefield Prison.

Frederick Henson, 23, serving 30 months for shop breaking, house breaking and larceny, failed to return from home leave to Stafford Prison.

Peter Cook, 29, serving 21 months for house breaking and larceny, absconded from Kirkham Prison, Lancashire.

Patrick Leonard Sutton, 26, serving three years for housebreaking, larceny and robbery, escaped from Chelmsford Prison, Essex, by scaling a "ladder" made of scrap metal. A second prisoner who escaped with him was recaptured within 10 minutes.

Husband, wife and brother shot in cottage

POLICE called to a cottage in Lower Foel Road, Dyserth, Flintshire, yesterday found Mrs. Helen Christopher, 30, her husband, Geoffrey, 46, and his brother Philip, 40, dead from gunshot wounds.

A neighbour said that Mrs. Elizabeth Mary Smith, 69, lived at Jasmine Cottage, with her daughter and her two grandchildren. Also living there was Philip Christopher.

"Mrs. Smith came rushing in this afternoon crying that her son-in-law had called. Mrs. Smith said that he told her to get the police. After she left the house she heard a third shot," said the neighbour.

At lunch time an elderly woman returning from her shopping in the village was stopped by a man and asked: "Where is Jasmine Cottage?"

'That's where they are'

After being told that it was 150 yards up the road he replied: "So that's where they are."

The two young Christopher children, Ian, eight, and Malcolm, 11, were taken to the home of the village doctor, Dr. D. L. Bourdillon.

The Christopher family took over the rented furnished cottage earlier in the year.

Egyptian MIG shot down

TEL AVIV, Wednesday

AN EGYPTIAN MIG-21 jet was shot down tonight in a clash with Israeli aircraft over Israeli-occupied Sinai, an Army spokesman announced.

According to the Israeli spokesman two Egyptian Mig-21s violated the ceasefire, and flew across the Suez Canal. He said they were some 10 miles east of the Bitter Lake when Israeli aircraft went up to intercept them.

In the short dog fight one of the intruders was shot down and was seen falling on the western bank of the Suez Canal. No parachute was seen dropping from the falling aircraft.

The Iraq delegate told the United Nations General Assembly today that if the United Nations fails to get Israeli troops out of occupied Arab territory a new outbreak of war is inevitable in the Middle East.—U.P.I. and Reuter.

Seven arrested in Spanish elections

MADRID, Wednesday. — Seven people were arrested in Tarrasa, near Barcelona, on charges of distributing leaflets "urging people to abstain from voting" in Spain's General Election.

Spaniards had showed little enthusiasm in the first democratic parliamentary elections for 30 years as political parties were banned and nearly all the 313 candidates are backers of the régime.—Reuter and U.P.I.

Docker died after handling bones

DUNKIRK, Wednesday.—Fifteen dockworkers have been in hospital, and another has died at Dunkirk since they worked in the hold of a British ship carrying ground bones from India several weeks ago, officials reported today.

Doctors are investigating the possibility that the dead man caught a disease prevalent in India and unknown in Europe.—A.P.

Threat to reluctant holidaymakers

Yorkshire Post York Staff

RAILWAY WORKSHOP employees who do not take the extra three days' holiday awarded last year were threatened last night with union pressure to make them do so.

Mr. George Barratt, general secretary of the Confederation of Shipbuilding and Engineering Unions, said after a meeting of the Confederation's railway shopmen's sub-committee that some workers who qualified for the extra holiday by ten years' service or more were not taking it.

The men were apparently prepared to work for extra money. There were isolated incidents of people not taking their annual holidays.

Mr. Barratt added: "We think the holidays should be taken. But the railway authorities don't seem prepared to issue an instruction.

"What is the use of us negotiating these extra days if they are not taken?"

Mr. Barratt added that if the railway authorities would not take action union pressure would have to be brought to bear. "We can do quite a lot," he said.

Paris police seek jockey

PARIS, Wednesday. — Police received an arrest warrant today and launched a large-scale search for William Pyers, the Australian jockey who won the Grand Prix de l'Arc de Triomphe in Paris last Sunday.

Pyers was sentenced in absentia to one year in gaol on July 4 by a Paris Court for a hit and run accident, but this afternoon was riding in races at Tremblay although police said they were still looking for him last night.—U.P.I.

end of the century it was printing an average of ten pages per issue, with twelve pages on Saturdays. Palmer died in 1903, after thirteen years of great accomplishment with *The Post.*

Under John Phillips, his successor, the paper continued to grow and prosper. The assistant editor was James Sykes, a modest and unassuming man, who was considered one of the best-rounded journalists in Britain. During this period, the editorial columns of *The Post* were distinctive and attracted attention throughout the country. Many of the editorials were contributed by Phillips himself, who was a "writing editor." The paper's news and commentary on foreign affairs and important national issues, such as free trade, were much admired and discussed. Phillips died in 1919, and was succeeded by Arthur Mann, who left a key post on the London *Evening Standard* to take the new position. Mann distinguished himself in many ways with *The Post,* but he perhaps is best remembered for his long and determined stand on British foreign policy during the 1930's.[6]

During the critical years prior to World War II, *The Post,* by its forceful expression of opinion, became one of the most generally respected journals of the day, even gaining considerable foreign readership. The paper insisted that it was only by means of collective action, through the machinery of the League of Nations, that European peace could be secured. In many cases *The Post* editorially rebuked Conservative leaders, an indication of the independence that characterized Mann's editorship. In fact, *The Post* criticized the Prime Minister repeatedly for the Government's casual attitude toward the ever more-threatening activities of Hitler and Mussolini on the continent. Its antiappeasement policy in the prewar period is one of its proudest stands, and one which, in restrospect, showed considerable understanding of the situation.

Even the *Manchester Guardian,* certainly not a paper to praise *The Post* without good reason, wrote in November, 1939:

> Soundness in judgement, tenacity of purpose, loyalty to principle, the courage to be unpopular . . . and even to offend the Party if the Party were not right; these qualities, which are the more precious for being rare, have marked *The Yorkshire Post* throughout the long controversy about British foreign policy which began with Mr. Chamberlain's Premiership. They represent something deep in the characteristic North, tough, earnest, individual. The country owes a debt for them to the old *Yorkshire Post.*[7]

In 1939 *The Post* absorbed its old rival, the *Leeds Mercury,* and early the next year Arthur Mann retired from his editor's chair and was replaced by William Linton Andrews who had edited the *Mercury* for several years previously. A man with a distinguished journalistic background, Andrews made the paper into one of the most critical British journals of the Second World War, one which offered constructive suggestions which were often adopted by Government departments. An example was the editor's proposal that men from the battle areas visit the war factories to tell them of their contributions to the fighting men.[8]

In the postwar period *The Post* continued to print its forceful comment on foreign affairs, to provide its readers with a variety of well-written news, both foreign and domestic, and to discuss and evaluate the state of music, art, and literature with a vitality and sophistication that has continued to command the respect of the intellectual community in Britain. Although it reserves its local and regional tone, it enjoys national and, increasingly, international reputation. It is a worthy Conservative answer to Manchester's *Guardian* and is a provincial daily with which London's *Times* should feel proud to be ideologically associated.

Sir Linton Andrews relinquished editorship of *The Post* at the end of 1960 after he had distinguished himself in that position for twenty-one years. He is undoubtedly one of the paper's most highly respected editors and one of Britain's more eminent newspapermen.[9] Today *The Post,* still a morning paper, is edited by J. E. Crossley and has a circulation of about 122,000. Along with Edinburgh's *Scotsman* and Manchester's *Guardian,* it stands at the top of Britain's provincial dailies in general quality and national prestige.

7

Profiles: Eastern Europe and the Middle East

Five additional profiles of European daily elite newspapers are presented in this chapter, three of them representing Communist journalism in the Soviet Union and Yugoslavia (*Izvestia*, *Pravda*, and *Borba*) and two of them exemplary of libertarian journalism on the eastern fringes of Europe—Finland's *Helsingin Sanomat* and Austria's *Die Presse*. Regardless of the national character of these papers, they are all elite journals with tremendous prestige and influence and have in common certain of the important characteristics which mark quality and prestige organs everywhere. Most of the best dailies of Europe are found in Western Europe and were presented in the last chapter; however, there are some notable dailies—varying considerably in the amount of control exerted upon them—which are published on the eastern periphery of Europe. It is with five of these journals that this chapter chiefly deals.

The Middle East is represented by only one newspaper—*Ha'aretz* of Tel Aviv, Israel. This does not mean that this area, spliced as it is into the fabric of Europe, Asia, and Africa, is without other good newspapers. It does mean, however, that only a few of them, exemplified by *Ha'aretz*, approach the quality of the other journals whose profiles appear in this book.

Borba
(YUGOSLAVIA)

Although there are variant opinions as to the liveliness, thoroughness, and objectivity of *Borba* (Struggle) of Belgrade, there is little doubt that in the context of the Communist world, the Yugoslav Communist Party's chief spokesman is among the very elite. The London *Times'* correspondent in Belgrade in 1965 said that *Borba* would be the choice of anyone of Eastern Europe who wished to be informed of the events of the world outside.[1] In comparison with the rest of the Communist press, its style and presentation of news, particularly in the area of foreign affairs, would be considered almost objective.

In page layout, typography, and general tenor, the morning daily (except Thursdays) reminds one more of the Western press than of the Communist press. *Borba* is especially strong in its international commentary and in its economic reporting and interpretation; but in spite of its serious subjects, it manages to relate its stories to the daily affairs of the citizens and is not loaded with dry statistics and unrelated bits of information.[2]

Although the paper was originally patterned after *Pravda* of the Soviet Union, it has come a long way in makeup, content, and orientation. It is certainly not a "typical" Communist Party daily newspaper, although it is still rather conservative in tone compared with some of the other 17 dailies of the country. Its official status is difficult to ascertain: although it was for many years the official organ of the Communist Party, it no longer considers itself that. Rather, it prefers the designation as the daily of the "socialist alliance." This permits it to give voice to unofficial viewpoints and to engage in controversy. Like other Yugoslav papers, *Borba* forms part of the most independent press of Eastern Europe. Much freedom exists (within Communist limits, of course), and only stories involving critical government policy or fast-breaking international events are likely to be "managed" in some way by the State. Criticism, of course, is never directed against Tito or against Yugoslavia's special brand of socialism. But compared with other Communist nations, the Yugoslav press, represented well by *Borba*, is highly critical, discursive, and intellectually lively.

Borba was founded in 1922 as a political sheet, representing the then outlawed Yugoslav Communist Party, but disguised as an independent newspaper. Its first seven years were activist and difficult: it urged disobedience and rebellion against the monarchy and against all political foes. It was from the first an advocate of a free press and waged a fierce editorial war against censorship; actually its reputation was made

★ ★ ★ ★

ГОДИНА XXXII — БРОЈ 277

Београд — Недеља, 8. октобар 1967.

Директор и главни и одговорни уредник Мома Марковић. Уређује редакциони колегијум. Рукописи се не враћају. Лист излази сваког дана.

ЦЕНА 30 ПАРА — НЕДЕЉОМ 50 ПАРА

ПРОЛЕТЕРИ СВИХ ЗЕМАЉА, УЈЕДИНИТЕ СЕ!

БОРБА

ОРГАН СОЦИЈАЛИСТИЧКОГ САВЕЗА РАДНОГ НАРОДА ЈУГОСЛАВИЈЕ

11. СТРАНА

Ко је „четврти човек“

ТИТУ УРУЧЕНА СУХАРТОВА ПОРУКА

Председник Републике примио јуче специјалног изасланика вршиоца дужности Председника Републике Индонезије министра Мохамада Јусуфа

Јуче пре подне председник Републике Јосип Броз Тито примио је специјалног изасланика вршиоца дужности председника Републике Индонезије генерала Сухарта, министра индустрије и енергетике Мохамада Јусуфа.

Министар Јусуф уручио је председнику Титу поруку вршиоца дужности председника Републике генерала Сухарта.

Пријему су присуствовали генерални секретар Председника Републике Владимир Поповић и југословенски амбасадор у Индонезији Будимир Лончар.

На пријему је био и индонежански амбасадор у Београду Ради Сухади.

(Танјуг)

Председник Тито у разговору са Мохамадом Јусуфом

Председник Тито примио пољску војну делегацију

Председник Републике и врховни командант оружаних снага СФРЈ маршал Југославије Јосип Броз Тито примио је јуче пре подне чланове војне делегације Народне Републике Пољске, коју предводи министар народне одбране маршал Марјан Спихалски, и задржао се с њима у пријатељском разговору.

Пријему су присуствовали државни секретар за народну одбрану генерал-пуковник Никола Љубичић, генерални секретар Председника Републике Владимир Поповић, главни инспектор ЈНА генерал-пуковник Раде Хамовић и начелник кабинета Врховног команданта генерал-потпуковник Петар Бабић.

* * *

Генерал армије Иван Гошњак, члан Савета народне одбране који замењује председника Савета у одређеним пословима, примио је јуче министра народне одбране Пољске маршала Марјана Спихалског и чланове пољске војне делегације. Том приликом Гошњак је предао одликовања којима је Председник Републике одликовао чланове пољске војне делегације.

Војна делегација НР Пољске са министром народне одбране маршалом Пољске Марјаном Спихалским отпутовала је јуче поподне после вишедневне званичне и пријатељске посете Југославији.

ЈОРДАНСКИ ПРЕМИЈЕР ЏУМА ПОДНЕО ОСТАВКУ

(Аман, 7. октобра, Ројтер) — Јордански премијер Џума поднео је данас оставку своје владе краљу Хусеину. Јордански краљ је прихватио ову оставку и мандат за састав новог кабинета поверио свом личном представнику Ал Талхунију. Џума је образовао владу 2. августа.

Сусрету Тита и чланова пољске војне делегације коју предводи министар одбране маршал Марјан Спихалски присуствовао је државни секретар за народну одбрану генерал-пуковник Никола Љубичић и више генерала ЈНА

ИНТЕРВЈУ ИНДИЈСКОГ ПРЕМИЈЕРА ИНДИРЕ ГАНДИ ДОПИСНИКУ ТАНЈУГА

ПРОШЛА СУ ВРЕМЕНА КАДА СУ ГРАНИЦЕ МЕЊАНЕ СИЛОМ

— изјавила Индира Ганди говорећи о кризи на Средњем истоку и наглашавајући да Индија поздравља иницијативу председника Тита

(Њу Делхи, 7. октобра, Танјуг). — Индијски премијер Индира Ганди изјавила је да ће приликом предстојеће посете неким европским земљама и УАР разматрати са лидерима тих земаља најактуелније међународне проблеме, али да са интересовањем очекује и разговоре о билатералним односима између Индије и тих земаља. Ову изјаву Индира Ганди дала је у интервјуу са дописником Танјуга у Њу Делхију Ладиславом Брунером уочи свога одласка у посету Београду, Варшави, Букурешту, Софији и Каиру. На путу у Варшаву, индијски премијер ће се зауставити у Москви.

Индира Ганди изразила је забринутост због ситуације на Средњем истоку истичући да се мир може обезбедити само повлачењем израелских снага на положаје од 4. јуна и правичним и часним решењем проблема палестинских избеглица. Пошто је поздравила

(Наставак на 3. страни)

СА ЗАСЕДАЊА ГЕНЕРАЛНЕ СКУПШТИНЕ УН

Синг и гледишта Ханоја

Изјава индијског министра одбране зазвучала као веродостојно преношење северновијетнамских ставова. — Да ли се у Вашингтону размишља о инвазији ДР Вијетнама?

(Од сталног дописника „Борбе“)

(Њујорк, 7. октобра) — Шеф индијске делегације на заседању Генералне скупштине

Наставак на 5. страни

Грчка под војним режимом

ОСЛОБОЂЕН ГЕОРГИОС ПАПАНДРЕУ

Поред бившег премијера на слободу је пуштено још осам посланика Уније центра

(Атина, 7 октобра) — Грчке војне власти ослободиле су данас бившег грчког премијера и лидера Уније центра Георгиоса Папандреуа. Папандреу се налазио у кућном притвору откако је у Грчкој у априлу ове године извршен државни удар.

Како јавља Ројтер, Министарство за јавни ред објавило је ноћас саопштење у коме се каже да влада укида сва ограничења у погледу кретања Папандреуа и још осморице бивших посланика Уније центра.

Међу онима који су ослобођени истовремено када и Папандреу налазе се и бивши атински градоначелник и министар унутрашњих послова у Папандреуовом кабинету Капотас и бивши министар за економску координацију у кабинету премијера Стефанопулоса Мицотакис.

У владином саопштењу такође се каже да ће питање ослобађања још 22 бивша посланика Уније центра бити стављено у надлежност комитета за безбедност који ће о томе донети одлуку.

Данас састанак Никезић-Ријад-Синг

(Њујорк, 7. октобра, Танјуг). — Државни секретар за иностране послове Марко Никезић састао се у току протекла два дана с министрима иностраних послова Норвешке, Мађарске и Турске. Никезић се такође састао са индијским министром одбране који предводи делегацију своје земље на заседању Генералне скупштине, затим амбасадорима Авганистана, Сирије, Совјетског Савеза и Сједињених Америчких Држава. У овој активности државног секретара средњоисточна криза била је у центру пажње.

Сутра у недељу, овде ће доћи до новог тројног састанка између државног секретара Никезића, министра иностраних послова УАР Ријада и индијског министра одбране Синга.

Уочи дебате у Бурбонској палати

Заједничка акција левих синдиката

Они подржавају предлог о изгласавању неповерења Помпидуовој влади

(Од сталног дописника „Борбе“)

(Париз, 7. октобра) — Што се више ближи уторак политичка атмосфера у Француској постаје све загрејанија. Већ подгрејана протеклом „недељом пољопривредника“, која је завршена билансом од преко 300 повређених, политичка температура прети да нарасте у следећој „недељи захтева“, коју од 9. до 14. овог месеца организују леви раднички синдикати, са Генералном конфедерацијом рада на челу.

У уторак 10. овог месеца у Бурбонској палати почиње општа дебата о фамозним владиним законодавним одредбама донесеним у току протеклог лета, а које сада треба да буду верификоване (или не) у парламенту. Поменуте две протестне недеље посвећене су управо тим одредбама.

Деголистичка већина и њена влада нису, изгледа, очекивале толико озбиљну, чак жучну, реакцију на какву су наишли њени „најлепши напори за даље побољшање економских и социјалних прилика у Француској“. Њих заједно је изненадио заједнички предлог Савеза француске левице о неповерењу влади, — уназад сматрајући тај гест чисто пропагандистичким, мање-више отпадничким маневром

Наставак на 8. страни

Заробљени полицајац

(Хонгконг, 7. октобра) — Један хонгконшки полицајац насилно је одведен данас преко кинеске границе, и од тада се о њему ништа не зна.

Како јавља Ројтер, полицајац се, на дужности, шетао једном улицом у близини линије која означава границу, када су га шчепала шесторица непознатих лица и пребацила с друге стране.

Месне власти скренуле су пажњу кинеској страни на овај „неодговорни и незаконити акт“, али нису добиле никакав одговор.

НЕСПОРАЗУМИ

Пето дете

МИЛАН БАЈЕЦ

Наивној представи да је стварање потомства државотворна делатност супротставља се сада исто тако наивна државотворност у виду покушаја да се законским регулисањем сређују ствари на том подручју. Реч је о алтернативном предлогу Одбора за социјално-здравствена питања Републичког већа Скупштине Србије да се дечји додаци за вишечланске породице подвргну дегресивној скали, с тим да пето дете остане без икакве државне помоћи. Својевремено се на једвите јаде пробило уверење да су новорођенчад ипак најпре ствар самих родитеља, па да отуд бар имућније породице треба једном скинути са државних јасала, тако да је дечји додатак најзад и постао оно што једино може да буде — чиста социјална помоћ. Али, ево, сада се покушава да се, по истој представи о „државној делатности“, једна обична социјала поново преобрази у нешто државотворно, само у овом случају у меру усмерену против претеране популације.

Југословени се нису ни раније множили ништа брже, док их је на то подстицао некадашњи општи и много издашнији дечји додатак. Догађало се једино то да понеки домаћин изгуби вољу за зарадом на радном месту, сматрајући ваљда да су му и приходи од деце довољни. Али, не изгледа ни сада вероватно да би предложена дискриминација петог детета у породици нешто нарочито утицала на популационе билансе. Догодило би се једино то да се без нарочите потребе удари по стомаку најсиромашнијих породица.

Дечји додатак није друштвено право, већ обична друштвена по-

ПРОБИЈЕН НАЈДУЖИ ЖЕЛЕЗНИЧКИ ТУНЕЛ НА БАЛКАНУ

Тунел „Буковик“ на траси будуће пруге Гостивар-Кичево дугачак је 7.048 метара. — Радове изводи београдска „Тунелоградња“

У Зајасу, недалеко од Кичева на траси будуће пруге Гостивар — Кичево, данас ће се скромном свечаношћу обележити пробијање најдужег железничког тунела код нас и на Балкану. Радови на тунелу званом „Буковик“, дугачком 7.048 метара почели су пре пет година. „Буковик“ гради београдско грађевинско предузеће „Тунелоградња“.

На градилишту које се сматра за једно од најтежих у нашој земљи, коришћена је најсавременија механизација. Захваљујући томе и залагању радника, досадашњи радови обављени су пре планираног рока. Ископано је 310.000 кубних метара материјала и уграђено 110.000 кубних метара бетона. Вредност обављених радова износи око 8,3 милијарде старих динара. Десет градитеља изгубило је животе пробијајући „Буковик“.

Извођач радова који је досад изградио велики број тунела на нашим пругама, путевима и на хидроелектранама, слави истовремено и петнаестогодишњицу рада.

Н. П.

СЕДНИЦА САВЕЗНОГ ИЗВРШНОГ ВЕЋА

Усвојени закључци о елементима економске политике у 1968.

Савезно извршно веће, под председништвом Мике Шпиљака, јуче је прихватило коначан текст закључака о привредним кретањима у овој и елементима економске политике у идућој години, који су донети на седници Већа 2. и 3. октобра.

Закључци ће се доставити Савезној скупштини за предстојећу дебату о привредним кретањима и економској политици у 1968. години.

ГРАЂЕВИНСКЕ МАШИНЕ „ЂУРЕ ЂАКОВИЋА“

РЕПОРТАЖА НА СТРАНИ 6.

as a champion of press freedom and as a government critic. The paper was banned after seven years, and most of its staff (young Communist intellectuals from Zagreb) were imprisoned for "crimes against the state." Among those imprisoned was Ognjen Prica, one of its first editors who had done much to give the paper its fighting spirit.[3]

In 1941 *Borba* began publishing again in the hills of the country, moving from one place to another with Marshal Tito's partisan fighters. When the Germans left Belgrade in 1944, *Borba* became the official Communist Party paper and as such was the most privileged and authoritative of the Yugoslav papers.

Borba published the first anti-Russian articles in 1948 when Yugoslavia was expelled from the Cominform, and for nearly six years it carried a column which waged a campaign against Stalin. It was during this period that it gained its international reputation as a Communist paper to be taken seriously. This was due both to a group of fine editors and contributors (such as Vladimir Dedijer and Milovan Djilas) and to the events which brought Yugoslavia to the attention of the Western press.

From a dull version of *Pravda* in its early days, *Borba* has changed its appearance and content more than any other Communist newspaper of Eastern Europe. It has its own distinctive style and character, and although it carries long, dull speeches in typical Communist fashion, its editorial commentary is pungent, colorful and to the point. More "hard" news (concrete day-to-day problems) appears and less and less abstract ideological discussion.[4]

Like other Yugoslav papers, *Borba* runs on a policy of what is called "self-management"—meaning that it must be self-supporting. This also means that competition in the press is growing and the papers must sell on their own merits.[5] *Borba* editors at one time used political controversy at home to sell papers, but this period in the 1950's soon ended and during the 1960's the paper has become more careful and has steered clear of controversial issues. Yugoslav journalists generally practice "self-censorship" in their domestic stories and these stories are without a doubt the dullest and least imaginative in the newspaper.[6]

Since about 1955, *Borba*, while toning down its internal coverage, has stressed international reporting. Its team of foreign correspondents is probably the best in Eastern Europe and its daily foreign affairs column called "Today in the World" is a well-informed and articulate commentary. Running about 10 to 16 pages a day, *Borba* presents a varied diet to its readers—commercial advertising, light features, comic strips, crossword puzzles, and light fiction. This light "Westernized" material is usually found on the last three or four pages, while the serious news and commentary of national and international affairs is collected in the first part of the paper.[7]

In spite of considerable sprightliness, *Borba* is a poor second in popularity to the lively *Politika* of Belgrade (circulation about 300,000 and with no links to the Party) and whereas *Borba*'s circulation in 1950 was 500,000, it had fallen to about 180,000 in 1965.[8] However, *Borba* does publish an edition in Zagreb also, and the combined circulation is in the neighborhood of 370,000.[9]

Ha'aretz
(ISRAEL)

Most Israeli newspapers are voices of trade unions, political parties, or other organizations or groups within the nation. Perhaps the most notable exception is the morning daily *Ha'aretz* (The Land) of Tel Aviv, a nonpartisan or independent paper that circulates all through the country. The paper's chief competition is *Ma'ariv*, an afternoon paper of the same city with the country's largest circulation of more than 100,000.[1]

In spite of competition afforded by *Ma'ariv* and other PM papers which display their editorial wares in a more interesting manner, *Ha'aretz* has continued its staid journalistic practices and has avoided lowering its standards in order to compete with its more colorful fellow dailies. Emphasis is given to foreign news, packed mainly into the first and third pages. Editorials appear on page two. *Ha'aretz* receives its foreign reports from its own correspondents and contributors in the world's leading capital cities and from the United States, British, French, and Jewish news agencies. This material is supplemented by articles from such papers as *Le Monde* and *The New York Times*.[2]

The oldest paper in the country, *Ha'aretz* was begun in 1919 when Tel Aviv was in its infancy and the Hebrew-speaking population of Palestine was only about 50,000. Until 1929, when Reuters of Britain began serving the country, *Ha'aretz* got the bulk of its news from Cairo by train, a day or so late. Just prior to and immediately after World War II when there was a mass influx into Palestine, and especially with the independence for Israel in 1948, *Ha'aretz* began to prosper.

The editor and publisher today is Gershom Schocken, son of a onetime owner of a big department store chain in Germany who turned the paper over to his son in 1939. Under Schocken's guidance *Ha'aretz* has become a true "information" paper, shifting away from the older policy of polemic journalism where news and views were practically indistinguishable.[3]

Ha'aretz's weekday edition of from 12 to 20 pages circulates some 40,000 copies, and the weekend (Friday) edition, running often to 60 and 70 pages, circulates about 50,000 copies.

Journalistic experience and specialized journalism academic training

הארץ

VOL. 49 / 14,652 / OCTOBER 3, 1967 / יום ג', כ"ח אלול תשכ"ז / שנה מ"ט / 30 אג'

למנויי הארץ

בשל גודלו של גליון הארץ ערה"ש תשכ"ח מחולק „הארץ" למנויים החל מיום ב' 2.10.67 בחלקים.

המנויים מתבקשים להריק את תיבות הדואר על מנת להשאיר מקום לקבלת יתר חלקיו ולצבור את הגליון בשלמותו.

בברכת שנה טובה

הארץ

מחלקת המכר והמנויים

חוסיין הגיע למוסקבה

ביירות: יחתום על עיסקת נשק עם בריה"מ

חוסיין מלך ירדן שהגיע לביקור בבריה"מ נפגש עם נשיא בריה"מ ניקולאי פודגורני (צילום רדיו של א.פ.)

התערבות בן חמדיה שנרצח מנעה חבלות נוספות במשק

עקבות החבלנים – לירדן; יריות באיזור שכם

מרשאל גרצ'קו יבקר בעיראק

נציג ירדן מזהיר את העצרת מ„התפוצצות נוספת" במזה"ת

דובר ישראלי: הגימה התוקפנית הירדנית מקנה עדיפות לשיקולי בטחון ישראל; שיחות בלתי־רשמיות לקראת כינוס מועצת הבטחון

„לה מונד": יתמזגו 5 ארגוני הטרור

שייך א־סייח צורף למשלחת ירדן באו"ם

ג'ונסון מברך לראש השנה

נאה

בגליון זה 12 עמודים – המחיר 30 אגורות

קהיר קוראת להגביר פעולות הטרור בישראל

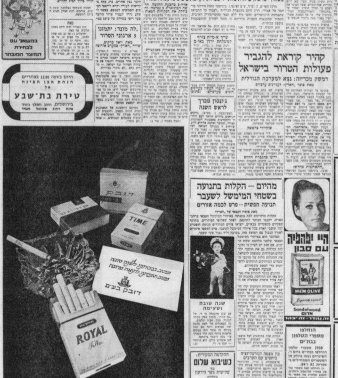

דמשק מכריזה: נצא למערכה הגורלית

מאת סופר „הארץ" לעניינים ערביים

בגליון ערב החג של הארץ

128 עמודים

סיפור מאת ש"י עגנון

התחנה האחרונה של מדעי היהדות — פרופ' ב. קורצווייל

לקראת ישראל תשכ"ח — פולס

ישראל במציאות החדשה — האלוף ח. הרצוג

מפריץ המשבר עד פריץ הקרבות

מדורי שחמט וברידג' ומוסף הארץ

ובו מוסף מיוחד — „השנה בתצלומים"

מהיום — הקלות בתנועה בשטחי המימשל לשעבר

תנועה חפשית — פרט לכמה אזורים

מאת סופרו הצבאי של „הארץ"

שנה טובה וטעימה

בון מצפה לנורמליזציה ביחסים עם הערבים

ההקלטה המקורית:

כשיבוא שלום

בפי שלישית גשר הירקון

הוחלפו מספרי הטלפון בבת־ים

2900 מספרי טלפון הוחלפו בבת־ים ביום ו'. השינויים נעשו בחלק מן המספרים המתחילים בספרות 82 ו־84.

משרד הדואר

יפה בן־עמי

איננה

ההלויה תצא מבית בן־עמי, שדרות ח"ן 9 נתניה, לבית העלמין הישן בנתניה היום, יום שלישי, כ"ח באלול תשכ"ז (3.10.67) בשעה 11.00 לפני־הצהרים

בית עובד בן־עמי

ביום ראשון, ד' תשרי תשכ"ח (8.10.67)

במלאות שמונה שנים לפטירתו של

בעלי היקר

אריה שנקר ז"ל

תערך אזכרה על קברו בבית הקברות הישן בתל־אביב, רחוב טרומפלדור, בשעה 4.00 (ארבע) אחה"צ.

רבקה שנקר

המשפחה

אזכרה

במלאות שמונה שנים לפטירתו של נשיאנו המנוח

אריה שנקר ז"ל

תערך ביום ראשון, ד' תשרי תשכ"ח (8.10.67) בבית העלמין הישן בתל אביב, רח' טרומפלדור, בשעה 4.00 (ארבע) אחה"צ.

חברי ההתאחדות, מוקיריו ומכבדיו יתיחדו עם זכרו.

התאחדות בעלי התעשיה בישראל

is not important to Schocken when he gets ready to hire a staff member. He prefers native intelligence, quick adaptability, versatility, and general erudition for his staffers. Only one reporter ever went to a school of journalism, and the chief editorial writers and the economic editor joined the staff with absolutely no former newspaper experience.[4]

Editorial sobriety is perhaps the most noticeable trait of *Ha'aretz*. Often it has played down reports which for one reason or another have captured the space and headlines of other Israeli papers. Although its front-page makeup could not be called dull, its inside pages are among the most stolid in the Middle East. *Ha'aretz* is a calm newspaper, never getting excited and always amassing substantial facts before launching into a controversial area. Without a doubt, it is the most reasonable, unemotional newspaper in the country, and perhaps in the entire Middle East.

Especially influential are the newspaper's economic and parliamentary reports and interpretive pieces. It is difficult to predict *Ha'aretz*'s policy regarding Government matters; it is its own master and makes its decisions one by one as it believes right. Although the paper generally supports the Government's economic position, it often opposes governmental policies relative to defense and national security. *Ha'aretz*, which calls itself "Independent Liberal,"[5] has fought consistently for better treatment of the Arab minority; it has crusaded for conservation of natural resources and for national beautification projects. It is also the leading press proponent of separation of Church and State.[6]

Of all the Israeli newspapers, *Ha'aretz* gives most emphasis to literary affairs. Its Friday literary section and those published on the eves of special holidays are some of the most noteworthy anywhere. The foremost Hebrew writers traditionally contribute poetry and fiction to its special literary pages.

With the exception of its weekend edition, *Ha'aretz* is aimed at the intellectuals, professionals, and businessmen of better-than-average education and sophistication. The Friday edition, however, provides articles and features which appeal to a much larger (and more entertainment-minded) audience. It compromised its general standards even more in 1963 when it initiated an illustrated magazine supplement, which is inserted in the Friday edition, its 48 pages laden with human interest pieces of all types—sports, entertainment, fashion, adventure, and crime.[7]

This concession to more popular tastes on the weekend, however, is the only one *Ha'aretz* has made. It is typical of the best in serious, sophisticated, well-informed journalism and its general tenor is unemotional and even at times almost scholarly. One should not get the idea that *Ha'aretz* is alone in Israel offering serious journalistic fare.[8] Even the livelier and more popular *Ma'ariv* (Evening) has few peers in the press among world newspapers of similar size (100,000 circulation) in its effort to provide accurate and timely information. For example, it keeps four permanent staff members abroad—in Paris, London, Washington, and New York.

So it is safe to say that although *Ha'aretz* typifies the best in Israeli quality journalism, it only reflects generally the overall seriousness and cosmopolitanism of the country's entire press. As Harry Golden of the United States has said, the Israeli press' attitude in general reflects the "outward-mindedness of a small country."[9]

Helsingin Sanomat
(FINLAND)

On Ludviginhatu (Ludvig Street), a short thoroughfare in Helsinki which is the Finnish equivalent of London's Fleet Street, *Helsingin Sanomat* dominates the press scene and continues its unswerving liberal course set at its founding in 1889. It is the country's biggest newspaper both in circulation (about 260,000 daily; nearly 280,000 on weekends) and in number of pages (often running 40 pages). The Finnish press, with few exceptions, is a party press and the connections are quite clear. *Helsingin Sanomat* is the main exception and prizes its independence of all political factions, although it has always fought hard for liberal and constitutional ideas.[1]

The newspaper is closely wrapped up with one family—the family of its founder, Eero Erkko, who started the paper under the name of *Paivalehti* (Daily News) "to let fresh winds blow through open windows into stuffy social and politicial conditions."[2] Finland was under Russian rule at the time. The paper immediately attracted progressive writers and artists who gave it such a vigorous tone that it is said to have become "not only a remarkable political event in its own right but also started a new phase in Finnish cultural life."[3]

When *Paivalehti* was suppressed by Russian officialdom in 1904, the *Helsingin Sanomat* was founded a few months later to take up the banner of its predecessor, and nothing but its name was really changed.

Eljas Erkko took over the direction of the paper in 1927 when his father's health failed. His dynamic personality dominated the newspaper until his death in 1965. He was one of the world's best-known publishers and was often referred to at home as "Finland's press king," and his paper as simply "the Erkkos paper."[4] Eljas Erkko greatly expanded the paper's coverage, began sending out special foreign correspondents, and signed news agreements with world agencies and important newspapers. It gets the news services today from *The New York Times*, *The Times* of London, *Dagens Nyheter* of Stockholm, and *Le Monde* of Paris.

Yleisestä rikoksentekijäin armahtamisesta lakiesitys

Yleisestä rangaistukseen tuomittujen armahduksesta annettiin perjantaisessa tasavallan presidentin esittelyssä lakiesitys eduskunnalle. Armahdusesitys koskee kaikkia rikoksentekijöitä, jotka ennen 1. syyskuuta tehdystä rikoksesta ovat joutuneet tai joutuvat kärsimään kansalaisluottamuksen menetysseuraamusta, sakon sovitusrangaistusta tai välitöntä kuritushuone- ja vankeusrangaistusta.

Armahduslakiesitys on valmisteltu itsenäisyyden 50-vuotisjuhlavuoden johdosta, ja hallitus ehdottaa, että se tulisi voimaan itsenäisyyspäivänä 6. joulukuuta tänä vuonna.

Esityksen mukaan elinkautista kuritushuonerangaistusta kärsivät tai sellaiseen rangaistukseen tuomittavat eivät saisi muuta lievennystä rangaistuksiinsa

(Jatk. siv. 12)

Pääministeri Rafael Paasio: — Valistuneisuus, vapaamielisyys ja myönteinen suhtautuminen kansanvaltaisen yhteiskunnan peruspyrkimyksiin ovat tukeva pohja toimittajan työssä.

Puun hintasuositus epätodennäköinen

Puunjalostusteollisuuden ja metsänomistajien suurten neuvottelukuntien yhteiskokouksessa tänään ratkeaa lopullisesti, syntyykö paperipuun hintasuositus vai ei. Kummallakin taholla suhtaudutaan varsin pessimistisesti myönteisen tuloksen aikaan saamisen mahdollisuuteen, koska näkemykset poikkeavat vielä tuntuvasti toisistaan. Hintasuositusneuvottelujen lopulliseksi määräpäiväksi oli asetettu 16. 9. MTK:n metsävaltuuskunta kokoontuu lauantaiaamuna.

Mikäli paperipuun hintasuositukseen ei nyt päästä, teollisuus pyrkii ostamaan puuta määräämillään hinnoilla.

(Jatk. siv. 20)

Pääministeri Rafael Paasio:

Lehdistö yhteiskunnassa tärkeämpi kuin aikaisemmin

— Lehdistön osuus nykyaikaisen yhteiskunnan monimuotoisessa organisaatiossa on tärkeämpi kuin aikaisemmin. Erityisesti kansanvaltaisessa yhteiskunnassa on lehdistöllä suorastaan ratkaiseva tehtävä kanavoidessaan mielipiteitä ja suorittaessaan yhteiskunnallisen kontrollin arvokasta ilmentämistä, sanoi pääministeri Rafael Paasio Sanoma Osakeyhtiön Opiston Toimittajakoulun ensimmäisen vuosikurssin avajaistilaisuudessa perjantaina.

Pääministeri korosti, että epädemokratiaa rakentavat suorastaan pelkäävät sallia lehdistölle vapauksia ilmaista kantaansa, esittää mielipiteitä, tuoda julki vaihtoehtoja päätöksenteoille.

Pohjoismaiden ensimmäisen yhden lehtitalon ylläpitämän toimittajakoulun avajaissanat lausui opiston johtokunnan puheenjohtaja, teollisuusneuvos Risto Kavanne. Hän selvitteli koulun tavoitetta kasvattaa toimittajakokelaasta pystyvä, ripeä, tietorikas, vastuuntunteva ja tunnustava lehtimies.

Lyhyeen avajaistilaisuu-

(Jatk. siv. 19)

Martti Peltonen

Merivoimien osastoa esitteli presidentin seurueelle toimitusjohtaja Olle Herold (vas.) Navigare-näyttelyn avajaisissa.

Tonniston nuorentaminen merenkulkumme tavoite

— Suomen kauppamerenkulun tärkeimpiä lähiajan päämääriä on tonniston jatkuva lisääminen ja ennen kaikkea sen nuorentaminen. Lisäksi meidän on puolustettava asemaamme omissa merikuljetuksissamme ja lisättävä osuuttamme kansainvälisissä tehtävissä, sanoi kauppa- ja teollisuusministeri Olavi Salonen avatessaan kansainvälisen merennäyttelyn Navigare 67:n Helsingissä perjantaina.

Suomen laivanrakennuksen ongelmien ratkaisussa ministeri Salonen totesi tarvittavan valtion tukea, etenkin kun suunnittelun ja tutkimuksen osuus laivanrakennuksessa kasvaa nopeasti. Tämän vuoksi meillä tulisi kehittää laivanrakennusteollisuuden ja varustamoiden yhteistä teknillistä tutkimustyötä ja tukea sitä. Lisäksi ammattikoulutuksen lisääminen on kokonaisuuden kannalta katsottuna kannattava taloudellinen sijoitus.

Tasavallan presidentti kunnioitti läsnäolollaan Messuhallin B-halliin järjestettyä avajaistilaisuutta, jossa oli lisäksi mukana valtiollisen ja taloudellisen elämän johtohenkilöitä, Suomessa vierailleva Englannin apulaiskauppaministeri sekä diplomaattikuntaa.

Näyttelyä käsitellään talousosastossa.

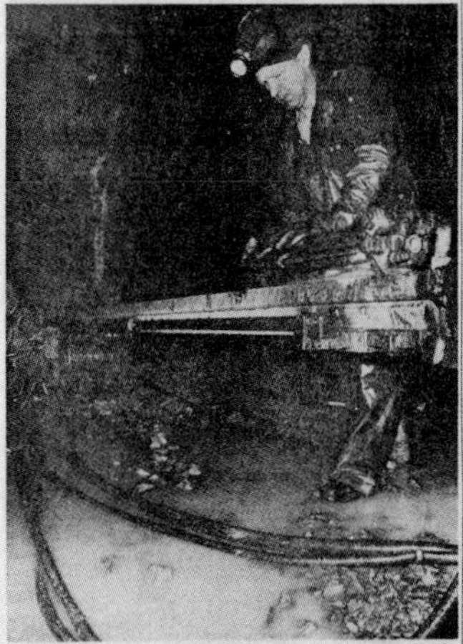

Unto Järvinen

Joukasta kotoisin olevalla kaivosmies Veijo Siivennoisella on kaksi toivetta: päästä maan pinnalle, päästä Suomeen.

Tapiola maailman paras USA:n kaupunkikilvassa

Amerikan arkkitehtiliiton asettamat asiantuntijat ovat valinneet Tukholman, Tapiolan ja skotlantilaisen Cumbernaudin esimerkeiksi maailman parhaasta kaupunkisuunnittelusta. Amerikkalaisen "alumiinikuninkaan" R. S. Reynoldsin muistoksi viime vuonna perustetun rahaston palkinnot, jotka jaetaan nyt ensimmäistä kertaa, myönnetään kaupungit suunnitelleille arkkitehtiryhmille.

Tulokset ja palkintolautakunnan arvostelut on julkaistu Amerikan arkkitehtiliiton julkaisussa "AIA Journal".

Asuntosäätiö nimesi kaksikymmentä henkilöä käsittävän ryhmän. — Amerikka-

(Jatk. siv. 18)

Tapiola, Cumbernaud ja Tukholma: esimerkit maailman parhaasta kaupunkisuunnittelusta.

Marsalkka Amer teki itsemurhan

Beirut, 15. 9. (Reuter) Sotamarsalkka Abdel Hakim Amer, joka äskettäin pidätettiin epäiltynä osallisuudesta presidentti Nasseria vastaan suunniteltuun salahankkeeseen, on tehnyt itsemurhan, kertoi Kairon radio perjantaina.

Sotamarsalkka Amer, 48, menetti Yhdistyneen arabitasavallan kakkosmiehen aseman viime kesäkuussa käydyn Israelin sodan jälkeen.

Kairon radio kertoi marsalkka Amerin tehneen itsemurhan ottamalla kahteen eri otteeseen myrkkytabletteja.

Nasserin oikean käden itsemurhasta tarkemmin sivulla 14.

Kekkonen käy jokaisessa vaalipiirissä — 20 puhetta

Alun kolmattakymmentä puhetilaisuutta on alustavasti suunniteltu presidentti Urho Kekkoselle, kun hän presidenttiehdokkaana aloittaa puhekierroksensa, joka ajoittuu tämän vuoden loppupuolelle ja ensi vuoden alkuun, kerrottiin Kekkosen vaaliliiton toimiston esittelytilaisuudessa perjantaina Helsingissä.

Puhekierroksen ohjelma on valmisteilla ja yksityiskohdat vielä lyömättä lukkoon, mutta Kekkosen kerrottiin käyvän puhumassa jokaisessa vaalipiirissä — eräissä useamminkin kuin kerran. Ahvenanmaalle hän ei kuitenkaan puhematkaansa ulota.

Neljän hallituspuolueen — sosiaalidemokraattien, keskustapuolueen, kommunistien ja sos.dem.liiton — edustajat selostivat vaaliliiton organisaatiota ja toimintaperiaatteita todeten mm., että Urho Kekkosen "kilpailijaehdokkaisiin suhtaudutaan hyvin asiallisesti". Vaalitaistelu pyritään pitämään nimenomaan presidentinvaalitaisteluna, puheenvuoroissa sanottiin.

Vaaliliiton toimintaperiaatteisiin kuuluu myös se "gentlemanni-periaate", etteivät tämän vaaliliiton osapuolet toimi vaalitaistelussa toisiaan vastaan.

Vaalitaistelun varsinainen lähtölaukaus on tarkoitukseena ampua 22. lokakuuta, jolloin annetaan julkisuuteen mm. Kekkosen vaaliliiton yhteinen julistus. Siihen mennessä valmistunee 30—40 minuuttia kestävä elokuva, jossa esitellään Kekkosen toimintaa presidenttinä valtiovierailuineen ja kotimaan matkoineen.

Samoihin aikoihin valmistuu myös jokaiseen suoma-

(Jatk. siv. 12)

Ummikko suomalainen Norrbottenin ongelma

Kiiruna, syyskuussa (Mauno Saari) Kaivosteollisuuden leimaama Pohjois-Ruotsi on monille sinne muuttaneille suomalaisille merkinnyt taloudellisen nousun symbolia. Malmintuoksuinen Kiiruna ympäristökylineen muodostaa kuitenkin nykyisellään osalle suomalaisista pelkän teollisen ghetton tai henkisen umpion, jossa ansaitaan kohtalaisesti, syödään, nukutaan ja tehdään paljon työtä.

Olkoonkin, että siirtolaisen juurettomuus on fraasi, se näkyy kovin selvästi suomalaiskylissä ympäri Norrbottenia.

Sen huomaa puolen kilometrin syvyisissä kaivoskäytävissä ja keskuksissa asuvien viihtymättömyydessä. Sosiaaliedut, vakituinen työpaikka ja kohtalaiset ansiot pitävät useimmat paikallaan, mutta umpioitumisen tunne, eristyneisyys saa monet tuntemaan olonsa suomalaismetsissä tilapäiseksi.

(Jatk. siv. 18)

Kolehtituotto 1,4 miljoonaa

Kirkoissa kannetut viralliset kolehdit tuottivat viime vuonna rahaa yhteensä n. 1,4 milj. mk, kerrotaan kirkkohallituksesta. Eniten myönnettiin kolehtivaroja kirkkomme ulkomaiseen ja pakolaisapuun, 216.000 mk, ja toiseksi eniten varattomille jumaluusopin ylioppilaille, n. 187.000 mk. Suomen lähetysseuran osuus kolehdeista oli n. 126.000 mk, sisälähetysseuran n. 104.000 mk ja merimieslähetyksen n. 68.000 mk. Kaikkiaan annettiin kolehtivaroja 42 eri kohteeseen.

Kirkon virallisia kolehteja kannettiin viime vuonna 34 sunnuntaina ja lisäksi kaikkina suurina kirkollisina juhlapäivinä. Muina pyhinä kerättyjen kolehtien tuotto menee kunkin seurakunnan oman toiminnan kustannuksiin.

Nigeria hyväksyi OAU:n välittäjäksi sisällissodassaan

Lagos, 15. 9. (Reuter) Nigerian liittovaltion hallitus on hyväksynyt Afrikan yhtenäisyysjärjestön ehdotuksen kuusihenkisen afrikkalaisvaltuuskunnan lähettämisestä Nigeriaan keskustelemaan 10 viikkoa kestäneen sisällissodan lopettamisesta.

Aluksi oli epäselvää, salliiko Nigeria kuuden Afrikan maan valtionpäämiehistä koostuvan valtuuskunnan pääsyn maahan, mutta asia selvisi Nigerian sotilasjohtajan kenraalimajuri Jakubu Gowonin ilmoitettua torstai-iltana, että valtuuskunta on tervetullut Lagosiin.

Biafran hallitus ei ole saanut virallista tietoa OAU:n välityspyrkimyksistä "joten me emme tiedä päätöksestä", sanoi maan Euroopan sotilashallituksen edustaja. Itsenäiseksi julistautuneen Biafran hallitus toimii mielellään yhdessä OAU:n ryhmän kanssa, kun sille ensin ilmoitetaan, mitä on tekeillä.

Many factors contribute to *Helsingin Sanomat*'s being Finland's leading newspaper. Probably the most important is its concern with serious news, a large part of it foreign (seldom less than eight solid columns a day).[5] The paper's network of foreign correspondents is large, with some twenty special writers and contributors in foreign capitals in addition to four staff correspondents permanently assigned abroad.

Another reason for its importance is its national character. Under Eljas Erkko, it became truly a national journal, going to the remotest districts every day. Its present circulation of some 260,000 is remarkable in a country where the total population is less than five million.

Helsingin Sanomat also carries more advertising than any other Finnish paper, and advertisers are so eager to use the newspaper's pages that the journal has no need for advertising salesmen. Display space is reserved weeks in advance of publication. *Helsingin Sanomat* is one of the few remaining great papers of the world to give over its entire front page to advertising. With the front page unavailable for news, the editors have made the main news page an inside right page opposite the editorial page. This helps draw attention to the editorials.[6]

The newspaper evidences an invigorating independence and progressive spirit in its editorial expression. Although it is never reluctant to present its opinions in clear and unequivocal language, it is ready to make other opinions available to its readers. This it does largely through a daily feature called "Press Voices" in which editorial opinions from other newspapers are given, these opinions representing all of the important parties of the country. The paper's own editorial policies are thrashed out at conferences of the top executives.[7] Most of the paper's views represent the middle way, although it has never been the mouthpiece of the political parties of the center.[8]

Helsingin Sanomat today finds itself, like other Finnish newspapers, in a position relative to the Soviet Union and to the West which calls for considerable journalistic skill and diplomacy. Steering a path through the middle of the ideological storms raging around it is no easy task for a nation or for a newspaper which desires to function freely and intelligently. Finland is managing to cope with these storms and to live with both ideological "camps." Its main newspaper, *Helsingin Sanomat*, speaks out daily with courage and freedom and thus serves the public by helping to preserve national independence and equilibrium. The paper today—under its two editors in chief, Aatos Erkko, son of Eljas, and Teo Mertonen—is perpetuating its tradition as a dignified and reliable journal.

Izvestia
(U.S.S.R.)

In a vast nation where the written word is very powerful and journalists enjoy a degree of prestige not enjoyed in other countries, *Izvestia* (News) stands out as one of the two most influential Soviet dailies. It not only wields tremendous power with the nation's leaders, but it claims the largest circulation in the world—more than eight million copies. It is the official organ of the Government—specifically of the Presidium of the Supreme Soviet and is printed in twenty-two cities scattered across the Soviet Union. Running four pages on weekdays and six on Sundays, it is published each evening except Monday. The regional editions, in most respects like the parent edition in Moscow, are printed from matrices flown from the capital. This standardized material is supplemented with local news by *Izvestia* writers in the "branch" areas.

The newspaper was begun on March 13, 1917, in Petrograd. The next year *Izvestia* moved to Moscow and its circulation grew rapidly. By 1924 its circulation was 354,000, and by 1932 had climbed to over a million and a half, a tremendous circulation at that time.[1] Its circulation remained around this figure until 1959 when Alexei Adzhubei, Khrushchev's son-in-law, became editor and put new life into the paper. Adzhubei, coming to *Izvestia* from the editorship of *Komsomolskaya Pravda*, the daily of the Young Communist League which he had invigorated, did much to make the dullest paper in the U.S.S.R. into one of the liveliest. Headlines became larger, articles shorter, pictures more in evidence, and writing briefer and crisper.[2] The Moscow edition changed from morning to evening and the pages were brightened by first-person reporting. A Sunday supplement called *Nedelia* (The Week), a tabloid pictorial complete with comics, cartoons, and short articles satirizing Western life, was instituted.[3] *Nedelia* today is also sold separately and enjoys great popularity.

In five years Adzhubei brought the paper's circulation to six million. After Khrushchev lost power in 1964, the new regime dismissed Adzhubei as editor of *Izvestia*. The new editor was Vladimir Stepakov, who was succeeded in late 1965 by Lev N. Tolkunov. Under these two editors the paper has remained lively and still reflects the changes brought about by Adzhubei. It is really impossible to ascertain *Izvestia*'s true circulation today. Many, and often rather widely varying, figures can be found (many recent estimates put it at nearly a million more than *Pravda*'s), but it seems safe to say that the paper prints more than eight million copies a day, making it one of the two or three largest newspapers of any kind in the world. Removal of newsprint restrictions may well bring the paper's circulation to more than ten million by the end of 1968. About two-thirds of *Izvestia*'s daily copies are mailed to subscribers, with the rest sold at kiosks and other central locations.

Izvestia correspondents are in twenty-two world capitals, all but four of them in non-Communist nations. In addition, it has roving reporters and foreign news analysts like Matveyev and Polyanov, whose readable columns resemble those of American columnists.[4] It also gets much material from *Tass*, the Soviet news agency and the newer feature agency, *Novosti*. *Izvestia* carries many of the same stories found in *Pravda*, the national daily of the Communist Party of the Soviet Union. But *Izvestia* gives more attention to relations of the U.S.S.R. with other governments and prints much news about elections and the workings of government machinery (both in the Supreme Soviet and in various Soviets of the Union). It is less concerned with theory than with the practical problems facing the country.

Articles are of many lengths, some running as long as 3,000 words, others as short as 150 to 200 words. The paper contains few hard, last-minute news items, although *Izvestia* means "News."[5] Most of its pieces educate or agitate, which is considered the prime function of a newspaper. Foreign news is found always on the first inside page; other than this, there are no permanent features. *Izvestia* carries very few editorials but rather concentrates on discussions (in which readers can participate), features (largely related to world affairs and Soviet national progress), and special essays written by intellectuals and high government officials. Also, a very important part of the contents is in the form of letters from readers.

Large numbers of letters pour into *Izvestia's* main office in Moscow's Pushkin Square. As far back as 1956 the paper received nearly 66,000 during the year. It is close to 350,000 at present. All of the letters are not published, of course, but they are read and those which are not printed are answered. A staff of about fifty, mostly women, handle the increasing flow of letters. All complaints (and there are many) are investigated. Through letters to *Izvestia*, and to other Soviet newspapers, the people can feel a part of the country's journalism. Editorial conferences (*letuchkas*) at *Izvestia* consider readers' letters several times a week to determine which ones will be used, and which ones should precipitate sending out a special reporter to look further into a situation. Letters are encouraged and *Izvestia* selects as many as possible which bring to light abuses, deal with moral matters, suggest improvements, and contribute in some way to national progress. In addition to writing letters, readers of *Izvestia* often visit the paper's "reception" department (adjacent to its "letters" department) to complain and discuss problems personally.[6]

Izvestia's pages are laid out in a lively manner. The diversification of typeface, occasional color printing, many photographs, and an aura of careful planning and dignity give the paper a responsible appearance,

ПРОЛЕТАРИИ ВСЕХ СТРАН, СОЕДИНЯЙТЕСЬ! [illegible]

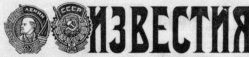

ИЗВЕСТИЯ

СОВЕТОВ ДЕПУТАТОВ ТРУДЯЩИХСЯ СССР

№ 187 (15581) Год издания 51-й | Четверг, 10 августа 1967 года | Цена 3 коп.

Большого успеха добились нефтяники Кубани. На буровой № 2 Тимашевского района достигнута глубина 6.207 метров. Бурение продолжается. На снимке (справа налево): бурильщик В. Гринь, помощник бурильщика Н. Джулай, механик Н. Головин и помощник бурильщика В. Называйко.

Фото О. Галушко («Известия»).

ТРУДОВОЙ РАПОРТ

ГОД РЕВОЛЮЦИИ 50

Меньше трех месяцев остается до знаменательной даты — 50-летия Советской власти. Среди тружеников Харьковской области все более широкий размах приобретает соревнование за выполнение взятых обязательств. О ходе соревнования рассказывают:

СТАТИСТИКА НОВОСТРОЕК

П. ЗМАГА, заместитель председателя облисполкома

— Одной из важных особенностей юбилейного соревнования является то, что наряду с пунктами о перевыполнении производственных заданий, улучшении экономических показателей коллективы предприятий наметили обширную программу по улучшению условий труда и быта. За полгода объем бытовых услуг в области увеличился по сравнению с соответствующим периодом прошлого года на 11,8 процента. Производительность труда на предприятиях управления бытового обслуживания выросла почти на 10 процентов. В области открыто 84 и реконструировано 25 ателье, мастерских и приемных пунктов службы быта. Введено в эксплуатацию комплексное предприятие химчистки одежды и стирки белья в новом жилом массиве Харькова — на Павловом поле, бытовые комбинаты в селах Рубежное Волчанского района и Николаевка Зачепиловского района.

Сельские населенные пункты, где нет стационарных мастерских, обслуживают сорок четыре передвижные автомастерские. За шесть месяцев проведено более трех тысяч выездов, принято заказов на сотни тысяч рублей.

В Харькове возводится универсальный магазин на Московском проспекте. Дом мебели, расположенный в новом жилом районе. На колхозном рынке строится крытый павильон из бетона и стекла на 850 торговых мест с гостиницей для колхозников.

К концу года, как и записано в наших юбилейных обязательствах, должен открыть свои двери Дворец культуры тракторного завода. Строится Дом быта, начато сооружение закрытого летнего катка, плавательного бассейна, мотеля для туристов, двух кинотеатров. Развернута подготовка к строительству цирка на 2.200 мест.

К началу нового учебного года в районах области войдут в строй 119 школьных помещений, 102 клуба, четыре кинотеатра, 230 магазинов на тысячу рабочих мест, строится 24 мастерские по бытовому обслуживанию населения.

Юбилейный год для харьковчан — год новостроек, новоселий.

МОЩНАЯ ТУРБИНА

Ю. КОСЯК, заместитель главного конструктора турбинного завода имени С. М. Кирова

— В обязательствах коллектива записано: «К 7 ноября разработать технические проекты паровой турбины мощностью в один миллион киловатт и паровых турбин мощностью 200 и 500 тысяч киловатт для атомных электростанций».

Могу сказать: эскизный проект турбины-миллионки выполнен досрочно. На Ленинградском Металлическом заводе начается ее сооружение.

Теперь о турбине К-220. Технический проект ее также выполнен досрочно. Мы приступили к выпуску рабочих чертежей. С опережением сроков идет разработка технического проекта турбины мощностью 500 тысяч киловатт.

ПЕРВЫЕ КИЛОМЕТРЫ

Г. МАКЕЕВ, редактор газеты «Темп» тракторного завода имени Серго Орджоникидзе

— Расскажу о том, как выполняется пункт обязательств об освоении нового типа трактора Т-150. В этой машине — будущее завода. Сейчас в опытно-экспериментальном цехе горячая пора: из шести тракторов, которые мы обязались выпустить к юбилею, два уже готовы. Они проходят испытания на полигоне. Конструкторы, инженеры-испытатели, трактористы внимательно следят за их работой. Предварительные испытания показывают, что Т-150 будет хорошим пахарем.

По-ударному трудятся на сборке коллективы старших мастеров П. Бурейко, П. Горянова и В. Алферова. В этих коллективах — высококвалифицированные рабочие, среди них много ветеранов завода.

Сегодня уже можно с уверенностью сказать: к юбилею Великого Октября будут готовы все шесть машин.

СОБЫТИЯ ДНЯ

ОБОЗРЕВАТЕЛЬ АМЕРИКАНСКОЙ ГАЗЕТЫ ПРИЗНАЕТ БЕЗНАДЕЖНОСТЬ АГРЕССИИ США ВО ВЬЕТНАМЕ

Подробности — на 2-й стр.

МИНИСТЕРСТВО ЭКОНОМИКИ ФРГ СООБЩИЛО, ЧТО ЗА ПОСЛЕДНЕЕ ВРЕМЯ УВОЛЕНЫ 145 ТЫСЯЧ ШАХТЕРОВ РУРА И СААРСКОЙ ОБЛАСТИ

В ВЕНЕСУЭЛЕ БОЛЕЕ 2 ТЫСЯЧ КРЕСТЬЯНСКИХ СЕМЕЙ ОСТАЛОСЬ БЕЗ КРОВА, ЗАТОПЛЕНЫ ПОСЕВЫ, ПОГИБЛО БОЛЬШОЕ КОЛИЧЕСТВО СКОТА В РЕЗУЛЬТАТЕ НАВОДНЕНИЯ, ВЫЗВАННОГО СИЛЬНЫМИ ЛИВНЯМИ

ВЗРЫВ РЕАКТОРА НА КРУПНОМ ХИМИЧЕСКОМ ЗАВОДЕ В РОТТЕРДАМЕ. УЩЕРБ — МИЛЛИОНЫ ГУЛЬДЕНОВ

Зарубежные новости

Высшие чины бундесвера и правительства ФРГ провели совещание по вопросу о выработке их новой военной концепции, которую канцлер Кизингер изложит президенту США на предстоящей встрече с ним. (Из газет).

БундесВЕРНАЯ любовь.

Рис. Бор. Ефимова.

ПО-ПРЕЖНЕМУ БЕСПОКОЙНО

КАИР, 9 августа. (По телеф. от соб. корр.). В Иерусалиме по-прежнему неспокойно. Хотя всеобщая забастовка закончилась, обстановка в городе остается напряженной. Усилены наряды полиции, но это не остановило распространения листовок, призывающих арабов не сотрудничать с оккупантами, не признавать израильскую аннексию арабской части города.

Поступили сообщения, что иерусалимский патриарх католической церкви отдал распоряжение закрыть свои приходы. Это сделано из-за того, что израильские солдаты совершили надругательства над некоторыми храмами. «Они содрали в одном из них дорогие украшения со стен, а в другие входили с собаками», — говорится в сообщении, полученном из Аммана. Кроме того, в другой церкви были похищены израильтянами золотые тиары.

В ответ на вчерашнюю всеобщую забастовку израильские власти закрыли ряд магазинов, которые вчера в знак протеста не работали. То же самое предпринято и в отношении транспортной компании. Магазины и лавки, которым запрещается торговать, израильские полицейские отмечают синим крестом.

В районе Наблус в Иордании вновь проведены аресты, особенно среди учителей-арабов.

Л. КОРЯВИН.

НАВСТРЕЧУ ОКТЯБРЮ

ХАНОЙ, 9 августа. (ТАСС). Здесь состоялось заседание комитета по подготовке к празднованию 50-летия Октября. В сообщении, опубликованном в газете «Нян зан», отмечается, что на совещании была подчеркнута важность пропагандистской и воспитательной работы среди всего населения ДРВ по изучению марксизма-ленинизма, изучению опыта Октябрьской революции и усиления сплоченности с Советским Союзом и другими братскими социалистическими странами.

НА КОНФЕРЕНЦИИ ОЛАС

ГАВАНА, 9 августа. (ТАСС). Вчера вечером завершили работу первая и четвертая рабочие комиссии первой конференции Латиноамериканской организации солидарности (ОЛАС). Первая комиссия приняла проект общей резолюции о революционной антиимпериалистической борьбе в Латинской Америке. Четвертая комиссия приняла сегодня вводную часть устава ОЛАС, проект которой был подготовлен специальной подкомиссией. Вторая и третья комиссии продолжают работу.

НЕ БЕЗ КОРЫСТИ

СТОКГОЛЬМ, 9 августа. (По телеф. от соб. корр.). Совершенно очевидно, что зарубежные круги, прежде всего западногерманские, усиленно подталкивают Швецию к вступлению в «общий рынок», далеко не в последнюю очередь заинтересованы в шведском уране.

Что же может случиться со шведским ураном, если Швеция войдет в состав «общего рынка»? Этот важный аспект проблемы поднял стокгольмская вечерняя газета «Афтонбладет».

Газета указывает, что присоединение Швеции к «общему рынку» в любой форме будет неизбежно означать присоединение и к Евратому, который скоро должен стать неотъемлемой частью структуры ЕЭС. Стало быть, продолжает газета, «согласно букве устава мы должны будем взять на себя обязательство поставлять наш уран, если это потребуется, общему агентству стран Европейского экономического сообщества, и даже не сможем ставить условий относительно его мирного использования».

Г. ДЕННИЧЕНКО.

В ЗЕРКАЛЕ МИРОВОЙ ПРЕССЫ

● **Многие зарубежные газеты в сообщениях из Вьетнама отмечают новые успехи в боевых операциях Армии освобождения Южного Вьетнама, в частности смелый налет патриотов на базу сайгонского военно-морского флота.**

● Румынские газеты освещают визит в Румынию министра иностранных дел Италии А. Фанфани.

● Югославская и египетская печать уделяет большое внимание начинающемуся 10 августа визиту в ОАР президента СФРЮ И. Броз Тито.

● Под заголовком «Суровые меры, принятые Израилем против арабского движения Сопротивления», ливанская «Аль-Гумхурия» рассказывает о расправе израильских оккупантов с участниками забастовок в Иерусалиме. Французская «Экоо» пишет, что поведение Израиля как оккупирующей державы вызывает сопротивление со стороны арабского населения.

Из обзора печати ТАСС за 9 августа.

ПЕЧЬ-АВТОМАТ

БАКУ, 9 августа. (ТАСС). С бакинского опытно-экспериментального завода в Куйбышев отправлена уникальная печь-гигант для особой термической обработки подшипников. Загрузку деталей производит механическая «рука» толкателя. Нужную температуру поддерживает специальный терморегулятор.

УКАЗ ПРЕЗИДИУМА ВЕРХОВНОГО СОВЕТА СССР

О награждении Горно-Алтайской автономной области орденом Ленина

За успехи, достигнутые трудящимися области в развитии народного хозяйства и в культурном строительстве, наградить Горно-Алтайскую автономную область орденом Ленина.

Председатель Президиума Верховного Совета СССР Н. ПОДГОРНЫЙ.

Секретарь Президиума Верховного Совета СССР М. ГЕОРГАДЗЕ.

Москва, Кремль. 8 августа 1967 г.

УКАЗ ПРЕЗИДИУМА ВЕРХОВНОГО СОВЕТА СССР

О награждении Джамбулской области Казахской ССР орденом Ленина

За успехи, достигнутые трудящимися области в развитии народного хозяйства и в культурном строительстве, наградить Джамбулскую область Казахской ССР орденом Ленина.

Председатель Президиума Верховного Совета СССР Н. ПОДГОРНЫЙ.

Секретарь Президиума Верховного Совета СССР М. ГЕОРГАДЗЕ.

Москва, Кремль. 8 августа 1967 г.

РЕЙД «ИЗВЕСТИЙ» РИТМ ПОТЕРЯН

Моторостроительный завод «Серп и молот» считается одним из ведущих предприятий. Вот почему каждая цифра плана в масштабах этого завода приобретает особое значение. План первого полугодия выполнен на [illegible]

[illegible] до 250 тысяч рублей.

Итак, направление выбрано правильное. Вопрос в том, насколько эффективно используется на заводе новое оборудование.

По данным последнего хронометража, во втором механическом цехе простои составляют 10,2 процента. Половина простоев — из-за неисправности станков и линий. Оборудование здесь очень точное, и доверять его можно только [illegible]

[illegible]

Бригада «Известий» по проверке юбилейных обязательств: А. МАКОГОНОВ, зав. областной газеты «Социалистична Харкивщина», А. ДРОБИТЬКО, Г. СЕМЕНОВ, В. ФАДИН, собств. корр. «Известий».

ХАРЬКОВ. (По телефону).

ИЗ ПОЧТЫ ЮБИЛЕЙНОГО ГОДА

ХРАНИТЬ ВЕЧНО

ИСТОРИК ЧИТАЕТ ПИСЬМА

В ноябре прошлого года («Известия» № 266) редакция обратилась к своим читателям с просьбой совместными усилиями написать «Летопись великой эпохи». Сотни писем с фотографиями, документами, воспоминаниями получила редакция. Многие из них были опубликованы на страницах газеты. Редакционной почтой заинтересовались сотрудники Государственного исторического музея СССР. Сегодня заведующий отделом письменных источников музея З. Н. БАКСТ рассказывает о некоторых материалах, присланных нашими читателями.

Прежде всего я хочу сообщить, что, с любезного разрешения редакции, наш музей принял на вечное хранение материалы, присланные в «Известия» сорока восемью товарищами. Они явятся предметом тщательного исследования. Но о некоторых из них хотелось бы сказать несколько слов уже сейчас.

П. Коломиец сохранил, казалось бы на первый взгляд, ничем не примечательную фотографию — празднование Первого мая 1917 года в одной из воинских частей Западного фронта. На фотографии снята большая группа солдат с плакатами. Тов. Коломиец сообщает одну любопытную подробность — плакаты помогли написать петроградские рабочие, приехавшие на фронт для агитационной работы. Теперь эта фотография стала интересным и редким экспонатом, показывающим влияние революционного пролетариата Петрограда на солдатские массы в период подготовки Великой Октябрьской социалистической революции.

П. Корж прислала сохранившийся у нее печатный листок «Стенная газета Куб. Чер. Роста» (Кубано-Черноморского отделения Российского телеграфного агентства) № 205 от 13 декабря 1920 года. В этом номере подробно рассказано об освобождении Крыма от врангелевских войск. Такого рода стенгазеты были широко распространены на местах в годы гражданской войны, но, к сожалению, не всегда сохранялись и теперь представляют большую редкость.

Иногда документ интересен не своим содержанием, а своей историей. Так, директор средней школы № 24 им. Ванды Василевской во Львове **И. Хомечко** прислал листовку, на которой в уменьшенном виде фототипически воспроизведен номер газеты «Известия Центрального Исполнительного Комитета и Петроградского Совета рабочих и солдатских депутатов», в котором был опубликован ленинский декрет о мире. С точки зрения изучения текста декрета о мире листовка ничего нового не дает. Но интересно другое. Листовка была найдена учениками школы среди старых польских и немецких книг. Она не похожа на книжную репродукцию. Это именно листовка, которая, возможно, была издана львовскими коммунистами в период нахождения г. Львова в составе панской Польши. Изучение истории этой листовки может приоткрыть интересные факты из деятельности Польской компартии, показать, как идеи Октября проникали в народные массы капиталистических стран.

Среди материалов, полученных музеем от редакции, имеются документы, рассказывающие о героизме коммунистов, их беспредельной преданности делу революции, кристальной моральной чистоте. Член партии с 1910 года, москвичка, врач **Т. Наджарова** прислала в «Известия» воспоминания об участниках большевистского подполья на Северном Кавказе. В них она приводит текст предсмертного письма Сурена Магуляна, члена армавирской подпольной группы большевиков.

Сурен погиб в застенках деникинской контрразведки, но его последнее письмо, написанное на клочке рубашки, дошло к друзьям. Как самую дорогую реликвию хранит Тамара Александровна этот клочок рубашки с выцветшими строчками письма.

«Милая Тамара. Посылаю последний товарищеский привет. Жду смерти, но чувствую себя бодро. Жизнь, в полном смысле этого слова, не изведанная для меня область. Не успел осуществить свои последние желания. Не должна ты мучиться и горевать. А из-за любви и нам — жить и работать и за нас. Сижу отдельно от Розы[1]. Она чувствует себя геройски. Всех осужденных к повешению — 16 человек. Пишу на рассвете, казнь состоится вечером.

Привет товарищам. Целую вас крепко. Сурен.

31 января 1920 года».

Через несколько дней продолжал:

«Милые друзья! Судьбе моей нужно было быть свидетелем смерти славных товарищей. Также мне без моей милой и славной Розы. Она погибла смертью храбрых, смело, без ропота и без страха она шла на эшафот.

Передайте матери Розы мой привет и успокойте ее. Мать такого славного, бесстрашного товарища не должна горевать и проливать слезы. Счастлива мать, имеющая таких дочерей. Сижу в секретке и третьи сутки жду своей участи. Из 16 — 7 товарищей повесят сегодня...

Последую примеру Розы и других товарищей и смело пойду к месту казни.

Прощайте. Будьте здоровы. Сурен. 5.II.1920 г.».

Воспоминания облекают в плоть и кровь такие общие понятия, как целеустремленность, энергия и энтузиазм строителей социализма и годы первых пятилеток. Почетный строитель **И. Цехмистренко** написал интересные и подробные воспоминания о создании первой плотины на Магнитогорском металлургическом комбинате.

Документы, составляющие личный архив, или, как говорят музейные работники, документы личного происхождения, представляют для историков большое самостоятельное значение. Очень важны они и для музеев.

Убедительная просьба к читателям «Известий»: бережно относитесь к своим личным архивам. Помните, для истории, — а она творится всеми и каждый день, — это бесценные реликвии, кто бы ни был их владелец — рабочий, колхозник, ученый, партийный или общественный деятель.

Сообщаем фамилии читателей, материалы и документы которых отобраны Государственным историческим музеем на вечное хранение.

А. Кравчуновский, Л. Курносова, Т. Наджарова, Л. Подвойский, В. Цивилев (Москва); **Н. Симанин, В. Шыров** (Ленинград); **Т. Верестовская, Н. Радевич** (Казань); **П. Кузнецов** (Удмуртская АССР, г. Воткинск); **П. Насонов** (Ульяновская обл., г. Инза); **Ф. Разницын, М. Ухов** (Челябинская обл.); **М. Ступак, О. Сыровчинская** (Новороссийск); **П. Шырков** (Ярославская обл.); **М. Зелинский, А. Иов, И. Цехмистренко, Н. Шереметьев** (Киев); **Г. Калинин, И. Хомечко, Н. Черковский** (Львов); **С. Борода** (Крымская обл.); **О. Гаврилишевская, Н. Трусова** (Днепропетровская обл.); **В. Гридин** (Одесса); **Р. Ерушева** (Чернигов); **Н. Казначко** (Луганская обл.); **П. Коломиец** (Черкасская обл.); **Е. Обрусникова** (Винницкая обл.); **Н. Подгородецкий** (Херсонская обл.); **Ф. Попов** (Полтавская обл.); **А. Пушкарь, С. Тищенко** (Донецкая обл.); **С. Ткаченко** (Ивано-Франковская обл.); **Ф. Чопенко** (Харьков); **Н. Виноградов** (Минск); **И. Роба** (Таллин); **П. Корж, Н. Морозова, Э. Хачфорин** (Баку); **В. Чантурия** (Сухуми); **С. Зимин** (Ташкент); **И. Минчин** (Самарканд); **А. Рябых** (Чимкентская обл.); **Н. Счастный** (Фрунзе); **Г. Усатенко** (Сырдарьинская обл.).

[1] Роза Каспарова, член партии с 1917 г., возглавлявшая группу большевиков-подпольщиков в г. Армавире, в которую входил Сурен Магулян.

yet one which does not repel the reader.[7] *Izvestia* tries to raise the cultural level of the Soviet people, an objective in common with the other big, national or "All-Union" dailies. Whatever is considered harmful, degrading or purely entertaining is not printed. Such subjects as crime, romance, social items, and human interest features do not find a place in the pages of *Izvestia.*

The paper publishes a steady diet of cultural and political items, readers' letters, serious essays and special announcements, all designed to keep the readers' minds on serious things. This, of course, is not enough from a Western point of view to make a good newspaper, but it is from the Soviet perspective. *Izvestia* typifies the best of the Communist elite newspapers and, without a doubt, has as much prestige and influence as any other daily of the world. In the context of the Soviet Union, it is a very important serious daily journal and from the Communist viewpoint is an outstanding contribution to "reasonable" world journalism.

Pravda
(U.S.S.R.)

The editorial said that the newspaper was an organ "to fight for a scientific approach to the management of the economy, for an improvement in the farms and methods of economic construction and for raising the level of Party and state discipline and of each official's personal responsibility for his job. . . ."[1] The editorial appeared in *Pravda* (Truth) and referred to the newspaper's main purpose for existence. To achieve these goals, the front-page boxed editorial (a standard feature) stated that the newspaper's tone must be calm and businesslike.

This seven-days-a-week paper, the organ of the Central Committee of the Soviet Union's Communist Party, is without a doubt the calmest, most businesslike, and most influential in the country and perhaps in the whole world. It stands at the apex of the Soviet press system and sets policy journalistically and disseminates official Party doctrine throughout the entire Union. There is an official quality and prestige associated with *Pravda* not found in other newspapers of the world, with the possible exception of Red China's *Jen-min Jih-pao* or Vatican City's *Osservatore Romano.*

Pravda is based in a spacious seven-story building, owned and operated by the State, on Pravda Street in the northwest section of Moscow. In the sprawling printing plant adjoining the main building are printed three other important all-Union dailies—*Komsomolskaya Pravda, So-*

vetskaya Rossiya, and *Agricultural Life*—as well as some twenty periodicals including the popular satirical fortnightly, *Krokodil*. Instead of large newsrooms, *Pravda* has its editorial sections broken up into several large and airy rooms in which staff members work in smaller, specialized groups or singly. Management of the paper is in the hands of an editorial collegium named by the Presidium of the Communist Party. Two main editorial departments, domestic and foreign, occupy the building with each divided into many sections. The home department is on the fourth floor and the foreign department takes up nearly all the third floor.[2]

About 150 people work in the home department, about a third in the readers' letters' section. The majority of the home-department staffers are specialists with university or technical school educations. In addition to this Moscow staff, *Pravda* has an extensive network of correspondents scattered throughout the Soviet Union; these correspondents work with local contributors in their areas in addition to sending in their own news items and *feuilletons*. All *Pravda*'s journalists are highly qualified ideologically as well as professionally.[3] They are dedicated party journalists and clearly understand what they are to do and why they are to do it. About 50 of the staff are women, some dozen of whom are actually writers. Their journalistic abilities are appreciated by the paper's executives.[4]

Pravda's foreign department, composed of four sections, relies mainly on its own correspondents stationed in more than twenty-five key places about the globe. It also gets much foreign material from the Soviet news agency *Tass*, which has exchange agreements with many other national agencies. The editors do not think it necessary with their limited space (usually six, sometimes eight pages) to subscribe to any of the big Western news agencies but have hinted that when newsprint becomes more accessible they will expand their foreign coverage.[5]

Although the circulation of *Pravda* is shrouded in some mystery, there is good reason to believe that it approaches seven million, making it one of the largest daily newspapers in the world. About a third of this circulation comes off its Moscow presses each night and the rest from about thirty major plants around the Soviet Union. Matrices are flown from Moscow to these other printing centers, making it possible for *Pravda* to be read in the most remote parts of the U.S.S.R.[6] Teletypesetting machines, being used now on a limited scale between Moscow and a few provincial points, will speed up this national publishing process and change the pattern when it is completed in the next year or two.

Pravda, as the "number-one" newspaper of the Soviet Union, typifies the best in Soviet journalism: pleasing, neat makeup and typography; an absence of sensational stories and pictures; well-written special articles on cultural subjects; interpretive articles on science written by outstanding scientists; pieces on literature by leading literary figures of

СЛАВЕН ПОДВИГ НАШЕЙ НАУКИ И ТЕХНИКИ!

Пролетарии всех стран, соединяйтесь!

Коммунистическая партия Советского Союза

ПРАВДА

Газета основана 5 мая 1912 года В. И. ЛЕНИНЫМ

Орган Центрального Комитета КПСС

№ 305 (17987) ● Среда, 1 ноября 1967 г. ● Цена 3 коп.

ПОСВЯЩАЕТСЯ ВЕЛИКОМУ ОКТЯБРЮ

РЕШЕНА СЛОЖНЕЙШАЯ ПРОБЛЕМА КОСМОНАВТИКИ

«Космос-186» успешно завершил полет

Сообщение ТАСС

31 октября 1967 года спутник «Космос-186» по команде с Земли завершил космический полет на 65-м витке и в 11 часов 20 минут московского времени осуществил мягкую посадку в заданном районе. Осуществление автоматической стыковки двух спутников и выполнение других научных задач, предусмотренных в программе полета спутника «Космос-186», закончено полностью.

Все системы, установленные на спутнике «Космос-186», на этапах поиска, сближения, причаливания и стыковки, а также при расстыковке, последующем полете и посадке на Землю продемонстрировали высокую надежность функционирования при решении принципиально новых для космонавтики задач.

Второй спутник «Космос-188» после расстыковки продолжает выполнение программы исследования космического пространства.

ЦЕНТРАЛЬНОМУ КОМИТЕТУ КПСС ПРЕЗИДИУМУ ВЕРХОВНОГО СОВЕТА СССР СОВЕТУ МИНИСТРОВ СССР

Мы, ученые, конструкторы, инженеры, техники и рабочие, принимавшие участие в создании и запуске двух искусственных спутников Земли «Космос-186» и «Космос-188», докладываем Центральному Комитету КПСС, Президиуму Верховного Совета СССР, Совету Министров СССР об успешном выполнении первой в мире автоматической стыковки и расстыковки двух космических кораблей на орбите.

Нас, как и всех советских людей, радует, что новый выдающийся вклад нашей социалистической Родины в дело освоения космоса осуществлен накануне 50-летия Великого Октября. Замечательные успехи советской науки и техники в покорении космического пространства стали возможны благодаря социалистическому строю, героическому труду всего советского народа, неустанным заботам и вниманию нашей партии и Советского правительства.

Новое достижение советской науки и техники мы посвящаем 50-летию Советской власти.

Заверяем Центральный Комитет КПСС, Президиум Верховного Совета СССР и Совет Министров СССР, что и впредь будем работать над решением сложных задач по дальнейшему мирному освоению космического пространства, самоотверженно трудиться во имя прекрасного будущего — коммунизма!

Ученым и конструкторам, инженерам, техникам и рабочим, всем коллективам и организациям, принимавшим участие в создании искусственных спутников Земли «Космос-186» и «Космос-188» и осуществлении выдающегося научно-технического эксперимента

Дорогие товарищи!

ЦК КПСС, Президиум Верховного Совета СССР и Совет Министров СССР горячо поздравляют ученых, конструкторов, инженеров, техников и рабочих, все коллективы и организации, принимавшие участие в создании, запуске и испытании искусственных спутников Земли «Космос-186» и «Космос-188».

Наша Советская Родина одержала новую выдающуюся победу в мирном освоении космоса.

Осуществление первой в мире автоматической стыковки и расстыковки искусственных спутников Земли на орбите — достойный подарок Советской Родине в канун 50-летия Великого Октября.

Новая победа в освоении космоса, как и успешный полет автоматической межпланетной станции «Венера-4», свидетельствует о дальнейшем развитии советской науки и техники. Все прогрессивное человечество вновь убедилось, каких замечательных успехов добился наш народ за годы Советской власти. Эти достижения — результат самоотверженного труда советского народа, который за короткий исторический срок превратил нашу Родину в могучую державу, идущую во главе мирового прогресса.

Советские люди горячо приветствуют славных ученых, конструкторов, инженеров, техников и рабочих, создавших замечательные искусственные спутники «Космос-186» и «Космос-188» и осуществивших беспримерный эксперимент в космосе.

Желаем вам, дорогие товарищи, дальнейших успехов в благородном деле по мирному освоению космоса, в решении задач, поставленных XXIII съездом КПСС.

Центральный Комитет КПСС — Президиум Верховного Совета СССР — Совет Министров СССР

ОТВЕТ СТАЛЕВАРОВ

ЧЕРЕПОВЕЦ, 31. (Корр. «Правды»). Весть о новой выдающейся победе советской космической техники быстро облетела мартеновский цех Северной Магнитки.

— Такое событие надо отметить «космической» вахтой,— решили сталевары В. Я. Козлов, В. О. Красавин, Е. С. Неваш, П. Т. Векшин, П. Ф. Измайлов и другие.

В эту смену было проведено много скоростных плавок. За сутки получено сверх задания много тонн великолепной череповецкой стали.

Задание пятилетки по объему товарной продукции решено выполнить к 5 декабря 1970 года.

Спасибо!

Великий праздник украшен новым примером могущества нашего народа. Спасибо нашим ученым. И мы не хотим отставать от них. На наших полях заложена такая основа урожая будущего года, что, кажется, раньше такой и не видели. Озимые зеленеют, как бархатный ковер, и сулят много зерна. Подкрепим своим трудом хлеборобов подвиг ученых.

М. ГОРДИЕНКО.

Председатель колхоза имени Калинина Зерноградского района Ростовской области.

Отличный эксперимент

На наших глазах совершаются новые этапы в освоении человеком космического пространства. Перед учеными, инженерами, техниками встают все новые сложные научно-технические задачи, решение которых требует большого комплексного труда представителей многих специальностей. К числу таких задач относилось и выполнение встречи и соединения искусственных космических тел, совершающих полет в космосе. Осуществление 30 октября первой в мире автоматической стыковки на орбите вокруг Земли двух советских спутников — крупное достижение в этом направлении.

Известно, что в США была проведена стыковка космических кораблей с ракетой-носителем при управлении экипажем корабля этим процессом. Однако полная автоматизация взаимного поиска на орбите двух космических тел, выполнение необходимых маневров для встречи и, наконец, непосредственного осуществления жесткого соединения, а потом и разделения представляет, несомненно, более сложную и перспективную задачу, успешное решение которой — новая победа научно-технической мысли.

Без выполнения подобного процесса невозможно мыслить о создании летающих в космическом пространстве обитаемых лабораторий, астрономических обсерваторий, периодическом их посещении персоналом и доставке оборудования и продовольствия.

Быть может, когда-нибудь понадобится при возникновении соответствующей ситуации послать на космический корабль вспомогательные средства или другой корабль для соединения с первым. Автоматическая стыковка повышает надежность проводимых в космосе экспериментов.

Немало замечательных успехов достигнуто в Советском Союзе за десять лет со времени запуска первого искусственного спутника Земли. Каждая из вновь возникающих в области космических исследований проблем требовала новых научных и технических поисков. А их результаты оказывают влияние на общее развитие техники и используются в самых различных ее областях. Космическая техника дала огромный импульс развитию радиотехники, дальней радиосвязи во всех ее видах, электроники, гелиоэнергетики, изысканию новых материалов, прогрессу других областей знания.

Осуществление автоматической стыковки, несомненно, существенно влияет на решение задач по автоматизации многих других сложных процессов, даже не относящихся непосредственно к деятельности человека в космосе.

Академик А. БЛАГОНРАВОВ.

ТРИУМФ СТРАНЫ СОВЕТОВ

Мир восхищен новым достижением Советского Союза в исследовании космического пространства

Новый выдающийся успех советской науки и техники в канун великого праздника Октября широко комментируется за рубежом. Печать, радио, телевидение десятков стран мира исключительно высоко оценивают успешную операцию первой в истории автоматической стыковки и расстыковки двух космических кораблей на орбите.

«Изумительная победа России», «Выход на порог новой эры завоевания Вселенной», «Триумф Страны Советов», «Великолепная демонстрация советской технической виртуозности», «Эпохальное событие в истории освоения космоса» — таковы заголовки газетных статей, заявления видных ученых, общественных деятелей различных стран в связи с новым космическим достижением СССР.

(Международные отклики на новое достижение советской науки и техники публикуются на 2-й странице).

УКАЗ ПРЕЗИДИУМА ВЕРХОВНОГО СОВЕТА СССР
ОБ УЧРЕЖДЕНИИ ОРДЕНА ОКТЯБРЬСКОЙ РЕВОЛЮЦИИ

Президиум Верховного Совета СССР **постановляет:**

1. В ознаменование 50-летия Великой Октябрьской социалистической революции учредить орден Октябрьской Революции.

2. Утвердить статут ордена Октябрьской Революции.

3. Утвердить описание ордена Октябрьской Революции.

Председатель Президиума Верховного Совета СССР Н. ПОДГОРНЫЙ.

Секретарь Президиума Верховного Совета СССР М. ГЕОРГАДЗЕ.

Москва, Кремль. 31 октября 1967 г.

Статут ордена Октябрьской Революции

1. В ознаменование 50-летия Великой Октябрьской социалистической революции учрежден орден Октябрьской Революции.

2. Орденом Октябрьской Революции награждаются граждане СССР, предприятия, учреждения, организации и другие коллективы трудящихся, воинские части и соединения, а также республики, края, области, города.

Орденом Октябрьской Революции могут быть награждены и иностранные граждане.

3. Награждение орденом Октябрьской Революции производится:

за активную революционную деятельность, большой вклад в становление и укрепление Советской власти;

за выдающиеся заслуги в построении социализма и строительстве коммунизма;

за выдающиеся достижения в области развития народного хозяйства, науки и культуры;

за особые отвагу и мужество, проявленные в боях с врагами Советского государства;

за выдающиеся заслуги в укреплении оборонной мощи Советского государства;

за особо плодотворную государственную и общественную деятельность;

за активную деятельность, направленную на развитие и углубление всесторонних дружественных связей между народами Советского Союза и других государств, укрепление мира между народами.

4. Орден Октябрьской Революции носится на левой стороне груди и располагается после ордена Ленина.

5. Орден Октябрьской Революции после смерти награжденного остается в его семье.

Секретарь Президиума Верховного Совета СССР М. ГЕОРГАДЗЕ.

Описание ордена Октябрьской Революции

Орден Октябрьской Революции изготовляется из серебра и представляет собой позолоченную, покрытую красной эмалью пятиконечную звезду на фоне серебряного лучистого пятиугольника.

В верхней части пятиконечной эмалевой звезды изображено знамя, покрытое красной эмалью, с надписью в две строки: «Октябрьская Революция».

В центре звезды расположен серебряный пятиугольник с изображением крейсера «Аврора». Пятиугольник оксидирован разными тонами.

В нижней части ордена помещены накладные серп и молот из золота.

Размер ордена между противолежащими вершинами эмалевой звезды 43 мм.

Орден при помощи ушка и кольца соединяется с пятиугольной колодочкой, обтянутой шелковой муаровой лентой красного цвета шириной 24 мм. Посередине ленты пять продольных голубых полосок.

Секретарь Президиума Верховного Совета СССР М. ГЕОРГАДЗЕ.

К сведению членов ЦК КПСС, кандидатов в члены ЦК КПСС, членов Центральной ревизионной комиссии КПСС, депутатов Верховных Советов СССР и РСФСР

Регистрация членов и кандидатов в члены ЦК КПСС, членов Центральной ревизионной комиссии КПСС, депутатов Верховных Советов СССР и РСФСР, прибывающих на совместное торжественное заседание Центрального Комитета КПСС, Верховного Совета СССР и Верховного Совета РСФСР, посвященное 50-летию Великой Октябрьской социалистической революции, производится 1 и 2 ноября с 10 часов утра до 8 часов вечера в помещении Кремлевского театра.

Телефоны: Б 4-27-77 и Б 4-32-05.

Только что был сварен традиционный «красный стык» на трассе крупнейшего в Сибири почти тысячекилометрового нефтепровода Усть-Балык — Омск. На снимке: герои строительства сварщики Павел Гордеев и Владимир Олексюк. Им, мастерам огненного шва, доверили сварить «красный стык» сибирского нефтепровода. Фото Н. Сапожникова. (ТАСС).

Председателю Революционного совета Председателю Совета Министров Алжирской Народной Демократической Республики
г-ну Хуари БУМЕДЬЕНУ

г. АЛЖИР

От имени народов Советского Союза, Коммунистической партии Советского Союза, Президиума Верховного Совета СССР, Советского правительства и от нас лично шлем дружественному алжирскому народу, Революционному совету, партии Фронт национального освобождения, правительству и Вам лично, уважаемый г-н Председатель, сердечные поздравления и наилучшие пожелания по случаю национального праздника Алжирской Народной Демократической Республики — праздника революции.

Отмечая вместе с алжирским народом тринадцатую годовщину со дня начала революции в Алжире, оказавшей столь большое воздействие на развитие национально-освободительного движения на африканском континенте, советские люди искренне радуются его успехам в деле упрочения независимости и суверенитета своей страны, продвижения по пути экономического и социального прогресса. Героический пример народных масс Алжирской Народной Демократической Республики, чьи революционные традиции и энергия являются залогом успешного созидания новой жизни в Алжире, заслужил признание и уважение народов других стран.

От всей души желаем алжирскому народу новых успехов в проведении важных социальных преобразований, в развитии национальной экономики и культуры, в совместной с другими народами борьбе за полное освобождение африканского континента от гнета и вмешательства сил империализма и колониализма, за ликвидацию последствий преступной израильской агрессии против арабских стран.

Выражаем твердую уверенность в том, что отношения дружбы и всестороннего сотрудничества, которые сложились между нашими странами и народами, будут и впредь развиваться и крепнуть в интересах алжирского и советского народов, во имя упрочения единства и солидарности всех стран, борющихся против империализма и колониализма, за мир, безопасность народов и социальный прогресс.

Л. БРЕЖНЕВ, Генеральный секретарь ЦК КПСС — Н. ПОДГОРНЫЙ, Председатель Президиума Верховного Совета СССР — А. КОСЫГИН, Председатель Совета Министров СССР

Москва, Кремль, 31 октября 1967 года.

РОДИНЕ — К ЮБИЛЕЮ

● КРАСНОАРМЕЙСК (Донецкая обл.). Новый мировой рекорд добычи угля из одного забоя установила бригада Анатолия Стеблова, работающая на шахте «Красноармейская». За тридцать один рабочий день она добыла 150.657 тонн угля, что на 28 тысяч тонн больше мирового достижения бригады Николая Гринды с шахты «Октябрьская». Бригада Анатолия Степанова ведет разработку пласта в 200-метровой лаве с помощью гидравлического механизированного комплекса «КМ-87».

● КЕМЕРОВО. Коллектив трижды орденоносного Кузнецкого металлургического комбината брал обязательство к 50-летию Октября за счет внедрения рационализаторских предложений сэкономить 3.200 тысяч рублей. Это обязательство успешно выполнено. Новаторы комбината за истекшее время года внесли тысячи предложений.

Прибытие делегации Демократической Республики Вьетнам

31 октября в Москву на празднование 50-летия Великой Октябрьской социалистической революции по приглашению ЦК КПСС, Президиума Верховного Совета СССР и Совета Министров СССР прибыла делегация Партии трудящихся Вьетнама, Национального собрания и правительства Демократической Республики Вьетнам. В составе делегации входят: Первый секретарь Центрального Комитета Партии трудящихся Вьетнама тов. Ле Зуан (глава делегации), член Политбюро ЦК ПТВ, заместитель премьер-министра и министр обороны ДРВ тов. Во Нгуен Зиап, член Политбюро ЦК ПТВ, заместитель премьер-министра и министр иностранных дел ДРВ тов. Нгуен Зуй Чинь, член ЦК ПТВ, заместитель председателя Постоянного комитета Национального собрания ДРВ, секретарь комитета ПТВ автономного района Вьет-Бак тов. Тю Ван Тан, кандидат в члены ЦК ПТВ, главный редактор газеты «Нян Зан» тов. Хоанг Тунг, кандидат в члены ЦК ПТВ, Чрезвычайный и Полномочный Посол ДРВ в СССР тов. Нгуен Тхо Тан.

На Внуковском аэродроме вьетнамских товарищей встречали: Генеральный секретарь ЦК КПСС тов. Л. И. Брежнев, член Политбюро ЦК КПСС, Председатель Совета Министров СССР тов. А. Н. Косыгин, член Политбюро ЦК КПСС, Председатель Президиума Верховного Совета СССР тов. Н. В. Подгорный, член Политбюро ЦК КПСС, председатель ВЦСПС тов. А. Н. Шелепин, член ЦК КПСС, заместитель Председателя Совета Министров СССР тов. В. Н. Новиков, член ЦК КПСС, министр иностранных дел СССР тов. А. А. Громыко, кандидат в члены ЦК КПСС, министр морского флота СССР тов. В. Г. Бакаев, член Центральной ревизионной комиссии КПСС, заместитель министра обороны СССР генерал армии тов. И. Г. Павловский, член Центральной ревизионной комиссии КПСС, заместитель заведующего Отделом ЦК КПСС тов. С. А. Баскаков, заместитель заведующего Отделом ЦК КПСС тов. О. Б. Рахманин и другие.

Делегацию встречали также глава Постоянного представительства Национального фронта освобождения Южного Вьетнама в СССР тов. Данг Куанг Минь, сотрудники посольства ДРВ и Постоянного представительства НФОЮВ в СССР. (ТАСС).

the nation; a variety of letters from readers; and the Soviet Union's most authoritative articles dealing with party theory and programs. Its editor is usually a very high Party member, its staffers are among the best in the U.S.S.R., and its reputation for giving the official "line" on all important matters makes it essential reading for the patriotic Soviet citizen. It is so important that it can be considered a special State institution.[7] All party ideological articles get priority in its pages; many of its articles are picked up and beamed across the U.S.S.R. by Radio Moscow or are transmitted to regional and local papers throughout the nation by *Tass*. Its main editorial is wired or broadcast in full to all major papers each day. As the "guardian of the Party line," *Pravda* takes a position on all questions of public life, and the other media follow its lead.[8] In short, the voice of *Pravda* is heard regularly throughout the whole land and, as it is one of the most-often quoted papers of the world, its influence is also international.

In 1962 *Pravda* celebrated its fiftieth anniversary. It had come a long way from its crude beginnings in 1912 in St. Petersburg as a Lenin-inspired underground paper. At first it had three staff members—Lenin and two others, and was published for a time as a tabloid. During its first dozen years it was often suppressed by the Tsarist Government, reappearing under different names until, after the Revolution, it moved to Moscow in 1918 to become the principal Party journal. It has grown steadily and rapidly and has had among its editors some of the Party's highest leaders—among them Stalin, Beria, and Shepilov. Many others have been among its most prolific contributors.

In recent years, one of the paper's most capable editors was Pavel A. Satyukov who did much to build up the paper's circulation and prestige during the Khrushchev era. After Khrushchev's sudden fall from power in 1964, Satyukov was replaced as editor by Alexei Rumyantsev who had edited *Kommunist* (the Party's main ideological magazine) and had held other important positions in Soviet journalism. During his short editorship, Rumyantsev editorialized under his own name for greater freedom of thought for scientists, writers, and other intellectuals.[9] He was replaced in 1965 by Mikhail Zimyanin, Soviet deputy foreign minister, who is taking a harder line against the United States, especially in regard to Vietnam.[10] He has also stopped agitation for more freedom for intellectuals; rather, he is tending to stress the need for a unity of thought and a support of Party policy by the intellectual community—at least in public expressions.

In spite of the new editor's step back from the courageous editorializing of his predecessor, there are indications that *Pravda* is liberalizing its policies in many areas. Regular "criticism sessions," for example, are held at weekly editorial conferences in which the previous week's issues of the newspaper are criticized, often severely, both from the point of view of content as well as writing style. *Pravda*'s coverage is compared with other big all-Union papers such as *Izvestia, Komsomolskaya Pravda,* and *Sovetskaya Rossiya.* The critics also analyze every article carefully for mistakes of all types, even the misspelling of names. If a writer or correspondent makes a mistake, he is reprimanded.[11]

Pravda staffers have begun openly discussing bottlenecks in news dissemination, unnecessary delays in printing late news items, and reader reaction to the content of the paper. They have even asked to be given responsibility to print certain news to "combat" the effects of the foreign press without waiting for the directives to come from the Party.[12]

Another liberalizing aspect is the fact that the letters chosen to appear in the readers' column (a standing section called "The Echo") are carrying more outspoken complaints. Writers increasingly are stressing need for better consumer goods, lashing out against public wrongs, and attacking minor bureaucracy, and discussing other facets of Soviet life not mentioned in print a decade ago.[13] Wrote *Pravda* in a recent editorial: "A reader's letter often becomes the beginning of a broad discussion on moral, philosophical, literary or economic themes."[14] More than 1,000 letters a day are received by *Pravda,* which tries to respond to, or investigate, every one in some way. The subjects of these letters run from very serious questions about domestic and international affairs to extremely personal matters. In addition to the letters, *Pravda* receives many of its readers who want to come to the offices to discuss problems and ask questions in person.

Pravda, in spite of its existence in a controlled society, is improving in many ways and deserves a firm place among the elite newspapers of the world. Its prestige and influence is probably not surpassed anywhere and the seriousness of its articles and the importance it gives to its readers should serve as good examples to daily journals everywhere. While "enslaved" from a Western point of view, *Pravda* proceeds carefully from day to day as it fulfills its responsibility to its society as it sees it and thrusts its influence ever deeper into the hinterlands of the vast Soviet Union.

Die Presse
(AUSTRIA)

On the heels of the Austrian uprising against authoritarianism and the fleeing of Metternich to England in 1848, a rash of bold and outspoken newspapers—nearly a hundred of them dailies—sprang up as a wave of freedom enveloped the country. Among these, and undoubtedly the most important, was *Die Presse* (founded 1848) published by August

Zang. A small (three-column pages) daily, it heralded the birth of modern journalism in Austria. This meant in large part that a free press took root, more cosmopolitan and literate, giving more emphasis to nongovernmental and objectively reported news.

Zang, who had been a professor of medicine at Wurzburg, was inspired to found *Die Presse* by the great success of *La Presse*, published in Paris by Emile Girardin and aimed to instill liberal concepts in a much larger segment of the populace. Political essays, which had dominated the Austrian press for many years, became scarce in *Die Presse* and the reader was presented ever-increasing quantities of national and international news.[1]

By 1850, with a return of authoritarian government, the nearly 100 dailies established several years earlier dropped to 20, and for the next decade the press remained throttled. In 1862, on a new wave of liberalism and a demand by the public for constitutionalism, a new press law did away with censorship and punishment for erring editors; *Die Presse* took a new lease on life and grew constantly. By 1851 *Die Presse*'s circulation was 13,000; by 1853, 17,000; by 1854, 23,000; and by 1859, 28,000.[2]

In September, 1864, *Die Presse* in effect became the *Neue Freie Presse* when it began under the new title with Dr. Max Friedlander and Michael Etienne, two editors of the original *Presse*, as the new directors. Little change was made in policy, content, or format; in reality, only the name changed. Under the editorship of Friedlander and Etienne, the paper became by far the best the nation had had, providing much well-written news, thoughtful commentary, excellent *feuilleton* articles. The *Neue Freie Presse* was the pacesetter in reviving an interest in cultural affairs and gained wide recognition outside Austria as one of the very best dailies in Europe.[3] By 1873 it had a circulation of 35,000, having risen from 4,000 at the time of its founding in 1864. Its staff totaled some 600, among them about 100 foreign correspondents.[4]

Friedlander died in 1872 and Etienne seven years later, and the paper passed into the hands of Moriz Benedikt, who actually ran the paper until 1920. He did much to modernize the plant, expand coverage, emphasize interviews, hire better-educated staffers, and was generally considered one of the dozen most powerful men in Austria, often being compared to Northcliffe of Britain and Hearst of the United States.[5]

Dr. Ernst Benedikt became publisher in 1920 and served in this position (also editor) of the paper until 1936. After World War I the *Neue Freie Presse* lost much of its circulation and struggled through the twenties and into the forties with serious financial problems. However it kept its general quality, and largely on the basis of its excellent *feuilleton* articles it was considered, along with Paris' *Le Temps* and *Journal des Debâts*, the best in Europe.[6] It still was strong in fiction, theater, music, and culture and, of course, economics where it had always excelled. The period between the two world wars might be called

Die „Milchminute“ kostet 3100 Schilling / S. 3 — Italiens Liebespaar Nr. 1 floh / S. 10

Preis 2 Schilling
Redaktion und Verwaltung
Inseratenannahme:
1190 Wien, XIX., Muthg. 2, Pressehaus
Tel.: 36 52 50 (Serie). FS.: 07-4110
Telegramme: Wienpresse Wien
Anzeigen-Stadtbüro:
Wien, I., Fleischmarkt 1 (63 32 60)
Vertrieb:
1140 Wien, XIV., Husterg. 3 (92 16 92)
Abonnement und Provinzverschleiß:
1010 Wien, I., Wollzeile 11 (52 69 63)
Erscheinungsort Wien
Verlagspostamt: Wien 1190 P. b. b.

Die Presse

Unabhängige Zeitung für Österreich

DAS WETTER:
Wechseld wolkig
Föhneinfluß
Teilweise nebelig
(AUSFÜHRLICH SEITE 5)

Jahrgang 1967 / Nr. 5879 — Wien, Dienstag, den 14. November 1967 — Gegründet 1848

Athenagoras nicht nach Wien

Patriarch muß seinen Besuch in letzter Minute absagen

Eigenbericht der „Presse“

WIEN (r). Überraschenderweise mußte der Besuch des Ökumenischen Patriarchen von Konstantinopel, Athenagoras, in Wien 18 Stunden vor dem erwarteten Eintreffen als Gast der Bundesregierung abgesagt werden. Als Grund wurde starke Übermüdung angegeben.

In einer amtlichen Mitteilung von Montag abend heißt es, daß Patriarch Athenagoras, der aus Anlaß der Verleihung des Ehrendoktorates der rechts- und staatswissenschaftlichen Fakultät der Universität Wien am 14. November in der Bundeshauptstadt hätte eintreffen sollen, Montag nachmittag über die österreichische Botschaft in London mitteilen ließ, er sehe sich wegen starker Übermüdung durch die bisherige, lange Reise veranlaßt, den vorgesehenen Besuch zu verschieben. Der Patriarch „wird den Besuch in Wien zu einem späteren Zeitpunkt nachholen, dessen Termin in Kürze vereinbart werden wird“, heißt es zum Abschluß des Kommuniqués.

Die Begründung der kurzfristigen Absage wäre, wie man in informierten Kreisen erfährt, an sich verständlich, denn das 81jährige Oberhaupt der Kirche von Konstantinopel und damit der Inhaber des Ehrenvorranges in der Orthodoxie ist durch die Besuche und Gespräche in Belgrad, Bukarest, Sofia, im Vatikan als Gast des Papstes, in Genf beim Weltkirchenrat und zuletzt in London bei Erzbischof Ramsey zweifellos stark beansprucht worden. Doch ist andererseits die erstaunliche Vitalität des Patriarchen bekannt und der Wunsch, direkt nach Istanbul zurückzukehren, erfolgte so plötzlich, daß Kombinationen über andere Ursachen Tür und Tor geöffnet sind.

Das Kommuniqué spricht von einem späteren Zeitpunkt, aber nicht von der ursprünglichen Regierungseinladung. Man hält es daher für möglich, daß Rücksichtnahme auf dringende türkische Vorstellungen Athenagoras im Hinblick auf die heikle Situation des Patriarchats zu einer Änderung seiner Dispositionen veranlaßt haben könnten, doch sind auch das im gegenwärtigen Augenblick nur Vermutungen.

Keine Hilfe für Draganovic

Intervention wegen Doppelstaatsbürgerschaft nicht möglich

Eigenbericht der „Presse“

WIEN (r.). Da der aus Österreich verschwundene Exilkroate eine Doppelstaatsbürgerschaft besitze, sei Österreich nicht in der Lage, in diesem Fall offiziell etwas zu unternehmen. Man werde sich jedoch weiterhin privat für sein Schicksal interessieren. Dies erklärte der österreichische Botschafter in Belgrad, Hartl, der „Presse“ am Montag. Der Botschafter dementierte Meldungen, wonach er das jugoslawische Außenministerium ersucht habe, Draganovic in Sarajewo aufsuchen zu können. Allerdings erklärte Außenminister Toncic am Montag im Budgetausschuß, ein Mitglied der Belgrader Botschaft sei angewiesen worden, mit Draganovic in Kontakt zu treten.

Draganovic hat zwar die österreichische Staatsbürgerschaft erhalten, von den jugoslawischen Behörden wird er aber weiterhin als Bürger ihres Landes betrachtet. In Fällen doppelter Staatsbürgerschaft gilt der Völkerrechtsgrundsatz, daß für solche Personen jeweils das Land zuständig ist, in dem sie sich gerade aufhalten. Nur beim Aufenthalt in dritten Ländern können beide Staaten intervenieren.

Angeblich soll Draganovic demnächst eine Pressekonferenz geben.

presse – telex

MASSIVE FORDERUNGEN

Für die Arbeitnehmer im Handel fordert die Gewerkschaft Lohnerhöhungen bis zu 16,7 Prozent. Dies wurde bei einer ersten Fühlungnahme der Sozialpartner mitgeteilt.
(Seite 2)

KOHLENREVOLTE

Ein schwerer Konflikt ist zwischen Premierminister Wilson und dem linken Flügel der Labour-Partei im Gange. Anlaß ist eine Revolte der Bergarbeitergewerkschaft gegen stärkeren Personalabbau.
(Seite 2)

MONSTERDIEBSTAHL

Beute im Wert von 70 Millionen Schilling machten Diebe bei einem Tresoreinbruch in London.
(Seite 10)

Funkbild: „Die Presse“/upi

DIE LETZTE STATION WAR LONDON

Der Ökumenische Patriarch von Konstantinopel, Athenagoras (links), ist von London — das Bild zeigt ihn dort im Gespräch mit Erzbischof Ramsey — direkt heimgekehrt. Den geplanten Besuch in Wien sagte er ab.

Keine Abwertung

Eigenbericht der „Presse“

WIEN (gr). Als „absoluter Unsinn“ werden an zuständiger Stelle Gerüchte über eine angeblich geplante Schillingabwertung bezeichnet, die auf ausländischen Finanzplätzen aufgetaucht sind und auf die schwierige österreichische Haushaltslage Bezug nehmen. Die österreichische Wirtschaftslage biete keinerlei Anlaß für derartige Befürchtungen, wird betont. Man hält es für wahrscheinlich, daß den Gerüchten Mißverständnisse im Zusammenhang mit der Unruhe um das Pfund Sterling (siehe Seite 7) zugrunde liegen.

Klaus: „Erst nach dem Budget“

Klarstellung der ÖVP zu Kombinationen um die Regierung

Eigenbericht der „Presse“

WIEN (ht). Über die APA gab Bundeskanzler und ÖVP-Obmann Klaus am Montagnachmittag folgende Erklärung ab: „Die Bundesregierung hat augenblicklich das Budget für 1968 im Parlament zu vertreten. Erst wenn das Budget mit den notwendigen Nebengesetzen beschlossen ist, ist für die Bundesparteileitung der ÖVP der Zeitpunkt gekommen, über das weitere Programm und über die daraus resultierenden notwendigen Maßnahmen Beschlüsse zu fassen. Im Zusammenhang damit wird auch darüber zu beraten sein, ob personelle Veränderungen in der Bundesregierung zweckmäßig sind. Daraus ergibt sich, daß alle in letzter Zeit verbreiteten Vermutungen und Kombinationen jeder sachlichen Grundlage entbehren.“ Diese Erklärung wurde veröffentlicht, nachdem eine „bündische Konferenz“ (Klaus, Withalm und die drei Bundesobmänner) die Situation beraten hatten, die nach den sonntägigen Äußerungen des Vizekanzlers entstanden war.

Mit der Situation — sowohl von Regierung und Partei nach den Herbstwahlen als auch der Problematik der Regierungsumbildung — wird sich heute, Dienstag, auch die ÖVP-Bundesparteileitung, zum Teil auch der ÖVP-Klub, befassen. Nächste Woche wird dieselbe Thematik von der Obmännerkonferenz der ÖVP (bündische und Landesobmänner) weiterberaten werden; diese hatte bereits in der vorigen Woche getagt.

In diesem Zusammenhang werden derzeit auch die Arbeiten am sogenannten Ministeriengestz intensiviert, das Klaus unmittelbar nach Bildung der ÖVP-Regierung angekündigt hatte, das aber bisher nicht recht weitergegangen ist. Es soll eine sinnvolle Zusammenfassung der Kompetenzen in den einzelnen Ministerien erreicht werden.

USA im Bann der Asienpolitik

Sato bei Johnson — Japan soll einen Teil der Verteidigungslasten übernehmen

Tel.-Bericht unserer Korrespondentin Marlene Manthey

WASHINGTON. Washington steht derzeit ganz im Bann der Asienpolitik. Am Montag führte US-Botschafter in Saigon, Bunker, ausführliche Gespräche im Weißen Haus, zu denen im Laufe der Woche sowohl der militärische Oberkommandierende, General Westmoreland, sowie der für die sogenannte Pazifizierung, also die zivile Befriedung und die weltanschauliche Ausrichtung der Südvietnamesen, verantwortliche US-Administrator Komer, zugezogen werden.

Zwischendurch werden Präsident Johnson und der japanische Ministerpräsident Sato im Weißen Haus konferieren, wobei es um weit mehr als nur die direkten amerikanisch-japanischen Beziehungen geht. Sato, der eine kompromißlose proamerikanische Politik verfolgt, so daß ihm seine Gegner vorwerfen, sich zu einem Werkzeug des US-Imperialismus in Asien zu machen, fordert von Washington die Rückgabe der seit dem Zweiten Weltkrieg besetzten japanischen Inseln. Washington hat schon durchblicken lassen, es könne Zusagen bezüglich der Bonin-Gruppe machen, das Problem der Riu-Kiu-Inseln stehe jedoch auf einem anderen Blatt. Dies gilt besonders für Okinawa, das seit 20 Jahren planmäßig zum stärksten US-Stützpunkt im Pazifik ausgebaut wurde und dessen strategische Bedeutung so wichtig ist, daß die USA nicht die Absicht haben, in absehbarer Zeit auf ihn zu verzichten.

Washington will im Gegenteil Japan stärker in seine Asienpolitik einbauen. Das Land, das wie kein anderes wirtschaftlich von der expansionistischen US-Asienpolitik profitiert, soll — so meint die amerikanische Regierung — einen Teil der Verteidigungslasten dort übernehmen und auch eine stärkere wirtschaftliche Hilfsrolle dort spielen. Denn Washington weiß sehr wohl, wonach der Umstand, daß die USA zwar längst eine asiatische Macht wurden, aber eben doch keine asiatische Nation sind, einer der Hauptgründe für die Rückschläge in Asien ist.

Japan durchlaufe zwar derzeit eine antiamerikanische Periode, doch rechnet Washington damit, daß dieses Sentiment durch das ständige Erstarken Chinas schließlich wieder neutralisiert werden wird.

Verfrühte Aufregung

VON HANS THÜR

Die Aufregung war groß, nachdem Vizekanzler Bock am Sonntag in einer Wirtschaftsbundversammlung zu den sich seit Tagen häufenden Kombinationen über die bevorstehende Umbildung des Kabinetts Klaus II Stellung genommen hatte. Er hat eine rasche Klärung verlangt und noch hinzugefügt, er habe schon vor längerer Zeit um Entlastung vom Ministeramt gebeten. Doch hob er auch hervor, daß Zeitpunkt und Umfang des Revirements einzig und allein Sache der Regierungspartei seien.

Diese Feststellung ging in der Überraschung darüber unter, daß gerade Bock das künstlich angewärmte Eisen anfaßte. Dabei hätte genau sie die Aufregung von vornherein dämpfen müssen. Denn Bock hatte ja nur abermals ausgesprochen, was seit Jahresbeginn auf dem politischen Terminkalender der ÖVP stand: Aus dem Kabinett Klaus II wird im Frühjahr 1968 das Kabinett Klaus III werden. Er, der seit einem Jahr bei jeder Revirementkombination als „abgeschrieben“ bezeichnet wird, hat aber auch allfällige Veränderungen erleichtert, indem er öffentlich feststellte, es zittere niemand in der Regierung um seinen Sessel, er, Bock, am allerwenigsten.

Die Labilität und Richtungslosigkeit, die die Volkspartei völlig unnötig seit den Herbstwahlen beherrschen, ließen allerdings nach der Bock-Rede die Gerüchtemühlen erst recht auf Touren gehen. Sie wurden diesmal jedoch unverzüglich gebremst. Bundeskanzler und Bundesparteiobmann Klaus hat nach Beratung mit Withalm und den bündischen Obmännern eine Klarstellung veröffentlicht: Zuerst das Budget samt Nebengesetzen, dann Erneuerung der Regierungsmannschaft. Das heißt aber, daß das Kabinett Klaus III kaum vor dem Februar das Licht der Welt erblicken wird — womit das Datum wiedergenannt ist, auf das sich bereits zu Jahresanfang die bündischen und Landesobmänner der Volkspartei geeinigt hatten; und das seit damals gewiß auch alle Mitglieder des Kabinetts Klaus II in ihren Kalendern stehen haben.

Ist damit dem Nervenkrieg um das Wann der Regierungsumbildung der Boden entzogen, so gewiß nicht dem um das Wie. Denn die Kanzlerpartei im eigenen Saft langsam zu schmoren, ist ein Rezept, mit dem noch jede Opposition versuchte, die Wähler in die eigene Garküche zu locken. Auf- und Abstiegskandidaten zu nennen, ist andererseits eine alte Methode, mit der die Gruppen und Grüppchen ihr Geschäft zu machen versuchen — und oft genug auch gemacht haben. Es steht also den derzeitigen Regierungsmitgliedern eine harte Zeit bevor, ebenso allen, die irgendwie als Ministerkandidaten angesehen werden können oder von denen irgendein Interessent fürchtet, daß sie von irgendeinem anderen ministrabel gemacht werden könnten. Die „Seelenmassage“ ist aber auch der Partei zugedacht, die am 6. März 1966 vom Wähler die Mehrheit für ein ganz bestimmtes Versprechen mit einem fest umrissenen Auftrag erhalten hat. Aber daß es ihnen immer wieder so ergeht, wußten schließlich alle, die sich in oder an die politische Arena begaben. Sie sollen deshalb auch jetzt gefälligst Nerven und kühlen Kopf bewahren.

Denn die Aufgabe, die von der Volkspartei mit der Zusammenstellung des Kabinetts Klaus III zu lösen ist, erscheint keineswegs gering. Es sind dabei viele Gesichtspunkte zu beachten, die einer großen Zahl von Politikern durchaus neu sind; wie ihnen ja auch das Feld des Alleinregierens selbst heute noch neu ist. Zunächst: Dieses Kabinett Klaus III ist von einer Partei und nicht von einer Koalition zu stellen, auch nicht von einer Koalition von Bünden und Landesorganisationen. Gewiß sind auch Bünde- und Länderinteressen durchaus legitim, doch haben sie am Ende und nicht am Anfang der Rangordnung ihren Platz. Aber noch bevor man nach den Männern sucht, müßte man die Ressorts richtig bauen. Zu viel ist da in der Zeit des Proporzhandels vermischt und verschoben worden. Hier hätte die Verwaltungsreform von oben ihren Platz. Es sind klare Sachgebiete zu schaffen und unnötige Regierungssessel abzubauen. Erst dann wird es sinnvoll sein, an die Männerauswahl zu schreiten, wobei neben der fachlichen und politischen Eignung wohl nicht zuletzt die persönliche zu beachten sein wird. Denn das neue Kabinett muß nicht nur konzeptiv, sondern auch kooperativ sein, soll es das erfüllen können, was die Volkspartei von ihm erwartet: die Lokomotive für 1970 zu sein.

Rekordetat der Stadt Wien

Hoheitsverwaltung und Stadtwerke geben 16,8 Milliarden aus

Eigenbericht der „Presse“

WIEN (g. t.). Die Gemeinde Wien wird im kommenden Jahr rund 16,8 Milliarden Schilling ausgeben: Das Budget der Hoheitsverwaltung sieht Ausgaben von 11,7, der Haushaltsplan der Stadtwerke solche von 5,1 Milliarden Schilling vor. Das präliminierte Defizit der Gemeinde ist mit 275 Millionen Schilling oder 2,4 Prozent geringer als der heurige Abgang, der mit 402 Millionen oder 3,8 Prozent veranschlagt worden ist. Das Defizit der Stadtwerke wird mit über 190 Millionen Schilling um rund 50 Millionen größer als heuer sein.

Das neue Rekordbudget der Bundeshauptstadt wird sowohl auf der Einnahmen- wie auch auf der Ausgabenseite eine Steigerung von über einer Milliarde gegenüber 1967 aufweisen: Die Einnahmen steigen von 10,2 auf 11,4, die Ausgaben von 10,6 auf 11,7 Milliarden. Bei den Landes- und Gemeindeabgaben ergibt sich mit rund 1,9 Milliarden Schilling keine Änderung, während sich die Einnahmen aus dem Finanzausgleich von 3,7 auf 4,1 Milliarden Schilling erhöhen werden.

Trotz den vermehrten Ausgaben wird die Stadt 1968 mit 2,7 Milliarden Schilling nur um knapp hundert Millionen Schilling mehr als heuer für Investitionen aufwenden. Die Personalkosten hingegen werden um etwa 200 auf 3270 Millionen Schilling steigen.

Im Gegensatz zum Rekordbudget der Hoheitsverwaltung wird der Wirtschaftsplan der Wiener Stadtwerke als prekär angesehen. Erstmals werden nämlich nicht nur die Verkehrsbetriebe — mit 500 Millionen —, sondern auch die Gaswerke und sogar die städtische Bestattung passiv sein. Das echte Defizit der Stadtwerke macht fast 350 Millionen Schilling aus, wird jedoch durch einen Zuschuß der Hoheitsverwaltung um 150 Millionen reduziert.

(Ausführlicher Bericht Seite 5)

Friedensschluß im Jemen

Royalisten und Republikaner vereinbarten Waffenstillstand

KAIRO (upi, reuter). Die Republikaner und Royalisten im Jemen sind in der Nacht auf Montag zu einem Friedensschluß gelangt und haben einen Waffenstillstand abgeschlossen. Damit scheint der seit fünf Jahren anhaltende Bürgerkrieg ein Ende gefunden zu haben. Beobachter werten diese Übereinkunft als bedeutenden Schritt zum Frieden in diesem südarabischen Staat.

Die Meldung hierüber wurde von der ägyptischen Nachrichtenagentur Mena unter Berufung auf den neuen jemenitischen Staatschef Iriani bekanntgegeben. Der Meldung zufolge sei der Kommandeur der royalistischen Streitkräfte, General Kassem Monser, außerhalb der Hauptstadt Sanaa mit 20 Vertretern der republikanischen Seite zusammengetroffen, wobei das Abkommen zustandekam. Mit einer solchen Einigung ist gerechnet worden, seitdem der ägyptische Staatspräsident Nasser und der saudiarabische König Faisal auf der arabischen Gipfelkonferenz in Khartum im September ein Ende des Bürgerkrieges vereinbart haben. Kairo hatte die Republikaner, Saudiarabien die Royalisten unterstützt.

Der neue jemenitische Staatschef Irianim erklärte zu dem Waffenstillstandsabkommen: „Das Abkommen und die Übereinkunft wurden im Interesse des Landes an einem Ende der Kämpfe erzielt.“ Indessen hat der neue jemenitische Regierungschef El Aini seine Besprechungen mit Präsident Nasser in Kairo beendet und ist auf dem Luftweg nach Sanaa zurückgekehrt. Über die Gespräche wurde nichts bekanntgegeben. Mehrere Mitglieder der Delegation, mit der El Aini nach Kairo gekommen war, sind in der ägyptischen Hauptstadt geblieben und werden heute, Dienstag, in andere arabische Länder weiterreisen.

Realismus am Roten Meer

I. m. — Wie rasch und reibungslos sich „Todfeinde“ einigen können, sobald die Drahtzieher, die hinter ihnen stehen, das Interesse an dem Konflikt verloren haben, beweist das jemenitische Beispiel. Fünf Jahre lang bekriegten sich in dem kleinen, rückständigen südarabischen Staat Republikaner und Royalisten. Die Republikaner freilich waren auf die 50.000 ins Land entsandten Elitesoldaten Nassers angewiesen und selbst diese konnten nichts gegen die fanatischen imamtreuen Bergstämme, die materiell von Saudiarabiens Monarchen Faisal unterstützt wurden, ausrichten. Nach dem Blitzsieg der Israelis konnte sich Nasser das Jemendebakel weder militärisch noch finanziell weiter leisten und so vereinbarte er mit Faisal den Frieden für den Jemen.

Das weitere lief mit beachtlicher Präzision ab: Nach Abzug der Ägypter wird Nassers Marionette Sallal gestürzt und eine Woche später vereinbaren Republikaner und Royalisten den Frieden. Was der neue jemenitische Regierungschef indes in Kairo mit Nasser sprach, wurde nicht bekannt. Hätte er Treuegelöbnisse abgegeben, wäre es in Kairo nicht versäumt worden, diese zu publizieren. Das neue Regime in Sanaa scheint selbstbewußter zu sein als jenes unter Sallal und dürfte auch die Lage realistischer einschätzen. Denn ohne Zugeständnis an die Royalisten wäre der Waffenstillstand nicht zustande gekommen. Realpolitik aber ist in Sanaa bisher noch nie betrieben worden. Sollte sie tatsächlich obsiegen, könnte man auf die Dauer des Friedens hoffen.

the paper's "literary" period, as this area of its contents took precedence over its general news coverage. In 1934 the circulation of the *Neue Freie Presse* was 43,000 counting both its morning and its evening editions.

The paper suffered greatly in general quality during the Hitler period as did all Austrian dailies, and it was significant that as the war ended the paper changed its name again and took a step back into the arena of independent and outspoken journalism. On January 26, 1946, the last year of the Second World War, the paper appeared as *Die Presse* once more, this time under the direction of Dr. Ernst Molden, who remained at its helm until 1953.[7] Molden, a strong-minded Swedish immigrant, continued the paper in the traditions of its predecessors but stamped his own personality on its pages. He began using articles contributed by leading governmental figures, university professors, and experts in various fields. It was, without a doubt, the leading serious, independent paper in Austria and it was taken seriously in high places. In 1953 the position of publisher went to Fritz Molden, Ernst's son, who continued to run the paper as his father had; his chief editor became Milan Dubrovic,[8] and later Dr. Otto Schulmeister, who guides the brilliant editorial staff today.

The paper is published today from a six-story "Presse-Haus" on the Vienna *Fleischmarkt*. Still considered a liberal newspaper with a cosmopolitan outlook, it has correspondents in London, Paris, Bonn, Rome, Buenos Aires, New Delhi, Tokyo, Stockholm, Cairo, Jerusalem, Warsaw, Zurich, and New York. It publishes each morning and its main appeal is still to the business community. It circulates some 53,000 copies daily and nearly 70,000 on Saturday.[9] Its makeup is attractive, neat, and conservative. Like most Austrian papers, it is well compartmentalized. It is the best informed on international affairs of all Austrian papers and has a large following among intellectuals of many types and among people of the upper-middle class. Its main competitors are the *Kurier* (biggest Austrian daily with about 280,000 circulation), *Arbeiter Zeitung* (Socialist paper of high quality), and the *Salzburger Nachrichten* (the best provincial daily and one of the nation's best).

8

Profiles: The Americas

Next to Europe, the Western Hemisphere (the Americas) has more outstanding elite newspapers than any other part of the world. North America, even without Mexico, accounts for the greatest number of these papers, but South America, or a little more inclusively "Latin America," is well represented by informed, literate, and sizable newspapers. The Western Hemisphere, in spite of its diversity and the fact that its press makes use of four languages (English and Spanish mainly, but also French and Portuguese), accounts for about one-third of the world's elite dailies.

Many general dailies besides the six presented in this chapter might have been chosen to represent the elite press of the Americas—such United States' papers as *The Washington Post, The Courier-Journal* (Louisville, Kentucky), or the *Milwaukee Journal*; such Canadian dailies as *La Presse* or *The Star* of Montreal; or such Latin American stalwarts as Mexico's *Universal*, Colombia's *Tiempo*, Argentina's *Nación*, Ecuador's *Comercio* or Chile's *Mercurio.* These are all very fine newspapers, and there are others. But it is believed that the six chosen for this chapter, and whose profiles appear on the following pages, serve as especially good examples of the elite press of the Americas.

Of the six dailies discussed in this chapter (in order of their respective countries' representation), three are from the United States, two are from Canada, and one is from Brazil. And, it should be noted that in Part II of this book four additional papers from the Americas are discussed—two from the United States (the *Los Angeles Times* and

The New York Times) and two from Latin America (*Excélsior* of Mexico City and *La Prensa* of Buenos Aires, Argentina).

The six dailies whose profiles follow are presented in this order: the United States' Baltimore *Sun*, *The Christian Science Monitor*, and *St. Louis Post-Dispatch*; Canada's *Globe and Mail* and *Winnipeg Free Press*, and Brazil's *O Estado de São Paulo.* Beyond the fact that these six are all very excellent newspapers, it is interesting that they represent diverse orientations in the "sane and serious" segment of the political spectrum. On such a continuum, from "liberal" to "conservative," the six papers would probably fall into this order: *Post-Dispatch, Winnipeg Free Press, The Christian Science Monitor,* Baltimore *Sun, The Globe and Mail,* and *O Estado de São Paulo.*

At any rate, the six are all rational representatives of the best journalism in the Western Hemisphere. Their diverse natures do not keep them from belonging to the same elite club, all of whose members must be serious, informative, concerned, catholic, and intelligent.

*The (*Baltimore*) Sun*
(UNITED STATES)

In 1963 the editor-in-chief of *The Sun* called his paper "the best unread newspaper in the world." And by 1968 little had changed to alter this description. The circulation of the patriarch of Baltimore papers was only 188,000 in 1963; it had risen only to about 195,000 in 1966 and was inching slowly toward 200,000 in 1967. This is a small readership for a quality newspaper, especially for one published in the midst of a large concentration of population. This is rather strange, also, for a well-established paper like *The Sun* which has always determined to be a *news*paper, and a good one. It may well be that this persistent emphasis on *news* is the very cause of its slow growth.

An analysis of the content of *The Sun* will show that it provides excellent national and international coverage. Its eight full-time foreign correspondents (in London, Bonn, Moscow, Hong Kong, Rome, New Delhi, Rio de Janeiro and Saigon) provide the paper with thorough and highly professional reports.[1] Their dispatches are seldom cut or changed, which led Louis R. Rukeyser, stationed in New Delhi, to say that "working for *The Sun* is a correspondent's dream. No other paper gives its men quite so much freedom."[2] Only since about 1955, when its London man was its only overseas correspondent, has *The Sun*'s foreign emphasis become truly notable. Charles H. Dorsey, Jr., managing editor until recently, was perhaps most responsible for the foreign expansion of *The Sun*'s coverage. He said in 1963: "We try to send abroad literate people able to think for themselves, and we leave them alone."[3]

The Sun's national coverage is outstanding also. With more than a dozen men in Washington, the paper provides its readers with insightful pieces of scope and depth rarely found in United States' newspapers. It may well be that such distinguished staff members as H. L. Mencken, Gerald W. Johnson, and Frank F. Kent of an earlier day had given the paper its "good image," but one cannot overlook such stalwarts of *The Sun* who since the 1930's have added luster to the paper's reputation—cartoonists like Edmund Duffy and "Moco" Yardley, reporters like Mark Watson, Paul Ward, and Price Day, and editorial writers like John Owens.

The local coverage of *The Sun* is generally considered its weakest area and this, perhaps, helps explain the low circulation figures. *The Evening Sun*, a livelier sister paper (with a much larger circulation) does a better job reporting the activities of Baltimore and the immediate vicinity. Perhaps another factor in keeping *The Sun*'s circulation low is the paper's physical drabness. Although this is often found among quality newspapers everywhere, *The Sun* appears to try harder than most to make its contents hard to read, and generally its pages look more Victorian than those of *The Times* of London. Pages are packed with news and the overall tone resembles a dull, gray, overcast day in late January. Page makeup, perhaps as it should be, is consistent in tone with the contents of the paper—aristocratic, ultrarespectable, old-fashioned, proud, and somewhat aloof. No other major American daily can match *The Sun* in its retention of this nineteenth-century aura. *Time* magazine rightly noted in 1964 that the style of *The Sun* was the style of Arunah Shepherdson Abell, who founded the paper in 1837 and whose descendants are still directing the newspaper.[4] There is still much about the paper that reminds one of mid-nineteenth-century journalism.

The reader who desires entertainment will not like *The Sun*. Although some features are printed, they are usually very serious and educational. *The Sun* assumes its readers to be intelligent, well-educated, curious, and thoughtful. Of all American dailies it perhaps caters least to popular tastes. Not only are its pages packed with reading matter, but the whole package is heavily impressive: a typical weekday edition runs 48 pages, with the mammoth Sunday issue often reaching 300 pages.[5] Paul A. Banker, who took over as managing editor in May, 1966, says that *The Sun* is mainly aimed at the better-educated, higher-income audience. He calls the paper "Independent Democratic" and says it is in the center on an ideological-political spectrum.[6]

Founded May 17, 1837, by Arunah S. Abell, a Rhode Islander, *The Sun* began as a four-page, four-column tabloid and was concerned mainly with providing news, "whether or not that news conforms to the editor's own prejudices and opinions."[7] Its stress on local news immedi-

The Weather
Mostly cloudy today, highest, 62. Partial clearing tonight, lows in the 40's. Yesterday's high, 59; low, 43.
(Details and Map, Page C 9)

THE SUN

Cambridge Militant Gets Year For False Alarm: C24

Vol. 261—No. 145—E | BALTIMORE, WEDNESDAY, NOVEMBER 1, 1967 | 46 Pages | 10 Cents

NATO MAKES NO PROMISES ON A-PACT

Move Approving U.S. Talks With Russia Is Noncommittal

By STUART S. SMITH
[Bonn Bureau of The Sun]

Bonn, Oct. 31—The North Atlantic alliance council today gave the United States its noncommittal approval for further nuclear nonproliferation treaty negotiations with the Soviet Union.

Washington will resume these talks on its own responsibility, official sources in Brussels stated.

No agreement between the United States and the NATO council yet exists on the proposed treaty's terms, it was added.

In recent weeks United States officials have repeatedly urged the Atlantic allies to indorse a single treaty draft text so they could face Soviet officials in Geneva with a strengthened hand.

Submit To Inspections

Thus far, however, this goal has eluded Washington, as today's announcement makes clear.

One of the principal difficulties is the refusal of the six Euratom nations to submit to International Atomic Energy Agency inspections, as the Soviet Union insists they should.

At today's council meeting United States officials promised the Euratom members that they will emphasize this point during future Geneva talks with the U.S.S.R. American sources stated. They added, though, that the Johnson Administration cannot pledge itself to achieving all treaty draft changes the Euratom nations think are necessary.

Last week West Germany, Italy and the three Benelux countries drew up five principles which they agreed the treaty should include. France, the sixth Euratom member, declined to participate as it will refuse to 'sign' any treaty to bar the spread of nuclear weapons in any event.

The United States believes that it understands the interests and concerns which underlie these principles, the officials stated following today's meeting.

The Euratom principles are:

1. All treaty control must be limited to fissionable material and cannot include nuclear installations devoted to peaceful purposes.

Regulated By Agreement

2. The control authority must be regulated in an agreement between Euratom and the International Atomic Energy Agency, which is a United Nations organization including Communist nations but not West Germany.

3. The Euratom—United Nations agreement must be limited to verifying already existing Euratom controls.

4. Euratom's nuclear material sources must in no way be jeopardized.

5. The agreement with the United Nations agency must not contain any so-called guillotine clause which would automatically subjugate Euratom to United Nations controls in case a treaty between the two agencies proves impossible to negotiate.

Many, if not all, of the Euratom principles are objectionable to the Soviet Union, which is using the entire matter as an excuse to attack West German policy.

Despite optimism in Washing-

(Continued, Page A 4, Col. 4)

AP Wirephoto
AFTER CEREMONY—Prince Charles and Princess Anne (right, hands clasped) look on as Prince Philip helps Queen.

LORDS' POWER WILL BE CUT

Queen Tells Peers About Laborites' Plans

By CHARLES V. FLOWERS
[London Bureau of The Sun]

London, Oct. 31 — Britain's Labor Government intends to curtail the remaining power of the House of Lords and either abolish or greatly reduce the voting rights of hereditary peers.

Queen Elizabeth made the announcement in the House of Lords today. The proposal was part of Prime Minister Harold Wilson's legislative program for the coming year.

In a curious annual rite, the monarch reads in the House of Lords a speech prepared for her by the Government.

Peers and members of the House of Commons attended the ceremony today that opened a new session of Parliament.

Deliberately Vague

The Queen's reference to the modification of the House of Lords was deliberately vague.

"Legislation will be introduced to reduce the powers of the House of Lords and to eliminate its present hereditary basis, thereby enabling it to develop within the framework of a modern parliamentary system," the Queen said.

The reform would amount to the biggest constitutional change since 1911, when the House of Lords was stripped of much of its power by the Liberal Government.

In the House of Commons later, the Prime Minister explained:

"We cannot . . . lay ourselves open to the charge that we are failing to modernize Parliament."

"An Anachronism"

Although the House of Lords serves well in improving legislation, he said, "it is an anachronism that a house with no responsibility to the electorate should have the powers it does."

"It is an indefensible survival of the centuries that one house should be based on the hereditary principle."

At present, there are 1,045 peers on the active roll of the House of Lords. Of these, 154 are "life" peers, appointed for outstanding service, and the

(Continued, Page A 6, Col. 1)

4 Red Mortar Shells Fired At Viet Inaugural Reception

By ROBERT A. ERLANDSON
[Sun Staff Correspondent]

Saigon, Oct. 31 — The Viet Cong fired four mortar shells into the grounds of Independence Palace tonight moments after Vice President Humphrey and Ambassador Ellsworth C. Bunker entered the day-long presidential inaugural reception.

The 80-mm. rounds damaged two official cars, slightly wounding the Vietnamese chauffeur of one of them.

There was only a slight stir among the milling 1,000-odd guests. A few moved toward the balcony for a better view. A military band continued playing.

Some thought the neatly spaced explosions were a cannon salute honoring the new Government. Others immediately realized it as incoming shell fire and moved away from the windows.

Police got a tip that the shelling came from a house in the riverfront area, but by the time they reached the scene the terrorists had tried to destroy their weapon with plastic explosives. Part of the house's roof fell in and the base of the mortar snapped. Officers found three unfired mortar shells in the rubble.

Police at the scene said the terrorists killed a 15-year-old neighbor who emerged from his house to investigate the noise. Officers said he was shot as two men fled from the dwelling to a motorbike waiting with a third man.

Vacant Two Months

Police said they learned the house had been vacant for two months until two men arrived this morning saying they planned repairs. They apparently smuggled the mortar in among tools.

The mortar attack on the palace at 7.22 P.M. was the beginning of a series of incidents tonight.

In others a ship reportedly struck a Viet Cong mine at

(Continued, Page A 2, Col. 3)

DOCKING CAPSULE LANDS IN RUSSIA

Partner Of Cosmos 186 Remains In Orbit

By BRUCE WINTERS
[Moscow Bureau of The Sun]

Moscow, Oct. 31—The Soviet Union today soft-landed the larger of the two space vehicles which were involved in an automatic docking operation 24 hours ago.

Tass, the official news agency, said the craft, believed capable of carrying a crew of five, was brought to earth in a "preset area" on its sixty-fifth revolution of the earth.

Others In Orbit

The other craft that took part in the historic rendezvous remained in space continuing a computerized research program, Tass said.

In addition to the second device involved in the docking, four other recently launched Soviet space vehicles, including

(Continued, Page A 6, Col. 2)

2 VICE PRESIDENTS TRADE PROMISES

Vietnamese Cohesion, U.S. Perseverance Pledged

By PHILIP POTTER
[Sun Staff Correspondent]

Saigon, Oct. 31 — Two vice presidents traded promises here today.

Vice President Humphrey told South Vietnam's leaders that despite minority dissent a majority of Americans supported the President's policies in Vietnam and that the Administration was determined to see the conflict through.

Vice President Nguyen Cao Ky promised Mr. Humphrey that he would work faithfully with President Nguyen Van Thieu, despite reports of friction between them, to build the nation.

Marred Only By Mortars

Mr. Humphrey had separate talks with the leaders after their inauguration today in ceremonies marred only by mortar shells falling on the grounds of the Presidential Palace at an evening reception. Rain had forced cancellation of an outdoor fete and only minor injury and damage was done.

The American Vice President was in the palace when the mortar shells landed just outside. Like some others, he thought they might have been salutes, and he showed no alarm.

American sources said his talks with Thieu and Ky earlier were quite productive.

Mr. Humphrey was told the new Government's top priorities were to be fighting corruption, reorganizing the military and civil administration, accelerating pacification and stabilizing the economy.

Ky Acknowledged

Ky acknowledged temperamental differences with the President, but said both were dedicated to the country's welfare. Although some had tried to make capital of imagined differences between them and tried to stir up trouble, he added there would be none. He said both would be in office

(Continued, Page A 2, Col. 2)

REFORMATION CELEBRATED

Divided Germans Honor 450th Anniversary

Berlin, Oct. 31 (AP)—The divided people of Germany today celebrated the 450th anniversary of the start of the Protestant Reformation.

In Wittenberg, now in East Germany on October 31, 1517, Martin Luther proclaimed his 95 theses that sparked the Reformation.

In West Berlin and West German cities, as well as other East German cities, church congregations honored the memory and spirit of Luther, the monk whose work changed the Christian world.

The East German regime had restricted the number of Western churchmen who could go to Wittenberg. The Church registry showed 211 Western guests, including only 39 from West Germany. The Church had hoped for 1,000 official delegates.

Among those attending were Dr. Eugene Carson Blake of the World Council of Churches and Dr. Frederick Schiotz, president of the Lutheran World Federation. The world bodies had protested what they called the severe visa restrictions on churchmen.

Luther's Grave

Bishop Gottfried Noth of Dresden, which is also in East Germany, recalled Luther's words: "The true treasure of the Church is the most holy gospel of the glory and grace of God."

In the castle church, where Luther posted his theses and where he is buried, Bishop Joannes Jaenicke of nearby Magdeburg pointedly called attention to the celebration of the anniversary in a Marxist environment. According to a church committee summation of his remarks, he said men's soul thirsts for God and this thirst is no humanistic program.

Noth and Jaenicke, as well as a Communist speaker at a state celebration, avoided strong statements. Church dignitaries were at the state gatherings and state functionaries attended the church services.

Fulbright Fights Viet Aid Claim

Washington, Oct. 31 (AP) — A State Department claim that 37 countries besides the United States are aiding South Vietnam "is very misleading, to put it mildly," Senator Fulbright (D., Ark.) said today.

Fulbright, a sharp critic of Johnson Administration Vietnam policy, told the Senate, "The old proverb that one cannot make a silk purse out of a sow's ear" applied to the department statement.

Fulbright told the Senate 16 of the 37 countries had given no help to South Vietnam since last year. Three others had provided no aid since 1965, he said.

In many instances among the 37 countries, Fulbright said, the aid they are giving is far less than their amount of trade with North Vietnam.

For example, the total amount of trade between Japan and North Vietnam in 1964-1965 was 39 times the amount of Japan's aid to South Vietnam, Fulbright claimed.

For Italy he said, trade with the North was more than ten times the aid to the South; New Zealand, eight times; the Netherlands, more than three times; Britain, more than double.

U.S. CONCEDES DRAFTING BID TO SPLIT G.M.

But Denies Decision To Petition Courts For Break-Up

Washington, Oct. 31 (AP)—The Justice Department conceded today that it has had in its files for sixteen months a rough draft of a proposal that could ask a court to order the break-up of the world's largest industrial corporation—General Motors.

However, department officials described the document as only a sample complaint drawn up as part of a lengthy investigation of the automobile industry. They said there has been no decision whether, if ever, the Government will petition the courts to order the break-up of G.M.

At the White House, George Christian, press secretary, said that "no matter of this kind has ever been brought to the President's attention," and added, "The President's alleged involvement in it is pure imagination."

Johnson's Dilemma

The Justice Department statements and the quick White House comment were reactions to a *Wall Street Journal* story that said President Johnson is in a dilemma over whether to file a suit against G.M.

The *Journal* said Mr. Johnson risks the enmity of G.M.'s 1,400,000 stockholders and outraging the business community if he proceeds with the suit. On the other hand, the *Journal* said, if he suppresses it, he risks enraging intellectuals, trade unionists and his own antitrust lawyers.

A Justice Department statement issued this morning said, "The automobile industry has been under study by the Antitrust Division for many years. The study is but one of scores of industry studies undertaken by the division. Many of these studies do not lead to litigation or even to the consideration of litigation."

Common Practice

The statement said that it is common practice during the course of these studies for lawyers to draft complaints and that such an internal draft "was prepared by an Antitrust Division lawyer in the automobile industry study" sixteen months ago.

A department statement issued later today said that neither evaluation nor processing of its automobile industry study has been completed and that "basic questions of legal theory remain unresolved at the staff level of the Antitrust Division."

In New York, a General Motors spokesman said James Roche, G.M.'s new chairman and chief executive officer, and Edward N. Cole, G.M.'s new president, would have no comment on the article.

Stock Fluctuated

In the wake of the story, General Motors stock fluctuated, closing off $3 from $85.50 to $82.50.

The department did not make the draft complaint public. The *Journal* story called it "104 neatly typed pages all in for-

(Continued, Page A 8, Col. 1)

Stock Market's 26.5 Million Deal Is Largest Ever

New York, Oct. 31 (AP)—The largest single stock transaction ever handled on the New York Stock Exchange occurred today in a deal valued at $26,519,000, the exchange said.

A block of 1,153,780 shares of Alcan Aluminium Limited traded at $23 per share, off $1.12.

The exchange said it was the largest transaction in terms of shares or dollars handled by any stock exchange.

Goldman Sachs & Co., brokers, handled the transaction for the buyer and seller. The firm declined to identify either

BENEFIT RISE IS SUPPORTED

Senate Group Tentatively Votes 15% Increase

By RODNEY CROWTHER
[Washington Bureau of The Sun]

Washington, Oct. 31—The Senate Finance Committee today tentatively agreed to a 15 per cent across-the-board boost in retirement benefits for the elderly, as proposed by President Johnson, and a minimum benefit of $70.

This was learned from committee sources, which made no official announcement, because the committee chairman, Senator Long (D., La.), wanted to poll a number of senators who were not present before formally disclosing the committee action.

The senators also agreed in the first round of votes on the Social Security revision bill, which they hoped to complete by Friday, to give certain elderly persons, aged 72 and over, $50 a month benefits, instead of the present $35 a month, and $40 a month voted in the House bill.

Above House Proposal

Today's tentative action on the level of benefits compared with a 12.5 per cent across-the-board increase voted by the House, and a $50 a month minimum.

The finance group's action came as the majority leader, Senator Mansfield (D., Mont.) told newsmen that before Congress can adjourn it must approve the Social Security revision measure "and a tax bill."

There is little doubt, now that the senators have begun voting on provisions in the Social Security bill, of the probability that it can be enacted.

Some Provisions Discussed

There remained today far more doubt about a tax bill, inasmuch as the President still has to convince the House Ways and Means Committee and in particular its chairman, Representative Mills (D., Ark), that substantial reductions in 1968 (current) spending are being achieved.

The committee, it is understood, has completed its consideration, but taken no tentative votes, on provisions that relate to health insurance, Medicare for the needy, child welfare services, child health and public assistance.

Many technical features of these parts of the bill were discussed at length in sessions attended only by a bare quorum of members, and some leas

(Continued, Page A 4, Col. 5)

PRESIDENT OPENS DRIVE FOR BILLS

Democratic Leaders In Congress Summoned To White House

By NATHAN MILLER
[Washington Bureau of The Sun]

Washington, Oct. 31 — President Johnson called Democratic congressional leaders to the White House today in an attempt to get passage of vital Administration bills snarled on Capitol Hill.

Presidential assistants declined to discuss the meeting except to say Mr. Johnson has not abandoned hope for his proposed 10 per cent income tax surcharge and that emphasis was placed on bills that have passed one House and not the other.

The meeting—described as a "review" of pending bills—was called after the President returned from his Texas ranch amid reports that Congress was contemplating a pre-Thanksgiving recess that would leave much important legislation unpassed.

Finish The Business

Today, Senator Mansfield (D., Mont.), majority leader, one of those invited to the White House, downgraded the possibility of an early recess, saying Congress would remain in session "until we finish all our business."

While most congressional observers believe the tax bill is dead for this session, Mansfield said the session should remain open until such legislation is acted upon. This would keep Congress in session until December.

Senator Dirksen (R., Ill.), the minority leader, also agreed that an adjournment by Thanksgiving "looks doubtful." He added that the adjournment date "depends on what legislation is dropped."

Preoccupied By War

Preoccupied by the war in Vietnam, President Johnson has done little of the lobbying that proved so successful in getting his Great Society programs through the last session, and what has been done, in many cases, has been ineffective.

George Christian, White House press secretary, has said the White House hopes for final approval of such bills as crime control, civil rights, truth-in-lending, Social Security, air pollution and anti-poverty.

Meanwhile, Senate and House negotiators had a second fruitless session on their widely differing versions of an interim spending bill while Senator Fulbright (D., Ark.) reported a similar impasse on the foreign aid authorization bill.

The House spending proposal includes language requiring President Johnson to cut from

(Continued, Page A 5, Col. 1)

Gary Candidate Asks Voting Halt

Hammond, Ind., Oct. 31 (AP)—Richard G. Hatcher, Negro candidate for mayor of Gary, Ind., asked a Federal court today to halt the November 7 election on grounds Negroes were being disenfranchised.

Hatcher, a Democrat, charged that a fair election was impossible.

Judge George N. Beamer, of the United States District Court, said a three-judge panel will be named by Chief Judge John S. Hastings of the Seventh United States Circuit Court of Appeals at Chicago to meet at 9.30 A.M. November 6, the day before the election, for a ruling on Hatcher's suit.

Claims Tampering

Beamer will be one of the three but the others were not named immediately. The panel will sit in the Northern Indiana United States District Court here.

Hatcher said more than 5,000 Negroes have been purged from the voting rolls and that 4,000 phony names of white people have been added. Unless this can be corrected, the complaint said, the election should be halted.

Joseph Radigan, the Republican candidate, branded the Federal suit "just another in a long

(Continued, Page A 7, Col. 4)

Analysis

Pope Takes Cautious View Of His Changing Church

By WELDON WALLACE
[Religion Editor of The Sun]

Rome, Oct. 31—Recent events at the Vatican have pointed up striking ways in which Pope Paul and his close advisers differ from Catholicism at large in their concept of the present-day Church.

Despite criticisms of the Pontiff—and one hears them frankly expressed—there can be no doubt that he earnestly and deeply seeks the good of the Church. During these past weeks, his devotion has been demonstrated in a particularly moving way by the taxing commitments he has kept despite a painful illness.

New Vantage Point

Yet a number of his actions and statements indicate he has not adjusted his thinking to important aspects of the new Church, as seen from the vantage point of the Ecumenical Council Vatican II.

What is the evidence of this?

A recent example was his use of the synod. In relation to it he stood as a solitary, supreme figure. The bishops acted in a framework so tightly circumscribed by the Pope that, except in an indirect way, the synod was not an expression of "collegial" authority—the council's image of Pope and bishops sharing in Church government.

More With Past

In his speeches, too, the Pope has shown a frame of mind more in keeping with the past than with trends today.

Addressing the synod at its formal opening, he sounded an alarm over "insidious dangers" threatening the Church

(Continued, Page A 8, Col. 5)

House Approves, 403 To 1, Law On Meat Inspection

By JAMES MACNEES
[Washington Bureau of The Sun]

Washington, Oct. 31 — The House today, by vote of 403 to 1, approved legislation strengthening and broadening the Federal Government's 61-year-old meat inspection services. The bill now goes to the Senate, which has held no hearings on the proposal.

Only Representative Price (D., Texas) voted no on final passage.

Otherwise Identical

Five hours debate on the measure turned greatly on assertions by proponents of the committee bill that a stronger substitute offered by Representatives Smith (D., Iowa) and Foley (D., Wash.), would infringe states rights.

The Smith - Foley substitute, otherwise identical to the committee-approved bill, would also have covered meat plants doing business intrastate whose gross annual sales totaled $250,000 or more.

On a teller vote on the Smith-Foley substitute, Maryland Representatives Fallon (D.), Friedel (D.), Garmatz (D.), Gude (R.) and Machen (D.) voted aye.

On final passage, only Representative Mathias (R., Md.), who was ill, failed to vote for the legislation.

Would Preserve Rights

Representative Poage (D., Texas), chairman of the House Agriculture Committee, which reported out the bill, declared the measure would "take care of whatever defects" exist under present law, without "destroying the rights or activities of any of the states of this union."

That state rights theme was reiterated during a full after-

(Continued, Page A 7, Col. 1)

On Other Pages

ately caught the public's attention and within a year it was selling 12,000 copies a day.

Abell, who was editor as well as publisher, thought that a newspaper should give the news and not be a political party supporter, a strange position for that day. He pioneered in news gathering, spending great sums of money on any project which promised to get his paper the news ahead of his rivals. *The Sun* was the first paper to send news by railroad, and developed relay horsemen to speed news to Baltimore long before the famed "pony express" was used in the West. *The Sun*, also, was among the first newspapers to use the telegraph.

Before the paper was a month old, it had received its first story (by mail) from a Washington correspondent. This was the beginning of a Washington bureau which has steadily grown and which has brought the paper much attention and many awards. During the Mexican War, *The Sun* provided some of the most notable war reportage; it even informed the President (on April 10, 1847) that the United States had captured the fortress at Vera Cruz, not only beating the mails with the news but also the official War Department couriers.

The paper had soon outgrown its original offices on Light Street and, after two years, had moved into a larger building in the center of town. Then later, in 1851, it was to move into the famous Sun Iron Building at Baltimore and South, where it would remain for the next half century.

During the Civil War, Baltimore was "occupied" by Federal troops and there was a soldier at the elbow of every editor. It is said that *The Sun* "conformed to the necessities of the situation" and "behaved so well that, of all the local newspapers, it was the only one which managed to come through the war without once being suppressed."[8] Just what that means is open to interpretation, but the fact is that *The Sun* did come through the war and difficult times intact. Since the paper was for the South but was against secession, it had problems getting and keeping readers during the war period.

Prior to his death in 1888 Abell gave control of the paper to his three sons, Edwin, George, and Walter. By that time it had come out of its war slump and was growing rapidly. In the period after the Civil War, mainly under the leadership of George Abell, *The Sun* fought vigorously against corruption of all types, but particularly against political machines and corrupt judges who had been appointed by them. The paper's campaigns during the last three decades of the nineteenth century did much to enhance its reputation.

Politically, *The Sun* has always been independent. In strongly Democratic Maryland, the paper (in 1895) supported a Republican gubernatorial candidate, and he won. Since that time, although the paper has usually sided with Democrats, it has felt free to support Republicans. In fact, it supported Republicans for President from 1940 through 1960.

In 1904 the Sun Iron Building was destroyed by fire, but continuous publication continued with *The Sun* being printed in Washington by *The Star.* After two months, production was moved back to Baltimore and temporary quarters. Two years later the staff moved into a new building at Charles and Baltimore. But it was not long before *The Sun* was cramped and needed a new building. The old Calvert Railway Station was purchased in 1949, demolished, and the cornerstone for the new Sunpapers Building at Calvert and Centre streets was laid. On the edge of the main business district today, it is a perfect site for the paper's ultramodern newspaper plant.

During World War II *The Sun* greatly increased its staff and its coverage. In 1966 on the writing-editing staff of *The Sun* alone, there were 160 journalists, all of whom had at least a college education.[9] Foreign coverage was given a big boost during World War II. A *Sun* staff member was the only correspondent for an individual newspaper present when the German Army surrendered at the end of the war, and three *Sun* correspondents watched the Japanese sign the surrender papers aboard the *U.S.S. Missouri.* Since 1925, *The Sun* and its journalists have received nine Pulitzer Prizes, as well as many other local and national awards.

Today *The Sun* continues in the traditions of Arunah Abell, regularly giving its faithful readers substantial and heady doses of news and editorials. The paper may well be an anachronism in United States where "cafeteria-journalism" (a little something for everybody in pleasant and colorful surroundings) has become the newspaper *Zeitgeist,* but the old *Sun* appears hardly to be aware of it.

The Christian Science Monitor
(UNITED STATES)

One of the most unusual daily newspapers in the United States, and without a doubt one of the best, is *The Christian Science Monitor* with headquarters in Boston. It is not a bulky daily "of record" packed with unsynthesized and long articles sprawling over numerous pages loaded with advertising; rather, it is a small (usually about twenty pages) tightly organized and well-written journal, stressing the significant, the serious, and the lasting aspects of the world's news and issues. In 1908 when *The Monitor* was founded by Mary Baker Eddy, its expressed purpose was "to injure no man, but to bless all mankind."[1] It was to be a well-edited paper which would appeal to the literate, concerned, and moral citizen. And it has been highly successful in both respects.

Mrs. Eddy's idealistic words launched a newspaper which was to transcend the religious movement which she began and become a general paper which would appeal to all readers who desire a rational, nonsensational approach to journalism. Although the politically independent paper is undoubtedly a great moral force in journalism, its morality is not ostentatious. The paper is professionally a good newspaper as well as a respected moral force.

Eric Sevareid, the well-known CBS news correspondent and commentator, has said of *The Monitor* that it takes "note of the world's ugliness, sin, and danger, but only briefly, as if to say 'all this shall pass' and order, sanity and goodness shall prevail."[2] Erwin Canham, editor of *The Monitor*, in a television interview in 1966, said that his paper "tries to present the nature of reality . . . to make a meaningful pattern out of a complex world."[3] It was his contention that the paper's policy was to take a positive approach and exploit the "underlying forces of unity" in the world. This paper, definitely, hopes to bring about a world community of reason.

The Christian Science Monitor does a good job of producing quality journalism. Every recent poll or survey has shown *The Monitor* very high in the ratings, both among American and foreign papers, and the paper has won literally hundreds of awards in many fields. Since its founding, it has never missed a day of publication. Its circulation today is right at 200,000 and its five daily editions go to readers in more than 120 nations. The paper is aimed mainly at serious students of public affairs and those seeking background on major issues in the world.[4] Its staff of writers and editors (nearly 200) is highly professional and well-educated. This level of education is rising steadily; the university degree is essential, and advanced degrees are becoming commonplace.[5]

Today *The Monitor* covers international news with seasoned writers on foreign affairs (about sixty). It has fifteen full-time staff foreign correspondents stationed in nine countries—London, Moscow, Paris, Bonn, Saigon, Tokyo, Hong Kong, Sydney, and Beirut. In addition, it has special correspondents in numerous other foreign locations. Some of its leading foreign correspondents in recent years have been William Stringer in London, John Cooley in Africa, and Harry Ellis in continental Europe.

Erwin Canham, editor-in-chief, has given a vivid picture of *The Monitor's* special kind of journalism in his book *Commitment to Freedom* (1958):

> *The Monitor* does not leave out news just because it is unpleasant, nor seek to throw a rosy glow over a world that is often far from rosy. To describe *The Monitor* as a "clean" newspaper is correct but incomplete. It also strives to expose whatever needs to be uncovered in order to be removed or remedied. It seeks to put the news in a sound perspective, giving greatest emphasis to what is important and reducing the merely sensational to its place in the accurate system of values.[6]

The Monitor, in many ways, is more like a quality European newspaper than an American one; it evidences the typical European careful selection in the editing process, as well as the ability to give its articles a sense of permanent value. It not only reports the news, but it puts the news in perspective and analyzes it—and all in relatively few pages of well-chosen articles and pictures so that the reader is not lost in a thicket of unrelated items.[7]

The Christian Science Monitor is one of the most widely quoted newspapers in the United States. Some 4,200 newspaper editors across the country read *The Monitor*, and it is used extensively in classrooms, especially in junior and senior high schools. It is in the libraries of more than 5,000 educational institutions, and more than 20,000 copies go daily to educators in the United States. It obviously is taken seriously by leaders in government; every day it is read by five associate justices of the U.S. Supreme Court, more than 90 per cent of the American Congress, 25 per cent of the members of the British Parliament, 21 diplomatic legations in Washington, D.C., and more than 140 American consuls in foreign countries, and the chief executives of several of the free world's leading nations.[8]

Three editions of *The Monitor* are printed in Boston at the main offices of the newspaper at 1 Norway Street. Another American edition is printed in Los Angeles, and one other is printed in London. Its Boston printing plant is one of the world's finest and the production quality of *The Monitor* is excellent. In 1965, although it had repeatedly won national awards for its makeup and typography, it underwent a complete face-lifting when its layout and typography were revamped. It became, with the March 1 issue, the first major American paper to go to a five-column layout for editorial matter throughout the paper, departing from the traditional eight columns found in most United States papers. Advertising, however, remained in eight-column format. The basic body type size was increased 20 per cent for better readability, and a more liberal use of photographs and artwork was instituted.[9]

The Monitor is well known for the quality of its writing. It has now, and always has had, many outstanding writers on its staff. Although Joseph C. Harsch, Roscoe Drummond, and William H. Stringer are probably the best known, there are many others. And among its editors are some of the most highly respected journalists in the United States. Erwin Dain Canham, editor-in-chief since 1964 (he was editor before that), holds honorary degrees from 21 colleges and universities and is generally regarded as one of the world's outstanding editors. DeWitt John, editor since 1964, had been a *Monitor* political reporter in Boston prior to World War II and had served on the foreign desk after the war.

Courtney R. Sheldon, managing editor since 1965, had previously been political writer, a Washington correspondent, and American news editor. Joseph G. Harrison, chief editorial writer, joined *The Monitor* in 1935 after studies in three American and two European universities.

THE CHRISTIAN SCIENCE MONITOR

BOSTON, THURSDAY, NOVEMBER 2, 1967 — *An International Daily Newspaper* — MIDWESTERN EDITION • 10¢

FOCUS on Europe

What's ahead . . .

Storm warnings are flying in Spain.

All signs point to a showdown between the Franco regime and a better organized, more aggressive opposition.

Strengthening this opposition has been the realization by a growing number of democratic-minded Spaniards that the government reform and liberalization they had hoped for are increasingly unlikely.

They are disillusioned by the way the new Constitution has been implemented; that only proregime candidates could take part in the recent parliamentary elections.

Main beneficiaries of this new mood of disillusionment are the Communists. Cold-shouldered up to now, they are coming to be accepted more and more by non-Communist opposition elements.

Communists in Spain are few in number. But they are well organized underground, are experienced, tough, and can draw on funds from abroad.

This being so, the winter promises more aggressive tactics. The Franco regime is expected to counter with equally tough repression.

⊖

It's true. The price of electricity really is going to fall in Western Europe.

At least that's what experts insist at the Organization for Economic Cooperation and Development in Paris.

Europe's electrical systems form a grid from Scandinavia to Spain and Sicily. Power exchanges across borders are common. But only now are the advantages of large-scale power production about to be realized.

A number of governments are drawing up mutual-assistance contracts to encourage use of superpower generating units. Giant orthodox thermal generating units are being developed. These will cut costs on their own.

Trends . . .

A new switch in East-West trade: The West now is the creditor.

East Europe used to supply more goods to the West than vice versa.

In the first half of this year Western exports to the East jumped by 24 percent. Increase in trade the other way round was only 4 percent.

The economic slow-down in West Europe accounts for part of it. But most of the difference is due to the new demands in the East for more and better consumer goods and greater freedom of choice.

⊖

Pipelines, like trade ties, are lacing Europe back and forth together.

The new Trans-Alpine Pipeline has just begun pumping 300,000 barrels of crude oil daily from Trieste on the Adriatic to refineries in southern Bavaria.

It's not only the sixth "big-inch" built in the last 10 years to meet rising demands for crude in Western and Central Europe. It's one step nearer an East-West linkup which could provide all Europe with a competitive but technically unified supply system.

The Russians already are pumping oil to Hungary, Czechoslovakia, Poland, and East Germany. Now they'd like to push branches into Western markets. A plan exists already to extend the pipe across Austria to Trieste.

But a more immediate possibility is an East-West pipeline bringing natural gas from Soviet Siberia into Western Europe. Italy has agreed. France is interested. Austrian negotiations are well advanced.

How and why . . .

Planners in Brussels are beginning to think that what is urgently needed is a Europewide reform of land tenure.

There are still thousands of peasants in Europe. Most farms are no bigger than 50 acres. Under modern conditions such farmers cannot make a living.

Europe's farm prices are high already by world standards. To give the small tillers of soil a fair return would mean prices too high for most other Europeans to afford.

Somehow the number of farms must be rapidly reduced—the size of the average farm be at least doubled.

⊖

His critics complain that Austrian Chancellor Josef Klaus gives too much time and attention to the East, too little to the West.

The Chancellor does not apologize. Austria, he feels, in her own self-interest is justified in promoting wider European cooperation, especially among the Danubian nations.

On his travels to the East this year, the Chancellor gained impressions that Hungary and Bulgaria both are primed and eager for wider contacts outside the Communist world.

For some time Hungary's Janos Kadar has spoken warmly of "Danubian cooperation"—economic partnership among Hungary, Austria, Czechoslovakia, and Yugoslavia.

Where to look

Jerusalem report

Israel pushes peace drive

Israeli Premier Levi Eshkol

. . . offers Arabs 'an agreed peace'

By Francis Ofner
Special correspondent of The Christian Science Monitor

Jerusalem

The Israeli Government has embarked on a major diplomatic campaign aimed at preventing an eventual deterioration of the current cease-fire into resumed hostilities with the Arab countries.

Israeli efforts are moving simultaneously in three fields:

- At the United Nations the Israelis are trying to explain that any resolution by the Security Council or General Assembly which encourages the Arab Governments to believe that the "clock can be put back to June 4" (the day preceding the six-day war) would be liable to move the situation away from peace. According to the Israelis, it would stimulate Arab thinking in the directions of revenge, guerrilla warfare, and belligerence.

- With regard to the great powers, the Israelis stress the dangers involved in what they see as the recently growing polarization of the East-West struggle around the Egyptian-Israeli conflict.

The issue may come up during Israeli Premier Levi Eshkol's meeting with President Johnson in Washington, unofficially scheduled for the end of December.

No similar talk between the Israeli head of government and Soviet leaders is foreseen since the Kremlin broke off diplomatic ties with Israel during last June's war.

- The Israeli Government is trying to convince the Arab Governments that it is as much in their interest as in that of Israel to have a cease-fire replaced by peace and not by war.

Defeats recalled

Reliance on the Soviet Union did not prevent the military defeat of Egypt and Syria in June, the Israeli argument runs. Nor is it likely that counsel from Moscow or Belgrade to "resist peace talks" will help the Arab nations to win back the lost territories, develop their countries, or raise their standard of living, Israel argues. But an agreement with Israel could contribute to such results, the Israelis say.

Mr. Eshkol's major policy statement to the Parliament Oct. 30 reflected government thinking along these lines.

Israel "will continue to observe the cease-fire as long as the other side does," the Israeli Premier said.

Direct talks urged

Israel's "fundamental aim of coexistence with the Arab states" remained unaffected by the war and its aftermath, Mr. Eshkol asserted.

Coexistence would be possible only if "an agreed peace" were reached, he said. But no agreed settlement was possible without talks between the conflicting sides, he added.

The fact that the Israeli Premier spoke of "an agreed peace" may

★ Please turn to Page 4

What follows the cold war?

By Saville R. Davis
Staff correspondent of The Christian Science Monitor

There is a fairly wide agreement among thoughtful students of world affairs, ranging from Washington to Moscow, on what could follow the cold war.

The East-West conflict would shift from the military arena to the political, in its primary emphasis.

Force would not drop out of the picture. But the big events would not be crises like those at Berlin and Cuba. Both sides would have learned to avoid them. Conflicts would tend to take place in small third countries, probably in the developing world, where the Communists demand revolution.

At this point the agreement ends. The big open questions begin, and the inquiring reporter finds that very few people are confident they have answers.

Questions pile up

What would the United States back in these smaller third countries? Strong-arm governments, that are dependably anti-Communist? Middle-ground regimes, promising evolution? Or a democratic form of revolution, to compete with that of the Communists?

What would the Communists offer those countries? Violent overthrow, and if so, how violent? To what degree supported from the outside?

Whether an East-West détente can follow the cold war hangs on answers that are not yet available.

Then come questions that are more specific and yet go deeper:

To Americans:

"Are you willing to take risks? Suppose an agreement is made to neutralize South Vietnam and it does go Communist. It wouldn't be easy to tell whether the elections were really fair or not. There would be a lot of suspicion that the Viet Cong was using invisible kinds of pressure.

"And suppose—it isn't impossible whatever one thinks about the domino theory—that another country in that part of the world decided it was no use, if the United States wouldn't back it with force, and gave in?

"It was hard enough for Americans to take Castro's seizure of power. How many Cubas could we stand? Latin America and Africa, as well as Asia, are full of unstable regimes. At what point would Americans cease to take the risk that free governments, or governments friendly to the West, could dip under Communist rule and come out once again?

"Would they decide, at some point, that this much was too much? Wouldn't the cold war return right then, in all its force and with armed interventions by both sides?"

To questions like these, this reporter has

★ Please turn to Page 7

Saigon divided

Viet bombing argued

By Elizabeth Pond
Staff correspondent of The Christian Science Monitor

Saigon

The decisions on bombing North Vietnam are being made in Washington, not Saigon. And, it appears from here, they are being made on American political, not Vietnamese military, grounds.

Both of these considerations work against any clear comprehension here of the thinking behind the step-up of bombing last week that struck Phuc Yen, North Vietnam's largest MIG airfield, for the first time, and intensified bombing of bridges and other targets inside Hanoi and Haiphong.

The best one can do from Saigon is to piece together an analysis that may or may not be applicable.

The bare facts are easy enough to come by.

As of the week of the Phuc Yen bombing, MIGs had shot down only 25 of the 720 American planes downed over the north, while American planes had shot down 95 MIGs.

However, the Pentagon noted a "significant recent increase" in MIG activity that downed six United States planes as against two MIGs in the two-month period from mid-August to mid-October. It was therefore decided, the Pentagon announced, to bomb Phuc Yen.

The last United States plane to be shot down by a MIG was lost on Oct. 9. Phuc Yen was bombed on Oct. 24 and 25.

The Phuc Yen strike means that five of North Vietnam's six MIG capable fields now have been bombed, and that except for any MIGs based at Gia Lam, Hanoi's combined

★ Please turn to Page 6

Inside...

UN takes annual look at Korean question

The UN General Assembly is taking its annual look at the Korean question. It has before it United States, Communist, and neutralist resolutions.

There is the usual tussle over whether or not to invite both Koreas to attend the debate.

Story: Page B16

Berkeley students press for more say on campus

Students at the University of California in Berkeley say they want to personally stoke the school's educational furnaces — or even rebuild them, if necessary. Some faculty members back the trend toward letting students have more to say.

Story: Page 7

Children's books say, 'Be yourself'

Children's books used to say, "Be good." Now some say, "Be yourself" —and do not necessarily mean the same thing.

There is an important line between avoiding "moralizing" and producing "a kind of moral vacuity," writes assistant book editor Patience M. Daltry in an article begining several pages of "Fall books for children."

Story: first page, second section

Pecan harvesters busy as squirrels

Pecans are big business in the southern United States. There are even mechanical shakers that grab a tree and send the crop to the ground all at once.

Story: Page 3

Associated Press Wirephoto

Anniversary trappings

Portraits of Soviet Communist Party Politburo members have gone up in Moscow for the Nov. 7 celebration of the 50th anniversary of the Bolshevik Revolution. The portraits include, from left, General Secretary Leonid I. Brezhnev, Premier Alexei N. Kosygin, and President Nikolai V. Podgorny.

He was a *Monitor* war correspondent from 1942–1945 and since the war he has traveled widely abroad. John Beaufort, a native Canadian who started with *The Monitor* as a copyboy in 1930, is features' editor. He has filled various news and feature assignments for the paper, was a war correspondent in the Pacific during World War II, and from 1946–1950 he was chief of *The Monitor*'s New York bureau. Mainly known as a drama and film critic, Beaufort lectures extensively on the theater. He became chief of the paper's London bureau in 1962, and was called back to Boston in 1965 to take over the important feature editor's position. He is in charge of a full range of features including Sports, Business and Finance, Travel, Books, Education, Arts-Entertainment, Real Estate, Automotive, Women Today, Family Features, and Home Forum (a page of essays and art).

These men, and many other writers and editors, give *The Monitor* its special character among American newspapers and make the reading of the paper a necessity for those who value sane, well-informed, and responsible journalism. There are critics who say that *The Monitor*, because it mainly emphasizes national and international news and views, should not be judged in the same context as other American dailies. It is true that the paper leaves most of the routine local incidents and all of the sensational stories to other newspapers; this, perhaps, is to its credit. It recognizes that it cannot be everything to all men, so it has set about being a reliable, cosmopolitan newspaper with a special national and world flavor. Not a "militant" quality paper like some others, such as the *St. Louis Post-Dispatch* or the *Winnipeg Free Press* of Canada, *The Monitor* steers a steady course forward with the times, upholding human rights and dignity and infusing in a calm way the best of rational journalism into a nation and world direly in need of it.

St. Louis Post-Dispatch

(UNITED STATES)

In many countries there is a tendency for cities located away from the seacoasts and far to the interior to be provincial, intellectually isolated, and unprogressive; furthermore, this image is projected to the newspapers of these interior cities. As a generalization it may be valid, but in the United States the city of St. Louis, Missouri, about as near the center of the nation as any metropolitan area could be, is a notable exception. Wide-awake, cultural, and intellectual, this city on the Mississippi River is undoubtedly among the four or five most sophisticated and cosmopolitan cities in the United States.

It is altogether fitting that such a city have a lively, informative, liberal, world-conscious daily newspaper—the *St. Louis Post-Dispatch.* The newspaper has grown with the city and has infused its progressive spirit and its concern for human rights and freedom into the city's citizens and its many readers throughout mid-America and in important places everywhere.

In 1878 the great Joseph Pulitzer,[1] a German-speaking immigrant from Hungary who was to become one of America's greatest publishers, bought the bankrupt *St. Louis Dispatch* and became its editor and publisher, merging it the same year with *The Post* to form the *Post and Dispatch.* The next year the name was changed to the present *Post-Dispatch.* Joseph Pulitzer was not long in instilling a liberal spirit into the paper and this spirit has guided the development of the paper to the present time. The new paper was a success from the start and its circulation rose rapidly as the public responded to its crusades and civic-improvement campaigns.

When Joseph Pulitzer retired from the newspaper business in 1907 at the age of sixty, the *Post-Dispatch* had already been in the hands of his son, the second Joseph Pulitzer, for about a year. The founder, however, continued to direct and dominate both the *Post-Dispatch* and the *New York World* (which he had bought in 1883) until his death in 1911. The second Pulitzer became president of the Pulitzer Publishing Co. in 1912, and like his father he emphasized the news operation of the *Post-Dispatch* and constantly poured memoranda upon his editors urging better journalism in all departments. He made suggestions, criticized, and actually did considerable writing and editing and generally contributed greatly to the paper's concern for careful news reporting and sharp editorial commentary.

From the first, the afternoon *Post-Dispatch* had valued intellectual freedom and no staff member was ever required to write a story which went against his beliefs. In 1948, for example, the editor of the editorial page, the editorial cartoonist and all but one writer in the department excused themselves from any comment on the Presidential candidacy of Thomas E. Dewey, who was supported by the paper.[2] Political independence has always been considered important to the paper. Since 1928, for instance, it has supported five Democrats and two Republicans for President. It might be called Democratic in the sense that it usually supports Democrats; it definitely may be called liberal, although it considers itself "in the center" ideologically.[3] This may seem somewhat confusing, because in the United States a newspaper which is as obviously liberal as the *Post-Dispatch* is commonly thought of as being "to the left" and not in the center. By being "in the center" may mean to the paper that it is only "moderately liberal," but even this would be contested by most of its readers.

What does the paper stand for? What are its main principles? The paper seeks solutions through negotiation of international (and national) disputes which threaten the people; it shares the concern of those everywhere whose liberty and equality are denied. It supports aspirations for better housing, education, and medical assistance. It is sympathetic with the objectives of trade unionism. It is "conservative in its jealous protection of Constitutional liberties deriving from the Bill of Rights."[4]

Further, it is concerned with the causes of minority groups, supporting demonstrations and methods of exploiting and publicizing social ills in the society. It is deeply dedicated to human dignity and liberty. In typical liberal fashion it is very much in favor of the United Nations, peace movements, student demonstrations for freedoms, social welfarism, extension of civil rights legislation, larger federal grants to states, and investigations of police excesses.

Since the beginning of American intervention in Vietnam, the *Post-Dispatch* has consistently criticized United States action. It has pointed out the dangers of escalation and derided American intervention as interfering in another nation's business, acting against the Geneva Convention, perpetrating atrocities in Vietnam, and generally reflecting an unrealistic and militaristic policy which makes it increasingly difficult to bring about world peace. Rather surprisingly, the *Post-Dispatch* does not advocate the recognition of Communist China by the United States or the Peking regime's becoming a member of the United Nations "under present conditions."[5]

The following is an interesting example showing the *Post-Dispatch*'s stand on one aspect of personal and international relations. In August, 1965, the paper carried a column by Max Freedman in which the highly respected writer for many United States papers and the Manchester *Guardian* criticized Martin Luther King for meddling in Vietnam. Freedman wrote from Washington that King was in danger of becoming the "Bertrand Russell of the United States" and like Russell, he was close to "putting off greatness and becoming a bore, an intruder where he has no business, and a busybody causing great mischief."[6]

The next day, the *Post-Dispatch* in an editorial entitled "The Prize for Absurdity," labeled Freedman's column "petulant" and "among the sillier comments of the season." The *Post-Dispatch* editorial pointed out that the "issues of war and peace in Vietnam are most definitely everybody's business, not a private preserve of self-acknowledged 'authorities,' and Dr. King's contribution is more than ordinarily welcome."[7]

The *Post-Dispatch* through the years has built up a reputation for excellent foreign coverage. Presently there are no foreign correspondents on a permanent basis with the paper, but there are usually one or two on specific assignments.[8] In spite of the recent restriction of *Post-Dispatch* foreign staffers, the reader of the paper gets a well-rounded view of world affairs from the news service stories (AP, UPI, *The New York Times* and *Chicago Daily News*) and from the paper's special writers abroad.

Important names in the paper's foreign correspondence stand out, names such as Clair Kenamore, Charles G. Ross, Raymond P. Brandt, and Julius Klyman in the years between the two world wars. During and after World War II foreign stories carried such distinguished *Post-Dispatch* by-lines as Richard L. Stokes, Theodore P. Wagner, Virginia Irwin, Sam Armstrong, E. A. Graham, Jr., Ralph Coghlan, Thomas R. Phillips, George Hall, Donald Grant, and Marquis W. Childs. In recent years Richard Dudman of the Washington bureau, and Donald Grant and Tom Yarbrough have written incisive articles about Latin America, Africa, and Europe. Marquis Childs, perhaps, has made more trips abroad than any other *Post-Dispatch* staffer and has reported almost every important European story since 1950.[9]

The *Post-Dispatch* today has a daily circulation of some 360,000 and a Sunday circulation of nearly 600,000. About 140 persons are on its writing and editing staff.[10] At least 90 per cent of these staff members have attended college, and about a dozen have advanced (graduate) degrees. Nearly half of these degrees are in journalism, most from the University of Missouri. *Post-Dispatch* staffers have attended some 75 colleges and universities, including Yale, Harvard, Oxford (England), Notre Dame, and Columbia. Three-fourths of the staff had experience on other newspapers before joining the *Post-Dispatch.*[11] The staff works in the paper's main building at Twelfth Boulevard and Franklin Avenue in St. Louis where editorial, business, and printing facilities cover an entire city block. In its printing plant is also printed its main competitor, the morning *Globe-Democrat*, which is about as conservative as the *Post-Dispatch* is liberal.

The editor of the *Post-Dispatch* today is Joseph Pulitzer, Jr., grandson of the founder. Editor of the editorial page is Robert Lasch, who was awarded the Pulitzer Prize for editorial writing in 1966. Actually the paper itself has received the Pulitzer Prize for outstanding accomplishments in journalism five times. This award, probably the most coveted journalistic award in the United States, is made annually by Columbia University in New York. In addition to these five awards, more than a half dozen staff members have received the Pulitzer Prize for outstanding service in various areas of specialization.

Besides the Pulitzer Prizes, the *Post-Dispatch* has won many awards and citations for its excellent journalism. It has been praised by many leaders of the United States. The late Adlai Stevenson said: "My views on the *Post-Dispatch* are simple: I regard it as one of the best papers on earth. I have read it all my life and, as long as I live, I intend to go on reading it."[12] Pierre Salinger, press secretary to the late President Kennedy, wrote during the Kennedy administration: "Ever since I have been associated with the President I know that he has read the *St. Louis Post-Dispatch* and has paid particular attention to the views expressed by that newspaper."[13] The American author, John Gunther, has called

ON TODAY'S EDITORIAL PAGE
More Mad Momentum: *Editorial*
The Negative Oath: *Editorial*
The Day the Aurora Opened Fire: *Mirror of Public Opinion*

ST. LOUIS POST-DISPATCH

CITY
Yesterday's Closing Stock Market Pages 6C and 7C

VOL. 89 NO. 307 — © 1967, St. Louis Post-Dispatch — TUESDAY, NOVEMBER 7, 1967 — 42 PAGES — 7c IN GREATER ST. LOUIS — 1.85 A MONTH, DAILY BY CARRIER

By Floyd Bowser, a Post-Dispatch Photographer

Construction Progress on Junior College Campus

Students and faculty members change classes at Meramec Community College as construction work continues. When completed, the campus at Big Bend boulevard and Geyer road in Kirkwood will provide room for 4500 full-time day students and an equal number of night students.

ENTRENCHED REDS ARE OVERRUN BY U.S. IN HIGHLANDS

BIG ICBM AMONG NEW WEAPONS IN RUSSIAN PARADE

Reds Give No Hint of Whether They Have Orbital Missile

MOSCOW, Nov. 7 (AP)—The Soviet Union today showed off six new weapons, including a huge intercontinental ballistic missile, on the fiftieth anniversary of the Russian Revolution.

The new red-nosed missile, more than 100 feet long, was displayed ahead of a missile shown on May day 1965 that has been claimed capable of striking from orbit.

Another new missile, with two stages hooked together, appeared to have a range of between 100 and 1000 miles. A new tactical missile was shown with a probable striking distance of 100 to 200 miles.

The Soviet navy showed a smooth, solid-looking missile with a blunt nose that probably was designed for launching under water.

Antiaircraft Weapon

Long silver antiaircraft missiles appeared on a tracked carrier as a new weapon. Official commentaries, apparently referring to a nuclear-headed missile shown in earlier parades, claimed for it the ability to knock down clusters of enemy planes.

The sixth new item in the parade of weapons through Red Square was an armored reconnaissance vehicle with a gun and a small antitank missile mounted on it.

Other weapons, seen in previous parades, were described as antimissile missiles.

Soviet commentators used the word "news" only once, saying a three-stage intercontinental rocket was power by a "new, highly efficient type of propellant." Tass, the official news agency, said that these rockets "need little time to be readied for firing and can be launched both from silos and other launching ramps."

The official accounts threw no light on whether the Soviet Union was testing an orbital bomb system. United States Secretary of Defense Robert S. McNamara said Friday that it was. During the two and a half years since the unveiling of thee orbital rocket, there has been no mention here of its being tried out in any way.

Official accounts of the parade today repeated the boast that the mammoth Soviet rockets—the biggest is about 115 feet long—"can deliver nuclear warheads of tremendous power." It was also claimed that "no other army in the world has such warheads."

Moscow television's commentator called attention to "an unusual special warhead" on one rocket which he said could destroy a large group of enemy planes in the air at a great distance from the Soviet Union.

U.S., Israel Criticized

The parade was preceded by the usual address by the Soviet defense minister, Marshal Andrei A. Grechko. He attacked the U.S. for its part in the Vietnam war, but in general his tone was milder than usual. He accused Israel of aggression, but said nothing about Communist China.

Soviet and foreign Communist leaders on Lenin's tomb watched the parade. The weather was crisp, clear, the tempearture in the 40s. Grechko urged the Soviet people to "increase their vigilance, to be always ready to defend the Socialist fatherland."

The Soviet army and navy,

TURN TO PAGE 8, COLUMN 4

Associated Press Wirephoto

Running for Cover

A First Air Cavalry Division trooper sprinting across a jungle clearing under fire of North Vietnamese regulars near Tam Ky, South Vietnam.

FLANK BROKEN AFTER COMPANY IS REINFORCED

Fighting May Herald New Offensive, Americans Believe

From Post-Dispatch Wire Services

SAIGON, South Vietnam, Nov. 7 — United States paratroopers and infantrymen, attacking at night, have overrun an intrenched North Vietnamese position in one of a series of new clashes in the central highlands. American intelligence officers think the fighting may herald the start of a dry-season offensive by the Communists in the jungle area.

Fighting back yesterday and today against heavy rifle and machine gun fire, U.S. troops reported killing 18 North Vietnamese in skirmishes near Dak To, 300 miles north of Saigon. U.S. Headquarters said 16 men of the U.S. 173rd Airborne Brigade were killed and 29 wounded.

About 500 American paratroopers called down rocket fire virtually on their own positions to smash Communist guerrillas closing in on them, U.S. spokesmen said.

Afraid of Hitting Men

"We put our rockets in so close at times that I was afraid we would hit troops, but they kept calling us in closer," said Capt. James Patterson, Mercer, Pa. He was the leader of the three helicopter rocket ships protecting the men of the 173rd Airborne.

Intelligence officers are predicting more bloody combat for the highlands area near the Laotian and Cambodian borders now that the monsoon rains are moving north. The forecast is based on reports of major North Vietnamese infiltration of the jungles in the first six months of the year.

The headquarters elements of five North Vietnamese divisions have been identified in the II Corps military area that includes the highlands.

A company of American infantrymen, sweeping through the area yesterday to assess the effectiveness of recent B-52 bomb strikes, came under heavy small arms and automatic fire from North Vietnamese regulars dug into well fortified positions.

Broke Through Flank

The clash continued until nightfall with Air Force fighter-bombers and Army gunship helicopters hitting the enemy positions. Then, three and a half hours after the initial contact, a second American company linked up with the first and together they broke through the Communists' flank and overran their position, U.S. spokesmen said.

This was the biggest of three skirmishes in the area southwest of Dak To.

Today, Communists lobbed four rounds of mortar fire into the companies' defensive positions and sprayed the perimeter with small arms fire, wounding two paratroopers.

American intelligence sources said a new North Vietnamese division, the Tenth, is known to be along the Cambodian-Laotian border, but has been avoiding serious contact with U.S. troops. The Communists are also believed to have infiltrated a complete new regiment, the 174th, into the Kontum region south of Dak To, in addition to an artillery battalion armed with 122mm. rockets and 120mm. mortars.

60 Rescued in Jungle

Also in the highlands, U.S. Army First Air Cavalry Division troops smashed into dense jungle today and rescued 60 montagnard mountain women and children. U.S. spokesmen said that the Viet Cong had kidnaped 238 of the highland folk yesterday and pressed them into slave labor in an effort to terrorize the countryside.

In the air, U.S. Air Force B-52 Stratofortresses dropped bombs today on Communist troops positions within seven miles of Loc Ninh, the Allied

TURN TO PAGE 8, COLUMN 5

MADISON SCHOOL CLOSED BECAUSE OF RACE TENSION

Dissension Is Laid to Extracurricular Activities

School officials closed Madison High School on the East Side today because of racial tension.

"It has now become a community situation," said Raymond Dragich, superintendent of Madison schools. "I'm hoping that we can bring all the resources of the community in to solve the problem."

The tension has grown out of demands of Negro students for fuller inclusion in extracurricular activities at the school, which has an enrollment of 750. About 40 per cent of the students are Negroes.

17 Refuse to Play

On Friday, the 17 Negroes on the Madison football team refused to play in a game because of dissatisfaction with the number of Negro cheerleaders at their school. Negro students have been boycotting the school cafeteria, and teachers said that attendance had fallen because of the dissension.

The decision to close the school wasm made at a meeting of Dragich, Madison School Board members and Francis Dant, principal of the school. Dant had recommended that the school be closed until some of the problems were resolved, Dragich said.

Yesterday a group of Negro leaders met with Dragich at his office. Meanwhile, white parents met with Dant in the school auditorium.

Mrs. Thomas Weston, president of a Madison area branch of the National Association for the Advancement of Colored People, expressed surprise at the school closing. She was unaware of the meeting of white parents. Separate meetings

TURN TO PAGE 8, COLUMN 2

FIVE COUNTY MUNICIPALITIES HAVING ELECTIONS

Three bond issue elections, an annexation proposal and an aldermanic contest will be decided in five St. Louis county municipalities today.

University City voters are deciding on a $730,000 bond issue for public improvements, including park land acquisition, Fire Department equipment, and a $400,000 municipal skating rink.

Bridgeton, in its first bond issue election since the city was founded 124 years ago, is seeking approval for bond issues of $400,000 for a city park and $300,000 for a new city hall. In St. Ann voters are being asked to approve $350,000 in bonds for street improvements. Voters there will also decide on whether to renew a 20-year franchise with Union Electric Co.

The annexation of 675 acres north of Bellefontaine Neighbors, consisting mostly of land belonging to the St. Louis State School and Hospital, is before voters in that city. Brentwood voters in the First ward will choose an alderman to replace George Ward, who resigned. Polls will be open from 6 a.m. to 7 p.m.

BUTTONS READY, ONLY THE MAYOR WON'T USE THEM

INDIANAPOLIS, Nov. 7 (AP) — Mayor John J. Barton's supporters were without campaign buttons in today's election. A campaign aid ordering the buttons told the manufacturer that they should read Barton only.

The maker followed the directions to the letter. The buttons say "Barton Only."

They will not be used for fear that voters might get the idea that the mayor did not want to be associated with the remainder of the Democratic slate.

REAGAN TO GET WHITE ELEPHANT NAMED 'GOP'

SACRAMENTO, Calif., Nov. 7 (AP)—Gov. Ronald Reagan and his wife are getting an elephant —a white one 15 months old and weighing 992 pounds.

The Reagans have decided to give it to Sacramento's Land Park Zoo. The elephant is the gift of Leka, son of the late exiled King Zog of Albania and a longtime admirer of Reagan, his assistant press secretary said.

Leka, who lives in Paris, offered the elephant to Reagan sometime ago.

Mrs. Reagan says "We have nicknamed it GOP."

Reagan is a Republican.

WALLACE'S GRANDMOTHER 100, HOPES HE'S PRESIDENT

MONTGOMERY, Ala., Nov. 7 (AP) — Former Gov. George C. Wallace's grandmother celebrated her 100th birthday and made a wish that she could live to see him president.

Mrs. Kate Frink Watson received a telephone call yesterday from her grandson.

"I hope you live another 100 years," Wallace said. He said Mrs. Watson replied, "I hope to live to see you president." Mrs. Watson lives in Graysville, Ala., with her daughter, Mrs. V. E. Thomas.

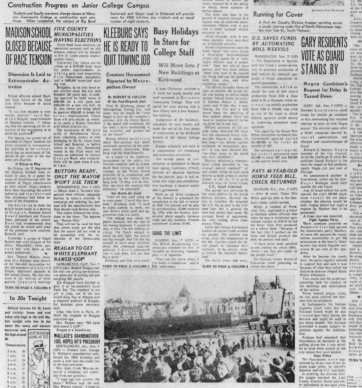

KLEEBURG SAYS HE IS READY TO QUIT TOWING JOB

Constant Harassment Reported by Metropolitan Owner

By ROBERT H. COLLINS
Of the Post-Dispatch Staff

Fred W. Kleeburg, owner of Metropolitan Towing Co., said today that he would be "very happy to give up the company's contract with the Police Board, if the board will reimburse me for what I have outstanding in my inventory and protect me on my leases."

Recent adverse publicity about Metropolitan has made continued operation of the company almost intolerable, Kleeburg told the Post-Dispatch.

As a result of the publicity, harassment by the public has become constant, and he is now more than willing to yield his contract to the Police Board provided he is reimbursed and protected on the leases, Kleeburg said. "If they will do that, they can have the contract this afternoon," he continued.

Not Worth the Grief

"Until all this stuff came up in your paper, I loved this business," Kleeburg said. "I used to enjoy coming to work, but now there's more grief and aggravation than it's worth.

"I'm talking now about the police business, not the rest of my towing business. I intend to stay in that. I'm not sobbing or crying. I'm Dutch enough to stand up and fight, but you're not big enough, and I'm not big enough to have done anything about this continued page-one publicity. I don't understand why it was done. It's not that big a plum."

Kleeburg said that as a result

TURN TO PAGE 8, COLUMN 1

Busy Holidays In Store for College Staff

Will Move Into 2 New Buildings at Kirkwood

A busy Christmas vacation is in store for many faculty and staff personnel at Meramec Community College. They will spend the time moving into a new library and a new humanities building.

Completion of the buildings, scheduled for next month, will mark the end of the first phase of construction at the Kirkwood branch of the Junior College District.

Classes presently are held in a combination of temporary and permanent structures.

The second phase of construction is scheduled to begin next spring, Lawrence O'Neill, director of physical facilities for the district, said. It will include new class and administrative buildings, a student center and a gymnasium.

Work on all three campuses of the district is scheduled for completion in the fall or winter of 1969. The district will be able to accommodate 32,000 students by 1970, with the student body divided about equally between night and day students. Present enrollment is about 10,000.

GOING THE LIMIT

LONDON, Nov. 7 (UPI) — The British Broadcasting Corporation's schedule for Nov. 18 includes an hour-long Japanese play — in Japanese.

"You lose the whole effect if you make a translation," said a BBC spokesman.

U.S. SAVES FUNDS BY AUTOMATING BOLL WEEVILS

WASHINGTON, Nov. 7 (AP) — The Department of Agriculture has found a money-saving way to automate production of boll weevils for research purposes, a House committee reported yesterday.

The automation, which reduced the cost of boll weevil production from $150 a thousand to $1 a thousand while increasing weekly production from 1500 to 250,000, was cited as one of the ways in which federal agencies saved money by improving manpower management.

The report by the House Post Office committee estimated that Government agencies saved $41,000,000 in the first six months of 1967.

The estimated savings for boll weevil automation were $45,000 in fiscal 1967 and $60,000 in the current fiscal year.

PAYS 48-YEAR-OLD HORSE FEED BILL, CHECK RETURNED

DURHAM, N.C., Nov. 7 (AP) — After 48 years, Texan Olin Miller paid his debt to the Durham county school system.

Miller, a resident of Plainview, Tex., explained in a letter to Durham school officials that when he was a vocational agriculture teacher in 1918-19 he fed his horse from feed produced on a school farm. "Because of the fact that I worked on the farm and helped produce the feed, no amount was paid.

"I have never been satisfied so am sending my check ($60), which I ask that you credit to the proper fund."

The Durham County Board of Education voted yesterday to return the check.

GARY RESIDENTS VOTE AS GUARD STANDS BY

Negro Candidate's Request for Delay Is Turned Down

GARY, Ind., Nov. 7 (UPI) — National Guardsmen stood ready for trouble as residents in this steelmaking city decided whether to elect its first Negro mayor. The election came after a bitter campaign marred by racial undercurrents and charges and countercharges of fraud.

Richard G. Hatcher, Negro member of the City Council, faced the challenge of white Republican Joseph Radigan in the race for mayor in this predominantly Negro city just east of Chicago.

An unannounced number of Guardsmen, called out by Gov. Roger Branigan, stood alert outside the city limits.

Just 12 hours before the polls opened, the city's 100,000 registered voters did not know whether the election would be held. Judges denied last night a request by Hatcher that it be postponed.

A close race was expected.

Fight Against Party

Much attention centered on Hatcher's bitter fight against the Democratic party. Hatcher, 34 years old, opposed the organization successfully to get the nomination in the heavily Democratic city where Negroes constitute 55 per cent of the residents.

After he became the candidate, the party regulars refused to support him and said it was because of what they called his failure to disavow alleged Black Power allegiance.

Two courts laid the guidelines yesterday both for conduct of the balloting and mobilization of the militia.

Three federal judges ruling on two suits ordered the election held as scheduled.

At Indianapolis, the Indiana Supreme Court ruled that the National Guard might be stationed near Gary during the election and might be used to put down trouble. The decision overruled a county judge's injunction against the mobilization.

Radigan had requested that Guardsmen be stationed at the polling places but it was decided to keep them outside of the city unless they were needed.

State Police

The Guardsmen were augmented by 25 per cent of the Indiana state police, by sheriff's deputies and by U.S. marshals.

In ordering the election held, the judges enjoined the Lake County Election Board and other defendants in two suits from prohibiting voting on the basis of race or color.

The court enjoined the de-

TURN TO PAGE 8, COLUMN 2

In 20s Tonight

Official forecast for St. Louis and vicinity: Sunny and cool today with high in the mid 40s; fair tonight with low in the upper 20s; sunny and warmer tomorrow with the high around 50.

Temperatures

1 a.m.	30
2 a.m.	28
3 a.m.	28
4 a.m.	28
5 a.m.	27
6 a.m.	26
7 a.m.	26
8 a.m.	28
9 a.m.	33
10 a.m.	*37

*Unofficial

Other weather information on Page 7A

UPI Telephoto

Russian 50th Anniversary Celebration

An intercontinental ballistic missile more than 100 feet long rolling past spectators in Red Square today.

NEWS INDEX

the *Post-Dispatch* the "most effective liberal newspaper in the United States."[14]

The *Post-Dispatch* won the University of Missouri School of Journalism Honor Award for distinguished journalism in 1932 and in later years six of its staff members also received these awards, among the most coveted in the country. Many other awards and citations have been received by the paper, typical of which is one in 1959 from the American Bar Association "for its contribution to public understanding of the nation's legal and judicial systems." It was an award given as a result of a series of six articles on the U.S. Supreme Court written by Irving Dilliard, one of the most distinguished editors who has ever worked for the *Post-Dispatch.*[15]

Although the news coverage of the *Post-Dispatch* is good, the news pages of the paper are not what gives the paper its special appeal or high esteem. There are probably many other papers in mid-America—such as the *Kansas City Star*, the *Des Moines Register*, the *Chicago Daily News*, and even its St. Louis competitor, the *Globe-Democrat*—which cover the news as thoroughly, or more thoroughly. What really distinguishes the *Post-Dispatch* is its articles of interpretation, background, and perspective, as well as its vigorous, well-written editorials.

The first page of the editorial section of the paper has for many years provided an example of the founder's request: "Never be satisfied with merely printing news." This is especially true of the Sunday edition where the whole page is given over to interpretive reporting and discussions of basic issues in the news. This page, under the direction of the managing editor, is called "the dignity page" by the staff. Such pages are common in the better European dailies, but hard to find in the press of the United States. Material is provided by various specialists of the newspaper's staff, by experts in various fields such as theology, education, and science, and by reprinting outstanding articles from other newspapers and from magazines and books. It is generally recognized as one of the best such pages in the country. Former President Harry Truman, with whom the paper often differed, said in 1961 of the page: "The Sunday editorial title section of the Post-Dispatch is one of the finest things I read. As a matter of fact, it is the first thing I read on Sunday morning."[16]

The *Post-Dispatch*'s editorial page, which follows the "dignity page," is distinctive also. While many American newspapers have abandoned forceful, provocative editorials, the *Post-Dispatch* continues to express frank and forceful opinion in an urbane and dignified style. It is this page, probably more than any other, that has given the *Post-Dispatch* its special place in American journalism. It comes to grips with disagreeable subjects and fights for causes which may be generally unpopular. Although its editorial positions usually follow the normal "liberal" line in the United States, an independent spirit marks the page and the reader is impressed by the originality and force of the editorials, even when they express a predictable position. Its editorial page cartoon has long been outstanding, and two of the truly great editorial cartoonists of the United States have been *Post-Dispatch* staffers, Daniel R. Fitzpatrick (until 1958) and Bill Mauldin (until 1962). Thomas A. Engelhardt does most of the cartoons today, the rest are reprinted from other papers.

The *Post-Dispatch* has often been compared to *The Guardian* of Britain and in many ways it is a good comparison. They are both highly literate, hard-hitting liberal dailies which make it their business to puncture pomposity and to point the way to rational solutions to human problems. They both detest bigotry in any form and lash out at extremists wherever they are found. In short, the *Post-Dispatch*, like *The Guardian*, prods and agitates its readers into grappling with important issues of the day. It is highly suspicious of emotionalism and endeavors constantly to expand reasonable discourse in the United States. There is little doubt but that it succeeds.

The Globe and Mail
(CANADA)

If Canada may be said to have a national newspaper, it is Toronto's *Globe and Mail*. Although its circulation is concentrated mainly in the central south and southeast, it is designed to appeal to readers in all parts of the country and is the only paper having national circulation on the day of publication. It has the largest morning circulation in Canada (close to 250,000)[1] and is usually considered the most influential and most respected of the nation's dailies.

The paper today maintains more out-of-province and out-of-country bureaus than any other Canadian paper, subscribes to more news services than any other, publishes its own weekly magazine and international edition, and takes pride in being Canada's "paper of record," devoting much space to texts of parliamentary debates, political manifestos, and the like.[2]

The Globe and Mail actually evolves from three newspapers: the *Globe* (founded in 1844), the *Mail* (1872), and the *Empire* (1887). Its founder is usually considered to be George Brown, a Scottish immigrant, who founded the *Globe*. Brown, through the paper, exerted great influence on the early development of Canada and helped bring about the Confederation. As architect of the Reform Party (later to become the Liberal Party), Brown used his paper to speak out for responsible government, individual freedom, and the desirability to preserve strong ties with Britain. So *The Globe and Mail* had a Liberal orientation in its early days, actually until it became "independent" in 1936.[3]

Sir John A. Macdonald, with Conservative Party financial backing, began the *Mail* in Toronto in 1872, and a second Conservative paper, the *Empire*, was founded in 1887 but was taken over by the *Mail* in 1895 to continue as the *Mail and Empire*. For almost forty years the *Globe* and the *Mail and Empire* competed in Toronto, the former reflecting Liberal thinking and the latter, Conservative. In 1936 the *Globe* (circulation 78,000) was bought from the Jaffray family (which had owned it since Brown's death in 1880) by George McCullagh, a former financial writer for the paper. In less than a month McCullagh had also bought the *Mail and Empire* (circulation 118,000) and the two papers were consolidated under the new name, *The Globe and Mail*.[4]

McCullagh breathed new life into the paper and its pages showed a spirit reminiscent of the days when the old *Globe* was edited by Brown. The new owner announced his paper's political independence at once, but it has only been since World War II that the paper has generally supported the Progressive Conservative Party. However, its editors criticize any government irrespective of party domination.

Harry G. Kimber, who had been general manager, became publisher when McCullagh died in 1952. Three years later the paper was bought by R. Howard Webster, a Montreal financier. In 1957, Oakley Dalgleish who had been editor for ten years became editor and publisher, and after his death in 1963, Webster took the title of publisher and named James L. Cooper editor-in-chief. In early 1966 *The Globe and Mail* became a part of the FP Publications Ltd., a newspaper group including seven other newspapers. The current philosophy of the paper was expressed in an interview in 1955 with Webster soon after he bought the paper: "Newspapers can do a wonderful amount of good and a certain amount of harm too. We hope *The Globe and Mail* will continue to contribute very much to the growth of Canada."[5]

Today the paper is probably the best example in the general Canadian press of a journal which, as one observer said in 1966, has "a calm and level-headed tone" thus causing it to "accurately mirror a calm and balanced nation."[6] This same writer called *The Globe and Mail* "Canada's superior paper," and placed the Montreal *Star* close behind it.[7] *The Globe and Mail's* chief editor, however, feels that the *Winnipeg Free Press* (see profile in this chapter) is the second best quality daily in Canada.[8]

Foreign coverage is considered very important at *The Globe and Mail*, and the paper maintains bureaus in three key cities—London, Washington, and Peking. The paper gets foreign news from such papers as the London *Times*, *The Observer*, *The New York Times*, *Le Monde*, and London's *Financial Times*. Its own news service from Communist China (established 1958) is the major (often the only) source of news from

The Globe and Mail

Mainly sunny
Toronto high 55
Details on page 2

124th YEAR, No. 36,768 | TORONTO, FRIDAY, OCTOBER 13, 1967 | 50 PAGES | TEN CENTS

No hint of compromise

Rusk says U.S. in peril if Vietnam abandoned

THERE WERE NO BLUES IN ST. LOUIS LAST NIGHT

While St. Louis team mobs Bob Gibson after the final play of the deciding World Series game, which Cardinals won 7-2 yesterday, umpire Augie Donatelli skips off with two of their caps for souvenirs. One belonged to Gibson, who won three games. — Story, pictures on Page 30. —AP Wirephoto

Bombing of North defended

By HEDRICK SMITH
© New York Times Service

WASHINGTON — Secretary of State Dean Rusk, replying forcefully to critics of Administration policy, yesterday warned that if the United States abandoned its treaty pledges to South Vietnam and Southeast Asia, it would "subject this country to mortal danger."

Mr. Rusk, in a departure from his usual calm tone spoke with obvious emotion during his 55-minute news conference yesterday. He contended that U.S. national interest was at stake in Vietnam because China poses a threat to non-Communist Asian nations over the next decade.

"If any who would be our adversary should suppose that our treaties are a bluff, or will be abandoned if the going gets tough," Mr. Rusk asserted in his opening statement, "the result could be catastrophe for all mankind."

Mr. Rusk was the third prominent leader to vigorously defend President Lyndon B. Johnson's policy this week in what is seen as an Administration counterattack on critics of its war policy. On Monday, John M. Bailey, the Democratic Party chairman, accused Republicans of playing "an opportunist game" on Vietnam, and Wednesday the House Speaker, John W. McCormack of Massachusetts, charged critics with giving comfort to North Vietnam.

Mr. Rusk gave no hint of compromise on the Administration's terms for peace or negotiations. He ticked off recent congressional proposals for peace initiatives—a pause in bombing North Vietnam, de-escalation of the bombing, action by the United Nations, or a new international conference at Geneva on Vietnam — and brushed them all aside as unworkable because of North Vietnam's opposition. He contended that North Vietnam was not interested in ending the war.

The domestic U.S. concern has coincided with pressure from many countries, including Canada, speaking at the United Nations, for another U.S. bombing halt to facilitate peace talks with Hanoi.

On Sept. 27 External Affairs Minister Paul Martin called on the United States to stop bombing North Vietnam as a first step toward peace negotiations.

He told the United Nations General Assembly: "It seems clear that all attempts to bring about talks are doomed to failure unless the bombing is stopped. This is a matter of first priority if we are to start the process of de-escalation and to open the door to the conference room."

Reminded of these proposals, Mr. Rusk said tartly he

RUSK — Page 2

Special status plans lack logic, Trudeau says

By ROGER NEWMAN
Globe and Mail Reporter

MONTREAL — French Canadians are misguided if they think they can have both a particular status for Quebec and a bigger voice in Canada's affairs, federal Justice Minister Pierre Trudeau says in a new book that is to be published here Monday.

Mr. Trudeau says that if Quebeckers opt for special status, they must accept that the French fact in Canada will be limited both jurisdictionally and politically to the province of Quebec.

His 227-page volume, Le Federalisme et la Societe Canadienne-Francaise, is a detailed outline of Mr. Trudeau's political philosophies and an explanation of how he came to form them. Using both new and previously published material, he addresses himself specifically to the French-Canadian people and attempts to define how their progress can best be achieved during the constitutional debate now in progress.

The Justice Minister says all present proposals for Quebec special status, whatever their form, contain a certain lack of logic.

"It is the following: how do you conceive a constitution that would give Quebec more powers than the other provinces — without reducing to nil Quebec's influence on Ottawa ... Those who hope to play on the two tables are not realists."

According to Mr. Trudeau, Quebec, if it became the national state of French Canadians, would have to renounce at the same time its demand for the parity of French with English at Ottawa and in the rest of the country. But if Quebec remains almost the same as the rest of the provinces, this option would not prevent French Canadians from organizing themselves as they wish in matters of provincial jurisdiction — such as social legislation, resources development and the civil code.

"Quebeckers would also have the right to be represented on the same level as all other Canadians," Mr. Trudeau says. "This option would permit them to require the parity of French with English in all federal institutions — and even to eventually negotiate this parity with the other provinces."

In Mr. Trudeau's eyes, the term "particular status," is a way for French Canadians to tell themselves that they are going to upset the constitution, while at the same time assuring the rest of the country that they will do nothing.

He compares particular status adherents to the French-Canadian intellectuals of the Thirties who advocated "corporatisme", the building of strong nationalistic community organizations, as the panacea for Quebeckers.

"Nobody at that time had the clairvoyance and courage to say that this was nothing but nonsense. In consequence, it was necessary to wait another 25 years for the only reform that counted: education. The net result today is that French Canadians, of all Canadian ethnic groups, are almost last in education, coming just before the poor immigrants who have just debarked from Sicily."

Similarly, he says, proponents of special status build elaborate structures and talk about constitutional reforms without any relation to reality.

"We are terribly lacking in direction. Rather than devoting ourselves to modifying our fundamental, intellectual, social and economic conditions, we are carried away by a legal superstructure idea—without even asking ourselves if it can work."

The 46-year-old Justice Minister, a lawyer and political economist says thought among provincial leaders has changed little in Quebec since the Thirties.

"Where they have changed, it is for the worse. The situations are no longer the same, but official French-Canadian thought has become even more monolithic and sterile. Its adherents are more intolerant; because I would not have thought that the use of dynamite in a free country can be construed as progress toward reason."

Mr. Trudeau's campaign against particular status is part of the new material in his book. A substantial number of chapters, however, are reprinted from his previous speeches and from Cite Libre, an intellectual Montreal magazine. Mr. Trudeau was a founder of this magazine

TRUDEAU — Page 2

Committee plans to study charges on Vietnam aid

By ANTHONY WESTELL
Globe and Mail Reporter

OTTAWA — The Commons Committee on External Affairs is to hold an investigation soon into charges that Canada is not providing adequate aid to South Vietnam, and that some of the medical equipment that has been shipped is defective.

External Affairs Minister Paul Martin agreed with Conservatives in the House yesterday that Dr. Michael Hall, the leading critic of the Vietnam aid program, should be invited to make his charges before the committee.

He added: "In fairness to the position and to the merits involved in the situation, I wish to say there is no foundation whatever for Dr. Hall's observations."

Mr. Martin has said that the committee can explore all the facts, and he claimed yesterday that the detailed program of medical aid to Vietnam would be a good indication that Dr. Hall's observations were not valid.

When Mr. Martin told the House that he would have "something to say at the appropriate time in the appropriate place" about Dr. Hall, Conservative MP Heber Smith (Simcoe North) told him to stop dealing in innuendoes.

Dr. Hall, a top-flight Toronto surgeon, served in Vietnam for several years. He was to have taken up an appointment as professor at the University of Hue but ended his contract with Canada's External Aid Office earlier this year when he could not make satisfactory arrangements with the Vietnam authorities about the job.

He has charged, in letters and broadcasts, among other things that Canada has:

— Sent $60,000 worth of butter to Vietnam, where the people do not eat butter;

— Sent $730,000 worth of flour, when the people eat rice;

— Insured that the foodstuffs are sold to the rich, rather than given to the poor, by insisting that the Vietnamese Government pay for them in local currency, which is reinvested in other aid projects;

— Failed to provide aid to civilian wounded;

— Failed to provide surgical teams;

— Sent defective hospital equipment.

When Conservative MPs raised questions about these charges in the Commons on Wednesday, Mr. Martin said the best place to deal with them would be before the External Affairs Committee.

Yesterday, he said he had already spoken to the chairman of the committee, Jean-Eudes Dube (L, Restigouche-Madawaska), to encourage an early meeting.

Meanwhile, an External Aid Office official denied yesterday that an External Aid spokesman had conceded Dr. Hall was right in saying some of the Canadian hospital equipment sent to Vietnam is unsuitable for Vietnamese needs. It mentioned canvas beds.

An official said yesterday: "We have not conceded anything. We have had no reports that there is anything wrong with the equipment. I've been out there and seen it, and I was told everywhere that it was fine."

He noted as a fact that Canada does not send canvas beds to Vietnam, they are made of steel and nylon.

These beds are part of the equipment for 10 emergency hospitals, which has been

CHARGES — Page 2

Your morning smile

The service station manager, sending his assistant out to fix a tire on a physician's car, advised him: "Diagnose the trouble as flatulency of the perimeter and charge him accordingly."

Soviet extends military service to schoolboys

By HENRY KAMM
© New York Times Service

MOSCOW — The Soviet Union announced and enacted into law yesterday an extension of military service and training to greater numbers of citizens, including high school boys, but coupled it with a one-year cut in the term of compulsory service.

The Defense Minister, Marshal Andrei A. Grechko, put the new measure before the Supreme Soviet, or parliament, in a speech calling for a higher degree of military preparedness. The fault, the marshal declared, lies with the United States.

He said: "The ruling circles of the United States, behind the screen of talk of peace and co-operation, are stepping up military preparations against the Soviet Union and other countries of Socialism that are creating dangerous hotbeds of war in various regions of the world."

The Defense Minister singled out Vietnam and the Middle East as such "hotbeds."

"It is only a strong growing military might, brought to the highest level, that can cool the bellicose ardor of aggressors and guarantee our country against possible hazards."

Earlier yesterday, the Supreme Soviet adopted a budget for 1968 that increased military spending by 15 per cent, from $16.09-billion to $18.5-billion.

The new draft law, adopted unanimously and without question by the 1,517 deputies, introduces compulsory preliminary military training to all secondary schools for the last two years of the 10-year course.

Marshal Grechko did not say what form the training would take, but the Education Minister, Mikhail A. Prokofyev, told the deputies that military officers would be attached to secondary school facilities to provide it.

Youths attending high school at night and working by day will be called to special military training centres.

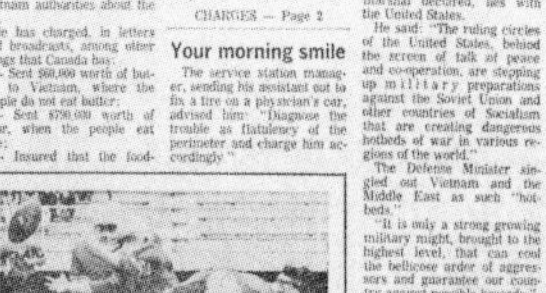

High school football—Page 31

24% to 50% pay increase sought

Guaranteed wage tops civic staff demands

By ALDEN BAKER

Two militant civic unions will demand from Metro today a guaranteed annual wage, general salary increases ranging from 24 to 50 per cent and no contracting out of civic work.

The current agreement with Local 79 and Local 43 of the Canadian Union of Public Employees expires in December. Local 79 represents office workers, staff of homes for the aged and foremen on outside jobs. Local 43 represents street cleaning, sewer and water plant employees.

Civic services were strained last November by a three-day strike by Local 43. Supervisory crews maintained services.

Wage increases of 15 per cent in some categories and 35 cents an hour in others were granted Local 43 in a retroactive 21-month agreement. A retroactive two-year agreement with Local 79 provided a 13½ per cent increase.

Officials from 35 other Metro civic union locals will meet Monday in the Lord Simcoe Hotel to indicate support to the two locals in their demands.

A union official said the meeting will present a strong united front seeking "an adequate wage and security."

For the past several months the mayors of the city and five suburban boroughs making up Mtro have been meeting as a committee to consider a uniform approach to bargaining.

Local 79 wants new fringe benefits to include maternity leave and paid holidays at Christmas Eve and New Year's Eve.

Maternity leave has been a matter of negotiation between employee and department heads. Civic workers are currently assured 10 paid holidays a year. Local 79 is asking payment of two-thirds of the cost of all welfare benefits, four weeks' holiday for employees with 10 years service, long service pay and doubletime pay for overtime in excess of four hours overtime worked in a day.

Both unions will likely push strongly for the right to refuse to cross the picket line of either union. Metro and the city last year asked the Ontario Labor Relations Board to declare that Local 79 was engaging in an illegal strike by refusing to cross Local 43 picket lines.

Counter-proposals will likely be presented by Metro and the city, most of them aimed at establishing control over the extent of fringe benefits.

Both unions plan to watch closely any attempt to apply economy measures that may reduce staff.

Old Massey Hall to be sold; will rise again in new location

Old Massey Hall — home of Toronto's fine music and of many rabble-rousing meetings — is going to be sold and a new Massey Hall built elsewhere.

A committee has been formed to plan the move, but no details have been decided. However, Mayor William Dennison says the city has some land next to the site of the proposed St. Lawrence Centre for the Arts and would be prepared to talk about the matter if approached.

Mavor Moore, general director of the centre, said he would be delighted to see a new Massey Hall built into a downtown cultural complex comprising O'Keefe Centre, St. Lawrence Centre, an opera house and a facilities building.

Less than a year ago, old Massey Hall was in line for a $1-million facelifting grant as part of the city's Centennial project but was squeezed out when money dried up.

Edward A. Pickering, joint chairman of the Massey Hall relocation committee, said yesterday that a new site has not been chosen and a study of costs has not been completed.

However, the new hall will seat about the same number (2,800), will serve the same function, and will be in downtown Toronto if possible.

In a statement released yesterday, Vincent Massey, a former Governor-General and still a Massey Hall trustee, is quoted as saying: "The Old Lady of Shuter Street has served Toronto well for over 70 years but she has had her day."

Mr. Massey, who is 80 laid the cornerstone of Massey Hall as a young boy. It opened on June 14, 1894.

The hall is run by a nonprofit trust, which pays no taxes on the land on Shuter Street near Yonge Street. The manager, Ross Creelman, said yesterday that the hall's yearly budget is about $80,000. It has been breaking even on its operations in most years.

Value of the hall and site is not known.

A spokesman for the architects, Mathers and Haldenby, said he doubted that a new hall could match the acoustics of the old one. "I don't think there has been a hall built anywhere in the world for 40 years as good as Massey Hall," he said.

Stocks lower as market follows N.Y.

Stocks yesterday suffered their most widespread declines in more than four months on the Toronto market, in the wake of weakness on Wall Street. Ford of Canada was down $2.75 to $166 and General Motors $2.12 to $90.

West Germans report ships under attack

THE HAGUE (Reuters) — Two West German fishing boats radioed early today that they were under fire from an East German warship in the Baltic.

3rd abduction into China is reported

HONG KONG (Reuters) — Another Chinese — the third in six days — was abducted across the border into China yesterday, a Hong Kong spokesman said.

He said four Chinese were arrested in the area where a police patrol saw two men lead a third across the shallow Shum Chun border river with his hands tied behind his back.

An army spokesman yesterday confirmed the British are using mines along the border to protect army posts.

Government control board

B.C. medical group rejects marijuana sale plan

From The British Columbia Bureau of The Globe and Mail

VICTORIA — A committee of the British Columbia Medical Association proposed yesterday that marijuana be distributed in Canada in much the same way as alcohol but the proposal was overruled by the association's general assembly.

The committee report said a marijuana control board, set up by the Government, would be a more appropriate legal control than present restrictions. But after prolonged debate at the general meeting in Victoria's Empress Hotel, the doctors approved only a watered down version of the report.

The doctors agreed that a more appropriate legal control of marijuana be sought but rejected the proposal for a marijuana control board. They also supported provincial legislation enacted this year to deal with LSD, striking out the committee's recommendation that LSD control remain under federal control.

The law governing marijuana is creating a new class of criminal among otherwise law-abiding people, the drug habituation committee report contended. "It may thereby produce more social disruption than could result from unrestricted use of the drug."

The seven-doctor committee found both marijuana and LSD being widely used in Vancouver.

"It should not be thought that (they) are indulged in solely by the so-called hippy element . . . (while) these drugs seem to be pillars of the hippy culture, there is evidence that marijuana particularly and LSD to a lesser degree are used by non-hippy or square people who are economically productive and derive from every social and economic stratum in society," the committee reported.

The committee underlined its belief that marijuana and LSD presented different threats and so should be subject to different controls. Any legal control must be consistent with the danger to be protected against, it felt.

"In contrast to marijuana, LSD is indeed a drug that poses some danger both to its user and to the community."

The committee concluded that marijuana, because it was both intoxicating and habituating (as opposed to addictive), should come under a control board that would regulate its distribution.

The committee decided that marijuana was probably no more harmful than alcohol to the user, though it questioned the need for another intoxicant in a society it considered well served by alcohol.

"However, it is not easy (to justify) classifying marijuana with the narcotics and for imposing the same stringent penalities."

LSD, as a basically dangerous drug of unpredictable effect, must be properly controlled, but not so tightly as to stifle research into the drug's potential as a valid therapeutic agent in medicine and psychiatry, the report said.

"Present legal controls and others projected may stifle research and let slip the opportunity to gain valuable and useful information about this strange, powerful and unknown substance."

The report recommended that LSD control remain under federal food and drug regulations, which permit its distribution to institutions for research by qualified investigators, but forbid any other distribution.

The B.C. Government this year enacted a law making LSD possession an offense, and requiring every citizen to report the location of any LSD known to him. But these laws have been attacked in the courts on constitutional grounds and their validity remains in doubt.

"It appears that this legislation was hastily conceived in an atmosphere of hysteria," the report said. The committee urged that a sensible education program be established for both the medical profession and public so that objective information on habituating drugs might be dispensed. It also proposed that facilities be set up in emergency departments of hospitals to treat those experiencing ill effects from use of any hallucinatory drug.

that country for many newspapers of the Western world. *The New York Times,* for instance, regularly uses this service of *The Globe and Mail.*[9]

The paper tries to present the news promptly and vigorously, with a reasonable balance, and in an unemotional and unsensational manner. It has a very substantial following among judges, lawyers, doctors, diplomats, clergymen, bankers, and teachers. Great emphasis is given to national and international general news, and to business and finance. To present this thorough and professional service, the paper employs 210 writers and editors.[10]

The paper considers itself today as independent politically, but it is by no means neutral. Ideologically, the paper is to the Right, but certainly to the thoughtful and calm Right. It is very careful to confine its opinions, which it gives with intelligence and clarity, to the editorial page. The writer keeps himself out of the news columns, which are backed by interpretive pieces written by specialists. The editorial page and page-opposite provide one of the most dignified and attractive two-page opinion sections among the world's elite newspapers.

The *Weekly Globe and Mail* was started in 1957, with a magazine supplement and other special features. A weekly overseas edition was begun the following year, printed for a time in London, but now in its own Toronto plant. In 1962 the paper added a Report on Business—a thrice-weekly section inserted in the regular paper but also circulated separately by airmail across the nation. The paper publishes five daily editions, with forty pages being the typical weekday size. A serious paper, excellently produced in all respects, *The Globe and Mail* well deserves its place among the world's elite dailies.

Winnipeg Free Press
(CANADA)

One sign of a healthy, intelligent, progressive newspaper is an intellectual independence and critical attitude stemming from a sound ideological position which is unencumbered by undue economic or political pressures. The *Winnipeg Free Press*, which has been called "Canada's Gadfly,"[1] manifests this independent and critical spirit. It has often admonished the Liberal Government in Canada even though it has a rich Liberal background, and it has ever fought to stay aloof from situations which would limit its editorial freedom.

Of all Canadian papers, the *Free Press* is perhaps most serious, both in its sober dress and restrained writing. It takes itself and its readers seriously, a fact which has led to its high place among North America's elite papers. The *Free Press* is at once powerful, respected, feared, and often hated.

It is not a large paper; at least a half-dozen dailies of Canada are larger in both circulation and number of pages. The *Free Press'* circulation is some 128,000 (with a separate weekly edition of some 400,000) and it is a thin paper compared to papers in Toronto and Montreal.[2] But no paper in the country has topped the *Free Press* as a champion of minority causes and a leader of informed and progressive national opinion. And no other paper is so consistently controversial or, as one writer has put it, "rough and cranky but always educated, fearless, and unrepentant."[3]

The *Winnipeg Free Press* was begun as the *Manitoba Free Press* by William Luxton in 1874 and struggled along until the 1880's when it took new life while the Canadian westward movement was at its peak.[4] It was during this period that John Wesley Dafoe came to Winnipeg as an Ontario farmboy. He was to become the great editor who would direct with great brilliance the "Old Lady of Carleton Street," as the paper became known, from 1901 until his death in 1944. Regarded generally as the finest editor Canada ever produced, Dafoe built the paper into what became "the Bible of Canadian prairies and the nation's thunderer."[5]

Dafoe edited the *Free Press* for forty years, infusing into the paper a respect for thorough news coverage combined with biting editorials.[6] He, more than anyone before or possibly since, gave the *Free Press* its special "personality" of brashness overlying a deep layer of serious and thoughtful calmness. He certainly gave the paper a character which made it a national newspaper, one which was essential reading for opinion leaders throughout the country.

When Dafoe died in 1944, Grant Dexter and George Ferguson jointly edited the paper for a short time. Ferguson left for Montreal to become editor of the *Star*, and Dexter returned to Ottawa and his main interest, reporting on Parliament. Tom Kent, a young Englishman trained at Oxford and on the *Manchester Guardian*, was brought in to edit the paper. He made some changes (such as reducing headline size on the front page) but did not essentially change the character of the paper. After five years, he left the paper to enter politics in Ottawa.[7]

Although the *Free Press* has changed somewhat since the days of Dafoe, it retains the essential character of what is sometimes called its Golden Age. It still influences public opinion, at least in Cabinet offices and diplomatic circles. Its editorials still pull no punches and deal with vital issues on a day-to-day basis. Its circulation is rising steadily. R. S. Malone,[8] today's publisher, fearing outside pressures, desires to keep the paper financially independent and sound. He has succeeded on both counts.

The *Free Press* is probably best known for its local and national news coverage. A three-man bureau is maintained in Ottawa which provides

GIVE THE UNITED WAY

Winnipeg Free Press

Final Edition

VOL. 75 — NO. 15 PRICE 10c WITH COMICS 15c WINNIPEG, MONDAY, OCTOBER 16, 1967 FORECAST: SUNNY; 35 and 55

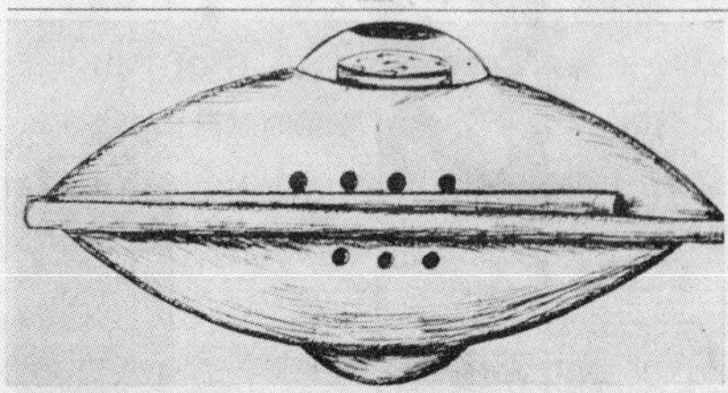

UFO Photo 'Best Yet' — RCAF

At right is arrowed photo of an unidentified flying object (UFO) taken by prospector Warren Smith of Calgary in southern Alberta. The RCAF says it is the best photo in its files and an enlargement shows a domed saucer, 40 feet across with blueish exhaust and 'quite large speed'. At left is Mr. Smith's sketch of the UFO which hovered near a forestry tower (he's made four sightings so far). He says the saucer had a green light around the rim and a rotating green light (arrows) in the upper bowl; when it flew off, the rim light went out, the dome light turned white and four blue 'exhaust' flames came from the rear.

Nasser Prepared To Start Talks With Israel Govt.

UAR President Willing To Negotiate Before Israeli Troops Quit Sinai Desert

By SIR DINGLE FOOT

LONDON (Special - OFNS) — Egypt's President Gamal Abdel Nasser is prepared to start talks between Egypt and Israel under United Nations chairmanship even before a withdrawal of Israeli forces from Sinai. This could be done, he suggests, in the framework of the 1949 armistice agreements.

He is also ready to accept an end of the state of war with Israel. But he insists that no settlement — including a reopening of the Suez Canal — can be concluded so long as Israeli troops occupy Egyptian territory. The president's peace policy links the passage of Israeli shipping through the Suez Canal with a solution of the problem of the Palestine Arab refugees in accordance with the UN resolutions calling for their return or compensation.

President Nasser hopes for a resumption of diplomatic relations with Britain followed by closer economic and cultural ties.

These were some of the main points which emerged during an hour's talk with President Nasser in Cairo last Thursday, the first interview he has given for publication since the Arab-Israel war last June.

President Nasser appeared relaxed and gave no impression of being sick or tired.

We discussed the possibility of a settlement between the Arab states and Israel. In Cairo now the formula most widely cited as the basis for settlement is "non-belligerency" (a formula which has already appeared in abortive UN resolutions this summer and in the mediation proposals put forward by Yugoslav President Tito).

President Nasser said that a beginning could be made by reviving the Egypt-Israel armistice agreement of 1949 which had in effect provided for non-belligerency. Under that agreement the carrying out of the armistice terms

—Continued

Please See READY Page 17

Damage By Spies Revealed

LONDON (Reuters)—London press reports say two British double agents working for the Soviet Union caused inestimable damage to Anglo-American interests in the post-war years.

The two agents—now both in the Soviet Union—were Kim Philby, a former top British intelligence official, and Donald MacLean, a former diplomat.

Vital information they are reported to have betrayed included American atomic secrets, negotiations on the North Atlantic pact, Korean War Strategy and plans for guerrilla subversion in Eastern Europe.

Philby, who fled to the U.S.S.R. in 1963, was formerly head of the Russian section of the British secret intelligence service and later worked in Washington as a liaison man between the British service and the Central Intelligence Agency.

The Sunday Times says his most impressive operation was in 1950, when he betrayed an

—Continued

Please See DAMAGE Page 6

Working On New Pill: MD

VANCOUVER (CP)—An American obstetrician says a pill is being developed which will enable women to end pregnancy up to a month after conception.

Dr. R. T. Pion, associate professor of obstetrics and gynecology at the University of Washington, said preliminary research already is underway in the Seattle area.

"Then the choice will be whether or not they want a child which has been conceived—not whether they will take a pill to prevent conception," he told a seminar sponsored by the Registered Nurses Association of British Columbia.

Dr. Pion said in an interview later he did not think such an action could be called abortion.

"It would be a pill to bring on menstruation."

He said a perfect contraceptive agent has not been found despite development of the birth control pill.

"Birth control pills can kill some women," he said. But he added that the number of women who die during pregnancy is greater than the number of women who die from taking birth control pills.

★ ★ ★

U.S. Holds Key

By OSGOOD CARUTHERS

CAIRO (Special-TPNS) — Egypt is hoping for a restoration of relations with Britain — and through that a possible shift in United States policy to a position more favorable to the Arabs in the Middle East crisis.

The feeling in Cairo today is that the crucial moment is approaching which will determine whether a formula for settlement of the crisis will be found in the United Nations or the situation will develop into one of dangerous desperation. And it is the firm conviction among all in authority here that the United States is the only power holding the key to this situation.

—Continued

Please See U.S. Page 6

Che's Dead: Castro

Bolivian Claim 'Bitterly True' Says Premier

HAVANA (CP) — Cuban Premier Fidel Castro announced Sunday night he has accepted as "bitterly true," that his former comrade in arms, Ernesto Che Guevara, is dead.

Castro made his acceptance in a speech beamed throughout Latin America that appeared to be the first step in a campaign to establish the Argentine doctor, said to have been killed in Bolivia, as a revolutionary hero and martyr.

He said "imperialism has a fear of Che after death." Guevara had been eliminated physically "but his example "can never be eliminated by anything or anyone."

The usually-flamboyant Castro, his voice subdued by emotion, accused the Bolivian army of murdering the 39-year-old Guevara after capturing him Oct. 8.

The death of one of the leading tacticians of the Cuban revolution was a "very hard strong blow to the revolutionary movement."

—Continued

Please See GUEVARA Page 15

A B C Circulation
City Zone [illegible]
Total [illegible]

NEARLY EVERYONE READS the FREE PRESS

THE STATE OF QUEBEC

Separatists Lose Round

Levesque Forced To Resign Liberal Party: Near-Independence Study Report Set Aside

By STAN McDOWELL

QUEBEC CITY (Staff) — Quebec Liberals rejected "separatism in all its forms" at their annual party congress which ended here Sunday.

Rene Levesque was forced to resign from the party and carry on alone his campaign for an independent Quebec in a Canadian common market.

And a report advocating the near-independence of a very broad special status for Quebec was set aside "for further study".

Nothing in the report, party leader Jean Lesage assured delegates, would become Liberal policy unless it were brought before a future Quebec Liberal Federation congress in the form of a resolution.

The number of votes in favor of the strongly anti-separatist resolution — too many to count accurately — was estimated at 1,200. Seven delegates voted against

—Continued

Please See LEVESQUE Page 10

★ ★ ★ ★ ★ ★

Better Without Levesque: Lesage

JEAN LESAGE

QUEBEC (CP)—Liberal leader Jean Lesage said Sunday night Rene Levesque's resignation will do more good than harm to the Liberal party.

Mr. Lesage told reporters he was not denying that Mr. Levesque was an active force within the party.

Suggested by a reporter that the party lost its greatest appeal to Quebec youth with Mr. Levesque's resignation, Mr. Lesage said:

"That remains to be seen."

Mr. Lesage said the number of resignations of disenchanted Liberals would not equal the number who will join the party because of Mr. Levesque's departure.

He said Mr. Levesque's influence across the province has diminished greatly and he had lost any influence in the party "because he was absent."

Mr. Levesque, former minister of resources and welfare, made only rare appearances at the legislature following the Liberal loss of power.

Reaction ranged from disappointment to delight within the

—Continued

Please See PARTY Page 17

★ ★ ★

RENE LEVESQUE

★ ★ ★

'Label' Angers Band

QUEBEC (CP)—Former Quebec Liberal Rene Levesque's little band of supporters at the annual meeting of the Quebec Liberal Federation insist that they are not separatists.

Most intend to quit the Quebec Liberal party, but no one interviewed during the weekend meeting said he would join either of Quebec's two separatist political parties.

—Continued

Please See 'LABEL' Page 15

★ ★ ★

Pearson Voices Warning

BANFF, Alta. (CP) — Prime Minister Pearson said Sunday night Canadians must face urgently the question of what price they are prepared to pay to maintain the unity of the country.

In a speech read in his absence here at the Conference on the Economics of Canadian Unity, the prime minister declared that, somehow, all of Canada must become as much of a homeland for all French-speaking Canadians as it is for all English-speaking Canadians.

—Continued

Please See PEARSON Page 17

★ ★ ★ ★ ★ ★

Kierans Cautions English On Vote

QUEBEC (CP)—Eric Kierans, president of the Quebec Liberal Federation, said Sunday night "it would be tragic" if the Liberals' vote against separatism were misunderstood in the rest of Canada.

Mr. Kierans began his presidential address to the closing banquet at the federation's annual meeting by addressing a message to English-speaking Canadians in other provinces.

"Confidence in Canada, overwhelming confidence in Canada, was voted in the last two years by the Quebec Liberals," he said.

The vote rejecting "separatism in all forms" represented not only the Liberal party or the Quebec people "but the entire French-Canadian nation."

"It would be tragic if this vote was misunderstood in the rest of Canada. The vote does not represent a defeat for the legitimate and just aspirations of the French-Canadians. . . ."

He listed these as preservation of the French-Canadian culture, recognition of the French language right across the country and the desire of French Canadians to administer more fully their own affairs within Confederation.

★ ★ ★

ERIC KIERANS

Land Firm Hit

Land-Switching, Blackmail Charged

TAMPA, Florida (AP) — Governor Claude Kirk has accused Gulf American Land Corp., of trying to blackmail him "to take the heat off" the giant development firm, trading in whose stock was halted on the American Stock Exchange.

The trading was halted by the exchange in New York shortly after a state investigating committee accused the company of a land-switch fraud in 1,300 Florida deals since 1963.

Governor Kirk said Gulf American tried to blackmail him with information it allegedly had about Florida's development commission chairman, C. Shelby Dale.

The Florida land sales board ended a long investigation with its order calling on Gulf American to show cause why its licence should not be revoked or suspended for misconduct reported by board investigators.

—Continued

Please See FLORIDA Page 15

Closure Likely Subject

OTTAWA (CP) — The announced intention of Dominion Steel and Coal Corp. to close its steel operations at Sydney, N.S., is likely to be a major topic when the Commons sits at 2:30 p.m. today.

The economic implications of the closing are so serious to the Cape Breton community of 34,000 that there could be demands for an emergency debate.

If such a move succeeded the House would put aside its regular business, which today is supposed to be consideration of a resolution proposing a one-cent increase in postage for letters mailed in Canada for delivery within the country.

—Continued

Please See CLOSURE Page 15

★ ★ ★

Saucer Reports Match Up

The picture of an unidentified flying object taken by an Alberta prospector appears to bear out a UFO-claim by a Falcon Lake man who said he was actually burned by a ship's exhaust.

Warren Smith of Calgary took "the best picture yet" of a UFO, which he described as being about 40 feet across, domed, with holes in the side and a bluish exhaust.

May 21, Steve Michalak, 50, of Falcon Lake, said he was burned by "a bluish exhaust." He described the UFO he saw as being about 35 feet across, protrusion on the top and a pattern of holes in the side.

The only difference in their descriptions was in their estimate of the size of the saucers, a difference of only five feet.

Cash, Jewels Stolen

NEW YORK (CP)—Three gunmen wearing Hallowe'en masks held up a cargo hangar of American Airlines at Kennedy Airport Sunday night and made off with $102,000 in cash and sapphires and rubies from the Far East.

The bandits appeared at the hangar, in a remote section of the sprawling airport, wearing masks with putty-style noses, eye glasses without lenses, and large moustaches.

The trio, armed with pistols, rounded up an unarmed guard and six freight clerks, then locked them in the hangar. The seven men were not injured.

Within 10 minutes the robbers sped away in a car with the loot—$80,000 in American currency in one packet, and four packages containing gems valued at $22,000.

It was the sixth big robbery at Kennedy Airport this year.

More than $123,000 worth of diamonds were stolen Sept. 23 from a Japan Air Lines Co. safe.

Nine gold bars valued at more than $23,000 were stolen Aug. 1 from the cargo offices of the Dutch KLM airline.

In one week in April a gold bar worth $40,000, $42,000 in currency, and $12,000 worth of semi-precious stones were taken in three separate thefts.

the paper with especially strong parliamentary coverage. Although the *Free Press* considers international news important and gives it special play, it has few full-time foreign correspondents. In fact, it keeps its own men only in London and Washington. Several specialists, however, are always ready to take foreign assignments when the paper feels there is a need, and the paper also uses expert correspondents (stringers) throughout the world.[9]

The editorial page is usually considered the best part of the paper. It is heavy reading, sometimes a little too argumentative even to the point of weariness. Two columns of editorials, and six others of assorted serious material, fill the page. "The Page," as it is called, is packed with material exclusively written for the paper, there being no syndicated articles permitted in this "sacred" area.[10] About three-fourths of the page's contents is written by staff writers, the other fourth by outsiders expressing a wide variety of views, many antagonistic to the paper's positions. According to Shane MacKay, former political writer and now the *Free Press* executive editor, "there does seem to be a general feeling that our editorial page is one of the most influential in Canada."[11] Editorials ("leaders") are the product of at least half a dozen men, all with foreign experience, university degrees, and some with graduate work. They are written carefully and researched well and are perhaps the most articulate and literate editorial expressions in North American journalism.

In international affairs the *Free Press* supports the United Nations and NATO, has advocated Canada's recognition of Red China, and has urged that the Peking Government be admitted to the United Nations as a full member of the Security Council. It calls for Canada to assume a more cosmopolitan viewpoint and lashes out at any attitude of neutralism or isolationism. And, as would be expected, it is highly critical of racism wherever it may be found and champions the causes of minorities everywhere. In many ways it is like the *St. Louis Post-Dispatch* of the United States. Shane MacKay, the executive editor, says the *Free Press'* political outlook is Liberal (he would surely say "liberal" with a small "l") but "more or less of the center."[12]

The *Winnipeg Free Press* is a good example of a paper which has managed to develop a cosmopolitan outlook without abdicating its local and regional emphasis. It certainly keeps its fingers on the pulse of the nation, not only providing its readers with a clear view of what is happening in Canada, but also stinging the national leadership in Ottawa with some of the most pointed and intelligent criticism provided by an elite newspaper anywhere in the world. If it is anything it is a "rational" paper, leading its educated readership through complicated arguments often resembling forensic exercises, rousing itself from time to time to roar and thunder in deeply felt indignation at man's inhumanity to man.

O Estado de S. Paulo

(BRAZIL)

What is often called "*The New York Times* of Latin America" or the "gray giant of Brazilian journalism" is a formidable daily published in São Paulo, the largest city of Latin America's largest country. *O Estado de S. Paulo* (The State of São Paulo), with a staff of 250 writers and editors and with full-time correspondents in eight foreign cities, has set a journalistic pace difficult to match in Latin America. Every weekday morning the paper circulates 180,000 copies and 250,000 on Sundays.[1] Only *O Globo* (The Globe),[2] an influential evening daily in Rio de Janeiro, is larger.

O Estado's highly paid and well-educated staff (all reporters have university degrees and at least six writers have doctorates; 95 per cent of all staff members are university graduates)[3] give the readers a journalistic package for their 30 cruzeiros (nearly three cents) probably provided by no other newspaper anywhere. A typical weekday edition carries 48 pages and the huge Sunday issue often runs to more than 150 pages. In these pages are found full texts of all major speeches and press conferences, translated articles from foreign papers, stories from five wire services, national news of all types, local items in profusion, and an abundance of advertising.[4]

In addition to its regular heavy fare of news, features, editorials, and interpretive pieces, the paper frequently runs special articles on a wide range of subjects, foreign and domestic. These, often continuing for a dozen or more issues in serial form, are well-written, well-researched and more thorough than most anything found in the country's magazines. *O Estado,* never writing down to its readers and considering itself mainly a journal for the intelligent, well-educated classes, prints many scholarly essays by intellectuals—notably leading literary figures and professors from the University of São Paulo.

"There is no doubt about it," said one rival Brazilian journalist from São Paulo in 1966, "*O Estado* is thorough and encyclopedic—actually filled with more reading material than a person can find time to read; it is the nearest thing in Latin America to *The New York Times.*"[5]

Most any survey of newspapers and their foreign news presentation will find *O Estado* at the top. A UNESCO study in 1953 showed that during a selected week in 1951 *O Estado* gave more foreign news than any of sixteen other important newspapers of the world.[6] And in 1960, the paper was found to be second only to *The New York Times* in space given to foreign news (*O Estado,* 200 column inches; *The Times,* 219 column inches) during a thirty-day period.[7] None of the eleven other

Diretor — Américo de Campos, 1875-1881; Francisco Rangel Pestana, 1875-1890; Julio Mesquita, 1891-1927; Nestor Rangel Pestana, 1927-1933; Plinio Barreto, 1927-1958

O ESTADO DE S. PAULO

JULIO MESQUITA (1891-1927)

Cap. e Int. de São Paulo: d. ú. NCr$ 0,20, dom. NCr$ 0,30. Assin. NCr$ 48. End. Rua Major Quedinho, 28. Tel.: 36-6931. End. Telegráfico ESTADO - Telex: 021-371 e 021-380.

DIRETOR: JULIO DE MESQUITA FILHO | ANO 88 | QUARTA-FEIRA, 16 DE AGOSTO DE 1967 | N.º 28.325 | DIRETOR REDATOR-CHEFE: MARCELINO RITTER

A Rosa de Ouro já está na Basílica

Oswaldo Marlrato — Enviado especial

D. Carlos Carmelo de Vasconcelos Motta, cardeal arcebispo de Aparecida, mostra ao povo a Rosa de Ouro

Dos enviados especiais e do correspondente do Vale do Paraíba

A Rosa de Ouro concedida pelo Papa Paulo VI á Basilica de Aparecida foi entregue ontem pelo legado papal, cardeal Amleto Giovanni Cicognani, ao cardeal arcebispo de Aparecida, Dom Carlos Carmelo de Vasconcelos Motta, em cerimonia solene realizada no Santuário da Padroeira do Brasil, á qual assistiram o presidente da Republica, o governador do Estado, ministros de Estado, chefes militares e altas autoridades eclesiasticas e civis.

A cerimonia teve inicio ás 9 e 50, com a chegada do legado papal á Basilica nova e foi encerrada com a celebração de missa solene, pelo representante de Sua Santidade. O programa do ato foi parcialmente alterado em consequencia da chuva — a entrega da Rosa de Ouro e a missa estavam previstas ao ar livre, nos fundos da Basilica, onde o espaço é bem maior, mas foram transferidas para a parte já coberta do templo. Apesar do mau tempo, dezenas de milhares de fiéis acompanharam toda a cerimonia.

Ao fazer a entrega da distinção, o cardeal Cicognani fez votos de que a Rosa de Ouro "seja a expressão do especial afeto do nosso Santo Padre para com a Virgem Maria, a quem insistentemente nós todos pedimos alcance benignamente do Senhor Jesus Cristo a prosperidade para a Santa Igreja e, para todo o mundo, o dom da paz".

OS DIGNITÁRIOS

O representante do Papa Paulo VI chegou a Aparecida procedente de São Paulo, acompanhado pelo governador Abreu Sodré e pelo cardeal Rossi. Após a cerimonia regressou a esta Capital, onde foi homenageado, á noite, com uma recepção no Palacio Pio XII.

O presidente da Republica, que cumprira rapido programa em São Paulo na véspera, pernoitou em Guaratinguetá e dali seguiu para Aparecida. Rumou depois para Franca, de onde viajou, no fim da tarde, para Brasilia.

EM FRANCA

O chefe do governo chegou a Franca ás 14 horas, para visitar a 8.a Exposição Agro-Industrial, onde lhe foi oferecido um banquete. Desembarcou, acompanhado pelo governador Abreu Sodré e pelo ministro Magalhães Pinto, no aeroporto da usina hidrelétrica de Estreito, a cerca de 50 quilometros da cidade.

Seguiu diretamente para a sede do Municipio, onde visitou rapidamente os "stands" da exposição. Durante o almoço, pronunciou breve discurso de improviso, fazendo referencias a sua experiencia de instalação do governo por uma semana no Nordeste e reiterando a disposição do governo de conhecer de perto todos os problemas que afligem a Nação.

Após o almoço o presidente da Republica regressou ao aeroporto de Estreito, percorrendo antes de embarcar as instalações da usina que ali está sendo construida.

O governador Abreu Sodré regressou a São Paulo no fim da tarde. (Pags. 13 e 14).

O povo rompeu cordões

Ao terminar a cerimonia liturgica, a imensa multidão, até então contida, rompeu os cordões de isolamento colocados nos dois lados da Basilica de Aparecida, formando um corredor, querendo dirigir-se em massa para ver a Rosa de Ouro. Ao mesmo tempo, saíam do interior da igreja o presidente Costa e Silva, sua esposa e outras autoridades, que se viram envolvidos pelos populares, mas logo auxiliados e protegidos por soldados do Exercito e da Aeronautica, que tiveram de abrir caminho quase á força.

O marechal Costa e Silva levou aproximadamente 15 minutos para vencer a pé um trecho de menos de 100 metros. Após deixar a grande area que circunda a Basilica, a comitiva presidencial novamente encontrou dificuldades, agora para atingir a via Dutra, pois o grande numero de veiculos e pessoas circulando atravancava as ruas da cidade. Atingida a rodovia, após 10 minutos, o presidente seguiu para Guaratinguetá, com um helicoptero sobrevoando o seu carro, durante todo o trajeto.

Mais de mil homens do Exercito, da Aeronautica, da Força Publica, da Policia Federal, da Policia Rodoviaria e do DOPS compuseram o rigido sistema de segurança do presidente da Republica. Para adquirir credenciais para trabalhar na area da Basilica, os jornalistas tinham de apresentar documentos de identificação e submeterem-se a uma revista pelos seus bolsos. Durante a cerimonia, no entanto, tiveram liberdade de movimentos, com poucas limitações.

30 páginas

e mais o

Suplemento Agrícola

Ultimatum a Mao Tsé-tung

HONGCONG, 15 (AFP) — O diario "Hong Kong Star" afirma hoje que o general rebelde chinês Cheng Tsaitao, que comanda as tropas da agitada Provincia de Wuhan, ameaçou Mao Tsé-tung com a guerra civil, afirmando em cabograma que enviou ao supremo chefe chinês: "Se você deseja a guerra, a terá".

Após informar que existem firmes indicações de que o general Cheng uniu suas forças ás do general Wang En-mao, comandante militar da Provincia de Sinkiang, onde estão os depositos nucleares chineses, o jornal diz que Cheng disse recentemente a Mao que não acredita em que o supremo chefe possa utilizar as armas atomicas.

Das fontes mencionadas pelo "Hong Kong Star" acrescenta-se que prossegue a luta em Wuhan, a qual se estende até Cantão. A informação acrescenta que quando o general Cheng foi convencido a abandonar seu comando em Wuhan impôs certas condições, que devem ser aceitas por Pequim. O diario acrescenta que Cheng continua, até agora, comandando suas forças.

Condições

Ao que se afirma, as condições que Cheng apresentou a Pequim e ao seu substituto, o general Seng Ze-wu, são as seguintes: 1) o general Seng pode trazer seus oficiais e um comissario politico, mas não tropas do Norte; 2) o general Seng deve fazer seu quartel-general em Hanyang, do outro lado do rio Wuchafe, onde tem seu quartel o general Cheng; e 3) antes de entregar o controle de suas forças, o general Cheng deseja saber que sucederá com o acordo celebrado entre ele e Chu En-lai, depois que o general pôs em liberdade dois reféns de Pequim, que havia detido.

Afirma-se que esse acordo incluía em seu preambulo as considerações de que Mao fôra conduzido a uma posição decorativa no regime, que Liu Shao-chi tinha renunciado e que fôra convocado o Congresso do Povo, para planejar o futuro do país.

O Exército em Cantão

HONGCONG, 15 (AFP) — O jornal "Sing Tao Yat-pao" afirma hoje que o XLI Corpo do Exercito chinês entrou em Cantão, para apoiar os partidarios de Mao contra os antimaoistas. Enquanto isso, prosseguem na cidade choques entre "guardas vermelhos" rivais, e há divisão entre as tropas comunistas e a policia.

Ver na 2.a página outras noticias da China.

Documento 'vietcong' em poder dos EUA

WASHINGTON, 15 (AP e AFP) — Um documento norte-vietnamita, atualmente em poder dos norte-americanos, revela que os Estados Unidos e a União Soviética tentaram formar, em 1966, no Vietnã do Sul, um governo de coligação integrado, em parte, por elementos comunistas.

Esta noticia figura num relatorio dirigido no dia 10 de abril de 1966 pelo secretario-geral do Partido dos Trabalhadores Norte-Vietnamitas (o PC), Le Duan, á Comissão Central do Partido Comunista Sul-Vietnamita.

Sob o titulo de "Negociações", Duan fala de um compromisso que os EUA teriam de propor á URSS. A França designaria o primeiro-ministro do gabinete de coligação. Um vice-primeiro-ministro seria nomeado por Washington e o outro seria um tal "senhor Tho", que poderia ser Nguyen Tho, principal dirigente "vietcong". Ao mesmo tempo, Anton Chelepin, então chefe dos Serviços de Segurança sovieticos, exortava Hanói a negociar.

Desmentido

Um porta-voz do Departamento de Estado declarou que sabia da existencia do documento em questão, mas desmentiu que os Estados Unidos tenham alguma vez tentado formar um governo de coligação no Vietnã do Sul com o apoio da União Sovietica. Acrescentou que o referido documento é um livreto que caiu em mãos dos norte-americanos durante o desenvolvimento da operação "Cedar Falls", no ano passado. Estava em poder de um oficial "vietcong" de graduação elevada ou intermediaria.

Interpelado pelos jornalistas, o porta-voz afirmou categoricamente: "Não temos e nunca tivemos a intenção de nos dirigir á União Sovietica, com o objetivo de estabelecer tal governo".

Posição de Saigon

Disse o porta-voz que os sul-vietnamitas não acreditam que um governo de coligação seja uma solução viavel. Como se recorda, o governo de Saigon considera o Vietcong um instrumento do Vietnã do Norte em sua agressão ao sul do Paralelo 17 e, por essa razão, recusa-se a qualquer dialogo a não ser diretamente com os dirigentes de Hanói.

Saigon faria uma ofensiva de paz

SAIGON, 15 (AP, AFP, UPI, ANSA e "Reuters") — Em circulos bem informados, comenta-se que a intensificação dos bombardeios ao Vietnã do Norte constitui a primeira parte de um plano conjunto para preparar a ofensiva de paz que deverá ser lançada pelo governo de Saigon que fôr eleito no proximo dia 3 de setembro.

Segundo se sabe de boa fonte, o plano foi decidido em julho ultimo pela Casa Branca. Após esta fase "dura", a ofensiva de paz em direção a Hanói será lançada espetacularmente por Saigon, "no momento propicio".

Ação secreta dos EUA

Tal ofensiva de paz de Saigon será acompanhada paralelamente por uma ação norte-americana, secreta, junto aos dirigentes da "Frente Nacional de Libertação". Essa ação secreta parece já estar em curso, segundo certos indicios.

Ver na 2.a página outras noticias do Vietnã.

B. Aires fará avião militar

BUENOS AIRES, 15 (AFP) — O jornal "Clarin" anunciou, em sua edição de hoje, que a fábrica militar de aviões da Argentina está projetando a construção de aviões a jato de treinamento avançado com patente francesa.

Segundo o jornal, "a Argentina, do mesmo modo que os demais paises latino-americanos, encara a possibilidade de produzir os equipamentos necessarios para suas Forças Armadas, pelo menos parcialmente, devido à recusa dos Estados Unidos em fornecer estes materiais".

Regis Debray fala à imprensa

CAMIRI, Bolivia, 15 (AFP e UPI) — O universitario francês Regis Debray, acusado de cumplicidade com os guerrilheiros castro-comunistas bolivianos, concedeu hoje uma entrevista coletiva à imprensa, no Cassino Militar de Camiri, onde se encontra detido. Ao contrario do uniforme de presidiario que lhe foi imposto no sabado e no domingo, Debray apresentou-se aos jornalistas trajando uma camisa de jersey azul, calças de côr clara, um sueter cinza e os cabelos cortados com maquina zero. A entrevista foi organizada pelo promotor do Conselho de Guerra, coronel Remberto Iriarte, que esclareceu aos jornalistas ser esta a ultima entrevista de Debray à imprensa, antes do seu julgamento a ser realizado, ao que parece, no fim deste mês, por um tribunal militar.

Debray negou, inicialmente, que tenha sido "instrutor" dos guerrilheiros bolivianos e lembrou que em 1963, viveu junto com os guerrilheiros venezuelanos, com os quais realizou um filme que foi apresentado na televisão francesa. Acrescentou que, por esse motivo, depois de permanecer varias semanas com os guerrilheiros bolivianos, apresentou-se voluntariamente em Muyumpampa, com todos os documentos em ordem.

Mais adiante, Debray declarou: "Fui torturado nos dois primeiros dias de minha prisão e fiquei inconsciente durante 48 horas na cadeia de Choreti". Acrescentou que os maus tratos que lhe foram infligidos quando foi preso, só foram suspensos com a intervenção de um chefe militar e que depois disso foi submetido a torturas morais.

Após reconhecer ser marxista e reiterar a sua admiração por Fidel Castro e Ernesto "Che" Guevara, Debray declarou que penetrou na zona de guerrilhas com o objetivo de encontrar e entrevistar "Che" Guevara, com o qual manteve contato aproximadamente quatro semanas. Reafirmou ter visto Guevara entre os guerrilheiros que operam no sudeste da Bolivia, em fins do ultimo mês de março, mas duvida que o ex-ministro cubano ainda esteja em territorio boliviano.

Logo em seguida, Debray reiterou que não participou jamais de atividades belicas e que não forneceu qualquer instrução tecnica aos rebeldes.

Ao concluir as suas declarações, Debray afirmou que entrou no país usando seu nome verdadeiro, mas que não disse às autoridades que a sua real missão era estabelecer contato com Guevara, porque isso o transformaria "em um agente da policia".

"Andres" e "Tania"

Prosseguindo em suas declarações, Debray afirmou ter conhecido um boliviano chamado "Andres", logo após ter chegado ao territorio da Bolivia. Este boliviano encarregou-se de apresentá-lo à misteriosa "Tania" que, por sua vez, levou-o até o local onde se desenvolvem as atividades de guerrilha.

De acordo com o pensamento das autoridades militares bolivianas, "Tania" é o pseudonimo da argentina Laura Gutierrez, que está ligada ao grupo guerrilheiro que recentemente entrou em choque com as forças governamentais.

Ver na página 7 o noticiário da América Latina.

Do enviado especial

D. Macedo levanta a imagem de N. S.ª Aparecida

Do enviado especial

A massa popular aguarda, diante do Santuário

North and South American dailies in the study came close to providing the foreign coverage of these two papers. Singling out *O Estado* for special praise for its international coverage have been the United Nations, the International Press Institute, and several American and European universities. *O Estado* has twelve foreign correspondents stationed in Washington, New York, Rome, Paris, Lisbon, Madrid, London, and Buenos Aires.[8]

This impressive Brazilian daily, a supporter of liberal democracy, was founded in 1875 by a group of seventeen men. Its slogan was "Representation and Justice."[9] For a time called *A Provincia de São Paulo* until its province became a state,[10] it was a good, but undistinguished, newspaper until it was bought by Julio de Mesquita. Since coming into the hands of the Mesquita family, the paper has constantly improved its coverage and has always played a strong part in affecting the political climate of the country. Editor Julio de Mesquita was succeeded in 1927 by his son, Julio, Jr., who was to become proprietor. Although aided well by his brother and six of their children, it is Swiss-educated Julio, Jr. who has given *O Estado* its special brand of excellence.[11] How highly he is regarded by fellow newspapermen of the Americas may be seen in the fact that he was elected president of the Inter-American Press Association at its 1966 meeting in Lima, Peru, succeeding Jack Howard of the United States' Scripps-Howard Newspapers.[12]

Although the paper considers itself "liberal," most outsiders usually refer to it as "conservative." Perhaps this is because in recent years it has fought so persistently against leftist tendencies in the country and against Communist attempts to infiltrate the government. Also, almost alone among the big Brazilian newspapers, it is a firm supporter of the United States in practically every aspect of its policy. *O Estado* also evidences a warm spot in its editorial heart for honesty, good manners, and European culture. It is also extremely "fat" with advertising and "dresses" extremely conservatively. In addition, it fights against permissiveness and relativistic ethics in both personal and government affairs. If this makes the paper conservative, then it is certainly that. *O Estado*'s critics in Brazil, and there are many, accuse the Mesquitas of having little concern for the masses, of being for the big businessman, and of generally defending the *status quo*.[13]

Julio de Mesquita, Jr. keeps a firm hand on the direction of the paper. As the director, he is mainly responsible for its total operation. His editor-in-chief is the highly professional and courageous Marcelino Ritter, undoubtedly one of the most versatile and most intelligent journalists in all of Latin America. *O Estado* is published in an ultramodern, 22-story building in the heart of São Paulo, Brazil's sprawling commercial city. Although most of the copies are distributed within São Paulo State, the paper has had a "national edition" since 1964 which is sold mainly in Rio and the capital city of Brasília.

Estado editors consider the *Jornal do Brasil* of Rio the second best daily of the country, with their own paper, of course, being the best. They feel also that O *Estado* greatly affects public opinion and gives the world a valid insight into the country's informed thinking.[14] Few persons, even its harshest critics, would take serious exception to that statement.

9

Profiles:

Asia, Africa, Australia

Although this chapter covers a tremendous segment of the world, it encompasses a very small number of elite papers. This small number is represented on the following pages by only six dailies. Two of them are Australian: *The Age* of Melbourne and *The Sydney Morning Herald.* (Others from Australia which might have been included are the *West Australian* of Perth and the excellent evening daily of Melbourne, *The Herald.*) India's *Hindu* of Madras, perhaps the most serious and lucid of the country, is another of the six. (*The Statesman* or the *Times of India*, two other excellent English-language dailies, would typify the elite press of India equally as well.)

Also included among the six is Cairo's *Al Ahram*, with little real editorial freedom but with considerable prestige in Egypt and the Arab world. Red China is represented by Peking's *Jen-min Jih-pao* (People's Daily), the rough equivalent of the Soviet Union's *Pravda* and *Izvestia* wrapped in one package. The Republic of South Africa, which has several excellent papers in English and Afrikaans, is represented by *Die Burger* of Cape Town, without a doubt the best of the Afrikaans papers. (The *Rand Daily Mail*, the most courageous and enterprising of the English-language papers, might have been included as the best example of the government-opposition press.)

These half-dozen dailies, then, represent Asia, Africa, and Australia. (A more lengthy profile in Part II discusses another excellent daily from Asia—Japan's *Asahi Shimbun.*) Students of the world's press might nominate a few additional papers from these regions for inclusion in this chapter, but it is highly doubtful that more than six others would make the grade. Certainly such dailies as the *Manila Times* of the Philippines, *Mainichi* of Japan, *Ta-kung Pao* of Red China, *Central Daily News* of Taiwan (Republic of China), or the *Cape Times* of South Africa are all important papers in their own ways and might have been chosen as representatives.

Explanations abound for the paucity of elite dailies in Asia and Africa: a multitude of languages and dialects, low literacy rates, scattered populations, underdeveloped economies, and unstable political systems. In spite of the fact that Australia has a generally healthy press system, its geographical isolation and small pool of well-educated or intellectual readers severely hinders the development of an elite press there.

The six profiles which are presented in alphabetical order on the following pages serve, not to indicate a judgment of the "best" of the elite papers of these areas, but to illustrate briefly the nature of some of the outstanding papers.

The Age
(AUSTRALIA)

Like all newspapers in this spacious and sparsely populated country, *The Age* is regionally based and its national news reflects its emphasis on its home city (Melbourne) and the state of Victoria. Although it does not strive for immediate national circulation (only the *Australian*,[1] begun in 1964, does), it is read in all the important places. Without a doubt it provides the best all-around news coverage in the country,[2] and although its reference to itself as "one of the world's top seven newspapers" is perhaps little more than a promotion gimmick,[3] its general quality is such that it commands a very respectable place among the world's elite newspapers. In Australia, *The Age* has several worthy competitors, notably *The Sydney Morning Herald* (the last profile in this chapter), the *West Australian* of Perth, and the *Herald* of Melbourne.

The Age, which today has a staff of some 1,000 working in offices of the modern 11-story building on Melbourne's Collins Street, has come a long way from the days when it was established as an eight-page, independent, liberal sheet in 1854. But in many ways, for example, a high respect for accuracy, a seeking after the truth, a liberal orientation in politics, and a serious tone, the paper remains little changed.

It has only grown. Today's editor, Keith Sinclair, has full editorial responsibility. He is permitted by the paper's board of directors to set and carry out policy within the confines of the paper's traditional tendency—which has been liberal, at times almost radical, since its founding in 1854 by two brothers, John and Henry Cooke.

The paper was bought for £2,000 from the Cookes by Ebenezer Syme in 1856. Later the same year his brother David became a partner.[4] Until 1908, the story of *The Age* was largely the story of David Syme; it was he who placed the mark of his ebullient, fearless, liberal personality most heavily on the paper. Under his leadership *The Age*'s circulation grew from a paltry 2,000 in 1860 to 38,000 in 1879, when the paper moved to new quarters in Collins Street. The Syme family has controlled *The Age* since 1856. When David died at the age of 80 in 1908, he left the paper in trust to his five sons. Today 60 per cent of the company, David Syme, Ltd. (a private company formed in 1948) is owned by the trust.[5]

Although *The Age* is largely an Australian newspaper, its overseas copies are read in academic and governmental circles as the most valuable press source for information on the country and its thinking. Its circulation is right at 190,000, all but about 15,000 in the state of Victoria. It is widely read and quoted in the government circles of Australia. It was Prime Minister Robert Menzies' favorite paper, and this in spite of the paper's frequent attacks on his conservatism. *The Age* was the first paper to publish verbatim stories of a prime minister's press conferences, and has helped break down the superciliousness with which the government traditionally treats the press in general.[6]

The Age considers itself politically liberal, but conservative in social attitudes. Its readers are in the top 25 per cent of the community in education and income, and its editors firmly believe that it influences public opinion in Australia "because it is the best-read newspaper among opinion leaders, according to independent surveys."[7] The only daily of the country which its editors feel is in the same class with it is *The Sydney Morning Herald.* Some authorities would probably name another paper, *The Herald* of Melbourne, which, in spite of its being an evening journal, maintains a very high overall quality.[8]

Although *The Age* probably covers the whole range of news as comprehensively as any other paper, its editors believe that it does its best job with politics and economics.[9] Professor Henry Mayer of Melbourne University tends to agree, saying that the person who wants the best "over-all news-content" would read *The Age*.[10] Staff members who write and edit total more than 120, with four of them being full-time foreign correspondents stationed in bureaus in London, Washington, Singapore, and Tokyo. In addition, *The Age* has access to correspondents from London's *Observer* and *Sunday Times*, and also to staff "stringers" in selected locations.[11]

The sound economic position of *The Age* permits it to concentrate on

THE AGE

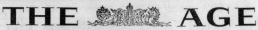

113th year of publication 24 Pages Melbourne Thursday September 7 1967 4c (Air 5c) 63 0341 (Classified 63 0301)

Australia cuts appeals to Privy Council

• Mr. Bowen

From ALAN BARNES

CANBERRA. — Australia yesterday took an historic step away from dependence on Britain when the Federal Government decided to abolish Federal appeals from the High Court of Australia to the Privy Council in London.

Most States are expected to follow suit and end once and for all the superiority of English Pirvy Councillors over the Australian judiciary.

Announcing the Federal Government's decision, the Attorney-General (Mr. Bowen) told Parliament: "This, the Government believes, is consistent with the growth of Australia as an independent nation.

"It is the logical first step towards making the High Court the final court of appeal for Australia."

The Government had sent warning of its decision to the British Government and all of the Australian State Governments, he said.

Mr. Bowen explained that the Federal Government's decision was only a first step, affecting only Federal law and relating mostly to constitutional matters.

He said that 44 such appeals had gone to the Privy Council in the past 21 years.

Appeal to the Privy Council on interstate matters — that is matters concerning the line of demarcation between Federal and State powers — would still be possibie.

But, he pointed out, such appeals only reached the Privy Council with the consent of the High Court, and the High Court had not given such permission since 1912.

High Court end

Thus, in effect, legal authorities explained, all Federal litigation now would end at the High Court.

However, over the past 20 years or so about 25 cases of appeal have gone direct from State Supreme Courts — mainly in New South Wales — to the Privy Council, and about another 20 cases in State jurisdiction have gone through the High Court to the Privy Council.

State legislation will be necessary to abolish this line of appeal to London.

Mr. Bowen said the Government had taken heed of the growing body of opinion in both the legal profession and among the public generally, that the stage had been reached where the High Court should start becoming the final court of appeal for Australia.

"It has been recognised for many years that each member of the Commonwealth is free to decide whether it wishes to discontinue appeals to the Privy Council," he said.

"Several Commonwealth countries, including Canada, India and Pakistan, have abolished the appeal altogether.

"The High Court of Australia enjoys a status equal to that of any other court in the English-speaking world."

Appreciated

Mr. Bowen said the Government appreciated the "learning and wisdom" which members of the judicial committee of the Privy Council had brought to appeals from the High Court since Federation.

"Many notable contributions to the working of our Federal Constitution have been made by their judgments," he said.

"I believe their Lordships' dignified, yet penetrating approach to cases has had a considerable influence on our own approach to appellate work in Australia," Mr Bowen said.

The Leader of the Opposition (Mr. Whitlam) said the public would welcome the decision to dispense with appeals to the Privy Council.

The retention of the appeals was inconsistent with Australia's status as an independent nation.

A survey taken in 1965 had shown that in 10 years the percentage of people favoring the High Court being the final court of appeal in Australia had risen from 65 to 81 per cent.

Those favoring retention of the Privy Council system had fallen from 22 to 10 per cent.

Prince writes to varsity NLF group

Cambodian Chief-of-State Prince Norodom Sihanouk, has sent a hand-delivered letter to the Melbourne University Labor Club advising it of a way to contact the National Liberation Front of South Vietnam.

• *Prince Sihanouk and (below) his letter-head*

The letter, written in French and bearing the seal of the State of Cambodia, was hand delivered to the club's letterbox in the Melbourne University Union.

Prince Sihanouk's letter was in reply to a request from a Labor Club on August 1 for the address of the diplomatic representative of the National Liberation Front in the Cambodian capital, Phnom Penh.

The letter reads: "Sirs, I have just noted your letter of the first of August and accede wholeheartedly to your request to enter into contact with our friends of the National Liberation Front of South Vietnam. Also I have sent to them that letter expressing your support in their just struggle against the American invaders."

The letter continues: "You could, henceforth, put yourselves in direct contact with the permanent representative of the National Liberation Front of South Vietnam in Cambodia at the following address: [illegible] Pan 52 Phnom-Penh."

Prince Sihanouk concludes: "I ask you to accept assurance of my keen sympathy."

The letter, dated August 26, was delivered via the Cambodian Embassy. With it was a note reading "With the compliments of the Royal Embassy of Cambodia, Canberra, A.C.T."

Bill's aim

A bill now before Parliament is aimed at preventing aid to the National Liberation Front, the Communist Party of North Vietnam or the Government of North Vietnam.

It follows moves by students at Melbourne and Monash universities to collect aid for the NLF.

Penalties under the new legislation provide for fines up to $2000 or two years gaol or both.

Despite a decree by the university administration, students at Monash University on Tuesday took up a collection for the NLF.

The students have been reported to the Vice-Chancellor (Dr J. A. L. Matheson), but as yet no action has been taken against them.

In the Senate yesterday, Senator Sim (Lib., WA) said the Government was acting against NLF aid because of [illegible] of the activities of "a few stupid students."

Senator McManus (DLP, Vic.) said those behind aid to the NLF were mature, politically sophisticated people.

The Adelaide University Labor Club tonight will consider a move to set up a committee to collect funds for the victims of U.S. bombing in both South and North Vietnam.

A similar meeting, held to discuss the issue a few weeks ago, ended when it was learnt the meeting was unconstitutional under the club's rules.

Two sorts to act on NLF aid students.—P. 16.

5 men charged on rock spree

Five men have received summonses over the five-month rock-throwing spree in Jennifer Street, Noble Park, earlier this year.

The men are all residents of Jennifer Street — the street where the barrage of stones was concentrated.

Two other men, not living in the area, will also be served with summonses.

They are charged on counts of throwing stones to the danger of persons and with discharging firearms in a populated area.

Jennifer Street residents formed themselves into a vigilante squad after rocks came hurtling down on their houses, breaking windows, near the end of March.

Night after night they were kept from sleeping by the barrage of rocks.

They slept with firearms at their bedsides, and often went out in parties at night in an effort to apprehend the "phantom."

Police patrolled Jennifer Street and the parallel Holtan Road for weeks on end —still the barrage did not stop.

Then midway through July the rock throwing stopped.

America's Cup, 1851-1967

Dame Pattie, in the final week of her preparation for the America's Cup challenge, is about to overtake America — a replica of the schooner which in 1851 defeated 14 British craft to start the Cup competition.

BELOW: Jock Sturrock, skipper of Dame Pattie, checks the yacht's rigging in Newport harbor.

Support grows for challenger

From MURRAY DAVIS

NEWPORT (Rhode Island), Sept. 6.

Many Americans here are now openly barracking for Dame Pattie to win the America's Cup, which starts next Tuesday.

They are "mad" with the cold reception they got when seeking a look at the defender, Intrepid.

While Dame Pattie's hull has been described as "ice blue," her crew are friendly and always ready to exchange a word with bystanders. Jock Sturrock does not discourage them.

The Labor Day holiday weekend found the challenger's jetty at Williams and Manchester jammed. It was in sharp contrast to the Intrepid's jetty, where a high wire fence and gatekeeper prevented unofficial callers.

The management of Intrepid's Newport shipyard last week posted a sign which showed "Intrepid" in big lettering, with "Newport Shipyard" beneath.

It had been up less than an hour when Intrepid's managers had it knocked down with the comment: "We don't want any more people around. It looks like advertising."

There seems to be much more humor in the relaxed Dame Pattie camp.

However, the atmosphere between the challengers and the defenders is decidedly chilly.

Mosbacher is reported to have received an apology from the Australian Consul - General (Sir Reginald Sholl).

No Dame Pattie spokesman was available for comment tonight, but the friction is believed to stem from the repeat flotation last issue.

This occurred on Friday when the Australian's made it clear they were not satisfied with the manner in which Intrepid was presented for her first measurement.

The America's Cup committee ordered a second measurement of both boats — insisting on the inclusion of certain winches and equipment on Intrepid.

The result — Intrepid was ordered to remove 104 lb. of lead from her ballast, while Dame Pattie was able to add just under 500 lb. to hers. Both boats lost 24 hours in the remeasure.

Labor drops ban on PMG rises

CANBERRA.—A protracted fight between factions of the Federal Parliamentary Labor Party ended yesterday when the party decided not to continue its opposition to the Government's increased postal and telephone charges.

The bill to increase charges later passed all stages in the House of Representatives, and will now go to the Senate.

The decision by the Labor caucus removed the possibility that the Government would use rejection of the charges as grounds for a double dissolution of Parliament and a snap general election.

Labor's decision — carried by 38 votes to 33 — was a victory of the party's parliamentary leader (Mr. Whitlam) who did not want to give the Government grounds for an election at this stage.

With the support of DLP and independent senators Labor originally had rejected the charges when they were first introduced in the Senate last May, and again when the Government tried to introduce some of the rises by way of regulation in June.

However, Mr. Whitlam urged that Labor should drop its opposition once the charges were reintroduced last month as part of the Budget and the Government was forced to justify the Post Office's need for the extra $44 million a year which the increases will raise.

Mr. Whitlam warned that the Government could use rejection of the charges in the Budget as grounds for seeking a double dissolution of Parliament and a general election.

Labor was not ready for a general election at this stage, Mr. Whitlam said.

This view was endorsed by the Labor caucus a month ago.

But subsequently the party's Federal president (Senator Keeffe) gave notice that he would move for the party's senators to "defer" the increases until control of the Post Office was removed from the Public Service and placed under an independent corporation.

Senator Keeffe and a solid block of caucus supporters argued that Labor should maintain a consistent attitude of opposing the charges, even as part of the Budget.

They argued that the Government was most unlikely to force an election on the issue, and even if it did, Labor was likely to win back some of the seats it lost at the polls last November.

"We have to fight the Government every inch of the way, trench by trench," Senator Keeffe told the caucus yesterday.

Additional pressure was brought to bear on the Labor parliamentarians by the recommendation from the ACTU that the charges should be opposed.

Later in the day, when the legislation to enforce the rises was introduced in the House of Representatives, Labor did not oppose it.

Taxation

The Opposition spokesman on PMG matters (Mr. Webb, Lab., WA) told the House the Labor Party did not object to the increased charges because they were now part of the Budget.

Mr. Webb said the Opposition had opposed the increased charges last May because it felt the Government was introducing taxation methods in the wrong way.

He repeated the Opposition's policy of pressing for the Post Office to be controlled by a corporation divorced from the Public Service Board and from Treasury control.

The increased charges are the same as those proposed when the Government first tried to get them approved by Parliament last May.

Crowd cheers as 2 shot

TOKYO, Sept. 6.

Two "counter-revolutionary" sympathisers of President Liu Shao-chi have been publicly executed before applauding thousands, according to Shanghai Radio.

The dead men — two of eight tried before more than 10,000 people in the big port city — were Shan Sun-lin, described as a "counter-revolutionary" and Liu Yung-ching, a "counter-revolutionary killer."

The radio said both were put to death on August 28. It did not say what had happened to the others.

It was the first officially circulated report of an execution of anti-Maoists since the start of the great proletarian cultural revolution in June 1966.

The two men were shot and "at the time thunderous applause was heard at the rally," the broadcast said.

Shan was described as a warden for the Shanghai prison during the pre-1949 days of nationalist rule.

The chief accusation against him was that since 1965 he "spread many [illegible] revolutionary handbills, wrote many anonymous letters, and carried out fanatic counter-revolutionary sabotage activities."

Hoodlum

Liu Yung-ching's crimes were more serious, the radio said. A hoodlum before the communists came, he "continued to revile and beat the masses" and apparently had borne a grudge against those who turned him in.

On August 15, he killed or wounded in revenge six persons who had exposed his crimes.

A Hong Kong newspaper reported today that the Chinese army was executing refugees caught trying to make their way from China's strife-torn southern province of Kwangtung to Hong Kong. — AAP.

Shark kills again

RABAUL.—A killer shark credited with snatching five victims off the coast of New Ireland struck again yesterday.

This time it killed a villager spearfishing in 12 ft. of water only 10 yards from the shore at Lambom Island, on the southern tip of New Ireland.

The fisherman, known only as Parang, managed to drag himself into a canoe moored nearby but died from loss of blood before he could be reached.

The attack was only a short distance from the spot where two schoolgirls were killed on successive days last year.

Villagers who saw the attack said they believed the same shark could be responsible for all the attacks.

The shark, known as "Big Fellow" and described as being between 10 and 20 ft. long and the diameter of a 44-gallon drum reportedly killed five children between August and November last year before disappearing from the New Ireland area.—AAP.

BARASSI the underdog

— BACK PAGE

TV-radio guide

WEATHER

CITY: Fine, mild, south-east winds. Expected top temp. 65 (yesterday 64).

Details — 14

STOP PRESS

De Gaulle arrives in Poland

[illegible] — AAP-Reuter.

quality in its journalism, and this is what it does. Here is the way Graham Perkin, the paper's assistant editor, put it in late 1966:

> *The Age* aspires to be a serious, "quality" newspaper. Because it has a secure advertising position—notably in "small" ads (it publishes the fourth highest volume of classified "small" ads in the world)—it can afford to be intent on quality rather than on popular appeal. It is absolutely independent in political outlook, in social philosophy. Major spending in recent years has been concentrated on foreign news coverage, on staff, on plant modernization and sophisticated communications facilities.[12]

Although *The Age*'s circulation is really quite broadly based, it is determined to keep its dignity. In its attempt not to vulgarize itself, it sets a tone which is more serious than that of any other Australian newspaper. It does attempt, however, to entertain and carries good comic strips and considerable social gossip. But while it does this, it tries to keep from offending the family reader. Its classified advertising (mentioned by Perkin above) is without an equal in the country; most of it appears in the large Saturday edition, which usually runs from seventy to eighty pages, or in its Wednesday edition which is almost as large.

The Age carries excellent editorials, and its feature articles and cultural pieces are probably without equal in Australia.[13] In addition, its special financial pages would be the envy of any daily in the world of similar size. *The Age* prefers to keep its news "straight," detached from the reporter's judgment and interpretation. International news and views are considered important by this paper which was the first in Australia to place a correspondent in Southeast Asia (1959) and to station one in Washington (1954).[14]

Although only about 25 per cent of the editorial staff are university graduates,[15] all must have attained university entrance level as a prerequisite to employment. Also, it is important to note that *The Age* trains every reporter very carefully. In the reporter's first year with the paper, the Cadet (as he is called) takes special courses in shorthand with reasonable proficiency expected. He is also enrolled at the University of Melbourne for the three-year, part-time course for the Diploma of Journalism. The Cadetship lasts four years, with salary raises each year plus other increases depending on the importance of reporting assignments. At the end of the four years, *The Age* reporter is considered a trained journalist, with shorthand skill, a university diploma, and practical training.[16]

What is the general nature of the newspaper produced by these reporters and other staff members? A typical issue is made up as follows: page 1 carries a good sampling of all the top news in a dignified and pleasing manner; page 2 is a forum with editorials, features, a news-of-the-day column and a letters-to-the-editor section, expressing mainly liberal viewpoints; page 3 begins a series of news pages (foreign news mainly on page 4) which goes through the financial section which often takes four pages; next come the women's pages, followed by the so-called "service" features—shipping, weather, and postal news. The daily magazine leads the paper's second section, followed by a wide selection of interpretive articles and features catering to all the family, classified advertising, and a comprehensive sports section.

In its large Saturday edition, *The Age* publishes a Literary Review which is considered by many to be one of the best of its type in the world. On Thursday is a 12-page TV-radio guide lift-out, and on Tuesdays and Fridays a bonus is presented in the form of a special children's supplement called "Junior Age." All of this is presented neatly on pages which are ten columns wide and measures 17½ x 23½ inches.[17]

A copy of *The Age* is a serious and comprehensive package. Its heavy general tone, however, is offset considerably by a lively makeup and the use of modern Bodoni type throughout. *The Age* manages to be at once a general family paper, a serious intellectual journal, and a sprightly political organ which "for more than half a century has frightened the life out of most politicians."[18]

Al Ahram
(EGYPT)

Al Ahram (The Pyramids) is a very important daily in Egypt and the Middle East generally because it is the closest of all the country's papers to the Government and virtually speaks for President Gamal Abdul Nasser. Editor of the Cairo daily is Muhammad Hassanein Haikal who is deeply, and almost alone among his fellow journalists, at the heart of events in Egypt. Considered generally to be an outstanding journalist, he is a long-time friend and confidant of Nasser since the period of intrigue and conspiracy prior to the 1952 coup which ousted King Farouk.[1] Many believe him to be closer to Nasser today than most of the Cabinet, a circumstance which imbues his paper with a prestige not found in the other journals of the country.

But even beyond the editor's personal contact with Nasser, *Al Ahram* would have a rightful claim to Egyptian press leadership, or perhaps on the press leadership of the entire Arab world. Without a doubt, its range of news coverage and discussion is outstanding, as is its production quality.

News coverage and discussion, of course, is much better in some areas than in others. For, like newspapers in other authoritarian countries, *Al Ahram* does not criticize the regime; nor does any other Egyptian paper for there has been little press freedom in the country since about 1958. Even by 1952 the Egyptian press had become a pale and nervous ghost of what it was in its colorful youth. Progressively *Al Ahram* and the rest of the country's papers have become propaganda instruments for the regime, manifesting from time to time some independent spirit, but falling ever more deeply into the web of governmental bribery and censorship.

Nasser recognizes the power of the press as an instrument for national progress and has actually encouraged or promoted literacy and press expansion. He is, in effect, trying "to remake the very character of his people."[2]

Controlling the communications media is important to Nasser, and he went about it seriously in 1960 when a law was passed reorganizing the press so as to make "the people" owners. *Al Ahram*, under this new nationalization of the press, found itself lumped with the Dar al Hilal publishing house (the country's biggest producer of periodicals) and Muhammad Haikal became a member of its council.[3] So today *Al Ahram* is essentially an arm of the Government, and together with the other journals of the country, is contributing to Nasser's controlled progressivism, which one writer has referred to as "justified as being the only alternative to chaos or Communism."[4] At any rate, as Nasser has assigned the Egyptian press the duty of serving as an instrument for national development so that the country can survive as an independent and modern nation, the press has accepted the assignment, willingly or unwillingly.

Al Ahram, which has sometimes been called by Americans "*The New York Times* of the Arab World,"[5] was founded in 1876 by two Christians, the brothers Salim and Bishara Taqla, who had left Lebanon to seek more freedom in Egypt. In Alexandria they began—but soon moved to Cairo—a small four-page paper which they named *Al Ahram.* They were followed by other Christian families from Syria, like the Sarrufs and the Nimrs, who were to make their imprint on Egyptian journalism. *Al Ahram* very early became the outstanding example of independent journalism and a purveyor of objective news reports instead of the common political harangues. It was followed, toward the end of the nineteenth century, by a great diversity of journals in many languages representing every conceivable point of view. Under British occupation, Egypt had the most intellectual, and certainly the most stimulating and lively, press in the Arab world.[6]

Pioneering among Egyptian newspapers in the building up of international news, *Al Ahram* very early stationed its own correspondents abroad. It also was among the first papers to emphasize local and national news of a nonpolitical nature. It still evidences many good journalistic characteristics: an excellent variety of news and features,

ملحق الجمعة

دار "الأهرام"

١٥ مليما

الإعلانات في القاهرة: دار الأهرام، ١٤ شارع مظلوم باشا — في الاسكندرية: دار الأهرام، ١٠ طريق الحرية

الاشتراكات: خمسة جنيهات مصرية لسنة كاملة، ٢٥٠ قرشا لستة أشهر، ١٢٥ قرشا لثلاثة أشهر، وتضاف مصاريف البريد بالنسبة للاشتراكات الخارجية

الأهرام

مؤسسا الأهرام سنة ١٨٧٥ : سليم وبشارة تقلا
جبرائيل بشارة تقلا (١٩١٢ - ١٩٤٣)
رئيس التحرير
محمد حسنين هيكل
السنة — ٩٢ — العدد ٢٩٢٩٢

١٦ صفحة

الجمعة
٢ يونية (حزيران) ١٩٦٧
2 JUINE 1967
Al-Ahram

أى دولة تحاول اقتحام خليج العقبة سوف تمنع من استخدام قناة السويس

دراسة هامة تجرى الآن ضمن خطة عامة لمواجهة تطورات الموقف المحتملة ومحاولات الضغط والاستفزاز

اذا حاولت أى دولة أن تقتحم خليج العقبة بالقوة فهى تقوم بعمل عدوانى ضد مصر ويحق لمصر بمقتضى معاهدة القسطنطينية ١٨٨٨ منعها من استعمال قناة السويس

أمر الى الطائرات المصرية المزودة بالصواريخ الموجهة أن تقوم بمتابعة تحركات حاملة الطائرات البريطانية "هيرمس" التى تعمل الآن فى البحر الأحمر

القاهرة تطلب أن يقوم كل رؤساء الدول الإسلامية بمناشدة شاه إيران أن يمنع شحن البترول الإيرانى الى اسرائيل وأن يصدر إعلانا بذلك

زكريا محيى الدين يطير صباح اليوم الى الجزائر لاجتماع هام مع الرئيس بومدين ويعود مساء اليوم

علم المحرر السياسى للاهرام أنه يجرى الان بحث موقف الدول التى قد تحاول بقطعها البحرية أن تقتحم خليج العقبة بالقوة لفتحه عنوة أمام الملاحة الاسرائيلية .

والراى المطروح للبحث هو انه يتحتم اعتبار مثل هذه المحاولة من جانب اية دولة تقدم عليها عملا عدوانيا عسكريا ضد مصر وشعبها وسيادتها الاقليمية ، الامر الذى يترتب عليه بناء على اتفاقية القسطنطينية سنة ١٨٨٨ منع سفنها من استعمال قناة السويس .

وعلم المحرر السياسى للاهرام ان الموضوع يجرى بحثه الان ضمن خطة يجرى الان وضعها لمواجهة تطورات الموقف ومحاولات الضغط والاستفزازات التى توجه الى الجمهورية العربية المتحدة بواسطة الولايات المتحدة الامريكية وبريطانيا .

طائراتنا المزودة بالصواريخ الموجهة تتابع حاملة الطائرات البريطانية هيرمس

طلب الى كل الدول الاسلامية بأن يقوم رؤساؤها بمناشدة شاه ايران وقف شحن البترول الايرانى الى اسرائيل

زكريا محيى الدين يسافر الى الجزائر اليوم

اطلاق النار على هليكوبتر اسرائيلية اخترقت مجال الاردن الجوى

تبليغ عراقى الى بريطانيا حول مستقبل تدفق البترول العربى

الافراج عن جميع المعتقلين السياسيين فى العراق

الملك فيصل يصل الى جنيف ويزور باريس غدا لمقابلة ديجول

خطاب لحسين فى جيش الاردن — الملك يزور المواقع الامامية

حكومة الاردن ومنظمة فلسطين تبدأ محادثات التنسيق بينهما

الاردن يستدعى سفيره فى المانيا الغربية

زوارق الطوربيد المصرية تابعت حاملة الطائرات الأمريكية الى أن خرجت من القناة

وزارة الدفاع الأمريكية تعلن أن الحاملة "انتربيد" ستواصل رحلتها للشرق الأقصى

٤ مدمرات سوفيتية تدخل البحر الابيض خلال ساعات

اجتماع مشترك لـ ٣ لجان فى مجلس الشيوخ الامريكى يحضره همفرى وراسك ومكنمارا لبحث الازمة

فرنسا تتمسك بحيادها فى الازمة والملاحة فى تيران

اسرائيل تعيد توزيع قواتها على خطوط الاردن

اسراب من طائرات العراق طارت الى الجبهة

فيصل يوقف شحن ذخائر للاردن بعد اتفاقية الدفاع المشترك بينها وبين مصر !

تحذير من الملك حسين الى جونسون

فضيحة جديدة تتفجر فى المانيا الغربية

بون تعطى اسرائيل ٢٠ ألف كمامة رغم معارضة وزير الدفاع

كيزنجر

كلمة للأهرام

سمعة ليبيا هى الموضوع !

الرئيس يستقبل السفير السوفيتى

تكتل غربى فى مجلس الامن ضد مشروع القرار العربى

مظاهرة فى ميونيخ ضد الشاه — تقذف سيارته بالبيض الفاسد

اجتماع لبحث الازمة بين جونسون وويلسون وبيرسون ؟

عقدة التواطؤ .. !

اليابان تعلن حيادها فى الازمة

notable cartoons, outstanding special articles on international subjects, and fine makeup and technical qualities. It subscribes to the services of the United Press International, Reuters, and other foreign news agencies. Its advertising is substantial in spite of the fact that it is limited, as it must be in a country where all large undertakings (including theaters) are nationalized. Its advertising consists mainly of state announcements and a few notices from foreign companies such as airlines. And, of course, there are many death notices and other assorted personal announcements in its columns.

Special supplements appear in the Sunday edition of the paper; among the most outstanding are those given over to literature and economics and to women's interests. Every Friday there is a magazine issue in which the paper's editor, Hassanein Haikal, presents a long, analytical piece often running an entire page. The London *Times*' correspondent in Cairo in 1965 said that this article "is always eagerly scanned for indications of the Government's attitude, though it equally deserves to be treated as accomplished political journalism."[7]

Al Ahram, certainly not alone among important world newspapers, frequently throws editorial barbs at the United States and sees it as a nation which tends to meddle in the affairs of other nations. For instance, in the spring of 1965, the paper commented:

> Successive reports of the landing of U.S. forces in Santo Domingo and of paratroopers in Vietnam, and the threat of aggression against Cuba, cannot be separated from Western policy toward the Middle East. The interconnection of the problems of the nations of the world has become a reality of our time. . . . No doubt the Arab East has become the prime target of the imperialist offensive. . . .[8]

And again in 1966 when Saudi Arabia's King Feisal visited the United States and had an official dinner in his honor cancelled by New York Mayor John Lindsay (because of the King's statement to the effect that if Jews support Israel he must consider them as his enemies), *Al Ahram* expressed outrage at the treatment of an outstanding Arab personage under a headline reading "Worst Treatment Accorded to Feisal in New York and Yet He Said Nothing."[9] *Al Ahram* is notoriously sensitive about Western "prejudices" against Arabs and sympathy toward Israel and takes every opportunity to point out cases which tend to substantiate this bias.

In the context of the Arab world, *Al Ahram* is prospering and growing. Its growth can be seen in that the circulation was right at 100,000 as recently as 1960; by the early part of 1967 it was inching up close to 150,000. Its large circulation (for an Arab paper), its modern facilities, its long-standing reputation in the Arab world as a notable journalistic institution, and the influence of its editor combine to make *Al Ahram* a dominant force in Egypt, North Africa, and the Middle East.

Important people in the Arab nations, and students of the Arab world in other countries, must still take the paper seriously; but it is its prestige as a reflector of Nasser's attitudes and not its lively independence of yesteryear, that keeps it in a prominent spot among the world's elite newspapers.

Die Burger
(SOUTH AFRICA)

The press of the Republic of South Africa may be said to be divided essentially into the English-language press and Afrikaans-language press. It is safe to generalize that the English papers are the better of the two groups, the more independent, the larger, the more enterprising, the more prosperous, and the more critical. The Afrikaans-language papers are the more reactionary, the more committed to the Nationalist Party, the more provincial, the more isolationist, and the smaller. There are good papers, however, among both groups and it is really dangerous, and unfair, to stereotype the South African press too hastily.[1] While it is true, for instance, that the Afrikaans press follows the government party rather slavishly, believing in "my government right or wrong" as one writer has put it,[2] there are periodic signs of intelligent journalism among its members.

One newspaper that provides a notable exception to charges of captive, thoughtless journalism among Afrikaans papers is *Die Burger* of Cape Town. Although it broadly supports Nationalist policies, it is often quite independent and deviationist, probing here, attacking there, questioning this point, refuting that point—a stance of some importance in a country with increasing press restrictions and a more sensitive government. And this independent spirit comes from a Government (Nationalist Party) paper, and not one of the opposition English papers exemplified by Johannesburg's excellent *Rand Daily Mail*, which is generally considered "the liveliest and most liberal" of the country's dailies and which in 1966 won the World Achievement Award of the ANPA (American Newspaper Publishers Association) Foundation.[3] The implication is this: in spite of a sensitive Government and many highly reactionary social practices,[4] the Republic of South Africa has the freest press on the entire African continent.

Die Burger was founded in 1915 at a time when the promise of Afrikaaner nationalism was not very bright. The founders of the paper, led by W. A. Hofmeyr, could little guess that the paper would play the large part it has in the nurture and consolidation of the South African

Nationalist Party. *Die Burger* literally means "The Citizen" in Afrikaans but the name reflects also the tough individualism of the first "free burgers" of the period when the Dutch East India Company controlled the land.

The first editor was Dr. D. F. Malan, who got the paper off to a good start, after considerable effort in getting out the first issue. In spite of the fact that poverty of journalistic experience among the small staff which produced the first issue on July 26, 1915 caused numerous problems, the paper did struggle through the early years under considerable financial strain and has survived without interruption to the present. *Die Burger* is, as Dr. Malan once said, "a child of grief and of hope." Its early period has been compared to that of Britain's *Daily Herald* (now under another name)—"a newspaper produced by campaigners rather than journalists, full of zeal, but perhaps not so well endowed with subeditorial talent."[5]

The paper's editorial talent has constantly grown and today *Die Burger* is able to feel comfortable in most any group of elite newspapers. Of all the Afrikaans newspapers of the country, it is easily the most highly professional: its writing is superb, and its typography, makeup, and production quality is perhaps superior to any newspaper on the entire continent. Its circulation (Monday through Friday) is right at 50,000, considerably smaller than its English-language companions in Cape Town—the *Cape Argus* (P.M.) with more than 100,000 and the *Cape Times* (A.M.) with nearly 68,000.[6]

Die Burger has the custom of printing the lead editorial every day from the *Cape Times*, and the English-language daily reciprocates. This in itself is significant and indicates something of the "openness" of both papers. Louis M. Lyons, former curator of Harvard University's Nieman Foundation, has written that only in Cape Town is "there any journalistic effort to bridge in some degree the communications barrier." He notes also that *Die Burger* is less narrowly partisan than the other Afrikaans papers and more professional in its operations.[7] Writing of the journalists he met at *Die Burger*, Lyons praised them as "a broadly informed professional group, more so than all but a few of the English language editors." He called Phil Weber, managing director of *Die Burger* "particularly impressive and his dynamic quality and rigorous standards are reflected through *Die Burger*."[8]

Today, the paper, having between 50,000 and 60,000 circulation, emphasizes South African and world politics, economics, art, and literature. It also gives considerable coverage to sports and to matters of feminine interest. It has about sixty writers and editors on its staff and, except in a few very special cases, insists on a university degree for its journalists. *Die Burger* has two full-time correspondents abroad, both in London.[9]

Although the paper was established as an opinion-forming paper supporting the Nationalist cause in politics and the Afrikaans move-

DIE BURGER
BY DIE POSWESE AS NUUSBLAD GEREGISTREER
KAAPSTAD, MAANDAG, 4 DESEMBER 1967. DRIE-EN-VYFTIGSTE JAARGANG. PRYS VIER SENT
LAASTE UITGAWE

HART IN S.A. OORGEPLANT

DIE PASIËNT | IN DIE HOSPITAALKAMER | DIE SKENKER

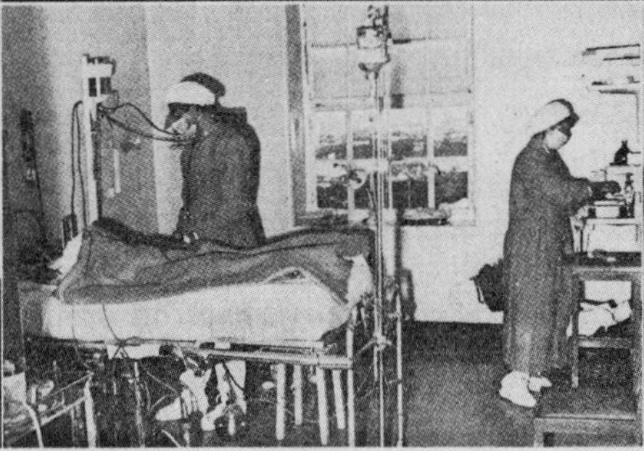

KAAPSE SPAN MAAK GESKIEDENIS

Pasiënt Glimlag ná 1ste Operasie in Sy Soort

MNR. LOUIS WASHKANSKY, 53-jarige sakeman van Seepunt (links op hierdie samegestelde foto), in wie se liggaam die hart van die 25-jarige mej. Denise Ann Darvall van Tamboerskloof (regs) gisteroggend vroeg in 'n dramatiese operasie in die Groote Schuur-Hospitaal oorgeplant is. In die middel lê mnr. Washkansky in die spesiaal toegeruste hospitaalkamer waar minstens een dokter en 'n verpleegster dag en nag by hom waak. Niemand sonder steriele teaterdrag word in die kamer toegelaat nie. Net nadat mnr. Washkansky die kamer binnegestoot was, het hy geglimlag. Sy toestand was verlede nag bevredigend.

„'n Wonderwerk!"

SOWAT drie weke gelede is aan mev. Ann Washkansky gesê dat daar net een manier is om haar man te red, en dit is om 'n nuwe hart in hom oor te plant. Gisteraand is die operasie gedoen en gisteraand het mev. Washkansky gesê: „Daar het 'n wonderwerk gebeur."

Gister het mev. Washkansky vertel van haar man se eerste hartaanval sewe jaar gelede, van sy stoed daarna en van die byna ondraaglike spanning waaronder die gesin geleef het van die oomblik dat hulle gehoor het dat 'n hartoorplanting op hul vader gedoen gaan word.

„Ek glo dat ons die beste en die mees toegewyde medici ter wêreld het," het mev. Washkansky, wat in Seepunt woon, gesê.

„Die nuus was net te groot vir my. Ek kan dit nou nog nie glo nie. Maar ek is trots dat die Suid-Afrikaanse medici die eerste is wat met so 'n delikate operasie slaag," het sy gesê.

'n Klompie familielede, onder wie mnr. Washkansky se broer en mev. Washkansky se twee susters, was gistermiddag by haar woning om die nuus met haar te deel. Sedert dit gisteroggend kort na middernag bekend geword het dat haar man geopereer gaan word, het familielede en vriende die hele nag saam met haar gewaak. Elke uur het hulle die hospitaal geskakel om na die vordering van die operasie te verneem.

Net na sesuur gisteroggend het hulle vir die laaste keer die hospitaal geskakel. Die operasie was pas verby. Mev. Washkansky se sy het net gehoor hy leef, die hart klop. Sy was so deurmekaar van vreugde en blydskap, vertel sy, dat sy nie geweet het wat om te dink nie. Sy kon dit net nie glo nie. Al wat sy weet, is dat 'n wonderwerk gebeur het.

Die 53-jarige mnr. Louis Washkansky het sewe jaar gelede die eerste hartaanval gehad. Vier jaar lank daarna het alles weer goed gegaan en kon hy met sy werk voortgaan.

Sowat 2½ jaar gelede het hy weer 'n ernstige hartaanval gehad. Dit het die hartweefsel sodanig beskadig dat dit die ander liggaamsdele begin aantas het. Al sy ledemate het begin opswel.

Op 14 September vanjaar was die hart so verswak, dat hy in die Groote Schuur-Hospitaal opgeneem is.

Hy is 'n wonderlike man, vertel mev. Washkansky. Deur al die swaar het hy nooit moed verloor nie en kon hy selfs in die hospitaal nog altyd 'n grappie maak. Gedurende sy verblyf in die hospitaal het hy altyd geglo dat hy sal lewe. Volgens die geneeshere is dit net sy sterk wil om te bly lewe wat hom so lank aan die gang gehou het, sê mev. Washkansky.

● VERVOLG OP BLADSY 9, KOL. 1 ●

'N WEERGALOSE PRESTASIE IN DIE MEDIESE GESKIEDENIS VAN DIE WÊRELD IS SATERDAGNAG IN KAAPSTAD BEHAAL DEUR DIE SPAN HARTCHIRURGE EN MEDIESE TEGNOLOË VAN DIE GROOTE SCHUUR-HOSPITAAL. HULLE HET IN 'N MIDDERNAGTELIKE OPERASIE VAN LANGER AS VYF UUR DAARIN GESLAAG OM DIE EERSTE HARTOORPLANTING OP 'N MENS TE DOEN.

Die man op wie die operasie gedoen is, is die 53-jarige mnr. Louis Washkansky, 'n sakeman van Seepunt. Sy hart was onherstelbaar beskadig en daar is elke oomblik vir sy lewe gevrees.

Die skenker was die 25-jarige mej. Denise Ann Darvall van Tamboerskloof, wat Saterdagmiddag noodlottig beseer is in 'n motorongeluk in Soutrivier.

Terselfdertyd is 'n nier van mej. Darvall in die Karl Bremer-Hospitaal op 'n jong Kleurlingseun oorgeplant. (Berig op bl. 7.)

Die hartoperasie was in elke opsig 'n volslae sukses. Vanoggend vroeg was mnr. Washkansky se toestand heeltemal bevredigend.

Die nuus van die geslaagde oorplanting was kort ná die operasie oor die hele wêreld bekend. Lof en gelukwensinge het uit alle oorde ingestroom. „Dit is werklik 'n groot prestasie," het dr. Michael Debakey, een van Amerika se voorste hartchirurge, gesê nadat hy die nuus verneem het.

Nou Ook Longe

'n Hartchirurg in Londen het die operasie as een van die merkwaardigste prestasies in die geskiedenis van oorplantings beskryf. Volgens hom baan dit nou die weg vir die oorplanting van nie net harte nie, maar van harte en longe in een operasie.

'n Ander Britse hartchirurg het dit as 'n „geweldige tegniese deurbraak" beskryf. „Almal wag nou om te sien wat in die volgende paar dae in Suid-Afrika gaan gebeur," het hy gesê.

Die kritieke stadium van die operasie het gisteroggend omstreeks 5.50 aangebreek toe die oorgeplante hart 'n elektriese skok toegedien is. Die vrees dat die hart nie sou begin klop nie, was ongegrond — dit het feitlik onmiddellik begin werk.

Triomf vir Barnard

Daardie oomblik was die verwesenliking van 'n ideaal wat die laaste tyd deur feitlik elke chirurg en tegnoloog ter wêreld wat met die oorplanting van organe gemoeid is, gekoester is. Dit was veral 'n triomf vir prof. dr. C. N. Barnard, adjunk-professor in die chirurgie en direkteur van chirurgiese navorsing aan die Universiteit van Kaapstad. Volgens sy hoof, prof. dr. J. H. Louw, hoogleraar in chirurgie, was dit 'n lewensideaal om 'n hart oor te plant.

Die operasie het 'n drama beëindig wat hom die afgelope veertien dae in die hospitaal afgespeel het. In daardie tyd het die hartspan heeltyds bystanddiens gedoen en geensen is toegelaat om Kaapstad te verlaat nie.

Hulle moes voortdurend by 'n telefoon bly sodat hulle ontbied kon word sodra 'n geskikte hart gevind word. In die loop van die twee weke is verskeie toetse op moontlike skenkers gedoen, maar elke keer is die een of ander tekortkoming in die hart van die skenker gevind. In een geval, die van 'n jong Kleurling wat in 'n motorongeluk gesterf het, is die operasie op die laaste oomblik uitgestel omdat sy hart nie aan al die streng vereistes voldoen het nie.

● VERVOLG OP BLADSY 12, KOLOM 1 ●

MEV. DARVALL

Denise Was 'n Stil Meisie, Sê Pa

DENISE DARVALL was 'n stil en teruggetrokke meisie. Sy het geen spesiale mansvriende gehad nie. Haar liefhebbery tuis was om na klassieke musiek te luister, het Denise se vader, mnr. Edward George Darvall van Tamboerskloof, gistermiddag aan Die Burger vertel.

Die gedroefde mnr. Darvall wat sy vrou en sy dogter in 'n motorongeluk verloor het, het gesê dat hy aan die dokters verlof gegee het om sy dogter se hart en niere te verwyder en aan iemand anders te skenk. Die verlof het hy Saterdagnag kort voor middernag gegee toe aan hom gesê is dat sy dogter besig is om te sterf.

WONDERLIK

„Denise was 'n wonderlike kind en baie geheg aan haar twee broers, Keith (14) en Stephen (17)," het mnr. Darvall verder vertel.

Sy het sowat vier maande gelede 'n nuwe motor gekoop en dit was in hierdie motor dat mnr. Darvall, sy vrou, Denise en Keith Saterdagmiddag op pad na vriende in Milnerton was toe die ongeluk gebeur.

● VERVOLG OP BL. 12, KOL. 4 ●

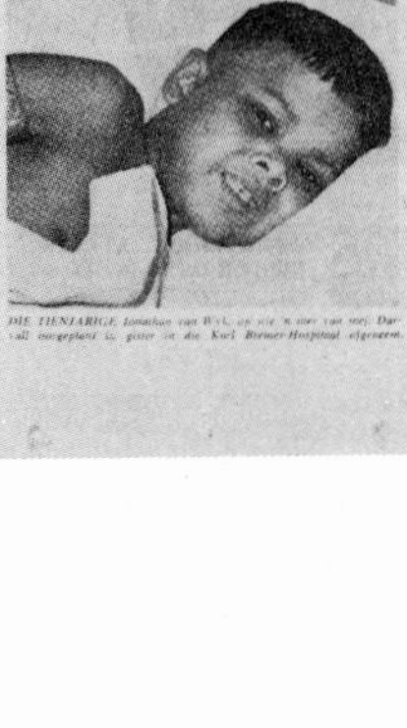

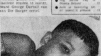

DIE TIENJARIGE Jonathan van Wyk, op wie 'n nier van mej. Darvall oorgeplant is, gister in die Karl Bremer-Hospitaal afgeneem.

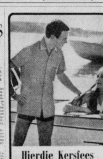

Ray en Cliff Keil Senuwees Op

WAS DAAR AL IETS SPANNENDERS?

Van VICTOR HOLLOWAY

JOHANNESBURG.

SATERDAG, 2 Desember 1967, verdien 'n spesiale plek in die annale van Suid-Afrikaanse sport. Daar was miskien al dae waarop Springbokke net sulke groot prestasies behaal het, maar ek glo nie dat al ooit spannender vertonings deur Suid-Afrikaanse sportmanne gelewer is as dié van Ray Moore en Cliff Drysdale op Ellispark nie.

Ek het nog altyd beweer dat daar geen spannender sport as Davisbeker-tennis is nie. Geen rugbywedstryd, krieketwedstryd, bokgeveg of wat ook al, kan ooit so met spanning belaai word soos 'n Davisbeker-wedstryd nie. Hierdie mening huldig ek sedert 1964, toe ek in die Roland Garros-stadion in Parys vir die eerste keer gesien het hoe anders Davisbeker-tennis is, anders as elke sport, ook Wimbledonse tennis.

Na die spel van Saterdag op Ellispark besef ek dat my vorige ondervinding van Davisbeker-tennis net 'n voorsmaak was van wat werklik in so 'n wedstryd kan gebeur.

WEGGEKYK

'n Kennis [illegible] die Moore-Orantes-wedstryd huis toe. Hy kon die spanning nie langer verdra nie. Hy het op die [illegible] vir die Drysdale-Santana-wedstryd gebly, maar in die laaste stel voor die rede het hy dikwels gemaak soos die vroue in die [illegible], weggekyk omdat die spanning te veel was.

En tog is het einde niet, of hoe sê die Hollanders? Die moontlikheid is daar dat vandag se voltooiing van die wedstryd tussen Drysdale en Santana 'n antiklimaks kan wees, maar moenie verbaas wees as daar nog twee stelle gespeel word wat aan die senuwees van elke sportentoesias in die land gaan knaag nie.

Drysdale se kans om sy eerste oorwinning in 'n stuk of agt wedstryde teen Santana te behaal, is nie te sleg nie, nie as hy speel soos hy Saterdagmiddag opgehou het nie. (Lees berig op bl. 34.)

ment generally, it has grown into a complete newspaper with all the modern services that a well-educated readership demands. According to P. J. Cillié, editor of *Die Burger*, the paper insists on the highest standards, journalistically and typographically. "We primarily serve the oldest and most sophisticated part of South Africa, the Cape Province, and are without doubt the most quoted newspaper in the country," the editor has said.[10]

Die Burger has had a stable continuity of ownership ever since its birth. This is considered very important for an elite paper, and Editor Cillié commented in a speech at the University of Cape Town (1966) that it is essential

> . . . for a quality newspaper, a paper of influence that all changes should happen gradually and that there should not be a sudden break with its best traditions. That, after all, is what gives it the status of an institution and adds to the sort of strength that can stand up to pressures of various kinds.[11]

Die Burger is proud of its heritage and its Nationalist political orientation; it is proud of the fact that, although it is ideologically to the Right it is a strong opponent of rightist extremism. It is definitely a sophisticated, well-informed newspaper which, in spite of its traditional ties with the Nationalist Party, often fails to follow the party line. Its editorial independence is cherished. Many of the paper's editors have been, and are, prominent in South African Government and education. Among the paper's contributors have been many of the most famous Afrikaans writers.

In conclusion, it is safe to say that *Die Burger* is well-written, well-edited, and well-produced. It is articulate and cosmopolitan, and aside from the fact that it has certain blind spots to Government excesses, stands as a good example of an elite daily in a country of many fine newspapers.

The Hindu

(INDIA)

Of the several outstanding English-language dailies of India, *The Hindu* of Madras enjoys an unrivaled reputation for reliability and concern for truthful and comprehensive news coverage. Other dailies like *The Statesman* and *The Times of India*[1] (and even the *Hindustan Times* and the *Indian Express*) are outstanding in many ways and can be called "national" newspapers, but *The Hindu* alone among them commands wide international respect as an authoritative expression of liberal and cosmopolitan attitudes. And among the serious voices of the English-language dailies, that of *The Hindu* is the most serious. A London *Times* correspondent, writing from Delhi in 1965, described its somber appearance by noting that its "heavy single columns march across the pages like Prussian guardsmen, grey and disciplined."[2]

Although *The Hindu* is very highly respected in India and the Far East and is perhaps the most comprehensive of the Indian dailies, it is doubtful that it contains "all that is worth knowing . . . within India or elsewhere in the world" as an Indian journalism professor wrote in 1966.[3] The paper does, however, regularly evidence that it has a great concern for accuracy, reliability, honesty, and authoritativeness. A wide assortment of national leaders and correspondents for foreign journals in Delhi read *The Hindu* regularly and carefully.[4] It is valued for its intelligent tone, its literate style, its progressive spirit, its cosmopolitan emphasis, and its forceful expression of opinion. From a historical perspective, *The Hindu* has played a notable part in the development of Indian intellectualism, the growth of a free-press philosophy, and the bringing about of Indian independence.[5]

Founded in 1878 as a weekly by an enthusiastic group of young intellectuals, *The Hindu* gave voice to the beginnings of nationalistic expression among middle-class Indians. From the beginning, the paper carried the people's grievances to the Government and early evidenced a social concern and an intolerance of public injustices which set it apart from most of the press and brought support from many quarters. However, the paper faced many troublesome years before it could gain financial stability.

In April, 1889, *The Hindu* became a daily, and since then it has been the "main daily purveyor of news to thousands of news-hungry people."[6] G. Subramanya Aiyer, who had guided the paper when it was a weekly, stepped out of the management position in 1889 and Karunakara Menon became editor. *The Hindu*, from its founding, had been an independent paper; but beginning in 1905, when its great editor-owner Kasturi Ranga Iyenger took over, an increasing identification with India's Congress Party was noted.

In the early years of the present century, the paper was especially active as a champion of the people's causes. These were important, formative years in India's independence movement and *The Hindu* made notable contributions to it, often flying in the face of Government opposition. Being an Indian-owned and nationalist paper it was often in trouble with the British authorities. But it kept up its intelligent journalism, never emotional or bitterly hostile, but more rightly "speaking to and even for British conscience" in calm, logical, yet sensitive, tones.[7]

The Hindu always maintained a dignified tone and forever sought fair play from all parties. Kasturi Ranga Iyengar and his writers wrote

THE HINDU

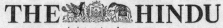

India's National Newspaper
REGD. NO. M 97
Vol. 91. No. 231.
Registered at G.P.O., U.K. & Ceylon as a Newspaper
MADRAS, SATURDAY, OCTOBER 7, 1967.
CITY 18 Paise 14 Pages
Price in Ceylon 18 Cents
Air Surcharge 4 Cents

India's Border Policy Commended Abroad—Desai

From Our Special Correspondent

NEW DELHI, Oct. 6.

Mr. Morarji Desai, Deputy Prime Minister and Finance Minister, who returned here this morning after his foreign tour, said that during his tour he was asked about the Sino-Indian border clashes. He felt that the general opinion abroad was that India was meeting the problem "properly and squarely."

Mr. Morarji Desai clarified that the statement he had made in Washington on the question of the recognition of Formosa did not run counter to the policy of the Government of India.

"My policy cannot be different from that of the Government of India", he said while talking to correspondents immediately on his return here this morning from a month-long foreign tour.

Our Bombay correspondent reports:

Mr. Morarji Desai, on arrival at the Santa Cruz airport this morning, told Pressmen that in respect of foreign investment there was some "reluctance" because of their "exaggerated picture" of our difficulties projected abroad.

When asked whether there would be any change in the policy governing foreign investment ... there was no need for a change now in the official policy governing foreign investments.

Mr. Morarji Desai, Deputy Prime Minister, who returned to Delhi on Friday from his foreign visit, talking to Pressmen at the airport.

—Wirephoto by our Staff Photographer

REPLENISHMENT OF IDA FUNDS

PTI reports:

S.S.P. Firm on Land Revenue Cut

Movement in U.P. Planned

NEW DELHI, Oct. 6.

The central leadership of the Samyukta Socialist Party is of the view that there can be no compromise on the party's demand for reducing land revenue on holdings up to 6½ acres by half and complete remission on holdings paying up to Rs. 5 in U.P.

This was the consensus at an informal meeting, attended by S.S.P. Ministers, M.Ps. and some Legislators from U.P., here to-day.

The central leadership feels that the question of land revenue was the "point of departure" for the party and the party will accept the challenge thrown by the U.P. Chief Minister.

Mr. Charan Singh has refused to accept the S.S.P.'s demand.

The State S.S.P. has decided to launch a movement from October 16 in support of its demand.

One of the central leaders of the party said here to-night it was definite that "we cannot continue in U.P. as we have been".

Whether the S.S.P. Ministers could resign and actively participate in the agitation or continue in the Ministry while the agitation goes on and force the Chief Minister to do whatever he thinks proper is the question yet to be decided.—PTI.

British Dockers Fight with Chinese Over Mao's Badge

TILBURY (England), Oct. 6.

Angry British dock workers refused to work on the Chinese freighter Hang Zhou to-day following a battle with Chinese crewmen.

Police broke up a mob of 60 longshoremen and Chinese who brawled on the River Thames dockside yesterday after a docker hurled a picture of Mao Tse-tung to the ground when it was pinned on him by a crewman.

Some dockers were bruised as they traded blows with lengths of timber with the Chinese. One Chinese was believed to have broken an arm and two had black eyes.

Indonesia Asked to End Ties with China

JAKARTA, Oct. 6.

Indonesian students to-day threatened to occupy the People's Chinese Embassy here unless the Indonesian Government broke off relations with China within three days.

The ultimatum delivered to the Foreign Ministry to-day, gives Foreign Minister Adam Malik three days after seeing the note to concede the demand. Mr. Malik, who has been attending the U.N. General Assembly, is due back in Jakarta to-day.

Some 300 students staged a demonstration before the Foreign Office to press their demand for severance of relations with China and the expulsion of all Chinese diplomats in Jakarta.

Nine Chinese diplomats and Chinese Embassy staff members at the same time staged a small demonstration of their own across town.

The Chinese, swathed in bandages covering injuries they received when the students sacked their embassy on Sunday morning, carried posters denouncing president Suharto's "Fascist Indonesian regime" and praising Chinese Communist Party Chairman Mao Tse-tung.

Their leader got into a heated argument with security officers of the Jakarta Garrison Command assigned to keep the Chinese under house arrest.

The Chinese spokesman argued vehemently against the treatment and requested permission for his people to visit the Indonesian Foreign Office to protest against their treatment.

The Indonesian troops refused to grant them permission. The six Chinese then shouted slogans like "long live Mao Tse-tung".

SUHARTO'S CALL

Meanwhile Acting President, General Suharto, to-day called for a "calm and quiet" consideration of the problem arising from the deterioration of relations with China.

But he gave no other indication of the Government's thinking on the incident in which 15 Chinese Embassy staffers and several Indonesians were injured, one of them fatally.

The students have also criticised the Government for allowing the Chinese to hoist the Chinese flag over the Embassy after the students had seized and burned the Chinese flag when they ransacked the Embassy.

Meanwhile China informed Indonesia yesterday it was sending a special aircraft to bring home its Charge d'Affaires and other members of the Chinese Embassy in Jakarta who were injured during a student attack on the Chinese mission last Sunday.—Reuter & UPI.

Rebel Nagas' Complaint Against Union Govt.

NEW DELHI, Oct. 6.

The underground Naga delegation to-day accused the Government of India of "insulting and humiliating" it and announced its sudden departure for Nagaland to-morrow morning.

Mr. Z. Ramyo, a member of the delegation, told newsmen here to-night that an official of the External Affairs Ministry had told it that the Prime Minister "will not be able to meet the Naga delegation" even though it was agreed at yesterday's meeting with Mrs. Gandhi that they would meet again. He said any refusal to meet them again might have "political considerations".

He said the deadlock after six rounds of talks continued.

The delegation would report "what has taken place here" to the Tatar Hoho (National Parliament) meeting "somewhere" in Shepoemaramgh district near Kohima on October 12, he added.

About the fate of the cease-fire agreement ending this month, he said the Nagas believed in peaceful methods for settlement of "all human problems".

The delegation had a two-hour meeting with Commerce Minister Dinesh Singh and other officials to-day.

He asserted that it was agreed "on both sides" at yesterday's meeting "that there would be an-

...

They were always welcome to stay as guests of the Government of India for as long as they pleased.

The Government had always treated them with every courtesy and consideration.

P.M. TO MEET TEAM

The Prime Minister will meet the underground Naga delegation to-morrow on the eve of her departure on a tour of the East European countries, it is learnt.

She could not meet the delegation on October 5 because of very heavy engagements.—UNI & PTI.

Mao's Plan for Asian Conquest

MOSCOW, Oct. 6.

A leading Soviet journalist has accused Chinese Party Chairman Mao Tse-tung of plotting to weld all Asia, including India and parts of the Soviet Union, into a new "Reich".

Foreign affairs expert Ernst Henry wrote in the weekly Literaturnaya Gazeta (Literary Gazette) that Mao was counting on a nuclear war wiping out one-third to one-half of mankind to help him create a "superstate" which might eventually embrace the whole world.

Henry wrote that Mao and his associates drew up a three-stage plan for world conquest in 1958 under the title "The Great Strategic Plan of Mao Tse-tung". Its motto is "The wind blows from the East," according to the article.—UPI.

Communist-led Kisans Attack Mirasdars: One Killed in Police Firing

MADRAS, Oct. 6.

In renewed agrarian trouble, one person was killed yesterday in a village in Mannargudi Taluk of Thanjavur District, when the police opened fire. According to the Inspector-General of Police, the police had to fire three rounds in self-defence when a mob of kisans attempted to attack them.

The Chief Minister, Mr. C. N. Annadurai, who gave the news to Pressmen said he was grieved to hear of the trouble. In an appeal, he said: "This being the harvest time, and since kuruvai crops cannot withstand delay of even two or three days, I request the kisans and other leaders, to whatever party they might belong, to co-operate in the harvesting, in the interest of the country and the people as a whole, postponing solutions to some of their grievances.

There has been agrarian unrest in this area for some time past and the current trouble arose between the Left Communist-led kisans on the one hand and caste-Hindus and Mirasdars on the other over wages. In the clashes five policemen and four caste-Hindus were reported to have been injured.

...

The Chief Minister said that the Government was always ready to hear the representations of kisans and would arrange tripartite talks about wages and other things. But the harvest should not be delayed or hampered, he emphasised. "Anyhow," he said, "it is a matter over which nobody can feel satisfied or happy. I am awaiting further and fuller reports."

The Chief Minister said that the taluks of Nagapattinam and Mannargudi were the troubled areas and Collectors had been holding talks from time to time with the Communist leaders over wages. In most cases, agreements had been arrived at. "I do not know exactly the reasons for the present trouble," Mr. Annadurai said.

DEMAND FOR HIGHER WAGES

Our Thanjavur Correspondent, who visited the scene of police firing, reports:

Pakkiri, a Left Communist Harijan, aged about 32 of Ramanuja Manali village died on the spot in the police firing. The trouble occurred in Poonthazhankudi, an interior village, seven miles from Tiruvarur, on the Tiruvarur-Mannargudi road.

It is said that the Communist-led kisans had been demanding 1½ marakals of paddy per kalam by way of wages for harvest and the land owners had been offering only 1¼ marakal.

On October 3, at a meeting of the land owners of Tiruvarur region held at Mangudi, an ad hoc committee was constituted to meet the land owners and labour representatives in villages wherever there was agrarian unrest to help bring about settlements for peaceful kuruvai harvest.

...

After completing the harvesting, the land-owners who had come to Karuppur from the neighbouring villages were returning to their respective villages. When they reached Poonthazhankudi at about 6 p.m. a few hundred kisans said to be led by Communists, are alleged to have accosted them from different directions and started pelting on them brickbats and stones.

A car of one Mr. Krishnamurthi Aiyar, Village Headman of Annavasal, who had also joined in the harvesting at Karuppur, was damaged. The driver is alleged to have been pulled out of the car and thrown into the channel nearby. Another person in the car was also allegedly assaulted. The attacking mob is also alleged to have hurled stones at the Sub-Inspector of Police, R. S. Pandiyan and Head Constable Natarajan and two other constables.

The sub-inspector, who had with him only one Head Constable and four constables, warned the crowd to disperse. But the crowd was stated to have become unruly and continued to pelt stones. Apprehending further danger, the Sub-Inspector pulled out the musket from a Constable and fired one round in the air. The mob still persisted in stone-throwing and the Sub-Inspector fired two more rounds, as a result of which Pakkiri died on the spot.

Meanwhile, Mohamed Ismail, a land-owner, who also participated in the joint harvesting by the Mirasdars, drove in the damaged car to Karuppur to telephone the police for further help. But he was also attacked.

TEA SHOP LOOTED

After sometime, the M.S.P. came to the spot and the crowd dispersed. A section of the frenzied ...

... Mr. C. G. Rangabashyam, Collector, to-day visited the affected places and Kalyanamahadevi village also. Mr. Rathnaswami, R.D.O., Mannargudi is conducting an enquiry into the firing incident.

A case has been registered against 94 persons.

The mirasdars from six villages told me this evening that they apprehended further trouble from Communists and unless a strong police protection was given harvesting is likely to be affected.

Soviet Nuclear Scientist Decides to Stay in West

EDMONTON (Canada), Oct. 6.

A leading Soviet nuclear scientist, Boris Dotsenko, disclosed here last night he has decided not to return to the Soviet Union.

Mr. Dotsenko, 41, who came to the University of Alberta a year ago on leave from his post as head of the Nuclear Laboratory at Kiev State University, said he wants to stay in Canada.—Reuter.

Status Quo on Sharing Krishna Waters Likely

FROM OUR SPECIAL CORRESPONDENT

NEW DELHI, Oct. 6.

The Prime Minister, Mrs. Indira Gandhi, is reported to have told the Chief Ministers of Andhra Pradesh, Mysore and Maharashtra that it would not be advisable to refer the dispute over the sharing of the Krishna waters to a tribunal.

...

On the other hand, the Prime Minister felt convinced that the projects to which the three States were committed under the 1951 agreement as well as the Hafiz Mohammed Ibrahim award should under no circumstances be held up.

...

Ultimately it was agreed by all the three Chief Ministers that an expert committee of engineers should go into this question and decide the exact availability of water from the Krishna.

...

The Prime Minister appealed to the Chief Ministers not to hold up any of the projects already committed to by the States. They should be allowed to be executed without any interruption. All the Chief Ministers have agreed to study the implications of this suggestion.

Indications are that the status quo in regard to the present arrangement for utilisation of the Krishna waters will be maintained.

PTI reports:

Later, the Prime Minister had separate meetings with the three Chief Ministers which observers regarded as an attempt to make them climb down from their known rigid stands.

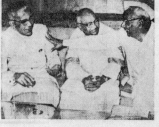

The Chief Ministers of Maharashtra, Mysore and Andhra, Mr. V. P. Naik, Mr. S. Nijalingappa and Mr. K. Brahmananda Reddi (from left to right) at the talks on river waters in New Delhi on Friday

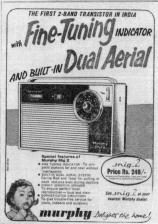

—Wirephoto by our Staff Photographer

Viet Nam War Unpopular, Admits Johnson

WASHINGTON, Oct. 6.

stinging articles at times, however, and their rhetoric of protest had its effect within the Government. The editor, who was quiet and reserved by nature, desired to pattern the appearance of *The Hindu* after *The Times* of London. [It is interesting that it was *The Hindu* which was the last Indian daily to take advertising off its front page (in 1958), as was *The Times* the last to do so in England (in 1966)]. It was mainly Iyengar who imbued the paper with its concern for accuracy. Although it could be called liberal politically, it was considered a conservative paper because of the slow and serious way it wrote and displayed its news and views.[8]

In 1921 *The Hindu* installed Linotype machines, rotary presses, and stereotyping facilities, having laboriously printed from handset type before. Information columns and new features were introduced and the paper expanded its readership rapidly during the twenties. Kasturi Ranga Iyengar died in 1923 and *The Hindu* was left to his two sons who were not as politically active as their father.[9] One son, Kasturi Srinivasan (who became editor in 1934) contributed significantly to the paper, making it a national institution and one of the great newspapers of the world. He admired Gandhi's methods, although he never failed to editorialize against them when he felt they were too extreme. He was one of the outstanding fighters for press freedom in Indian journalistic history.

After India won its independence in 1947, Kasturi Srinivasan was instrumental in forming an independent nationalist news agency for India. As a result of his work, the Press Trust of India was formed in 1949 and he became its first president. Actually PTI was not quite independent and operated as a kind of junior partner to the Reuters agency of Britain; in 1952, however, it achieved complete independence and became a full-fledged national news agency.[10]

Throughout the 1950's the prestige of *The Hindu* grew as it established a far-flung foreign correspondent network and extended its coverage into remote regions of India. The paper's editorials, largely written by K. P. Viswanatha Iyer, began to draw attention at home and abroad. Many outstanding journalists worked for *The Hindu*—B. Shiva Rao, K. Balaraman, K. S. Shelvankar, S. K. Gurunathan, and H. Venkatasubbiah. Srinivasan died in 1959, leaving behind a great newspaper and a reputation as one of the very greatest newspaper editors of modern India. From his son, who died soon after becoming editor, the editorship was passed to a senior member of the staff, S. Parthasarathy, who is editor today.

The Hindu is designed mainly for the educated class, and its circulation of some 136,000 (large for India) gives some indication of the concern for serious reading matter which exists among the sizable educated population of South India. Without a doubt southern India receives special emphasis in the columns of *The Hindu*, but the paper's reportage from Delhi is outstanding both in quantity and in quality.

News from all state capitals may be found regularly in the paper's pages. So, although it is a southern-based paper, *The Hindu* does a creditable job of representing the entire nation. London's *Times* has described it as "a national voice with a southern accent."[11]

Although the paper prints substantial amounts of foreign news and has several full-time correspondents stationed outside India, its foreign news coverage does not match in comprehensiveness and insightfulness its local and national coverage. One reason for this may be a space shortage: the paper usually has no more than twelve or fourteen pages, nearly half of which carry advertising. It might be said that *The Hindu* looks like *The Times* of London and sounds like *The Guardian*,[12] and it is the combination of the tradition and spirit of these two British dailies in *The Hindu*'s pages which has given it its special prestige and potency in Indian society. There is little doubt but that the paper is the most highly respected and influential daily of India, and (considering its size and resources) one of the truly great papers of the world.

Jen-min Jih-pao

(RED CHINA)

Perhaps the morning *Jen-min Jih-pao*[1] (People's Daily) of Peking should not be considered at all in this book. In a way it is not a newspaper, being more of a governmental bulletin board or organ of political agitation and propaganda for the Communist regime of China. Quite likely it contributes little to "a world community of reason"; however, as one writer said in late 1966, it probably "reaches more people directly or indirectly than any other publication in the world today" and in a country of some 750 million citizens it is "the ultimate voice of authority."[2]

The paper has been called "a colossal bore"[3] and perhaps it is; but no one can deny its influence and wide prestige in Communist China where almost everyone who is important in the society reads the paper. It is primarily an instrument of the power elite and resorts at times to exaggeration, half-truths, and outright falsification. Even the U.S.S.R.'s *Izvestia*, not noted for strict objectivity itself, has accused *Jen-min Jih-pao* of "slander and inexcusable lies."[4]

Long political and ideological editorials and official news releases filling the paper's usual six (some days, four, and other days, eight) pages form the main journalistic diet for the leading elite of the nation and serve as a guide for other Chinese journals.[5] About four of these pages contain editorials and "news," and some two carry cultural material, features, and state advertising.[6]

While the Chinese consider *People's Daily* a national paper, in reality it is not because of the country's great distances and poor transportation facilities. However, it is safe to say that the paper's influence is felt throughout the land and copies filter to important opinion leaders on a national scale. Each regional city (*e.g.*, Shanghai, Canton, Wuhan, and Chungking) has its own important party paper to supplement *People's Daily*.

As it is with Communist Party papers the world over, *People's Daily*'s circulation is shrouded in considerable mystery. Very likely, however, by 1967 it was well over two million. Circulation figures, in any event, would belie actual readership. Issues of the paper are posted at most city intersections in glass-enclosed "holders"; the paper is read aloud in factory and farm; selections from it are sent out to other communication media by the Government's news agency *Hsin-Hua* (New China); its editorials are often read over the People's Broadcasting Station (Radio Peking), and its directives are chalked on thousands of blackboards in village schools. *People's Daily*, the official organ of both Party and Government, regularly carries articles by the most prominent of the nation's leaders, often by Premier Chou En-lai and Party Chairman Mao Tse-tung.[7]

The tremendous impact of this leading Chinese Communist daily is indicated by the following brief excerpt from French correspondent Robert Guillain's book, 600 *Million Chinese*:

> I have seen the pedicab boy, the street sweeper, the mother of a family, stop in front of the famous paper in the public places where it is hung, and try laboriously to decipher its difficult texts. I have heard it read in public, for the benefit of college students; it comes over loud-speakers for train travelers. More often still a lecturer reads it to the illiterates who still abound among the adult population. . . .[8]

If any newspaper of the world is more serious and monotonous than those in the Soviet Union, it must be *People's Daily*. No light "human interest" material in the Western sense is found on its pages; there are no comics, no gossip or scandal, no reports from courts or items about murders, robberies, or other criminal activities. A few short fictional pieces and, from time to time, poems will be printed; these usually have a political theme or moral. Cartoons or caricatures appear frequently; these are well-drawn and usually downgrade the West, but increasingly are antagonistic toward the Soviet Union also. The makeup is quite subdued, but not so dull as most of the paper's contents. A Frenchman, writing in 1966, called the makeup or layout of the pages good, clear, and dignified.[9] A London *Times* correspondent had said a year earlier

人民日报

1948年6月15日创刊 第7051号 1967年10月29日 星期日 夏历丁未年九月廿六

毛主席语录

我全军将士必须时刻牢记，我们是伟大的人民解放军，是伟大的中国共产党领导的队伍。只要我们时刻遵守党的指示，我们就一定胜利。

（《中国人民解放军宣言》）

一切行动听伟大统帅毛主席的指挥

——6037部队党委领导“三支”“两军”工作的经验

解放军报编者按：6037部队高举毛泽东思想伟大红旗，旗帜鲜明，立场坚定，坚决支持左派广大群众，为人民建立了新的功勋。他们的经验值得大家学习。

6037部队支左工作经验，最重要的就是他们“跟上”跟得紧，“靠下”靠得近。

“跟上”，就是紧跟毛主席，紧跟毛泽东思想，紧跟以毛主席为首的党中央，紧跟毛主席的伟大战略部署。对毛主席和以毛主席为首的无产阶级司令部发出的一切指示，句句照办，步步紧跟。遇到问题，及时请示报告。

“靠下”，就是依靠真正的无产阶级革命派，依靠群众，遇事多和群众商量，勤作调查研究，坚信最聪明、最有才能的，是最有实践经验的群众，甘当群众的小学生。

这样，做好“三支”“两军”工作就有了根本保证。

“三支”“两军”工作，是我们伟大领袖毛主席交给我军的极其光荣而艰巨的政治任务。在支左中，做出了显著成绩的部队，要谦虚谨慎，不骄不躁；犯过错误的部队，要勇于改正，轻装前进，虚心向支左好的部队学习。在同一地区支左的部队，要互相学习，互相帮助，互相支持，并肩前进。我们一定要斗私批修，“跟上，靠下”，把支左工作搞得好上加好，决不辜负伟大领袖毛主席对我们的期望。

在史无前例的无产阶级文化大革命运动中，6037部队高举毛泽东思想伟大红旗，坚定地支持无产阶级革命派，取得了“三支”“两军”和部队革命化建设的双胜利，为人民建立了新的功勋。最近，他们热烈响应、认真学习伟大领袖毛主席发出的**要斗私，批修**的伟大号召，总结了前一阶段支左工作的经验。部队党委认为，要搞好支左工作，最最重要的就是要以“**斗私，批修**”为纲，做到跟上靠下：对上，紧跟伟大统帅毛主席，一切行动听伟大统帅毛主席的指挥；对下，紧紧依靠真正的无产阶级革命派和广大革命群众，紧紧依靠部队广大指战员，拜群众为师，向群众学习。这是搞好支左工作的根本，也是我军革命化建设的根本。

对毛主席的指示句句照办，步步紧跟

林副主席说：“这次无产阶级文化大革命，最高司令是我们毛主席。毛主席是统帅。我们在伟大统帅的指挥下，好好地听我们统帅——毛主席的话，文化大革命一定能顺利发展，一定能取得伟大胜利！”一年来，6037部队所以能做好“三支”“两军”工作，在无产阶级文化大革命中为人民建立新功，就是靠对伟大领袖毛主席的绝对信仰，无限忠诚。

在这场史无前例的无产阶级文化大革命中，部队党委对毛主席的指示，有的理解得比较快，有的暂时不理解或不完全理解，但是，他们牢牢记住一条：绝对坚信毛主席，无限忠于毛主席，对毛主席的一切指示，句句坚信，步步紧跟，百分之百地照办，百分之百地执行。文化大革命初期，红卫兵小将“杀”向社会，起初他们看不惯，当看到毛主席一次又一次接见红卫兵，坚决支持革命小将的伟大榜样以后，他们就坚决扭转自己的看法，和革命小将站到一起。当毛主席亲自主持制定的“十六条”公布之后，他们以这个伟大文件为武器，认真地分析了青岛市的革命形势，认清了党内一小撮走资本主义道路当权派的真面目，就坚决支持无产阶级革命派起来造反。去年九月，青岛市党内一小撮走资本主义道路当权派，为了挽救其彻底灭亡的命运，极尽造谣污蔑之能事，对革命的领导干部王效禹同志进行了极其恶毒的人身攻击。当时部队党委对王效禹同志并不了解，当看到毛主席对青岛问题的批示后，坚信毛主席的批示是无比正确的，就坚决和王效禹同志站在一起，全力地支持王效禹同志和青岛市的无产阶级革命派。今年一月二十二日，青岛市无产阶级革命派在王效禹同志领导下，向党内一小撮走资本主义道路当权派夺权时，部队党委当天夜里就作出决定，支持这个夺权。可是一夜间，全市贴了许多反对夺权的大字标语，部队内部议论纷纷。面对这种情况，党委组织大批机关干部，深入到青岛市各群众组织中去，进行了广泛的调查，然后组织大家带着调查来的情况，学习毛主席有关阶级斗争的论述，用阶级分析的方法进行了热烈讨论。最后大家认定：青岛市的党政财文大权过去确实被党内一小撮走资本主义道路当权派篡夺了，这个权应该夺回来；参加夺权的是无产阶级革命派，这个权夺得对。认识一致了，行动就坚决了，因此在支持夺权斗争中，尽管遭到谩骂、围攻甚至殴打，机关上下也毫不动摇，一支到底，在最紧急、最关键的时刻，为青岛市的无产阶级革命派撑了腰。

及时向毛主席的无产阶级司令部请示报告

6037部队党委认识到，尽管我们努力学习毛泽东思想，领会毛主席的革命路线，但我们的思想觉悟和认识水平总是有一定的局限性。只有我们伟大领袖毛主席站得最高，看得最远，最有预见性，只有毛主席的无产阶级司令部，能够掌握全局，洞察运动的发展趋势，对各种问题作出最准确、最妥善的处理。因此，他们在“三支”“两军”工作中遇到重大问题时，总是坚决地、及时地向以毛主席为首的无产阶级司令部请示报告。

他们认为请示报告，不仅仅是上下关系、工作制度的问题，而且是对待以毛主席为首的无产阶级司令部无比坚信，对待无产阶级文化大革命高度负责的问题。今年一月二十二日，部队党委得到青岛市无产阶级革命派夺权的消息后，便以严肃认真、高度负责的精神，立即召开紧急会议研究决定，一面积极支持，一面把夺权情况和自己的行动计划汇报给上级。当接到中央文革的指示后，他们连夜印发到部队，传达给全体干部、战士和职工、家属，做到人人皆知，家喻户晓。中央文革的指示，传达了毛主席的声音，给这个部队的广大指战员带来了极大的鼓舞和力量。

请示报告，不是推卸责任，也不是把困难上交，而是革命的需要，是无产阶级革命的纪律。他们在支左过程中，对毛主席的最新指示和党的方针政策的贯彻执行，以及对一些重大问题的处理，都能采用电话、电报、书信、派人或者负责同志亲自去面谈等方法，及时汇报情况，请示工作。在请示报告之前，都进行充分的调查研究，提出自己的见解和打算，供上级参考。他们派到山东省昌潍地区的支左部队，对于打开局面的每一个较大的行动计划，都事先向山东省革命委员会和王效禹同志作详细的汇报，经过批准之后再执行。这样，就避免了走弯路，犯错误。他们体会，在文化大革命中，各地区的革命形势发展不平衡，进展有快有慢，反复有大有小。因此，加强请示报告，及时使下情上达，上情下达，既便于下头紧跟上头，也便于上级了解下情，适时加强领导。

（下转第二版）

印尼反动派破坏中国印尼两国关系的滔天罪行

社论

以苏哈托、纳苏蒂安为首的印尼法西斯军人集团，在干了一连串野蛮的反华暴行之后，悍然要求中国关闭驻印尼的大使馆和领事馆，撤回驻印尼的使领馆全部人员。我国政府已发表严正声明，强烈谴责印尼反动政府的反华行径，决定暂时关闭驻印尼大使馆和领事馆，并且撤回使领馆全部人员。中国人民对于印尼反动派破坏两国关系的滔天罪行，表示最大的愤慨和最强烈的抗议！

印尼反动派疯狂反华，已经到了登峰造极的程度。然而，它却倒打一耙，叫嚷什么是中国“蓄意恶化两国关系”。你们想用凭空捏造的无耻谎言来推卸自己的罪责，这是绝对办不到的！

中国印尼两国关系恶化到目前这种地步，完全是印尼反动政府一手造成的。印尼法西斯军人集团在一九六五年十月发动反革命政变后，就有计划地多次掀起狂暴的反华排华浪潮。它在全国范围内开动宣传机器，对中华人民共和国和中国人民最敬爱的伟大领袖毛主席，进行恶毒的诬蔑、诽谤和攻击。它出动大批武装军警和暴徒，野蛮袭击我国驻印尼代表机构达四十三次之多，前后达七十名中国外交人员遭到毒打和掳击。它非法霸占我国代表机构的办公处所和宿舍，肆无忌惮地侵犯我国代表机构的外交特权。它对旅居印尼广大爱国华侨进行了灭绝人性的种族主义迫害，焚烧华侨房屋，掠夺华侨财产，捣毁华侨商店，把成千上万的华侨关进集中营和监狱，大批华侨惨遭杀害。印尼反动政府恣意践踏国际关系的最起码的准则，制造了国际关系史上少有的法西斯暴行。你们的血债累累，罪恶昭彰，怎么能赖得掉呢？

不仅如此，印尼反动政府还同被中国人民唾弃的政治僵尸蒋匪帮明目张胆地进行勾结。它同蒋匪帮官员频繁接触，并且公开叫嚷要“承认”蒋匪帮。这是对七亿中国人民的严重政治挑衅，是蓄意破坏中国印尼两国关系的铁证。

以苏哈托、纳苏蒂安为首的印尼反动派疯狂反华，破坏中国印尼两国关系，这是由他们的反动阶级本性决定的，是他们这一小撮法西斯军人集团执行卖国、独裁、反共、反人民、反革命政策的必然结果。

这个法西斯军人集团，是印尼封建地主、官僚买办资产阶级的总代表，是最腐朽、最残暴、最反动的势力，是屠杀革命人民的刽子手。他们一上台，就进行了大逮捕、大屠杀，血洗了千岛之国。他们对印尼人民进行了敲骨吸髓的压榨和穷凶极恶的掠夺，使印尼人民处于水深火热之中。为了转移国内人民的视线，印尼反动政府就乞灵于反华排华。

这个法西斯军人集团，是地地道道的卖国贼，是美帝苏修所豢养的忠实走狗。他们的法西斯政权，本来就是在美帝国主义策划的反革命军事政变中建立起来的。他们一上台，就大肆拍卖印尼的独立和主权，向美帝苏修乞讨美元和卢布。他们加紧卖身投靠美帝苏修，就必然地要充当美帝苏修的反华走卒。

印尼反动派日益变本加厉地疯狂反华，是美帝苏修在背后策动的，是它们最近一个时期在亚洲掀起的反华浪潮的一部分。印尼反动政府反华愈是猖狂，美帝苏修就愈加起劲地为它输血，给它打气。美帝国主义已经计划今年将给予印尼反动派八千万美元的贷款。苏修也答应印尼反动派延期偿还十二亿美元的巨额债款和利息。美帝和苏修还不断地向印尼反动派提供军事“援助”。印尼反动派破坏中国印尼两国外交关系，就是适应美帝苏修的需要。

建立在血腥统治基础上的印尼法西斯政权，是极端不稳定的。它在国内面临严重政治经济危机，困难重重，就象坐在火山口上一样，惶惶不可终日。它完全依赖美帝苏修的支援过日子，并且拚命拉拢“马来西亚”拉赫曼集团、台湾蒋介石匪帮等等最腐朽的一些反革命渣滓来为自己壮胆。它对革命的中国害怕到了极点，视之为眼中钉、肉中刺，因而蓄意破坏中国印尼两国的外交关系。这恰恰反映了它的虚弱性。

印尼反动派中断中国印尼两国的外交关系，这丝毫无损于中华人民共和国，绝对阻挡不了毛泽东思想的万丈光芒，破坏不了中国印尼两国人民之间的伟大的战斗友谊。在长期反对帝国主义、殖民主义的斗争中，我们两国人民一直是互相支持，互相鼓舞。中国人民在伟大毛泽东思想指导下，一贯积极支持印尼人民的反帝反殖斗争。我国驻印尼大使馆的全体外交人员，遵循伟大领袖毛主席的教导，在支持印尼人民的革命斗争，加强两国人民之间的战斗友谊方面，也作出了积极的贡献。印尼反动派破坏中国印尼两国人民传统友谊的阴谋，是绝对不能得逞的。印尼反动派对印尼人民和中国人民犯下的滔天罪行，一定要彻底清算！

侨居印尼的广大爱国华侨，是中华民族的好儿女，是中国人民的亲骨肉。长期以来，他们同印尼人民友好相处，在反抗帝国主义侵略的斗争中，患难与共，并肩战斗。广大爱国华侨为了维护祖国的尊严，维护自己的正当权益，维护中国印尼两国人民的友谊，同印尼反动政府进行了英勇顽强的斗争。不少华侨以自己的鲜血和生命写下了气壮山河的英雄诗篇。他们的斗争是正义的，印尼人民和全世界人民同情和支持他们，伟大的社会主义祖国坚决支持他们。中国政府已经严正宣布：不管印尼反动政府破坏了两国关系，中国政府和中国人民将继续采取一切必要和可能的措施，保护华侨的正当权益。我们坚信，广大爱国华侨一定会更高地举起毛泽东思想伟大红旗，更加紧密地和印尼人民团结在一起，为粉碎印尼反动政权的种族主义迫害而斗争到底。

我们伟大领袖毛主席说：“**一切内外黑暗势力的猖獗，造成了民族的灾难；但是这种猖獗，不但表示了这些黑暗势力的还有力量，而且表示了它们的最后挣扎，表示了人民大众逐渐接近了胜利。**”印尼反动派对印尼人民所作的种种迫害，必将促使印尼人民更广泛更剧烈的革命，加速印尼人民革命高潮的到来。有着光荣的革命传统的印尼人民，目前正在重新集结力量，展开新的战斗。他们从血的教训中深刻地认识了伟大领袖毛主席教导的“**枪杆子里面出政权**”这一颠扑不破的真理，决心走中国革命的道路。我们坚信，不管印尼人民在前进的道路上还会遇到什么样的困难和曲折，革命的潮流是势不可挡的。黑暗终将过去，曙光就在前头。灿烂的阳光必将普照印尼的大地。最后的胜利一定属于英雄的印尼人民！

that the most spirited and vigorous thing about the paper was its "title-piece" (nameplate), indicating that nothing very positive could be said about the paper's appearance.[10]

People's Daily deals almost exclusively with "big" issues—national and international events—and leaves local news to the country's some 200 provincial dailies. The main news in the paper is largely concerned domestically with national progress in all fields, and internationally with unfavorable aspects of events related to its ideological foes (whether the West or another Communist nation). Wide coverage, for example, is given to activities of the National People's Congress or to important speeches by important party leaders. The war in Vietnam is regularly covered, with anti-American aspects (such as the killing of civilians) played up. Strikes and racial demonstrations in the United States get good play in *People's Daily*.

The paper constantly criticizes the United States for being in Vietnam and for progressively escalating the war. Notice the "line" it takes in an editorial in 1965, which is typical of its anti-American position:

> U.S. imperialism has repeatedly attacked the Democratic Republic of Vietnam, adopting a swashbuckling posture as if it would not hesitate to risk a bigger war. In point of fact, it is outwardly strong but inwardly brittle; it is weak and jittery despite its fearful appearance.[11]

And its attacks on the Soviet Union, especially since the middle of 1965, have been getting worse. In November, 1965, *People's Daily* charged that the "new leadership of the CPSU has conducted an incessant and massive campaign to inflame anti-Chinese sentiment at home and has sent its people abroad on anti-Chinese missions."[12] In December of the same year an editorial in the paper asserted that the Soviet Union's leaders were "hatching a big plot for a general attack on China and a general split in the international Communist movement and the social camp."[13]

The editorials of *People's Daily* are often reprinted in other Chinese papers and journals throughout the country. They represent the "official line" at the time and are necessary reading by Communist leaders. The editorials deal with a wide range of questions—foreign and domestic, political and cultural, economic and philosophical. Editorials tend to concentrate on one subject over a long period, often for several months, before dropping it for another. Frequently these editorial campaigns will be touched off by a letter from a reader which appears in the paper's popular "letters" column.[14]

People's Daily is often said to have been founded in the caves of Yenan province in 1948; but actually that paper was the *Liberation Daily* whose title was appropriated by the important party paper in Shanghai. It was rather in the Hopei province toward the end of the civil war in

1948 that *Jen-min Jih-pao* was established as the main party paper, moving to Peking in April, 1949.[15]

People's Daily has played a significant role in the new literacy campaign by urging the adoption of a simplified ideogram-language for the printed mass media and by sponsoring programs which required that the paper be read aloud to others. The paper has led the way in certain important newspaper makeup practices designed to simplify reading and make the paper more "functional." For example, headlines in *People's Daily* may be run either vertically or horizontally, and the body type (the actual text or story matter) is displayed from left to right across the page in Western fashion. This is a big departure from the traditional Chinese pattern of displaying stories right to left and vertically on the page.[16] In spite of simplified writing and more elemental "conceptographs" in the press and increased literacy drives in the schools, the literate segment of China's approximately seven hundred million would probably be no more than twenty million.

Today *People's Daily* stands as the outstanding journalistic voice of Red China, with its some three hundred editorial staff members enjoying a preferential position as the elite communicators, seven days a week, of their government's message to their countrymen and to foreigners. From its efficient East German presses housed in a modern plant on Peking's Chang An Street, come copies of a journal, which, although perhaps bizarre as a newspaper in the Western sense, is making a great impact on Chinese society and is providing a means for outsiders to study the thinking of the Peking regime.

The Sydney Morning Herald
(AUSTRALIA)

Whereas *The Age* of Melbourne is perhaps the prime representative of liberalism in the Australian daily press, it can be said that *The Sydney Morning Herald* exemplifies conservatism. The *Morning Herald* is an old paper; in fact, it has a longer history than any other Australian metropolitan paper published today. Founded in 1831 as the *Sydney Herald* (a weekly), it became a daily in 1840 and added "Morning" to its name two years later.[1] It was under John Fairfax, who guided the paper's destinies from 1841 until his death in 1877, that the paper was molded along staid conservative lines.

In a way *The Sydney Morning Herald* is a composite of England's *Times* and *Daily Mail*, for it combines the traditional serious and comprehensive news and views presentation of the former with an appeal

LATE EDITION

FORECASTS (for 24 hours from 6 a.m.): CITY: High cloud. Warm. Windy. Exp. max. temp. 80 degs. N.S.W.: Mainly fine. Warm in N., windy in S., with a cool change and isolated showers.

The Sydney Morning Herald

Monday, October 2, 1967

SUN: Today rises 5.32, sets 5.58. MOON: Rises 4.37 a.m., sets 4.4 p.m. TIDES (Fort Denison): High, 6.51 a.m. (4ft 8in), 7.2 p.m. (5ft 8in). Low, 12.43 a.m. (6in), 12.38 p.m. (8in).

No. 40,496 Telephone 2 0944 One Hundred and Thirty-seventh Year of Publication 32 PAGES & TV Guide PRICE 5c

China Embassy sacked by Djakarta mobs

DJAKARTA, Sunday.—Mobs of students today sacked the Chinese embassy and injured nine diplomats.

The Chinese fought back with broken bottles and knives as more than 1,000 club-swinging youths raided the embassy before dawn.

The attack followed the accidental deaths last night of three Indonesian students when a soldier guarding the beleaguered embassy jolted the trigger of his cocked sub-machine gun.

Only a few soldiers were posted outside the embassy during today's raid and they offered no resistance.

Students belonging to two militant student fronts, Kami and Kappi, blocked streets to the Embassy and rammed through the gates in a truck about 3 a.m.

They pulled out filing cabinets, radio equipment, printing presses, furniture and other material from embassy buildings and set the loot afire.

Several embassy cars were pushed into the bonfire.

The students then went for the diplomats.

They dragged nine embassy personnel out of their quarters and beat them as Indonesian troops looked on, United Press International says.

The diplomats fought back with broken bottles and knives and severely injured at least three of the students.

TREATED

The pillaging lasted about five hours. Then the students left as quickly as they arrived, leaving an Indonesian flag fluttering in place of a big red banner raised to celebrate China's National Day.

Troops picked up the injured diplomats and took them under heavy guard to a military hospital.

Students said the raid was in revenge for the attempted Communist coup two years ago in which six of the nation's top military officers were murdered.

The attack followed an assault on the embassy last month when a mob pillaged Chinese buildings and traded shots with embassy personnel. That attack brought relations between Indonesia and China close to the breaking point.

• Irian rebel plan squashed, Page 3.

RUSSIA: 1917 TO 1967

The "Herald" publishes on Page two today the first of two fascinating and authoritative articles on Russia today—what its people think of the past and what they hope for the future.

This year is the 50th anniversary of the Russian Revolution, and a team of 12 specialist reporters from the "New York Times" under the direction of Harrison Salisbury spent weeks in Russia preparing the articles.

The second article will appear tomorrow.

Two N.S. soldiers killed in Vietnam

CANBERRA, Sunday.—Two Australian soldiers, both National Servicemen, were killed and one wounded when Vietcong ambushed a vehicle in Phuoc Tuy province, Vietnam, early yesterday.

The men killed were Private Leslie James Weston, 22, married, of Bundaberg, Queensland, and Private William John Brett, 21, single, of Armidale, N.S.W.

Private Noel Stuart Harald, 30, single, of Yeppoon, Queensland, who was wounded, is in a very serious condition. All next of kin have been notified.

The three men were all members of C Company, 2nd Battalion, Royal Australian Regiment.

The ambush occurred when two vehicles were moving from Dat Do, south of the Australian Task Force base, to a checkpoint at the Horseshoe fortified outpost.

The Vietcong, using claymore mines, automatic rifles and grenades, ambushed the leading vehicle and fled.

Three magazines from a Soviet-manufactured automatic rifle were found in the ambush area.

• Some complaints on poll accepted—P. 3.

Bomb kills two policemen

ROME, Sunday. — Two policemen carrying a terrorist bomb away from a crowded train yesterday were killed when it exploded in their hands.

The explosion shook the town of Trento, capital of Alto Adige in the South Tyrol where German-speaking extremists are demanding a union with Austria.

LATE NEWS

Bookmakers face payout of $500,000

Doubles bookmakers face payouts of at least $500,000 if either the favourite Gala Crest or second favourite General Command wins today's Metropolitan at Randwick.

Both horses have been coupled for these amounts with Cabochon, winner of the first leg, the Epsom Handicap, at Randwick two days ago.

They also would have payouts of around $300,000 if Prince Gram, Bore Head, El Gordo or Auto Filou should win.

One Sydney punter has Gala Crest running as the second leg of a double worth $20,000.

The bookmaker who laid the bet said it was the first he had taken on the Epsom-Metropolitan double.

PRICE CUT

Another Sydney punter has front-runner Hambledon going to win him $50,000.

Bookmakers last night cut Gala Crest's price from 4-1 to 7-2, and forecast he could be at 3-1 on the course.

Former Queensland jockey Peter Gumbleton, who has yet to win a race at Randwick, will fly from Melbourne this morning to ride Gala Crest.

Gumbleton is bringing his wife over to bring him good luck.

He said in Melbourne last night: "If Des Lake can bring his mother from Melbourne to see him win the Epsom, then I can bring my wife over to see me win The Metropolitan."

"Herald" selections for The Metropolitan (13f), timed to start at 3.40 p.m., are: GALA CREST, 1; GENERAL COMMAND, 2; AVENIAM, 3.

• Race preview, page 26.

CLASH ON SIKKIM BORDER

DELHI, Sunday.—Chinese troops opened fire on Indian soldiers on the Sikkim-Tibet frontier today and intermittent firing is still going on, an Indian Defence Ministry spokesman said.

Indian troops returned fire.

The Chinese troops used recoilless guns and mortars, he added.

The shooting was at Cho La Pass, about three and a half miles from Nathu La, on the border.

The Nathu La Pass was the scene of five days of fighting between Indian and Chinese troops last month, with estimated heavy casualties on each side.

Indian casualties of that clash have not been announced, but are believed to be more than 45 dead and 60 wounded.

(A.A.P.-Reuter)

Troops shell Nigerian rebel capital

LAGOS, Sunday.—Federal forces are shelling Enugu in Biafra and are concentrating on the outskirts of the town "for the final punch."

The Federal Information Commissioner, Chief Anthony Enahoro, said today that fighting was raging near the capital of secessionist Nigeria.

Leader of the Biafrans, Lieutenant-Colonel Odumegwu Ojukwu, in a radio broadcast called on Enugu's 60,000 inhabitants to defend the city at all costs.

(A.A.P.-Reuter)

Mirage jet still missing

NEWCASTLE, Sunday.—The wreckage of a Mirage jet fighter which crashed into mountainous country near Gloucester last Monday night still had not been found tonight.

Rider's death

FORBES, Sunday.—A 28-year-old rodeo rider, Robert Harridan, of Bombala, was fatally injured yesterday when he was thrown from a bucking horse and kicked in the head at Warroo Rodeo.

THREE ASKED TO ITALY

The Prime Minister, Mr Holt, and the Minister for External Affairs, Mr P. M. C. Hasluck, have accepted formal invitations to visit Italy.

President Giuseppe Saragat, of Italy, issued the invitations yesterday at the end of his State visit to Australia.

The Italian Foreign Minister, Professor Amintore Fanfani, who accompanied Mr Saragat on his Australian tour, also formally invited the N.S.W. Premier, Mr Askin, to visit Italy.

A spokesman for the Premier's Department last night said Mr Askin was visiting relatives over the weekend and could not be reached for comment on the invitation.

In a joint communique yesterday Mr Holt and President Saragat said the President's State visit had offered an excellent occasion to consolidate the friendship between the two countries.

"It was felt that it would prove of mutual benefit to increase contact at all levels between the representatives of the two countries," the communique said.

More than 2,000 people were at Kingsford Smith Airport, Sydney, yesterday to farewell President Saragat, when he boarded the chartered Alitalia jet for his return flight to Rome.

Before boarding the aircraft, he thanked Australians for the warm welcome he had received in "this very hospitable and generous country."

• President flies home, Page 5.

The Geoghegan brothers of Liverpool, Leo (right) and Ian, receive the trophies which were later taken away from them after a check of lap scores in the Gallaher 500.

GARDEN PRIZE WINNERS ON DISPLAY

Thousands of people took advantage of fine spring weather during the weekend to visit more than 30 gardens entered in the "Herald" metropolitan garden competition.

Cars brought people from as far as Newcastle, Wollongong, Cessnock, Walgett and Woy Woy. One group hired a taxi from Katoomba to see the prize-winning displays.

Five major prize-winners alone raised more than $1,500 for charity. Some others had not counted their takings last night.

In addition many owners of gardens which won zone prizes or were highly commended are opening their gardens for charity.

Almost 3,000 people who visited the championship winning garden of Mr and Mrs R. J. McNiven, of Edgecliffe Esplanade, Seaforth, formed a continuous stream in the narrow street outside their home.

CHARITY

Mrs McNiven had to ask police for "no parking" signs to prevent cars blocking the street.

More than $700 was raised from adults' entrance fees at her home for the Far West Children's Home, Sydney auxiliary.

"You'd swear blind St George was playing the grand final out here with the number of people and cars about," said Mr J. Prideaux, of Gold Street, Blakehurst. Mr Prideaux's garden was part of the good neighbour section first prize winner.

He said carloads of people were arriving from as far away as Wollongong to see his garden and those of his neighbours, Mr and Mrs A. F. Christie and Mr and Mrs L. A. Middleton.

The three families who shared the good neighbour first prize, raised $380 for the St. John of God Hospital, Richmond.

Garden owners reported little or no damage to their displays.

Eighty-degree temperatures are expected to draw "bumper" crowds to the colourful displays, most of which will be open to the public again today.

Some of the prize-winning gardens also will be on display next weekend.

• Gardens on display today, Page 21.

Admirers crowd the a... ...arden of Mr and Mrs R. J. McNiven, of Edgecliff Esplanade, Seaforth, yesterday.

Campaign against holiday offenders

In the first two days of the holiday weekend police throughout N.S.W. arrested 51 motorists and booked another 1,485 for traffic offences.

The State-wide traffic campaign will continue today with all available police on duty to control the flow of holiday traffic back to the city.

Traffic snarls repeatedly brought holiday motorists to a halt on the Pacific Highway leading out of Sydney yesterday morning.

From early morning until noon police worked to sort out two lines of north-bound cars trying to converge into a single line at Mount Kuring-gai.

11 KILLED

About 1,600 cars an hour were running into the bottleneck, where several accidents earlier in the morning already had caused chaos.

Eleven people have been killed in N.S.W. road accidents so far this weekend.

The toll brought total deaths on N.S.W. roads so far this year to 829, eight more than in the same period last year.

Fine, warm weather is expected to continue today, with freshening north-westerly winds and a top temperature of 80 degrees in Sydney.

The Leader of the Federal Opposition, Mr E. G. Whitlam, will lead the Eight Hour Day march from the Town Hall to Redfern Oval at 10.30 a.m. today.

Main sporting events will be racing at Randwick, second round of the cricket, metropolitan tennis championships at Strathfield, speedboats on Kogarah Bay from 10.30 a.m. and motor cycle racing at Mount Panorama, Bathurst.

• Road toll report, Page 9.

Death of Mr O. J. Syme

MELBOURNE, Sunday.—Mr Oswald J. Syme, former chairman of David Syme and Co. Ltd., publisher of the "Age," died in the Freemasons Hospital, East Melbourne, today, aged 89.

He was the last surviving son of the late David Syme, one of the founders of the "Age" 113 years ago.

• Obituary, Page 4.

Placings mix-up in 500 car race

By Our Motoring Editor

BATHURST, Sunday.—The Ford Falcon GT co-drivers Harry Firth and Fred Gibson were tonight declared provisional winners of the Gallaher 500 Saloon Car Race after nearly four hours of doubt about who had actually won.

At the end of the race it was the Geoghegan brothers, of Liverpool, who received the checkered flag, the winner's laurels, sashes and champagne.

But when official provisional results were issued about 7.30 tonight, Firth, of Victoria, and Gibson, of Sydney, were named the winners.

Ian Geoghegan lodged a protest which may be heard next week.

The secretary of the Australian Racing Drivers' Club, Mr Jack Hinxman, said the change had been made following a re-check of the official lap scores.

He said that Firth and Gibson had not protested.

As it now stands, the Geoghegans are placed second outright, followed by Doug Chivas and Max Stewart, in an Alfa Romeo GTV, with Kevin Bartlett and Laurie Stewart also in an Alfa, in fourth place.

Almost everyone in the estimated crowd of 20,000 was surprised when the checkered flag fell first on the Geoghegan car.

Leo Geoghegan, who was driving the Ford Falcon GT at the finish, was in some doubt as to his position.

"I thought I may have been in the lead," he said.

• Race record, more pictures Page 7.

'Pill' emerging as major child poisoner

CANBERRA, Sunday.—Forty-six children under five were poisoned by contraceptive pills during the first six months of the year, the Minister for Health, Dr A. J. Forbes, said today.

"It appears that contraceptive pills are emerging as a major cause of poisoning among young children," he said.

Dr Forbes was releasing details of some of the 1,909 cases of accidental poisoning to children under five which had been reported to the National Poisons Service in the first half of the year.

Poison case reporting began on a national scale in January.

Dr Forbes said only eight of all the poisoning cases had been fatal, but long-term illness had resulted in many cases.

Most of the reported cases were due to poisoning by medicinal preparations being left around the house within easy reach of children.

There were 795 cases of poisoning by medicinal preparations including pain-relieving drugs (mostly aspirin) 119 cases, sedatives 73, tranquillisers and anti-depressants 67, and anti-histamines 59.

Household preparations such as bleaches, disinfectants, detergents and other cleaners accounted for 374 poison cases.

Pesticides, of which a large number were domestic fly sprays, were responsible for another 204 poisonings. Kerosene and similar solvents were involved in 176 cases.

Dr Forbes urged that all drugs be carefully disposed of once a course of drug treatment was completed.

This was particularly important for attractive, brightly coloured, sugar-coated tablets which had been specially prepared for use by young children.

"They cannot be expected to distinguish them from sweets which many of them are permitted to eat freely," Dr Forbes said.

Dr Forbes also recommended that potentially dangerous household preparations such as kerosene, substances containing kerosene, disinfectants, fly sprays, and pesticides should be kept out of the reach of young children at all times.

New-born baby saved from rubbish heap

MELBOURNE, Sunday.—A naked newly born boy, blue from cold, was found abandoned on a rubbish heap in a lane at suburban Huntingdale today.

He was nearly dead from exposure when admitted to the Royal Melbourne Children's Hospital after a high-speed dash by police.

Police have launched an extensive search for the mother, who they fear is in urgent need of medical treatment.

'ON A HEAP'

Tonight the baby, named Simon by other children at the hospital, was back to a healthy pink.

Doctors said he weighed 6lb 2oz and was a fine, healthy boy.

Simon owes his life to his lusty voice—his cries were heard by Mr Ned Hall, of Ross Street, Huntingdale.

Mr Hall was walking along Ross Street when he heard the cries coming from the lane at the rear of his home.

"For a few minutes I couldn't work it out and then I saw the baby lying on a heap of rubbish and ashes," he said.

"I got a real shock—he was lying there with not a stitch on and crying his head off."

Mr Hall's sister, Mrs Annette Darlo, a mother of two young children, ran outside with a blanket and wrapped the baby in it.

"I must have had the touch because he stopped crying and I held him while the police were called," Mrs Darlo said.

But when Mrs Darlo handed Simon over to the police, he started crying again and finally they had to ask her if she would come with them to the hospital.

Police blocked off streets and redirected traffic as the police car, carrying Mrs Darlo and Simon, made the dash to the hospital.

His temperature was 11 degrees below normal when he arrived at the hospital.

He will stay at the hospital for a few days until he recovers. A decision will then be made on where he will be sent.

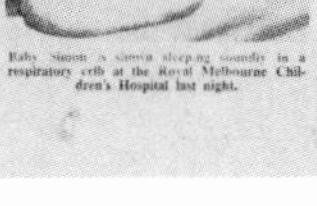

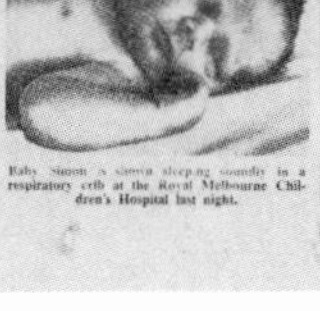

Baby Simon is shown sleeping soundly in a respiratory crib at the Royal Melbourne Children's Hospital last night.

TWO DIE IN DAM TRAGEDY

MELBOURNE, Sunday.—A middle-aged couple drowned after their car rolled into a storage dam at Yallourn, 90 miles east of Melbourne, today.

Police were called when a passing motorist noticed the roof of a car partly submerged in the dam.

The dead couple were Archibald McLachlan, 63, of Eastern Hostel, Yallourn, and Estel Curtis, 43, of Western Avenue, Newborough.

Police said the couple were sitting in the car, which was parked in a parking area alongside the dam, when it rolled down a slight embankment into the water.

Sleeping man dies in bedroom fire

MELBOURNE, Sunday.—A middle-aged man died when fire gutted his bedroom in an apartment house in suburban Armadale early today.

The fire is believed to have started in the man's room while he was asleep. His name was not released tonight.

Firemen were called to the blaze soon after 3 a.m.

Substation-Officer G. A. Mather fell through a charred section of a ceiling while fighting the fire and was taken to the Alfred Hospital.

COLUMN EIGHT

INDIGNATION. A sign-post at Sandringham, on Botany Bay, reads: "The Department of Civil Aviation is spending taxpayers' money to keep birds away from Australian airports. For safety sake please don't encourage birds to this area by feeding them."

Yesterday three seagulls perched atop the sign, tilted their heads as though to read it—then flew straight to sea.

\+ + +

LIFE in the doghouse, 1967 style. Positions Vacant small ad.: "Girl for Dog Kennel. Live-in."

\+ + +

PARLEZ VOUS? Federal Ministers are not noted for their linguistic ability, but some try hard. The former Minister for Immigration, Mr Hubert Opperman, could make a competent speech in colloquial French—learnt while pedalling France's highways as the world's No. 1 cyclist. His successor, Mr Billy Snedden, is studying Spanish and essayed it a few times on a recent overseas visit.

When addressing visiting Italian journalists, the Minister in charge of tourist activities, Mr Don Chipp, spoke in what he described as "my very bad Italian." The visitors appeared to understand—or were too polite to say they did not.

\+ + +

SOFT SELL. California has the distinction, among other things, of having given the world the Hippies. Now its Wine Advisory Board recommends wine with hospital meals "to produce a state of euphoria—and reduce patient complaints—a phenomenon which is particularly welcomed by hospital staffs."

\+ + +

UP-TO-DATE. Those P.M.G. boys never forget. Mr R. M. Cooper, headmaster of Canterbury Boys' High School, was notified by the department of the school's new telephone numbers. The letter was addressed to Mr E. J. Rourke, the school's first headmaster and "father" of Canterbury, who retired in 1932 and died in 1950.

\+ + +

CROWNED. When the A.M.P. switched to computers, policy holder Henry Victor King emerged as "KING HENRY V." Mr King, businessman, travel agent and motel owner, of Port Lincoln, South Australia, lives at Kingscourt—just to complete the illusion.

\+ + +

SEA CYCLIST. The Japanese cargo vessel Fugo Maru, now visiting Sydney, is a big bulk-carrier — so big that when it moored off Cremorne Point a crew member rode a bicycle along the deck to get to the windlass from his accommodation right aft.

INSIDE

Printed and published by John Fairfax and Sons Limited, of Jones Street, Broadway, ... Postal address, Box 506 G.P.O. Sydney, 2001. Registered at the General Post Office, Sydney, for transmission by post as a newspaper.

to a larger audience found in the latter. In the United States, the *Los Angeles Times* and the *Chicago Tribune* would seem to combine characteristics which fuse in the dual nature of the *Morning Herald.* Undoubtedly the most dignified of Australian newspapers in its makeup, the paper spreads its contents about with great reserve and care. The main front-page story is positioned in the upper-left corner (following British practice) and it usually carries a large picture at the top center of its front page. Its pages, like many other Australian newspaper pages, carry ten columns, making them wider than the more common European and American pages of eight (or six) columns.

Letters to the editor are important to the newspaper. So are editorials ("leaders") which are very lively and readable and which have helped the paper gain the reputation of being "a gadfly to complacency."[2] The news columns emphasize law, police activities, and accidents (mainly for the "popular" tastes), and a heavy coverage is given to politics, economics, and foreign affairs for the more serious segments of the readership. Literary articles and book reviews in *The Sydney Morning Herald* are especially good.[3] Its criticism of the arts in general is considered the best in Australia, and especially noteworthy is the paper's weekly (Saturday) magazine and book review section.[4]

Although the *Morning Herald* does not give the proportional stress to international news given in such papers as the *Neue Zürcher Zeitung* of Switzerland or *Le Monde* of France (or even the *West Australian* of Perth), it does provide good foreign coverage. Certainly it compares well with *The Age* and the Melbourne *Herald,* both outstanding world-oriented papers. By Australian standards the bureaus of the *Morning Herald* in New York and London are large, and its interpretive pieces on international relations received from these two places especially are excellent. Most of the paper's foreign news comes from the Australian Associated Press (AAP); additional news from abroad filters in from its own correspondents and stringers and from special news services.

The *Morning Herald* sees itself as a special type of Australian paper and one with a unique quality. For example, it says:

> The aim of the *Herald* is to provide a full, comprehensive, and responsible service to the minority whose tastes require it, while also giving it, in substance and form, suitable to the vast numbers of modern newspaper readers who demand a "popular" Press. . . .[5]

Following this formula, the paper has made itself acceptable to a large segment of Australians, and its circulation of more than 300,000 is quite substantial for the country. In many ways its general appeal and serious demeanor reminds one of Denmark's influential conservative *Berlingske Tidende.*

John Fairfax in the 1850's and 1860's molded the *Morning Herald* into the important institution it is today. It has grown steadily since, always substantially controlled by the Fairfax family,[6] and maintaining its conservative orientation.[7] The newspaper filled its front page with classified advertising until 1944 when it was replaced with news; in this respect it predated its English colleague, *The Times*, by twenty years. Symbolizing the urbanity of the paper today is a regular column ("Column 8") signed "Granny" (a term often used to refer to the paper itself) which appears on the right side of the front page. It is one of Australia's most popular columns and manages to combine a sophisticated commentary on the news with gossipy items.

One of the persons who during recent years has been most influential at the *Morning Herald* has been Rupert Henderson. He was managing director until 1964 and presently is a member of the board. Present board chairman, Warwick Fairfax, has said that Henderson, who has been with the paper about a half century, "is entitled to be regarded as the outstanding newspaperman of his generation."[8] The senior staff members of the *Morning Herald* are all outstanding Australian newspapermen—competent, literate, cosmopolitan, and experienced.

The Sydney Morning Herald is published in one of the most modern newspaper plants in the world at Broadway and Wattle Streets, Sydney. Its age, its forceful articulation of opinion, its dignity of presentation, and its concern with well-rounded news coverage have combined to make the *Morning Herald* one of the elite newspapers of the world.

PART II

Selected Elite: A Closer Look

This second section of the book, in one way, is simply a continuation of the profiles of elite papers which have been presented in Chapters 6 through 9. However, there are reasons for keeping the fourteen which follow separate, and not including them in appropriate slots in the preceding four chapters.

First, there is the simple fact of the writer's bias or his preference for these particular fourteen papers. Although they may not be the best in every way of the world's elite papers, they are believed to contain certain characteristics and special potential for influence which are absent (or less potent) in most of the other leading elite papers. Certainly these fourteen do not form a homogeneous "group"; their natures are diverse, but they seem to objectify the most salient features of the elite press. When they are considered together they tend to blend their distinctive tones into a full-bodied orchestration of world journalism.

Second, there is no doubt but that these fourteen dailies would rank very high in any list of the world's most influential and most serious newspapers. They are in many respects, and with few exceptions, of a very high order of elite newspapers.

For these reasons, admittedly largely subjective, are the following profiles presented. About the only way they differ from those in Part I is that they are treated more intensively, with the hope that they will offer a fuller and more meaningful view of particularly important papers and will illumine certain areas of elite journalism generally.

The fourteen profiles which follow represent ten nations and four continents. In no way does the order in which they are presented indicate an attempt at ranking them. They appear according to major geographical region (continent) in the order of that region's representation in the profiles. Therefore, the nine European papers lead off, followed by Latin America's two papers and by the two from the United States. Finally, the one from Asia is presented.

Profiles, then, come in this order: The British papers, *The Guardian* and *The Times*; Denmark's *Berlingske Tidende*; France's *Le Monde*; West Germany's *Frankfurter Allgemeine* and *Die Welt*; Switzerland's *Neue Zürcher Zeitung*, and Italy's *Corriere della Sera* and *Osservatore Romano* (Vatican City). Next come the Latin American dailies, Mexico's *Excélsior* and Argentina's *La Prensa*; the United States' dailies, *Los Angeles Times* and *The New York Times*, and finally, Japan's *Asahi Shimbun*, representing Asia.

The fact that all fourteen are from the non-Communist world may, of course, indicate further bias on the writer's part. This is certainly not denied, and, with the exception of Vatican City's *Osservatore Romano*, all of the newspapers exemplify the best in free and pluralistic journalism which, from the writer's Western libertarian perspective, would seem to be most valuable in bringing about a world community of reason.

10

British Elite: Two Paths

Respect for tradition, a deliberateness in analyzing possible courses of action, civility and respect in taking issue with opponents, a love for thoroughness, a caustic and sly humor, spirited debate, subtle innuendo and delicate phrasing, firm resolve yet flexibility of action, a love for pomp and ceremony and the trappings of class hierarchy yet a feeling for the common man. These attributes, contradictory in many respects, may well describe the complex person who calls himself British, and to a very great degree they are reflected in the two outstanding British quality daily newspapers—*The Guardian* and *The Times*.

Quite likely no country but Britain could have two elite dailies so different yet so much alike as these Big Two of England. Together they represent or personify the British character and the best in the nation's journalism.

Where *The Guardian* is brash and liberal, *The Times* is staid and conservative; where the former is a gadfly, the latter is a defender. But despite such differences the two dailies have this in common: They are both trying to provide Englishmen with serious, relevant news and views and to keep journalistic dialogue on a sane and rational plane.

While *The Guardian* considers itself Britain's conscience, *The Times* views itself as a solid rock of traditional English thought and virtue that provides a stabilizing influence in a chaotic world. Where *The Guardian* is nonconformist, *The Times* is conformist. Where *The Guardian* eagerly casts about for a cause or a foe to attack, *The Times* rolls quietly on seeking to pacify rather than to agitate. It might well be said that the

Big Two are opposite but complementary sides of the most valuable British journalistic coin: Rational Leadership.

These two morning national dailies, as representatives of the best in British journalism, retain their individual personalities, although they continue to grow and change. They maintain their balance, dignity and, most important of all, their rationality as they seek to keep abreast of the complexities of the modern world. Both speak to a well-educated, concerned audience in a conversational tone that inspires confidence and dispels emotionalism. Both papers are proud of their past and confident of their future. Things are happening to both papers: In 1952 news was put on the front page of the *Manchester Guardian* for the first time, and then the paper dropped the "Manchester" from its nameplate in 1959, started a separate edition in London, and has become a national paper. *The Times* threw off its traditional front-page advertising in favor of news in May of 1966, revamped its typography and layout, and found itself on much more solid financial ground when Lord Thomson of Fleet bought into it in the fall of 1966. It has made significant progress since.

Britain, and especially London, has excellent newspapers (both daily and weekly) other than *The Guardian* and *The Times—The Daily Telegraph, The Financial Times*, and *The Observer*. But the Big Two dailies best represent what is most outstanding in the nation's journalism: spirit, intelligence, and stability. Although both papers tend to slip from journalistic grace from time to time, and although other British papers on occasion evidence more enterprise or skill or insight in dealing with certain events or issues, the Big Two elite dailies continue to exemplify quality journalism at its vigorous, literate, and rational best.

On the following pages of this chapter the two papers are viewed more closely, first *The Guardian* and then *The Times* (for alphabetical reasons only). Necessarily they must be treated rather superficially here, which is rather a pity for their histories are extremely rich and their current journalistic practices should offer inspiration to the budding journalist and challenge to the hardened veteran wherever they may be found. But perhaps a cursory look at the imposing duo will help illumine two great British dailies and serve as a stimulant to further interest in these quite different, yet amazingly similar, British newspapers.

The Guardian

The Guardian, publishing today simultaneously in London and Manchester, is not a newspaper to which one reacts neutrally. This is the way it has always been since its founding as a small Manchester weekly in 1821. The paper has served as a catalyst to the nonconformist British conscience and has represented the most informed and intelligent sector of British progressive, liberal thought. As T. S. Matthews has said, *The Guardian* "keeps reminding its readers that civilization exists and is worth saving."[1]

With a total daily circulation (for its four editions) of 285,000, *The Guardian* is liberal with a small "l" and is designed mainly for "intellectuals, thinkers, lively minds, and businessmen." It considers its strongest areas "depth" foreign news, articles with "social conscience value," and political news. Some 120 editors and writers, mostly university graduates, work to achieve the paper's special kind of quality. Twenty foreign correspondents round out the paper's coverage and give it a cosmopolitanism for which it is universally noted.[2]

The Guardian has been called "Britain's nonconformist conscience, literate, scatty,"[3] and it does, indeed, see its role "as admonishing and instructing the national conscience."[4] T. S. Matthews lauds it as "a daily compendium of modern and current history and politics, theoretical and applied science, economics, contemporary literary and art, and on occasion . . . archaeology, ancient history, philosophy, and engineering as well."[5] It has a vision of itself equally as flattering as that seen by Matthews. In 1966 its self-description noted that it was an analytical ("analyzes news like no other paper"), careful ("looks carefully at everything of importance in the world"), and important paper. It sees itself also as a serious paper ("never sensational and tries not to be superficial"), an honest paper ("doesn't mold facts to suit its line"), and one that is opinionated but truthful ("although it has strong opinions, they are not allowed to get in the way of truth").

It also sees itself as a paper with social-awareness ("has great humanity, cares about social problems"), and with high writing standards ("great attention is given to the English that is written for it, grammatical standards are set extremely high"). It is concerned with intellectual content but values lighter material also ("ideas count for a lot but the entertainment value of newspapers is not lost sight of"), and it believes it is highly significant ("to read *The Guardian* is to get to the heart of things").[6]

In 1931 the *Manchester Guardian*, as it was then called, received an Honor Award "for distinguished work in journalism" from the University of Missouri School of Journalism. The citation, presented by Dean Walter Williams of the world's oldest school of journalism, commended the paper for "its defining by unremitting practice for the profession everywhere those journalistic virtues of reliability and authority; for its brilliant battle for liberalism, for sympathetic understanding of the points of view of other people and other nations, for its courageous fight for peace, and for its sensitiveness to moral ideas."[7]

The Guardian, without a doubt, is a national institution in Britain, and along with its more conservative counterpart, *The Times*, has made a significant impact on British society. *The Guardian*, although considering itself the paper of highest quality ("the best") in Britain, bestows second place on *The Times*, while admitting that "frankly *The Times* gives a wider news coverage on certain occasions."[8] *The Guardian* considers *The Times* somewhat "pompous and censorious, timid, snobbish and orthodox,"[9] and, while it sees its own role as "admonishing and instructing the national conscience," it views *The Times* as "the servant of the Establishment."[10]

C. P. Scott, the paper's greatest editor, once said that a newspaper's "primary office is the gathering of news" and that "at the peril of its soul it must see that the supply is not tainted," for, as he added: "Comment is free, but facts are sacred."[11] Today *The Guardian* has perhaps forsaken to some degree Scott's emphasis on news, for less than half of its nonadvertising space is filled with news—the rest with something else (criticism, commentaries, predictions, interpretation, political polemic). The concern in *The Guardian* appears to be not on news but on this "something else" and various of its critics, like British journalist Henry Fairlie who is one of the bitterest, believe it has ceased to function as a newspaper.

Fairlie, for example, writing in the British intellectual monthly *Encounter* in 1966, wrote *The Guardian* off with these blistering words:

> It has almost ceased to function as a newspaper altogether. Its news coverage, foreign and domestic, is spasmodic and never complete; its comment is always unexhilarating, and normally unilluminating; its feature pages are an acknowledged disaster . . . its writing, generally, is arch when it is not simply incompetent. It is without form, without substance, and without purpose: a disgrace to radical journalism.[12]

Fairlie's criticism, although it seems unduly harsh, does reflect a rather general attitude among both liberals and conservatives (especially those connected to the press and broadcasting) in Europe.[13] In 1966, at least, there was rather general feeling that *The Guardian* had slipped considerably in recent years and that it was a rather pale and tame image of its former self. Other press commentators, however, do not agree. For instance, Karl E. Meyer, in a long analysis of the British press in the United States' *Esquire* magazine, at the same time that Fairlie was downgrading *The Guardian,* had this to say of the paper:

> *The Guardian* is to the English nonconformist conscience what *L'Osservatore Romano* is to the Vatican. Since the Boer War, the paper has been dissenting with robust regularity. Its opposition to Britain's Suez adventure cost it thousands of readers. Under Alastair Hetherington, soft-spoken, boyish and North Country in manner, *The Guardian* continues to afflict the powerful and has differed from U.S. policy in Vietnam.[14]

Regardless of particular appraisals both positive and negative of *The Guardian,* it is obvious that the paper is still very much a force to be reckoned with, and has counted among its staff members in recent years names of great import in world journalism—Norman Shrapnel (Parliament reporter and one of the most admired stylists and reporters in Britain), Gerard Fay (London editor and expert on the Far East), David Low (the famous New Zealand-born cartoonist), Richard Fry (German-born financial editor), Alistair Cooke, Max Freedman, and Richard Scott (United States correspondents who are among the paper's popular writers), and others such as Hella Pick, George Hawthorne, Peter Jenkins, Ian Aitken, Terence Prittie, Darsie Gillie, Victor Zorza, and Normand Crossland.

In a study made of American and English dailies and their use of foreign news in 1966, *The Guardian* was found to give over 16.7 per cent of its news space to foreign news.[15] This, obviously, is a substantial proportion and shows that the paper retains its cosmopolitan outlook. This percentage, although behind *The Times'* 20.8 per cent, was considerably larger than America's *Washington Post* (12.6 per cent) and only slightly behind *The New York Times* (17 per cent).

Regardless of certain indications of disillusionment with *The Guardian* by some critics, surveys show that readers value the paper most for its lack of bias. Perhaps its strongest following (in Britain, at least) is in the universities, and surveys have seemed to substantiate this. One study has shown that *The Guardian* is read by one-third of all British university students, and that it is the daily paper which most students read and buy regularly.[16] *The Guardian* is widely read in intellectual circles in other countries also, especially in the United States. Actually it is the small-format *Manchester Guardian Weekly* that has the great overseas readership. In the United States the *MGW* is the most widely read foreign paper imported into the country. *The Guardian* has no Sunday edition and the *MGW*, an anthology of its best stories, fills this weekend need, with about half of its copies going abroad.

The Guardian today values its overseas coverage as much as it does its overseas audience. It maintains staff correspondents in New York, Washington, Paris, Bonn, Geneva, East Africa, and at the United Nations. It also has local correspondents in almost every country; from all these comes a steady flow of foreign news and interpretive pieces to supplement normal agency reports. A team of staff members in both Manchester and London are ready at all times to fly to any spot in the world at a moment's notice. Domestically, *The Guardian* keeps main offices or bureaus in Bristol, Birmingham, Leeds, Newcastle on Tyne, and Glasgow. In addition, local correspondents or stringers are in every major town and city of Britain.

Today's *Guardian* is a very different newspaper from the small four-page weekly first issued on May 5, 1821, by John Edward Taylor, son of a Manchester Unitarian minister. At this time, the only dailies in Britain were in London, provincial cities and towns not having the potential readership to support anything but weeklies. *The Guardian* faced great local competition at the time of its birth; six other weeklies were already publishing in Manchester. But in spite of this, *The Manchester Guardian* (the "The" was dropped in 1952 and the "Manchester" in 1959 with the "The" being restored) was a success from the outset. Perhaps one reason was that it gave more emphasis to editorials than did the other papers.[17]

John Taylor, the founder, was an ardent Liberal and active member of the Reform movement. He and a dozen of his friends intended the new paper to aid the Liberal cause, but it was not to be confined to this. A prospectus published prior to the paper's first issue, stated in part:

> It will zealously enforce the principles of civil and religious Liberty, in the most comprehensive sense of those terms; it will warmly advocate the cause of Reform; it will endeavour to assist in the diffusion of just principles of Political Economy. . . . The Foreign Intelligence of the week will be regularly and succinctly detailed, whilst particular attention will be paid to Parliamentary Debates. . . .[18]

Two years after the first *Manchester Guardian* was issued, it was selling 1,750 copies each week, and the next year the sales doubled. After twelve years the paper had Manchester's largest circulation—nearly 4,000.[19]

In 1855 when the stamp duty on newspapers was abolished, daily morning papers sprang up rapidly in the provinces. The *Manchester Guardian* became one of the first of these and dropped its price from twopence to a penny. Thereafter, the paper grew rapidly in circulation, coverage, and prestige. Until 1861, it went through a series of editors and that year J. E. Taylor II became editor. At this time *The Guardian*, with a circulation of more than 20,000, was becoming well known as a sound and thoughtful provincial daily. In 1870 it had its own war correspondents in the Franco-Prussian War—three with the French and one with the Germans.[20]

A young Oxford graduate was to join *The Guardian* in 1871, a person who was destined to stamp his personality on the paper and give it a worldwide reputation. He was Charles Prestwich Scott. Before coming to *The Guardian* to work for his cousin, J. E. Taylor II, he had worked briefly as an apprentice journalist at *The Scotsman* in Edinburgh. Scott was with *The Guardian* but a year when he was appointed editor. At the time he was only twenty-five years old.[21] Scott was determined to improve the quality of the paper. He pounced immediately on sloppy writing, and wrote at one point: "People talk of 'journalese,' as though a journalist were of necessity a pretentious and sloppy writer; he may be, on the contrary, and very often is, one of the best writers in the world. At least, he should not be content to be much less."[22] Scott gathered an outstanding group of journalists around him such as John Masefield, William Archer, Laurence Housman, J. M. Keynes, Arthur Ransome, Arnold Toynbee, J. M. Synge, and W. T. Stead.[23]

Taking particular interest and pride in the editorial page, Scott considered himself the keeper of the paper's conscience—a conscience which he desired to make the conscience of Britain itself. He was quick to instill in his staff the conviction that *The Guardian* was not like other papers, that it was a special kind of paper, in a class unto itself. Scott enforced his high ideals with severity. He demanded good writing and deplored articles exhibiting only "smartness" and "trick of words . . . made to atone for lack of thought."[24] Speaking of the paper's duty, he said that it must have "courage and fairness, and a sense of duty to the reader and community" and that its "primary office is the gathering of news," stressing that "at the peril of its soul it must see that the supply is not tainted." Scott's desire for fairness is evidenced in his famous words: "Comment is free, but facts are sacred. Propaganda . . . is hateful. The voice of opponents . . . has a right to be heard. . . . It is well to be frank; it is even better to be fair."[25]

The Guardian was bought by Scott in 1907 after the death of J. E. Taylor. Scott was then sixty, his wife had just died; he made the paper his whole life and remained engrossed in its direction for the next twenty-four years. Jumping early into the political fray, Scott involved his paper in the great issues beginning in 1886 with the "Irish question" (the Home Rule issue), which *The Guardian* supported in the face of much opposition. Its stands often made the paper unpopular. During World War I, for example, during a highly nationalistic period, *The Guardian* presented the minority views of internationalism and pacifism.[26]

In 1921 when the paper was a hundred years old and Scott had been editor-in-chief a half-century, all of Britain, regardless of ideology or party, congratulated him. Lloyd George called him "the noblest figure in modern journalism." *The Observer* called him "the greatest and in every way the best of all recorded editors." *The New York Times* said

Autumn books, pp. 9-12

CHESTER BARRIE SUITS FROM KENDALS MAN'S SHOP

THE GUARDIAN

37,710 Manchester Friday October 6 1967 Price 5d

Please Remember YOUR LOCAL CHILDREN'S CHARITY
The Boys' and Girls' Welfare Society, 16-18 Queen Street, Manchester 2.

LTA goes it alone on Open tennis

By DAVID GRAY

The Lawn Tennis Association made the most momentous decision in its 80 year history at a council meeting in London yesterday by recommending the abolition of the distinction between amateurs and professionals in this country in defiance of the rulings of the International Lawn Tennis Federation.

Risking ban

Britain may try again in Salisbury

With the Rhodesian Front and Labour Party conferences out of the way, it now seems likely that the Commonwealth Secretary, Mr George Thomson, will include Salisbury in his visits to African capitals in the next few weeks.

Our political staff report from Scarborough that there is no desire among Ministers to raise expectations of a new round of "Tiger-style" talks with the Smith regime and that contacts with Mr Smith in the current exchange of letters between the two capitals have given no ground for hope that the regime is ready for meaningful negotiations.

Sir Humphrey Gibbs, the Governor of Rhodesia, is known to be anxious for a new initiative towards a settlement.

Dr Kaunda accuses Britain, Rhodesian nickel projects, Obstacles to Minister's tour, page 14.

Zambia's offer

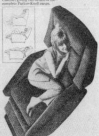

Frustrated export at Liverpool Docks. Report, page 2.

Dockers ignore strike call from Mr Dash

BY OUR OWN REPORTER

Attempts to persuade the rest of London's dockers to join the 6,000 on strike at the Royal Group of docks failed yesterday.

The militancy of Mr Jack Dash, leader of the unofficial port workers' liaison committee, ended in face. He led a march of 4,000 strikers from the Royal group to the West India and Millwall docks, intending to hold a prostrike mass meeting. But the 4,000 found the West India men at work: no one had told them about Mr Dash's meeting. At Tilbury Mr Dash did have his meeting—during the lunch break—but the Tilbury men then returned to work.

Into dry dock

Held to ransom

Common Market overtures backed by Labour Party

From JOHN TORODE, our Labour Correspondent—Scarborough, Thursday

The Labour Party is now solidly, but far from unanimously, in support of the Government's overtures to the Common Market.

Report	page 5
Comment	8
William Davis	15
More expansion plans	22
Peter Jenkins	22

Essential issues

Full employment

Chinese and dockers clash after Mao insult

Marines to protect Aden withdrawal

Aden, October 5

Jobs policy 'courageous'

Buenos Aires, October 5

Mr G. Brown confronts Mr G. Brown

From JOHN PALMER

Scarborough, Thursday

Pressure for invasion of North Vietnam, page 13

Trawlers get corned beef warning

By our Correspondent

Hovercraft link

Envoy's talks with de Gaulle routine

EFTA concern, page 17

Flying Yorkshiremen

On other pages

MR MARSH, the Minister of Power, has been asked to intervene in the exchange between the Coal Board and the Central Electricity Generating Board ... 3

AIRCRAFT programme "proceeding exactly as planned"; or is it "under the axe"? ... 8

Archestratus	6
Arts	7
Chess problem	21
Crossword	21
Finance and Industry	15 & 16
"GUARDIAN" INQUIRY: Drink and driving	4
Home news	2-5, & 22
Horner	2
Jenkins's column	22
Leaders and letters	8
London letter	7
Overseas news	13 & 14
Sport	20 & 21
TV and radio	2
Weather forecast	22
Women	6

Classified advertising

Appointments: Senior and Executive	17 & 19
Public	4, 17, 18, & 19
Full index	2

Cotton MPs protest at snub

By our own Reporters

MPs' letter

Little cheer, page 15

Biafran leader 'fleeing'

Lagos, October 5

that "for many years the *Manchester Guardian* has been regarded both at home and abroad as the most influential newspaper in England."[27] Scott was to die eleven years after these accolades.

During C. P. Scott's editorship, his oldest son John Russell Scott was business manager of the paper. It was he who built up the paper's financial reserves until he was able to buy the *Manchester Evening News* in 1924. (The two papers have remained editorially autonomous ever since.) When the elder Scott retired in 1929, he was succeeded as editor by his younger son, Edward T. Scott. C. P. Scott died in 1932 and a few months later Edward T. was drowned in a boating accident.

The chief editorial writer of *The Guardian*, W. P. Crozier, was appointed editor and served in this capacity for the next twelve years. When he died in 1944, Alfred Powell Wadsworth, again the chief editorial writer, took over the editorship. As T. S. Matthews has said, "Scott had made *The Guardian* a great paper: Crozier had kept it going. Wadsworth developed it and made it better than ever."[28] A friendly and aproachable man, Wadsworth was called "A. P." by most of the staff. He had been a journalist for four decades when he became *The Guardian*'s editor. He encouraged the light touch, and the paper's style became more contemporary and colloquial than it had ever been. It was said that Scott made righteousness readable but Wadsworth also made it witty.[29] He died in 1956 when he was sixty-four.

It was then that Alastair Hetherington became editor. His editorship began only a week before the Suez Crisis. He had previously been the paper's foreign editor. Before coming to *The Guardian* he had worked for the *Glasgow Herald* in his home town, and for a time in Hamburg for *Die Welt.* In character with *The Guardian's* past, Hetherington opposed Britain's Suez adventure, a stand that for a time cost it thousands of readers.[30] In 1964 the editor moved to new headquarters in London, at 192 Grays Inn Road, but he has since made frequent and regular visits to the old Manchester offices at 3 Cross Street.

The Guardian is owned by the Scott Trust which has control of all voting shares in the publishing company. A few nonvoting, fixed-dividend shares remain in public hands but they represent only a small part of the paper's capital and the fact is that the newspaper is run in a nonprofit-distributing manner. The Trust holds the shares and is the proprietor of the newspaper. Members of the Trust are three grandsons of C. P. Scott and three senior employees of the paper. Laurence Prestwich Scott is chairman and joint managing director of the Manchester Guardian and Evening News Ltd.[31]

Editorially *The Guardian* today is as liberal and radical as it was in its early days. Its executives, however, want to make sure that the terms "liberal" and "radical" are understood. They say, for example, that it is not Liberal in the sense of being attached to the Liberal Party, a party to which it has never been officially connected. It also gives encouragement and support to the Labour Party and even at times to the Conservatives "when the policies and performance of either party merit them."[32]

"Radicalism" to *The Guardian* means "holding the most advanced views on political reform by democratic methods." It is the underlying radicalism applied to all of life which *The Guardian* believes makes it possible for the paper to support no party officially and yet avoid the danger of being uncommitted or indifferent.[33] Although considering itself "radical," it also considers itself ideologically "center-left."[34] Its editorial stand, quite consistent with left-liberalism, is in part one advocating Red China's admission to the U. N., the United States' recognition of Red China, nuclear disarmament, American withdrawal from Vietnam, a strong British and world opposition to Rhodesia and South Africa, and better relations generally with Communist nations. This position, unpopular in many quarters, shows that the paper has not broken the basic liberal-radical journalistic ties with the earliest days of its history. Although it has changed, and is changing, it remains very much the same. In this respect it is like its older and better-known rival of the quality press—*The Times* of London.

The Times

Early in 1968, *The Times* of London, under the stimulating ownership of Roy Thomson and the progressive editorship of forty-year-old William Rees-Mogg, had boosted its circulation to more than 350,000 and had become more lively and controversial. It has managed to keep its highly respected image of reliability, civility, and dignity while changing into a better-balanced newspaper. Even before Thomson bought it in late 1966, *The Times* had undergone some notable changes—dropping advertisements from its front page, for example, and generally making its appearance more modern and attractive.[35]

Toward the end of 1966 it was announced that Thomson (Lord Thomson of Fleet) was in effect the new owner of the paper with 85 per cent of the stock. Gavin Astor of the family which had owned the paper since 1912, would have the other 15 per cent. Thomson insisted right after the purchase, and has insisted since, that the paper will be free and in the hands of the editor. He said: "All my life I have believed in the independence of editors, and the new editor-in-chief (Denis Hamilton) has been guaranteed absolute freedom from interference."[36]

Probably one of the biggest changes in the "new" *Times* is the leader (editorial) page. The editorials are more incisive, more forceful, more controversial than ever before. Most of them are written by Editor Rees-Mogg, journalist, broadcaster, and economics expert.

Denis Hamilton is editor-in-chief. He had been the editor of the *Sunday Times* (a quality weekly) for five years. He promises to increase coverage, enlarge the paper's scope and size, and get more correspondents. With the coming of Thomson to *The Times*, the paper's scholarly Sir William Haley,[36a] editor since 1952, moved up to board chairman.[37]

Other than possibly adding more pages and expanding the already wide national and foreign coverage, there is little reason to believe that Hamilton will bring about any startling changes. The paper is as it has been for most of its history: dignified and polite, uncluttered and well-edited, with excellent writing generally and editorials which are highly polished and deceptively sharp.

The Times has won innumerable honors and awards for its quality journalism. One of these, and one which expresses the typical world-wide reaction to the paper, was the Honor Award for Distinguished Journalism given *The Times* in 1933 by the University of Missouri School of Journalism. The paper was commended for "its impartiality, its learning, its courage, and its incorruptible English honor; for its completeness and accuracy, its urbane and cultural editorial page . . . ; for its polished special articles, its excellent financial reviews and its world outlook."[38] And, in 1958, reflecting its continuing prestige, a critic called *The Times* "sedate, unsensational, well-mannered, impeccably turned out" and standing for the "sober, phlegmatic, matter-of-fact side of the British character."[39]

It has ever stood in the highest journalistic circles of the world, and, despite certain weaknesses which critics have always delighted in pointing out, it is perhaps the one paper which most readily comes to mind when thoughts turn to quality daily journalism.

The newspaper that is *The Times* today began as a small sheet in 1785. Actually it was called *The Daily Universal Register* for three years, when its founder and editor, John Walter, changed its name to *The Times*. At that time Walter was content to publish commercial news and scandal and little more.

John Walter II, the founder's son, took over the paper at the beginning of the nineteenth century. He had a different approach to journalism than his father, desiring that the paper serve Britain's rapidly rising middle class and that it be more than an outlet for notices, both commercial and sensational. With his famed editor, Thomas Barnes, who took over the editorial reins in 1819, he developed *The Times* into an important organ of public opinion and political influence. It was under Barnes that *The Times* won its reputation as the "Thunderer." Barnes was the man who perfected the technique which would continue to serve the paper well—continuing contact with the right people. In 1815 the circulation was 5,000; six years later it had doubled.

By the time *The Times* came under the editorship of the great John

LATE LONDON EDITION
TUESDAY OCTOBER 10 1967
NO. 57,068 SIXPENCE

THE TIMES

IN BUSINESS NEWS:
PRIVATE DOLLAR
SHARES PLAN

Rolf Hochhuth yesterday: "Information placed in Swiss Bank".

Author of Churchill play booed

BERLIN, Oct. 9.—Rolf Hochhuth, the German playwright, was booed when he appeared on stage after the world premiere of his controversial play *Die Soldaten* (The Soldiers) here tonight.

The play by the 36-year-old writer dramatizes Sir Winston Churchill's part in ordering the bombing of German towns during the war.

Earlier Herr Hochhuth, at a press conference, said that his research had also produced enough circumstantial evidence to assume that British intelligence carried out a wartime political murder with Sir Winston's approval.

He confirmed that the play implies that Sir Winston ordered the murder of General Vladislav Sikorski, the Polish leader, though it does not say so in so many words.

One British questioner today demanded: "Can you really imagine Sir Winston Churchill could order such a murder? I cannot."

Herr Hochhuth replied: "I respect your view, but I can."

He said the play was a call for an international air war convention. His main aim was to attack

Oswin Trilling, whose full review appears on page 7, writes: "The Soldiers . . . is not calculated to appease its enemies."

area bombing of civilian populations.

His interest was aroused in the death of General Sikorski, leader of the wartime Polish Government-in-exile who was killed in an air crash off Gibraltar in 1943, by confidential information, which had now been deposited in a Swiss bank, he said.

Herr Hochhuth said he did not regard the decision as a lighthearted one because he had great respect for Churchill as the greatest warlord of our century. He had been faced by the necessity of waging war against Hitler. "War against Hitler cannot be fought with the civil law book", he said.—*Reuter*.

A dispute over certain passages in a new book about the death of General Sikorski became known yesterday.

The book *Accident: Death of General Sikorski* by David Irving, is published by William Kimber.

A statement in the personal columns of *The Times* yesterday said the author "is not responsible for matter interpolated into page 192, 193, second half of 229, 230 and first half of 231. Nor does he support the views expressed therein".

Mr. William Kimber, managing director of William Kimber, later issued the following statement:—

Test pilot's theory of crash cause

"I am personally responsible for the interpolations in the text of *Accident: Death of General Sikorski* by Mr. David Irving from which he has today in a public announcement dissociated himself, despite the fact that he had earlier authorized their inclusion.

"All the matter in question derives from Wing Commander Roland Falk, who at the time of the accident was chief test pilot at the Royal Aircraft Establishment, Farnborough, and was called as an expert witness at the court of inquiry. . . .

"The passages give an account of what Wing Commander Falk believes to be the most likely explanation of the crash."

Mr. Kimber adds that the court found that the pilot, Mr. Edward Prchal, was in no way to blame for the accident.

Our Berlin Correspondent writes: Mr. Irving explained tonight in Berlin that he authorized the publisher to make cuts and alterations to avoid libel suits. The authorization did not mean, however, to give the publisher the right to insert in the last four pages a theory of which Mr. Irving disapproved.

BRITAIN DROPS SPECIAL LINK WITH US

New stage on way to Common Market

One further step in Britain's advance towards the Common Market was taken by the British Government yesterday when Lord Chalfont, who has special responsibility for the day-to-day negotiations, declared that Britain does not lay claim to any special relationship with the United States.

Lord Chalfont spoke on television after returning from Brussels to London for consultations with Mr. George Brown, the Foreign Secretary, on the progress of Britain's application to join the European Economic Community.

CHANGED PATTERN OF ATLANTIC ALLIANCE

By A. M. RENDEL, Diplomatic Correspondent

Lord Chalfont spoke on television last night about an interview published yesterday in the Roman Catholic newspaper, *L'Avvenire d'Italia*, in which he had stated that Britain laid no claim to a special relationship with the United States—and would do so even less when she became a member of the European Community.

"Our relationship", he had said, "will be Europe's relationship. It will continue to be close in many fields such as defence, politics, trade and technology, and the Atlantic alliance will continue to be the basis of Britain's security, but there will be a place here, as in other fields, for a more specifically European point of view."

Lord Chalfont here seemed to range the British Government on the side of those who would develop the Atlantic alliance in future by building up the "European pillar".

Much in common

In his television interview Lord Chalfont said that this was not really a change in policy. The so-called special relationship had for some time been changing in character, just as foreign policy had changed as Britain concentrated more upon the affairs of Europe.

"We still have", he said, "a great deal in common with the United States"—for example, the enormous advantage of a common language—but in future the relationship had got to be less and less a special relationship between Britain and the United States and more and more a relationship between the United States and Europe, of which Britain was going to be a member sooner or later.

Everyone should remember that unless Britain could help to strengthen Europe "we are going to be taken over by America." Britain, therefore, was seeking a European identity—a place in Europe enabling it to stand up as an equal partner with the United States.

Lord Chalfont also said that President de Gaulle was anxious that Britain should not press her application too hard and was arguing that the time was not yet ripe for Britain's entry: but the British Government had to convince him that the British were genuine in their bid to enter the European Community.

He believed that some of the fears behind the British application were now coming home and that they might give the General occasion to think again.

Misleading idea

Lord Chalfont's statement on the special relationship is fully in line with what the Foreign Office has been saying less officially for some time. In the diplomatists' view Britain's links with the United States, arising from language, common law, and many traditional attitudes in common, will always be close, but the idea of any organic special relationship has long since been misleading and the phrase itself is widely regarded as something of a millstone, hampering a sound appreciation of the real relations of Britain both with the United States and with Europe.

The next moves had already been discussed yesterday evening by Mr. George Brown and Lord Chalfont, who had returned from Brussels in the late afternoon, after talks there with M. Jean Rey, the chairman of the Brussels Commission, in the light of the publication of the commission's report. Mr. Wilson is also being kept closely informed.

Britain replies on sterling, page 5.

Tories will want a full explanation

By DAVID WOOD, Political Correspondent

Although Lord Chalfont must have made sure of Mr. Wilson's and Mr. Brown's approval before asserting and later justifying that Britain lays no claim to a special relationship with the United States, it is the first time it has been so baldly stated in public as part of the preparations for a European negotiation.

Some Tory politicians will want to question Mr. Wilson and Mr. Brown to make sure that Lord Chalfont has stated not his personal view as the Minister who will be responsible for any negotiations in Brussels with—or against—the French, but the collective opinion of the Cabinet.

There is nothing politically exceptionable in the explanation Lord Chalfont offered in a television interview last night. His was a form of words that in itself does acknowledge a special relationship at present. But the explanation follows the logical line of the British application to join the Market since the early days of Mr. Macmillan's attempt. It is no less the logic of American policy in Europe.

Nevertheless, senior Ministers continue to claim or to suggest that there is a special relationship between Washington and London that on occasion is of great importance to Britain. There is nothing organic about it, of course, but British Ministers value it for the immediacy of understanding and the promptitude of fellow feeling that has helped to ease a variety of British problems month by month and year by year. Nobody should doubt that Mr. Brown set a very high value on the invitation he had to visit President Johnson for intimate personal talks during his recent visit to the United Nations.

When British Prime Ministers and Foreign Ministers find themselves as sympathetically received and understood in the capitals of the Six as they are in Washington, what is called the special relationship between the United States and Britain will begin to seem as irrelevant, or out of date, as Lord Chalfont has now stated it to be.

Mr. Arthur Leary, area organizer of the N.U.V.B., who was dismissed yesterday, addresses Vauxhall workers.

Union ousts Vauxhall militant

BY A STAFF REPORTER

Mr. Arthur Leary, east Midlands area organizer of the National Union of Vehicle Builders, and the most militant of the full-time union officials concerned in the Vauxhall Motors pay dispute, was summoned before his national executive in Manchester yesterday and summarily dismissed from office.

Mr. J. E. Orford, assistant general secretary of the N.U.V.B., said: "Mr. Leary was told that his employment was terminated with immediate effect. This has nothing to do with his handling of the Vauxhall dispute. It is concerned with another matter entirely."

An N.U.V.B. shop steward said last night: "Whatever the executive may say, we know he has been sacked because he was the only union official with the guts to stand up to Vauxhall's American management. The men at Vauxhall's will not stand for it. They will either walk out or tear up their union cards."

Mr. Leary, a full-time N.U.V.B. official for 13 years, said last night: "They have accused me of circulating a document critical of the executive on changes in rules—a document every other official circulated. It seems they want to get rid of me but I'm not finished yet."

But he appealed to the men to stay at work and not lose more money by walking out.

MP shocked

Mr. Robert Maxwell, Labour M.P. for Buckingham, said he was shocked at the union's decision, taken at a time when the pay and productivity talks with Vauxhall had reached a critical stage.

He feared the union would lose several thousand members at Luton and Dunstable as a result.

Mr. Leary has been at odds with his executive since early last month, when he refused to condemn a work-to-rule and overtime ban at the Vauxhall factories.

BAR TRADE CUT BY TESTS

BY A STAFF REPORTER

Drinking drivers were hard to find in the West End last night. As one landlord put it: "The screw has been turned and until people find the way to loosen it they will be wary."

Of 34 people approached in six public houses, only four admitted being in charge of cars. And one of them was drinking pineapple juice.

Three points about the introduction of breathalyser tests appeared to be uppermost in the minds of many motorists: the seeming unfairness of an inflexible law, the effect on individual liberty, and the feeling that when the novelty wears off things will be much as before.

Public houses throughout the country reported a drop in business yesterday. Many licensees in the Nottingham area said last night that trade had been lower than normal by between 50 and 75 per cent. Car parks were almost empty.

The start of the tests brought falls of up to 1s. in brewery shares on stock markets yesterday. Scottish and Newcastle fell by this amount to 65s. 6d. The smallest drop, by 1½d. to 22s. 4½d., was in Guinness.

Sweden is considering scrapping the breathalyser test because it is "alarmingly inaccurate". Sweden's chief professor of forensic science, Professor Roger Bonnichsen, said on independent television last night that they hoped to replace it with something much better.

Absconder fined, page 2.

Gay Brewer pays caddie £1,000

Al Fyles, of Southport, Lancashire, who caddied for Gay Brewer, winner of the £19,754 Alcan golfer of the year championship at St. Andrews yesterday, collected about £1,000 for his week's work.

Brewer, who beat Billy Casper by four strokes in a play-off, said he did not think he could have played the course without Fyles's help. "I paid my caddie $2,500 (about £900) when I won the United States Masters title and $20,000 earlier this year. Al will get more than that", said Brewer.

Peter Ryde—Page 13

Expo crowd boo princess

MONTREAL, Oct. 9.—Princess Margaret and Lord Snowdon were booed and shouted at by an angry crowd of Expo 67 exhibition visitors today.

The incident occurred at the Czechoslovak pavilion. Hundreds of visitors had stood in driving drizzle for up to three hours, waiting to see the pavilion when the news was given that it was being closed for the duration of the Princess's visit.—*Reuter*.

Attlee memorial appeal

BY OUR POLITICAL STAFF

Sir Robert Bellinger, Lord Mayor of London, is to launch a national appeal to establish a memorial foundation in memory of Lord Attlee.

Announcing this yesterday in a statement from 10 Downing Street, the Prime Minister said the appeal was being launched at his invitation and with the support of the leaders of the other parliamentary parties.

A funeral service for Lord Attlee will take place tomorrow at the Temple Church, E.C. It will be followed by private cremation at the South London Crematorium.

Arkle to have X-ray

BY A STAFF REPORTER

Arkle, the steeplechaser whose career was put into jeopardy last December when he fractured a bone in the hoof of a foreleg, is to have an X-ray examination this week. Veterinary surgeons will then decide whether he can return to racing.

Even if Arkle is given the all-clear it will be a long time before he races. At present he is confined to his stable at the Irish home of his owner, Anne Duchess of Westminster. "He has not been out at all. No one has any idea yet about when he will be fit to race", a member of the duchess's staff told *The Times* last night.

Welsh poet dies

SEATTLE, Oct. 9.—Mr. Vernon Watkins, aged 61, the Welsh poet, died here last night while playing tennis at Washington University, where he was visiting Professor of English.—*Reuter*.

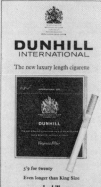

Obituary, page 10.

Farewell to Sir Malcolm

From HENRY STANHOPE—Stamford, Lincolnshire, Oct. 9

Carnations in the form of a treble clef, the promenaders' tribute.

Sir Malcolm Sargent was buried today with dignity, and just a little pomp and circumstance in the town where he grew up.

Perhaps more than any other conductor of his generation Sir Malcolm played music for the people; and it was the people who flocked to his funeral.

Thousands from this lovely old town came to the church of All Saints or stood silently in the mellow streets to pay their last respects to Stamford's only freeman and its most famous son.

People queued for up to two hours for the 450 seats in the fifteenth-century church. Loudspeakers relayed the service to 250 others in St. John's Church near by, where Sir Malcolm once pumped the organ and sang in the choir, and to 3,000 standing in the town square.

On the green bank of the churchyard 200 wreaths splashed colour on to the grey afternoon. There were roses and pinks from the Duke and Duchess of Kent, "Edward and Katharine", flowers from Mr. Edward Heath, from Sir John Barbirolli, Lady Beecham, from the Festival Hall, the Albert Hall, all of Britain's leading orchestras and choirs, and from Miss Erica Iole, "a young fan aged 11".

One, a wreath of white carnations in the shape of a treble clef, was "from his children, the promenaders".

The Archbishop of York, Dr. Coggan, a personal friend, read the lesson from the First Epistle to the Corinthians and an extract from Bunyan's *Pilgrim's Progress*. Choristers from Peterborough Cathedral sang Brahms's anthem "How lovely are thy dwellings", Handel's "Since by Man came Death", and Walford Davies's "God be in my head and in my understanding".

Sir Thomas Armstrong, president of the Royal Academy of Music, played an organ voluntary before the service started.

It was in a sense Sir Malcolm's last concert. He planned the music for it several months ago and thus it was carried out, down to the last detail.

The family mourners included his son, Mr. Peter Sargent, and his wife, and their sons, Nicholas, aged 14, and Simon, aged 13, and Sir Malcolm's sister, Miss Dorothy Sargent.

Ché Guevara dead in Bolivia clash

Castro lieutenant among guerrilla casualties

VALLE GRANDE, BOLIVIA, Oct. 9.—Ernesto "Ché" Guevara, the former Cuban revolutionary leader, was killed in a clash between Bolivian Army troops and guerrillas, it was officially announced here tonight.

The announcement was made by the commander of the Eighth Bolivian Army Division, Colonel Joaquin Zenteno Anaya.

He said that Guevara was one of the six guerrilla casualties of the clash yesterday near this south-eastern Bolivia town. Guevara's body was awaiting a helicopter to move it out to Camira or La Paz, the colonel added.

Guevara, the former right-hand man of Dr. Fidel Castro, the Cuban Prime Minister, and regarded by some as the leading intellectual force behind Castro's Government, disappeared from the Cuban political scene two and a half years ago and his whereabouts had been a mystery since then.

Three captives

Earlier today the Army High Command in La Paz said Guevara was presumed to be among the guerrillas killed or wounded in the clash, in which five soldiers were killed and four wounded.

The clash took place near the town of Higueras, 130 miles north of Army anti-guerrilla headquarters in Camira and 21 miles north-east of here.

The guerrilla casualties were believed to include three dead and three wounded captives.

Scores of people gathered at the local airport earlier today when reports circulated that Guevara was among the casualties and that the bodies of the dead guerrillas would be brought here for identification.—*Reuter*.

Legend of "Ché" Guevara, page 8.

Lions Rugby team for Rhodesia

BY A STAFF REPORTER

The British Lions will play Rhodesia at Bulawayo during their South African Rugby tour next spring and summer. This unanimous decision by the four home Rugby unions tours committee was announced yesterday by Mr. J. G. M. Hart, secretary of the committee.

The Commonwealth Office said last night that such a visit could not take place "without giving the impression that relations between Britain and Rhodesia are not affected by the illegal declaration of independence".

The tour was bound to cast doubt in Rhodesia and throughout the rest of the world on the seriousness of British policy towards Rhodesia.

There are no regulations to stop British sportsmen playing in Rhodesia. Oldham Athletic, the Football League club, were not deterred from doing so this summer by a statement from Mr. George Thomas, Minister of State for Commonwealth Affairs.

However, when Yorkshire rejected their invitation from the Rhodesian Cricket Association last month, their secretary, Mr. John Nash, said that they had done so "in view of the political pressure which has been exerted".

Leading article, page 9.

Ship in trouble off Alaska

KODIAK, ALASKA, Oct. 9.—The 8,137-ton United States cargo ship *Panoceanic Faith* radioed today that she was sinking 870 miles south-west of here with 43 passengers and crew aboard.

Five ships and two coastguard cutters were racing to the scene and a C-141 cargo plane carrying four 20-man life rafts also joined the massive rescue operation.—*Reuter*.

Danish princess expects baby

COPENHAGEN, Oct. 9.—Princess Margrethe, heir to the Danish throne, is expecting a baby next May, the Court announced today. The princess, who is 27, married Prince Henrik of Denmark, aged 33, in June.—*Reuter*.

ON OTHER PAGES

T. Delane in 1841, it had established itself as a social and political power and was respected throughout the country. Under Walter II it had begun to concentrate on foreign news and had correspondents on the Continent. When Walter II took over, *The Times* was a small four-page paper; when he died in 1847, six years after his editor, Barnes, it had grown to twelve large pages.

When the new twenty-four-year-old editor, John Thadeus Delane, took over in 1841, *The Times* had become the semiofficial spokesman for the government itself, irrespective of what party was in power. Under Delane the paper improved its position, and it was said that there was no state secret safe from its hard-working reporters. *The Times*, at mid-century, was the largest and most influential daily in the world. Abraham Lincoln said he knew of nothing, with the possible exception of the Mississippi River, more powerful than *The Times*.[40] Disraeli spoke of two British ambassadors in every world capital—one sent by the Queen and one by *The Times*. In 1856 the British Government learned of the Russian acceptance of peace proposals ending the Crimean War by reading *The Times*.[41]

Delane himself did very little writing, but he stamped his ideas on the whole paper. He passed on everything that went into its columns and had a flair for turning colorless articles into journalistic masterpieces. He more than any of his predecessors understood the impact of a newspaper on political thinking and used *The Times* skillfully in this area. Governmental leaders, foreign and domestic, sought his friendship.[42] Although Delane is generally praised and considered the greatest of all British editors, there are those who feel he is overrated. One of these is Brian Inglis who, writing in London's *Spectator*, shows another view of Delane. He accuses Delane of "getting infatuated with ministers and doing exactly what they told him." And what is probably worse, Delane is said on occasion to have permitted the ministers to write editorials for the paper.[43]

Regardless of Delane's actual importance to the paper, the fact is that *The Times* made some notable contributions during the nineteenth century. Probably the greatest of these was the paper's infusion into British journalism of the idea that a newspaper was independent, responsible to public opinion and not to government.[44] *The Times* expanded its national coverage greatly, introduced important production equipment, and employed the world's first war correspondent, William Howard Russell. It is said that Russell's critical reports of British management of the Crimean War helped bring down the Cabinet in 1855 and led to a needed Army reorganization.[45] Without a doubt the second and third quarters of the nineteenth century were the Golden Age of *The Times*. The reporting of the Crimean War boosted its circulation from 50,000 to 70,000. Although Russell's reports angered the Army and Government, little could be done about *The Times* since it had developed such a powerful following among opinion leaders throughout the country.[46] The paper scored another first during the Crimean War by collecting funds for charitable purposes—in this case money for the British wounded in the war.[47]

The age of Delane lasted from 1841–1877, but the drive of the great editor slackened during his last years and with it the great period of *The Times*. In 1877 Delane was succeeded as editor by Thomas Chenery, who was followed by George E. Buckle in 1884. From 1848 John Walter III was publisher; when he died in 1894, he was succeeded by Arthur Walter.

In 1908 *The Times*, which had been suffering financially and was about to go under, was purchased and rescued from its economic slump by Alfred Harmsworth (Lord Northcliffe). Arthur Walter died in 1910 and was succeeded by his son, John Walter IV, as chairman of The Times Publishing Company. For the new owner, Lord Northcliffe, the purchase of the influential paper was the fulfillment of a long ambition. But Northcliffe did not fit well with *The Times*; as hard as he tried, he could not change the paper significantly as he had such papers as the *Daily Mail*, and for the first time he was frustrated by a journalistic failure. He even brought in Geoffrey Dawson as editor to try to get some order into *The Times*, but he really was his own editor, meddling in every department just as he had been doing on his *Daily Mail* and the *Mirror*. Lord Northcliffe died in 1922, and it is generally thought that because of his tendency to personally supervise everything and his affinity for sensation, he would have ruined the paper's reputation had he lived much longer. To his favor, it must be said that he did make some much-needed changes in *The Times*' organization and increased efficiency in certain departments. And what is most important, he managed to keep the paper financially solvent.

Geoffrey Dawson had followed Buckle as editor, but in 1919 he had left *The Times* after a dispute with Northcliffe, and Henry W. Steed was made editor. On Northcliffe's death in October, 1922, *The Times* passed into the hands of John Jacob Astor who, in association with John Walter IV, set up a Trust to run the paper. Dawson returned to the paper as editor and remained until 1941. He was followed by R. M. B. Ward and then W. F. Carey. In 1952 Sir William Haley became editor of *The Times* and by 1966 had given the paper new life and had brought back to it much of the prestige it had enjoyed in pre-Northcliffe days.

Since 1952 the reputation of *The Times* has grown steadily, although its financial condition has not always been what its owners would wish. Although the paper under Sir William Haley did not abandon its traditional values, it did change, brightening somewhat both its physical appearance and its contents. Haley came to *The Times* from the British Broadcasting Company where he was director-general; he moved to the editorship of the paper at the right time, for the image of the old "Thunderer" was in need of repair. It was often referred to as the

"Whimperer" and its circulation had dropped to 230,000. Haley, while editor, consistently attempted to give the paper more spirit, but without de-emphasizing the traditional insistence on truth and careful reporting. *The Times*' reputation in this area has been well-stated by a German journalist: "It prefers to wait twenty-four hours, and to be beaten by competitors, rather than publish a doubtful report. It has its reward: at home and abroad a *Times* report is considered correct until the opposite is proved. My personal ten years' experience as correspondent in London has shown me how rarely *The Times* is in error."[48]

Haley, on becoming editor, insisted on accuracy and the truth. Often referred to as "the doyen of London editors," he made some cosmetic changes in the Old Lady of Printing House Square, such as introducing photographs, simplifying the nameplate, taking advertisements off the front page. Perhaps his most important change was to instill a new vitality into the editorials, many of which he wrote himself.

British journalist and critic, Henry Fairlie, commenting on *The Times*' editorials under Haley, wrote that "at their best—which usually means when Haley has written them himself—the leading articles . . . are perhaps the most articulate editorialising" in either Britain or the United States. He said that they have "a primitive force, which sweeps one through them, even when one disagrees with what they say, and leaves one feeling six inches taller."[49]

Haley, who actually began his career as a telephone copytaker on *The Times* in 1920, has given the paper a new vigor, edge, and first-class news reporting. Although *The Times* gives few by-lines and still insists on a large degree of anonymity, certain of its staffers such as Louis Heron (Washington correspondent) are recognized leaders in British journalism. Haley probably did more than any previous editor to improve the quality of its foreign coverage. An American content analysis of British papers in 1966 showed that *The Times* devoted 20.8 per cent of its news space to foreign news, and a year before another study showed its foreign news took up 19.65 per cent of its non-advertisement space.[50] Certainly this indicates great emphasis on foreign coverage and, at least from these two studies, shows that the proportion of foreign news in *The Times* is increasing.

Haley, who has spearheaded this increased foreign coverage, has been called "a curious bird, withdrawn, relentless, a latter-day Victorian, a product of self-help—he left school at 16—with a boundless appetite for work and a strong streak of puritanism that came out in his biting Profumo leader, 'It *is* a moral issue.' "[51]

Although Haley may be a "latter-day Victorian" and proud of *The Times*' tradition, he is no reactionary in his journalistic philosophy. Note these words from a speech he gave in 1965:

> For a newspaper to have a sense of responsibility did not mean it should blindly accept that authority was always right,

> however well-meaning. Responsibility was not a hesitation to be revolutionary, a preference for the official over the unofficial or for accepted ideas over those seemingly unacceptable. It was an honest searching for truth. . . . The press should be part of the general educational process that is going on all the time.[52]

The Times is still a paper of the Establishment—the government, the nobility, the ruling class—but it is definitely independent and not a Conservative spokesman as it is often accused of being. Sir William says it is ideologically "in the centre" and that it is designed for "the intelligent readers of all classes."[53] Surveys have shown that at least 70 per cent of those listed in *Who's Who* read the newspaper. "*The Times* is a record," according to Haley. "It has a duty not only to its readers of today but to those of a century hence."[54] Although Haley left his editor's chair in the early days of 1967, his influence is still felt throughout the paper.

As it has been through the years, *The Times* today is recognized for its thoughful and interpretive articles, for its calm and rational discourse, and for its thorough news coverage, although it is highly selective compared to *The New York Times*. It has often shown remarkable foresight in seeing the future importance of an event or a speech and has recognized the importance of "ideas" long before "newsworthy" activities emerged from them. A good example of this journalistic "intuitive reporting" was *The Times'* printing of a speech by Dean Acheson setting forth the idea for the Marshall Plan weeks before General Marshall ever announced the plan at Harvard University. According to James Reston of *The New York Times* the London *Times* was the only paper in the world to carry Acheson's speech.[55]

The Times assumes the reader is already well-informed and wants new information and interpretation to fill in the gaps. All news stories are treated with a certain detachment and in a respectful manner. Like its respected namesake in New York, *The Times* has long been considered a "newspaper of record." However, in recent years it has abandoned this effort and less and less often does it print in full an important speech or document, or every minor appointment in every remote corner of the world. But, as one writer has said, "by becoming less of a 'record,' it has to be admitted, it has seemed to become more of a 'newspaper.' "[56] Commonly running twenty pages an issue, *The Times* averages about 50 per cent of its total space in advertising. An average of twenty-two stories appear on its front page.[57]

Personal advertisements, although no longer on page 1, are still very popular in *The Times*. They are readable, humorous, lively—"a surprise a column inch . . . cannot be surpassed."[58] Letters to the editor, probably the best in the world and for at least a century the paper's most popular ingredient, are as excellent as ever and give insights found nowhere else in Britain. They are as "finely turned as antique silver," one writer has said, with a tone which is "punctilious," a style of "elaborate understatement."[59] Of the "Times Literary Supplement" it has recently been said that "in no other city surely is there an equal . . . in terms of breadth and depth of criticism. Current books in Russian, French, Italian, and German are reviewed as if they had been published locally, and the caliber of the unsigned reviews is the more remarkable when one learns that a front-page article, running perhaps to 3,000 words, will net the author a fee of as little as 75 dollars."[60]

There are many persons who are wondering if *The Times*, now that it has fallen into the press empire of Lord Thomson of Fleet, will lose much of its old freedom and quality. Thomson himself, of course, has promised to keep out of the paper's editorial matters and his experience with *The Scotsman* of Edinburgh and other papers in and out of Britain tends to indicate that he is sincere. Denis Hamilton, his editor-in-chief at *The Times*, believes that the paper is as free as it ever has been and that with its new capital it will reach a far larger audience in the next few years. Contrary to some, Hamilton envisions no loss of quality for the paper. He has said that Lord Thomson is "best in dealing with quality papers" and that the merger of *The Times* and *The Sunday Times* was natural as both papers had been editorially alike for years and were both serious papers believing in independence for editors.[61]

Lord Thomson has shown that he does know how to keep a newspaper a "quality" journal and at the same time boost its circulation and make it more appealing to a wider readership. *The Times* is changing. Stories are not as long as they were; they are more crisply written. A separate financial section has been added, and women's news and features are taking on more importance.

William Rees-Mogg, the editor, recognizes that his newspaper has been regarded as the voice of the British people in the past and wants to continue this tradition "when we feel we have a clear national function in speaking out." But, he says, "Normally *The Times* is just acting as any other independent newspaper, and we do not want to feel constantly weighed down with national responsibility."[62] Many observers have commented on what they feel is a "move to the left" by *The Times*. Rees-Mogg denies this, saying that the paper is simply following the "healthy non-conformism" of previous editors. "Perhaps the main difference is not so much what we say now as the way in which we say it."[63]

Rees-Mogg exemplifies the new *Times* as progressive, questioning, energetic, and intelligent. He is helping change the paper, but he believes that much of the material of the old *Times* should be retained in the new. And this is what *The Times* of London is today: the old institution, its noted traditions intact, leaping forward with new vigor toward a new and more imposing place in the world's journalism.

11

Berlingske Tidende:

A Soft Voice in Denmark

More than two centuries of history surrounds the three-story building and the newspaper it houses on Copenhagen's narrow Pilestraede. *Berlingske Tidende* (Berling's Times) moved into this building in 1765, having been founded sixteen years earlier (1749) by an immigrant German printer, Ernst Henrich Berling. Since its establishment it has remained in the hands of Berling's descendants, standing today as the world's oldest family-owned paper. Its powerful, though soft, voice has had a great impact in a country where there have been many important newspaper voices. *Berlingske Tidende* is a worthy example of the best of the nation's press, a press that has traditionally been of a high type—serious, responsible, interesting, and relevant.

Perhaps to a greater degree than in any other country, the Danish newspapers have taken on the personality or character of their land and people. They are friendly yet reserved, bright yet serious, intriguing yet distant. A certain charm surrounds them and, as is true with the Dane and his cities and towns, makes them hard to resist. Although British and German journalism has had some effect on the country's press, Danish newspapers have developed their own distinctive character, at once popular and serious. *Berlingske Tidende* perhaps offers the best example of this special Danish press trait; other papers may evidence at times as much seriousness, and often more verve, but none can really muster as much prestige as Berling's historic paper.

Denmark is a small country and no newspaper is able to cater to only one select segment of the population. So newspapers serve two purposes: to give people what they *want* to read and at the same time to give them what they *ought* to read. In effect Danish papers are "omnibus" journals, presenting something for everybody in the family, but always with good taste and with emphasis on the family. This leads to a healthy, wholesome press devoid of the sensational aspects of the popular papers of England or France. Although "entertaining" features take an important place in Danish papers, the overriding tone is one of responsibility and seriousness, of open-mindedness and tolerance. The provincial papers have retained the traditional political interests to a far greater degree than have the Copenhagen papers, leading some to call the capital's papers "journals of news" and the provincial papers "journals of views." This, of course, is an oversimplification for all Danish papers combine news and views and are rather heavily tinged with politics.

Newspapers such as *Faedrelandet* and *Dagbladet, Nationaltidende* and *Aftenposten, Dagens Nyheder* and *Morgenbladet, Politiken,* and *Jyllandsposten* have chiseled their names deeply into Danish history. The names of famous journalists such as Carl Ploug, Carl Bille, Christen Nielsen, Christian Ferslew, Herman Bang, Chresten Berg, and Viggo Hørup lighted up the nineteenth-century scene with their intellects and personalities. In this century journalism has made further imprints upon the nation through such newspaper stalwarts as Henrik Cavling, Frejlif Olsen, Emil Wiinblad, and Vilhelm Lassen, to name only a few.

But in the midst of these proud names must be placed that of the *Berlingske Tidende*, which as it developed through the years was ever a pacesetter and a serious competitor for the entire press. And, of course, the name of its founder, E. H. Berling, stands high among the pioneers of Danish journalism.

In Denmark today where more than fifty dailies have disappeared since 1945, *Berlingske Tidende* appears more firmly entrenched than at any time since its founding by Berling in 1749. It has the country's largest circulation, some 172,000 each morning and nearly 335,000 on Sunday,[1] and the most stable financial position. It is not only a Danish institution but a national habit. Dr. Vincent Naeser, main stockholder of the paper and great-great grandson of the founder, has called the *Berlingske Tidende* "an absolutely decent paper," and "one which reflects the Danish mind."[2] Its chief editor, Terkel M. Terkelsen, refers to it as having great impact on Danish public opinion through its serious, consistent, and moderate editorial policy.[3]

What accounts for *Berlingske Tidende*'s influence and prosperity? Tradition, of course, is one factor; for example, Hans Christian Anderson was a regular contributor to its pages. And, so far as is known, no other paper has been published so long under the ownership of the same family. But there are many other, more direct, reasons for its current status: its virtual monopoly among Denmark's papers of classified advertising; its heavyweight editions which resemble American dailies, giving extensive coverage to a wide range of subjects; its traditional accessibility to the affairs of the Royal Family and to Government generally; its ability to adapt to general governmental drift to the left without forsaking its basically conservative stance; its long experience in newspaper finance which gives it a sense of stability and security; and finally, its thorough and reliable news coverage and dignified, responsible appearance in format and typography.

Berlingske Tidende appeals to the middle- and upper-class readers mainly offering something for every member of the family in typical Scandinavian manner. Its varied assortment of serious material and entertainment would make it quite different from ultraserious dailies like France's *Le Monde* or Switzerland's *Neue Zürcher Zeitung.* Denmark, with its small population of some four million, cannot support exclusively "serious" papers or "popular" papers; or, perhaps, it might be said that the Danes are as bored with too much froth as they are with too much seriousness in the papers.[4] Editor Terkelsen says that his paper's readership is distributed among all sectors of the public; however, he points out that "as the country is too small to support highly specialized newspapers, the appeal of *Berlingske Tidende* is regarded as all embracing within the Danish community."[5] This makes it possible for the paper to provide outstanding national and foreign news and serious opinion and interpretive pieces while at the same time giving considerable space to popular (but family-type) features. This is certainly not exclusively the case with the *Tidende*, being quite common throughout Scandinavia, but it is rather unusual in the world's elite press except in a few other important newspapers such as Japan's *Asahi Shimbun.*

Today *Berlingske Tidende* is a regular-size-format paper seven columns wide. Editions of the paper usually run more than thirty-six pages on weekdays and often close to seventy on Sundays. Its page makeup is horizontal and on its front page it usually carries one or two large photographs. Its pages, like those of most Scandinavian dailies, are glued at the fold. Many cartoons are used throughout the paper, most of them being serious or satirical editorial expressions. At least one page of each issue is devoted to the theater; two pages, to sports; one page, to society; one page to puzzles and radio-television listings. Generally a photograph or two is used on the paper's attractive, clean-cut editorial page. Opposite the editorial page is a page of columns and interpretive articles. Each edition contains a complete section of small advertisements.

International news is considered very important by the editors of the *Tidende.* It maintains its own correspondents in Washington, New York, London, Bonn, Brussels, Moscow, Stockholm, and Oslo; it also subscribes to the London *Times'* News Service, *The New York Times* News Service, the Associated Press and the national Danish news agency, Ritzau. The paper's network of correspondents is larger than that of

Telefon (01) 15 75 75
219. årgang nr. 261

Berlingske Tidende

Grundlagt 1719 af E. H. Berling

Torsdag 21. september 1967
44 sider

Dansk-norsk-svensk initiativ i Europarådet

Grækenland er anklaget

Også Fællesmarkedet overvejer at træffe forholdsregler mod Athen-styret

Folket har mistet friheden, men kun midlertidigt, siger Athen

Fra vor udsendte korrespondent. STRASBOURG, ONSDAG AFTEN

Grækenland, der var det første land, som indklagede en anden stat for Europarådets menneskerettighedskommission, fik i eftermiddag selv en sag for i Strasbourg.

De tre skandinaviske landes faste stedfortrædere ved Europarådet, deriblandt den danske minister Mogens Warberg, og repræsentanter for de tre landes udenrigsministerier — fra Danmark den kommende leder af den politisk-juridiske afdeling, udenrigsråd Janus Paludan — afleverede til Europarådets generalsekretær, Peter Smithers, tre enslydende klager over, at den græske regering havde tilsidesat en række fundamentale bestemmelser i den konvention til sikring af menneskerettighederne, som Grækenland selv har underskrevet — og ydermere selv i to tilfælde har anklaget England for ikke at respektere på Cypern.

Støtte fra Benelux

Det skandinaviske initiativ vil, efter hvad der oplyses, ikke alene blive støttet af de tre Beneluxlande, men også af Island. Og i eftermiddags blev det under forhandlingen i fællesmarkedslandenes Europa-parlament af den tyske socialdemokrat Ludwig Metzger hilst stærkt velkommen, at de tre skandinaviske lande havde taget initiativet til, at menneskerettighedskommissionen nu søger at genskabe demokratiske tilstande i Grækenland.

give anledning til alvorlig bekymring. På baggrund af denne situation og for at leve op til de mål, som Europarådet har nedlagt i sin status, har den danske regering efter omhyggelige overvejelser og med den rådgivende forsamlings Grækenlands-resolution tidligere på året in mente besluttet at indgive en klage mod den græske regering. Ved at gøre dette har den danske regering ikke gjort andet end at tage i anvendelse det maskineri, som Europarådet — i øvrigt enestående på dette område blandt internationale organisationer — har oprettet til beskyttelse af menneskerettigheder og fundamentale friheder — og som Grækenland selv har skrevet under på og ved tidligere lejligheder selv har påberåbt sig.

Svar fra Athen

Endnu før den skandinaviske klage var blevet officielt afleveret, havde Grækenlands faste repræsen-

Fortsættes side 2. (1

DANSK STAND LUKKET

Den danske stand på handelsmessen i Saloniki er lukket af dens leder, Flemming Andersen, i protest mod, at en dansk pige, der var beskæftiget på messen, er blevet anholdt af det græske sikkerhedspoliti. Anholdelsen skyldes en manglende underskrift på et underordnet papir. Messens græske leder, Stavros Antoniadis, har forgæves bedt Flemming Andersen møde op for udstillingskomiteen og afgive forklaring. Antoniadis har derefter besluttet, at den danske stand skal forblive lukket udstillingsperioden ud.

Ydermere antydede Europa-kommissionens præsident, Jean Rey, at de nuværende politiske tilstande i Grækenland vil kunne få alvorlige følger for samarbejdet mellem Grækenland og Fællesmarkedet inden for den gældende associeringsaftale.

Grækenland har selv været klager

I det brev, der fra stats- og udenrigsminister Jens Otto Krag ledsagede den 12 sider lange »klage«, hedder det, at »den nuværende situation i Grækenland ikke kan undlade at gøre indtryk på min regering som dybt tragisk og i sandhed

Sø-hotel-projektet i Sortedamssøen med adgang fra Østerbrogade.

Hotel i Sortedamssøen

Projekt til 45 millioner

Til Københavns Magistrat er indleveret et af de mest utraditionelle forslag, der længe er set. Et internationalt selskab ønsker at opføre et hotel på pæle ude i Sortedamssøen med indgang fra Østerbrogade og parkering under vandet. Ideen er arkitekt Max Louws. Han har tidligere gjort sig tanker om et sø-hotel.

Ideen blev opfanget i udlandet, arkitekten har på halvanden måned udarbejdet planen i detaljer; det store spørgsmål er nu: vil Københavns Kommune sælge en del af søen til konsortiet?

Det utraditionelle hotelbyggeri kommer til at koste 45 millioner kroner. Foruden hotel med 406 sengepladser bliver der flere restauranter med plads til 3.000 gæster og offentlige haveanlæg.

Konsortiet har travlt. Man vil helst i gang til foråret 68. Siger København nej, bygger man i stedet for i Stockholm. Se mere om projektet side 19.

b-j.

VEJRET

Svag til frisk sydlig vind, vekslende skydække og regn- eller tordenbyger. Maksimumtemperaturer i dag mellem 11 og 13 grader.

Med kurs mod Canada – Med gode rejseønsker fra kongeparret og tronfølgerparret i går eftermiddags af sted fra Københavns Lufthavn med DC-8'eren »Olav Viking« til Canada på officielt besøg. Prinsesse Margrethe var iført en marineblå kjole og rød hat, og prins Henrik viste sig for første gang med Eden-hat. Læs Povl Westphalls reportage side 9. (Foto: Aage Sørensen).

G. L. Christrup efter de nye oplysninger i Vagn Jensen-sagen:

Ønsker en fhv. minister afhørt

Erklæring fra departementschef Mogensen og svar fra G. L. Christrup

Departementschef Eiler Mogensen, Undervisningsministeriet, udsendte i går over Ritzaus Bureau en erklæring som svar på den artikel i Berlingske Aftenavis i lørdags, som lod formode, at departementschefen havde en divergerende hukommelse vedrørende et møde med hrs. G. L. Christrup i 1964, tilsyneladende afhængigt af, om han udtalte sig i eller uden for en retssal.

Departementschefen understreger, at der ikke er nogen uoverensstemmelse mellem hans forklaring til undersøgelsesretten i den verserende Vagn Jensen-sag og hans udtalelser til Ministerialforeningens formand, ekspeditionssekretær Rasmus Reeh, i telefonen den 27. september i fjor.

Det var Rasmus Reehs opfattelse at den pågældende telefonsamtale, at departementschefen fuldt ud vedkendte sig erindringen om det omstridte møde, skønt telefonsamtalen fandt sted mellem to retsmøder, hvor departementschefen under vidneansvar erklærede, at han intet huskede om det.

Departementschefens i går udsendte erklæring har omgående givet kontorchef Vagn Jensens bisidder, hrs. G. L. Christrup, anledning til en offentlig opfordring til den fhv. undervisningsminister K. Helveg Petersen, nu nedrustningsambassadør, om at oplyse, om det var ham, eller evt. det i 1964 nedsatte ministerudvalg, der havde foranlediget, at departementschef Mogensen henvendte sig til højesteretssagføreren med forslag om, at Vagn Jensen lod sig sygemelde, hvorefter han ville få bevilget afsked med fuld pension. Højesteretssagføreren finder det hensigtsmæssigt, at forklaringer om dette forhold afgives i en retssal.

Departementschef Mogensens erklæring, udsendt i går eftermiddags, lyder således:

»I et interview i Berlingske Aftenavis den 16. september, som har været gengivet i store dele af dagspressen, har Ministerialforeningens formand, ekspeditionssekretær Rasmus Reeh, givet udtryk for, at jeg undet en telefonsamtale med ham

Fortsættes side 2. (2

Det mægtige skib løber af stabelen og ud i vandet.

En ny »Queen«

England betaler for at bevare traditionerne

Fra vor korrespondent
LONDON, ONSDAG AFTEN.

Under helt overvældende interesse og national begejstring, der i hvert fald var en gammel søfartsnation værdig, blev det største britiske passagerskib siden krigen i dag søsat fra det berømte John Brown skibsværft vest for Glasgow. Dronning Elizabeth var skibets gudmoder og gav det navnet »Queen Elizabeth II«, et navn, der i øvrigt vil irritere skotterne, der aldrig har villet anerkende, at dronning Elizabeth I også var deres dronning.

Det ny skib er på 58.000 ton og skal sættes ind på den nordatlantiske rute, hvor det afløser den 33 år gamle »Queen Mary« på 81.000 ton, der i disse dage er på den sidste tur til New York. Det ny skib, der står ud på sin jomfrutur om halvandet år, afløser også »Queen Elizabeth«, der er fra 1938.

Cunard-selskabet fik en ekstra navngivningsgave fra den britiske regering i aftes, da man bevilgede et ekstra lån på 120 millioner kr. til selskabet, der i forvejen havde fået 350 millioner kr. i lån til skibet, der i alt er kommet til at koste 590 millioner kr. Cunard har i årevis tabt penge på de to gamle »dronningers« passagertrafik, og der er ikke større chancer for, at det ny skib kan tjene penge på ruten. Sidste år havde Cunard et tab på 150 millioner kr. som helhed, og man venter et betydeligt underskud også i år. Man indrømmer kun nødtvungent, at de store passagerskibe ikke kan klare sig i konkurrencen med flyvemaskiner.

Der er udtrykt en del kritik af den store statsstøtte. Hvis skatteydernes penge skal sættes i projekter af dette format, burde det så ikke være i succesrige foretagender med fremtidsudsigter i stedet for i et urentabelt prestigeprojekt, har man spurgt.

p.m.

Tilståelse i bankkuppet

Den ene italiener lægger kortene på bordet

Den ene af de tre italienere, der sidder fængslet for bankrøveriet i Lyngby, aflagde i går eftermiddags fuld tilståelse. Italieneren, den 27-årige repræsentant Corrado Magliozzi, blev straks fremstillet i Lyngby Ret, hvor han gentog tilståelsen. De to øvrige italienere nægter fortsat kendskab til røveriet.

Corrado Magliozzis tilståelse faldt, efter at han havde været til afhøring hos to italienske kriminalkommissærer. De to politifolk er sammen med en kriminalassistent fra Interpols afdeling i Rom taget til Danmark for at konstatere, om de tre fængslede italienere kan sættes i forbindelse med en række bankrøverier i Rom.

Tilståelsen blev i aftes holdt hemmelig af politiet i Lyngby. Berlingske Tidende erfarede dog, at italienerens tilståelse kom efter kun få minutters samtale med de to italienske kriminalkommissærer, der er kommet hertil fra henholdsvis Turin og Milano. Da Corrado Magliozzi havde fortalt om sin andel i forbrydelsen, blev der straks berammet et retsmøde.

Det var politimester Erik Bech selv, der mødte som anklager i Lyngby Ret. Retsmødet var kortvarigt, og der kom intet frem om Corrado Magliozzis motiv til at deltage i bank-røveriet. De to øvrige fængslede i sagen nægter fortsat. De vil formentlig i løbet af i dag blive forelagt deres landsmands tilståelse.

Bankrøveriet fandt sted den 15. september i Kjøbenhavns Privatbanks Nybrovej-afdeling i Lyngby. Tre morklædede mænd bevæbnet med en maskinpistol og en pistol holdt bankpersonalet op og røvede 6.000 kroner. De fleste af pengene tabte røverne dog under flugten.

Politiløjtnanter

Under røveriet blev bankbestyrer Carl Hansen slået ned og hårdt såret af den ene røver. Alt disponibelt mandskab blev straks sat ind i jagten på røverne, og et par timer efter blev Corrado Magliozzi og hans to landsmænd pågrebet i en lejlighed i Glostrup. I lejligheden blev der fundet en adskilt maskinpistol og en pistol. Disse våben nægtede de alle tre kendskab til ved anholdelsen og senere i grundlovsforhøret.

Foruden de tre italienske kriminalfolk, der allerede er kommet til Danmark i forbindelse med bankrøveri-sagen, har to løjtnanter fra det italienske rigspoliti, La Carabinieri, bebudet deres ankomst.

p.

Dronning Elizabeth og prinsesse Margaret vinker.

En ekstra stemme til Krag – Se side 2

any other Danish paper and, consequently, the coverage of foreign news is regarded as outstanding considering the size of the country and the newspaper.

Berlingske Tidende also carries full reviews of literature, and opens its columns to discussions on economics and all matters related to the community and national life. Since it is a paper of general appeal, it carries a substantial sports section and in addition offers much material of interest to women. In its large Sunday edition the paper runs an article called "Free Forum" in which leading personalities of five political parties (Communists are absent) express their opinions on a number of subjects. Other matters of general interest are discussed in "Letters to the Editor" and in a daily signed article (*kronik*) in which the writer is allowed to advance his viewpoint however contrary it might be to the *Tidende*'s editorial position.[6]

What about the educational level of the editorial staff? It varies, of course, depending on the duties involved. Generally the staffers fall into two categories: (1) specialists, who hold an academic degree, and (2) others, who have learned journalism by apprenticeship. All trainees in journalism presently undergo courses at the Journalist High School which has the cooperation of the University of Aarhus. There are two courses, each lasting three months, within the normal apprenticeship period of three years.[7]

Berlingske Tidende is widely considered[8] and considers itself as independent, although many persons persist in linking the paper to the Conservative Party.[9] Perhaps it is closest to that party in its basic editorial position, but this does not mean that it is against the program of the Social-Democratic governments which seem to be fairly well established in the country. The paper is officially described as independent conservative, which the editors call "essentially liberal in character in view of the political set-up in Denmark."[10] Aside from considerable semantic obfuscation of such language, the fact remains that the paper is critical of the economic policy pursued by successive Social-Democratic governments, but often is in agreement with the foreign policy, especially as it pertains to support for NATO and the United Nations.[11]

Labels, by and large, are unimportant in respect to the *Tidende*; such terms as "liberal" and "conservative" are certainly unclear unless one understands well the context in which they are used. Newspapers—serious, rational ones at least—are like persons: too complex and too dynamic to be adequately classified. For example, the editors of *Berlingske Tidende* were recently asked if their paper advocated the recognition of Red China by the United States. Terkel Terkelsen, one of the chief editors, replied in these words:

> We follow the principle never to advise foreign countries on foreign policy which they should pursue. Consequently, we do

> not expressly advocate recognition of Red China by the United States, though it would appear desirable if political events were developing in such a way that diplomatic relations between Red China and the United States could be established.[12]

Although many persons both right and left politically will undoubtedly consider this statement an example of political "hedging" and editorial evasion, in reality its wording and tone reflect much about the newspaper. This seems a perfectly sensible stance for the *Tidende*, an indication of its thoughtful, moderate position and its "center" orientation in the Danish political spectrum. In short, it is a calm, reasonable position. The paper, quite unlike "conservative" papers in the United States, favors Red China being a member of the United Nations and from time to time supports programs and positions which would be anathema to conservative American dailies like the Richmond (Virginia) *News-Leader* or the *Chicago Tribune*.

The story of this outstanding Danish newspaper began when, in January of 1749, a forty-one-year-old immigrant German printer named Ernst Henrich Berling acquired a vacant newspaper license in Copenhagen and began publishing a sixteen-page semiweekly. Originally called the *Københavnske danske Post-Tidender*, the paper had the exclusive privilege of using the Royal Mail for the distribution of its some 800 copies. Berling, as printer for the King (Frederik V) obtained certain other privileges for his paper; for example, a monopoly on official news and advertising.[13]

The *Post-Tidender* came out on Tuesdays and Saturdays and quickly prospered and grew. Foreign news in the first years was mainly translations from German which came principally from Hamburg sources. News of Copenhagen was stressed, however, in these early days; births, marriages, deaths, ship sailings and arrivals, and financial items were used regularly in the paper. When Ernst Berling died in 1750, only a year after he started the paper, he left his publishing business to his two sons. The paper grew rapidly and the original building having become too small, the *Post-Tidender* moved to a larger and better site in 1765. Here in the heart of Copenhagen on the Pilestraede it has flourished ever since. As the paper has grown it has expanded its facilities and today it takes up a full block of buildings, but the old house into which it moved in 1765 remains the hub of its activities.

Like most other Danish papers, Berling's journal was State-privileged for about a century and a half. This situation, while economically good for *Berlingske Tidende*, led at times to Government interference in the paper's policies. In 1776 the press gained full freedom (from University censorship) which it kept for three years. A Government decree in 1799, following press excesses, clamped on heavy restraints especially in the areas of political and economic discussion, and throughout the first half of the nineteenth century *Berlingske Tidende* and the other papers filled their pages chiefly with entertainment, literature, and news of the theater. In the late 1820's the paper published as often as four times a week, and from 1831 generally came out daily, and from 1841 regularly every weekday, and from 1844 both in the morning and evening. In spite of Government restrictions on the press during this period, *Berlingske Tidende* passed some notable mileposts. In 1851 a Press Act irrevocably introduced freedom of the press. (In 1938 a new Press Act reaffirmed press freedom but emphasized press "responsibility" and called for every paper to have a legally "responsible person," usually the editor, who would be responsible for all anonymous contents of the paper.)

One of the outstanding editors of *Berlingske Tidende* in the nineteenth century was Mendel Levin Nathanson who made many contributions to the paper's excellence. It was he who began the literary *feuilleton* and dramatic reviews in Danish journalism with contributions from leading literary figures such as Hans Christian Anderson. Nathanson called the public's attention to interesting facets of politics and drew new readers. While Nathanson was editor and Carl Berling (the founder's great-grandson) was manager (from 1738–1858) the circulation grew from 1,400 to nearly 10,000—more than twice that of any other Copenhagen paper. It was Nathanson who began a morning edition (1844) which was at first mainly an advertisement paper. During this period, or most of it, the *Tidende*'s attitude was conservative but far from progressive, and as one writer has said, its semiofficial character made for "cautious, level-headed, and reliable journalism."[14]

In 1881, at the time when a new rotary press was installed, the morning edition was converted into a fully independent and complete newspaper, losing its "supplementary" or "subordinate" status to the main evening paper. By 1900 the morning paper's circulation was about 15,000 with the evening paper staying at some 9,000 where it had been in 1860. *Berlingske Tidende* broke all connections with the Government in 1901 and showed that it could survive well as a fully independent paper, competing on completely equal footing with all other Danish papers. *Berlingske Tidende* began its Sunday edition in 1913, bringing to its readers a wide range of material and a colored magazine section of size and quality previously unknown in the Danish press. It was this same year that the paper made a great beginning toward better journalism in many areas, largely because it acquired a new editor-in-chief: Christian Gulmann.

Coming as he did after a period of minor achievements and uninspiring journalism, Gulmann's contributions seem especially significant. It is safe to say that he probably did more than any other to make *Berlingske Tidende* into a real, full-ranged newspaper. He started the Sunday edition mentioned above, instituted the interview story, published the first photograph, and built the morning edition (today's *Berlingske Tidende*) into its present superiority over the evening edition. Gulmann was largely responsible for building up the paper's foreign coverage and enlarging the staff generally. Poets and authors were brought onto the staff. It was Gulmann's desire to make the *Tidende* into a paper which combined the reliability of the London *Times*, the literary quality of *Le Journal* of Paris, and the wide scope and appeal of London's *Daily Express*. He had largely achieved this when he died in 1934. Without a doubt he was one of the *Tidende*'s greatest editors and one of the most versatile of all Danish journalists.[15]

In the first few years of the 1900's the newspaper's circulation was around 20,000, and by the end of the First World War it had climbed to right at 50,000. Growth continued steadily during the interwar period and by 1938 *Berlingske Tidende*'s circulation stood at a little more than 125,000. In the early 1930's, shortly before war was to engulf Europe, one of the *Tidende*'s greatest writers on international affairs became well known. His name was Nicalai Blaedel and he had begun his journalistic career as a firm supporter of the Liberal Party, writing for *Politiken*. He shifted his position, however, and joined the Conservative Party in 1927 and worked first for *Dagens Nyheter* and then with *Berlingske Tidende*.

Blaedel was probably the most brilliant and lucid writer on international affairs in Danish journalism history. At the time the Nazis were gaining power in Germany, he constantly tried to inform the Danish public of Hitler's true nature and aims. He wrote some of the most insightful and predictive articles about what was happening in Germany published anywhere in the European press. He repeatedly warned his readers about the Nazis and stressed that events in Germany were only the prelude to a tragic event which would involve Denmark.[16]

What Blaedel wrote came to pass and Denmark was occupied by the Germans. *Berlingske Tidende*, among other Danish papers, was permitted to publish by German authorities, but under close scrutiny, of course. (In addition to its regular edition, the *Tidende* published an underground paper.)[17] Even under German censorship, *Berlingske Tidende* lost no opportunity to snipe at the Nazis, but always subtly and obliquely. For example, the story is told about a Wehrmacht officer who demanded news of the activities of his regimental band printed in *Tidende*; he was informed that he must pay ten kroner for the "advertisement."[18]

Recognizing the great traditions and journalistic accomplishments of *Berlingske Tidende*, the University of Missouri School of Journalism awarded the paper one of its Honor Medals in 1961. The award was made in recognition of the paper's "vigorous international fight for basic freedoms and its continued defense of freedom of speech and printed word against all attacks, its fairness in its editorial comments, thus providing its readers with an intelligent orientation to current problems, and its reliable Danish and world news presentation." Dr.

Vincent Naeser, in accepting the medal, said that the *Tidende* was "proud to join your international honored brotherhood of sworn defenders of the Freedom of the Press and Human Rights."[19]

There is no doubt but that *Berlingske Tidende* stands at the apex of Danish quality journalism. Its main competitor is Copenhagen's morning *Politiken* (circulation about 140,000 weekdays), a livelier paper known for its excellent writing and literary traditions. A Liberal paper, it was founded in 1884 by Viggo Hørup, one of the very great writers and journalistic figures of Denmark.

Berlingske House also publishes a noon paper, the *B.T.* (founded in 1916), a sort of New York *Daily News* which averages nearly fifty pages an issue. However, compared to the New York tabloid, *B.T.* never uses poor taste in its liberal sprinkling of pictures; seldom if ever does it carry crime or murder pictures. *B.T.*'s circulation is about 168,000, making it next to its morning parent *Berlingske Tidende* the largest daily paper in the country. The House of Berlingske also publishes a more serious and sophisticated evening edition called *Berlingske Aftenavis* (*Berling's Evening News*), having only a small circulation of about 22,000. The company, in addition to these three Copenhagen daily papers, publishes two weeklies and one monthly radio-TV magazine.[20]

Peter Andersen is managing director of Berlingske House. The two chief editors are Svend Aage Lund and Terkel M. Terkelsen. The managing director is responsible for the overall economic administration of the three dailies, the two weeklies, and the monthly magazine. The chief editors are responsible for the editorial side of all papers and periodicals, but each publication has its own editor who is the "responsible person" by law for the content of his publication. Each Berlingske newspaper and periodical has its separate editorial staff.[21]

Berlingske Tidende wants the public to understand the value of newspapers to society and to public education in general. To this end, the paper printed a special color supplement of sixty-four pages in the fall of 1965 devoted to the functions of a newspaper in modern Danish society. It showed graphically what the *Tidende*, at any rate, was doing every day, covering subjects from politics to art, science, and economics and showed clearly the newspaper's role in a modern pluralistic society.[22] *Berlingske Tidende* is a proud paper, a confident journal, one which never rests on its historic traditions and laurels or on its current press leadership. Rather it pushes on day after day into new journalistic frontiers with dignity and reasoned self-assurance, speaking in a clear but quiet voice to its faithful and intelligent readers.

12

Le Monde: Looks Are Not Everything

Without a doubt the most unremorselessly intellectual of the world's elite newspapers and the one which has made fewest concessions to "modern" journalism is Paris' evening *Le Monde* (The World). Despite its small circulation and dull makeup, it has earned the respect of serious press critics everywhere for its depth reportage, thoughtful opinion, and uncompromising concern for spiritual and intellectual values. *Le Monde,* with a circulation right at 300,000 and an additional 100,000 added on days of big news, publishes two or three editions a day.[1]

Le Monde likes to keep its pages, headlines, and type small and its ideas large. It is an undersized and underweight six-column tabloid paper running from sixteen to twenty-four pages, with what are probably the grayest, most monotonous pages of any newspaper in the world. But looks are not everything, and the reader gets plenty to read—if his eyes are good enough and his intellectual curiosity strong enough to propel him through the fields of tiny type unrelieved by even an occasional illustration. The usual news and commentary are printed in seven-point type, with eight-point (most newspapers' regular body type) used only for a few stories needing special emphasis. *Le Monde* even uses footnotes in some stories; these are set in six-point type.

One of the most serious dailies in the world (along with Zurich's *Neue Zürcher Zeitung* and Frankfurt's *Frankfurter Allgemeine*), *Le Monde* concentrates on world news and commentary, supplemented by weighty political and economic analysis. Although a tabloid (in size),

Le Monde eschews sensational contents of any kind and any resemblance between it and what is generally thought of as "tabloid" journalism is purely a matter of page size. It is the only tabloid paper in the world duller in appearance than Switzerland's *Neue Zürcher Zeitung* (see chapter 14). Anyone but the ultraserious reader would surely find *Le Monde* almost unnecessarily dull. In fact, there is actually a saying that is often heard in French newspaper offices: "as boring as *Le Monde*."[2]

No photographs appear in *Le Monde*, certainly a factor which gives the paper a claim to distinction. The paper's position is, contrary to the old Chinese proverb, that a good verbal description is worth far more than a picture which takes up valuable space and distracts the serious reader. Jacques Sauvageot, *Le Monde*'s administrative director, says that the practice of not printing pictures did not begin as a principle; rather, he recalls: "We inherited the equipment of the prewar newspaper *Le Temps*, which happened to have the oldest presses in Paris, dating back to 1911, and by 1944 they were very old indeed. They simply couldn't print satisfactory photographs."[3] Sauvageot's statement notwithstanding, *Le Monde*'s director Hubert Beuve-Méry prefers to stress *policy* as the main reason for the absence of pictures in *Le Monde*. The paper is a "word-oriented" news-journal, Beuve-Méry, says, and since the reporting is very good, there is no need for photographs.[4] "The reader today has enough pictures forced upon him from every side; we believe that the *Le Monde* reader appreciates us sparing him more of them. We believe that our reports are clear and can hardly be helped by the kind of pictures usually presented by newspapers," the publisher, and founder, of *Le Monde* adds.

The newspaper's editors are highly selective in their determination of what is "fit to print." How consequential is it, nationally and internationally? This seems to be the main determinant. Ultraseriousness: the tone for everything. Beuve-Méry says that the paper stresses politics, economics, philosophy, and literature more than other types of material.[5]

Whereas the straight news reports of certain happenings are often quite short, the interpretation and backgrounding of these events wander through columns and columns of small type. Often whole texts of treaties, speeches, resolutions, trial proceedings, and official pronouncements are printed *in toto*. Although the paper certainly can be called a *news*-paper, attempting to observe objectivity in its news stories, it still retains much of the older French journalistic nature—that of a "views" paper. It is above all a paper of interpretation, of speculation, and realistic conclusion. *Le Monde*, like several of the other outstanding elite papers of the world, has an uncanny ability to foresee developments, to predict, and to offer reasons, often days or weeks before headlines burst out with news stories.

As one writer has said, *Le Monde* is heavy with analytical writing "at the expense of the 'All-we-want-is-the-facts-Ma'am' school."[6] But it

VINGT-QUATRIÈME ANNÉE — N° 7066 — 24 PAGES ★ ★ ★ — DIMANCHE 1er et LUNDI 2 OCTOBRE 1967

Le Monde

Rédaction, Administration : 5, r. des Italiens, Paris-IXe. — Directeur : Hubert BEUVE-MÉRY

0,40 F

Algérie, 0,45 D.A. ; Maroc, 0,50 dir. ; Tunisie, 50 m. Allemagne, 0,50 DM ; Autriche, 4,50 sch. ; Belgique, 5 fr. ; Danemark, 1,50 kr. ; Espagne, 6 pes. ; Grande-Bretagne, 1 sh. ; Italie, 100 l. ; Luxembourg, 5 fr. ; Norvège, 1,50 kr. ; Pays-Bas, 0,50 fl. ; Portugal, 5 esc. ; Suède, 1,25 kr. ; Suisse, 0,40 fr. ; U.S.A., 50 cts.

Tarif des abonnements page 3

C.C.P. PARIS N° 4207-23
TELEX PARIS N° 22813
Ad. télégr. : JOURMONDE-PARIS
Tél. : PRO (770) 91-29

LES PROBLÈMES MONÉTAIRES ET ÉCONOMIQUES INTERNATIONAUX

Rio ou la morale de l'ambiguïté

Comme dans un ballet bien réglé, la figure finale de l'assemblée de Rio a réuni tous les protagonistes, l'air satisfait. A l'unanimité, ils ont adopté les résolutions proposées, notamment celle qui avait déjà été pratiquement rédigée à Londres à la fin du mois d'août dernier. Mais les jeux de scène qui ont précédé la chute du rideau montrent bien que des affrontements nouveaux se préparent lorsqu'il s'agira de mettre à exécution les décisions de Rio. Quelle morale tirer de cet étonnant dialogue de sourds qui a eu lieu dès les premiers jours entre M. Michel Debré et M. Fowler, et de la suite des événements ?

Il est clair que les « droits de tirage spéciaux » n'ont pas la même signification en anglais qu'en français. Pour M. Debré, il ne peut s'agir que de crédits (la preuve en est qu'ils sont remboursables à 30 %). Pour M. Fowler, nous sommes en présence de monnaie (puisque, pour 70 %, ces droits de tirage ne sont pas remboursables).

Entre l' « or-papier » des Américains et l' « étalon-or » des Français il n'y a pas de passerelle, l'opposition est irréductible. Mais il faut bien vivre, et les uns comme les autres — sans rien renier de leurs choix — savent qu'en matière monétaire le plus dangereux est encore de brusquer les choses.

Une autre querelle était plus sérieuse ou plutôt moins dogmatique : c'est celle qui s'est élevée à propos du parallélisme entre les modifications à apporter aux statuts du Fonds monétaire et la mise en place du nouveau système de liquidités additionnelles. Les Européens entendaient, on le sait, disposer d'un droit de veto, et ils ont obtenu satisfaction, dès Londres, à propos des décisions sur les droits de tirage, ce qui était bien la moindre des choses puisqu'ils étaient les gros créanciers du monde occidental. En revanche, on ne sait pas encore s'ils auront la possibilité de faire pièce aux Américains sur d'autres mesures à prendre au sein du Fonds, comme l'augmentation des quotas, les opérations sur l'or, la réforme du statut du personnel, etc. Les Six doivent en discuter entre eux en novembre. Malgré la bonne tenue du front européen à Rio (les Allemands notamment ont constamment appuyé M. Debré), les Américains ne désespèrent pas de constater bientôt une nouvelle faille sur ce point dans la C.E.E., les Italiens ayant paru en effet (par reconnaissance pour le soutien que la lire a reçu jadis de Washington ?) beaucoup plus réservés.

Mais sur les cent huit pays du Fonds monétaire une dizaine seulement étaient intéressés par ces querelles byzantines. Les liquidités additionnelles, qui permettront peut-être un jour de dégager un ou deux milliards de dollars par an de ressources supplémentaires, iront pour les huit dixièmes aux pays riches, puisque la répartition sera proportionnelle à la contribution de chaque Etat au Fonds monétaire. C'est là un scandale pour l'esprit, et l'on comprend que M. Michel Debré, comme l'an dernier à Washington, ait insisté cette année à Rio sur la nécessité de mettre sur pied des mécanismes de stabilisation des cours de matières premières, avec l'aide des institutions de Bretton-Woods. Cette fois, on va mettre sérieusement le sujet à l'étude. Ce propos est sans doute moins ambitieux que celui de la « monnaie-marchandises » préconisée par MM. Kaldor, Tinbergen, de Largentaye, Mendès France, mais il part du même sentiment qu'une injustice fondamentale est à réparer.

Sur ce chapitre aussi règne une certaine ambiguïté. Quelques mauvais esprits anglo-saxons n'hésitent pas à dire que c'est pour s'attirer dans les votes les bonnes grâces du « tiers monde » que le ministre français des finances a fait ses propositions. D'un autre côté, les Sud-Américains s'émeuvent d'un projet qui tendrait à favoriser surtout les Africains. C'est à New-Delhi, en février, que ce vaste sujet sera traité au fond.

La commission de Bruxelles souhaite l'ouverture de négociations avec Londres « dans les formes les plus appropriées »

Le point fondamental est celui du statut de la livre

Très attendu, le rapport de la Commission des Communautés européennes, sur la demande d'adhésion de la Grande-Bretagne et de certains autres pays au Marché commun, a été adressé, vendredi, aux gouvernements des Six. Le 20 septembre, à Strasbourg, M. Jean Rey, président de l' « exécutif » de Bruxelles, avait déjà, avec précaution, levé un coin du voile devant les parlementaires européens sur les idées qui avaient guidé les travaux de la commission. « Le temps est venu, disait-il notamment, de commencer ces négociations, car ce n'est vraiment qu'avec nos partenaires européens, la Grande-Bretagne et les autres pays intéressés qu'il serait possible d'approfondir convenablement l'ensemble des problèmes et de constater si nous sommes arrivés au moment où cette immense étape peut être franchie. »

Cette philosophie, ou plus exactement cette manière d'envisager l'ouverture des pourparlers avec les Anglais, se trouve développée dans les conclusions du document qui vient d'être envoyé aux ministres. Il est bien entendu que la Commission ne propose pas d'ouvrir les négociations pour une adhésion à tout prix de la Grande-Bretagne, mais, « en vue de lever les incertitudes qui subsistent notamment sur certains points fondamentaux... », d'approfondir comme il est nécessaire les problèmes mis en relief par le présent document et rechercher si des solutions peuvent être trouvées qui permettent de sauvegarder la cohésion de l'ensemble.

La Commission ne dit rien, au reste, sur le style de ces négociations, qui devraient s'ouvrir « dans les formes les plus appropriées ». Elle manifeste, on le voit, une grande prudence, et nul doute que des hommes comme MM. Raymond Barre et Jean Deniau, membres français de l'organisme bruxellois, ont poussé beaucoup en ce sens.

Il est trop tôt pour savoir si cet avis plein de nuances aura l'heur de plaire au gouvernement français. Jusqu'ici, on ne cachait guère à Paris que n'importe quelle réunion autour d'une table avec les Anglais était indésirable, en tout cas prématurée. Le général de Gaulle craint visiblement de s'engager dans un processus au bout duquel, si vraiment il juge qu'il faut laisser à la porte les Anglais pour des raisons politiques, il n'aura plus à sa disposition que le veto dont il s'est déjà servi le 14 janvier 1963. Mais le veto *a priori* serait-il plus facile à faire passer ? Ne risquerait-on pas, ce faisant, de provoquer un grave ébranlement de cette Communauté qu'on veut précisément aujourd'hui préserver dans toute sa pureté ? En deux mots, les Anglais ne sont-ils pas plus dangereux au-dehors que dans la C.E.E. ?

En mettant l'accent dans son avis sur les obstacles formidables qu'il faudrait lever pour que la Grande-Bretagne puisse entrer sans que l'élargissement des Communautés soit payé par l'affaiblissement de leur dynamisme, la Commission manifeste en tout cas que « rien n'est joué ». Comme le disait récemment un haut fonctionnaire français de Bruxelles, « ce n'est pas au moment où la mayonnaise de l'Europe européenne est en train de prendre (et on l'a bien vu par exemple à Rio) qu'il faut risquer de la faire tourner ».

PIERRE DROUIN.

(Lire la suite page 16, 1re col.)

LES PRISES DE POSITION SUR LE CONFLIT VIETNAMIEN

Le président Johnson se dit prêt à rencontrer le président Ho Chi Minh

Bien qu'il se soit déclaré prêt à rencontrer le président Ho Chi Minh, c'est un discours « dur » qu'a prononcé vendredi soir à San-Antonio, devant deux mille parlementaires américains, M. Lyndon Johnson. Rarement, en effet, le chef de la Maison Blanche avait posé en termes aussi nets les buts de guerre des Etats-Unis au Vietnam : c'est de la « survie » des Etats-Unis qu'il s'agit, a-t-il affirmé. Un tel enjeu laisse peu de marge à d'éventuelles discussions avec Hanoï, que le président se déclare cependant prêt à favoriser par une suspension des bombardements.

UN TISSU DE CONTRADICTIONS

De notre correspondant particulier ALAIN CLÉMENT

Washington, 30 septembre. — Une fois franchi un certain seuil d'exaspération, il est vain d'attendre d'un chef d'Etat attaqué à l'extérieur et à l'intérieur comme l'est M. Johnson qu'il fasse montre d'une logique irréfutable. Il n'y a donc pas lieu de s'étonner qu'on puisse ramasser à la pelle les contradictions dans le discours-programme prononcé vendredi à San-Antonio par le plus illustre des Texans. D'un côté, il s'est affirmé plus que jamais décidé à faire front « *à tous les gangsters, quelle que soit leur idéologie* », de l'autre il se déclare prêt — aux applaudissements de l'assistance — à rencontrer demain s'il le faut le président Ho Chi Minh, en évitant toutefois d'indiquer quel pourrait être leur terrain d'entente.

Le ton général du discours de M. Johnson fait douter de l'utilité d'un tel dialogue. Car si les Etats-Unis sont vraiment au Vietnam à seule fin d'écraser « *l'agression* », de décourager une fois pour toutes « *l'appétit de conquête et l'expansionnisme communiste* », si la clef de leur « *engagement* » n'est pas le seul désir d'assurer le droit du Vietnam du Sud à son autodétermination, mais la volonté de faire prévaloir « *la sécurité de la nation américaine* » et, au-delà, d'étouffer dans l'œuf une troisième guerre mondiale, peut-être même une conflagration nucléaire, on ne voit pas pourquoi ils devraient en fin de compte accepter un compromis forcément boiteux et précaire. La seule « *sécurité* » concevable dans cette perspective planétaire, est une victoire militaire sans bavure sur un Vietnam exsangue au Nord comme au Sud. Le président Johnson n'a pas hésité à invoquer à l'appui de ce jusqu'au-boutisme la caution du général Eisenhower, lequel avait pourtant tout fait, malgré un langage qui ne le cédait en rien quant à l'inflexibilité à celui de son second successeur, pour ne pas enliser le prestige et la puissance de son pays dans le bourbier vietnamien.

De même est-il vain pour un président aussi critiqué que M. Johnson de jurer que les dissensions intestines du peuple américain ne doivent pas induire Hanoï à croire que la guerre ne sera pas poursuivie avec la dernière vigueur. Elle le sera certainement... tant que M. Johnson sera à la Maison Blanche et se persuadera que le seul moyen d'y rester est de prouver qu'il ne se laisse pas intimider par la vague de mécontentement et d'incrédulité qu'il soulève.

(Lire la suite page 2, 1re col.)

PAUL VI OFFRE SA « COLLABORATION » A M. THANT POUR METTRE FIN A LA GUERRE

Le pape Paul VI a fait parvenir le 22 septembre un appel à M. Thant, lui demandant de reprendre ses efforts en vue d'une solution du conflit vietnamien. Paul VI se déclare prêt dans cette lettre, qui a été transmise au secrétaire général de l'O.N.U. par Mgr Alberto Giovanetti, observateur du Saint-Siège auprès des Nations unies, à offrir sa collaboration « sous toute forme qui pourrait être utile » *pour mettre fin à ce* « triste conflit qui cause tant d'anxiété au monde ».

« *Le Saint-Père connaît et apprécie l'intérêt et le souci du secrétaire général des Nations unies concernant la menace que la continuation du conflit vietnamien porte à la paix du monde,* déclare le message pontifical reçu mardi par M. Thant et rendu public vendredi. *Le Saint-Père a toujours suivi et continue de suivre avec une profonde inquiétude la situation dans le Sud-Est asiatique et il a accueilli avec une satisfaction profonde les nouvelles selon lesquelles, en ces jours, de nouvelles initiatives sont en cours, ou sont projetées, afin de trouver la base d'une solution honorable et pacifique du conflit.*

» *Le Saint-Père désire assurer le secrétaire général des Nations unies qu'il apporte, comme toujours, ses encouragements aux efforts des hommes de bonne volonté en faveur de la paix, et qu'il est disposé à leur offrir sa collaboration sous la forme qui pourrait être utile,* poursuit le message.

» *Le Saint-Père nourrit l'espoir que le secrétaire général des Nations unies usera de sa grande influence pour éliminer les obstacles et surmonter les difficultés afin de hâter le jour où les armes auront été déposées, et où le peuple du Vietnam pourra se consacrer dans la sérénité, la liberté et l'indépendance, à la reconstruction de sa patrie. Le Saint-Père invoque l'abondance des faveurs divines sur cette tache noble et généreuse* », conclut l'appel, auquel M. Thant n'a pas encore répondu. Cet appel est signé par le cardinal Cicognani, secrétaire d'Etat du Vatican.

Peu après la publication du message pontifical, M. Dean Rusk s'est montré surpris par l'allusion de Paul VI à « *de nouvelles initiatives* » de paix et aurait indiqué en privé qu'aucun sondage de paix n'est actuellement en cours. Au Vatican on fait seulement remarquer que le texte pontifical a été rédigé avant que l'Union soviétique ne fasse connaître qu'elle avait décidé d'accroître son aide au Nord-Vietnam. On ajoute à ce sujet que, dimanche dernier, Paul VI a fait preuve d'un grand pessimisme lorsqu'il s'est adressé de sa loggia aux fidèles. Le pape avait alors déclaré, après avoir fait allusion à certains espoirs : « *Au lieu de cela, nous avons maintenant la sombre perspective de nouveaux armements et de nouveaux combats.* »

SAGESSE ET SERVITUDES DE LA SENESCENCE

La vieillesse a changé dans tous les pays évolués, où le vieillissement des populations — notion mathématique — s'est accru régulièrement depuis la révolution industrielle du dix-huitième siècle. Aux quelques patriarches respectés des temps jadis se sont substitués des millions de retraités dont la collectivité assure tant bien que mal la survie, en vertu des notions actuelles de solidarité sociale.

Dans le même temps, cette survie s'est prolongée, car si le vieillissement démographique s'est accru, la sénescence — notion physiologique cette fois — recule, ou peut reculer grâce aux progrès de la médecine et plus précisément de la gérontologie, qui n'est une discipline distincte que depuis 1950.

L'homme d'aujourd'hui peut, s'il est bien informé et s'il bénéficie de tous ces progrès, conserver jusqu'au terme de sa vie l'intégrité de ses fonctions ou de ses aptitudes physiques ou mentales. Mais l'inutilisation de ces aptitudes, rançon de l'inaction et de la solitude, favorise leur involution et ces déclins séniles qui ne relèvent plus, comme on le croyait jadis, de la fatalité, mais sont autant de tragédies personnelles, et qui imposent aux collectivités des charges financières écrasantes.

L'Etat ne peut à lui seul remédier à l'isolement des vieillards, ou à la ségrégation trop souvent pratiquée à leur égard ; leur intégration dans la société exige le développement d'un certain sens communautaire et surtout la substitution d'un esprit d'initiative, d'une solidarité active, à l'esprit de revendication et aux conceptions actuelles, aliénantes et passives du « droit à la sécurité ».

Les deux visages, individuel et collectif, médical et socio-démographique, du vieillissement ne peuvent être dissociés ; tous les travaux publiés depuis quelques années montrent que leurs imbrications sont étroites et qu'ils exigent une étude commune, de laquelle pourrait naître l'élaboration de cette véritable « politique de la vieillesse » que préconisait déjà il y a cinq ans le rapport Laroque, mais qui ne soulève encore, ni en France ni dans d'autres pays voisins, l'intérêt qu'elle mérite.

Cette politique est l'affaire de tous, pour ses implications économiques et sociales ; elle est aussi, par ses incidences médicales et psychologiques, l'affaire de chacun, et c'est sous ce double aspect que nous nous efforcerons d'en définir les bases.

I. — VIEILLARDS D'HIER ET D'AUJOURD'HUI

Par le docteur ESCOFFIER-LAMBIOTTE

Les vieillards ont connu, durant de longs siècles, et dans presque toutes les sociétés, une situation privilégiée tenant, pour l'essentiel, à la double singularité de la richesse et de la rareté.

Depuis l'origine des temps, et jusqu'au milieu du XVIIIe siècle, les populations humaines se caractérisaient en effet par une mortalité infantile effroyable (40 %), une espérance de vie moyenne par conséquent très brève (vingt-cinq à trente ans pour les Grecs et les Egyptiens, trente-sept ans pour un groupe social entre tous favorisé, celui des empereurs allemands du XVIIe siècle) et la très faible proportion relative des hommes qui atteignaient ou dépassaient soixante ans. L'étude des registres paroissiaux et des dénombrements fragmentaires semble indiquer que les sexagénaires ne représentaient pas plus de 4 à 6 % de la population dans les villes (Italie des XVe et XVIe siècles) et une proportion plus faible encore des habitants des villages. La plupart d'entre eux appartenaient à la catégorie « des eupatrides, des bien-nés et des bien-nourris » ; le froid, la faim, la maladie et parfois les solutions plus expéditives encore suggérées par l'image classique du cocotier, ou par Platon et Cicéron pour les esclaves ou les travailleurs âgés, se chargeaient d'éliminer chez les pauvres l'espoir ou l'angoisse de la vieillesse.

(Lire la suite page 9, 1re col.)

A NOS LECTEURS

Les journaux quotidiens ont désormais la faculté de fixer librement leur prix de vente.

Cette mesure, souhaitée depuis longtemps par la profession, permet aux quotidiens français, parisiens et régionaux, d'augmenter de 10 centimes leur prix de vente.

« Le Monde », pour sa part, sera mis en vente lundi au prix de 50 centimes. Nos lecteurs doivent savoir que les recettes nettes de vente ne couvriront, même à ce nouveau prix, qu'un peu plus de la moitié du prix de revient, le complément provenant des recettes de publicité.

S'il est souhaitable que le quotidien reste accessible à tous, sans distinction de fortune, nous croyons que l'indépendance financière, condition de l'indépendance sur tous les autres plans, est un impératif absolu, et nous savons que les lecteurs du « Monde » partagent cette conviction.

Les abonnements en cours seront naturellement servis jusqu'à leur expiration et les nouveaux tarifs, qui n'entreront en vigueur que le 1er novembre, seront calculés de façon à réduire, pour nos abonnés, l'incidence de l'augmentation.

AU JOUR LE JOUR

Si toi aussi tu m'abandonnes

Ce n'est ni un communiste, ni un neutraliste, ni un partisan du Vietcong, qui demande aux Américains un peu plus d'indépendance pour le Vietnam et les menace d'un nouveau Dien-Bien-Phu s'ils s'obstinent, mais le général Thieu en personne, c'est-à-dire, de fait et de droit, le représentant de la seule autorité qui, par sa demande d'assistance, puisse justifier la présence des Américains au Vietnam.

La chose n'est pas nouvelle. Les classiques du western montrent qu'un vrai redresseur de torts peut se passer même de l'assentiment des gens qu'il libère des méchants. La coopération de la victime n'est pas nécessaire pour un sauvetage. Il suffit seulement qu'elle se tienne tranquille, et si elle se débat, un sauveteur bien avisé lui impose le calme, au besoin par la manière forte.

En somme, tout le problème est de savoir s'il faut attendre que Hanoï soit complètement détruit pour commencer à bombarder Saigon.

ROBERT ESCARPIT.

appears that this formula—mixing facts with their interpretation—is what has given *Le Monde* its special attraction. Another press observer has called *Le Monde* "a daily anthology of think pieces."[7] The paper is calm, unhurried, and placid, appearing to hang above the battle, surveying the area very thoughtfully before entering the fray with its arsenal of rational journalism. In a country where the purely political press is rapidly disappearing, *Le Monde* never shirks straightforward political comment and consistently represents an intelligent left-of-center line.[8]

Le Monde readers probably know what has happened, for their radio, television, and the morning papers have already told them. What *Le Monde* readers desire is the why and how of the news and the paper's editors and writers proceed to furnish these "extras." Because of the small type, the compact headlines, the absence of photographs, and sparse (but expensive) advertising, *Le Monde* writers have the space and leisure to supply thoughtful, well-researched essays and stories. The paper sees itself as something of a continuing higher education. "Having taught Public and International Law for eleven years, I conceive, above all, a newspaper to be a medium of teaching that concerns itself with current events," says Beuve-Méry. "Maybe this is the reason why in spite of *Le Monde*'s austerity and absence of pictures it has increasingly had more young as its readers."[9]

Le Monde got its start after the Nazi occupation of Paris had ended in 1944. The new Government under General de Gaulle desired a voice —a newspaper which would be respected at home and abroad. De Gaulle realized that a new press would be helpful in a quick re-establishment of France as an important nation in Europe; he desired a press free from much of the prewar corruption and untainted by collaboration with the Vichy Government. It has even been said that another reason de Gaulle wanted a new highly respected paper was that he hoped it would reflect his own views and purposes.[10]

The prewar *Le Temps*, a conservative daily which had been a supporter of the Munich Pact, was expropriated and de Gaulle proceeded to build *Le Monde* on the foundation of the old Paris daily. *Le Temps* had been considered one of Europe's best dailies prior to World War II and was especially good at the turn of the century and through the first three decades of the 1900's. It was a kind of "semiofficial" mouthpiece of government (in the sense of an "Establishment" paper), and was France's most quoted paper. It began losing prestige in the late 1920's when it took political subsidies and by 1931 had sold out its physical assets to a combine of coal and steel interests.[11]

Hubert Beuve-Méry was chosen as the new director of *Le Monde,* and he and his staff put out the first issue of the paper from the old *Le Temps* building and presses in December, 1944. The new daily inherited many of *Le Temps*' old staff members, its neo-Gothic nameplate (logotype) design, its ultraserious tone, and its basic typeface. When asked to head the new paper, Beuve-Méry recalls that he agreed "only if we could be independent, without subsidies of any sort, public or private."[12] His terms were accepted and he became the first *Le Monde* editor, a post he still holds.

On the front page of the first issue, an article informed the reader that:

> A new daily appears: *Le Monde*. Its main ambition is to assure the reader of clear, real information, fast and complete. But in our times one cannot be satisfied with merely observing and describing. People are drawn along a flood of tumultuous and tragic events of which every man, whether he wants it or not, is as much the author as the spectator, the beneficiary and the victim. . . . What is needed is a revolution—a revolution by law—in order to triumph; a revolution that will restore, by the union and creative effort of all the French that are worthy of this name, French grandeur and freedom.[13]

After only about a year, *Le Monde* was successful, with a circulation of at least 150,000 and a reputation as an independent and reliable newspaper. It had begun selling outside France, and was clearly established as a journal directed at an intelligent, well-educated, and liberal audience.

At first *Le Monde* was criticized by the Left as a thinly disguised organ of the trusts. The Right, especially highly placed Army officers, attacked the paper and Beuve-Méry as "cryto-Communist" during the fighting in Indo-China and Algeria—in both issues *Le Monde* was ahead of the public in calling for negotiated settlements.[14] At one point in the Algerian trouble, terrorists protesting *Le Monde*'s liberal stand on Algeria's independence, exploded a bomb near the paper's building, injuring several employees. Although copies of *Le Monde* were confiscated several times in Algeria, this never happened in France, although such action was threatened repeatedly. *Le Monde* favored de Gaulle's efforts to bring about order at the end of the Algerian crisis. It also supported his return to power in the December, 1958 referendum, making it clear that it agreed with his aims but often disliked his means. For example, it supported his ambition to make France a respected and strong nation again, but found his insistence that France have an atomic bomb shocking.[15]

Le Monde's progress to an undisputed place of leadership among Europe's elite dailies owes much to Hubert Beuve-Méry, its founder and directing editor. The paper has grown better as "Beuve," as his staff members call him, has struggled for political and financial independence. He has been the strong and vital force behind *Le Monde*. Born in Paris of poor parents in 1902, Beuve-Méry had a hard struggle to secure his education and gain his journalistic reputation. At the age of twenty-six he went to Prague (in 1928) where he taught at the French Institute, becoming a few years later the Prague correspondent for the great pre-World War II Paris daily, *Le Temps*. He resigned in 1939 when his political opinions did not agree with those of the editors of *Le Temps*. In World War II he served first in the French Army and later in the Resistance, where, working for the underground, he took the pen name "Sirius" under which he still writes a stinging column.

Today Beuve-Méry, whose scorn for money and its corrupting influence is well known, supervises the paper very closely. Each morning he arrives at the grim old *Monde* offices and plant off the Grande Boulevard (at 5–7 Rue des Italiens) and holds a "standing" conference with his top editors, often lasting about an hour. There is a give-and-take on major issues and general suggestions are discussed. Also Beuve-Méry assigns the theme of the daily "foreign bulletin," which appears in boldface type in the left column of the front page, to a specialist. Only this unsigned essay, in effect an "editorial," represents *Le Monde*'s position on an important foreign issue.[16]

The retail sale of *Le Monde* is carried out through the services of Nouvelles Messageries de la Presse Parisienne (News Delivery Services of the Parisian Press) which handles the distribution of all but two of the Parisian papers. The foreign sales are handled by the Departement Etranger Hachette (Foreign Department of Hachette publishing firm). *Le Monde* publishes the following weeklies: *Le Sélection Hebdomadaire* (a twelve-page edition for subscribers only), *Le Monde Diplomatique*, and *Lc Monde des Philatélistes*.

Although many persons think *Le Monde* "reflects the enlightened official opinion,"[17] this is not the case. In fact, according to one writer it is far more often *Le Figaro* that has revealed the precise opinion of the Ministry.[18] The question is frequently asked: "What is *Le Monde*'s political orientation?" This cannot be easily answered because of the extreme independent attitude prevailing at the newspaper; there is a constant desire on the part of the paper's editors to be honest and objective. This attitude precludes the paper's tying itself to a particular "position" in an unyielding way. Giving a political label to *Le Monde* is made more difficult by the great diversity of opinions and tendencies of the paper's collaborators or contributors. Many persons still accuse *Le Monde* of being a Communist paper and others are just as convinced that it is conservative and bourgeois. Generally, however, *Le Monde* is considered liberal, left-of-center, and internationalist. Beuve-Méry calls its political orientation "social liberalism or liberal socialism, as you will, to reconcile as much as possible liberty with justice."[19] Certainly the paper is pacifistic, ever in favor of rational discussion and arbitration. Its editorial position advocates the recognition of Red China by the United States because it believes that "it is vain, dangerous, not to recognize what exists." It also favors Red China being a member of the United Nations, for "if the presence of China in the U.N. is dangerous, its absence can be even more so."[20]

Le Monde is to politics and international relations what London's

Financial Times and New York's *Wall Street Journal* are to finance. Political analysis and news, along with international affairs and parliamentary reportage and a good leavening of literary and cultural material will account for some 50 per cent of the nonadvertising space in an average issue.[21] Such an issue will run on the average sixteen pages, with about half the total editorial content dealing with foreign affairs. Advertising, bringing in some 52 per cent of the paper's total income, accounts for only about 20 per cent of the total space.[22] *Le Monde* often delves into aspects of international reporting neglected by most other papers. In 1958, for example, the Asian Conference of the International Press Institute noted that the degree of interest in China shown by European and American papers bore little relationship to the importance of the Peking regime for the Western world. The conference noted that out of nineteen important newspapers of the Western world analyzed, only one, *Le Monde*, gave "good background material to illuminate the current news."[23]

Le Monde carries no comic strips, no cartoons, no puzzles, no contests, and does not consider social events or sports very important. It does print a listing of events (roughly equivalent to the Court Calendar of London), and carries summaries of new laws and regulations, a complete stock-market report, and several pages of financial news. These features give it a certain aura of officialdom in the manner of the London *Times*, but it certainly does not speak for the Government. It is, on the contrary, one of the most independent dailies in the world, and nobody is quite sure who will be the next target of its barbed editorial arrows. As *Le Monde* sees it, its loyalty is only to the truth as determined by its intelligent and conscientious staff.

This staff consists of only eighty writers and editors. But their morale is high and they are well-educated, most holding degrees in law, economics, philosophy, and literature.[24] About a fourth of these staff members were with *Le Temps* before World War II. *Le Monde* staff members have great pride in the paper and not many leave it. Back in 1956 a new paper called *Le Temps de Paris* was founded and admitted that it would try to take readers away from *Le Monde*. Financed by wealthy industrialists, the new paper had plenty of money with which to try to lure *Le Monde*'s staff members away, often salary increases of 200-300 per cent, but only one left *Le Monde*. *Le Temps de Paris* died within three months.[25]

From the beginning, Beuve-Méry collected a team whose common characteristics were youth (or youthful spirit) and intellectual curiosity. Many of them were short on experience, but were long on talent. Special knowledge, not journalistic knowledge, was what they had, and this was what Beuve-Méry wanted. Today *Le Monde* is staff-owned, with Beuve-Méry holding the major interest.

Over the years *Le Monde* has established a very efficient and knowledgeable reportorial staff that includes men of eminence in every field;

for example, Emile Henriot, the literary critic, is one of France's most renowned novelists and playwrights, and Jacques Fauvet, a leading political writer, has published three first-rate political books in France, England, and the United States.[26] Writers have great freedom; copy is not changed to fit policy. Staff members can be found on both the political Left and Right, with perhaps most on the Left. A close look at *Le Monde* will show that opinions of all political orientations are included. One writer recently commented that perhaps this wide range of opinion leads to an "unevenness" in the paper's editorial profile.[27] This may well be true, but it is this "unevenness" or pluralism of viewpoints which sets *Le Monde* apart from most rigid political papers.

Le Monde has twenty-four foreign correspondents stationed in "the large and medium-sized capitals: Washington, New York (U.N.), Montreal, London, Moscow, Rome, Brussels, Warsaw, Belgrade, Athens, Istanbul, New Delhi, Rabat, Algiers, Tunis, Dakar, Rio de Janeiro, Buenos Aires, etc."[28] Some of the best of *Le Monde*'s foreign correspondents are Ronald Delcourt (Bonn), Alain Jacob (London), Phillippe Ben (New York), and Henri Pierre (Moscow). The paper also has its specialists and special envoys who are sent to "trouble spots" of the world or to cover special events.

The readers of *Le Monde* are well-educated and well-informed. Raymond Manevy, former editor of *Paris-Soir* (1931–1942) and later President of the Centre de Formation des Journalistes, defined *Le Monde* as the paper that "recruits its readers generally from the University, the Court, the Administration, Industry and Banking" and one whose "readers like serious news and neglect the *faits divers*."[29] The paper seems to appeal mainly to younger age groups—from twenty to about fifty-five; in fact, readers who are under fifty comprise three-fourths of *Le Monde*'s readership. Most of the readers live in towns and cities, and a big majority are from the middle- and higher-executive groups.[30] In addition to readers among executives in commerce, industry, finance, the paper appeals chiefly to university professors and students and to members of the liberal professions. *Le Monde*'s audience is composed largely of what the British call "the Establishment"—the elite capable of forming opinion and institution policy.[31]

Although *Le Monde* is generally considered the best French daily, it comes under periodic heavy criticism. Perhaps this is to be expected of any concerned, vital elite newspaper, and especially one which concentrates on politics and world affairs. In the case of *Le Monde*, it seems that attacks grow and multiply in proportion to the paper's prestige. Typical example: The weekly *Europe-Magazine* of Brussels, on January 26, 1965, questioned the objectivity of *Le Monde*, pointing out several alleged mistakes in the French daily's article about the political situation in Belgium, and concluding that "it is displeasing to see a foreign paper, that wants to pass as serious and well-informed, spreading assertions that can only poison the atmosphere of Belgium." The

Belgian journal continued: "If the stories of *Le Monde* on South-East Asia, the Middle East, and Latin America are as deformed as those pertaining to our country, the least one can say is that they are subject to doubt."[32]

Beuve-Méry himself, as well as his paper, comes under occasional attack. Usually it centers on his immense power. One French writer has asked: "What gives Mr. Beuve-Méry this power? How can he justify it?"[33] The German magazine *Zeitungsverlag und Zeitschriftenverlag* in its August 6, 1965 issue, writes that although *Le Monde* theoretically has a democratic structure with participation of its editors in editorial policy, the powerful personality of Beuve-Méry has managed to impose an authoritarian regime in that he "considers it his natural rights" to determine the contents and policies of the paper.[34] Keeping himself generally above the fray, Beuve-Méry repeatedly insists that his paper is free and independent and strives constantly to be "a public service."[35]

Regardless of the criticisms of *Le Monde*, there is no doubt but that the paper occupies a unique and exceptional place in France: "an irreplaceable national institution," as the Manchester *Guardian* has called it.[36] *L'Express*, the outstanding weekly news magazine of France, has summarized beautifully the value of *Le Monde*:

> Whatever the personal value of H. Beuve-Méry and of his paper, the fight he leads would only have an anecdotic interest if it did not represent today one of the last lighthouses that light for France the road of intellectual courage, sternness of spirit and of political morality.[37]

No serious, courageous elite daily anywhere, attempting to establish a world community of reason, could hope to be more than one of these "last lighthouses" in the midst of world journalism.

13

West Germany's Serious Duo

Although West Germany (The Federal Republic of Germany) has many excellent daily newspapers, two stand out as the best examples of serious, quality journals which circulate throughout the Bundesrepublik and have large foreign circulations. These are Frankfurt-am-Main's *Frankfurter Allgemeine* and Hamburg's *Die Welt*. Only they, of the country's more than six hundred main dailies, can claim to be national newspapers. Their main competitor is Munich's liberal *Süddeutsche Zeitung*, and although it does have some readers outside southern Germany, its circulation is concentrated in the State of Bavaria. The once prestigious Berlin press, largely because it finds itself in an island city surrounded by Communist East Germany, has no dailies of elite status to compete with those in such cities as Hamburg, Frankfurt, and Munich.

West Germany's press is predominately composed of a large number of local newspapers (average circulation: 10,000), and the educated and well-informed German reads two papers—his local paper for local news, and one of the two big elite national dailies.

The *Frankfurter Allgemeine Zeitung* (or the *FAZ*, as it is often called) will be discussed first in this chapter. It was founded in 1949 by pre-World War II German journalists, and was influenced by the world-renowned old *Frankfurter Zeitung* which died with Hitler's regime. More traditionally "German" than *Die Welt* but somewhat similarly oriented politically, the *FAZ* retains much of the writing style and outward appearance of the quality German dailies of the 1920's and 1930's. *Die Welt*, born as a licensed British-type paper in the British occupation zone in 1946, is much livelier and modern in its writing and makeup techniques.

Both papers are well-informed, intelligent, and serious, and are more often quoted at home and abroad than any other West German daily. Each daily sees the other as its chief competitor in the country's elite press; *FAZ* editors believe their paper is the best and *Die Welt*, second best. *Die Welt* editors would reverse the order.

A writer for the London *Times* has written that if a German university professor were stranded on a desert island and asked to select the one newspaper he would like to read, he would probably pick the scholarly *FAZ*. If he were a businessman or a politician, his choice would almost surely be *Die Welt*. Perhaps it is safe to say that *Die Welt* stresses politics in the manner of France's *Le Monde*, while the *FAZ* attempts a broad coverage with a tendency toward economics like Switzerland's *Neue Zürcher Zeitung*. Both West German dailies, however, are well-balanced journals offering a broad diet for the serious reader.

Frankfurter Allgemeine

Although it was founded only in 1949 just when the licensing of German newspapers was lifted by the Occupation Authorities, the *Frankfurter Allgemeine Zeitung* (Frankfurt General Newspaper) is one of a seemingly vanishing breed of sedate old newspapers that emphasize content, not appearance. There is probably no other newspaper in the world today more dignified in its typography and makeup or more serious and careful in its writing than Frankfurt-am-Main's prestigious daily.

The *FAZ* (a common designation) came into being when the German Federal Republic was only beginning and, in effect, there were no German newspapers. Immediately the *Frankfurter Allgemeine*'s founders, dedicated journalists from the prewar era,[1] set about creating a daily newspaper, independent of outside authorities which "was to work and speak—both inside and outside the country—for the whole of Germany."[2] The *FAZ*'s subtitle, which it still bears ("Newspaper for Germany"), reflects the journal's basic aspiration.

As the West German nation was struggling to regain its equilibrium and the native press was on the threshold of explosion, the *FAZ* made its appearance and was immediately embraced by Germans hungry for their own type of journalism. The war had shattered the thriving and healthy German press of pre-Hitler years. Highly respected dailies like the *Berliner Tageblatt*, *Vossische Zeitung*, *Deutsche Allgemeine Zeitung*, and the revered old *Frankfurter Zeitung*, among the best newspapers in the world as the 1930's began, were all gone. In 1949 only a few dailies existed in what is now the Federal Republic, and these were papers started by the British, Americans, and French in their respective occupation zones.

With the birth of the Federal Republic and the ending of licensing in 1949, the press immediately took life and began to grow. In the British zone alone, 150 journals sprang up within one month, and similar beginnings were made throughout the country. Most of the growth was centered in the small regional or local papers (*Heimatpresse*), with circulations concentrated in their immediate vicinities. None of the very early newspapers declared its intention to reach a readership in all parts of the country. To fill this gap the *FAZ* appeared November 1, 1949, founded by a group of men who had worked on the old *Frankfurter Zeitung*. Its aim: to provide the country with a supraregional journal and to be as good as, or better than, the famous old *Frankfurter Zeitung*.

With the *FAZ* began a supraregional press in the Federal Republic which would try to provide the kind of national news and comment to which Germans had been accustomed before the war. In the first edition, the *FAZ* defined its mission in these words: "The truth of the facts must be sacred . . . strict objectivity in its coverage . . . fair treatment of opposing viewpoints . . . the preservation of the ideals of freedom and justice, which our profession shall serve."[3] An editorial in a later edition was more specific in declaring the paper's intentions:

> The object of the enterprise is to preserve the light of freedom from the many outside forces. We despise chauvinism; we don't place the nation above humanity! But we love equally as little the dishonorable role of national imprisonment. Mainly because we (the German people) do not recognize ourselves as Europeans, we need not be an inferior member in the European community. Germany cannot be excluded from the great ideals of freedom and justice.[4]

Many of the staff members of the *FAZ* had served on the old *Frankfurter Zeitung* which had stopped publication in 1944 on Hitler's orders; until then it had been permitted to publish with considerable freedom by Goebbels for propaganda purposes since it was still read rather widely outside Germany. A group of its former staff members had gathered in Mainz during the occupation years to establish the *Allgemeine Zeitung* there.[5] When the *FAZ* was founded in 1949, many of these old staffers returned to Frankfurt-am-Main to work for the new paper. Officially, there is no formal connection between the two papers, although it is obvious that the present staff is proud of the connection, however tenuous, for in many of the promotional booklets and brochures, the *FAZ* uses the slogan "The young international newspaper with an old tradition."

Frankfurter Allgemeine

ZEITUNG FÜR DEUTSCHLAND

D-Ausgabe / Dienstag, 3. Oktober 1967 — Herausgegeben von Nikolas Benckiser, Bruno Dechamps, Jürgen Eick, Karl Korn, Jürgen Tern, Erich Welter — 40 Pfennig / Nr. 229 — D 2954 A

Wilson kämpft mit der eigenen Partei um den EWG-Beitritt

Starker Widerstand auf dem Labour-Kongreß in Scarborough / Gewerkschaftsführer Cousins Sprecher der Opposition / Fünf Bedingungen

hö. SCARBOROUGH, 2. Oktober. Der 66. Jahreskongreß der Labour Party ist am Montagmorgen in Anwesenheit von Premierminister Wilson, Außenminister Brown und anderer Kabinettsmitglieder in dem nordenglischen Seebad Scarborough nach der üblichen bürgermeisterlichen Begrüßung von dem Jahresvorsitzenden Boyd eröffnet worden. Boyd, der sich gegen einen kommunistischen Rivalen um die Nachfolge des in den Adelsstand erhobenen Präsidenten der Metallarbeitergewerkschaft, des jetzigen Lord Carron, bemüht, hielt in seiner Ansprache die Mitte zwischen Loyalität und Kritik, zwischen der Verteidigung der Regierung und der maßvollen, aber deutliche Warnung, sie solle etwas tiefer „in den geheimnisvollen Dschungel der willkürlichen Festsetzung von Preisen und Profiten, der Machenschaften der Börse" und ähnlicher Übel dringen. „So manchem schlechtbezahlten Arbeiter scheint es, daß die Regierung bei den Gewerkschaften Boxhandschuhe, bei den Fabrikanten, Groß- und Einzelhändlern aber Samthandschuhe benutzt." Im Ton seiner Rede und in ihrem moralischen Appell verriet Boyd, daß er nicht nur Gewerkschaftsfunktionär, sondern auch aktives Mitglied der Heilsarmee ist, die zusammen mit den Freikirchen weit mehr Einfluß in der Geschichte der Labour-Bewegung gehabt hat als Karl Marx.

Premierminister Wilson kämpft auf diesem Jahreskongreß, wenn man der britischen Presse glauben wollte, nahezu um seine politische Zukunft, so wie das in der gleichen Kongreßhalle vor sieben Jahren Gaitskell, sein Vorgänger in der Labour-Führung, getan hat. Gaitskell, der damals von den Neutralisten geschlagen worden ist, ohne daß Wilson einen Finger zu seiner Verteidigung gerührt hätte, hat nach seiner schweren Niederlage den Delegierten zugerufen, er werde so lange kämpfen, bis die damals von Cousins geführten Neutralisten besiegt seien.

Es ist nicht ohne Ironie, daß der von Wilson in sein Kabinett aufgenommene Cousins nach seinem protestierenden Rücktritt nun auf dem diesjährigen Kongreß gleich zweimal Front und Fronde gegen Wilson anführt. Der erste Angriff richtet sich gegen die Wirtschaftspolitik des Wilson-Kabinetts, die an diesem Dienstag von Schatzkanzler Callaghan gegen ihre zahlreichen und auf der Konferenz mit Millionen von Stimmen versehenen Widersacher verteidigt werden muß. Die zweite und, international gesehen, wichtigere Attacke richtet sich gegen den Beitritt Großbritanniens zum Gemeinsamen Markt, über den am Donnerstag diskutiert wird.

Beim Vorspiel dieses zweiten Angriffes hat der bisherige Handelsminister Jay in Scarborough bereits vor der Eröffnung des Kongresses eine Rolle gespielt, die völlig klar gemacht hat, daß die Beitrittsgegner nicht nur in der Labour-Bewegung in diesem sonst so unscheinbaren, stillen und einsamen Mann einen fürchtenswerten Streiter gefunden haben. Wie ernst Wilson Jay, den er aus seinem Kabinett entlassen hat, und die neu aufgeflammte Gegnerschaft gegen den Beitritt nimmt und nehmen muß, verrät die vom Gesamtvorstand mühsam hergestellte Resolution, die dem Kongreß zur Annahme vorgelegt wird. Sie ist auch so nur mit sechzehn gegen drei Stimmen bei zwei Stimmenthaltungen angenommen worden.

Der Text der langen Erklärung lag noch nicht vor, als Jay auf einer Kundgebung gegen den Beitritt sprach. Aber er hatte es bei seiner Kenntnis dessen, was sich im letzten Jahr im Kabinett abgespielt hat, nicht gerade schwer, zu erraten, was darin stehen werde. Jay bestritt von vornherein, daß sich an den vom Parteikongreß von 1962 beschlossenen fünf Bedingungen, von deren Erfüllung der britische Beitritt abhängig gemacht werden soll, irgend etwas von Belang geändert habe, so daß sie heute keine Hindernisse mehr seien.

Die ganze Resolution des Labour-Vorstandes aber steht und fällt mit der Behauptung, die Situation habe sich seit 1962 so geändert, daß ein Beitritt jetzt ohne Verletzung dieser Bedingungen möglich sei. Um ganz sicher zu gehen, daß in der Debatte am Donnerstag keine Unklarheit bestehen wird, was es mit diesen Bedingungen auf sich hat, ist von Cousins eine Resolution eingebracht worden, in der „die Labour-Regierung aufgefordert wird, auf geeigneten Sicherungen für die britischen Interessen in der Agrarpolitik zu bestehen, um Erhöhungen der Lebensmittelpreise zu vermeiden und damit das Versprechen des Premierministers in Bristol im Wahlkampf von 1966 einzuhalten". (Fortsetzung auf Seite 4, Spalte 6.)

Ein König im Kreml

N. B. König Hussein von Jordanien ist mit einem Gefolge von Mitarbeitern zu einem viertägigen Aufenthalt in Moskau eingetroffen, wo er mit allen protokollarischen Ehren einschließlich der dem Staatsoberhaupt zukommenden 21 Salutschüsse begrüßt wurde. In unserer durch Gewöhnung gegenüber politischen Reisen abgestumpften Zeit ist dieser Besuch wohl geeignet aufzufallen; zuverlässige Informationen über Absichten und Erfolge des Zusammentreffens Husseins mit den Politikern des Kreml muß man abwarten.

Die Sowjets haben sich zwar längst daran gewöhnt, wann immer ihre politische Linie das zweckmäßig erscheinen läßt, auch mit gekrönten Häuptern unbefangen Umgang zu pflegen. Es ist aber noch nicht so lange her, daß gerade dieser Monarch in Moskau als „Kreatur des Imperialismus" mißachtet wurde; und als er mit Nassers Bruderkuß auf der Wange und als der Hauptbetroffene der arabischen Niederlage den Anspruch darauf erworben hatte, von Schimpfwörtern verschont zu werden, fand doch alle Welt es ganz natürlich, daß Hussein (oder seine Abgesandten) nicht zu den Pilgern gehörte, die nach dem Fünftagekrieg in dichter Folge nach Moskau aufbrachen. Die Scheidung der arabischen Staaten in „konservative" und „progessistische" war auch durch die gemeinsame Front der Araber gegen Israel nicht verwischt worden, ja sie zeichnete sich fast noch schärfer ab, denn man suchte dem konservativen, westlich orientierten Element in der arabischen Welt die Schuld an der Katastrophe zuzuschieben. Inzwischen ist die ägyptische Politik zurückhaltender geworden; sie sucht sich gelegentlich an eine der Wirklichkeit Rechnung tragende politische Lösung heranzutasten — die Information der Zeitung „Al Ahram", über die heute berichtet wird, ist ein Anzeichen dafür.

In dieser Situation vollzieht sich der Besuch Husseins. Der Kreml dokumentiert mit dem Empfang des Königs, daß er seine Nahost-Beziehungen nicht allein vom Sozialreform-Eifer der Staaten und Regierungen abhängig macht. Es könnte für Moskau interessant sein, in dem kleinen Staat am Jordan, der eine erstaunliche Lebenskraft beweist und der nicht nur auf englische und amerikanische Subsidien angewiesen sein möchte, auch Fuß zu fassen. Auch Überlegungen über den Frieden im Nahen Osten werden eingeschlossen sein, so sehr Moskau darauf bedacht sein wird, eine Labilität zu erhalten, die ihm Mitsprache und Einwirkung im Nahen Osten sichert, vielmehr die Möglichkeit für sie erweitert. Mit einem unmittelbar vorangegangenen Besuch in Kairo hat sich Hussein abzusichern gesucht. Gewiß bedeutet diese Moskau-Reise mehr als eine pittoreske Kuriosität.

Viele Wenn und Aber in Brüssel

Die Kommission zu den Aufnahmeanträgen / Der EWG-Ministerrat berät

Gz. LUXEMBURG, 2. Oktober. Unter dem Vorsitz von Bundeswirtschaftsminister Schiller haben in Luxemburg am Montagnachmittag eineinhalbtägige Beratungen des EWG-Ministerrats begonnen. Im Mittelpunkt des politischen Interesses stand der Bericht, den der Präsident der Europäischen Kommission über die Stellungnahme der Kommission zu den vorliegenden Beitrittsanträgen von Großbritannien, Irland, Dänemark und Norwegen gegeben hat. In Brüssel und den europäischen Hauptstädten sickerten bruchstückweise weitere Einzelheiten über die Stellungnahme durch, die jedoch dem seit einigen Tagen bekannter Tenor der Stellungnahme nicht mehr Wesentliches hinzufügen können.

Wenn auch der positive Grundzug der Stellungnahme der Kommission kaum bestritten werden kann, so sind im Laufe der Diskussion, insbesondere auch über die Schlußformel, zahlreiche „Wenn und Aber" eingebaut worden, die in England wohl als enttäuschend empfunden werden.

Die wirtschaftspolitischen Überlegungen und insbesondere die Frage nach der Rolle des Pfundes in einer erweiterten Gemeinschaft nehmen einen dominierenden Einfluß ein. Hier scheint der Einfluß des französischen Vizepräsidenten, Professor Barre, recht stark gewesen zu sein. Es sei unmöglich, so wird festgestellt, Übergangsmaßnahmen zu vereinbaren — die einen späteren Beitritt unterstellen —, wenn nicht die britischen Maßnahmen zur Herstellung eines dauerhaft gesicherten Gleichgewichts bekannt seien.

Die Kommission regte sogar an, Großbritannien möge im Hinblick auf einen späteren Beitritt dann mit der Gemeinschaft über diese Maßnahmen und ihren zeitlichen Ablauf verhandeln. Der Umstand, daß das Pfund eine Weltreservewährung ist, macht es nach Meinung der Kommission notwendig, die Gesamtheit der Währungsbeziehungen im Rahmen des Commonwealth gründlich zu erörtern. Es sei undenkbar, daß im Rahmen einer erweiterten Gemeinschaft das Pfund eine Sonderrolle spiele.

Die Kommission weist ferner darauf hin, daß eine vergrößerte Mitgliederzahl die Konfliktmöglichkeiten mehre und daß unter Umständen dafür Sorge getragen werden müsse, daß die Vorschrift über die Einstimmigkeit im Ministerrat, die jedem Staat ein Vetorecht gebe, oder auch die Nutzung von Schutzklauseln nicht mißbraucht würden. Die Rolle der Kommission, die dann vierzehn Mitglieder umfassen solle, dürfe nicht angetastet werden. Die Frage der Gewichtung der Stimme im Ministerrat sei lösbar; entscheidend sei, daß der Dynamismus und der Zusammenhalt in der Gemeinschaft nicht verringert würden.

Der Ministerrat dient ferner der Vorbereitung der Tagung des Assoziationsrates EWG — Türkei, der in der kommenden Woche in Ankara tagt. Die Beziehungen haben sich gut entwickelt, und der Rat ist im Begriff, bestimmte Einfuhrkontingente für die Türkei zu erweitern. Ernsthaft erörtert werden soll die Frage, ob und unter welchen Umständen im kommenden Jahr über den im Assoziationsvertrag vorgesehenen Beginn der eigentlichen „Übergangsphase" verhandelt werden soll, an deren Ende dann eine Zollunion stünde.

Ehmke Nachfolger von Schütz?

R. BONN, 2. Oktober. Bundesaußenminister Brandt muß sich, nachdem sein Staatssekretär Schütz Regierender Bürgermeister in Berlin werden soll, bald um einen neuen Staatssekretär bemühen. Es scheint verständlicherweise festzustehen, daß dieser Posten weiterhin mit einem Sozialdemokraten besetzt werden soll. Die Partei fühlt sich nach der Regierungsumbildung in Bonn noch immer so sehr zu kurz gekommen, daß ihr Vorsitzender Brandt nicht ohne sehr starke Widerstände keinen Sozialdemokraten zum Nachfolger von Schütz berufen könnte. Der gegebene Nachfolger wäre unter diesen Umständen der ehemalige Botschafter Duckwitz, der im Auswärtigen Amt großes Ansehen genießt und der SPD angehört. Doch Duckwitz mußte schon eine Berufung auf einen hohen Botschafterposten vor kurzem auf Anraten seines Arztes ablehnen. In dieser Situation wird jetzt mehr und mehr von dem Staatssekretär im Bundesjustizministerium, Ehmke, gesprochen. Ehmke ist Professor der Rechtswissenschaft und ein sehr aktiver sozialdemokratischer Politiker. Brandt und Ehmke kennen sich seit langem.

Rebellen erwarten entscheidende Schlacht

bb. ACCRA, 2. Oktober. Die ostnigerianischen Rebellen rüsten sich in ihrer Hauptstadt Enugu zur entscheidenden Schlacht, von der, wie der Rebellenführer Ojukwu über den Sender Enugu erklärt, das Leben des Achtmillionenvolkes der Ibo abhängt. Die etwa 60 000 Einwohner der Stadt sollen Straße um Straße, Haus um Haus gegen die Bundestruppen verteidigen, die ihrerseits bereits vor einer Woche bis auf zehn Kilometer an Enugu herangerückt sind und sich auf den Einmarsch vorbereiten. Ojukwu hat nur den Kindern und ihren Müttern erlaubt, sich von Enugu nach Süden abzusetzen. Es ist aber nicht klar, ob der seit neun Tagen unsichtbare Ojukwu selbst noch in seiner Hauptstadt sitzt oder sich nicht schon in das 130 Kilometer südlich gelegene Ausweichquartier bei Umuahia zurückgezogen hat. Von dort ist die Straße weiter nach Süden bis Harcourt noch sicher, wo sich, wie Sprecher der Zentralregierung in Lagos sagen, das einzige unzerstört gebliebene Flugzeug der Rebellenluftwaffe als Ojukwus letzter Ausweg befindet. Reste der Rebellen haben um die Ortschaft Agbor im Ibo-Gebiet Mittelwestnigerias eine starke Verteidigungsstellung bezogen. Dort halten sie eine aus drei Richtungen anrennende Brigade von 3000 Mann Bundestruppen fest, so daß diese nicht über den Nigerfluß setzen und ebenfalls auf Enugu vorrücken kann. Auch von der Insel Bonny vor Port Harcourt, die schon im Juli von Bundestruppen besetzt worden war, werden Kämpfe gemeldet.

Bonn verzeichnet Mißstimmung über „etablierte Parteien"

SPD und CDU von dem Bremer Wahlergebnis enttäuscht / Keine Auswirkungen auf die Bonner Politik

R. BONN, 2. Oktober. Das Ergebnis der Wahl in Bremen hat mit dem Verlust der absoluten Mehrheit der Sozialdemokraten bei einem äußerst geringen Gewinn der CDU die beiden großen Parteien enttäuscht. Die Sozialdemokraten bemühen sich zwar, wie der gesamtdeutsche Minister Wehner, ihre Stimmenverluste insbesondere auf lokale Verhältnisse zurückzuführen. Allgemein wird in Bonn darauf hingewiesen, daß der Nachfolger des sehr beliebten, vor zwei Jahren zurückgetretenen Senatspräsidenten Kaisen an der Spitze der bremischen Regierung nicht dessen Ausstrahlungskraft hätte haben können. Aber die Größe des sozialdemokratischen Stimmenschwunds läßt sich allein mit der Abwanderung früherer Kaisen-Wähler nicht erklären. Zudem sind die SPD-Verluste nicht der großen Oppositionspartei in Bremen, der CDU, zugute gekommen.

So heißt es bei den großen Parteien in Bonn, die Wahl in Bremen habe gezeigt, daß Wähler, die mit der Regierungsarbeit der einen von ihnen unzufrieden seien, nicht zur anderen gingen, wenn diese in der Opposition sei, sondern die radikale Opposition wählten. Man dürfe die Augen nicht verschließen vor einer sichtlichen Mißstimmung vor allem jugendlicher Wähler über die „etablierten Parteien". Zu dem Unbehagen könne auch die in Stadtstaaten oft besonders sichtbare Parteipatronage beitragen. Diesem Mißvergnügen verdanke die NPD ihren Aufstieg, die meistens aus Protest gewählt werde.

Der Sozialdemokratische Pressedienst hat am Montag geschrieben, natürlich sei das Ergebnis der Wahl enttäuschend. Man habe zwar mit Verlusten gerechnet, aber doch geglaubt, die absolute Mehrheit behalten zu können. Immerhin behalte die SPD mit 50 von hundert Sitzen die beherrschende Position. Alle anderen Parteien hätten die absolute Mehrheit der SPD brechen wollen, inwieweit die Bremer Sozialdemokraten selbst dazu beigetragen hätten, alle Speere auf ihre Brust zu richten, müsse geprüft werden.

Ob sich die Bonner Politik entscheidend auf das Wahlergebnis ausgewirkt habe, werde einer gründlichen Untersuchung bedürfen. Der stellvertretende Sprecher des SPD-Vorstandes sagte dazu, das Wahlergebnis sei vor allem unter örtlichen Gesichtspunkten zu sehen, und werde sich nicht auf die Bonner Politik auswirken. Auch der stellvertretende Bundespressechef unterstrich, daß das Wahlergebnis in Bremen keine Absage an die Große Koalition gewesen sei. Sie habe auch der Opposition in Bonn, der FDP, keinen Auftrieb gegenüber der letzten Bundestagswahl gegeben.

Der Deutschland-Union-Dienst zeigte sich mit der Stimmenzahl der CDU recht zufrieden und führt den Gewinn der FDP auf die örtlichen Gegebenheiten zurück. Für die NPD habe der ganz überwiegende Teil der ehemaligen Wähler der Deutschen Partei gestimmt. Ganz rechtsstehende Kräfte könnten auch die DFU gewählt haben. Viele dieser radikalen Wähler hätten sich durch eine gefühlsbedingte Protesthaltung bestimmen lassen.

Dehnkamps Position

dr. BREMEN, 2. Oktober. Das Ergebnis der Wahl wird wohl, so nimmt man in Bremen allgemein an, Auswirkungen auf die SPD-Führung in der Hansestadt und vermutlich auch auf die Zusammensetzung des künftigen Senats haben. Unmittelbar nach der Veröffentlichung des vorläufigen Endergebnisses hatte Bremens Regierungschef, Bürgermeister Dehnkamp, angekündigt, die SPD werde personelle, organisatorische, politische und sachliche Konsequenzen aus dem Wahlergebnis ziehen. Die Bremer SPD sucht nach dem oder nach den Schuldigen für ihre schwere Niederlage, die von niemandem bestritten wurde. (Fortsetzung Seite 4, Spalten 2 und 3.)

Anerkennung – die Frage scharf gestellt

Von Ernst-Otto Maetzke

Der Bundeskanzler hat in seinem jüngsten Brief an den Sowjetzonen-Ministerratsvorsitzenden dessen Hauptverlangen nach der Hinnahme der bestehenden Verhältnisse in Deutschland durch ihre verbriefte Anerkennung beiseite gelassen. Das heißt freilich nicht, daß die Forderung Stophs, des SED-Politbüros und der sowjetischen Führung nicht zur Kenntnis genommen worden wäre. Das immer starrsinnigere Beharren der Kommunisten auf „Anerkennung" als Voraussetzung irgendwelcher politischer Übereinkünfte hat vielmehr in der Bundesrepublik zu nützlichen Erkenntnissen geführt.

Klar geworden ist vor allem, worum es sich bei dieser Forderung überhaupt handelt. Keineswegs nämlich um juristische Formalien, beispielsweise den Verzicht auf Rechtsverwahrung oder die Preisgabe von Rechtsvorbehalten oder -titeln im Gefolge einer normativen Fixierung der bestehenden Zustände in Deutschland. Begriffen worden ist statt dessen in den letzten Wochen hierzulande, daß es sich bei der kommunistischen Anerkennungs-Forderung um eine ausschließlich politische Frage handelt. Die lange Zeit so bequeme juristische Verbrämung des Problems funktioniert nicht mehr. Und die handlichen juristischen Formeln, die der Bundesrepublik das Recht auf eine annehmbare Lösung der Deutschland-Frage zuzusprechen schienen, sind, samt allen „Doktrinen", die aus ihnen hergeleitet wurden, als untaugliche politische Instrumente erkannt worden. Sie waren es im Grunde immer.

Man ist dem Parteichef der Sozialistischen Einheitspartei der Sowjetzone zu Dank verpflichtet, daß er für solche Klarheit gesorgt hat. Seitdem er der kommunistischen Forderung nach Anerkennung konkrete politische Inhalte gab, kann sie niemand mehr als Kaprizierung auf juristische Finessen mißverstehen. Unter „Anerkennung" versteht die kommunistische Seite jetzt erklärtermaßen die „Nichteinmischung" in die „inneren Angelegenheiten" des von ihr beherrschten Teiles Deutschlands. Auf diese klar verständlichen politischen Kategorien hätte die Diskussion um die „Anerkennung" vernünftigerweise schon vor Jahr und Tag zurückgeführt werden müssen. In Ulbrichts Rede zur Hundertjahrfeier des Erscheinens des ersten „Kapital"-Bandes von Karl Marx wird solche „Nichteinmischung" zum ersten Mal ungeniert gefordert, und in dem Vertragsentwurf, der dem letzten Brief des Zonen-Ministerpräsidenten an den Bundeskanzler beilag, taucht der Begriff wieder auf.

„Anerkennung" soll also künftig heißen (und hat übrigens auch in der Vergangenheit nichts anderes bedeutet), daß man verspricht, an den Zuständen in Deutschland nicht mehr rütteln zu wollen. „Anerkennung" besagt nach erklärter kommunistischer Meinung ausdrücklich, daß man Abstand davon nehme, angesichts der Teilung des Landes politisch noch irgend etwas bewirken zu wollen. Was jenseits von Mauer und Stacheldraht auf deutschem Boden geschieht, soll anerkanntermaßen den „inneren Angelegenheiten" der kommunistischen Machthaber zugerechnet werden, die nur sie selbst etwas angehen. Damit ist erfreulicherweise der Kern der vielumstrittenen Anerkennungsfrage freigelegt. Die deutschen und die sowjetischen Kommunisten haben sie endlich so scharf gestellt, wie sie im Grund von Anfang an gestellt war.

Wie wird man sie beantworten? Glücklicherweise erleichtert die kommunistische Berufung auf die angeblichen „inneren Angelegenheiten" die Entscheidung wesentlich. Wer fortan nach den Möglichkeiten der Anerkennung der deutschen Sowjetzone fragte — auch in der Bundesrepublik gibt es solche Fragesteller —, weiß jetzt genauer als vordem, daß er danach fragt, ob die Angelegenheiten der deutschen Sowjetzone die Bundesrepublik und ihre Bewohner künftig etwas angehen sollen oder nicht. Alle weiteren Anerkennungs-Überlegungen sind von der Bejahung oder Verneinung dieser Grundfrage abgeleitet. Wer fürderhin meint, daß ihn die Verhältnisse im anderen Teil Deutschlands etwas angingen, hätte der „Einmischung" das Wort geredet, hätte sich der unbefugten Mitsorge im Sinne einer „Anmaßung" schuldig gemacht und hätte die Anerkennung damit verweigert.

Mit solcher klaren Sicht des Problems hat man auf alle juristischen Krücken verzichtet. Auch auf die vordergründige Ausflucht, daß die Anerkennung der „Existenz" der kommunistischen Herrschaft über einen Teil Deutschlands gar kein Problem sei, da sie jeder Vernünftige ohnedies in Rechnung stelle. Dafür hat man größere Freiheit im Umgang mit diesem Herrschaftssystem auf deutschem Boden gewonnen als bisher. Daß Kiesinger seinen Staatssekretär als Gesprächspartner der Zonen-Machthaber benannte, ist ein sichtbarer Beweis dafür.

In puncto Anerkennung ist damit allerdings für die deutschen und sowjetischen Kommunisten wenig gewonnen. Am Prinzip der pflichtmäßigen, unentwegten Einmischung der Bundesrepublik in die deutschen Angelegenheiten jenseits der innerdeutschen Grenze hat sich kein Jota geändert. Jeder politische Kontakt mit den Verantwortlichen des anderen Teiles Deutschlands ist vielmehr eine Manifestation aktiver Einmischung, ein Zeugnis aktiver Mitsorge um das Schicksal der Nation.

Die Verhältnisse in Deutschland hinzunehmen, wie sie sind, jedem Änderungswillen abzuschwören, ist undenkbar. Daß von kommunistischer Seite ein solcher Schwur gefordert wird, macht die Deutschland-Frage ausweglos. An der sowjetischen Führung wäre es, diesen Zustand zu ändern, an dem offensichtlich sie selbst ebenfalls leidet.

Kiesinger macht Urlaub

O. D. BONN, 2. Oktober. Bundeskanzler Kiesinger macht gegenwärtig einen kurzen Urlaub in Bebenhausen bei Tübingen. Er nahm daher auch nicht an der Sitzung des Fraktionsvorstandes der CDU/CSU am Montag in Bonn teil. Doch will Kiesinger am Donnerstag für einen Tag nach Bonn kommen, um an einer Sitzung des Wirtschaftskabinetts über den Leber-Plan teilzunehmen. Der Fraktionsvorstand der CDU/CSU hörte am Montag einen Bericht des Fraktionsvorsitzenden Barzel zur politischen Lage und befaßte sich außerdem mit dem in dieser Woche anstehenden parlamentarischen Arbeitsprogramm, auch mit einem groben Zeitplan bis Weihnachten, wobei besonders die vorliegenden Großen Anfragen zu berücksichtigen waren.

Hussein in Moskau

F.A.Z. MOSKAU, 2. Oktober. König Hussein von Jordanien, der sich in der Vergangenheit oft sowjetische Kritik gefallen lassen mußte und als „Marionettenkönig" bezeichnet wurde, ist am Montag mit allen protokollarischen Ehren zu einem viertägigen offiziellen Besuch in Moskau empfangen worden. Wie von sowjetischer Seite zu hören war, soll der Besuch der Stärkung des Friedens und der Sicherheit im Nahen Osten, der Beseitigung der aus der „israelischen Aggression" entstandenen Folgen sowie der künftigen Entwicklung der sowjetisch-jordanischen Beziehungen dienen. (Siehe Seite 4.)

Spaethen will nicht mehr kandidieren

F.A.Z. FRANKFURT, 2. Oktober. Der Vorsitzende der Deutschen Angestellten-Gewerkschaft (DAG), Spaethen, will auf dem Bundeskongreß der Gewerkschaft vom 9. bis 13. November in Berlin nicht mehr für das Amt des Vorsitzenden kandidieren. Nach einer Sondersitzung des DAG-Führungsgremiums am Montag in Hannover wurde mitgeteilt, Spaethen habe diese Entscheidung aus Rücksicht auf seine Gesundheit getroffen. Spaethen, der 58 Jahre alt ist, war seit 1960 Vorsitzender der DAG.

Tarifpartner tagen in Frankfurt

FRANKFURT, 2. Oktober (UPI). Der Vorstand der Industriegewerkschaft Metall und der Vorstand des Gesamtverbandes der metallindustriellen Arbeitgeberverbände (Gesamtmetall) sind am Montag zur gleichen Zeit in Frankfurt zusammengetreten. Während von der Gewerkschaft erklärt wurde, die Vorstandssitzung sei rein routinemäßig, ließen die Arbeitgeber wissen, der Gesamtmetall-Vorstand sei im unmittelbaren Zusammenhang mit der gleichzeitigen Tagung der IG-Metall-Führung zusammengetreten. Die Gleichzeitigkeit der Sitzungen hatte am Wochenende Spekulationen über ein neues Spitzengespräch der Tarifpartner hervorgerufen. In Frankfurt hat ebenfalls am Montag die dritte Verhandlungsrunde für den Lohntarif der 340 000 Beschäftigten der Metallindustrie in Hessen begonnen.

Besuch aus Indien

O. D. BONN, 2. Oktober. Der stellvertretende indische Ministerpräsident und Finanzminister Desai wird an diesem Dienstag zu einem dreitägigen Besuch in Bonn erwartet. Außer Unterredungen mit dem Bundeskanzler am Donnerstag und Bundesaußenminister Brandt, die im wesentlichen der Vorbereitung des noch nicht genau festgelegten Besuchs Kiesingers in Indien gelten, sind auch Besprechungen mit dem Minister für wirtschaftliche Zusammenarbeit, Wischnewski, vorgesehen. Am Mittwoch wird ein Kapitalhilfeabkommen unterzeichnet.

Ostblockreise Indira Gandhis

d. w. NEU-DELHI, 2. Oktober. Indiens Ministerpräsident, Frau Indira Gandhi, wird, wenn nicht innenpolitische Verwicklungen — etwa im Zusammenhang mit der in diesen Tagen erwarteten Regierungsumbildung in Westbengalen — in letzter Minute zu einer Änderung ihrer Pläne zwingen, am 8. Oktober zu einer Osteuropareise aufbrechen. Sie wird Warschau, Belgrad, Sofia und Bukarest offizielle Staatsbesuche abstatten.

The *FAZ* of today does remind one of the old *Frankfurter Zeitung*. The gray front page, bare of any pictures or color, with its neat columns of dignified type, prepare the reader for conservative news coverage and editorial policy. Judging from appearance alone, the *FAZ* bears a close resemblance to its old prewar namesake.

Die Tat, a highly respected Swiss daily, was quick to note the strong resemblance between the *FAZ* and the prewar quality paper. It wrote, in 1949, of the *FAZ*'s front page "with its quiet, sophisticated and reserved layout that shies from that of the tabloid, and moreover, the inside pages with outstanding predominance of the intelligent, polished and learned commentaries of daily news and a quiet intellectual distance to other wordly matters—all this would remind one of the *Frankfurter Zeitung*."[6]

The *FAZ* of today reminds the German more of the prewar quality newspaper of his country than does any other in the Federal Republic. It even persists, in some of its headlines, in using the old German text type which was common in pre-Hitler Germany. The *FAZ* is, without a doubt, the heaviest and most serious in makeup and writing of any newspaper in Germany, and with the possible exception of *Le Monde* or Zurich's *Neue Zürcher Zeitung*, there are no dailies in the world more staid in appearance or academic in content. Although the *Frankfurter Allgemeine* does use some pictures on its inside pages, they are not large. Stories, not pictures and large headlines, dominate in the *FAZ*. Pages and pages of closely set type under conservative one-line headlines face the *FAZ* reader. These pages are neat and well planned and the stories are presented in horizontal rectangles for easy reading. The dress of the *FAZ* is definitely in keeping with its total character of seriousness and thoroughness. A special section (on slick paper) called "Bilder und Zeiten" does carry large pictures; included only in the Saturday edition, this section usually runs six pages and features quality photographs, profiles, literary essays, and other cultural articles.

Other special sections are carried on certain days by the daily. Each Monday a financial section, largely international in nature, is carried. A science supplement appears each Tuesday, while "Today," on Wednesdays, deals with depth stories and analyses of political events. Every two weeks, on Thursday, is printed a travel section which contains no travel advertisements. On Sundays appear a pictorial *feuilleton* page, a woman's page, a literary page and a discussion page.[7]

The reader of *FAZ* can usually predict where in the paper he can find certain types of reading material. Usually, the first four pages are filled with world news and commentary. Sometimes, serialized novels appear across the bottom of the second page. Page 5, when it is not given over to foreign news also, contains sports items, as does the sixth page. More news, relating to Germany's dealings with foreign nations, appears on the seventh and eighth pages under the regular title "Deutschland und die Welt." Page 9, the next to last page in the first section, is typically given over to letters to the editor, with the section's back page carrying advertising.[8]

In the eight-page second section, in addition to pages of advertising, the reader usually gets two pages of financial and economic news and views, a page of letters to the editor, and a single *feuilleton* page. (It should be noted, however, that the brevity of the *feuilleton* offerings in the regular edition does not tell the whole story. Regular supplements, and occasional special ones, provide more detailed criticism and reviews of the theater, movies, the literary and music world.) A six-page special supplement (science, literature, travel) usually is included with the regular edition just described.

The daily edition of *FAZ* hovers around twenty to twenty-eight pages, and the weekend (Saturday) edition ranges from fifty-four to sixty-six pages. The big Saturday edition contains, like the other editions, a heavy emphasis on political, economic, and cultural news. It is only that the reader gets much heavier amounts of it. This Saturday edition contains a beautifully printed rotogravure section, filled with literary articles, book reviews, special features such as personality sketches, and many fine photographs. Without a doubt, this section (mentioned earlier) called "Bilder und Zeiten" (Pictures and Times) is one of the finest such sections to be found in a newspaper anywhere.

To cover the field of news, and to cover it in its thorough and expert manner, the *Frankfurter Allgemeine* has nearly 150 writers and editors.[9] About 75 of these are in the main editorial office in Frankfurt, and are assigned to these main departments: politics, economics, *feuilleton*, local and area news, and sports. Also in the main office is a cartoonist, two photographers, and a fashion specialist.[10] Besides the paper's full-time staff more than 450 journalists in various places in Germany and abroad are regular contributors. In addition, more than 500 specialists, reviewers, and critics are at the newspaper's disposal with contributions in their own fields.[11]

The *FAZ* has forty-five foreign correspondents, about sixteen of whom are full-time staff members.[12] Permanent bureaus are established in London, Paris, Washington/New York, Athens, Brussels, Buenos Aires, Moscow, New Delhi, Pretoria, Stockholm, Tokyo, Warsaw, Vienna, Zurich, Nairobi, Madrid, Beirut, and Rome. And the paper has stringers in some twenty-five other important cities of the world.[13]

A few of the many outstanding foreign correspondents for the paper, all with doctoral degrees, are the following: Jan Reifenberg and Frederick Rosenstiel, Washington; Paul West and Heinz Höpfl, London; Karl Jetter and Hans Weseloh, Paris; Harald Vocke, the Middle East; and Hermann Pörzgen, Moscow.

Supplementing its foreign news coverage are the wire services of the Associated Press, United Press International, Deutsche Presse Agentur, Reuters, and other national press agencies through exchange agreements. About 50–60 per cent of the foreign news of the paper is credited to the *FAZ*'s own reporters—identified by the reporter's initials at the beginning of the story. Editorials and major news stories on the front page usually carry full by-lines.

The *FAZ* is organized as a nonprofit, limited liability company (*Fazit-Stiftung*). Controlling the majority of shares in the company and serving as curators are Franz Böhm, Alex Haffner, Max Schmid, Friedrich Sieburg, and Erich Welter. The board of publishers is composed of Welter, Nikolas Benckiser, Bruno Dechamps, Jürgen Eick, Karl Korn, and Jürgen Tern. These publishers also own stock in the *FAZ* as do business managers Werner Hoffmann and Victor Muckel, the publishing house Adolf Fraund of Wiesbaden, and the music publisher B. Schott's Sons of Mainz.[14]

Circulation of the *Frankfurter Allgemeine* has reached almost perfect geographical distribution throughout West Germany, including West Berlin, with about 51 per cent circulating in the area north of the Main River, and 49 per cent reaching the area south of the river. Its daily circulation is right at 300,000 with the week-end edition, on Saturday, climbing to about 340,000. This circulation compares favorably with its two closest rivals for a national quality circulation—*Die Welt* of Hamburg and *Süddeutsche Zeitung* of Munich, both with daily circulations of over 200,000 and Saturday circulations of about 300,000.

Professor Dr. Erich Welter, *FAZ* editor, says his paper is designed primarily for the intelligentsia, businessmen, politicians, academicians, and educated people of all classes. He classifies the newspaper as "liberal" but says it is ideologically in the center.[15] The *FAZ* is probably thought of most often, however, as a conservative paper; in fact, it is regularly alluded to as an independent conservative journal.[16] Its editorial position is one which does not favor Red China's admission to U.N. membership, and it is against the United States recognizing the Peking Government. Dr. Welter, one of *FAZ*'s founders and earlier a noted journalist on the staff of the old *Frankfurter Zeitung*, feels that the Frankfurt paper today is West Germany's best (highest quality) daily and lists *Die Welt* as second best.[17]

One mark of an elite newspaper is its international readership. Some 20,000 daily copies, or about 7 per cent of its total circulation, are distributed abroad. The quality of the foreign readership is also important, and the *FAZ* has looked into that. In a study conducted in 1965, for example, the *FAZ* determined to find out to what extent the paper is read as a financial journal abroad. Results showed that of the Swiss businessmen contacted, 31 per cent read the paper's economic section regularly and another 31 per cent read it on an occasional basis.[18] It is interesting to note that the *FAZ* was the only German newspaper with an economic section mentioned in the replies, indicating, to some degree at least, the paper's influence in one predominantly German-speaking country.

Another study, conducted by *Time* and *Life* magazines in 1963, aimed at determining the newspaper with the greatest and most regular readership in the Common Market. Of 1,176 questionnaires sent out, 447, or 38 per cent, were returned. To the question "Which daily do you read regularly?" the *FAZ* was first with 29 per cent of the replies. In still another survey, conducted by the Institute of Market Research in Europe in 1963, businessmen ranked the *FAZ* sixth in all newspapers read, but singled it out as the only economic daily read every day.[19]

No professional journalism schools exist in West Germany, only *Zeitungswissenschaftliche Institute* (Institutes of Newspaper Science), and their subject matter is closer to what one *FAZ* editor calls "sociology of communication than it is to professional journalism."[20] According to Jürgen Tern, one of the executives of the *Frankfurter Allgemeine*, his paper considers practical experience, as well as academic training, very important. The great majority of the paper's staff members and correspondents are university graduates, according to Tern, and there is no bias for or against any of the German universities which he says "are more or less on one level." The *FAZ* expects three main things of its writers and editors: integrity, sincerity, and good judgment. "Writing ability is presupposed," says Tern.[21]

The *Frankfurter Allgemeine* is often considered the voice of German industry and business, and without a doubt it gives the most thorough economic coverage in the Federal Republic. But it has also built a reputation for astute political reportage, and its scientific articles are among the best in world journalism. Like most of the newspapers in modern West Germany, the *FAZ* is unattached to any political party and takes pride in the fact that it speaks as an independent, and often critical, voice. Criticism, however, is not one of its strong points; rather than risk falling into sensationalism through criticism, it has chosen to largely "stand aside" and record objectively.

Today's *FAZ* is a worthy successor to the old *Frankfurter Zeitung*. It is superserious. As well as giving a great amount of its own commentary on national and world affairs, it summarizes the more important world comment. The accent is always on accuracy and care; there is little of the colorful reporting which is found in such elite papers as the London *Times, Dagens Nyheter, Asahi Shimbun,* or even in its own West German colleague, *Die Welt*, which we shall look at now.

Die Welt

In contrast to the gray, austere *Frankfurter Allgemeine* is *Die Welt* (The World) of Hamburg, a daily which manages to combine the dignity and quality of traditional serious German journalism with a modern dress and lively demeanor. Like the *FAZ*, it is a national newspaper and a leading international representative of the best in West German daily journalism. *Die Welt*, subtitled "Unabhängige Tageszeitung für Deutschland" (Independent Daily Newspaper for Germany), is published in Berlin and Essen as well as in Hamburg. A quick look at its pages is enough to see that while it is quite different from the *FAZ* and the pre-World War II elite German dailies, it is imbued with the same dignified tone and aura of civility.

Die Welt was founded as a twice-a-week newspaper under British occupation authorities in Hamburg on April 2, 1946, and quickly gained a reputation for objective and comprehensive news coverage. In a few months it had nearly 500,000 circulation in two editions—one in Hamburg (about 325,000) and the other in Essen (about 175,000). Controlling officer was Col. H. B. Garland of the British army. Hans Zehrer, a highly respected German journalist and novelist, was managing editor, and Albert Lubisch was publishing manager.[22] For a brief time Zehrer held the editorial reins, but left the paper because of political differences. The position went to Rudolf Küstermeier, who probably had the greatest impact on the paper prior to 1953 when it was bought by Axel Springer, and Zehrer returned as chief editor.[23]

In 1947, with the start of a Berlin edition published in the old Ullstein Publishing House,[24] the circulation of *Die Welt* was over 600,000, and by 1949 it had reached an unheard-of figure of one million. On July 1, 1949, it began publishing as a daily, and had foreign bureaus in London, Paris, Amsterdam, Vienna, Salzburg, Stockholm, Copenhagen, Zurich, Rome, and Madrid. It had become a true national (*überregionale*) newspaper, and although it lost much of its circulation when it went daily, it began at once a slow but constant growth which has persisted to the present.[25]

Licensing ended in 1950, the British authorities stepped out of *Die Welt* and the paper became a German company. Three years later 75 per cent of the company's shares were bought by Axel C. Springer, a Hamburg publisher who was to become West Germany's largest newspaper owner.[26] It is said that Springer paid one million dollars for the paper, and with its purchase, the youthful businessman-journalist (only forty-one) became the biggest publisher of newspapers and periodicals in the Federal Republic.[27]

Prior to buying the paper and getting into the quality publishing field, Springer had, for example, launched the highly successful *Hamburger Abendblatt* (in 1948) and two years earlier had started a weekly broadcasting magazine called *Hör zu* (Listen), which has grown to be the country's largest magazine with about 4.5 million circulation. Today Springer's press empire, consisting of a variety of newspapers, has a total daily circulation of some 20 million copies, or about 30 per cent of West Germany's newspaper copies.[28]

Although conservative in many respects, *Die Welt* has always been progressive in its journalistic practices. By 1955 it was the first German newspaper with three printing plants (Hamburg, Essen, and Berlin), and was the first to link its publishing sites with teletypesetter machines. It had been the first German paper to use Telefoto, receiving a picture of the Helsinki Olympics in 1952.[29] *Die Welt* has always been in step with the latest innovations in journalism; it has been willing, and still is, to deviate from established patterns of doing things and to experiment. With such a progressive spirit, it has come to be a completely new kind of elite newspaper in the German press context.

Die Welt today may not carry as many long, interpretive articles on as many different topics as the *Frankfurter Allgemeine*, but its news coverage is perhaps more comprehensive. Its manner of writing is clear, direct, and lively, with an emphasis on short sentences. Also indicating the infusion of British and American journalism into the paper is its practice of giving the most important facts of a story in the opening paragraph. Unlike the *FAZ*, whose stories often ramble along for several columns, *Die Welt* prefers to present shorter, crisper stories, and more of them. It also differs from its Frankfurt competitor in that it shies away from the heavy academic approach and from any form of intellectual mannerisms. This does not mean that it popularizes its contents; it simply seeks to make its writing readable as well as significant and its appearance attractive as well as dignified.

Die Welt has a high goal for itself: "Supplying news from all parts of life, from all over the world—political, economical, cultural, scientific and sports news, and to submit this news comprehensively, precisely and quickly; providing readers with the possibility of finding their own way; helping them to form an opinion of their own by furnishing comments and opinions, interviews and critical viewpoints."[30] The paper's executives realize that the attainment of such a goal is extremely difficult, but emphasize that *Die Welt* never stops in its effort. Commenting further on the paper's aims, a *Welt* official says:

> In the world of newspapers we want *Die Welt* to be a prestige symbol standing for intelligence and culture, for responsible thinking, initiative and success. We want *Die Welt* to be considered as a paper of unparalleled integrity, of comprehensive, fast and reliable news reporting, of courageous and responsible commentary. Its voice must be authoritative and disciplined, its style lively yet timely and serious and trustworthy.[31]

From its beginnings in 1946 it has sought to live by these principles. And its editors have made it into a distinct kind of German paper, more lively and lighter than most but still sophisticated and dignified. It has, perhaps more than most other German newspapers, sought to make a distinction between news and opinion, to keep its editorializing in editorials and personal columns, and its news isolated in news columns.

Although it occasionally slips into the old German practice of mixing news and its writers' views, it at least attempts to keep them apart and clearly labeled.

Die Welt is the nearest thing in Germany to a national paper, and nobody doubts its wide influence in government circles. According to John Tebbel, journalist and professor of journalism,[32] *Die Welt* enjoys a greater reputation abroad than it does at home. Tebbel believes that students and younger readers feel *Die Welt* is too conservative. The newspaper, however, does not consider itself conservative, preferring to simply call itself "independent and above party lines."[33] There is little doubt, however, that *Die Welt* is, like the *FAZ*, what can rather accurately be called "independent conservative."[34] The correspondent in Bonn of the London *Times* has described *Die Welt* as "conservative to the marrow, but with a strong social progressive influence."[35]

There is no hint of pretension in *Die Welt*, and it tries to talk clearly to all of its readers, and especially to politicians, businessmen, and teachers, with the hope of influencing their views. Joachim Freyburg, head of the paper's Information Department, says that *Die Welt* is aimed primarily at "opinion leaders in politics, economics, science and cultural life."[36]

In addition to being read everywhere in the Federal Republic, *Die Welt* is circulated in more than 120 countries of the world. It is the only German newspaper to have a special air edition; mainly intended for foreign readers, it is printed on extra-thin paper. *Die Welt* prints ten editions daily from plants in Hamburg, Essen, and Berlin. Besides the routine daily editions of the paper, *Die Welt* is noted for the excellent occasional special issues which it publishes. Examples of such special editions were these: (1) the superbly written and illustrated thirty-two-page "special tribute" to Konrad Adenauer which came off *Die Welt's* presses the day after the Chancellor died in the spring of 1967, and (2) a small tabloid-size edition of twelve pages called "Zeitung des Jahres" (Newspaper of the Year) which described the paper's being honored in the United States in May, 1967, and gave background information on *Die Welt* and on the University of Missouri where the honor was bestowed.

A typical daily edition of *Die Welt*, running twenty to thirty pages, carries several pages of general national and world news, and these regular pages: Opinion, Politics (usually two pages), Reportage, Letters from Readers, Science, Economics (often four or five pages), Sports, and *Feuilleton*.

In addition to the regular departments just named, *Die Welt* carries during an average week these extras: on Monday, a special page "School and the University"; on Tuesday, a page given to automobiles called "Motor"; on Wednesday, a page of basic world issues "Forum of the World"; on Thursday, the excellent literary magazine supplement called "Die Welt der Literatur" (a twelve-page section founded in March,

Theater-Festspiele am Lido (Feuilleton)

Monatsabonnement 6,00 D-Mark zuzüglich 1,60 D-Mark anteilige Zustell- und Versandgebühren bei Zustellung durch die Post oder durch Träger. Auslandsabonnement 13,00 D-Mark einschließlich Porto. Der Preis des Luftpostabonnements wird auf Anfrage mitgeteilt. Die Abonnementsgebühren sind im voraus zahlbar.

DIE WELT

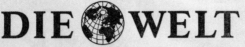

UNABHÄNGIGE TAGESZEITUNG FÜR DEUTSCHLAND

Verlag DIE WELT, 2 Hamburg 36, Kaiser-Wilhelm-Straße 1, Tel. 34 10 19, FS 021 11 49, 1 Berlin 61, Kochstraße 50, Tel. 03 11/6 10 81, FS 018 07 06, 43 Essen, Sachsenstraße 36, Tel. 021 41/24 71, Fernschreiber 080 73 41, 6 Frankfurt (Main), Froschenallee 71—81, Telefon 06 11/33 50 85, FS 041 24 49. Gültige Anzeigenpreisliste Nr. 36 vom 1. Januar 1967

Freitag, 13. Oktober 1967 — Ausgabe N — C 7108 A — Nr. 239 · Preis 40 Pf

Postministerium wird aufgelöst Stücklen Generalpostmeister?

Kiesinger: Noch vor der Wahl – Barzel und Schmidt drängen

Von unseren Korrespondenten

Schr./St. **Bonn**, 12. Oktober

Die Umwandlung des Bundespostministeriums in ein bundesbahnähnliches Unternehmen mit einem Generalpostmeister an der Spitze soll noch vor den nächsten Bundestagswahlen vorgenommen werden. Bundeskanzler Kurt Georg Kiesinger ließ am Donnerstag mitteilen, daß er an der Koalitionsvereinbarung festhält, die diesen Wandel ins Auge gefaßt hatte. Dabei war abgesprochen worden, daß Richard Stücklen, der Vorsitzende der Landesgruppe der CSU, erster Generalpostmeister werden soll.

Dollinger

Stücklen

Foto: AP/dpa

Kiesinger steht wegen der Postfrage in engem Kontakt mit den Vorsitzenden der Koalitionsfraktionen, wird aus Regierungskreisen versichert. Die Initiative dafür, daß das seit der Koalitionsbildung schlummernde Problem über Nacht für Bonn wieder akut wurde, wurde von den Fraktionsvorsitzenden Rainer Barzel und Helmut Schmidt ergriffen. Sie verständigten sich in der vergangenen Woche darüber, die Frage im Sinne einer schnellen Lösung voranzutreiben.

Ein Sprecher des Bundespostministeriums sagte am Donnerstagabend auf Anfrage, daß Minister Werner Dollinger ein Gutachten über mögliche Umwandlungen des Ministeriums vorliege, und er beabsichtige, dem Bundeskanzler „in absehbarer Zeit" hierüber Vortrag zu halten. Er werde „im nächsten Jahr" einen Vorschlag über die künftige Form des Ministeriums vorlegen.

Im übrigen verwies die Presseabteilung des Ministeriums auf eine Rede, die Dollinger am Donnerstag in Düsseldorf gehalten hat. Hier nannte der Minister drei Möglichkeiten einer Organisationsform, falls das Ministerium aufgelöst werden sollte:

1. Umwandlung in eine Körperschaft des öffentlichen Rechts.

2. Bildung einer Generaldirektion nach dem Vorbild der Bundesbahn.

3. Bildung einer Aktiengesellschaft und damit verbunden, eine Teilprivatisierung.

Die Parlamentarier dagegen wünschen einen Status für die Post, der der Bundesbahn entspricht. Sie hoffen, daß dann stärker als bisher moderne finanz- und betriebswirtschaftliche Gesichtspunkte zur Geltung kommen. An Stelle des Ministers Dollinger und der zwei Staatssekretäre Hans Steinmetz und Helmut Bornemann soll nach ihren Wünschen ein auf fünf Jahre gewählter Vorstand treten, gebildet aus dem Generalpostmeister und Vorstandsmitgliedern.

Hintergrund des Drängens der Fraktionsvorsitzenden auf Umwandlung der Post bildet das Unbehagen an dem zu großen Umfang des Bundeskabinetts. Während der Koalitionsverhandlungen wurde über eine Verringerung der Zahl der Ministersessel um vier bis sieben verhandelt. Die Ressorts Post, Bundesschatz, Wohnungsbau, Familien, Vertriebene, Gesundheit und Entwicklungshilfe wurden dabei erwähnt. Koalitionspolitische Gesichtspunkte machten damals die Absicht zunichte. Übrig blieb lediglich die Vereinbarung, das Bundespostministerium noch in dieser Legislaturperiode in einen Wirtschaftsbetrieb umzuorganisieren.

SPD-Fraktionsvorsitzender Helmut Schmidt hat vor kurzem noch einmal öffentlich eine Verringerung der Zahl der Ministerien gefordert.

Gerade deshalb wird aus den Koalitionsparteien heraus jetzt gedrängt, die Postfrage zu lösen. Dabei geht die SPD davon aus, daß die Zahl der Bundesminister sich damit um einen verringert, also die CDU/CSU keinen Ersatzmann für den ausscheidenden Werner Dollinger in das Kabinett entsenden wird.

Altersversorgung für Abgeordnete

Beschluß des Bundestagsvorstands

Von unseren Korrespondenten

St. **Bonn**, 12. Oktober

Vom kommenden Jahr an soll für alle Abgeordneten des Bundestages eine Altersversorgung eingerichtet werden. Diesen einstimmigen Beschluß hat am Donnerstag der Vorstand des Bundestages gefaßt.

Noch ist unklar, in welche Form die Altersversorgung gekleidet wird. Es gilt als möglich, daß aus den Diäten jedes Abgeordneten eine Rücklage geschaffen wird, es wird aber auch erwogen, über den Weg einer Versicherung Sondervereinbarungen zu treffen.

Der Bundestagsvorstand will offensichtlich Mittel für die Altersversorgung aus dem Einzelplan 2 des Bundeshaushaltes beschaffen. Er bezog sich bei seinem Beschluß auf den „Auftrag des Grundgesetzes".

In Artikel 48 des Grundgesetzes heißt es: „Die Abgeordneten haben Anspruch auf eine angemessene, ihre Unabhängigkeit sichernde Entschädigung." Eine Reihe von Härtefällen hat in den vergangenen Jahren immer wieder neue Anstöße zu Vorschlägen für eine Altersversicherung der Parlamentarier gegeben. In Bonn ist bekannt, daß auch der Tod des SPD-Fraktionsvorsitzenden Fritz Erler zu diesen Fällen rechnet.

„KP nach wie vor verfassungsfeindlich"

Von unseren Korrespondenten

H. K. **Ulm**, 12. Oktober

Die Kommunistische Partei kann nach Ansicht der Länderinnenminister nicht zugelassen werden. Auf ihrer Konferenz in Ulm vertraten sie — in Anwesenheit von Bundesinnenminister Paul Lücke — den Standpunkt, die KP gelte nach wie vor als verfassungsfeindlich. Sie sei eine in ihren Zielen auf die Beseitigung der demokratischen Ordnung gerichtete Organisation.

Aussicht auf Zulassung habe nur eine mit der demokratischen Ordnung der Bundesrepublik übereinstimmende Partei. Auf das theoretische Problem, ob es eine westdeutsche KP geben könne, die diese Voraussetzung erfüllt, gingen die Minister wegen des inneren Widerspruchs dieser Konstruktion nicht ein.

Die in Baden-Württemberg diskutierte Frage der Bewaffnung der Polizei mit Handgranaten bleibt weiterhin offen. Die Innenminister wünschen hier einheitliche gesetzliche Vorschriften in allen Ländern. Zur Gemeindefinanzreform wollen die Innenminister möglichst bald die Vorstellungen der von Bonn eingesetzten Kommission erfahren.

Kreml sondiert Sicherheitsfrage

Brandt empfängt Zarapkin

Von unserem Korrespondenten

Schr. **Bonn**, 12. Oktober

Bundesaußenminister Willy Brandt hat am Donnerstag den sowjetischen Botschafter Semjon Zarapkin empfangen, der ihm mündlich und schriftlich den Standpunkt der Sowjetregierung zu verschiedenen Aspekten der europäischen Sicherheit vortrug.

Brandt informierte anschließend Bundeskanzler Kiesinger über Verlauf und Inhalt der knapp einstündigen Unterredung, um die Zarapkin nachgesucht hatte. Die amtlichen Stellen schweigen sich bisher über den Inhalt der sowjetischen Vorschläge aus. Hinweise, daß übertriebener Optimismus fehl am Platz sei, lassen jedoch bezweifeln, daß Moskau einen Tag vor der außenpolitischen Debatte des Bundestages positiv auf den Appell Brandts von der vergangen Woche reagiert hat.

Die Frage des Gewaltverzichts und der europäischen Sicherheit durch gleichzeitige Verringerung von Truppen hatten zu den 14 Punkten gehört, in denen Brandt vor einem Vierteljahr die möglichen Themen deutsch-sowjetischer Gespräche zusammengefaßt hatte. Deutsch-sowjetische Verhandlungen zu diesem Punkt scheinen sich noch nicht abzuzeichnen. Auf jeden Fall ist jedoch ein deutsch-sowjetisches Gespräch, wenn auch nur zögernd und nicht sehr produktiv, in Gang gekommen. Das ist die Meinung von Diplomaten in Bonn.

Es war am Donnerstag noch offen, ob die Regierungserklärung Brandts vor dem Plenum des Bundestags am Freitag neue Aufschlüsse über die sowjetische Haltung geben wird. Zu den deutschen Gesprächsvorschlägen für die Frage der europäischen Sicherheit gehörte der Vorschlag eines völkerrechtlich verbindlichen Gewaltverzichts und die Frage einer Truppenreduktion in Ost und West. Auch das Thema Atomsperrvertrag gehört dazu.

Jean Rey schweigt über sein Gespräch mit de Gaulle

Paris, 12. Oktober (AFP-dpa)

Der französische Staatspräsident Charles de Gaulle hat am Donnerstagnachmittag den Präsidenten der Europäischen Kommission, Jean Rey, zum erstenmal seit dessen Wahl als Nachfolger Walter Hallsteins zu einer dreiviertelstündigen Unterredung empfangen. Wie schon bei seinem Antrittsbesuch in Bonn weigerte sich Rey, über das Gespräch Auskunft zu geben. Es dürften dabei aktuelle Probleme der EWG-Politik, darunter die Beitrittsanträge Großbritanniens und anderer Länder, erörtert worden sein.

Druck auf Gehälter für leitende Angestellte

Eigenbericht der WELT

Wg. **München**, 12. Oktober

Merklich zurückhaltender als im Vorjahr waren Betriebe und Verwaltungen in den ersten sechs Monaten 1967 bei Anforderungen von Angestellten in gehobener und leitender Position.

Den 15 600 Vermittlungsaufträgen standen, wie aus einem Bericht der Bundesanstalt für Arbeitsvermittlung und Arbeitslosenversicherung über die Tätigkeit ihrer Zentralen und regionalen Fachvermittlungsstellen hervorgeht, 18 600 Arbeitsgesuche von entsprechend qualifizierten Bewerbern gegenüber. In 3700 Fällen konnte bis Ende Juni die Vermittlung erfolgreich abgeschlossen werden.

Anfang Juli 1967 hielten sich die bei den Fachvermittlungsstellen vorliegenden Stellenangebote und Arbeitsgesuche mit jeweils rund 12 000 die Waage. Die gebotenen Gehälter sind, wie die Bundesanstalt betont, in vielen Fällen niedriger als 1966.

In den einzelnen Berufssparten gab es teilweise erhebliche Unterschiede. So waren 2000 Ingenieure der einzelnen Fachrichtungen gefragt, während 4900 Bewerber einen neuen Arbeitsplatz anstrebten, darunter zahlreiche junge Ingenieure, die nach Abschluß ihrer Ausbildung eine Anfangsstelle suchten.

In der Fachrichtung Techniker und technische Assistenten lagen Ende Juni bei 1800 Stellenbewerbungen nur 900 Angebote vor.

Arbeitsminister besorgt über Entlassungen bei Glas

Nachrichtendienst der WELT

München, 12. Oktober

Sehr überrascht über das Ausmaß der geplanten Massenentlassung bei der Hans Glas GmbH, Dingolfing, war das bayrische Arbeitsministerium. Arbeitsminister Fritz Pirkl will darauf hinwirken, daß die Zahl der Entlassungen so niedrig wie möglich gehalten werden kann.

Im bayrischen Wirtschaftsministerium wird darauf verwiesen, daß die angekündigte Entlassung von 1000 Arbeitskräften seit Herbst vorigen Jahres eine „ausgemachte Sache" sei. Wäre der Staat auf diese Bedingung von BMW nicht eingegangen, hätte sich das Unternehmen nicht zu der Sanierung bereit gefunden, und Dingolfing wäre überhaupt in Frage gestellt worden.

Finnmark abgewertet

Von unserem Korrespondenten

-ey. **Helsinki**, 12. Oktober

Völlig überraschend hat die finnische Reichsbank unter dem Eindruck steigender Arbeitslosenziffern, nachlassender Produktion und schnell schwindender Devisenvorräte die Finnmark um 31,25 Prozent abgewertet. Der neue Wechselkurs der Finnmark beträgt jetzt 4,20 Finnmark für einen US-Dollar und 1,05 Finnmark für eine DM. Die Finnmark ist zuletzt 1957 um 39 Prozent abgewertet worden.

Wirtschaft: Finnland

Politikerin aus dem Orient auf dem Balkan

Die Nationalhymnen beider Länder erklangen auf dem Belgrader Flughafen, als die indische Ministerpräsidentin Frau Indira Gandhi zu einem dreitägigen offiziellen Besuch in Jugoslawien eintraf und von Staatschef Tito begrüßt wurde. In einem mehrstündigen Meinungsaustausch über alle wichtigen weltpolitischen Fragen nahm die Nahost-Krise und der Vietnam-Krieg besonders viel Raum ein. Auf einem Bankett versicherte Frau Gandhi, Indien unterstütze die Bemühungen Präsident Titos um eine Entspannung im Nahen Osten. Eine bedingungslose Einstellung der amerikanischen Luftangriffe auf Nordvietnam könne das Kriegsende näherbringen. Foto: DIE WELT/UPI

Gegenangriff der Anhänger Johnsons

Kongreßsprecher McCormack wirft Vietnam-Kritikern Verrat vor

Nachrichtendienst der WELT

Washington, 12. Oktober

Während bisher in der inneramerikanischen Vietnam-Debatte vor allem die Gegner und Kritiker der Regierung zu Worte kommen, sind jetzt die Anhänger Präsident Johnsons zum Gegenangriff übergegangen.

In einer leidenschaftlichen Rede vor dem Abgeordnetenhaus verurteilte John McCormack, der Sprecher des Hauses, in scharfer Form die Regierungskritik von Kongreßmitgliedern und warf ihnen vor, die Nordvietnamesen in ihren Aggressionsabsichten zu ermutigen. Er fühle sich zu seiner Rede provoziert durch die strategische Analyse des nordvietnamesischen Verteidigungsministers General Giap, der die inneramerikanische Opposition als „wertvolles Zeichen der Sympathie" bezeichnet hatte.

Zuvor hatte schon der demokratische Abgeordnete Celler (New York) die „Schmähexzesse" der Regierungskritiker verurteilt. Auch Außenminister Dean Rusk hat in die Diskussion eingegriffen und die Vietnampolitik Präsident Johnsons mit allem Nachdruck verteidigt. Damit zeichnet sich mehr und mehr eine Gegenkampagne der Regierung ab. In einer Grundsatzerklärung bekräftigte Rusk das amerikanische Engagement in Vietnam und betonte, daß dort die Sicherheit der Vereinigten Staaten auf dem Spiel stünde gegen ein mit Atomwaffen ausgerüstetes China. Er fühle sich durch die in Südvietnam erzielten Fortschritte ermutigt, wenn auch der Friedenseintritt nicht bestimmt werden könnte.

Während McCormack im Kongreß sprach, wandte sich der demokratische Senator Fulbright im Senat mit beißender Kritik gegen die Befürworter der Vietnam-Politik Johnsons. Er griff die Äußerung des republikanischen Fraktionsvorsitzenden Everett Dirksen auf, der zur Verteidigung Johnsons erklärt hatte, die USA schützten in Vietnam das „heilige Gebäude der Freiheit". Dieser endlose und erfolglose Krieg, meinte Fulbright, habe nicht dazu beigetragen, die Freiheit im eigenen Lande zu stärken. Im Gegenteil habe er eine ungesunde Atmosphäre der Verdächtigungen und Beschuldigungen sowohl innerhalb der Regierung wie im ganzen Lande entstehen lassen. Die „große Gesellschaft" sei zu einer „kranken Gesellschaft" geworden.

Moskau: Vorrang für Konsum-Güter

Oberster Sowjet billigt auch neues Wehrdienst-Gesetz

Moskau, 12. Oktober (dpa-AP)

Am dritten Tag seiner Sitzung verabschiedete der Oberste Sowjet am Donnerstag einstimmig die Wirtschaftspläne für die nächsten drei Jahre, in denen erstmals die Konsumgüter-Industrie Vorrang erhalten hat, und den Staatshaushalt in Höhe von 123,6 Milliarden Rubel (rund 543 Milliarden DM). Davon sind 16,7 Milliarden Rubel (rund 73 Milliarden DM) für die Verteidigung ausgewiesen.

Am Nachmittag wurde ein neues Wehrdienstgesetz angenommen, das Verteidigungsminister Andrej Gretschko vorgelegt hatte. Es sieht die Kürzung der aktiven Wehrdienstzeit um ein Jahr und die Einführung einer obligatorischen vormilitärischen Ausbildung für alle Jugendlichen vor. Die Wehrdienstzeit für Armee und Luftwaffe soll nur noch zwei Jahre, für die Marine drei Jahre betragen. Das Einberufungsalter wird einheitlich auf 18 Jahre festgelegt. Aus der Rede des Marschalls ging nicht hervor, ob die Kürzung der Wehrdienstzeit die Zahl der sowjetischen Streitkräfte — die auf 3,5 Millionen Mann geschätzt wird — verringern wird.

In seiner Rede, in der er die Änderungen des Wehrdienstgesetzes begründete, beschuldigte Gretschko die USA, „unter dem Deckmantel des Geredes von Frieden und Zusammenarbeit" die Kriegsvorbereitungen gegen die Sowjetunion und andere sozialistische Länder zu verstärken und „gefährliche Kriegsherde in verschiedenen Teilen der Welt" anzulegen. Den „imperialistischen Mächten" machte er den Vorwurf, die internationale Lage verschärft zu haben und die Gefahr eines neuen Weltkrieges zu steigern. Es wurde damit gerechnet, daß die Sitzung des Obersten Sowjets noch am Donnerstag zu Ende geht.

Lateinamerika tritt für Deutschland ein

Brandt dankt für Unterstützung des Selbstbestimmungsrechtes

Von unserem Redaktionsmitglied

ra. n. **Hamburg**, 12. Oktober

Das Verständnis der lateinamerikanischen Länder für die Lage des geteilten Deutschlands und ihre Unterstützung für das Selbstbestimmungsrecht des deutschen Volkes hat Bundesaußenminister Willy Brandt am Donnerstagabend in Hamburg gewürdigt.

In einer Festrede zum Ibero-Amerika-Tag, der aus Anlaß des Jahrestages der Entdeckung Amerikas durch Columbus gefeiert wird, dankte Brandt den Südamerikanern für ihr Eintreten für den deutschen Standpunkt bei den Vereinten Nationen. Argentiniens Außenminister habe erst kürzlich wieder die Beendigung der deutschen Teilung gefordert.

Die Ansichten der Bundesregierung zum Atomsperrvertrag würden in ähnlicher Weise von Brasilien und anderen lateinamerikanischen Staaten geteilt, hob Brandt hervor. Durch eine „Vertiefung des politischen Gesprächs" sollte die Partnerschaft mit Lateinamerika gefestigt werden.

Der Bundesaußenminister versprach, Bonn werde in der EWG weiter eine Politik der „Wahrnehmung lateinamerikanischer Interessen" verfolgen. „Im Rahmen unserer Möglichkeiten" werde die Bundesrepublik auch mithelfen, die sozialen und wirtschaftlichen Probleme des Subkontinents zu lösen.

Brandt setzte sich für eine Verstärkung der kulturellen und Handelsbeziehungen ein und sagte, die technische Hilfe sollte den Schwerpunkt in der Zusammenarbeit mit Lateinamerika bilden.

Wirtschaft: Lateinamerika

Brenner erwartet Mehrheit für Streik

Schlichtung auch in Hessen

Von unserem Korrespondenten

-pfl. **Frankfurt a. M.**, 12. Oktober

Auch in Hessen hat die IG Metall am Donnerstag die Tarifverhandlungen für die Metallindustrie als gescheitert erklärt. Damit muß auch in diesem Bezirk eine Schlichtung eingeleitet werden.

Der Frankfurter Bezirksleiter der Gewerkschaft, Hans Eick, sagte dazu, die Erregung unter den hessischen Metallarbeitern sei angesichts des laufenden Abbaus von Sozialleistungen ohnehin kaum noch einzudämmen. Der Arbeitgeberverband erklärte zu dem Vorgehen der IG Metall, die Gewerkschaft sei trotz des neuen Angebots der Arbeitgeber vom Vortage offensichtlich nicht ernsthaft bemüht gewesen, eine Verschärfung des Konflikts zu vermeiden.

Otto Brenner, der Vorsitzende der IG Metall, ließ in einem Gespräch mit der WELT keinen Zweifel an seiner Auffassung, daß bei der Urabstimmung in Nordbaden und Nordwürttemberg am 19. Oktober die Mehrheit der Metallarbeiter ihre Bereitschaft zum Streik erklären werde.

(Fortsetzung Seite 6, Spalten 4 und 5)

„Comet Mark IV" stürzte mit 66 Insassen ins Meer

Zeichnung: Werner Schmidt

Nachrichtendienst der WELT

Nikosia, 12. Oktober

Ein Passagier-Flugzeug vom Typ „Comet Mark IV" stürzte am Donnerstagmorgen mit 59 Passagieren und sieben Besatzungsmitgliedern an Bord 160 Kilometer südöstlich von Rhodos und 250 Kilometer westlich von Zypern ins Mittelmeer. Alle 66 Insassen kamen ums Leben. Bis zum Mittag waren 22 Leichen geborgen worden.

Die vierstrahlige Maschine, die der britischen Luftfahrtgesellschaft „British European Airways" (BEA) gehörte, war in London gestartet; sie machte in Athen eine Zwischenlandung und flog dann in Richtung Nikosia weiter.

Seite 22: Piloten

Mehr Straftaten

Nachrichtendienst der WELT

Hamburg, 12. Oktober

In den ersten acht Monaten dieses Jahres ist die Kriminalität in den meisten Bundesländern im Vergleich zur gleichen Zeit des Vorjahres stark gestiegen. Das ergab eine Umfrage der Nachrichtenagentur dpa.

In Niedersachsen nahm die Zahl der Straftaten um 17 Prozent, in Rheinland-Pfalz um 10,3 und in Hessen um 8,8 Prozent zu. In Niedersachsen war die Zunahme der Verbrechen erschreckend: Die Zahl der Fälle von Mord und Totschlag stieg um 38,2 Prozent.

Seite 7: Kriminalität

Im Süden noch heiter

Nachrichtendienst der WELT

Hamburg, 12. Oktober

Während im Norden und Westen der Bundesrepublik an diesem Freitag mit Schauern gerechnet werden muß, wird es in Süddeutschland noch meist heiter und überwiegend niederschlagsfrei bleiben. Die Temperaturen: im Norden und Westen 15 bis 18, im Süden bis 24 Grad.

1964); on Friday, an extra page called "Arts Market," and on Saturday a special section called "Intellectual World" carrying contributions from all fields of cultural and intellectual life. Also, on Saturday, is a special business page with commentary and analysis of economic and financial problems throughout the world.[37]

On Sunday, there is a separate and complete newspaper, with its own staff, published by the Verlagshaus Die Welt; it is called *Welt am Sonntag* (World on Sunday) and, like Britain's weekly *Observer* or Switzerland's weekly *Weltwoche*, is an outstanding political newspaper.[38] This national weekly, founded in 1948 and edited by Bernhard Menne, is printed and distributed from plants in Hamburg, Berlin, Essen, and Frankfurt-am-Main. It averages thirty-six pages, has a circulation of about half a million, and sends copies to eighty foreign countries. The Berlin and the Hamburg editions of *Welt am Sonntag* have their own local sections. The quality of this paper is so great that many leading journalists, professors, theologians, and political figures contribute to its pages. Willy Brandt, for example, has written for it, as have such German intellectuals as Prof. Helmut Thielicke, Dr. Thomas Dehler, and Prof. Wilhelm Röpke.[39] Dr. Wolfgang Bretholz, the diplomatic correspondent for *Welt am Sonntag*, is generally recognized as one of the best writers on international affairs in Europe.

Die Welt pays particular attention to foreign news and has thirty full-time correspondents stationed in these cities: Athens, Beirut, Brussels, Calcutta, Los Angeles, Washington, London, Madrid, Milan, Moscow, Nairobi, Paris, Prague, Rome, Singapore, Stockholm, Tokyo, Vienna, Zurich, and Valparaiso. Some of these correspondents, like veteran Heinz Barth, now stationed in Washington, are among Europe's best reporters. *Die Welt* also sends special correspondents to all crisis spots, and relies on the Associated Press, the United Press International, Agence France-Presse, and many part-time stringers abroad for much of its foreign material.[40]

Chief editor of *Die Welt* is Dr. H. F. Gerhard Starke, who took over the top editorial position when Hans Zehrer, who had guided the paper to its prestigious place in world journalism, died in August, 1966. Zehrer had announced in June that he would retire in August, 1966, and Dr. Starke was named as his successor. It was a grim coincidence that the noted editor who had been with *Die Welt* since 1953, would die the month he would have retired.[41]

Zehrer's successor came to *Die Welt* from Cologne where he was administrative director of the "Deutschlandfunk" (German Radio). Born in 1916, he was educated at Leipzig and Geneva where he studied philosophy, sociology, history, and journalism. He received his Ph.D. from Leipzig University in 1939, and until 1945 was on the editorial staff of Berlin's *Deutsche Allgemeine Zeitung*. From 1946 until 1949 he worked for two journals in Munich, and in 1949 he became head of a political department of "Nordwestdeutscher Rundfunk," where in 1956 he was elected chief editor and head of the political section. He was soon widely known for his political commentary on Saturdays called "From Week to Week." In August, 1961, he was made head of "Deutschlandfunk," whose programs are chiefly beamed at foreign countries and into the Soviet Zone of Germany.[42]

Dr. Starke is known as a conservative, hard-line anti-Communist. This, in addition to *Die Welt*'s hiring in 1966 of two conservative columnists, William S. Schlamm and Winifred Martini, has caused some German press observers[43] to be convinced that the paper is veering rapidly to the Right. The volatile and bombastic Hamburg-based news magazine *Der Spiegel*, often a bitter critic of *Die Welt*'s publisher, sputtered in 1966 that "liberal judgments are no longer in *Die Welt*."[44] A careful analysis of *Die Welt* in 1965 (under Zehrer) and in 1967 (under Starke), however, reveals no discernible shift, and there is no reason to believe that Dr. Starke is not carrying on in the same independent spirit that marked the paper under his predecessor.

Chief Editor Starke is assisted by a couple of managing editors or *Stellvertretende*, as they are called, who are special representatives of the chief editor. These two, both noted journalists, are Hans-Wilhelm Meidinger and Dr. Heinz Pentzlin. Until late 1966, Ernst J. Cramer was also among this group. He is now the head of the central planning bureau for the entire Springer organization and one of Axel Springer's most trusted advisers.

Another important executive of *Die Welt* is W. Joachim Freyburg, long-time staff member and presently head of the Information Department. Herr Freyburg is the man who publishes an excellent sixteen-page monthly house organ for *Die Welt* (called *Verlagshaus Die Welt: Nachrichten für unserer Mitarbeiter*), and who is in charge of an elaborate public relations or information program. Now that *Die Welt* and two other Springer newspapers (*B.Z.* and *Berliner Morgenpost*) are published from the sumptuous new 25 million dollar plant (opened October 6, 1966) only a few yards from the Berlin Wall, Freyburg works out of Berlin offices as well as his old headquarters in Hamburg. Springer's new building, rising twenty-two stories high, is on the Kochstrasse in the heart of Berlin's old newspaper quarter where famous pre-World War II publishers such as Ullstein, Scherl, and Mosse had their newspaper plants.[45]

Axel Caesar Springer, *Die Welt*'s publisher, is proud of the quality and reputation of his paper and is determined to interfere as little as possible in its editorial matters.[46] He has expressed his credo, briefly, as follows: "Newspapers should be interested in, but not take the place of politics. Newspapers must explain, illuminate, censure or support political developments. The newspapers' task is to caution or to stimulate. Newspapers are supposed to state their case, but they should never try to take the place of politics, lest they destroy politics."[47] He also has emphasized that it is his firm conviction that "the responsibility of a publisher must follow in the traditions of Peter Zenger and Thomas Paine, in combatting any threat to freedom of expression."[48]

Although it is only natural for Springer's strongly held sympathies and antipathies to inevitably influence *Die Welt* to some degree, the fact that the paper is the product of a team of three or four senior men rather than of one editor, and that its operations and policies are watched over by *Stiftung Die Welt* (Die Welt Foundation) which owns the remaining 25 per cent of the shares, gives the newspaper far more freedom than is enjoyed by the four other daily papers, two Sunday papers, five magazines, and a variety of trade publications, all owned by Springer.

Die Welt's persistence in maintaining lofty principles, a good staff, a dedication to accurate and serious journalism, and an impressive circulation (some 280,000 on weekdays; more than 300,000 on Saturdays),[49] has assured it a high place among the world's elite dailies. This is attested to by the opinion leaders who read it, by the important libraries which receive it, by the regularity with which it is quoted in the world's press, and by the consistency with which it lands in a listing of the world's best daily newspapers.

Since its founding in 1946, *Die Welt* has received many honors and special recognitions for its general excellence. One of the latest in its series of awards came on May 5, 1967, when it was the foreign recipient of an Honor Medal "for distinguished service in journalism" given by the University of Missouri's School of Journalism. The award, one of the most valued given in the United States, prompted many letters and telegrams of appreciation and congratulations from important persons throughout Europe.[50] Making the trip from Berlin to accept the award and to make a speech during the School of Journalism's "Journalism Week" was Axel Springer, accompanied by Ernst J. Cramer. Joining Springer in Columbia, Missouri, for the ceremonies were Heinz Barth of *Die Welt*'s Washington bureau, and Uwe Siemon-Netto of the Springer News Service's New York office.

In way of conclusion, the text of the Honor Citation, presented *Die Welt* along with the special Honor Medal, is quoted below. It can serve as a brief summary statement of why the newspaper has a place in the small group of the world's elite dailies. The Citation, presented to Herr Springer by Dr. Earl F. English, dean of the Journalism School, follows:

> To *Die Welt* of the Federal Republic of Germany, in recognition of:
>
> its daily example of literate and significant journalism by which it provides its elite readership, domestic and foreign, with extensive news coverage, thoughtful commentary, and astute insights—all presented in an attractive yet dignified manner;
>
> its concern for national and international stability and confidence, and its determination, under the leadership of its

publisher, Axel Springer, to break down walls of ignorance, prejudice and fear that divide the Germans into two nations and the rest of the world into many hostile camps;

its responsible, well-educated and articulate writers and editors, who, largely inspired by their long-time chief editor, the late Hans Zehrer, and by his successor in 1966, Dr. H. F. G. Starke, have consistently endeavored, since the newspaper's founding at the end of World War II, to raise the nation's political, moral and intellectual level.[51]

14

Neue Zürcher Zeitung: Quality Journalism, Swiss Style

Out into the quaint but busy streets of Zurich three times each day roll trucks on their way to deliver copies of the *Neue Zürcher Zeitung*, a product representing the most uncompromising kind of "quality journalism."

The *NZZ*, as it is widely called, is actually more than a daily newspaper; its three daily editions—morning, noon, and evening—are in effect three entirely different newspapers with no overlap among the editions. At the outset it should be emphasized that this German-language paper is unique among world elite journals: it has the general attributes of a quality paper, but it has developed in a very special, and very Swiss, manner. It is quite different as a newspaper and it takes great pride in this distinctiveness which has made it into a European institution and an international symbol of journalistic excellence and achievement. From its lofty press pinnacle in its neutral and freedom-loving country, the *NZZ* views all the world with a cold and intellectual detachment that has no equal among the world's quality journals.

Throughout its history it has avoided "scoops" and has shunned any form of sensationalism, even to the point of using perhaps the smallest headlines (actually labels) and headline type of any newspaper anywhere. It digs for background material, checks and double checks for accuracy, and is likely to slough off the "hottest" wire stories onto some inside page to make way on page 1 for a long, perhaps even full-page, interpretive piece by one of its own correspondents. Its long reports ramble across whole pages, broken only by an occasional one- or two-column crosshead. The casual and nonmotivated reader will quickly retreat from its heavy, ultraserious, coldly intellectual pages, realizing that they are intended for those whose backgrounds and interests call them into a journalistic experience resembling a leisurely study of a textbook on contemporary society rather than a reading of a daily newspaper.

The *Neue Zürcher Zeitung* (New Zurich Journal), of all the world's elite papers, is probably the most individual, the most serious, the most responsible, and the most cosmopolitan. From a modest local sheet founded in 1780, the *NZZ*, following its formula of undiluted quality, has developed into one of the world's best newspapers, and in many ways easily *the* best. Most of contemporary journalism's "rules" and principles are broken by the paper which proudly produces its knowledgeable and heuristic journalism while eschewing the gaudy gimmicks of its less prestigious cousins with much larger circulations.

An earmark of the *NZZ* is its thoroughness. Whether a particular article deals with an international economic trend, a political coup in Latin America, an important trial in Berne, or a leak in a Zurich sewer system is no matter; the reader can feel assured that the article has had the attention of some of the keenest minds and best writers in Europe. Sensationalism is not in the newspaper's vocabulary: to be sensational would be an affront to the paper's traditions and an insult to its readers. Its well-educated correspondents, about whom more will be said later, are stationed in strategic spots throughout the world. Probably they, more than anything else, give the *NZZ* its particular tone. Knowledgeable in the ways of eliciting "meaning" from their sources instead of surface "facts," these correspondents are probably unrivaled today by any foreign correspondents in the world. Encouraged by the newspaper's tradition of erudition and freedom, these men write freely—in the way they feel they can best get through to their readers. They are not encumbered by any journalistic "5-W" form for the introductions of their stories, nor by a rigid "inverted pyramid" story structure so beloved by American newspaper editors. They write as they like, without worrying that the copydesk will tamper with their product; and the length of a story is strictly a matter of their own judgment and conscience.

The newspaper's outstanding foreign editor, Dr. Fred Luchsinger,[1] wrote in 1965 on being asked what he thought about the importance of his paper in Swiss and European thought: "We know that our paper is read rather carefully and extensively in many political and diplomatic, also in business and financial, circles where the German language is known. We do not give it too much thought. Our main interest is to inform as responsibly as we can; what the influence of such information may be, is not a matter which regards us primarily."[1a]

Norbert Muhlen, a writer for the United States' *Reporter* magazine, an observer who does not have reason to be as modest as Dr. Luchsinger, credits the quality of the paper to its great staff. He wrote in 1959 that the "moral conscientiousness of editors and writers to whom newspapering is not a job but a profession and who turn out a modern newspaper . . . helps explain why today Swiss newsmen are among the world's best, why they are content to write (without by-lines) for the *NZZ* and why the *NZZ* is a truly great European institution."[2] Muhlen added that the *NZZ* aims precisely at being an "all-inclusive, trustworthy three-times-a-day encyclopedia of current events." Its wide Swiss and foreign audience of highly educated and intellectually motivated opinion leaders seem to like it.

In a survey conducted in 1964, a panel of twenty-six internationally oriented American journalism professors chose and ranked the world's leading dailies;[3] the *NZZ* ranked fourth (after *The New York Times*, *The Times* of London, and *The Guardian* of Manchester/London), and a panel of seven Syracuse University journalism professors named the *NZZ* the best newspaper in the world.[4] The Syracuse panel based its opinion on the size of the world reportorial staff, stylistic quality, journalistic courage, and editorial independence and decency.

The *Neue Zürcher Zeitung* is highly regarded by other elite papers, a coveted distinction for any serious contender for a top spot in the world's quality press. *Dagens Nyheter*, the great Stockholm daily, has carried a special article contending that "one can literally follow the development of the world in the *NZZ*, from Bolivia to Nepal, from the Gold Coast to Iceland. . . . It always presents trustworthy information opening new horizons." And *The Times* of London, never one to throw laurels around carelessly, has said that the *NZZ* is "equal in stature to the most distinguished organs of the big countries."[5]

Willy Bretscher, *NZZ* editor-in-chief since 1933,[5a] once said of his paper that it was trying to create "a spiritual safety zone, a well-defined refuge for human beings and eternal human ideas."[6] For this reason the paper has been able to hold out against modern sensationalism. The editor said: "We want to show that it is not necessary to subscribe to a method which will lead to the inevitable self-destruction of the free press."

Important leaders in diverse spots as Willy Brandt in West Berlin and Walter Lippmann in the United States regularly take heed of what the *NZZ* has to say. The paper has always appealed to serious and intelligent world leaders. For example, during World War II Bernard Berenson, a critical and astute student of the world press, expressed in the

Samstag, 4. November 1967 — Der Zürcher Zeitung 188. Jahrgang — Fernausgabe Nr. 303 Blatt 1

Neue Zürcher Zeitung

und schweizerisches Handelsblatt

Wöchentlich 7 Ausgaben

Redaktion: Falkenstraße 11, Zürich

Verwaltung und Druckerei: Goethestr. 10 • Telephon 051/3271 00

Briefadresse für den Auslandvertrieb: Hauptpostfach, 8021 Zürich

Streifband-Abonnemente:

			3 Mte.	6 Mte.	12 Mte.
Ausland, Streifband		sFr.	31.50	58.—	109.—
Deutschland	bei unseren Vertretungen	DM	25.50	47.—	89.50
England		£	2.13.0	4.16.0	9.0.0
Frankreich		fFr.	34.—	62.50	115.—
Italien		Lit.	4 000.—	7 300.—	14 000.—
Oesterreich		S	180.—	330.—	600.—

Postabonnemente in Belgien, Dänemark, Deutschland, Finnland, Italien, Luxemburg, den Niederlanden, Norwegen, Portugal, Schweden

Einzelnummernpreise:

Belgien	bFr. 6.—	Italien	Lit. 60.—
Deutschland	DM —.60	Niederlande	hfl. —.50
England	1/3 d	Oesterreich	S 3.50
Frankreich	fFr. —.50	Schweden (Luftpost)	Kr. 1.—
		Spanien Pes.6.50 (Luftp.)	10.—

Annoncenpreise und Zahlungsmodalitäten für jedes Land sind zu erfragen bei der Annoncenabteilung der Neuen Zürcher Zeitung, Postfach 215, 8021 Zürich

Die Frage einer Vietnaminitiative in den UN

Positive Aufnahme der Anregung Mansfields

W. I. Washington, 2. November

Der Versuch *Senator Mansfields*, den Drang der Vietnamkritiker nach «Aktion» zu befriedigen und zu nützen und ihn in Richtung einer Resolution über eine amerikanische Initiative in den Vereinigten Nationen zu lenken, scheint von der Regierung Johnson positiv gewertet zu werden.

Goldberg vor der Senatskommission

Botschafter *Arthur Goldberg* erschien heute vor der Außenpolitischen Kommission des Senats, um den Gedanken Mansfields zu unterstützen. Er gab einen Abriß seiner bisherigen Bemühungen um den Vietnamkonflikt in den UN, die alle ergebnislos verliefen, und legte auch eine lange Liste von *Erklärungen Hanois und Pekings* vor, in denen eine «Einmischung» der Weltsicherheitsorganisation mit Verve abgelehnt wird. Goldberg gab seiner tiefen Enttäuschung über das negative Resultat aller bisherigen Versuche Ausdruck; aber er versicherte, daß er sie fortführen werde. Die Mansfield-Resolution könne ihm dabei helfen als Ausdruck der Stimmung im Senat und im Repräsentantenhaus.

Um die Wiedereinberufung der Genfer Konferenz

Das UN-Verfahren, das in Gang zu bringen dem Präsidenten anheim gestellt wäre, würde nach Goldberg nicht die materielle Behandlung der Vietnamfrage zum Gegenstand haben, sondern den *Wiederzusammentritt der Genfer Konferenz*, sei es in der vierundfünfziger, sei es in der zweiundsechziger Zusammensetzung. Diese Konferenz würde sich dann mit der Substanz des Problems befassen.

Verschiedene scharfe Kritiker des Johnsonschen Kurses, so zum Beispiel *Senator Fulbright*, der Vorsitzende der Kommission, erklärten, daß sie die *negative Haltung der Sowjets* in dieser Frage einfach nicht verstehen könnten. *Senator Gore* aus Tennessee hob wahrscheinlich den springenden Punkt hervor, als er darauf hinwies, daß die Formel «Zurück zum Genfer Abkommen von 1954» von den Kommunisten eben anders verstanden werde als in Washington. Aehnlich wie Benjamin Cohen vor einer Woche vertrat auch Gore den Standpunkt, es gelte von vornherein die Position der *Nationalen Befreiungsfront* in den allfälligen Konferenzverhandlungen zu klären. Goldberg erwiderte ihm, die Vereinigten Staaten würden sich einer Vertretung der Nationalen Befreiungsfront nicht widersetzen und erforderlichenfalls auch für sie eintreten.

Allgemeiner Konsens

Zur Abwechslung schienen alle Herren der Kommission von dieser Sitzung *hochbeglückt*. Senator Mansfield gab wohl dem allgemeinen Konsens Ausdruck, als er erklärte, die Resolution habe den Zweck, der Welt zu beweisen, daß die Vereinigten Staaten alles getan hätten, um die Weltsicherheitsorganisation einzuschalten — was ja auch ihrer Verantwortung entspreche. Selbst wenn nichts dabei herauskomme, sei die Anstrengung positiv zu werten. «Schaden kann es nicht. Wir haben nichts zu verlieren, sondern nur zu gewinnen.»

Die Mansfield-Resolution wird nun wahrscheinlich ihren Weg durch die beiden *Kongreßhäuser* machen. Der Präsident wird dadurch zu nichts verpflichtet, und vor allem kann er den Zeitpunkt und die Umstände der amerikanischen Initiative im Sicherheitsrat bestimmen. Die Politiker im Kongreß aber werden sich sagen können, daß sie nicht nur geredet, sondern auch etwas «getan» hätten, um ihren Friedenswünschen Ausdruck zu geben.

Appell Johnsons an die Demonstranten

Washington, 2. Nov. (UPI) Präsident Lyndon Johnson appellierte am Mittwoch auf einer überraschend einberufenen Pressekonferenz in Washington an die Vietnam-Demonstranten, bei ihrem Auftreten zu bedenken, was die *nordvietnamische Propaganda* aus diesen Protesten, die nicht zum Frieden beitrügen, mache. Johnson betonte: «Wir werden weiterhin für *begrenzte Ziele* kämpfen, um die Ausdehnung des Krieges zu vermeiden, die Aggression abzuschrecken und die Selbstbestimmung zu schirmen.» Er glaube nicht, daß die Demonstranten den Marineinfanteristen an der Pufferzone zwischen Süd- und Nordvietnam hülfen oder zu einer Lösung beitrügen. Auch von Personen außerhalb der Regierung, die sich eifrig mit der Frage befassen, was an der amerikanischen Kriegspolitik in Vietnam falsch sei, erwartet der Präsident «keine großen unvorhergesehenen Entwicklungen». Die *kritischen «Außenseiter»* sprächen und handelten ohne hinreichende Information, ohne Kenntnis der Berichte von den Frontkommandanten und ohne die Verantwortung, die der Regierung auferlegt sei. Eine Lösung des Krieges käme eher, wenn diejenigen, die an der Heimatfront stehen, die gleiche Urteilskraft und Festigkeit an den Tag legten, wie sie die Amerikaner in Vietnam zeigten.

Kommunistische Konsolidierungsbestrebungen in Vietnam

Kr. Hanoi, stolz auf die angeblichen Abschüsse von über 2400 amerikanischen Flugzeugen, lehnt nach wie vor starr alle Verhandlungsvorschläge ab und verkündet laut seine Erwartung eines militärischen Sieges über Amerika im «Volkskrieg». Doch mehren sich die Zeichen, daß der Krieg immer mehr an der *Substanz* Nordvietnams *zehrt* und der von der Führung herausgestellte Optimismus nicht unbedingt den Realitäten entspricht. Aus der nordvietnamischen Parteipresse ist neuerdings zu entnehmen, daß gegenwärtig Anstrengungen zu einer gewissen Konsolidierung der innenpolitischen und wirtschaftlichen Lage unternommen werden. Nach dem Massenaufgebot und den improvisierten Notmaßnahmen von Anfang 1965 zur Abwehr der amerikanischen Luftangriffe und zur verstärkten Unterstützung des Vietcong strebt die nordvietnamische Führung gegenwärtig eine *«Normalisierung» des Verteidigungszustands* an.

Die neuen Maßnahmen zeigen ein doppeltes Gesicht: sie dienen einerseits der Umstellung auf einen «langdauernden Widerstand», anderseits sollen sie Vorbereitungen für einen raschen Wiederaufbau nach Kriegsschluß treffen, als ob Hanoi trotz gegenteiligen Behauptungen nicht mehr mit einer längeren Kriegsdauer rechnen würde. Das Hauptaugenmerk richtet sich dabei auf die *Wiederherstellung von Autorität und Kontrolle* der Partei. Dezentralisierung, Verlagerung der Betriebe, Evakuierung der Städte und Umstellung der Wirtschaft auf lokale Produktion gingen nicht ohne Beeinträchtigung des hierarchischen Gefüges der herrschenden Partei ab. Zahlreiche Funktionäre, so bemängelte kürzlich das Parteijournal «Hoc Tap», hätten sich allzusehr auf Produktion und Verteidigung konzentriert und dabei den «Parteiaufbau» vernachlässigt. Um dieser *Gefahr des «Lokalismus»* zu steuern, wurde befohlen, daß die Parteikomitees die absolute Kontrolle über Verteidigung, Administration und Wirtschaft wiederherstellen müssen. Zu diesem Zweck sollen in der Parteiorganisation die *Bezirkskomitees* gestärkt werden und anstelle der übergeordneten Provinzkomitees die eigentliche politische Leitung übernehmen.

Angespannte Menschenreserven

Als zweites dringendes Problem stellt sich für die nordvietnamische Führung das Haushalten mit Menschenkräften, deren Reservoir für Verteidigungsaufgaben, Transport- und Reparaturarbeiten und den Einsatz in Südvietnam nahezu ausgeschöpft ist. Das Politbüromitglied *Le Than Nghi* gab im Juli offen zu, «daß der Krieg einen Teil unserer Produktionskräfte zerstörte, einige Schwierigkeiten in der sozialistischen Industrialisierung verursachte und zu einer Ueberbeanspruchung der Arbeitskräftereserven führte». Er wandte sich gegen Ermüdungserscheinungen, einen verbreiteten Fatalismus und die Furcht vor noch größeren Entbehrungen.

Nach der partiellen Mobilisierung vor einem Jahr scheint jetzt ein gewisser Abbau der eingezogenen Truppen im Gange zu sein, das heißt ihre Umteilung zur Volksmiliz und Verwendung für Produktionsaufgaben in den Dörfern. Parteiführung und Regierung faßten eine Reihe von Beschlüssen, um die Ausbildung von dringend benötigten technischen Kadern zu fördern. In ideologischen Erörterungen taucht dazu das Argument auf, daß ohne «technische Revolution» und ohne Aufbau der sozialistischen Wirtschaft die Industriemacht Amerika nicht «aus eigener Kraft» geschlagen werden könne. Es wird auch zugegeben, daß die bisherige Organisation von Arbeit und Produktion der Kriegssituation nicht mehr gewachsen sei, die Führung aber keine Lösung für dieses brennende Problem gefunden habe.

Die Parteizeitung «*Nhan Dan*» sprach am 9. August von «ernsten Versorgungsschwierigkeiten» und forderte größere Sparsamkeit im Verbrauch und Sorgfalt bei der Verwendung ausländischer Hilfe. Bemerkenswert sind auch Anweisungen an die Parteifunktionäre, die nationalen *Minderheiten* in den Berggebieten sowie die religiösen Minderheiten der Buddhisten und Katholiken mit Samthandschuhen zu behandeln, was darauf schließen läßt, daß Hanoi mit seinen Minderheiten nicht geringere Sorgen hat als Saigon.

Giap zwischen «Tauben» und «Falken»

Auf außenpolitischem Gebiet ist Hanoi sichtlich bestrebt, das Gleichgewicht zwischen *Moskau* und *Peking* zu wahren. Die durch einen Parteierlaß eingeleitete Massenbewegung zur Feier des sowjetischen Oktoberjubiläums wurde genau ausbalanciert durch Veranstaltungen zum Gründungstag der Volksrepublik China am 1. Oktober. Kein Ereignis wurde aber in Nordvietnam so gefeiert wie die Explosion der ersten *chinesischen Wasserstoffbombe*, die nicht wenig zur Versteifung des Durchhaltewillens beigetragen hat. Die Energien Nordvietnams erhielten außerdem materielle und propagandistische Stärkung durch die eben abgeschlossenen *Verträge* über unentgeltliche Militär- und Wirtschaftshilfe mit China, der Sowjetunion und anderen kommunistischen Ländern, einschließlich Albaniens, die als eine Art «kollektiver Gegeneskalation» gepriesen werden.

Die mit dem Pendeln zwischen Peking und Moskau zusammenhängende Auseinandersetzung von «Falken» und «Tauben» innerhalb der nordvietnamischen Führung geht weiter, auch wenn sie nicht die gleiche Publizität wie die auf der andern Seite erhält. Die früheren Forderungen nach «raschem Sieg» oder nach dem offenen Eingreifen der nordvietnamischen Armee im Süden sind zwar verstummt; das Militärjournal «*Quan Doi Nhan Dan*» setzte sich im September aber weiterhin für «Klassenkampf und gewaltsame Revolution» ein und bezeichnete den bewaffneten Kampf und die «Verstärkung der revolutionären Streitkräfte» als einzigen Weg zum Sieg. Seit dem Tod des Führers der prochinesischen «Falken» und Kommandanten des Vietcong, *General Nguyen Chi Thanh*, ist der nationalkommunistische General *Vo Nguyen Giap* wieder stärker in den Vordergrund getreten. Es heißt auch, daß ein Vertrauter von Giap, Generalmajor *Hoang Van Thai*, das Kommando der nordvietnamischen Truppen im Süden als Nachfolger von Thanh übernommen habe.

Revidierte Strategie im Süden

General Giap veröffentlichte Mitte September in der Parteizeitung «Nhan Dan» eine große Artikelserie über die militärische Lage in Vietnam, die sich deutlich von der bisher verfolgten strategischen Konzeption seines Gegenspielers Thanh unterscheidet. Anstelle der von Thanh vor zwei Jahren befürworteten und geleiteten «Generaloffensive» *großer Einheiten* im Süden, die Giap jetzt kritisiert, vertritt der nordvietnamische Verteidigungsminister eine Kampfführung mit *kleineren* Einheiten der Hauptstreitkräfte, die nach seinen Worten «nicht immer die gleiche Stärke wie der Gegner haben müssen». Giap erhebt dazu die Forderung nach einer Verbesserung der bisher vernachlässigten Zusammenarbeit von Infanterie mit Artillerie, Kommando-, Pionier- und Luftabwehrtruppen. Giap ist also keineswegs für eine Rückkehr zur ersten Phase seiner Guerillataktik, faßt aber doch eine gewisse «De-Eskalation» ins Auge, auch wenn diese nicht als das von Johnson erwartete Gegensignal gemeint sein dürfte. Wenn Giap jetzt von dem Uebergang von «quantitativer» zur «qualitativen» Kriegführung spricht — er sagt dazu: «Es ist besser, weniger Gefechte mit guter als viele mit schlechter Taktik zu führen» —, so läßt sich aus seinen Ausführungen die Absicht herauslesen, daß Nordvietnam den Fluß seiner Truppeninfiltration nach Südvietnam drosseln und seine im Süden stehenden Truppen statt mit zusätzlichen Divisionen durch *technische Spezialeinheiten* ergänzen will.

Giap beschreibt lang und breit die bisherigen Siege des Vietcong und leitet daraus die Voraussage ab, «daß die Möglichkeit einer vollständigen militärischen Niederlage für eine Million Mann amerikanischer und Marionettentruppen eine Realität zu werden beginnt». Die Amerikaner hätten in ihrem «lokalen Krieg» die Initiative verloren und befänden sich in einer Sackgasse. Eine weitere Intensivierung des «lokalen Kriegs» würde Amerika vor innere Schwierigkeiten wie vor die Gefahr eines globalen Krieges stellen. Giap warnt seine Seite aber auch, daß die inneramerikanische Opposition gegen Johnson nicht überschätzt und daß weder eine Aenderung der amerikanischen Politik nach den Präsidentschaftswahlen von 1968 noch eine «Revolution im Lande des imperialistischen Aggressors» erwartet werden dürfe. Die Entscheidung könne nur durch einen Sieg auf

Umfang 96 Seiten

Inhaltsübersicht

following words (from his Diary) an evaluation of the *NZZ*, which would prove as appropriate today as when he wrote them:

> . . . the Swiss [newspaper] dispassionately looks around the circle of the earth, espying what can interest a humanized man, under present conditions. Nothing escapes its observation and its humane as well as rational comment. I know no other daily so universally well-informed. . . .[7]

Fred Luchsinger, chief editor of the *NZZ*, has said that his paper wishes "to inform a public interested in world and home affairs, mainly political and economical, as broadly and with as much background as we possibly can."[8] News, according to Dr. Luchsinger, dominates the paper's columns, but the *NZZ* is accustomed to following problems and developments in various parts of the world "even when there is no sensational news coming from them." The newspaper's foreign editor recognizes that to American eyes the *NZZ* may not draw a sharp distinctive line between straight news and news analyses; this is quite understandable, he says, because "since we think that news and its background belong together we do not separate them very strictly." Dr. Luchsinger, who for many years was the paper's noted Bonn correspondent, emphasized that the main task of the correspondents "is *to explain* the facts which, of course, does not mean to give their subjective views on them."[9]

Dr. Luchsinger was expressing what *Time* magazine said about the *NZZ* in 1955 when it reported that the Swiss paper's editors feel that "a fact in itself doesn't mean anything; it's what you think about the fact that matters." The interpretation of the facts, said *Time*, has made the *NZZ* "the most influential and widely respected daily published on the continent."[10] Comprehensive reporting, together with the editorial impression created by the forbidding stretches of body type, might cause the uninitiated *NZZ* reader to level a charge of dullness at the paper. A British journalist has something to say in this respect: "This reporting in breadth and depth does not make for dullness. On the contrary the *NZZ* is a most readable paper, full of life, variety and color and it is a measure of these qualities that even the local Swiss news is presented in a way that will attract the foreign reader who has little personal interest in those matters."[11]

Although the *NZZ* is published in a neutralist social environment and has built up a worldwide reputation for fairness, it does not refrain from expressing opinions. It has definite opinions, and it presents them clearly and courageously; this is one reason it has grown to greatness. Further, the newspaper considers it as its duty to judge events, not only on a day-to-day basis, but to assess trends and developments over a long timespan. Its political interpretations, diagnoses, and analyses have proved especially alert and intelligent, even though they have occasionally been wrong. The editors know that the paper's political stands do not always please their readers; this is the way they would have it. Even those readers in opposing political camps (who would not want to dispense with the *NZZ*) recognize that the paper discusses political controversy in an open and invigorating manner. The *NZZ* takes sides, although its staff tries very hard not to do so at the expense of thoroughness, balance, and truth. In short, it considers itself a journal of opinion as well as a newspaper; a serious interpreter of facts as well as a conveyer of facts, a catalyst to serious dialogue, and a journal of reason.

The political and ideological orientation of the *Neue Zürcher Zeitung* is rather difficult to assess. Each of the paper's readers, wrote the London *Times* in 1965, must decide for himself whether the *NZZ* is more liberal- or conservative-minded. It is undoubtedly a liberal paper "in the European sense," which is not exactly the same thing as being liberal in the American sense. *The Times'* commentary on the paper goes on to say that "it is an unorthodox kind of party newspaper, springing from its historical association with the Radical Party and the 1848 Swiss regeneration."[12] Chief Editor Luchsinger says that ideologically the *NZZ* is "in the center" but should be considered liberal in "the European sense"—near the Radical (Freisinnig-Demokratische) Party of Switzerland."[13]

The paper, for example, is very strongly anti-Communist, a good friend of the United States, very distrustful of Britain's Labour Government, a proponent of free capitalism, and a supporter of German rearmament. It is very skeptical about the possibilities of permanent coexistence. It has been much less critical of (in many ways it has supported) United States foreign policy in Vietnam and in other world trouble spots than most of the other non-American quality papers.

Being the independent and thoughtful journal that it is, the *NZZ* does not follow *any* ideological "line." It judges only as it sees things and does not try, as is the case with many newspapers, to make its editorial decisions fit a predetermined position. In this respect, it is indeed a *true* liberal paper, not a journal shackled to a predictable editorial position.[14] "Thus," wrote *The Times* of London, "just after the war it was, by Anglo-Saxon standards, a convinced participant in the cold war, fearing Soviet hegemony in Europe had replaced Hitler's, but now it favours the efforts towards independence among the east European countries (on which it is excellently informed)."[15] When asked in the summer of 1965 if the paper thought the United States should recognize Red China, Dr. Luchsinger responded: "Not of our concern; no matter of primary importance for the time being."[16] This answer would suggest that although the *NZZ* addresses itself to a multitude of international problems, it deals with those it feels are truly vital and does not waste its time building journalistic straw men.

Dr. Luchsinger, in a letter to the writer, has summed up his feelings about the importance and general orientation of the *NZZ* in these words:

> As for the importance of our paper for Switzerland we may draw your attention to the fact that we live in a system of direct democracy where the people (the male population) has to decide itself in referendums on laws, financial commitments, etc. of the state. This implies, on the newspapers of the country, the necessity of extensive public discussion of pending issues. We try to lead these discussions as expertly as we can, which often means by letting the experts speak out. In these discussions we usually take sides. In this, we continue the tradition of the Swiss political press which is, if not bound to be loyal to this or that party, at least in most cases in sympathy with one or the other of the parties. Being liberals, we are in most cases, but by no means in all, more or less in agreement and sympathy with the views of the party representing Swiss Liberalism.[17]

In addition to its great impact on Swiss thought and life, the *NZZ* has tremendous prestige in continental Europe and expanding influence overseas. Its circulation, far from large when compared to many popular papers of Europe, is sizable for an elite paper. In 1965 it stood over 240,000, some 80,000 copies for each of its three daily editions. There is also the overseas edition, the so-called *Fernausgabe*, incorporating much news from the other editions, which circulated about 20,000 copies. The three main editions are in reality separate newspapers, without any editorial overlap.

During a week, more than 1,300,000 copies are printed on the modern rotary presses. Close to 65 million copies of the *NZZ* are printed in an average year, and during one year (1962) nearly 1.8 billion pages of text were offered to its readers. The *NZZ* is primarily a subscription newspaper, having very little appeal for the hurried reader stopping at the street-corner kiosk. The paper is prospering, with most of the profits turned back into the editorial and mechanical departments. Although three hundred Swiss citizens own stock in the *NZZ*, none is allowed to own more than thirty shares, thus assuring continuance of the paper's independent policy and freedom from economic pressures.

The *Neue Zürcher Zeitung* is widely read in government and financial circles, and by all kinds of intellectuals. It is *the* quality paper for the Swiss, and also has a large readership among important leaders in West Germany, who have excellent elite papers of their own (*e.g.*, *Die Welt* of Hamburg, *Frankfurter Allgemeine* of Frankfurt, and *Süddeutsche Zeitung* of Munich). Since German is rather widely known among the educated persons of Europe, the *NZZ* projects its influence into most all

European countries, even into Eastern Europe. For instance, more than a thousand copies go daily behind the Iron Curtain.

Abroad, as at home, it is for a sophisticated audience, not for those readers who want short and hastily written snippets of news and large doses of entertainment. Mainly dealing with politics, economics, literature, and technology, the *NZZ* aims at those who have the interest, the time, and the intelligence to expose themselves to a dispassionate analysis of a subject presented in well-turned sentences that seriously dissect a topic and expose its inner workings. *NZZ* editors feel that the paper has great influence on public opinion in Switzerland and that it gives the world a valid insight into informed thinking on basic issues.[18]

One way the *NZZ* has projected its influence outside the German-speaking world is through the *Swiss Review of World Affairs*, a monthly English-language magazine which selects and translates the *NZZ*'s most significant longer articles. Founded in 1951 by Dr. Urs Schwarz, a foreign editor of the *NZZ*, at the suggestion of some American friends of the newspaper, the journal has proved to be a great success. The *Swiss Review* is airmailed to all parts of the world, some copies reaching almost every country. Its greatest circulation (about 50 per cent) is in the United States. Over 15 per cent goes to other overseas areas, about the same percentage to European countries, and the remainder is regularly read in Switzerland by persons who find it convenient as a summary of the comprehensive *NZZ*, or for language reasons.[19] It is generally considered by political scientists and others interested in depth reporting of international affairs to be one of the best-informed journals in the world.

The correspondents of the *NZZ* are chiefly responsible for the paper's unique kind of quality. They are not hurried collectors of *news items*, interested only in sending back to their paper an unsystematized hodge-podge of stories. Rather, they unobtrusively and patiently wait, watching and listening, for information which can be used to give the reader a balanced view of economic and political developments and trends.[20] Some 50 full-time (four in the United States) and 160 part-time correspondents are interested, not so much in writing "a story" but an aspect of *the* story. Even the paper's headlines reflect this orientation: they are worded in such a general way that no one "story" is heralded; rather they serve as a "theme" placed over the correspondent's piece, which is left to be judged by the reader—and disagreed with if the reader is so inclined.

One British writer,[21] commenting on the importance of *NZZ* correspondents in 1959, wrote that they "enjoy full freedom of expression and seemingly unlimited space, and are able to write without fear of sub-editorial massacre." And, he adds: "They are fortunate in addressing an audience which needs no coaxing into reading serious articles by having them cut up into snippets and adorned with catchy headlines."

Here is what Willy Bretscher, former editor in chief of the *NZZ*, says about the paper's correspondents:

> The *NZZ's* principal source of information is its network of correspondents, in the spirit of its tradition and pursuing a special kind of reportage used by few other newspapers: A kind of reportage which constantly strives to present individual news reports subordinated to the larger context of the total picture and thereby giving them the proper proportion.[22]

One may wonder how this type of reporting can avoid falling into dangerous journalistic pits of pure subjectivism and tedentiousness. Herr Bretscher does not consider this a particularly important problem on his newspaper. He says:

> The solution of this problem is comparatively simple. It lies first of all in the professional and human qualities of the reporters, in their integrity and independence; it consists furthermore in the fact that these reporters fulfill their task as citizens of a small neutral nation which has no irons of its own in the fire of international politics, which pursues no specific policies which could come into conflict with the aims of other nations but whose national interests are linked to the highest interests of all other peoples, with the interest of mankind in the preservation of the peace, in the moral and material reconstruction of the world, in the protection of freedom and human rights.[23]

According to Dr. Luchsinger, chief editor, most of the *Neue Zürcher Zeitung*'s staff members have full university training, two-thirds of them holding doctors' degrees in history, law, economics, or literature.[24] The foreign correspondents for the paper are extremely well-educated and well-informed; they are probably the best in the world. Most have doctorates in the areas of their writing assignments and are considered specialists in their fields. In the United States, for example, is Dr. Werner Imhoof, one of the most astute and knowledgeable political analysts in the world. Stationed in Washington, D.C., he is the *NZZ's* chief United States correspondent; he is aided by Dr. Rudolf Schlesinger and Dr. Walter Hoeffding in New York, specialists in economics and technology. Men like Drs. Eric Mettler and Hans Egli in London, Drs. H. E. Tütsch and Salomon Wolff in Paris, Drs. Theodor Wieser and Hans Zimmermann in Bonn, Dr. Otto Frei in Berlin, Dr. Max Beer with the United Nations (New York), and Dr. Fritz Sonderegger with the United Nations (Geneva) are responsible for the *NZZ*'s being held in such high regard in the area of foreign affairs—especially in politics and economics, thought by the editors to be of prime importance in modern reporting.

All of the *NZZ's* foreign bureau chiefs and most of their assistants have doctorates and are specialists in the areas they are writing about. In addition to the regular staffs stationed in main world centers, the *NZZ* has nearly two hundred additional collaborators or stringers who report regularly from Europe, South America, South Africa, North Africa, Eastern Asia, and Australia.

Commenting on the rather offbeat types of articles used by the *NZZ* and the paper's deviation from general reportorial practices, Dr. Luchsinger says, "We do not think too much abut how many or what people might be interested in what story." Since the interests of the Swiss and foreign readers of the paper are quite diverse, Dr. Luchsinger feels that the *NZZ* "can be sure to have readers for analyses even of those parts of the world which are not in the center of the news, for instance developing Africa and Latin America."[25] This is the philosophy that has led the *NZZ* actually to keep ahead of the "news" for often it has led its readers to understand, even to anticipate, the conditions that suddenly thrust an area into the world's spotlight.

"In other words," writes Dr. Luchsinger, "if we have a good and well founded study on Kenya or on Afghanistan we do not hesitate to present it to our public, even if it does not have a so-called news value. But, of course, the center of gravity of our writing and of our interest is Europe, the Atlantic world and its problems, the East-West situation and, for the time being, Vietnam."[26] In 1968 the paper's news and commentary on Vietnam and Southeast Asia was especially thorough and it is safe to say that its coverage of Latin America and Eastern Europe was as good as that found in any other newspaper.

The amount of international news and views presented to the reader of the *NZZ* is phenomenal. Statistical studies made by the International Press Institute from October, 1952 to January, 1953 showed that the *NZZ* carried nearly twice as much foreign news as its nearest competitor among twenty-three newspapers from eight countries. The second highest was an unidentified British paper. Moreover, the percentage of foreign material to total nonadvertising text was one-third higher than its nearest competitor (an unidentified French paper).[27]

It might be well at this point to take a look at an issue of the *NZZ* during 1965 to get an idea of the general content and emphasis. The foreign edition (*Fernausgable*) for Friday, July 30 is an issue of forty-eight pages (four sections of twelve pages each). The pages measure roughly 19 x 13 inches (a *kleinfolio* or "tabloid" format), with four columns to the page.

The entire front page is given over to a discussion of the Vietnam situation with special attention given the comments of President Johnson in his news conference. One small article from London completes the front page; it deals mainly with Radio Moscow's reaction to the President's remarks. One small picture (two columns wide) is tucked down in the lower left-hand corner (often there is no picture on the front page) giving a general view of President Johnson talking to reporters in the White House.

In keeping with the paper's light use of illustrations, only three pictures appear in the whole edition of forty-eight pages: one of the press conference just mentioned, one of Averell Harriman and Tito of Yugoslavia conferring in Belgrade (on page 3),[28] and one of the Dutch royal family on holiday in Porto Ercole, Italy.

The first section contains most of the foreign news—nearly a hundred rather short (one to four inches) foreign items from the services of United Press International, Agence France-Presse, Reuters, and Deutsche Presse Agentur. These stories originated in forty different cities of the world, from the big national capitals to places like Ba Gia (South Vietnam) and Americus, Georgia (U.S.A.) and are concise and well-edited. In addition the *NZZ* offers its readers fourteen longer analyses, often running a column or more, datelined Washington, Paris, Bonn, London, Buenos Aires, Rabat, Frankfurt, Brussels, Toronto, and The Hague.

In the second section are found a wide assortment of serious essays, and news analyses pertaining mainly to Swiss affairs. Section 3 deals mainly with Canton Zurich, giving the Swiss reader a thorough orientation to the situation in his community, especially from a political and economic perspective; this section also contains discussions of music, literature, and art in a couple of pages known as "Feuilleton." The fourth ("Handelsteil") section is given over to economics with emphasis on foreign and international finance.

The *NZZ* is not only a good contemporary paper; it has always been good and is proud of its history. "It will not be possible for us to report the news, as so many other papers do," said Johann Heinrich Füssli in the first issue on January 12, 1780, "before it has happened."[29] And since that day, the *NZZ* has approached the news more from the historian's perspective than from that of the journalist. At first the paper was called simply *Zürcher Zeitung* and it was not until July 1, 1821 that it added the "Neue" to its title, making it the *New Zurich Journal*.[30] In addition, it began to publish three times a week instead of one. Three years later, however, it reverted to a biweekly. The *NZZ* has been published daily since January 1, 1843. It began twice-daily publication in 1869, moving to new quarters and beginning to appear three times a day in 1894.

Since 1945 the paper has extended its foreign coverage most significantly. After the war it began sending some of its most gifted writers to the Near East, India, North and South Africa and other important regions where the paper had no full-time correspondents. The *NZZ* had no regular correspondent in the United States until after World War II. Its monthly *Swiss Review* in English has come out since 1951, and in 1946 the paper made a significant typographical change when it changed its headline and body type from the old German Gothic to a more modern and legible Latin face.[31]

Ever since Füssli assumed the paper's first editorship, the *NZZ* has had a series of outstanding editors. Probably the most notable, and certainly the ones who occupied the editor's chair the longest periods, were Dr. Peter Felber (1849–1868),[32] Prof. G. Vogt (1878–1885), Dr. Walther Bissengger (1888–1915), and Dr. Albert Meyer (1915–1929). Willy Bretscher, undoubtedly the most illustrious editor of the journal, held the position until 1968.

The newspaper has been editorially "cold and deep"[33] since its founding, and has approached its reportorial responsibilities in a leisurely and independent manner. In 1789, for example, it reported the Bastille's fall a week after it had happened. And in 1805 the paper briefly told of the French fleet's defeat at Trafalgar and pointed out: "In the first moments of such events, one is inclined to exaggerate conditions. It ought therefore be better to wait for reports which are written in cold blood and come from safer sources."[34] Because of this kind of care and restraint, the paper has been listened to when it has spoken out.

As early as 1930 the paper warned of the Nazi threat, bemoaning the rise of Hitler and offering detailed analyses of what was happening in Germany. And after the war began, the *NZZ* continued to warn of the totalitarian peril and provided what was probably the most objective and thorough analysis of German activities until the war was over. During the war, the Germans repeatedly threatened to invade and occupy Switzerland unless the *NZZ* and other Swiss papers stopped reporting on Germany in such a critical (*i.e.*, truthful) manner.[35] Under the able direction of Herr Bretscher who was then fairly new in the editor's position, the *NZZ* continued to speak as Germany's conscience, withstanding numerous pressures from the Nazis. The *NZZ* was banned in Germany from 1934 onwards because the paper had reported that it was Goering, not the Communists, who had set fire to the Reichstag. However, the German Government subscribed to two hundred copies of the *NZZ* each day for its own information. Although the paper was firmly established as a great newspaper before World War II, its reputation abroad was further fostered by its insightful analysis of the months of Nazi preparation for the war, by the wealth of its information and its wartime comments.[36] Since 1945 its prestige has been even greater, due largely to its ever-increasing coverage and analysis of the world during the "cold war."

Each day when the paper's staff members report to work in the five-story building at Falkenstrasse 11 and its conscientious foreign correspondents sort and interpret a multitude of stories, they must all feel a touch of pride and even awe to work for such a noble and notable institution. Certainly they have reason to know that their paper is a responsible voice of reason, enlarging its horizons daily and shrinking the limits of world irrationality.

Under the terrible international tensions of the cold war, Willy Bretscher has observed that the world's people must be able to have confidence in the press—a press that observes attentively and dispassionately what is happening, and gives the people the truth. For the *NZZ* "giving the truth" means two things: "that the press does not irresponsibly soothe and lull the people to sleep, as it would be doing if it kept silent about or minimized present dangers; but it also means that the press may not disturb or needlessly frighten the people, that it must avoid dramatizing events with unbridled sensationalism and thus distorting the picture of reality."[37]

"Accuracy, wide scope, and thoughtfulness" have been called the journalistic qualities most valued by the *NZZ*.[38] With such a formula, which does seem to epitomize the paper's philosophy, the *NZZ* has become one of the greatest, if not the greatest, journalistic voices of the modern world. William Guttmann, a British journalist, has gone so far as to say that "it is no exaggeration to say that this Swiss newspaper is as informative on British politics and diplomacy as the average British daily—and, on such topics as Britain's finance and commerce, even more so."[39]

In spite of many of its traditional nineteenth-century newspaper practices both physically and editorially, the *NZZ* is a forward-looking, progressive newspaper. It is liberal in the truest sense of the word, and from its pedestal of influence sets a high standard for all newspapers everywhere seeking to climb the steep and rigorous path to uncompromising quality. It is an elite paper among elite papers, not content to rest on its past achievement, for it recognizes that the world is becoming ever more complex, frustrating, and dangerous. Who better than Willy Bretscher could express the *NZZ*'s sentiments as it looks into the bleak and uncertain future?

> An old newspaper, the NZZ will continue to carry on its guardian's office in reporting the truth carefully and conscientiously three times a day. Thus do we wish to contribute to the enlightenment and information of a public opinion capable of enduring the war of nerves which world history is waging today against all of us.[40]

15

Italian Elite: Two Faces

Italy has very few elite newspapers. In fact, after one has named three —or at the most four—dailies, he is left with a rather mediocre group of some 110 others which have little or no national reputation and certainly none outside Italy. The elite press is centered mainly in three cities—Milan, Turin, and Rome. Undoubtedly the best elite daily is Milan's great *Corriere della Sera,* with national distribution and a long tradition of thorough, serious, and independent journalism.

The *Corriere* is also the largest of the Italian elite with a daily circulation of at least 500,000. (Its nearest quality rival, *La Stampa* [*q.v.*, Chap. 6] of Turin claims a circulation of nearly 350,000, and *Il Messaggero* of Rome, a good paper but aimed at a lower intellectual audience, has some 360,000.)

In addition to these, and a few other dailies like *Il Resto del Carlino* of Bologna, there is one other daily which must be mentioned: *L'Osservatore Romano.* A special kind of paper and one about which very little has been written, it deserves a place with *Corriere della Sera* as one of the country's most prestigious dailies. It is undoubtedly among the most respected and most widely quoted of all newspapers, both in Italy and abroad.

L'Osservatore Romano, published daily in Vatican City, is definitely the "other face"—the serene, authoritative face—of Italy's quality press and is one which is looked to for guidance and enlightenment and for special insights into Vatican thinking. Although it prints a wide range of serious general news, it is through this semiofficial status as the

Vatican spokesman and reflector of papal thinking that it wields its greatest influence and commands close attention by opinion leaders throughout the world.

The *Corriere della Sera*, a proud old Italian paper published in the bustling atmosphere of one of Europe's largest commercial centers, illustrates the very best in general quality journalism and presents the strained, competitive face of the Italian elite press. *L'Osservatore Romano*, on the other hand, published in the serene, unhurried shadows of St. Peter's, is another face of Italian elite journalism—stately and moral with tremendous prestige due largely to its connections. Both of these papers are highly literate, cosmopolitan, and rational. Both are highly respected in and out of Italy. Both are important papers with interesting philosophies and colorful histories. It is well that they be examined here, if but briefly. First, let us look at Milan's *Corriere della Sera.*

Corriere della Sera

Italy's newspapers are largely political journals, attached in some way to a political party and slanting their contents to fit some ideology. Papers not owned by political parties belong to what is called the *stampa d'informazione* (the information press) and they are considered "independent." However, in Italy, as is really true to a degree in all countries, independence is a relative quality. Independent papers are usually owned by leading industrialists to whom the newspaper is a subordinate interest, and often its integrity is influenced by the owner's commercial considerations or his desire to retain the goodwill of government.

The most notable exception to the rule of owner interference is *Il Corriere della Sera*, with headquarters in Milan and such a widespread circulation in Italy that it is considered the country's only national newspaper. Although owned from its earliest days by the Crespis, a rich and socially prominent Italian family, the paper is as independent as any newspaper can be. One of the most influential newspapers in Europe, the *Corriere* has a staff of the most responsible Italian journalists and correspondents in most of the important capitals of the world.[1]

Il Corriere della Sera, although today a morning paper, was established March 5, 1876, six years after Italy's unification, as an evening paper in Milan. Later, when it changed to morning publication, it retained its old name, *The Evening Courier*. It is one of the oldest extant newspapers of Italy, for very few papers founded at the time have survived two world wars and the great upheavals which have struck

Italy since the 1870's. It is a self-supporting paper, since its daily circulation of 500,000 copies (Sundays more than 600,000) and its lucrative advertising revenue make it possible to publish at a profit. The *Corriere* is the leading publication of a publishing group which includes an evening paper (circulation about 170,000), the largest Italian mass weekly (over a million copies), a women's weekly (460,000 copies), a children's weekly (335,000). All these publications are estimated to be read in Italy by more than 10 million people.[2]

Although about 85 per cent of its readers are in the northwestern part of Italy, the *Corriere della Sera* is a national paper with distribution to every region, even to the offshore islands. Nearly half of the copies go to readers in the cities with more than 100,000 population. As to socioeconomic class, 21 per cent of *Corriere*'s readers are in the upper class and 48 per cent are in the middle class.[3] The paper comes out every day (the Monday edition gives major space to sports, especially soccer which is Italy's national sport) and with increasing frequency contains twenty-four pages an issue. In addition to two large local staffs, in Milan and in Rome, the *Corriere* has more than six hundred correspondents reporting from throughout the country.

The paper has twenty-six full-time foreign correspondents in some twenty important foreign cities. London, Paris, New York, and Bonn each have three men. Two of its most notable foreign correspondents are Vero Roberti in Moscow and Giorgio Sansa in Paris. Its special war correspondent in Vietnam, Egisto Corrati, has provided some brilliant reportage in recent years and has been wounded in fierce fighting which he was covering. In addition to its full-time correspondents in other countries, the *Corriere della Sera* has a large group (from twenty to twenty-five) of traveling correspondents called *inviati speciali* (special envoys); this group contains the most famous names in Italian journalism and their reports come regularly from all over the world. These are not only good reporters, but are excellent writers. Probably one of the best of these *inviati* in the paper's history was Luis Barzini (1874–1947), whose travel stories and war dispatches were so good that he gained an international reputation.[4] The *Corriere* gets its foreign news from its own correspondents, from the Italian news agency ANSA (Agenzia Nazionale Stampa Associata) which also transmits Reuters and Agence France-Presse services, and from the news services of the United States.

The *Corriere* prints a special foreign edition on airmail paper with the result that in every part of the world, from London to New York, from Stockholm to Tokyo, from Buenos Aires to Johannesburg and Sydney, it is possible to buy the most recent copy of the newspaper. This edition usually runs sixteen pages. A few of the *Corriere*'s most outstanding writers, and there are many, are Indro Montanelli (regular portraits of world figures and literary articles), Augusto Guerriero (foreign politics), and Libero Lenti (the financial page).[5] The paper's contributors include scientists, economists, judges, sociologists, and men of letters. Every day it prints a special page, dealing with a single subject or with a particular interest: a women's page, a young people's page, or a page on motoring, agriculture, or literature. It normally carries but one editorial, placed in customary Italian fashion on the front page and signed by the writer. The paper gives especially good coverage to business and financial news, both national and foreign.

Before Italian unification, the Italian press was very largely literary. This old literary interest is still quite evident in the better papers, especially in the *Corriere*. Actually this paper pioneered in what has become almost an Italian journalistic institution: the *terza pagina* or "third page" which serves as a sort of cultural department carrying different types of articles including essays, analyses, travel pieces, reviews, and discursive or interpretive pieces. Articles by famous authors and by specialists in particular fields, very often university professors, are regularly found on the "third page." This page in the *Corriere* is probably the best such page in the Italian press. Editor Alfio Russo says that all men who represent important segments of Italian society want to write, and usually do, for *Corriere*'s third page.[6]

Another characteristic, and perhaps the main one, of the "third page" is the opening article called the *elzeviro* (from the name of the typeface in which it has traditionally been printed) running usually two full columns down the left side of the page.[7] This is usually a light literary article, but with serious overtones. These *elzeviri* are considered among the best in the country and are often included in literary anthologies. Among the outstanding *elzeviro* writers of the *Corriere della Sera* are Indro Montanelli, Emilio Cecchi, and Alberto Moravia.[8] The paper's entire "third page" and especially the *elzeviro* reflects an orientation which has characterized the journal since its earliest days.

Il Corriere della Sera was founded in 1876 by Eugenio Torelli-Viollier, a Neapolitan publicist who learned journalism from the great French novelist, Alexandre Dumas. The paper began modestly, with a capital of some 30,000 lire gathered by some young men of the upper-middle class in Milan. It had its editorial offices in one room in the Galleria di Milan, which is now the historical center of the city and just a few steps from the famous La Scala. The paper was printed from a small office in the basement from a crude press.

Politically the *Corriere* joined the ranks of the liberal Right and fought courageously to preserve its freedom of opinion. Gradually the Crespi family, which still owns it, bought up all the *Corriere's* stock. Torelli-Viollier, as editor, was always free in editorial matters. In the early days, in fact, the paper expressed opinions that were contrary to the industrial interests of the owners.[9] This editorial freedom of the editors of *Corriere*, begun by Torelli-Viollier, has continued to the present.

Benigno Crespi, a cotton manufacturer and the first Crespi owner, acquired new and modern offices for the *Corriere* near his house in Via

Anno 92 - N. 240 - L. 60 (Arretrato L. 120)

Milano, Mercoledì 11 ottobre 1967 - L. 60

CORRIERE DELLA SERA

I COLONNELLI DI ATENE

Augusto Guerriero

PER STABILIRE LE CAUSE E I RIMEDI AL BANDITISMO

IL GOVERNO FAVOREVOLE ALL'INCHIESTA SULLA SARDEGNA

Propone che sia svolta da quindici deputati e quindici senatori nel limite di un anno - Martedì alla Camera dibattito sull'episodio di Sassari - Nuove interrogazioni parlamentari - Due proposte di legge dei liberali

Tempo lungo o breve?

Le decisioni del magistrato

Ugo Indrio

Favorevole al divorzio

Il direttivo dei deputati socialisti

CON L'ADESIONE DI OTTANTAQUATTRO STATI

Johnson firma il trattato per l'uso pacifico dello spazio

Invito all'Unione Sovietica a unirsi all'America per sostituire all'era di competizione spaziale un'era di cooperazione - Un programma di sforzi coordinati per l'esplorazione dei pianeti - Il discorso dell'ambasciatore russo Dobrinin

DAL NOSTRO CORRISPONDENTE

Nuova York, 10 ottobre.

Ugo Stille

La ratifica a Mosca

DOPO TRENTUN ANNI

SI È VOTATO IN SPAGNA con un'alta percentuale degli iscritti

L'opposizione denuncia, nella provincia di Madrid, pressioni in favore dei candidati del «Movimiento», «atonia generale» e «assenza di passione» - Una organizzazione deficiente - Strettissime le rose dei candidati

Madrid: il generale Franco, capo dello Stato, vota nel seggio elettorale di El Pardo dove ha la sua residenza. (Tel. Associated Press)

DAL NOSTRO INVIATO SPECIALE

Madrid 10 ottobre, notte.

Alfredo Pieroni

Continua in seconda pagina

L'ANNUNZIO AL SOVIET SUPREMO

Aumentate del 15 per cento le spese militari dell'URSS

E' il più forte aumento dopo il '61 - Ma altre cospicue somme del bilancio militare restano nascoste sotto altre voci - I piani economici per il prossimo triennio - Resta precaria la situazione agricola

DAL NOSTRO CORRISPONDENTE

Mosca 10 ottobre, notte.

Pietro Sormani

Pietro Verri in the center of Milan. He bought new machinery, hired new staff members, and the paper grew rapidly. From its initial circulation of 3,000 copies, the *Corriere* reached 50,000 in 1887 and 100,000 in 1898.[10] Copies of the paper were already filtering into all the principal European cities where the *Corriere* was considered not only the reflection of the thinking of Italy's leading economic center, but of Italian public opinion in general.

Torelli-Viollier, the founder and first editor, died at the end of the nineteenth century and the editorship went into the hands of various leading journalists of the *Corriere* for a time. One of these was the well-known architect and writer Luca Beltrami, who designed the principal *Corriere* building which is still used in the Via Solferino. The new building which houses the *Corriere* and its evening companion, *Corriere d'Informazione*,[11] was dedicated in 1904. At that time the editor was Luigi Albertini, who is remembered as a man of excellent character and demanding in his journalistic expectations.

Luigi Albertini became editor and also a junior partner in 1900 when Italy was still stunned by the assassination of King Umberto by an anarchist in Monza. Albertini desired to turn the paper into a truly national newspaper and to expand its circulation.[12] He achieved his wish and under his editorship the paper's circulation rose to 400,000 by 1920. He constantly clashed with the Fascists who were beginning their rise to power because of his strong opposition to the politics of Mussolini and to the new laws of his party which were restricting press freedom. He persistently refused to sign a Fascist card, and was eased out in 1921, to be replaced by his brother, Alberto. During the editorship of Luigi Albertini the first weekly publication of the "Corriere della Sera" group was started in 1899, *Domenica del Corriere*, which because of its excellent photographs was immediately very successful. (Today the *Domenica del Corriere* is still the foremost weekly in Italy with a circulation of more than a million. The second weekly started by Albertini in 1909 was *Corriere del Piccoli*, a children's paper. Today it has a circulation of 400,000 and is Italy's oldest and biggest children's magazine.)

In 1929 Alberto Albertini was followed in the paper's editorship by A. Borelli (until 1943) and then by A. Amicucci (until 1945 and Italy's total defeat in World War II).[13] Between 1925 and 1944 the *Corriere* followed the Fascist line but lost much of its former appeal, losing out to Mussolini's own paper, *Popolo d'Italia*. Its circulation dropped during the period from close to 600,000 to nearly 300,000.[14] In 1945 when Italy was finally freed from the Germans, the press once again published in freedom, and new journals sprang up to replace the Fascist papers. The old independent papers like the *Corriere* and *La Stampa* of Turin were restored to their former owners by the Military Government. Within a year the *Corriere* had pushed its circulation up to near 450,000. For about a year after the fall of Mussolini's regime the editor was Mario Borsa, a former *Corriere* staff member. He was succeeded in 1946 by Guglielmo Emanuel who served until 1952. Then came M. Missiroli to the editorship to hold the position until 1961 when the present editor, Alfio Russo, took over.[15]

Since World War II the *Corriere* has progressed steadily in every way and has equaled, if not surpassed, its prewar quality. Its present editor, Alfio Russo, has done much to enhance its reputation at home and abroad. He became editor on October 15, 1961, having spent the previous nine years as editor of Florence's *La Nazione*. A scholarly and gentlemanly Sicilian, Russo had worked for the *Corriere* as a special correspondent in Paris from 1947–1952. Under his editorship the *Corriere's* circulation has risen about 20 per cent and its reputation has grown correspondingly.[16]

Alfio Russo writes often on political subjects and follows carefully the entire editorial production of the paper. In fact, he is even found occasionally in the composing room bending over a type form. He seldom leaves the paper until 2 or 3 A.M., after he is sure everything is in order. Russo desires to be a real editor, and not just a "figurehead" editor as is often the case in Italy. He has a special affinity for good writing and has done much to improve the general level of journalism in all sections of the paper. "We want beautiful writing, beautiful and precise words, and good grammar," he has said. "In addition, we demand typographical excellence." Not yet sold on American-type journalism education, Russo believes that "the best journalists come from the humanistic studies."[17]

Russo wants to make it clear that he has complete editorial freedom. Neither the Crespi family nor its representative on the paper (General Manager Egidio Stagno[18]) try to direct the *Corriere*'s editorial policy. Italian editors, according to Russo, have much more freedom than their counterparts in many other countries. The Italian editor, at least on the *Corriere*, follows his own line independently of the owner or general manager. Russo and Stagno have a weekly conference and submit periodic reports to the owners.[19]

Il Corriere della Sera is usually thought of as "conservative." Editor Russo calls it "liberal," and points to its long history of independence and struggle for basic freedoms. He even recalls that the *Corriere,* before it was taken over by the Fascists, was one of the greatest foes of Mussolini and his party. The *Corriere* also evidences liberal tendencies by being for a united Europe, for NATO, for the United Nations, and for internationalism generally.[20] Russo perhaps would call the paper's position as being on the "liberal Right," a position which would seem quite accurately to describe it.

On the other hand, the *Corriere* evidences certain conservative tendencies: it has an affinity for the *status quo,* especially in economic matters, and is a staunch foe of Communism. "We believe communism is against the human community, and we are against any reform measures which might introduce communism," Editor Russo says.[21] The paper was called "conservative" in 1961 by Frank Brutto, an authority on the Italian press.[22] It was listed as *droite* (right), in contrast to *La Stampa* of Turin which was called *centre gauche* (center left) in an International Federation of Journalists' bulletin.[23]

Regardless of what label might be given to the paper, one can definitely say that the *Corriere* is a serious, progressive, moderate, and well-informed daily. It is a cultivated journal which does not write down to its readers. Although it does carry certain features which are popular with the Italian masses, it consciously strives to keep the general tone of its contents high, or as Russo says, "to always remain authoritative, sincere, intelligent, and elevated in style."[24] When asked in 1966 to name the three or four best daily newspapers in Europe, Editor Russo quickly listed *The Times* of London, the *Neue Zürcher Zeitung* of Switzerland, and *Le Monde* of Paris. Then, with a smile, he added: "And, of course, the *Corriere della Sera!*"

L'Osservatore Romano

A daily newspaper, which shares in a special way the immense prestige and influence of Milan's *Corriere della Sera* but which is about as different from it as any paper could be, is *L'Osservatore Romano* (The Roman Observer) of Vatican City. Without a doubt, *L'Osservatore* is one of the most important newspapers in Italy, although its circulation is not impressive. Its great influence rests mainly on the fact that it is the official (or at least "semiofficial") voice of the Pope, and as such it is very often quoted nationally and internationally. It is a journal, which one writer has said, "regards news through the perspective of history rather than in terms of deadlines."[25]

Published in the Vatican's well-equipped printing plant, the *Osservatore Romano* is issued six times a week, while a more comprehensive companion paper called *L'Osservatore della Domenica* (The Sunday Observer) fills in on Sundays. The *Osservatore Romano*'s language is Italian, but it often uses other languages (especially Latin) in printing papal utterances in full on its front page. It is not a large paper (usually eight to ten pages), but its pages are packed tightly with body type and compact headlines, and the paper is read carefully by leaders in the Roman Catholic Church and by observers of Vatican opinion everywhere.

Nobody seems to know exactly what its status is: some feel it is "official" and others think it is "unofficial." It calls itself "unofficial,"

PRIMA EDIZIONE

LIRE 60

L'OSSERVATORE ROMANO

GIORNALE QUOTIDIANO POLITICO RELIGIOSO

UNICUIQUE SUUM NON PRAEVALEBUNT

Anno CVII - N. 210 (32.587) CITTA DEL VATICANO Lunedì-Martedì 11-12 Settembre 1967

Gratitudine paterna di Paolo VI alle manifestazioni augurali dei fedeli

La preghiera per le grandi intenzioni della Chiesa

Notizie sulla salute del Santo Padre

Questa mattina lunedì, alle ore 11,30, è stata diramata la seguente informazione:

Il Santo Padre ha trascorso una notte tranquilla.

La temperatura continua ad essere normale.

Nel pomeriggio di ieri domenica, Sua Santità ha celebrato la S. Messa nella Sua Cappella privata, ed ha ricevuto, per la trattazione degli affari più urgenti, il Sostituto della Segreteria di Stato, S. E. Monsignor Giovanni Benelli.

Alle ore 22,30 di sabato 9 settembre veniva diffuso il seguente comunicato:

Il medico personale di Sua Santità, Prof. Mario Fontana, invitato a formulare il suo giudizio diagnostico in merito alla indisposizione del Santo Padre, ha rilasciato la seguente dichiarazione:

«Il processo morboso febbrile ...

(Fotografia Felici)

Non è mancato

Ottime le fotografie della Luna trasmesse oggi dal «Surveyor 5»

Nonostante l'imperfetto funzionamento di una valvola del comando dei razzi frenanti l'approdo, avvenuto nelle prime ore della mattinata, è stato impeccabile

PASADENA, 11.

I risultati del referendum di Gibilterra

GIBILTERRA, 11.

Il Primo Ministro siriano ha formato un nuovo Governo

Con un decreto del Ministero dell'istruzione sono state nazionalizzate tutte le scuole private — Colloquio fra Atassi e il Ministro degli esteri irakeno

DAMASCO, 11.

IL SINODO EPISCOPALE

but there is no doubt that it reflects the Pope's thinking. Professor Ignazio Weiss, probably Italy's foremost journalism historian and student of the press, calls it an official journal at least in all articles pertaining to the Vatican; he refers to the rest of its contents as unofficial.[26] One thing is certain: the Pope is the owner if not the editor, and as the only daily published in Vatican City it undoubtedly is careful not to expound ideas or carry news which the Pope would find objectionable.

Most writers like to duck the issue by calling the paper "the Vatican newspaper." One or two may go so far as to devise a term like "official unofficial paper." Others will refer to it as the "Pope's own paper," giving the pontiff the status of publisher. Italians customarily refer to it as "the paper of the Pope." Actually, the Vatican has an official paper, a fortnightly called *Acta Sedis Apostolicae* (Acts of the Apostolic See), a sort of papal counterpart to the United States *Congressional Record.*

Raimondo Manzini, *Osservatore's* current editor, does not regard his paper as an official organ. As he sees it, everything it publishes is opinion and reporting, the only exception being "Nostre Informazioni" (Our News), an official front page column listing papal audiences, major nominations and appointments and the like. "*L'Osservatore* is not the voice of Vatican City. It is one voice of many voices from within and without—all of them of one faith," Manzini has said.[27] The editor who preceded Manzini, the late Count Giuseppe Dalla Torre, said shortly before his retirement that the *Osservatore Romano* is "a Catholic newspaper in which the Holy See publishes its official bulletins. Nothing else."[28] At any rate, Catholics are not bound in conscience to accept the views of the publication. The argument about official status can never be neatly resolved. Suffice it to say, the paper is "of the Vatican" and is the most reliable means of ascertaining the thinking of those closest to the Pope.

The Vatican has owned the paper outright for many years and it was founded with the aid and blessing of the Pope. Official pronouncements of the Pope first appear verbatim in its pages. The editor, whose official title is "Director," is appointed by the Pope. Advertising and circulation income are obviously less than production costs, hence Vatican subsidization can be presumed. All of this certainly gives the paper an aura of an "official" journal.

L'Osservatore Romano has seen persecutors and dictators come and go. In war as in peace it has presented news and opinion with a serenity and sense of history one would expect from an organ published in the shadow of St. Peter's. "According to *L'Osservatore Romano*" is a phrase newspapers use to mean Vatican gospel, and the paper's pen has been described as the "papal sword," especially now that the Pope has no armies. The paper's influence far outstrips its modest circulation which is in the neighborhood of 60,000 daily.[29] Leading churchmen around the world take the paper; also many other opinion and political leaders read it; Charles de Gaulle, for instance, is a subscriber. Even the Kremlin has a subscription. World leaders want to know the opinions of the Vatican and the Pope, for it is their hope that the Catholic Church, a neutral in world affairs, will help to tip world opinion in favor of their particular country or cause. The paper is widely quoted throughout the world—from the pulpit, from the press, and from radio and television.

Begun on July 1, 1861, *L'Osservatore Romano* originally had no intention of being a Vatican voice. It had a clear purpose of putting forward the Church's case in the struggle against anticlericalism which was going on at the time, whereby the Pope would lose his temporal dominions to the new Italian state. It identified itself then, as now, as a political-religious newspaper. It was founded through the wishes of Pius IX, at the urging of two political refugees who became the first editors—Nicola Zanchini, a lawyer, and Giuseppe Bastia, a journalist. This duo had come to Rome from their native Romagna where their Catholic zeal had brought them into conflict with the Piedmontese authorities who had replaced papal rule there.

The papal Undersecretary of the Interior, Marcantonio Pacelli (grandfather of the future Pope Pius XII), who had himself been thinking of starting a new Church paper, liked the idea and supported Zanchini and Bastia in their plans.[30] The name *L'Osservatore Romano* was taken over from a newspaper which had ceased publication some ten years earlier.[31] The purpose of the paper was to "refute the calumnies being launched against Rome and the Roman Pontificate, to record everything worthy of note that happened during the day in Rome, to recall the unshaken principles that are the basis of Catholicism, to instruct in the duties the people have toward their country and to urge and promote the reverence owed to the Pontiff and Ruler."[32]

The official backing of the paper by the Church was kept secret, the reason perhaps being to keep the paper free from censorship of the Vatican itself or to give the Vatican a voice without Vatican officials knowing it was the voice.[33] The two editors were given as much freedom as possible by the government and by the Church, which at this time were almost one and the same. Ownership of the paper, disguised but real, had to remain with the Ministry of the Interior. The editors were, in effect, subsidized.

After a few years, the newspaper was doing poorly and Augusto di Baviera, secretary of the papal editorial staff, became editor and restored the paper to economic health. He was succeeded by a lawyer from Bologna, Gianbattista Casoni. The paper began what has been called its "golden era" when Giovanni Crispolti was appointed editor by Pope Leo XIII. Up to that time, the paper actually was owned by private individuals who were faithful and devoted to the Holy See, and also was subsidized to a large degree. Pope Leo XIII in 1890 decided to buy the paper, paying off all mortgages and other debts.[34]

Pope Leo appointed Casoni, a zealous Catholic, editor. The new editor is said to have given this account: "The pope said to me: 'Everybody has his paper, the Holy See must also have its own. I have called upon you to take the direction of the paper. . . . Be independent of everybody; you are answerable only to me and my secretary of state.' "[35]

In November, 1929, after the Concordat with Mussolini (the Lateran Pact whereby Vatican City was set up as an independent state), *L'Osservatore Romano* moved from its quarters in Rome to a new printing plant within the newly created Vatican City, not only to be more directly responsible to the Pope but to be safer from the ever more destructive and vicious groups of Fascists.[36] The paper, still regarded as the official voice of the Vatican, became less openly combative in the area of politics and more concerned with religion and the defense of the Church's rights.[37]

L'Osservatore in the early 1930's was the only Italian paper operating with substantial freedom from Fascist control. The invasion of Finland by Russia was condemned by the paper as an act of wanton aggression and a warning to all the world that the latent designs of Moscow for expansion outside Russia were finally unmasked. The paper's warning of the implications of the German troops' crossing into Poland without declaring war was not nearly so forceful but the event was reported with a note of sadness even though the editors were aware that even this would antagonize Mussolini and his friend, Hitler.[38]

A clash between the *Osservatore* and the Fascists was bound to occur since Mussolini's party increasingly attacked the Church and advocated social changes which the Vatican newspaper could not permit to pass unchallenged. Leader in the paper's running fight with the Fascists was Count Giuseppe Dalla Torre, probably the most famous of the eight men who have edited the *Osservatore*. (His forty-year tenure had begun in 1920 when he joined the paper as a fiery young Catholic journalist from Padua, and it ended in 1960 when he retired at the age of seventy-five with the title of director emeritus. He died in October, 1967.) Dalla Torre was a persistent thorn in Mussolini's side, and never permitted the paper to refer to him as "Il Duce." The paper was constantly harassed by the Fascists and Dalla Torre was threatened with arrest for lack of cooperation; the editor boldly answered by referring to Hitler as an "antichrist."[39]

When Hitler came to Rome in May, 1938, Pius XI left for his summer residence at Castel Gandolfo to avoid contact with him. *L'Osservatore*'s typical between-the-lines comment was that the Pope preferred the air of Castel Gandolfo to that of Rome. The paper then proceeded to completely ignore Hitler's visit.[40] It was in 1939, the year the former Cardinal Pacelli became Pope Pius XII, that the Fascists began beating newspaper delivery men in the streets of Rome. Priests found reading the paper were also beaten, and newspaper sales in the streets were prohibited at the beginning of 1940. When Italy entered the war in

June, 1940, the mailing of the Vatican paper was halted for three months. An announcement appeared in the paper saying that it would halt publication. For some reason, the beatings stopped and mailed copies began getting through; the paper never really missed publication.[41]

During the course of the Second World War only the Vatican paper printed a daily column impartially reporting war news, trying to be impartial in its reportage. The circulation zoomed to some 350,000 as Italians were eager to read Allied communiques. The *Osservatore* became Mussolini's greatest irritant within Italy. Dalla Torre was once waylaid outside St. Peter's by Fascists and barely escaped injury. For weeks thereafter he made his way home through a route entirely inside the 108-acre Vatican State.[42] When Rome was liberated by Allied armies toward the end of the war, *L'Osservatore Romano* carried the news on the last page, while headlining a religious ceremony on page one. A writer on Vatican affairs explained: "I don't think the editor . . . intended to snub the conquerors of Rome. It was just his tactful way of reminding his readers that wars are won and lost, empires crumble, regimes rise and fall, but the Church goes on forever because her power is spiritual and not material."[43]

Dalla Torre was replaced in 1960 by Raimondo Manzini, who had edited Bologna's influential Catholic daily, *L'Avvenire*, for thirty years. Upon becoming editor of the *Osservatore*, Manzini said, "I don't want this to be a paper read only by priests, a sort of bulletin of the Holy See."[44] He began immediately to make the paper more readable. He spruced up the layout, began running livelier pictures, and added new features dealing with matters of general interest. He has more than doubled the staff, from some thirty to about sixty, and has many correspondents in various regions of Italy to send in news of their areas. He has also assigned a few correspondents to foreign capitals and plans to continue expanding the paper's foreign coverage.[45]

Each Pope has dealt with the paper differently. When Benedict XV ascended to the papacy, he controlled the paper rather strictly. He used to mark every morning some passages in either blue or red depending on whether he approved or disapproved. Sometimes he would even send handwritten instructions to the editor. Pius X and XI also sent written instructions to the paper on occasion. When the paper observed its 75th year, Pius XI ordered a world Catholic Press Exposition to be held in Vatican City; it was held and termed very successful. Leo XII laid down the modest aim for the paper that "if it cannot always be first with the news it would be nice at least for it not to be always last."[46] Pope John XXIII instructed the paper to stop calling him by his exalted titles and to refer to him simply as the Pope or the Pontiff.[47]

The views of the current Pope are not difficult to determine, for he had quite a bit to say about the paper in its centennial edition when he was unaware he would be the next pontiff. As state secretary, he had received the criticism often lodged against the *Osservatore*, and in answering some of this criticism in 1961 he made some of the most lucid statements about the paper to be found anywhere:

> We have little in comparison with other big papers, but what we have is good. . . . Our news perhaps is too dignified, too polished, too quiet; readers are not thrilled. It is a serious newspaper. . . . The emphasis is on editorials rather than on news. It doesn't want to give news, but it wants to create thought. It is not enough for it to relate events; it wants to comment on events. . . . In this paper the journalist is an interpreter, a teacher, a guide. . . . The paper appeals more to specialized people—to the politicians, to scholars, to devout persons and not to the mass of the readers. . . . No other paper can see more, can tell more or can give a better orientation towards educating people to truth and charity. It is the "paper of the pope."[48]

Besides the long columns devoted to accounts of religious ceremonies, the texts of papal speeches and pronouncements by other Church dignitaries, *L'Osservatore* does carry a considerable amount of commentary and opinion. It has recently begun printing occasional columns of criticism on radio, television, movies, and the theater, concentrating mainly on the moral aspects of the works. The paper deals more with religion and less with politics, especially Italian politics, and avoids highly controversial political issues when possible. It is certainly less polemical than it was under Dalla Torre when it tended to relish a fight with the Communists and the Nenni Socialists.

Makeup of the newspaper can be described as restrained or modern conservative. Multicolumn headlines surrounded by ample white space represent an attempt at modern horizontal makeup. Pages are seven columns wide. Features and special articles of analysis often run long, giving the paper large masses of gray. Italic type, not the most readable, is often used as body type; in fact, as much as one-third of the front page may consist of italic body type (fortunately 10-point in size instead of the more common 8-point). By-lines or writers' identification lines, when used, are generally printed at the end of a story. Pictures, when they appear, are usually large and are placed near the center of the page. The front page may have as few as four stories or as many as twenty-five. One issue taken at random carries stories from Caracas, London, Tokyo, Bucharest, Washington, Bonn, Paris, Geneva, Lisbon, Vienna, and Cape Kennedy.[49]

In addition to its main Italian daily editions, *L'Osservatore Romano* is published as a weekly in French and Spanish editions. The French edition was begun in late 1949 under the supervision of the man who is today Pope Paul VI. It was organized as a French-language edition to serve France, Belgium, Switzerland, Canada, and the Near East. The weekly is edited in the Vatican and printed in Paris.[50] The Spanish-language weekly edition began in 1951 under the sponsorship of a society in Buenos Aires called "Petrus" in order to bring Latin American Catholics closer to the Vatican. Material for this edition is prepared in Rome, sent by air to Buenos Aires, and printed there for distribution in Latin America, mainly in Argentina, Uruguay, Chile, Bolivia, and Paraguay.[51]

Even if the *Osservatore* were printed only in Italian, or even Latin, it would have considerable influence and impact throughout the world. It would be quoted often and widely (as it is); it would serve as a source of ideas for articles in many languages; it would filter into dozens of languages of the world and would make itself heard through sermons, conversations, and the written word wherever Vatican thinking and activities are considered important. It is possible that the paper could have greater impact if it were more like other newspapers or if it were published in many other languages, but it is doubtful. As it is, *L'Osservatore Romano* gains prestige from the very fact that its circulation is restricted and its character is extremely stolid and serious. It is highly probable that the paper would lose something very important if it were to pattern itself after the "newspapers of the world," even those of high quality.

16

Two Spokesmen for Latin America

With the exception of a few small and scattered French and English newspapers, the press of Latin America is Ibero-American. And, excluding the Portuguese-language press of Brazil, the Latin American press is predominantly Spanish. Throughout the sprawling region from the United States-Mexican border to the southernmost tip of South America, Spanish-language newspapers form, along with radio broadcasts in Spanish, the one big common denominator in mass communication.

In spite of widespread illiteracy, vast distances and poor transportation, generally inferior production equipment, many repressive governmental press policies, and staggering economic problems, the Latin American press contains many fine newspapers. Poor ones dominate, to be sure, but considering the tremendous barriers facing the press in Latin America, it is surprising that the region has been able to produce the many quality newspapers that it has.

By and large, the best newspapers are concentrated in six countries —Mexico, Colombia, Peru, Chile, Argentina, and Brazil. Any major area of the world would be fortunate to have outstanding dailies such as *El Universal*, *Novedades*, and *Excélsior* of Mexico City; *El Tiempo* of Bogotá; *El Comercio* of Lima; *El Mercurio* of Santiago de Chile; *La Nación* and *La Prensa* of Buenos Aires, and *O Estado de S. Paulo* (see Chap. 8). They are prime representatives of the serious, progressive press of Latin America. They are newspapers which are concerned about quality journalism and are determined to establish themselves firmly in the world's elite press. As representatives of the best in Latin American journalism, they all speak for the most progressive elements in their respective societies.

Two of them—*Excélsior* of Mexico City and *La Prensa* of Buenos Aires—are worthy representatives of the entire Latin American elite press. *Excélsior*, founded only in 1917, typifies the progressive and dedicated philosophy of journalists who determined to adapt modern American journalism and economics to the traditional newspaper practices of Spain. And, *La Prensa*, through its long and distinguished history in which it has become a leading social institution and bulwark against tyranny, offers an inspiring pattern for other Latin American dailies.

Excélsior

Mexico is said to be a country of contrasts. This is certainly true of its newspapers which range from the crudest little hodgepodge weeklies and dailies to the big modern dailies of Mexico City, Guadalajara, and Monterrey. In the capital city, the hub of the country's political, intellectual, and social life, are several very fine dailies. But it is *Excélsior*, the largest and most complete, that stands as Mexico's leading quality newspaper. Its main competitors are *Novedades* and *El Universal*, also capital dailies offering serious journalism to a well-informed and cosmopolitan readership.

By the end of 1967, *Excélsior's* daily circulation was right at 125,000 and its Sunday circulation had exceeded 130,000. The newspaper is usually considered a cooperative with its key staff members owning shares in the company.[1] This fact, according to its late director general, Rodrigo de Llano, is one reason why *Excélsior* has such "a high degree of staff morale."[2] It was also de Llano's belief that any newspaper "with a serious purpose, high ideals of objectivity and integrity will draw to it writers and other staff members of high quality."[3]

Rodrigo de Llano, who died January 31, 1963, has been called one of the "giants of Mexican journalism"[4] and was extremely active in the Inter-American Press Association and other international groups. It was really under his leadership that *Excélsior* reached its high position in the world of journalism. Much credit, also, is due Gilberto Figueroa who, as general manager until his death in 1962, ran the paper with great skill and foresight and participated in editorial decisions.

Under the direction of de Llano, *Excélsior* was known as the "farthest to the right" of all Mexico City newspapers. Admirers said it had great influence on public opinion, while its critics called it "middle-class reactionary, nationalistic, and antirevolutionary." Mexico's Communists said that it was pro-United States of American, pro-Franco, antiliberal, and anti-Communist. It was also called pro-Church, antilabor, Right Wing, procapital, and usually antigovernment.[5]

Since the deaths of de Llano and Figueroa, *Excélsior* has veered away from the older conservative position. In fact, many readers, as well as a number of newsmen in Mexico City, have noted "leftist" tendencies in the paper's new leadership. Bruce Underwood, head of journalistic studies at Temple University in Philadelphia who did an exhaustive study of the Mexican press in 1965, admits the change in policy has taken place but believes the present orientation of *Excélsior* is "moderate."[6]

The newspaper was founded in 1917 by twenty-eight-year-old Rafael Alducin, who laid a foundation upon which a quality journal could be built. Alducin was not long in making the paper's editorial section the best in Mexico, with articles that reflected the thoughtful, moderate viewpoint of the reasonable segment of the country's intellectuals.[7] On his death, his widow took over the management of *Excélsior*, the first case in Mexico of a woman having such a position on an important paper. The newspaper's building, which was begun by Alducin on Bucareli Street, has now been expanded and runs all the way through to the beautiful Paseo de la Reforma. *Excélsior*, since its founding, has kept abreast of new journalism technology; for example, it was the first paper in Mexico to install rotogravure presses and the first to use Ludlow machines to set headlines.[8]

Excélsior has been called "an institution in Mexico, like *The New York Times* in the United States, the London *Times* in England and *La Prensa* in Argentina."[9] Calling itself the "Newspaper of National Life," *Excélsior* is universally respected among Mexican journalists and other Latin American readers for its serious tone and thorough news coverage. The fact that it is published in the capital and has the nation's largest circulation enhances its tremendous prestige. It is usually considered the nearest thing in Mexico to a "national" newspaper, and although a general interest paper, it circulates mainly among the high social and educational class.

According to Dr. Marvin Alisky, director of Arizona State University's Institute of Latin American Studies and perhaps the foremost United States authority on the Mexican press, *Excélsior* is sold all over Mexico every day. "For example," he says, "one can see copies, just in by air-mail, being sold rapidly at Nogales (on the United States border), Tijuana, Ciudad Juarez and Nuevo Laredo, and news dealers save copies for good customers as it goes quickly."[10] He further states that no other daily has the national distribution that *Excélsior* enjoys in key cities, state capitals, and in libraries. Most anywhere in the country, Alisky says, "one finds it in the offices of government officials, teachers, business leaders, labor leaders, and also in most upper-class homes."

While providing excellent national coverage, *Excélsior* does not neglect foreign news; in fact, it presents proportionately more foreign news than do the major daily papers of the United States.[11] Twenty-five foreign correspondents of the newspaper are stationed in New York, Washington, Madrid, Paris, Bonn, Rome, and London. In addition to reports from its correspondents, it provides much foreign material from the Associated Press and from the French Agence France-Presse.

The newspaper's average of sixty pages daily are packed with a wide assortment of national and world news. The pages are attractively made up, and the typography and general quality of printing is on a par with the best in American newspapers.

A popular letters-to-the-editor column called "Foro" often consumes an entire page and is open to a diversity of opinions and political positions. The fact that a heavier dose of writing by Left-Wing journalists has been appearing since about 1964 seems to help bear out the contention that *Excélsior* is becoming more "liberal" in its orientation. At least, its opinion pages have become more pluralistic and, perhaps, considerably more interesting. A great amount of space is given to personal articles or "essays" of many types, and the attempt to play down crime and small-scale scandals indicates that traditional European journalism of the Spanish variety is still deeply rooted in *Excélsior*.[12]

The large Sunday edition, and especially the special supplement called "Diorama de la Cultura," offers examples of well-written, thoughtful historical and literary essays that in many countries would appear only in monthly or quarterly magazines or journals. The literary base which forms the bulk of the special "features" in *Excélsior* is a reflection of the traditional idea that quite serious, academic or "qualitative" pieces have a rightful place in the newspaper press. At present, some of the best writing being done in Mexico can be found on the pages of *Excélsior*.[13] A light popular supplement, "Sunday Magazine," also appears with the Sunday edition; it is filled mainly with features about sports and movies. Another eight-page Sunday section, in rotogravure, deals with tourism, while another (usually four pages) is largely given over to historical and religious articles. A twelve-page color comic section is also contained in the Sunday edition.

The interpretive or background articles in *Excélsior* are perhaps of higher quality than are the news stories. In fact, there are some students of the Mexican press who are rather cautious in their comments about the accuracy and objectivity of Mexican-written news stories. Dr. Alisky, for example, says that perhaps the only Mexican daily that presents objective reporting is the English-language daily of Mexico City, *The News*.

Iníciase en Italia la Semana Cultural Mexicana

(Ver 1a. y 2a. columnas)

EXCELSIOR
EL PERIODICO DE LA VIDA NACIONAL
Registrado como artículo de segunda clase en la Administración de Correos el 18 de marzo de 1917

AÑO LI — TOMO V | FUNDADOR RAFAEL ALDUCIN | DIRECTOR GENERAL MANUEL BECERRA ACOSTA | MEXICO, D. F.—MARTES 17 DE OCTUBRE DE 1967 | GERENTE GENERAL J. JESUS GARCIA | NUMERO 18,496

Nuestro Crecimiento, de los más Rápidos del Mundo: Ortiz Mena

Yáñez y Fanfani, en las Inauguraciones

Cabal Imagen de Nuestro País, Mediante Diversas Exposiciones

Por JOSE TORRES, corresponsal de la AP

ROMA, 16 de octubre. (AP)—México inició hoy una serie de actos para dar a conocer al pueblo italiano diversos aspectos de su cultura a través de la pintura, la bibliografía, la artesanía, la cinematografía y la música.

Al inaugurarse hoy la primera semana cultural mexicana en el Instituto Italo-Latinoamericano, el secretario de Educación de México, licenciado Agustín Yáñez, subrayó la importancia del acontecimiento.

"México ofrece a Italia un espejo que quizás, en alguna medida, le devolverá una imagen inédita. Al mismo tiempo que le entrega la experiencia singular de un pueblo que precedió a otros por caminos revolucionarios..."

Yáñez, el Ministro italiano de Asuntos Exteriores, Amintore Fanfani y embajadores, altos funcionarios del gobierno y muchos invitados, estuvieron presentes en el acto inaugural de la semana.

Esta consta de una exposición de pintura, una del libro y otra de artesanía popular, todas ellas en el Instituto, una reseña cinematográfica, un ciclo de conferencias y conciertos de música mexicana.

El acto se abrió con unas palabras del presidente del

SIGUE EN LA PAGINA NUEVE

Pide Rusia Ayuda a Jodrell Bank

Quieren que Rastree su Astronave que Debe Llegar Mañana a Venus

LONDRES, 16 de octubre. (AP)—Los hombres de ciencia rusos pusieron hoy en alerta a la estación receptora de Jodrell Bank, en la Gran Bretaña, para que ayude a seguir el rastro de su artefacto espacial Venus IV, a causa de su "extraordinaria importancia y significado".

El profesor Sir Bernard Lo-

SIGUE EN LA PAGINA DOCE

DON MANUEL Espinosa Yglesias, durante su discurso a los participantes en la II Convención del Sistema Bancos de Comercio.

EL SECRETARIO de Hacienda abordó temas de trascendencia nacional al contestar las preguntas formuladas por los convencionistas.

EL LIC. JUAN Sánchez Navarro, expuso la labor realizada por el Sr. Espinosa Yglesias al frente del Consejo del Banco de Comercio.

Hablo en la Junta de Bancos de Comercio

Auge del Ahorro que Beneficia a la Economía

Ningún Peligro de Inflación Avizora el Secretario de Hacienda

Por ADRIAN VILALTA, reportero de EXCELSIOR

El ahorro interno crece en México más rápidamente que la capacidad de uso del mismo y los bancos y el Estado han tenido que promover, conjuntamente, operaciones para que estos recursos no queden estériles y en cambio beneficien a la economía general del país.

El secretario de Hacienda, licenciado Antonio Ortiz Mena, hizo esta declaración ayer, al contestar las preguntas que le formularon varios banqueros —en realidad, agricultores, ganaderos, industriales y comerciantes— que participan en la II Convención del Sistema Bancos de Comercio.

Ortiz Mena, anunció, además:

I) No hay peligro de inflación y el país ha crecido, en los últimos tres años, a una tasa promedio del 7%, una de las más elevadas en todo el mundo.

SIGUE EN LA PAGINA ONCE

Notable Alza del Ingreso per Cápita

Espinosa Yglesias Expone en Cifras el Vertiginoso Progreso

Llevamos treinta y cinco años de transformación continua en un México vertiginoso que "se ha habituado al progreso", ha demostrado que el dilema entre desarrollo y estabilidad es falso y que probablemente alcanzará este año una producción de 300,000 millones de pesos, equivalentes a 325 dólares por habitante (6,562 pesos) —75% más que hace 10 años— que sitúa al país al nivel de varias naciones europeas.

Manuel Espinosa Yglesias, presidente del Banco de Comercio, así lo afirmó ayer, en la inauguración de la II Convención del Sistema Bancos de Comercio ante el secretario de Hacienda y centenares de convencionistas de toda la República y observadores de la banca de 10 países extranjeros.

Anunció que el Banco de

SIGUE EN LA PAGINA DIEZ

URSS: Utopía y Realidad

Auge de la Genética

- ★ La Rehabilitación de Timofeyev
- ★ Lysenko, Favorito de Stalin
- ★ La Pléyade de Premios Nobel

(La Genética, proscrita en la época de José Stalin, durante la cual prevalecieron las ideas de Lysenko, favorito y protegido del dictador, cobra fuerza insospechada en la Unión Soviética en un renacimiento que hace abrigar profundas esperanzas de nuevos logros. La radiación y sus influencias sobre las características hereditarias de los hombres, los animales y las plantas, recibe atención especial de los sabios. En éste, segundo de sus tres artículos, Walter Sullivan aborda ese y otros interesantes temas.)

Por WALTER SULLIVAN,
Especialista en Asuntos Científicos de "The New York Times"
exclusivo para EXCELSIOR
(c) por The New York Times News Service

— XII —

La primavera pasada, una delegación de la Academia Nacional de Ciencias de los Estados Unidos fue a Moscú para entregar a Nikolai V. Timofeyev-Tessovsky el premio Kimber de Genética.

George B. Kistiankowsky, químico de Harvard, quien concibió la idea para provocar la explosión que hizo estallar la primera bomba atómica, antiguo consejero del Presidente Dwight D. Eisenhower y ex miembro del Ejército Ruso Blanco, leyó la cita en la que se explicaban los merecimientos de Timofeyev-Tessovsky para hacerlo digno del galardón que se le había concedido. Se puso en brazos del sabio ruso un ramo de flores y Nikolai N. Blokhin, presidente de la Academia Soviética de Ciencias, estaba a punto de dar fin a la ceremonia, cuando se adelantó una mujer.

Había ido desde el Instituto de Timofeyev-Tessovsky, en la cercana Obninsk, para presenciar la entrega del premio. En cuanto captó la atención de los presentes esa mujer se lanzó a hacer un elogio del viejo genetista, quien había salido de la Unión Soviética en la década de los años veintes y quien llegó a ser una de las principales figuras del Instituto Max Planck para la Investigación del Cerebro, en Berlín. Cuando el Ejército Rojo se apoderó de esa ciudad, el genetista fue arrestado y enviado a Siberia. Sin embargo más tarde se le rehabilitó.

SIGUE EN LA PAGINA DOCE

Inventario de Suelos, Urgente

Resulta Indispensable Para la Planeación, Dicen en una Junta

La Sociedad Mexicana de la Ciencia del Suelo afirmó ayer, al abrir su tercer congreso nacional en el auditorio del Centro Nacional de Enseñanza, Investigación y Extensión Agrícolas de Chapingo, que es imperioso iniciar el levantamiento de un inventario de suelos en todo el país, en el que puedan basarse trabajos de planificación agrícola, distribución de tierras, otorgamiento de créditos y aún el cobro de cuotas de riego e impuestos.

La propuesta fue hecha por el doctor Ramón Fernández González, presidente de la SMCS, después de haber informado que sólo han sido estudiadas, con cierto detalle, alrededor de 10 millones de hectáreas, de las cuales sólo de dos millones de hectáreas hay estudios completos.

Dijo también que en las zonas erosionadas se ha observado que las capas duras que se han quedado expuestas pueden ser convertidas en suelos agrícolas. Los métodos que pueden ser usados, afirmó, deberán ser motivo de estudios para aumentar la velocidad de recuperación y la reducción de costos. En estas áreas, dijo, generalmente se

SIGUE EN LA PAGINA CATORCE

D. O. Hablará Ante la O. E. A

Lo Hará a Petición de los Dirigentes de ese Organismo

WASHINGTON, 16 de octubre. (AP)—El Presidente de México, Gustavo Díaz Ordaz, hablará en la Organización de Estados Americanos, con ocasión de su visita a esta capital los próximos días 26 y 27.

Unos funcionarios norteamericanos dijeron que el programa de la visita está en preparación, y no se publicará hasta que sea aprobado por Díaz Ordaz.

Se tiene entendido que la sugerencia de que hable en la OEA fue hecha por algunos miembros de la organización interamericana.

También hablará en una sesión conjunta del Congreso de los Estados Unidos. Se anticipa que probablemente pronunciará ambos discursos el 27, pues el primer día de la visita lo dedicará a distintas ceremonias en su honor y a conversaciones privadas con el Presidente Lyndon Johnson.

Frentes Políticos

- ★ Nulificarán Elecciones en Veracruz
- ★ Irregularidades en Varios Municipios
- ★ Defiende el PPS a Empleados Comerciales

Por FRANCISCO CARDENAS CRUZ

En por lo menos media docena de municipios de Veracruz, las elecciones de alcaldes efectuadas el día primero del actual, serán nulificadas.

Irregularidades en los comicios, destrucción de boletas electorales, repudio a los candidatos y amenazas en algunos pueblos que pueden degenerar en hechos de sangre, son algunas de las causas.

Tierra Blanca, Tlacotalpan, Lerdo de Tejada, Coatzintla y Juchique de Ferrer y dos más, son las poblaciones en donde, en vez de alcaldes, habrá Concejos Municipales.

El corresponsal de EXCELSIOR en Jalapa, José Luis Hernández Sosa, informó lo anterior, anoche.

Del caso de Playa Vicente, donde se ha llegado al extremo de amenazar con nulificación de elecciones o actos violentos, Hernández Sosa indicó que figuran entre los que dictaminarán hoy los dipu-

SIGUE EN LA PAGINA NUEVE

Seguirá el Alerta en el río Lerma

En esa Cuenca y en Chapala Persiste el Peligro, Dice R. H.

El ingeniero José Hernández Terán, secretario de Recursos Hidráulicos, dijo ayer que en lo que falta del año continuará el estado de alerta en el río Lerma y en el Lago de Chapala, debido principalmente a que continúan las lluvias en la zona y al alto nivel que ha alcanzado el agua.

Para evitar el peligro de desbordamientos e inundaciones, trabajan un millar de hombres con equipo suficiente para proteger con roca los bordos, precisó.

El funcionario señaló lo anterior al salir de su acuerdo con el Presidente Díaz Ordaz, a quien dio un pormenorizado informe de la situación.

Dijo, por otra parte, que los agricultores del norte y del

SIGUE EN LA PAGINA NUEVE

III Competencia Internacional

Los Vencedores de Ayer

Estos fueron los triunfadores en las distintas pruebas finales efectuadas ayer y correspondientes a la III Competencia Deportiva Internacional:

Atletismo

800 metros planos, hombres: J. P. Dupresne, Francia, 1' 48" 8/10.

3,000 metros steeplechase, hombres: Gastón Roelants, Bélgica, 8' 37" 8/10.

Salto de altura, hombres: V. Gaurilov, Unión Soviética, 2.13 metros.

Lanzamiento de la bala, hombres: Randy Matson, Estados Unidos, 19.87 metros.

100 metros planos, mujeres: Miguelina Cobián, Cuba, 11" 4/10.

400 metros planos, mujeres: C. Cooke, Estados Unidos, 52" 4/10.

SIGUE EN LA PAGINA CATORCE

Calendario Para Escuelas Oficiales

La Secretaría de Educación Pública, a través de su departamento de Estadística Escolar, dio a conocer el calendario de trabajo en escuelas oficiales, para el periodo 1967-1968, que se iniciará el 21 de noviembre.

A este calendario se sujetarán también las actividades de escuelas particulares incor-

SIGUE EN LA PAGINA NUEVE

Pronostican Lluvias Para Esta Noche

Ayer, la temperatura máxima en la capital fue de 23.1 grados y la mínima de 12.

El Servicio Meteorológico Nacional informó ayer que el huracán "Priscila" se encontraba a 330 kilómetros al

SIGUE EN LA PAGINA CATORCE

Horario Estricto Para Espectáculos

En lo sucesivo, cualquier evento deportivo, en local abierto o cerrado, deberá efectuarse en el día y la hora anunciados en la propaganda, haga o no mal tiempo.

Esta determinación de la Oficina de Espectáculos del Departamento del Distrito Federal, en relación a la función de box efectuada el sábado

SIGUE EN LA PAGINA NUEVE

Proyectan Explotar el Carbón de Coahuila Para Generar Electricidad a Bajo Precio

Por EDUARDO GARCIA JEAN, enviado de EXCELSIOR

MONCLOVA, Coah, 16 de octubre.—La explotación de los yacimientos carboníferos del Estado de Coahuila permitirá generar energía eléctrica a más bajo precio; crear nuevas fuentes de trabajo y ahorrar recursos no renovables derivados del petróleo.

La Comisión Federal de Electricidad, según informó su director, licenciado Guillermo Martínez Domínguez, está en la etapa de experimentación y opera la planta termoeléctrica "Venustiano Carranza", ubicada en Nava, Coahuila.

El funcionario ve con optimismo este proyecto en el que trabajan en forma coordinada el Instituto Nacional de Recursos no Renovables, la Secretaría del Patrimonio Nacional, Altos Hornos de México y la Fundidora de Fierro y Acero de Monterrey.

Los técnicos de esas dependencias y empresas exploran la cuenca carbonífera de Coahuila para cuantificar su riqueza y posibilidad de explotación. Al término de este estudio, y sopesadas las conveniencias económicas, Altos Hornos de México y la Fundidora de Monterrey aprove-

SIGUE EN LA PAGINA ONCE

Ingresó el Banco de Culiacán al Grupo del Banco de Industria y Comercio

En días pasados se formalizó la operación por la cual el grupo del Banco de Industria y Comercio, S. A., adquirió una importante participación en el capital del Banco de Culiacán, S. A., que pasa así a formar parte del consorcio financiero en el que figuran igualmente, el Banco General de Monterrey, S. A., el Banco General de Tamaulipas, S. A., el Banco del Sur, S. A., Promotora de Industrias, S. A., Financiera General de Monterrey, S. A., Seguros Atlas, S. A., Fianzas Atlas, S. A., y el Banco Inmobiliario Atlas, S. A.

SIGUE EN LA PAGINA NUEVE

Elaborating further on Mexican reporting, Alisky says:

> Sometimes *The News'* parent newspaper, *Novedades*, and often *Excélsior*, meet U.S. standards of care and accuracy. But there are times when these dailies join the tabloids and lesser papers to run foolish speculation-type sensational stories of little lasting significance. In 1965, all the Mexican dailies except *The News* ran the foolish story from Chihuahua that police were rounding up several hundred Communists. I was in Chihuahua City and the number was exactly eight young men. Even the AP and UPI bit on that one and ran stories to the States based on the scare version. *Excélsior* is less quick to jump to such conclusions and less guilty than most other Mexican papers to run sensational stuff, and it does have the decency to later run a second story stating that the first one was groundless and that investigation proved that the facts had not been reported in full.[14]

Critics who point to well-known weaknesses in the Mexican newspapers generally, and they would apply to some extent to *Excélsior*, are justified in saying that salaries are too low, that editorial staff members must often have several jobs in order to enjoy an adequate income, that gratuities from outside sources are accepted by reporters, that opinion often slips into the news columns, and that the press is not as free as it could be. Salaries for editorial employees are low in Mexico, but they are far better than in many Latin American countries. It should be noted, however, that salaries on papers like *Excélsior* and *Novedades* are considerably better than they are on many of the capital dailies. In spite of the fact that some of *Excélsior*'s staffers may get some income from other employment, it is safe to say that the general quality of writing and editing on the paper is as good as, and in most cases better than, that found in other leading dailies of Latin America.

The leading executives of *Excélsior* are Manuel Becerra Acosta, director general; José de Jesús García, general manager; Victor Manuel Verlarde, assistant director; Filiberto Massa, administrative officer; Arturo A. Sánchez Aussenac, editor-in-chief; Luis A. Ros, production manager; Armando Rivas Torres, copydesk chief, and Carlos Díaz Gonzáles, advertising manager.[15] Carried still in the staff box of each edition are the names of the two deceased journalistic leaders, de Llano, director general from 1924 to 1963, and Figueroa, general manager from 1934 to 1962.

Outstanding reporters for *Excélsior* in recent years have been Pedro Pablo Camargo, Luis Ochoa, Alardo Prats, Miguel Angel Alvarez, Raúl Beethoven Lomeli, and Carlos Denegri. Among the many brilliant columnists of the paper these names must be mentioned: Mauricio Fresco, J. Fernando Mendoza, Bernardo Ponce, Aldo Baroni, Augusto Assia, Gena Pastor, Diego Cordoba, and Pedro Gringoire. *Excélsior* has two of the best editorial cartoonists in Latin America, Rafael Freyre Flores and Abel Quezada.

When Rodrigo de Llano died in 1963, he was succeeded as director general by Manuel Becerra Acosta, who had served as managing editor for many years and whose sophistication and dedication to quality journalism made him a logical choice for an important position. It is interesting that Becerra Acosta considers the newspaper as "liberal," although it is generally referred to in the Mexican context as "conservative."[16] This may be explained by tricky Latin American semantics in which a "liberal" newspaper (to a United States observer) may, in the context of Latin America, be actually thought of as "conservative." At any rate, it does not help much to find that Becerra Acosta, while calling his paper "liberal," pronounces it ideologically *"derechista"* (rightist).[17]

According to Becerra Acosta, his paper is aimed at the upper classes and definitely has a great influence on Mexican public opinion. He also, quite naturally, considers *Excélsior* the best (highest quality) daily in Mexico, but refrains from saying what other one he considers second best. The paper, he points out, has some two hundred writers and editors, all well-educated and "able to handle complex world issues with skill and sophistication."[18]

In describing *Excélsior*, Becerra Acosta has said that it forms part of the "cream of the Mexican and the world press for various and important reasons," among which he lists its long tradition and its respect for "men of all social classes, of all cultural levels, and of all political positions."

Concluding this discussion of *Excélsior* and giving a good insight into the newspaper's character and the journalistic standards of its director general, is the following verbatim short commentary written in late 1965 by Becerra Acosta:

> It is not by chance that Excélsior enjoys its undeniable public acceptance. Years of struggle, many years, were taken to build an organ that has as its principles objective information, independent commentary, defense of moral principles, wherever these are found.
>
> Excélsior, serious in its news, responsible on each of its pages, is not dishonest nor is its honor, good faith, or the solidarity of its editorial opinion ever doubted.
>
> It has banished, since its founding, ignoble campaigns, petty goals. Consecrated to the interest of the common good, it has always had an obligation: to add to the general strength in order to build a better country, without forgetting that one of its primary functions is the daily chronicle—often frightful—of covering international events. Preoccupied above all with Mexico, it understands, nevertheless, that the world has restricted, and today isolated progress is not possible nor is an isolated life. This, combined with a sense of national responsibility, is what gives a universal character to the paper.

> I think—I am convinced—that the writers, columnists and editors of Excélsior contribute to the excellence of the paper because they respond intellectually and morally to the world around them.
>
> I don't want to mention some of the best of our staff members because it would establish an inevitable discrimination. But it is enough to say that we have essayists, reporters, novelists, economists and sociologists of continental reputation, and in some cases, of well-earned universal fame.[19]

La Prensa

From impressive quarters at Avenida de Mayo 567 in Buenos Aires, is published a daily newspaper that perhaps as much as any other in the world has held unswervingly to the lofty idealism of its founder. *La Prensa* has followed its founding spirit of independence and service to such a degree that its policy has served as a challenge to every government of Argentina and an inspiration to freedom-loving people everywhere.

La Prensa (The Press), perhaps the best-known of all Latin American dailies, was founded in 1869 by Dr. José Clemente Paz, who said in the first issue that "Independence, respect for the private citizen, reasoned criticism of public officials but not of their individual personalities, will form our creed." Further, he editorialized that "truth, honor, freedom, progress, civilization" would be the newspaper's goal.[20] From the first it was announced that *La Prensa* would not accept Government subscriptions, and that any attempt to influence the impartiality or independence of the paper would be regarded as offensive.[21]

Early in its history *La Prensa* began offering free medical and legal services to all, set up a huge library for the public, gave free advice to farmers and industrialists, and established a school of music. The paper became in a real sense a social institution in Argentina and became respected throughout the world as an enterprising, truthful and courageous newspaper.[22] Its independence and that of its staff members became traditional, and fifty years after its founding, it was able to write:

> This newspaper may have committed errors in some of its judgments on men and affairs during its long term of life; but its independence, its serenity, its ethical purpose, its institutional and patriotic doctrine, no one may deny.[23]

But in order for the paper to reach the prestige it had come to enjoy after fifty years, its founder and his son, Ezequiel P. Paz, had to go beyond simply standing for high ethical principles; they had to make *news* the heart of *La Prensa*. The early Argentine press consisted chiefly of philosophical discussions and political polemic. Very early Dr. Paz recognized the importance of news. He realized that his paper had to do more than deliver dull sermons and foresaw a new day coming for Spanish-language journalism. Dr. Paz insisted on a high standard of accuracy, and was the first Argentine publisher to divorce news from views and to thwart the rule of the editorial department by the business department.[24]

With José C. Paz, the paper's founder, the basic concept of *La Prensa* —and the whole Argentine press to some degree—swung away from a strictly political orientation to one more independent and geared to news presentation. The Paz family rejected, generation after generation, many offers of public office in order to keep themselves and their newspaper free from political pressures.[25] While *La Prensa* was growing into the largest and most prestigious Spanish-language newspaper in the world, it was meeting stiff competition from another serious daily, *La Nación* of Buenos Aires, which had been founded in 1870 by Bartolomé Mitre and which was destined to be *La Prensa*'s closest rival for elite status through the years, even until today.

La Prensa had set a new example for Argentine and all Latin American journalism. As Herbert Matthews of *The New York Times* has written: "All the best in Argentine life was reflected in *La Prensa*'s pages. It became the symbol of which the humblest Argentine was proud because he knew that wherever free journalism was respected, *La Prensa* was honored."[26] The paper became well-known all through the world and was quoted as the authoritative voice of Argentina or of Latin America in general.

Typographically, *La Prensa* was serious and sedate and, unlike many contemporary Latin American dailies, gave no suggestion of sensationalism. This policy has persisted through the years, and although news replaced classified advertisements on the front page in the 1950's and a few modern makeup techniques have been instituted, *La Prensa* today still reflects something of a stodgy, old-world conservatism in its appearance.

In 1898, Dr. Paz handed his highly successful paper over to his son, Ezequiel Pedro Paz, who at the age of twenty-seven began forty-five years as publisher and chief editor of *La Prensa* without being absent a single day from his office. A man of intense energy and tremendous sense of responsibility, Ezequiel Paz, like the great C. P. Scott of Britain's *Guardian*, lived for and with the newspaper constantly. He worked in all departments of the paper, reading proofs, and even helping in the composing room at times. He was a firm advocate of accuracy, objectivity, and balance in the news columns.

There has probably never been a journalist in Latin America, or anywhere in the world for that matter, who has held higher journalistic

LA PRENSA

METEOROLOGICAS, Página 12 — CAPITAL Y ALREDEDORES — HOY: Bueno, templado [illegible]. Máxima alrededor de 21 grados. MAÑANA: Bueno, [illegible]

Año XCVIII — Nº 33.539 — Edición de 28 páginas — Precio $ 20 | Primera Sección | BUENOS AIRES, SABADO 12 DE AGOSTO DE 1967 | Dirección y Administración: Av. de Mayo 567 - Tel. 33-1001/1

Analizó el gabinete el presupuesto para 1968

Fueron tratadas también la licitación de El Chocón y la política de subsidios

El teniente general Juan Carlos Onganía presidió en la mañana de ayer una reunión de ministros en la cual, entre otros temas, se consideraron "la orientación y las bases del presupuesto nacional para 1968", según la información que fue suministrada posteriormente por la Secretaría de Difusión y Turismo.

En la reunión, que se inició a las 8.25 y finalizó a las 12.45, participaron los ministros de relaciones exteriores y culto, doctor Nicanor Costa Méndez; de interior, doctor Guillermo Borda; de economía y trabajo, doctor Adalbert Krieger Vasena; de defensa, ingeniero Antonio R. Lanusse, y de bienestar social, doctor Julio Alvarez, y el secretario general de la Presidencia de la Nación, general Héctor Repetto.

Los temas tratados

Durante la primera hora de las deliberaciones, estuvieron presentes también el secretario de trabajo, señor Rubens San Sebastián, y el subsecretario de economía, ingeniero Raúl Ondarts, quienes, al retirarse, expresaron a los periodistas que habían concurrido para exponer algunos temas relacionados con sus respectivos departamentos de Estado, aun cuando no precisaron cuáles eran.

Pocos minutos antes de las 13 abandonaron el despacho presidencial los ministros de economía y trabajo, y de defensa, y anunciaron que la reunión había finalizado.

El doctor Krieger Vasena adelantó que se habían analizado las directivas generales del presupuesto de 1968.

A su vez, el ingeniero Lanusse, interrogado por los periodistas, negó que hubiera sido considerada la proyectada ley anticomunista.

Información oficial

Finalizada la reunión, que se efectuó en el despacho presidencial, el director de prensa de la Secretaría de Difusión y Turismo, doctor Enrique Nores Bodereau, dio a conocer una información, en la cual se expresa que, en ella, "se consideró en primer término y fundamentalmente, la orientación y las bases del presupuesto nacional para 1968".

"A este respecto —agrega la información oficial— los participantes hicieron una larga exposición sobre los programas que ejecutarán en el año próximo. Este tema abarcó la mayor parte de las deliberaciones y, a continuación, se trató la política oficial a seguir en el otorgamiento de los subsidios que acuerda el Poder Ejecutivo a diversas instituciones, los cuales se realizan ahora con intervención del Ministerio de Bien-

(Continúa en la pág. 6, col. 8)

Los rebeldes del Congo crearon su propio gobierno

Darían 10 días de plazo a Mobutu para dimitir y liberar a Tshombé

Bukavu (Congo), 11 (UP) — Los mercenarios blancos victoriosos crearon hoy un gobierno de "salvación nacional" del Congo encabezado por el coronel Leonard Monga.

En el cuartel general de los mercenarios, situado en Bukavu, Monga anunció que daría plazo de 10 días al presidente congoleño Joseph Mobutu para renunciar y poner en libertad al ex primer ministro Moise Tshombe de su cautiverio en Argelia.

La emisora oficial congoleña difundió una declaración de Mobutu de que no negociará con los rebeldes, a quienes la radio calificó como "esos insignificantes".

El ministro de relaciones ex-

(Continúa en la página 2, col. 8)

Provocó China a los Soviets

Moscú denunció que la Guardia Roja abordó una embarcación en Dalny

Moscú, 11 (UP) — La Unión Soviética denunció hoy oficialmente que una turba de la Guardia Roja de China comunista abordó un buque ruso, "capturó" a su capitán y "trató de atropellar" a los tripulantes.

El anuncio está contenido en una enérgica nota de protesta entregada al encargado de negocios chino en esta capital, y distribuida por la agencia de noticias soviética Tass.

El anuncio dice que el incidente, ocurrido el miércoles en el puerto de Dalny, fue "una provocación preparada".

"En una flagrante violación de las normas reconocidas de derecho internacional y cometiendo actos arbitrarios e ilegales, las autoridades chinas retuvieron la motonave soviética Svirsk y capturaron al capitán", dice la nota.

El mismo día, se agrega en la denuncia, una turba de unos mil ciudadanos chinos se congregó cerca del barco y muchos subieron a bordo y trataron de maltratar a los tripulantes.

Pekín reclama unidad en el ejército

Hong Kong, 11 (UP) — El régimen de Pekín urgió hoy a las fuerzas armadas que se mantengan fieles al jefe del partido Comunista chino, Mao Tse-Tung. Agregó que solamente el apoyo militar podía evitar que el partido y el Estado "cambiaran de color político".

Este llamamiento apareció publicado en el órgano oficial de Pekín, el "Diario del Pueblo", a raíz de informaciones según las cuales se utilizaban tropas para aplastar a la oposición surgida contra Mao en la lucha por el control del poder en China.

Junto con una exhortación similar formulada por el ministro de defensa Lin Piao, el diario indicó su preocupación por la lealtad de los 2.500.000 hombres que tienen en las fuerzas armadas.

Con informaciones sobre violencia procedentes de diversas regiones de China, incluyendo Cantón, Shanghai, Chekiang y Mongolia interior, es obvio cuánto puede depender Mao de sus fuerzas armadas.

Pero se supo que hubo un gran deterioro de la lealtad entre las fuerzas armadas, y al mismo tiempo circulaban rumores diversos.

El mes pasado, en la ciudad central de Wuhan hubo un levantamiento contra el régimen de Mao, y estas fuerzas se opusieron a los intentos del gobierno de aplastar la revuelta.

Anteriormente, el diario derechista "Hong Kong Star" informó sobre deserciones en masa de las tropas regulares en la provincia de Kuang Tung, agregando que los desertores se habían sumado a las fuerzas rebeldes de Kuang Tung.

¿Conferencia militar?

Según Radio Pekín, Lin Piao se estaría preparando para una conferencia militar en Pekín y citó estas palabras suyas:

"Debemos oponernos a todos aquellos que van contra la línea de pensamiento de Mao". Aparentemente, Lin es el heredero de Mao.

El "Diario del Pueblo", según dijo la agencia oficial noticiosa Nueva China, hizo un llamamiento para que se destruya el cuartel general "de los burgueses", el cuartel general de quienes están contra Mao, tales como el presidente Liu Shao Chi.

Hoy temprano el diario independiente de Hong Kong "Ming Pao" dijo que se declaró la ley marcial en la ciudad sureña de Cantón para poner término al derramamiento inútil de sangre entre grupos rivales de la Guardia Roja que interpretan diferentemente a la "revolución cultural".

Bombardeo a un vital puente de Norvietnam

En su ataque, la aviación estadounidense desafió a la artillería antiaérea roja

Saigón, 11 (UP) — La aviación estadounidense desafió hoy el intenso fuego de 2.000 cañones antiaéreos que rodean a Hanoi y bombardeó por vez primera en la guerra el vital puente de Doumer, precipitando su tramo central sobre las aguas del río Rojo, según anunció un portavoz militar norteamericano.

Radio Hanoi dijo que millares de habitantes de esta capital buscaron "ordenadamente" los refugios antiaéreos durante el ataque, pero no mencionó los daños causados al puente, cuya importancia es fundamental para las comunicaciones ferroviarias y motorizadas entre Vietnam del Norte y la China comunista.

Tres aviones derribados

La emisora afirmó que tres aparatos norteamericanos fueron derribados en acción, dos de ellos mientras atacaban "zonas residenciales en el centro de Hanoi", pero la información no fue confirmada por las autoridades militares estadounidenses.

El puente de Doumer está situado apenas unos dos kilómetros y medio al norte de la capital norvietnamita. Corre a lo largo de más de 1.500 metros y empalma con una pequeña isla superpoblada en medio del río.

Objetivo del ataque

El bombardeo formó parte de una nueva ofensiva norteamericana tendiente a cortar las rutas por las cuales China comunista envía sus materiales y equipos bélicos a Vietnam del Norte.

El puente no sólo conecta a Hanoi con las vías férreas del nordeste y el noroeste, ambas ligadas con China, sino que también constituye la principal conexión entre esa ciudad y el aeropuerto municipal de Gialam.

Dicho aeropuerto nunca ha sido bombardeado, si bien se sabe que numerosos interceptores Mig tienen allí su base, pero ninguno de esos cazas de construcción soviética alzó esta vez vuelo para combatir a los aparatos atacantes.

Las únicas defensas mencionadas por los pilotos que participaron en la operación fueron las de los dos millares de cañones antiaéreos que defienden la capital comunista, muchos de ellos emplazados precisamente en una posición para proteger el estratégico puente y el aeropuerto vecino.

Frustran un atentado

En Saigón, entretanto, la policía anunció que había descubierto una banda terrorista del Vietcong, deteniendo a dos expertos comunistas en explosivos, poco antes de que pudiesen volar un edificio central donde viven y trabajan altos mandos de las fuerzas norteamericanas destacadas en Vietnam.

La policía agregó que de haberse consumado ese atentado podrían haber muerto o resultado heridos prácticamente centenares de militares norteamericanos y civiles survietnamitas que se hallaban en la zona.

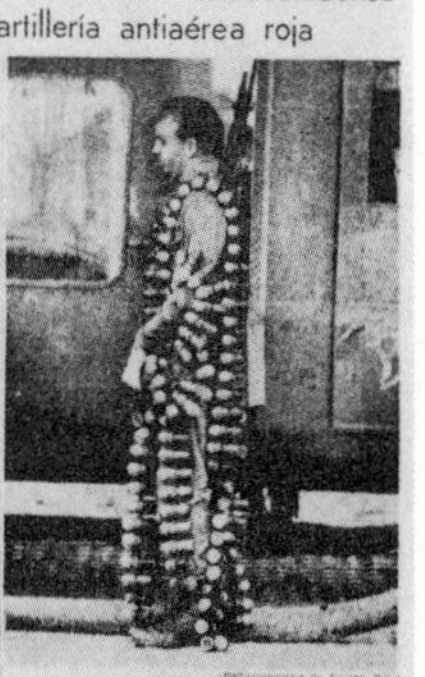

(Radiotelefoto de United Press)

Este hombre, trasformado en un arsenal ambulante, lleva una banda con proyectiles de 40 mm. El soldado pertenece a la compañía 334 de helicópteros, cuyo base está en Bien Hoa, Vietnam del Sur

Mons. Fulton Sheen pide que EE.UU. se retire de Vietnam

Nueva York, 11 (UP) — Monseñor Fulton J. Sheen, obispo de Rochester (Nueva York), instó ayer al presidente Lyndon B. Johnson a que haga un gesto de conciliación único en la historia mundial, retirándose de la guerra en Vietnam.

En una entrevista grabada para el programa "El mundo de la religión" de la Columbia Broadcasting System (CBS), el prelado afirmó que hablaba sólo desde el punto de vista cristiano sin intervenir en la discusión de los aspectos políticos y militares del conflicto. Monseñor Sheen hizo su primera solicitud por el retiro unilateral de los Estados Unidos de Vietnam en un sermón pronunciado el 30 de julio pasado.

Amenaza de las autoridades de Quebec, Canadá

París, 11 (UP) — El primer ministro de la provincia de Quebec, Daniel Johnson, amenazó esta noche con independizarla del resto del Canadá si no se reforma la constitución del país, dando a los francocanadienses de Quebec "más libertad".

"De ser esto imposible, nos apartaríamos y eso sería independencia", expresó Johnson en una entrevista en francés por la red de televisión oficial del gobierno.

Johnson elogió al presidente de Francia, Charles de Gaulle, que desató una ola de protestas del gobierno de Ottawa en julio último al gritar "Viva Quebec libre", durante su breve visita a Montreal. La frase es una consigna del grupo separatista francocanadiense que desea formar una república aparte en el territorio provincial de Quebec.

Anunciará el Papa importantes reformas

Ciudad del Vaticano, 11 (UP) — El papa Paulo VI anunciará grandes reformas en el Sacro Colegio de Cardenales, la Secretaría de Estado y el Vicariato de Roma, en un documento que será distribuido la próxima semana, según se supo hoy.

Fuentes autorizadas del Vaticano afirmaron que el Pontífice revelará sus planes para la publicación de este documento dentro de las próximas 48 horas y cuyo contenido se hará público el 18 de este mes.

El documento o "motu proprio" incluirá las reformas a las tres ramas principales de la Curia Romana: el Sacro Colegio de Cardenales, la Secretaría de Estado, a cuyo cargo se hallan los asuntos internos e internacionales, y el Vicariato de Roma, que administra la diócesis romana.

A San Martín de los Andes viajó el presidente

Asimismo visitará el 23 del corriente la provincia de Córdoba

El presidente de la Nación, teniente general Juan Carlos Onganía, viajó ayer por vía aérea a Neuquén, en compañía de su esposa, señora María Emilia Green.

La partida del avión presidencial ocurrió a las 14.10 desde el Aeroparque de esta capital y la Secretaría de Difusión y Turismo no proporcionó ninguna información oficial sobre el viaje.

El primer magistrado pasará un corto período de descanso en la zona de San Martín de los Andes, donde reside una hija suya, y se supo que probablemente regrese a esta capital el domingo por la noche o el lunes próximo por la mañana.

Asimismo se informó ayer en la Casa de Gobierno, que el teniente general Onganía visitará en los días 22 y 23 del corriente, la provincia de Córdoba.

No pudo establecerse en cambio, si ese viaje comprenderá también la provincia de Santiago del Estero, como se había pensado en un principio.

La llegada a Neuquén

Neuquén — El avión presidencial en que se trasladó el teniente general Onganía llegó a Junín de los Andes a las 18.2. Desde allí el presidente y sus acompañantes prosiguieron viaje en automóvil hacia la localidad de San Martín de los Andes.

Durante su permanencia en aquella población, el primer mandatario se alojará en el domicilio particular que el teniente primero Enrique Antonio Peña, esposo de una de sus hijas, ocupa en el barrio de oficiales del regimiento de caballería de montaña 4, Coraceros General Lavalle, donde presta servicios. Esa unidad se halla ubicada a 4 kilómetros aproximadamente de San Martín de los Andes, sobre el camino que une a esa localidad con el lago Lolog. A su vez, el barrio de oficiales se encuentra en un lugar más elevado de la zona, a un kilómetro de los cuarteles.

Es propósito del teniente general Onganía descansar en aquella residencia hasta mañana, en que regresará a la capital federal.

El gobernador de la provincia, ingeniero Rodolfo Rosauer, se trasladó ayer por vía aérea a San Martín de los Andes para aguardar la llegada del presidente de la Nación.

Varios bancos dan ya créditos personales

En otros se estudia todavía el nuevo régimen instituido

En fuentes bancarias oficiales se explicó anoche la demora de los bancos en hacer conocer sus planes para conceder créditos personales, que fueron autorizados por la circular 5788 (Bancos) del Banco Central. Díjose al respecto que esas instituciones de crédito han sido sorprendidas por la decisión de la repartición oficial mencionada, que anteriormente no permitía en absoluto la concesión de este tipo de préstamos para consumo y exigía declaración de bienes antes de aprobar cualquier operación crediticia.

Bancos que lo otorgan

Se dijo también que cuatro instituciones de Buenos Aires han comenzado o se aprestan a conceder esos préstamos. Tales bancos son el de Galicia, el Holandés Unido, el Argentino de Comercio y el City Bank. La primera de estas instituciones, que ya ha confeccionado los formularios en los que se solicitarán los créditos, ha concretado alrededor de 1.000 de estas operaciones, dentro de las condiciones de la circular B-378 (30 meses de plazo, un interés del uno por ciento mensual sobre el monto total de la operación, que nunca podrá superar los 350.000 pesos por firma y en el total de los bancos, entre otras), exigiendo un aval y la existencia de un empleo con ciertas condiciones de estabilidad.

El sistema en los Estados Unidos

Con respecto al City Bank, esta institución ha sido la primera en los Estados Unidos en lanzar este tipo de financiación de consumo, utilizando cheques de viajero para la cancelación de los pagos mensuales, y publicando en los diarios los formularios de pedido, para que los interesados los remitan por correo. Se indicó que este grado de simplificación puede obtenerse gracias al uso de equipos electrónicos que procesan toda la información recibida en corto tiempo, y que en el total de préstamos concedidos, sólo llegaría al uno o uno y medio por ciento el monto de los incumplimientos.

Señalóse también que es más difícil la falta de pago en los pequeños deudores que en las grandes empresas financiadas, por la misma cuantía de las operaciones.

Otras posibilidades

Se dijo también que en los próximos dos meses la mayoría de los bancos otorgarán estos créditos, quedando excluidos del sistema tan sólo los más pequeños, que no cuentan con suficientes fondos en giro.

Finalmente se indicó que existe la posibilidad de que algún banco adquiera empresas financiadoras de adquisiciones para consumo a fin de usar la estructura de aquellas en las operaciones indicadas. De cualquier manera, se dijo, los bancos que concederán créditos por montos cercanos al tope permitido, no serán competencia para esas empresas, cuyo tope parece estar por debajo de 100.000 pesos en la mayoría de sus operaciones.

Será liberada la importación de papas

Objetan la medida los productores de Tucumán

La Secretaría de Agricultura y Ganadería, dio ayer a conocer una información en la que hace referencia a la determinación del gobierno de facilitar la importación de papas, a fin de que el aumento de la oferta gravite atemperando el alza de los precios.

Para ello se eximió al producto de los derechos de importación que lo gravan, hasta el 15 de octubre próximo.

Indicóse que se asegura así el mantenimiento de márgenes satisfactorios para las existencias aún en poder de los productores a la vez que no interferirá en la comercialización de las nuevas cosechas que comienzan en noviembre.

La medida fue determinada por las intensas y generales heladas producidas en el mes de junio último, que provocaron la pérdida casi total de hortalizas con la consiguiente alza de los precios.

Objeciones a la importación

Tucumán — Aspectos relacionados con la producción de pa-

(Continúa en la pág. 6, col. 1)

Presentaría Rusia una moción de desarme en común con los EE. UU.

Moscú indicó esa disposición, y William Foster iría en breve a Ginebra para tratar el caso con A. Roschin

Ginebra, 11 (UP) — Fuentes autorizadas revelaron hoy que la Unión Soviética indicó su disposición a presentar juntamente con los Estados Unidos un proyecto de tratado contra la proliferación de las armas nucleares.

Un portavoz norteamericano agregó en medio de la conferencia del desarme, donde están representadas 17 naciones —entre ellas, el Brasil y Méjico—, que el jefe de la delegación estadounidense, William C. Foster, regresará este fin de semana de Wáshington, a fin de tratar los detalles finales con su colega soviético, Alexei A. Roschin.

Foster viajó a Wáshington el miércoles último, para comparecer ante el Senado de su país, pero dijo que regresaría a esta ciudad en cuanto los soviéticos mostrasen su disposición a presentar el proyecto conjunto de tratado.

El mismo portavoz señaló que los soviéticos no ocultaron su disgusto por el viaje del negociador norteamericano, debido a que la aceptación del Kremlin, según indicaron, podía llegar en cualquier momento.

Antecedentes

Los Estados Unidos y la Unión Soviética habían alcanzado un acuerdo en principio sobre el pacto desde hace varios meses, pero su presentación a la conferencia del desarme se mantuvo en suspenso debido primero a las disensiones manifestadas en el campo occidental y luego a la demora que tales disensiones ocasionaron en los rusos.

Círculos allegados a la conferencia afirmaron que la presentación formal del proyecto podría efectuarse durante la sesión del martes próximo.

En su estado actual, en realidad, el proyecto no impide inmediatamente que nuevas naciones adquieran armamento nuclear, pues su texto ha quedado incompleto al dejar en blanco el discutido artículo tercero, relacionado con las seguridades de su cumplimiento.

El control

Tanto los Estados Unidos como la Unión Soviética desean que la ejecución del pacto contra la proliferación nuclear sea controlada por el organismo de las Naciones Unidas para la energía atómica, cuyo asiento se halla en Viena.

Los países integrantes del Mercado Común Europeo, sin embargo, objetan ese tipo de control, arguyendo que afecta su soberanía y ofreciendo en cambio que la vigilancia sea efectuada por la comunidad europea de energía atómica (EURATOM), idea que Rusia rechaza por considerar que ello equivaldría a que los europeos se controlasen a sí mismos.

Las potencias neutrales no nucleares, en fin, exigen una compensación por su renuncia a esas armas, mediante algún sacrificio de las naciones nucleares, como por ejemplo algún indicio de que éstas no seguirán fabricándolas. El proyecto

(Continúa en la página 2, col. 7)

Tomóse equipo en Bolivia a los guerrilleros

Fue en recientes choques sostenidos con los insurgentes

La Paz, 11 (UP) — Las tropas bolivianas se apoderaron de abundante material bélico en los recientes choques con los guerrilleros en las cercanías de Ñancahuazú, al este del país, según informó el comando de las fuerzas armadas.

Un guerrillero fue muerto en un encuentro cerca del lugar llamado El Oso. El comando agregó que el ejército no tuvo ninguna baja en los choques que se prolongaron por espacio de una semana y que forman parte de la operación antiguerrillera Cynthia.

Derrotados los insurgentes, los soldados registraron la zona y encontraron un depósito de armas y otros materiales. La lista incluye lo siguiente.

Armas: ocho fusiles Garand, 30 fusiles Máuser, 18 metralletas, 23 carabinas, cuatro ametralladoras livianas, un mortero, 32 cargadores de metralletas, 10 lanzagranadas, 14 bayonetas, un calculador de distancia para mortero.

Munición: 4.511 tiros de fusil, 1.770 cartuchos para metralletas, 211 para ametralladora, 37 granadas para morteros, 30 granadas de fusil, 142 granadas de mano, 26 cartuchos de dinamita y tres rollos de alambre de púa.

Además fue tomado un importante equipo de ropas y otros enseres.

El anuncio no mencionó las marcas de las armas, excepto los Garand y Máuser, que forman parte del equipo militar boliviano.

Las fuentes militares declararon que esto constituye un duro golpe para los guerrilleros, que no tienen medios de reabastecerse de armas.

Las conversaciones del mariscal Tito y Nasser

Consideraron la situación actual en Levante y la "agresión" israelí

El Cairo, 11 (UP) — El presidente Gamal Abdel Nasser y su colega de Yugoslavia, Josip Broz (Tito) aplazaron esta noche la segunda etapa de sus conversaciones formales sobre la situación del Medio Oriente.

No se suministró explicación alguna por la decisión.

Anoche Tito había cancelado su cena informal con Nasser indicando que se hallaba "fatigado" por el viaje aéreo desde Belgrado hasta esta capital.

El presidente yugoslavo, quien tiene 75 años de edad, recibió últimamente instrucciones médicas para que restrinja sus actividades en razón de su edad y los efectos de los achaques que le afectaron hace casi un año.

Se tenía entendido que los dos mandatarios, sin embargo, reanudarían probablemente sus conversaciones a última hora de la noche, tras cenar juntos en la residencia suburbana de Nasser.

Un portavoz oficial informó que la primera etapa de conversaciones duró hoy dos horas y abarcó la situación actual del Medio Oriente, la "agresión" israelí y sus consecuencias, así como también la reunión de emergencia de las Naciones Unidas.

(Continúa en la página 3, col. 1)

(Radiotelefoto de United Press)

El presidente Tito, de Yugoslavia (izquierda), aparece junto al mandatario egipcio al iniciar ayer la primera de sus conversaciones formales, que se realizan en el palacio de Koubbeh, en El Cairo

EN OTRAS PAGINAS

INFORMACIONES:

	Págs.
El contralmirante (RE) Carlos Alberto Sánchez Sañudo habló ayer en el Instituto Popular de Conferencias	7
La Corte dispuso en un fallo que no procede indemnizar a quien es despedido por estar jubilado	13
Fueron dictadas nuevas normas acerca de ciertos trabajos insalubres	9
Celébrase hoy el 161er. aniversario de la Reconquista de Buenos Aires	8
Viaja hoy a Washington una misión para negociar sobre doble imposición	8
Rindióse homenaje a San Martín en el Museo Histórico Nacional	9
Inaugúrase hoy la 67ª Exposición Ganadera de Rosario	15
Renunciaron a sus cargos el jefe y subjefe de la policía de San Juan	4
Inauguráronse en Viedma, Río Negro, las Primeras Jornadas Patagónicas de Derecho Procesal	4
Son aplicadas desde ayer en Buenos Aires las medidas de racionalización administrativa	5
Reuniéronse en Corrientes gobernadores del nordeste	4
Las autoridades de Córdoba dieron un nuevo comunicado sobre el atentado cometido el jueves último	4

	Páginas		Páginas
Agropecuarias	25 y 27	Informe del interior	4 y 8
Artes plásticas	7	Instrucción pública	14
Bolsa y comercio	3, 15 y 27	Meteorológicas	12
Cartas a La Prensa	8	Navegación	14
Conferencias de hoy	7	Palabras cruzadas	12
Culto católico	14	Policía	[illegible]
Deportes	18 y 21	Radiotelefonía y TV	26 y 27
El día social	8	Servicio aéreo	14
Entidad. ciencia. y literar.	[illegible]	Teatros, mús. y cine	23 y 26
Farmacias de turno	14	Tribunales	13
Fechas históricas	20	Universitarias	12
Femeninas	[illegible]	Artes, ciencia,	14 a 24 y [illegible]
Hace 50 años	14	Turismo	[illegible]
Hipódromos	19, 21 y 23	Remates	25

COMENTARIOS EDITORIALES: (Pág. 8)

Sigue el aumento del costo de la vida: *Sigue en forma alarmante el aumento del costo de la vida, y lo más grave es que nada autoriza a pensar en una evolución favorable del proceso mientras no aparezcan soluciones capaces de contener la inflación.*

El exceso de requisitos en recibos de remuneraciones: *Ante el cúmulo de exigencias para preparar los recibos para los pagos de remuneraciones del personal, una entidad rosarina ha señalado con sobrada razón la necesidad de que se les devuelva a dichos documentos su finalidad específica, que ha quedado desvirtuada por una serie de exigencias ajenas a su propia naturaleza.*

Declaraciones de un dirigente negro: *Las incongruencias expresadas por un dirigente negro en la reunión de la OLAS son una muestra del nivel intelectual y moral de la misma. La mentira y la calumnia puestas al servicio de la tiranía y la subversión.*

standards and ideals than Ezequiel Paz. A kind of personal creed, which he wrote, was adopted in 1926 by the First Pan-American Congress of Journalists, and in October, 1950, was approved as the official creed of the Inter-American Press Association. It is felt that this creed, reflecting to a considerable degree some of the reasons for *La Prensa*'s success, should be quoted here:

> To inform with accuracy and truth; to omit nothing that the public has a right to know; always to use an impersonal and correct style without detriment to the gravity or to the force of critical thought; to reject rumors and such statements as "it is said" or "it is asserted" in order to affirm only that about which one holds a conviction supported by proofs and documents; to consider that the omission of a news article is preferable to its erroneous or unjustifiable publication; to take care that in reporting news the writer does not allow his personal viewpoint to slip in, because to do this constitutes commentary, and the reporter or chronicler should not invade the field reserved for other sections of the daily; to remember before writing how powerful an instrument of diffusion one has at one's disposal and to bear in mind that harm caused to an official or to a private individual by false imputation can never be entirely remedied by nobly conceded clarification or correction; to maintain a lofty calmness in polemics and not to make any statement which we might have to retract the next day; and finally, to inscribe in letters of gold in a prominent place, clearly visible about the work tables, the words of Walter Williams, distinguished North American newsman: "Nobody should write as a journalist what he cannot say as a gentleman."[27]

Ezequiel P. Paz retired in 1943 and was succeeded by Alberto Gainza Paz, the son of the founder's daughter, who took over the paper at a very tragic time in Argentine press history. A revolution was under way which set up a *de facto* government in the country, lasting until 1946. In that year a permanent government was established under the authoritarian President Juan Perón. Wishing to bring the press under his control as soon as possible, Perón lost no time in establishing a centralized office of information in charge of all official news, and in 1944 he issued a decree which limited the activities of the press and restricted the duties of newspapermen. Soon all journalists in the country had to register with the Government or be barred from journalism. Perón's regime also obtained the right to determine the salary and type of job for each Argentine newspaperman.[28]

Gradually the Government took over the distribution of newsprint and finally became the sole distributor. The number of pages in all newspapers was set by the Government. In spite of these measures *La Prensa* managed to thrive and to assert its traditional independence.

An independent newspaper was not what Perón wanted—especially not a journal with the wide popularity of *La Prensa*. All during these years, until 1951 when it finally fell into the hands of Perón, *La Prensa* suffered a constant campaign of abuse as did a few other antigovernment papers. Perón urged readers and advertisers to boycott the newspaper, and the building of *La Prensa* was attacked several times by armed crowds, the police always arriving too late to keep order.

Posters throughout Buenos Aires told of the paper's "unpatriotic nature" and expressed the Government's wish that it be ignored; loudspeakers from across the street from *La Prensa* blared forth daily insults; official Government newspapers poured abuse and lies on the newspaper; police would stop *La Prensa* delivery trucks, often several times in one block, to fine the drivers or caution them about some minor point. In 1947 *La Prensa* was asked to pay import duties on newsprint going back to 1939 on the grounds that much of this paper had been used for advertisements instead of information. Threatening telephone calls were made to the newspaper offices and Dr. Gainza Paz was arrested at one point without being told the charge. In November, 1950, the Government ordered circulation of all papers cut by 20 per cent. Then, in January, 1951, the final blow fell: the Union of News Vendors (Government-controlled) began putting pressure on *La Prensa* to eliminate its own circulation system and put this in the hands of the union. *La Prensa* could not accept this and other union demands.[29]

Violence flared, a *La Prensa* employee was shot and union men laid siege to *La Prensa*'s plant and employees were not allowed to work. The paper appealed for police protection, but police simply disregarded incidents of violence against *La Prensa*, and legal action was taken against the editors of the newspaper because of these "violent incidents." It was after this that Perón's Government took over the paper and turned it into another Perónista organ. A bill to expropriate *La Prensa* passed both chambers of the Congress easily. After the final "free" edition appeared (Jan. 26, 1951), a Government crew quickly put up large pictures of Juan and Eva Perón inside and outside the *La Prensa* building and prepared for a new day of Perónist publishing.

Dr. Alberto Gainza Paz and many members of the old staff slipped to safety outside Argentina. Between January 26, 1951 when *La Prensa's* free voice was silenced, and December 21, 1955 when the paper was restored to its old owners, it was published under the direction of the Perónista regime. This paper which before its captivity by Perón had circulated some 400,000 copies daily, sank to less than 200,000 under its Perónist management; and probably a third of this circulation was forced subscriptions to governmental offices.[30]

With news replacing the traditional classified advertising on the front page, *La Prensa* reappeared on February 3, 1956 under the direction of Alberto Gainza Paz. This February 3 issue of twenty-four pages appeared as number 29,476, ignoring the five years that had elapsed since Gainza Paz published number 29,475 in 1951. Dr. Gainza Paz immediately set about restoring the paper to its position of dignity and leadership in Argentina. He wrote the author recently that since he started publishing again his main concern has been "to publish the best paper possible."[31]

He went on to say:

> I knew that many young readers had come into the newspaper reading age while our paper was absent and that I could not rely only on prestige and the usually short memory of those who had suffered under the dictatorship. That is why I did my best to rebuild the paper keeping its standards of accurate and unbiased reporting, full coverage of news and strong and independent editorial policy. I feel we have succeeded.[32]

The bulk of the editorial staff is composed of old *La Prensa* employees who stayed loyal and never worked for the Perón publication, or of new men, many of whom had no previous journalistic experience. Today the writing and editing staff numbers about 250 in Buenos Aires and some 400 all through Argentina. The paper also has five full-time correspondents stationed in Montevideo, New York, Paris and Madrid, and, in addition, has many special writers in strategic cities of the world.[33] Perhaps its two best-known foreign correspondents are Manfred Schönfeld in London and José Antonio Mendía in Paris. The paper today gives good coverage to world affairs, often running as many as 30 columns of foreign news an issue.

A content analysis of leading Argentine dailies in 1964 by Paul Hoopes showed that *La Prensa* carried more foreign news than any other (except the English-language *Herald*), with *La Nación* running a close second. It also indicated that each of the dailies studied (*La Prensa*, *La Nación*, and *The Herald*) printed more foreign news during the three-month study period than did the average American newspaper in 1959 and 1961, ten Mexican dailies in 1962, and seven South American newspapers in 1959.[34] Hoopes also found from his study that *La Prensa* was "democratic in principle, internationally pegged and the front-runner among its contemporaries." It is interesting, also, that he found *La Nación* "nationalistic, Catholic and resentful of the reduced power position of Argentina in Latin America."[35]

The *La Prensa* of today, while still dignified, is livelier and brighter than before, and the style of writing is not quite as pedantic as that which marked the paper's pre-Perón era. It still specializes in foreign news and commentary and is known for its interpretive and thorough news stories. Its editorials are well-written and erudite, but one recent critic, Dr. Mary A. Gardner of Michigan State University, contends that the post-Perón *La Prensa* is not writing "the hard-hitting editorials on controversial political issues" which one expects of such a highly respected publication.[36]

The average issue of today's *La Prensa* runs twenty-eight pages, usually in two sections. The first section contains most of the foreign and domestic news and the editorial section. A wide assortment of news and features is found in the second section along with most of the advertising. In an analysis of the contents of *La Prensa* in 1964, Wayne Wolfe found that the paper devoted the most column inches to the following categories in this order: government-politics, economics, entertainment, accidents, sports, miscellaneous, social problems, culture, science and medicine, and human interest.[37]

La Prensa's pages have eight columns, and the makeup is essentially horizontal with frequent four-column headlines. There is usually at least one picture on the front page with illustrations used rather sparingly throughout the inside pages. The Sunday edition of *La Prensa* normally contains two feature or "essay" sections with high-quality pictures and superlative feature stories dealing with travel, history, science, art, and literature.

Although the newspaper has not re-established itself as the important national institution it was before 1951, it is making great strides in that direction. For example, the old public service organizations are again in operation. On one floor there is a free medical clinic where anyone, not only subscribers, can receive treatment of almost any type. In 1962, twenty-two doctors treated close to 10,000 persons each month.[38]

On another floor the public library, containing nearly 50,000 volumes on law and medicine, gets almost constant use from 2:30 to 11:30 P.M. each weekday. Nearby is a team of attorneys giving free legal advice during five periods a week. Lectures, sponsored by the newspaper, are held in a 200-seat lecture hall on a higher floor.

The news and advertising departments of *La Prensa* are in the beautiful old building on the Plaza de Mayo, almost directly across from the *Casa Rosada*, the Argentine White House. The mechanical department is in a recently modernized and expanded plant about a half-mile distant, and the two buildings are connected by pneumatic tubes. A very efficient operation in its entirety, the smoothly coordinated plant is largely due to Máximo Gainza, the son of Dr. Gainza Paz and the manager of *La Prensa*.

In step with modern technology and with great respect for its revered old traditions, *La Prensa* is going quietly forward, slowly and with dignity resurrecting its old image. Its daily circulation is approaching 280,000 and its Sunday circulation is right at 350,000. Perhaps it is not as prestigious as it was in the golden days of Ezequiel Paz, but it is still able to take immense pride in the fact that it has held to the ideals of its founder and has never ceased in its attempt to provide the most intelligent and serious journalism possible for its loyal readers everywhere.

17

The Times: Los Angeles and New York

The two newspapers whose profiles appear on the following pages will probably be considered by many readers to be strange companions for a single chapter. Quite possibly some readers will be unprepared or unwilling to even accept the idea of the *Los Angeles Times* having a place in a book on elite newspapers. And, why, others may ask, is the Los Angeles daily treated first in the chapter?

A word of explanation, therefore, is in order. Those who shudder at the thought of the *Los Angeles Times* being among the elite newspapers simply add credence to the old saying that a poor reputation dies hard. They are remembering the old L.A. *Times*, a paper more interested in a narrow Republicanism and conservatism and in the size of the annual profit than in quality, pluralistic journalism. They have not read the paper since about 1960, so they do not know of the tremendous strides the West Coast paper has made in all departments, nor do they know of the mammoth effort and great expenditures by the paper to build up a superior writing and editing staff. If they have seen the "new" *Times*, they will not find it surprising that it should rank among the elite.

As to why it is included in this chapter with the aristocrat of the American press, *The New York Times*, the reason lies chiefly in an arbitrary decision by the author. If there is a paper on the West Coast which comes closest to being like *The New York Times*, it is the *Times* of Los Angeles. It is the West Coast's biggest and wealthiest daily; it is the most thorough; it has the largest and best-paid staff, and it is certainly the fastest improving. In the author's opinion, it ranks among the three or four best dailies in the United States.

And, finally, for those who may wonder why it is taken up before *The New York Times,* the answer is simple: Alphabetically, it comes first.

Few readers would challenge the right of *The New York Times* to be among the world's elite dailies. Probably most critics (at least in the United States) would name it first. Its reputation is very good. In fact, its reputation throughout the world probably exceeds reality as much as the *Los Angeles Times'* reputation falls short of reality. Good reputations, once established, are as difficult to change as are bad ones. This is not to imply that *The New York Times* is no longer worthy of its fine reputation; on the contrary, the newspaper is without a doubt better than it has ever been. It is simply to say that the general public is as prone to continue thinking a newspaper great, without reading it, as it is to think a newspaper poor or mediocre without reading it.

The New York Times is a great newspaper. There is little doubt about that, regardless of what criteria of evaluation one may use. Its reputation matches its performance.

The *Los Angeles Times* is also a great newspaper. After studying it carefully, the author has no qualms about treating it here, or, even in lumping it in the same chapter with *The New York Times.*

Both newspapers are improving, the *Los Angeles Times* probably more rapidly and noticeably. *The New York Times* just rolls along like the Mississippi River, slow and easy, while its Los Angeles counterpart is rushing forward with typical Western energy and verve. Both dailies are published in vigorous metropolitan centers and there is every reason to believe that they will continue to grow and improve.

Los Angeles Times

As every journalist knows full well, an image or stereotype is hard to shake from the public mind. Newspapers themselves are not immune from this human tendency to project a certain "image." The *Los Angeles Times* for about the first eighty years built up and perpetuated an image of stodgy conservatism. It was a paper which generally was not considered progressive or even very fair in its editorial positions. Otis Chandler, today's publisher, would not even deny this, although he might not put it quite so bluntly.

Chandler recalls: "We tended to be very conservative, and we used to bias the news—we didn't print both sides of labor-management disputes, we wouldn't print much Democratic news, we were narrow in our religious coverage. . . ."[1]

Chandler became publisher in 1960 at the age of thirty-three and since then the *Times* has experienced what is perhaps the most notable metamorphosis in American newspaper history. Times were changing swiftly in 1960 and fortunately Chandler saw what must be done. He did it and the *Times* began to dissipate its old image. By 1964, the West Coast newspaper, which had always been thought of as a good example of provincial journalism, had won a citation from journalism educators for enhancing "public understanding of great national and international issues by providing thoughtful, searching background articles by respected, competent Washington and foreign correspondents."[2]

In 1967, the *Times'* daily circulation had risen from about 525,000 (in 1960) to 850,000 and its Sunday circulation from some 900,000 to about 1,200,000. It was the third largest in the United States every weekday (from fourteenth largest in 1956), following the *New York News* and the *Chicago Tribune*. On Sunday it ranked fourth after the *New York Daily News*, *The New York Times*, and the *Chicago Tribune*.[3]

The great growth in quality, as well as in circulation, is due largely to Otis Chandler and to his chief editor, Nick B. Williams. Emphasis now is squarely on the writing and editing staff, and the overall improvement in all editorial departments probably cannot be matched in American journalism history. Chandler has seen to it that news coverage, both domestic and foreign, qualitatively and quantitatively, is emphasized, and has gone a long way in demolishing the paper's traditional image as a spokesman for ultraconservatism.

The *Times'* Washington bureau has jumped from three men in 1963 to at least a dozen today. As late as 1962, the paper had only a single foreign correspondent. Today it has fourteen foreign bureaus, and domestic coverage is excellent, with major bureaus in Atlanta, Chicago, New York, Houston, San Francisco, and Sacramento.[4] In 1962 the *Times* and the *Washington Post* announced that they had reached an agreement "to exchange Washington, foreign, and regional interpretive news."[5] This service has greatly improved the serious coverage of the *Times*.

Most observers agree that the *Times* is now an excellent newspaper and one which continues to improve faster than most other elite dailies. The *Times* is still Republican, but it is not nearly so dogmatic in its conservatism as it was before 1960. Although it supported Barry Goldwater with reservations in the 1964 Presidential election, it had given its support to liberal Republican Nelson Rockefeller in the primary election. The paper was careful to note that it opposed Goldwater's stand "on the civil rights law, the nuclear test ban agreement, the sale of U.S. grain to Russia, and the control of tactical nuclear weapons by NATO field commanders."[6]

The *Economist* of London, which had through the years harshly criticized the *Times* for its conservatism, in 1965 called it "by all odds the best California newspaper—most complete, and soundest in news judgment and honest in presentation."[7] The *Economist* added: "It has built up a good staff, gives its specialists more space than any other western paper and covers what it writes about in depth." As the London magazine saw it, this was quite surprising because "a few years back it was a shoddy sheet of extreme right-wing viewpoint and with a Hollywood divorce focus for its news measurement."[8]

After the *Times* had won a Pulitzer Prize for its coverage of the Watts riots in the summer of 1965, even the ultraliberal *Frontier* magazine of Los Angeles (now consolidated with *The Nation*) had some kind words for the daily, noting the "sharply improved quality of reporting" and the fact that "news coverage, local, national and international, has been vastly increased under an editorial budget that has doubled to $8 million in the past six years."[9]

Nick Williams, the *Times* editor who, with Otis Chandler's approval, directed the paper's bid for editorial excellence, has said that he used a three-point guideline for bringing the paper from provincialism to its present quality status: (1) upgrading staff whenever possible when staffers left for other jobs or retired, (2) seeking better editorial personnel—"the men or women we wanted for particular spots, even though the better staffers cost substantially more money," and (3) adding new and better talent for jobs which were not yet open or for which there was no vacancy.[10]

According to Williams, the *Times* seeks "to be a serious, opinion-leading newspaper by daily addressing itself to the issues facing Los Angeles, California, the U.S. and the world."[11] These issues are discussed by an editorial board comprised of the publisher, editor, managing editor, the editorial writing staff, and representatives from the political, financial, foreign and national staffs. Here is a sounding board from which emerge the *Times'* editorials.[12]

As to the paper's impact on public opinion, Ted Weegar, the assistant managing editor, gave the following example in the summer of 1966:

> Following the Watts riots of August, 1965, the *Times* said editorially on numerous occasions that solutions to the race problem lay in the area of increased contacts with the city officials and the Negro community, and vigorous implementation of the poverty program. The *Times'* position was not warmly received. The mayor and the chief of police were not in accord with our stand. But the paper steadfastly stuck to its viewpoint and stuck to it pretty much alone. Indeed, the newspaper found itself the only voice in the community at a time when the city desperately needed to hear from all its elements. Now, however, a year hence, other opinions are ar-

> riving at the editorial stand we took then. There has been some progress in race relations, and the road ahead is a long one, but the way was blazed by the *Times*.[13]

The *Times'* improvement in foreign coverage has been almost unbelievable. Within two years after Otis Chandler took over the publisher's chair from his father the paper was well on its way to becoming one of the very few internationally significant dailies in the United States. In addition to strengthening the Paris bureau in 1962, the *Times* created in Tokyo a Far Eastern bureau, in Rio de Janeiro a Latin American bureau, a bureau in Mexico City, another in Hong Kong, and a United Nations bureau in New York. In 1963 other bureaus were established in London, Vienna, Bonn, and Rome. The next year another bureau was opened in Moscow, and still another in Saigon. In 1966 bureaus were begun in Bangkok, Buenos Aires, and New Delhi. Other bureaus were planned to open in 1968.[14]

The foreign correspondent for the *Los Angeles Times*, like many of his counterparts on the best European dailies, is not bound by deadlines, nor is he under pressure to file every day. Reminiscent of correspondents for the *Neue Zürcher Zeitung*, he digs in depth and takes his time providing interpretation for events. He is interested in the "why" as much as the "what" of the story.[15]

There is evidence that the *Times*, probably more than any other United States paper, seeks experts for its foreign bureaus and men who will be permitted to stay in one area long enough to obtain the most valid picture possible. One observer has commented that being a correspondent for the *Times* "is the closest one can come to a career service" in journalism since the days when a London *Times* correspondent enjoyed such a status. Highlighting the fantastic job the *Times* has done in improving its foreign coverage, this observer adds: "When one considers that it costs the *Times* an estimated $50,000 to establish a bureau and to maintain it (double the cost for Vietnam) it indicates that the *Los Angeles Times* has lost its parochial outlook (if it ever had it) and is dedicated to the enormous task of providing its readers a truly world-wide view."[16]

Many persons have contended that the *Times'* expansion and general improvement was forced by *The New York Times'* attempt to establish a West Coast edition in 1962. Otis Chandler denies this and says that his paper began its major editorial overhaul in 1959. "The entire program was under way long before '*The New York Times*' decided to test the temperature out West," he said in 1964. "Let me at last put this argument to rest by stating that our program was more than 75 per cent completed prior to their first announcement of their intention to start their Western Edition."[17]

The *Los Angeles Times* today is a big paper, often running more than two hundred pages in its weekday editions. It consumes more newsprint than any other American daily, and accounts for at least 20 per cent of all newsprint used in the eleven Western states.[18] The *Times* contains a number of outstanding editorial features, including suburban sections which compete well with new papers springing up around the city, a comprehensive business and finance section, a complete separate Sunday opinion section with interpretive features of a serious nature, a daily editorial section offering viewpoints from a wide range of the political spectrum, a tabloid-size magazine (*Calendar*) which focuses on drama, art and literature, and a new (begun 1966) rotogravure magazine (*West Magazine*) in the Sunday *Times*.

In 1966 the *Times* instituted two significant changes. It converted its rather stodgy eight-column pages to a modern, six-column format, with column rules eliminated. On page 2 the paper began a full-page news summary, providing readers with a concise and comprehensive roundup of the major news developments in all the principal news areas. The *Times* carries special background or interpretative articles which in general quality rank with the world's best journalism. Typical of such "series" articles was a group in 1966 by John Randolph called "South Koreans in Vietnam"; in 1964 a series on "The Press and the Courts" by Gene Blake; "Are We Losing Our Mobility?" by Ray Herbert (1965); "The View from Watts" by Jack Jones (1965); "Southern California A.D. 2000" by Sterling Slappey (1966), and "The Okinawa Occupation" by Arthur J. Dommen (1966).

The "Opinion" section, appearing in the Sunday edition, is one of the best such departments in world journalism. Usually a twelve-page section, it gives the serious reader a wealth of interpretation, background, and opinion on local, national, and world issues. Representative of the thoughtful and informative "depth" pieces in the section are these four which appeared in 1966: D. J. R. Bruckner's "The Mob—a Common Aim and a Common Soul," giving insights to various mobs and the response of the police to them; Bob Jackson's "Easy Gun Purchases Linked to Constitution," discussing a growing problem; Martin Bernheimer's "Music Depreciation in Our Public Schools," a description of a de-emphasis of "cultural" subjects in Los Angeles schools; and Robert S. Elegant's "The Essence of China's New Revolution" which describes the goal of Peking's leaders.

Blandly stereotyped articles from the wire services have been disappearing rapidly from the *Times*, replaced by exclusive stories from the paper's growing network of correspondents and its specialized in-depth reporters. The *Times*' own editorials, under the direction of veteran *Times*-man James Bassett, steer a moderate course. They usually oppose extremist candidates and take a responsible, or at least unemotional, position on the big issues of the day. Says Otis Chandler: "We cannot afford to be merely an organ of Republican thinking."[19] Some of the

Los Angeles Times

LARGEST CIRCULATION IN THE WEST, 861,350 DAILY, 1,212,983 SUNDAY

VOL. LXXXVI † SEVEN PARTS—PART ONE CC WEDNESDAY MORNING, NOVEMBER 1, 1967 114 PAGES

DAILY 10c

BEFORE PARLIAMENT—Queen Elizabeth II is helped by husband, Prince Philip, from the throne in the House of Lords after the opening of Parliament. She wears the imperial state crown. Flanking couple are children, Prince Charles, 18, and Princess Anne, 17, at far right.
UPI Wirephoto

Two Major Blazes Reported Curbed

Dying Winds and Rising Humidity Aid Fire Battle

BY JERRY COHEN
Times Staff Writer

Dying winds and rising humidity aided fatigued fire fighters late Tuesday in containing two of Southern California's disastrous brush fires.

Ringed were the blazes in Orange County and near Malibu.

In San Diego County, where three fires still burned out of control, the community of Poway was reported out of danger.

But two new brush fires sprang up briefly in Los Angeles County.

One began about 1:35 p.m. in Soledad Canyon 15 miles north of Newhall and crews cleaning up Malibu hotspots were sent there.

The other flared up nearly an hour and a half later in Bootlegger Canyon north of Soledad and resulted in at least one death.

Unidentified Body Found

Fire crews reported finding two charred automobiles and one body in the Bootlegger Canyon blaze and authorities fear there may be more dead. The unidentified body was found in one car, a Jeep, and both vehicles were parked near a burned-out shack.

Both new fires burned only a small amount of acreage and were contained by nightfall.

Earlier, a fire fighter died battling the blaze in Riverside County's San Jacinto Valley, the second death there since flames broke out Sunday.

A brief flareup in the northeastern section of Latigo Canyon caused concern for a time among the 750 men on Malibu fire lines, but it was quickly doused.

Although arsonists were suspected in several of the blazes, cause of the Malibu fire was ruled accidental. County Fire Capt. Lee Forman said a new high tension line being strung by work crews suddenly snapped and, while the wire was not charged, the metal strands sparked on a rock and set off the blaze.

The Malibu fire, which resulted in

Please Turn to Page 21, Col. 1

MERCURY SOARS INTO 90'S; OCEAN AIR TO COOL AREA

BY LEONARD GREENWOOD
Times Staff Writer

Temperatures soared into the 90s Tuesday in many parts of Southern California as low humidity from a diminishing Santa Ana prolonged the fire hazard.

But the Santa Ana will end today, cold air will start coming inland from the sea, humidity will rise, and by weekend, there is a good chance of showers all along California's coastal belt, forecasters said.

Palm Springs' temperature hit 97 degrees Tuesday, and it was 93 at Pasadena, San Gabriel and Santa Ana. Burbank and Torrance had 92, and in central Los Angeles it was 90.

As the Santa Ana continued to weaken, humidity rose slightly to between 10 and 20%, after unusually low readings of 1 or 2% Monday.

Warm weather will continue today. Most parts of the Southland can expect the same temperatures as Tuesday, and in the desert, readings may be 2 to 3 degrees higher,

Please Turn to Page 26, Col. 1

Parliament Told of Labor Plan for Curb on House of Lords

BY ROBERT C. TOTH
Times Staff Writer

LONDON — The Labor government, speaking through Queen Elizabeth, announced plans Tuesday for radical reform of the British House of Lords, oldest, largest and perhaps most anachronistic body of its kind in the world.

"Legislation will be introduced," she said in the government-written speech at the opening of Parliament, "to reduce the powers of the House of Lords and to eliminate its present hereditary basis—thereby enabling it to develop within the framework of a modern parliamentary system."

Silence greeted the announcement as the queen addressed the jointly assembled lords and members of the House of Commons in the ornate Victorian chamber of the House of Lords.

Heath Attacks Reform Proposal

Later, Conservative leader Edward Heath attacked the proposed reform in Commons as a "sop to the left wing" of the Labor Party and a "diversion" from the high unemployment and other economic ills facing the government.

Prime Minister Harold Wilson, expanding on the queen's words slightly, said his government hopes to get cooperation on the reform from the opposition parties, but if not, it would push through the changes within a year.

Indications are that the number of lords sitting in the House will be slashed from the current 1,045, less than 200 of whom regularly attend, to about 300.

The most important remaining power of the Lords, which has been whittled away progressively since they were first summoned by Edward I in 1295, is to delay passage of a bill by one year. Wilson wants this cut to six months, sources said, to reduce the chance of important

Please Turn to Page 16, Col. 1

Humphrey Narrowly Escapes Mortar Attack by Viet Cong

Shells Explode in Saigon Palace Grounds Just After Vice President Arrives at Reception Given by Thieu

BY WILLIAM TUOHY
Times Staff Writer

SAIGON—A high-level diplomatic reception given by newly inaugurated President Nguyen Van Thieu at Independence Palace Tuesday night was interrupted by a Viet Cong mortar attack on the palace grounds.

The attack occurred just after Vice President Humphrey had entered the brightly lighted national executive building.

The attack apparently was designed to coincide with the Vice President's arrival.

On hand in the huge reception room of the palace when the mortar rounds exploded with sharp concussions were President Thieu, Vice President Nguyen Cao Ky and most emissaries from the 23 nations who sent delegates to the presidential inauguration Tuesday morning.

Although the windows shook, the band played on and the reception and a later dinner went off as scheduled.

Three Rounds Hit Grounds

As the guests maintained an attitude of composure, at least three 60-mm. mortar rounds landed in the palace grounds, the closest about 50 yards from the main building.

One shell hit about 10 yards from the car of Rear Adm. Kenneth L. Veth, commander of U.S. naval forces in Vietnam. The shell hit in the soft, wet earth.

Steel fragments flew, slightly wounding the admiral's driver and damaging the car.

The wounded driver was taken to the hospital, blood staining his uniform. Adm. Veth had already entered the palace.

Another shell hit about 25 yards away. Fragments ruptured the gas tank of the car of Maj. Gen. Douglas Vincent, military commander of Australian forces in Vietnam.

Gen. Vincent was also in the palace, but his driver, Cpl. Juan Cruz, saw the shell explode. "I only

Please Turn to Page 18, Col. 1

Israel Will Bolster Navy Soon to Meet Egyptian Challenge

BY DAVID LARSEN
Times Staff Writer

TEL AVIV—The Israeli navy will soon be bolstered by the addition of new vessels, it was learned Tuesday.

Sources described the new craft as a type of ship which will be able to provide the answer to anything Egypt has on the seas.

A number of the new vessels are scheduled to be delivered soon. The ships are being built in another country in conformity to Israel's needs.

The ships, it is said, will be as much a threat to Egyptian shipping as Egypt's missile boats are to Israel.

Security regulations do not permit a full discussion of this addition to the Israeli arsenal, but it is apparently what the commander of the navy was referring to when he addressed a class of graduates at the naval college in Acre.

Extensive Reinforcements

On that occasion, just nine days before the sinking of the destroyer Elath, Brig. Gen. Shlomo Erel said the navy would shortly be "very extensively reinforced" to enable it to safeguard the country's shore more efficiently.

The new ships will not be equipped with missiles of the type which sank the Elath. For one thing, such hardware is not available from any Western arsenal, as far as is known.

Even so, it was pointed out, should Egypt be planning to use its missile boats with any regularity in the future, Israel would not want to counter with missile vessels of its own.

The oversized torpedo boats which launched the four rockets from Port Said are small, fast and are bad

Please Turn to Page 12, Col. 3

Jordan Deal to Buy 36 Starfighter Jets From U.S. Shelved

BY TOM LAMBERT
Times Staff Writer

WASHINGTON — The United States and Jordan have decided to set aside an agreement under which the Arab nation was to have bought 36 F-104 jet Starfighters from this country, it was learned Tuesday.

"The F-104 deal is dead," an informed source said.

The decision to shelve the transaction, agreed upon last year, reportedly stemmed from a recent American-Jordanian conclusion that Jordan could neither buy, fly nor maintain the supersonic F-104s.

Instead, Jordan's King Hussein reportedly hopes to try to obtain enough British-made Hawker Hunter subsonic jet fighters to replace the 26 in his air force which were wiped out in last June's Arab-Israeli war. Hussein already has acquired about 10 Hunters.

The Soviet Union reportedly has offered Hussein up to 50 MIG fighters, (type unknown). But he is said to be reluctant to turn to Moscow for warplanes if he can obtain them in the West.

Refuses Soviet Weapons

Unlike other Arab nations such as the United Arab Republic, Syria, Iraq and Algeria, Jordan has refused Soviet arms offers in the past and has obtained its military equipment from Western countries.

Because of that policy, plus Hussein's generally pro-Western attitudes and his relative moderation since the Arab-Israeli war, some U. S. officials were distressed when Jordan was omitted last week from a list of six Middle Eeastern nations named to receive "selected items" of American military aid.

Jordan's omission reportedly resulted from resentment by some senators over Jordan's participation in the Arab-Israeli war.

Israel, Libya and Morocco were named last week to receive American warplanes—48, 10 and 6 respectively. Those nations plus Saudi Arabia, Lebanon and Tunisia also will receive other American military equipment. The planes and other items had been ordered here before the Arab-Israeli war but were held

Please Turn to Page 12, Col. 1

FIRE LINE BUCKET BRIGADE

Malibu Residents Swing Wet Sacks, Rugs to Save Homes

BY CHARLES HILLINGER
Times Staff Writer

Gunny sacks and old rugs soaked in water saved a dozen homes from fire in the Malibu area, residents said Tuesday.

"We've been through this several times before. We knew what to do. We got the gunny sacks and old rugs ready," said Mrs. Julia Gaylord of 29057 Pacific Coast Highway.

Her house in the Zuma Mesa Estates area near Point Dume is a half mile from the highway.

Mrs. Gaylord said when the fire moved toward the homes Monday she and other women in the community went into action.

"We could have run for our cars, driven away and let our homes burn to the ground, but we stayed and fought it.

"We poured water in buckets, pails, pots, pans—in anything we could find. Then we ringed our homes with the containers of water waiting for sparks to fly on our property."

As embers showered the area, the residents used the sopping sacks and rugs to beat out small fires around homes and on roofs.

It was impossible to save two of them—the $70,000 residence of the Anthony Sanchez family at 6300 S. Zuma Mesa Drive, and the $50,000 home of the John C. McKeown family at 29053 Pacific Coast Highway.

But the destruction would have been much greater if it hadn't been for the gunny sacks and old rugs.

Mrs. Ruth Dunning of 29055 Pacific Coast Highway credited two 18-year-old boys, Jeff Long and Dick Zeider, with saving her expensive home.

The boys stood off the fire that

Please Turn to Page 24, Col. 3

UAW Threatens Local Strikes if GM Tries to Build Stockpile

DETROIT (AP)—A top United Auto Workers official said Tuesday the union will permit strikes at some General Motors plants if the auto maker prepares for a possible companywide walkout by scheduling too much overtime.

UAW Vice President Leonard Woodcock told newsmen he advised the company of the union's plans at a contract bargaining meeting requested by the UAW. It was the first meeting of union and company negotiators at the main table since Sept. 19.

Woodcock, who heads the UAW's GM department, said the corporation would be informed when such a local strike would start and when it would be over. Such a walkout, he said, would be proportionate to the length of overtime worked.

He said the union has evidence that GM stepped up its assembly schedule after an agreement was reached with Ford Motor Co. He said 21 of GM's 23 auto assembly plants worked overtime Saturday.

A UAW source said the union fears that GM could be planning to stockpile a huge backlog of 1968 cars so it could ride out a lengthy shutdown if there is a strike.

General Motors has the right to have employes work overtime, Woodcock said, "but when one day of work now can mean two days of loss in a strike imposed by the

Please Turn to Page 11, Col. 1

FEATURE INDEX

STATE SEEKING SMOG AMENDMENT SUPPORT

Exclusive to The Times from a Staff Writer

WASHINGTON—The California congressional delegation was busy Tuesday rounding up support in the House for restoration of an amendment to an air pollution bill that would permit California to set auto emission standards without federal approval.

House debate on the bill, originally scheduled for today, was delayed until Thursday.

Details and a photograph of Los Angeles during a smog siege that was displayed on the House floor appear on Page 1, Part 2.

CALLS ROCKEFELLER, ROMNEY IDIOTS

GOP Official May Campaign for Wallace

BY JACK NELSON
Times Staff Writer

SACRAMENTO—George C. Wallace's third-party presidential pitch got a restrained reception from Sacramento's prestigious Comstock Club Tuesday. But there were sparks of enthusiasm, including a Republican Party official's declaration that he might campaign for the former Alabama governor.

The club of business, professional and government leaders was polite but generally cool as Wallace delivered his stock speech. He drew scattered applause for attacking liberals, federal bureaucracy and peace demonstrators and for advocating states rights and stronger support for police and private property rights. About half the crowd of 800 stood and gave him a brief ovation at the end.

Later at a night rally at the El Dorado Hotel here, an overflow crowd of more than 2,000 applauded the same speech.

One Comstock club member, John L. Milliken, an auto dealer and member of the County Republican Committee and the GOP State Central Committee, called Wallace "one of the great Americans" and said:

"If the Republicans nominate an idiot like Rockefeller or Romney, I'll definitely resign from the committees and campaign for Wallace."

Milliken declared that he knows other Republican officials who feel the same way.

"I'm local chairman of the United Republicans of California, the strongest conservative Republican organization in the state," he said, "and we all feel that way."

Although the great majority of about 30 club members interviewed by newsmen said they would not vote for Wallace under any circumstances, many expressed admiration for him and several said they had an open mind about whether they would vote for him.

One club member who did not attend Tuesday's session, Gov. Reagan, told a Capitol press conference he thought Wallace could get the required 66,059 new party registrations to qualify him on the ballot as the American Independent Party's

Please Turn to Page 10, Col. 1

THE WEATHER

Fair today and Thursday. Winds light and variable in mornings and nights, becoming westerly 10 to 15 m.p.h. in afternoons. Light smog. High today, 86. Low Thursday, 53. High Thursday, 82; low, 53. High Tuesday, 90; low, 60.

Complete weather information on Page 22, Part 1.

sanest and most moderate editorials to appear during the violent riot-ridden summer of 1967 appeared in the *Los Angeles Times*.

In addition to its own wide range of columns and editorials, the *Times* gives the reader in its three-page editorial section a potpourri of syndicated columns. Publisher Chandler tries to maintain a political balance, dividing his columnists into three main classes: liberal, moderate, and conservative. Among the liberals are such writers as Walter Lippmann, Robert Hutchins, and Drew Pearson; among the moderates are Roscoe Drummond, Stewart Alsop, and Max Freedman; and among the conservatives are Russell Kirk, Barry Goldwater, and William Buckley, Jr. Otis Chandler knows it is always difficult to categorize a newspaper ideologically; he admits the paper is Republican-moderate, but insists that it can only be described as "independent" politically.[20]

The *Times* and its staff members have won many awards through the years; most important are five Pulitzer Prizes, including two for public service. Latest of these, for local reporting, was awarded in May, 1966, for coverage of the riots in Watts. There is little doubt that with the excellent journalistic talent which the paper is collecting, it will receive an increasing number of honors.

How did this newspaper evolve to its present position of prestige and respect? Actually, the *Times* has always, ever since its founding in December, 1881, been an important institution in Southern California and has played an important part in the development of the city and the area. The founder and first publisher was General Harrison Gray Otis.[21] When Otis died in 1917, his son-in-law, Harry Chandler, became publisher. In 1922 the *Times* opened the first newspaper-owned radio station, and six years later became the first newspaper to make use of airplanes for newspaper delivery. The present five-story Times Building was built in 1935. The paper won its first Pulitzer Prize "for disinterested and meritorious public service" in 1941.

Norman Chandler, who had gradually been assuming his father's responsibilities, became publisher upon Harry Chandler's death in 1944. Under the new publisher's direction, the *Times* developed a more balanced physical expansion, became a leading force in Southern California's cultural development. In 1959 Norman Chandler began the present phase in the development of the Times-Mirror Company—a program of planned diversification in the fields of printing, publishing, education, and the graphic arts. Relinquishing direction of the *Times* itself in 1960 to devote his full time to the Times-Mirror Company as president and board chairman, Norman Chandler passed the title of publisher to his son, Otis.

It has mainly been under Otis Chandler, since 1960, that the *Times* has witnessed its greatest change. A new long-range program of improvement in all departments has been instituted which has resulted in new sections for the paper, expansion and improvement of the staff, opening of some twenty new domestic and foreign news bureaus, and the founding of the *Los Angeles Times-Washington Post* News Service.

Today the *Times* is published from a three-building complex in Times Mirror Square in the Los Angeles Civic Center. Covering an entire city block, the modern facilities cost some 63 million dollars. The paper's composing room has 84 typesetting machines, and electronic data processing equipment is used for much of its typesetting work. The 96 press units have an hourly capacity of up to 540,000 copies of a 64-page paper. Special color presses print the full-color Sunday comics and other special color material.[22]

Although the paper quite evidently has shifted from a rather firm conservative position to a moderate one, many of its stands still reflect conservative orientation. For instance, the paper generally supports President Johnson's position in Vietnam, and on the matter of admitting Red China to the United Nations it has advocated finding ways for China to start a dialogue with the outside world, but has not suggested United Nations membership. Nor has it advocated United States recognition of Red China, although it constantly supports the start of meaningful conversation.[23]

The *Times* bases its overall editorial policies on two major premises:

1. The maintenance of the concept of individual liberty through watchful vigilance at home and abroad.
2. The preservation, as an essential to the concept of individual liberty, of the free enterprise system in the United States and wherever else, and to the extent that, the wishes of other peoples permit it.[24]

This basic platform of the *Times* has always been its guiding editorial principle. Under successive publishers and editors it has been modified somewhat, but it has persisted as the foundation for the paper's policy. Although the shift has been toward more moderate positions, many of them well into the liberal camp, the *Times* stands firmly by its two major premises.

Whatever may be thought of the *Times* or its publishers from the paper's beginning, it must be said that the journal has been the primary interest of a family of considerable vision, who for four generations have firmly believed in the future of Southern California and have dedicated their newspaper to the enlightenment of the populace. With this vision the paper has been economically successful; in turn, its management has seen fit to substantially return its profit into broad improvement of the product.

The *Los Angeles Times*, in addition, has had wise editorial guidance which understands that a newspaper is in the public domain and is blessed with constitutional guarantees of freedom which in turn carry heavy responsibilities. This responsibility has been assumed and discharged without question. The *Times* is not standing still; it is improving in every way, always reaching for a firmer hold on journalistic quality. Although its "new image" and reputation is still not firmly entrenched in the United States, much less throughout the world, the paper deserves and has received a place among elite newspapers.

The New York Times

In the midst of a rather unfashionable and run-down corner of New York City, at 229 West 43rd Street, is found the graceless grimy-faced fourteen-story building that houses *The New York Times*, a paper that is solidly "in" the world's elite press and has been for a long time. This is a proud, almost arrogant, newspaper whose daily circulation of over 900,000 goes to a special leadership audience around the world.

With the exception of *The Wall Street Journal* or *The Christian Science Monitor, The New York Times* is the nearest thing in the United States to a national newspaper.[25] In spite of the fact that its attempted Western regional edition failed in late 1963, *The Times* manages to have readers in every state and in nearly 85 per cent of all counties of the fifty states. The failure of the West Coast edition perhaps showed that no United States paper can circulate nationally as in Japan or Britain because most advertising is local and out-of-town circulation does not seem to attract advertisers. Even so, *The Times* does circulate limited numbers of copies throughout the country. Its Sunday edition, especially, with a circulation of about 1.5 million, has wide national (and international) readership with at least one-third of the Sunday copies going outside New York City. The Sunday paper's circulation is constantly growing in spite of a late 1967 per-copy price increase from 50 to 60 cents beyond the metropolitan area.[26]

In late 1967 *The New York Times* was planning an afternoon edition, having already established itself more firmly in Europe by cooperating with *The Washington Post* in publishing the old and respected *Herald Tribune* edition in Paris. One can always expect to find a copy of *The Times* in leading libraries and governmental offices throughout the world. It is not only a national organ in one sense, but goes a long way —as do most elite newspapers published in a major language—toward being an international newspaper.

The New York Times, certainly the biggest in total operations of United States papers and one of the three largest in circulation, sits serenely in the primary spot of American daily journalism. Not everybody likes it, but nobody can ignore it. It leads all papers of the world in its widespread collection and publication of news and views. It averages sixty-two pages daily, and more than one and a half million words flow into its New York offices every day from fifteen news services, some two hundred foreign correspondents (about a fourth of them full-time), and hundreds of writers throughout the United States.

It is best known as a "newspaper of record" and, while most commentators speak of its quantity, there is no doubt but that the general quality of its journalism ranks with the best of the world. It is not as careful in its typography as dailies such as *Pravda*, not as unpretentiously interesting in its prose as *The Times* of London, not as tediously tnorough in certain stories or as well-documented as *Le Monde*, and not as scholarly and serious as Switzerland's *Neue Zürcher Zeitung* or West Germany's *Frankfurter Allgemeine*, but it goes further in combining the worthy characteristics of all these great papers than any other single daily in the world.

Most anything any reader might want in a newspaper, with the exception of journalistic froth, can be found in *The Times*. As critic Dwight Macdonald has written in *Esquire*, it is only when one who is accustomed to the paper must do without it for some time that he "begins to appreciate the feast it provides."[27] The great bulk of material printed and the complexity of the huge operation often results in hasty editing and inadequate proofreading, especially in the early editions which go to nearly 12,000 American towns. One example of this can be noted in a May 10, 1966 edition, where on the same page (50 C) the identical story appeared twice but under different heads. One head read "Cesar Leon Makes Debut as Guitarist"; the other read "Cesar Leon Makes Guitar Solo Debut." Giving additional emphasis to this tautology was the fact that the stories appeared in adjacent columns, side by side. But things seem to settle down in the final editions of *The Times* and the final product reflects the overall quality of the newspaper.

The Times' international reporting has always been considered one of its strongest areas. Adolph Ochs had, since the early 1920's, determined to make the newspaper's foreign coverage the best in the world. Whether it has become the world's best is perhaps debatable,[28] but there is no doubt but that successive publishers have shared Ochs' concern with foreign reporting. By 1924 *The Times* was carrying so much foreign news that its own radio station was set up to receive press messages directly from Europe, and soon after, from other parts of the globe.[29]

A roster of outstanding foreign correspondents for *The Times* would require many pages. However, it might be well to mention a few who have represented the paper with great ability and dedication through the years: Walter Duranty, Clarence Streit, Wickham Steed, Frank Kluckhohn, Tillman Durdin, Wythe Williams, George Barrett, Herbert L. Matthews, Harrison Salisbury, Homer Bigart, A. M. Rosenthal, Henry Lieberman, Tad Szulc, Paul Hofmann, and David Halberstam.[30]

An American press critic, John Lofton, in appraising *The Times'* foreign coverage in 1963, used the Berlin "crisis" of two years earlier as an example. While most American papers were exaggerating the situation and presenting a rather hopeless picture, *The Times* was, according to Lofton, attempting "to put the situation in perspective by reporting events suggesting the possibility of negotiation" and to present its readers with "front page stories about diplomatic efforts to avert a military clash."[31]

A. T. Steele, commenting on *The Times'* coverage of China in a book on that country written in 1966, was especially laudatory of the newspaper's reporting. He called its coverage "probably pre-eminent in the field,"[32] saying that in a check made of a dozen United States papers during March, 1964, he found that *The Times* led all in amount of space given China, with *The Washington Post* running a fairly close second.[33]

David Halberstam, who received a Pulitzer Prize for his Vietnam coverage in 1963, has said that he was careful to maintain an independent position. "While we were sympathetic to the aims of the U.S. government, we had to be critical of the representatives of our government who created a policy of optimism about the war that simply was not justified."[34] The next year, in his book *The Making of a Quagmire,* Halberstam stressed that the "staunch backing" given him by *The Times* was indispensable in his pessimistic reports from Vietnam about the progress of the war. "I was always supported by the great strength of the paper which backed a young reporter despite unrelenting and insidious pressure," he wrote, referring to attempts by officials in Washington to get *The Times* to tone down Halberstam's stories. "It was a hard way to learn how a great newspaper operates under fire, but it was a very good lesson."[35]

Halberstam was said by many in the United States to be too critical of American policy in Vietnam and biased in his reports. Much the same type of charge was hurled at Harrison Salisbury of *The Times* in 1967 when, on a trip to North Vietnam, he wrote that United States aircraft were bombing residential areas of Hanoi.

The New York Times has an enviable record in its international reporting and is generally considered very strong in this area. It is hardly strange, however, that some critics feel otherwise. Typical of these is George Lichtheim, a long-time British journalist and now a United States professor and press analyst. He thinks *The Times* is greatly overrated, saying that a person interested in international affairs who "has himself at some stage been a member of the journalistic profession, will wonder how *The Times* ever managed to get itself included in the list of the world's leading newspapers."[36] He proceeds to criticize the paper's writing, its objectivity, its accuracy, and asserts that "the plain fact of the matter is that as a reliable source of information about the world outside America's borders, *The New York Times* is inadequate and misleading."[37]

Sir Francis Williams, a British press historian and journalism critic, agrees with Lichtheim in many respects, and has called *The Times* "the Great Pedestrian of the Press," saying that it is a good paper but not a well-written or well-edited one. Such statements are easily found in the United States and abroad, but regardless of the popularity of downgrading *The Times*, most critics are reluctant to close their criticisms without some such words as these from Francis Williams: "Despite its sins of commission, it really does stand as a monument to serious-mindedness and honest intent."[38]

Quite often one hears unfavorable comments about *The Times'* editing, which one American university professor of political science recently called "chaotic, with just everything thrown in anywhere without any evidence of careful consideration." Critic Dwight Macdonald has pointed to what he termed the paper's "intellectual mediocrity" and has said that the reader has to do "a lot of digging" through the facts of a copy of the newspaper "to sort them out in the welter of *Times* verbosity and to find out what they mean"—in other words "do the work which the editors should have done."[39]

The Times is often referred to as "the good, gray *Times*." This is not only due to its typography and makeup which is rather old-fashioned and uninteresting, but also to its editorial policies. Although the editorial policy of late has veered toward liberalism, however moderate, and the paper has dressed up its editorial page somewhat, most critics seem to think that its editorials are still rather dull and cautious. Politically, *The Times* has supported only six Republican Presidential candidates in the present century. Generally its criticism of the United States' involvement in Southeast Asia and the nation's China policy indicates its swing toward liberalism; with this swing has come a livelier editorial demeanor —but nothing really startling.

The Times as a newspaper really defies classification. It is a kind of composite of all newspapers, aiming to some degree at all audiences, except, perhaps, those seeking the lurid and sensational journalism sought by readers of such papers as New York's *Daily News*, London's *Daily Mirror*, or Hamburg's *Bild*. Its thoroughness, which seems to be its chief distinction, justifiably warrants its oft-heard label "The Paper of Record." Its columns are often clogged with complete texts of speeches, full reports of congressional activities, stories attacking important events from every conceivable angle. *The Times* even printed the complete 296,000-word Warren Commission Report the day after it was released.

Here is what one American newspaper editor, Robert C. Notson of the Portland *Oregonian*, says about the thoroughness of *The Times*: "*The New York Times* is unique in its field. Both in completeness and authority it sets a high standard. Newspaper editors, as well as other readers, find in it a great resource. As nearly as a newspaper can be, it is a history of one day in the world of events."[40]

Because of this thoroughness, the paper is highly respected in the

"All the News That's Fit to Print"

The New York Times

LATE CITY EDITION

Weather: Fair and somewhat colder today, tonight and tomorrow. Temp. range: today 50-40; Sunday 61-41. Complete U.S. report on Page 93.

VOL. CXVII . . No. 40,119 NEW YORK, MONDAY, NOVEMBER 27, 1967 — 10 CENTS

AT LEAST 250 DIE AS HEAVY FLOODS HIT LISBON AREA

Record Rains Fall All Day and Most of the Night—Most Traffic Is Halted

HIGHER TOLL IS FEARED

Up to 6 Feet of Water Flows in Capital, Swamping Cars —Hundreds Are Homeless

Special to The New York Times

LISBON, Nov. 26 — A record rainfall and floods during the night killed about 250 people in the Lisbon area. Many others were missing. The floods plunged the region into darkness and disrupted communications.

A total of 176 confirmed dead was reported in a special noon issue of Lisbon's leading newspaper, Diário de Notícias. At least a dozen children were among the victims.

Worst hit was the town of Quintas, about 20 miles north of Lisbon, where 81 bodies were found in the ruins of flood-wrecked homes. More casualties were feared at the town, which is on the banks of a stream near the bullfighting town of Vila Franca de Xira.

Marines Called In

The marines were called in to help firemen struggle against the floodwaters at the village of Odivelas, north of Lisbon, which is still isolated. Firemen reported 42 dead and about 100 missing in the area.

This morning, President Américo Deus Rodrigues Thomaz visited the worst-hit parts of the Lisbon area, where flimsy shacks were uprooted, walls torn down and roads cut.

Traffic in the capital was hopelessly congested, and public and private services were almost at a standstill. Hundreds of people were homeless.

It rained all day yesterday and most of the night, but the heaviest downpour lasted from 6 P.M. until midnight, when three and a half inches of rain fell.

The rainstorms and heavy fog paralyzed Lisbon's airport yesterday and most flights were rerouted to Barcelona and to Madrid.

In the heart of the capital as much as six feet of water

Continued on Page 8, Column 4

Floods From Record Rains Deluge Central Portugal

Associated Press Cablephoto

A young girl salvaging a TV set from ruins of her home in a suburb of Lisbon yesterday

Yale Seeks $388-Million In a Record Fund Drive

By JOSEPH G. HERZBERG

Special to The New York Times

NEW HAVEN, Nov. 26—Yale University is seeking $388-million in the next 10 years, the largest fund-raising goal ever established by a university. In his annual report, made public today, Kingman Brewster Jr., Yale's president, said the university would seek money from individual donors —"the several hundred members of each generation whose assets would allow them to be philanthropists of capital significance."

Until the Yale announcement, the highest total sought by a university was Columbia's drive begun last year for $200-million in three years.

Of the $388-million that Yale seeks, $146.5-million would be used for new or expanded capital facilities and $241.5-million would be added to the Yale endowment, which is now at $503.5-million. A successful fund drive would bring the endowment near $750-million, plus appreciation.

'Hand-Tailored' Learning

Mr. Brewster said that the need for a large infusion of funds was dictated by a determination to keep Yale's quality high, and by the competition among universities for talent, both in faculty and students.

"Yale," Mr. Brewster said, "will strive to keep life and learning hand-tailored rather than pre-cut—more a product of interest than of conformity to administered routine."

Mr. Brewster also expressed a determination that Yale remain relatively small. A 10-year projection of Yale enrollment shows that the present enrollment of 8,475 (4,100 undergraduate and 4,257 graduate

Continued on Page 56, Column 1

BMT-IND CHANGES BEWILDER MANY

Transit Authority Swamped With Calls From Riders as New System Starts

By EMANUEL PERLMUTTER

Thousands of subway users swamped Transit Authority switchboards with questions, others wandered underground in confusion and some made test runs yesterday as changes in services went into effect.

The new system will get its first working-day test today.

"I'll muddle through, that's the advantage of being a New Yorker," commented Frank Derwin, a 23-year-old law student, when he learned at the Times Square BMT station that the Brighton express no longer stops there.

Several thousand extra employes will be on duty at the subway stations on their off-hours today to give guidance to travelers, but many of the system's four million passengers tried to get a jump on avoiding confusion.

Two Million Maps Issued

During much of yesterday, the 66 phone lines at the authority headquarters, 370 Jay Street, Brooklyn, were backed up with calls coming in at an average of 500 an hour.

From 9 A.M. to 7 P.M., more than 8,500 calls were received from information-seekers, the authority said.

The authority had issued about two million multicolored, pocket-sized maps outlining the eight changed routes, but they seemed to confuse rather than help many passengers.

The authority also has installed 934 maps in subway stations. The maps — 5 feet high and 4 feet wide—depict in eight colors the routes of subway lines under the new plan.

At the Times Square BMT

Continued on Page 49, Column 1

2 HELD IN ATTACKS ON 3 ELDERLY MEN

Suspects Are Seized Shortly After West Side Mugging

By LAWRENCE VAN GELDER

Two suspects in a series of knifepoint muggings of elderly men yesterday were seized by the police within minutes after they allegedly hurled a 78-year-old victim down a flight of steps after robbing him of $18.

A short time later, the police said, three victims positively identified the two, Leon Joseph Goslin, 27 years old, and Willie Mack, 20, as the men who had attacked them in separate incidents within one hour yesterday morning on the West Side.

The muggings took place against the background of a series of similar attacks in recent weeks in the area.

Early Saturday morning, a 22-year-old Jersey City State College senior, James Looby of 38 Kelly Boulevard, Bayonne, N. J., died of a stab wound in the heart inflicted after he refused a request for cigarettes at 70th Street and Amsterdam Avenue.

Last Sunday seven persons were attacked in a wave of muggings in the same neighborhood, and on Nov. 13, Meyer Davis, the society bandleader, was mugged while walking on 48th Street between Fifth Avenue and the Avenue of the Americas.

Many residents of the West Side expressed fear yesterday. In Lincoln Center, a guard said persons cutting through the area to reach [illegible] on Amster-

Continued on Page 54, Column 3

BASE NEAR DAKTO ASSAULTED BY FOE

Kontum Camp Also Shelled —B-52's on Deepest Raid in North, Strike Pass

Special to The New York Times

SAIGON, South Vietnam, Monday, Nov. 27—North Vietnamese troops poured heavy mortar fire yesterday on an artillery base near Dakto and the Special Forces camp in Kontum, 40 miles to the south.

B-52 bombers made their deepest penetration by a few miles into North Vietnam to attack truck convoys moving through the upper Mugia Pass, 100 miles north of the border, under cover of rain and fog.

Sharp fighting also flared up again in the Conthien area.

The loss of a Marine Intruder fighter-bomber on Saturday was announced, bringing to 756 the number of [illegible] lost in the North.

In the fight a mile west of the strongpoint at Conthien and less than a mile from the demilitarized zone, elements of the First Marines reported having killed 22 enemy soldiers in a four-hour battle. Seven marines were killed and 16 wounded, 13 of whom required medical evacuation.

The Conthien area has been

Continued on Page 11, Column 1

U.S. Tanker With 37 Missing Off Japan

By United Press International

SASEBO, Japan, Monday, Nov. 27 — An American oil tanker radioed this morning that she was on fire and taking water, and that the 37-man crew was abandoning ship.

An air-sea search of at least eight hours for the vessel, the Cleveland, revealed only an oil slick. There were fears that the 10,626-ton ship had sunk.

The tanker sent two S O S messages. The first, at 3 A.M. (3 P.M. Sunday, New York time), said a fire was raging in the engine room. The "abandoning ship" message came later.

Both messages were received at the United States Navy base in Sasebo on the western coast of Kyushu, Japan's southernmost island. The vessel gave its position as 12 miles southwest

Continued on Page 93, Column 5

KENNEDY ASSERTS JOHNSON SHIFTED U.S. AIM IN VIETNAM

Says Brother's Policy Has Been Changed—Humphrey Defends Saigon Military

By PETER GROSE

Special to The New York Times

WASHINGTON, Nov. 26—Senator Robert F. Kennedy said today the Johnson Administration had turned away from the Vietnam policy of President Kennedy and had forgotten the moral responsibility at stake in the war.

"We turned, we've switched," he said, and consequently the moral fiber of the United States had been "seriously undermined."

The New York Democrat was interviewed on the Columbia Broadcasting System's "Face the Nation" television program.

He acknowledged a share of responsibility for Vietnam policy decisions during his brother's Administration.

"If there are mistakes that have been made, I have been involved in those mistakes," he said. "But perhaps, if you admit mistakes, you are a little wiser than you were when you were committing them."

Compares Two Policies

Comparing Kennedy Administration thinking with the policy of President Johnson, Senator Kennedy said:

"First, we were making the effort there [in Vietnam] so that people would have their own right to decide their own future, and could select their own form of government, and it wasn't going to be imposed on them by the North Vietnamese, and we had the support of the people on South Vietnam.

"Now we turned, when we found that the South Vietnamese haven't given the support and are not making the effort."

On a later television program, "Meet the Press" of the National Broadcasting Company, Vice President Humphrey disputed one of Mr. Kennedy's points.

South's Role Questioned

Supporting his charge that the South Vietnamese were not "making the effort," Senator Kennedy asked:

"Why, for instance, in the battle of Dakto, hasn't it been the South Vietnamese Army that has gone up that hill? Why hasn't it been the South Vietnamese army that has been on the demilitarized zone and stayed there? Why does it always have to be the Americans?"

Mr. Humphrey replied:

"My answer, of course, would be that the South Vietnamese army has been at Dakto, and has been at the DMZ, and in fact some of the most courageous fighting of this war has been by some of the units

Continued on Page 15, Column 1

Leaders Disagree on Vietnam War

Senator Robert F. Kennedy on 'Face the Nation' yesterday

Associated Press Wirephoto

Vice President Humphrey appearing on 'Meet the Press'

7 Nations' Banks to Press For a Stable Gold Market

By CLYDE H. FARNSWORTH

Special to The New York Times

BRUSSELS, Nov. 26 — The governors of seven central banks, forming the so-called Gold Pool, met secretly in Frankfurt this afternoon to "insure orderly conditions" after a week of feverish speculative activity.

A communiqué issued in Washington and made available here said the seven central banks had enough gold and foreign-exchange reserves to guarantee the fixed price of $35 an ounce for gold.

The public declaration was viewed as a major attempt to bring reason to bear in the highly agitated markets.

[President Johnson returned from Texas to Washington for a meeting with Secretary of the Treasury Henry H. Fowler Monday on the gold speculation.]

The Gold Pool was formed after similar speculation in 1960 pushed the price of gold in the London bullion market to more than $40 an ounce.

The central banks in the pool are those of the United States, Britain, Belgium, the Netherlands, Italy, West Germany and Switzerland.

The seven central banks combined have slightly over $27-billion worth of gold—more than enough to meet any conceivable speculative demand and hold the price.

The statement issued tonight indicated that the seven were prepared to throw those resources into the fight to maintain the gold price—and, therefore, the existing pattern of exchange rates among the leading currencies.

In the past, such joint efforts by the major countries have succeeded in stopping speculative attacks on currencies. There has been no precedent since World War II for the present gold-buying wave, but so far its volume is less than $500-million.

France was one of the original members of the Gold

Continued on Page 79, Column 3

VANCE ARRIVING IN ANKARA TODAY; A DECISION LIKELY

Greeks Are Said to Agree to Withdrawal of Some Regulars From Cyprus

TURKS DARKEN 3 CITIES

They Are Reported Ready to Ease War Preparations if Athens Starts Pullout

By SYDNEY GRUSON

Special to The New York Times

ANKARA, Turkey, Nov. 26—Cyrus R. Vance, President Johnson's special envoy, will return to Ankara from Athens tomorrow morning for what diplomats here expect to be the decisive meetings with Turkish leaders in the crisis over Cyprus.

He is believed here to have obtained Greece's agreement to the immediate withdrawal of some of her regular army forces from Cyprus. This has become Turkey's first condition for a peaceful settlement of the crisis, which was sparked by the deaths of 28 Turkish Cypriotes fighting against Greek troops 10 days ago.

It was not yet known here whether the Greeks had dropped their insistence that Turkey simultaneously demobilize some of her forces, which have been on a war footing for the last week. A Turkish invasion fleet is ready in the southern ports of Mersin and Iskenderun.

Return Is Quick

The fact that Mr. Vance is returning here so quickly indicated to observers that he had persuaded the Greeks that Turkey will not give in on this point. Mr. Vance flew to Athens yesterday after his second round of talks with Turkish leaders.

The Turks are prepared to lessen their visible readiness for an invasion of Cyprus only after Greece begins or announces the start of the withdrawal of her regulars.

In an appeal Friday to Turkey, Greece and Cyprus, Secretary General Thant called for the "ultimate withdrawal from the island of all non-Cypriote armed forces other than those of the United Nations."

Under the 1960 Zurich and

Continued on Page 3, Column 1

EGYPT RULES OUT BASES FOR SOVIET

Declares Peace With Israel Possible, but Not Treaty

By ERIC PACE

Special to The New York Times

CAIRO, Nov. 26—The chief spokesman for the United Arab Republic said today that it would not permit the Soviet Union to establish military bases on Egyptian soil.

The spokesman, Dr. Mohammed H. el-Zayyat, made the declaration at a news conference in which he also said that Cairo would welcome Gunnar Jarring, the new United Nations envoy; had ruled out a peace treaty—but not peace—with Israel, and had formally proposed a new meeting of Arab leaders.

Answering reporters' written questions, Dr. el-Zayyat said: "We are against giving bases to anyone and certainly against giving bases to the Soviet Union or the United States or any country."

The question had been prompted by persistent reports that the Soviet Union has asked Egypt to permit the establishment of military facilities.

Dr. el-Zayyat's answer, however, did not rule out the possibility that Cairo might allow Moscow to have a naval refueling station or other facilities if, in the Egyptian view, they did not constitute a base.

The Egyptian Government has not yet disclosed whether or how it will otherwise repay the Soviet Union for the

Continued on Page 32, Column 4

The Growing Farm Exodus: Land Loses Its Hold

By DOUGLAS E. KNEELAND

Special to The New York Times

CRESTON, Iowa — The bright November sun high in the southwest was a false promise. The wind rustling the dried stalks of a hilltop cornfield in Dodge Township 10 miles northeast of here bore the taste of winter.

Paul Kline, bundled in heavy work clothes, his cap pulled over his ears, shut off the motor of the red tractor that had been cutting swaths through the corn with a two-row picker.

Standing up, he squinted into the sun, then swung his arm in a slow arc.

"I can count up six vacant houses," he said, "from right here, from where I can see."

What is happening in Dodge Township in Union County, Iowa, is happening in farm areas throughout the country — an apparently unending migration to urban areas that has been going on for more than half a century.

The Department of Agriculture estimates that last year just under 11.6 million persons, or less than 6 per cent of the population, were living on farms. This represented a loss of 768,000 from 1965.

Bill Kesler for The New York Times

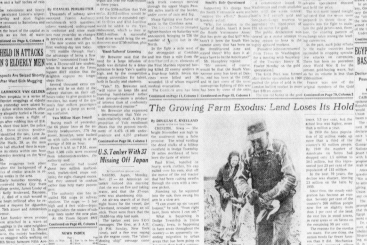

Mr. and Mrs. A. V. Severien on their farm in Union County, Iowa, pick ears of corn that their tractor missed earlier.

From 1960 to 1966, the department reported, the average annual loss of farm population was 804,000, a rate of 5.9 per cent. During the nineteen-fifties, the rate was lower, 5.3 per cent, but the actual loss was higher, more than a million a year.

In 1910 the farm population of 32 million made up more than a third of the country's 92 million people. By 1940 the number of Americans on farms had dropped only 1.5 million to 30.5 million, but this represented just 23 per cent of the population of 132 million.

In the next 10 years, the decline was sharper, leaving 23 million on the farm by 1950.

Since then, the steady emigration has become an exodus. Seventy per cent of the country's 200 million people now live on slightly more than 1 per cent of the land; the rest live in small towns, in rural areas or on farms on the remaining 99 per cent.

The reasons for the exodus are many. For one thing, the nation needs far fewer farmers than it did. Mechanization and improved tillage methods have produced a system so efficient that a single American farmer now feeds and clothes nearly 40 of his countrymen, com-

Continued on Page 72, Column 4

universities and colleges of the United States. It is found in practically every academic library and is read by more than half of the college presidents. On the campuses of Harvard, Yale, Chicago, and the University of California at Berkeley, for example, it sells nearly 5,000 copies daily.

Besides its popularity in the academic community, *The Times* is important among those interested in the arts and intellectual affairs generally. Its economic coverage is impressive, with financial and business news filling some dozen pages on the average day. *The Times* prides itself on its many specialists. Some of them are John Cogley, religion editor; Fred Hechinger, education editor; Hanson Baldwin, military editor; Walter Sullivan, science editor; and Craig Claiborne, food editor.

The influence of *The New York Times* on United States national politics and its large readership in Washington has been well-documented.[41] A *Times* associate editor and long-time Washington correspondent, James B. Reston, has often spoken of the paper's concern with thoroughness and accuracy, especially in its political reporting, and has pointed to its responsibility to the serious, intelligent reader.

"Our primary responsibility," Reston once said, "is not . . . to the commuter reading the paper on the train. Our primary responsibility is to the historian of fifty years from now. Unique among newspapers, *The Times* is prime source material—and we must never poison the stream of history."[42] In spite of some critics who feel at times that *The Times* does "poison the stream of history," most students of the press would agree that the paper is the prime newspaper source for academic persons. Usually it is not the contents of *The Times* which is faulted, but the packaging of the material. But, as one recent commentator has said, until a utopian paper comes along "which is able to present *The Times*' coverage in a more attractive package, *The New York Times* will remain the nation's premier newspaper."[43]

The New York Times has a staff in Washington of some thirty men and women and provides a heavy reading diet of political news. It is usually considered excellent in its coverage and its stories filter into many American papers through *The New York Times* News Service. A British critic (the Washington correspondent for the London *Times*), however, sees some weaknesses in the New York paper's capital coverage. Chief of these is that the Washington bureau "is prone to give too much attention to almost imperceptible changes in Government policy, and the members compete with one another for prominence in the paper."[44]

Some 370 "reporters and writers" in its home office in New York form the backbone of *The Times*' news operation. In addition, a dozen regional correspondents send in their dispatches from various parts of the United States, and some 50 full-time foreign correspondents serve the paper from all the important news centers of the world. It is probably safe to estimate that the total editorial staffers putting out the daily and Sunday *Times* number more than a thousand.

The *Times* has sometimes been called the "Fifth Estate" since it serves as a kind of model or standard against which other American papers are judged. Most United States publishers and editors, all priding themselves on their individual contributions to journalism, would probably deny this, but one does not have to be around any daily newspaper office very long before he is aware of this "*New York Times*-consciousness" which exists. Although many editors consider the editorials of *The Times* "too timid and dull," editorial comment in a large segment of American newspapers reflects the influence of the New York daily's editorial page.

There is no doubt but that the editorial page of *The Times* has grown more lively in the last few years. John B. Oakes, who heads the staff of editorial writers who work in a series of tenth-floor offices surrounding a reference library, believes that *The Times* should make it clear as to where it stands on any major subject. He feels it is the paper's duty to enter any public controversy, and *The Times* is doing so more forcefully all the time. At least 20,000 letters and telegrams are received by the editorial-page staff every year, and leaders in almost every field of human activity daily deluge the "Ivory Tower," as the editorial writing department is often called, with calls, all seeking to take issue with something *The Times* has written, or to praise its comments, or to enlist its influence.[45]

The great newspaper which is *The New York Times* began back in September, 1851, as a rather crudely printed journal in a city of half a million. A journalist, Henry J. Raymond, and two financiers, George Jones and Edward B. Wesley, saw a need for another inexpensive paper in the New York field. With Raymond as editor and Jones as business manager, the *New York Daily Times* was born as a large-size four-page paper, selling at one cent a copy.[46]

Although the printing was of poor quality at first (attributed to a new press), it was very well edited with a front page packed with foreign and local news. In little more than two months its circulation had done a little earlier. According to the United States' foremost jour- expenses forced the paper in its second year to increase its subscription price to two cents, as Bennett's *Herald* and Greeley's *Tribune* had done a little earlier. According to the United States' foremost journalism historian, Frank Luther Mott, *The Times* may be considered the "culmination and highest achievement" of the inexpensive newspaper movement which began with the New York *Sun* and other papers in the early 1830's.[47] Editor Raymond determined from the first to make the paper appeal to a highly intelligent audience and one which would, like Greeley's *Tribune*, take a high moral tone. But, as the late Dr. Mott has said, *The Times*, in addition to its moral tone and conservatism, was predominantly a *news*-paper, presenting the reader a well-balanced and heavy diet of news—especially foreign news.[48] Thus, it may be said that Raymond set the basic pattern for *The Times* to follow throughout its history.

Between 1884 and 1896 *The Times* was in a period of decline, largely because it was growing too stodgy and old-fashioned in a newspaper world being turned upside down by Joseph Pulitzer. Jones died in 1891, and Charles Miller and associates bought the paper from the Jones family in 1893. Editor Raymond had died back in 1869 and his successors were unable to fight successfully the forces which were undermining *The Times*. In spite of the paper's general quality and high moral standards, the paper had fallen on bad times. By 1896 it was losing at least a thousand dollars a week, staff morale was low, and there was no doubt but that a rejuvenation was badly needed or the paper would disappear. The circulation had slowly dropped to 9,000, not very impressive when compared to the morning *Journal*'s 300,000.[49]

The man who came out of the Tennessee hills to bring new life to the faltering *Times* was Adolph Simon Ochs, not yet 40, who left his *Chattanooga Times* to set in process what was probably the greatest newspaper miracle the country had seen.

"Here I am in New York ready to negotiate for the leading and most influential newspaper in America," Ochs wrote exaggeratedly to his wife in March, 1896. "The supreme gall of a country newspaperman burdened with debt."[50]

Ochs may have been in debt and burdened with inexperience in big-city journalism, but he had exactly what *The New York Times* needed: an intuitive business sense, faith, and imagination. While retaining the emphasis on sobriety and reliability, Ochs went even further in stressing news. He eliminated fiction (*The Times* had been running short stories), increased business news significantly, and started a weekly book section. He instituted a Sunday magazine, and chose a slogan—"All the News That's Fit to Print"—which is still used by the paper. In 1898, with the circulation at 25,000, he cut the price of the paper from three cents back to a penny. Within three years *The Times* was back on firm footing with a circulation of 102,000.

One of the best journalistic moves Ochs made in these early years was to hire a new managing editor: a sharp-minded young intellectual named Carr Van Anda who had been working for the *Sun*. The principle of sparing no expense to get and print the news began under Van Anda's editorship and has endured to the present.

Van Anda, like Ochs, believed in what he called "hard" news, thoroughly and accurately presented. A tireless worker, he often stayed at the office all night. He was there at 1:20 A.M. on April 15, 1912, when a distress signal came in from Newfoundland that the pride of Britain's passenger fleet, the *Titanic*, was in trouble. The new ship, believed unsinkable, had hit an iceberg and was in some kind of danger. But was it really serious or just a narrow escape? Van Anda could not tell from the short and garbled message. Although he was generally considered a conservative and a cautious man, like Ochs, Van Anda gambled on the unthinkable: that the *Titanic* was sinking.

He threw his staff into action; the story was approached from almost every conceivable perspective. Some reporters put together lists of famous persons on board; others turned out features about the ship and other important passenger liners; still others did stories on similar sea disasters. In other words, Van Anda and *The Times* went all the way with the story; they played it big. At other newspapers, editors were more skeptical, more cautious, inserting such words as "rumored" here and there. Van Anda's three-column headline mirrored the sureness that has marked *The Times* through its history:

NEW LINER TITANIC HITS AN ICEBERG;
SINKING BY THE BOW AT MIDNIGHT;
WOMEN PUT OFF IN LIFEBOATS;
LAST WIRELESS AT 12:27 A.M. BLURRED

Officials of the White Star Line which owned the *Titanic* had been releasing optimistic statements all during the day of April 15, and did not confirm Van Anda's story until the evening of April 16. Van Anda's final edition, which went to press about three hours after *The Times* had received the first brief wireless report, had stated flatly that the *Titanic* had sunk. This was perhaps a great risk on Van Anda's part and his "deductive journalism" may have shocked many, but it remains as one of the great against-a-deadline news-coverage feats in all journalism.

The Times excelled in depth news coverage during World War I, and printed the full text of the Versailles Treaty—a full eight pages of type. Throughout the twenties and thirties the paper kept up its tradition of thorough coverage, presenting long, accurate stories, many of which other papers either ignored or played in summary fashion. In 1935 Ochs died of a cerebral hemorrhage and his paper was left in the hands of his son-in-law, Arthur Hays Sulzberger, who was publisher until 1961 when he became board chairman. He was followed by another son-in-law, Orvil E. Dryfoos, who died unexpectedly in 1963.

Arthur Ochs Sulzberger (or "Punch" as he is widely called), the thirty-seven-year-old son of Arthur Hays Sulzberger, became the new publisher, the youngest *The Times* had ever had. "Punch" Sulzberger has made many changes in the newspaper, not all of which have been popular with leading staff members. He shifted many of the top executives around and changed titles in several instances. Turner Catledge, who had been managing editor, became executive editor with supreme editorial power. Lester Markel, long-time Sunday editor, became an "associate editor" as did James ("Scotty") Reston of the Washington bureau. Harrison Salisbury, noted foreign correspondent, was given the title of "national editor." Clifton Daniel, who is married to former President Truman's daughter, became managing editor. Tom Wicker replaced Reston as Washington bureau chief. These and other changes were made mainly between 1962 and 1964.[51]

"Punch" Sulzberger is reappraising *The New York Times*, making changes and asking questions about traditional practices. He is concerned about the makeup, the typography, the quality of reporting and editing, the competition of television—in short, all aspects of the newspaper. *The Times* has changed greatly since 1963, but it has managed to maintain so much of its old character and appearance that only the most sensitive readers have been aware of the metamorphosis. *The Times* is, in effect, still *The Times*.

18

Asahi: No Coddling for the Masses

Some five million Japanese buy copies of *Asahi Shimbun*[1] each morning, and nearly four million more copies go to these same readers in the evening. Although the morning and evening editions are separate newspapers, they are usually subscribed to as a "set" and in this way Japan's largest newspaper produces close to nine million copies a day, making it (along with the Soviet Union's *Izvestia*) the largest daily in the world. It is conservatively estimated that *Asahi* has a readership of about twenty million adults and young adults every day.

Asahi and its two main daily competitors of Japan—*Mainichi* and *Yomiuri*—command mass sales without stooping to sensationalism on a scale found in many other nations. *Asahi*, especially, provides its mass readership with serious, intelligent journalism and is usually considered the best-informed and most intelligent of the Big Three. While providing the masses a wide assortment of reading material, *Asahi* makes certain that it does not coddle them. *Yomiuri*, the most "popular" or entertainment-oriented of the three leading national dailies, is pitched at a much lower level of readers. *Mainichi* hits between them. All three papers have daily circulations of more than five million, a fantastic situation for a single nation. *Asahi* stands out as the most prestigious of the Japanese papers and has shown itself the leader in technical innovation and new features.

Asahi in Japan means more than a newspaper; it includes radio and television broadcasting, the publication of some two hundred books every year and a great diversity of magazines. In spite of its size and varied activities, the paper is not a dangerous monopoly endangering any other enterprise or restricting the public's capacity to receive diverse news and views. Japan has a pluralism of communication voices which would be difficult to match in any other country. *Asahi* is only the largest of nearly half-a-dozen national papers. Nor is *Asahi* a "cannibal" that gobbles up local newspapers, for there are some one hundred local Japanese papers that are strong and vigorous and enjoy high prestige among the daily press and have great reader loyalty.

A very large staff works for *Asahi,* more than 7,500 persons. About 2,000 of these are in some type of writing or editing position; another 4,000 are split about equally between the printing and business departments. Administrative personnel, special publications staff members, and miscellaneous workers account for the other 1,500 positions.

Asahi is published from plants in five cities—Tokyo (started 1888), Osaka (1879), Seibu (1935), Nagoya (1935), and Sapporo (1959). The first four of these rank as "head offices" with Sapporo (capital of the northern island of Hokkaido) considered a "branch" office. Well over a hundred different editions are published throughout the country each day. In Tokyo alone there are eight main editions in the morning and four in the evening.[2] Subeditions, printed in many locations throughout Japan, reinforce the printing potential of the main *Asahi* plants in the five cities named above.

Although *Asahi* appeals to the masses, it has managed to capture the "elite" among Japanese readers at the same time. It has found a formula which permits it to offer quality material to the intellectuals and entertainment to the average Japanese reader. One writer has compared *Asahi* to the best among Tokyo department stores where an "exclusive boutique linked to a Paris couturier is set amid a vast range of sound quality ware and where there is no bargain counter."[3]

The paper is a serious, quality newspaper, and in spite of its mass circulation, has managed to keep this reputation. It covers its stories in depth. Like most Japanese papers, *Asahi* is drab and gray in its makeup, running a few small photographs. It is more concerned with reporting every fact at the expense of lively writing. Politicians and administrators find the paper's up-to-date news necessary reading. Its editorial, which usually runs on page 2, is normally an exhaustive analysis of some basic issue; it is so exhaustive, in fact, that seldom does it reach a definite conclusion.

Immense production problems face *Asahi,* among which is the cumbersome way in which Japanese is still written (with a minimum of 2,304 characters in Chinese, Japanese, and Roman—plus numerals).[4] Local copy is handwritten, but *Asahi*'s pioneering of telephoto transmission of handwritten copy and the introduction in 1960 of *kanji* character teletype machines and even the facsimile radiophoto transmission of entire newspapers to be printed in Hokkaido (1959), have made possible great advances. Although *Asahi* did not pioneer in fac-

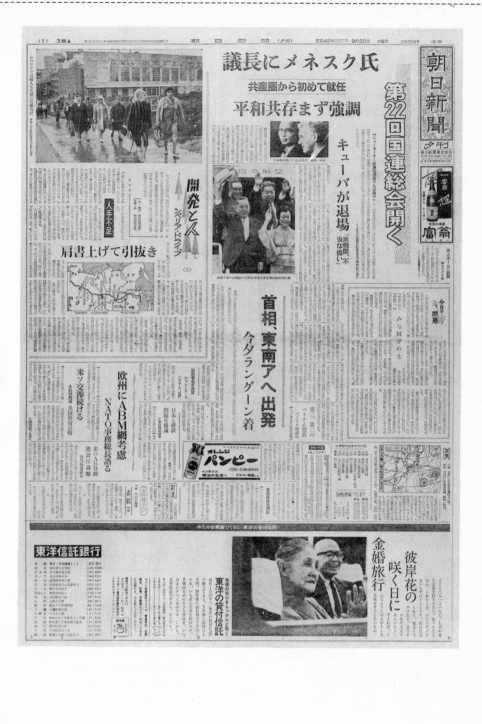

朝日新聞
夕刊
朝日新聞東京本社

第22回国連総会開く

議長にメネスク氏

共産圏から初めて就任

平和共存まず強調

ウ事務総長（左）とメネスク議長＝AP

【ニューヨーク＝長谷特派員十九日発】

キューバが退場

「米税関、不当な扱い」

首相、東南アへ出発

今夕ラングーン着

シベリアでは婦人らも大切な労働力だ

開発と人　シベリア・ドライブ　〈1〉

人手不足

肩書上げて引抜き

欧州にABM網考慮

NATO事務総長語る

米のABM網建設は遺憾

米ソ交渉続ける

ABM問題　米国務省言明

日本と借款問題を協議

今日の問題　みな同学の士

訂正

素粒子

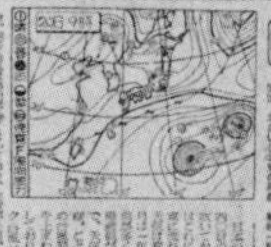

simile transmission, it was the first to use it successfully on a regular basis. Up to eighteen pages of a separate paper are radioed by microwave as full-size photos from Tokyo to Sapporo in Hokkaido (about 500 miles) where high-speed rotary offset presses print the edition from the negatives received.[5]

To provide its readers with the latest, most accurate, and fullest national and international coverage, *Asahi* has close to three hundred bureaus in Japan and nineteen others overseas—in Washington, New York, London, Paris, Geneva, Bonn, Moscow, Cairo, New Delhi, Bangkok, Hong Kong, Naha, Peking, Seoul, Saigon, Jakarta, Honolulu, San Francisco, and Los Angeles.[6] In addition, it subscribes to twenty-four different news agencies, including Reuters, AP, AFP, NANA, Soviet News, Central News Agency, *Le Monde*, *The Observer*, *The New York Times*, and London *Times*. The paper has a foreign desk of about forty men, each of whom is a specialist in at least one other language.[7]

As a news-gathering organization *Asahi* has few peers either in the quantity or quality of its staff. Only one in eighty university graduates applying for jobs pass the paper's own entrance examination, probably the most difficult such test in the world. It includes a graduate-level translation exercise (covering either German, French, Chinese or English). Each applicant must also write a long essay and a digest of a complicated speech, and must take a comprehensive test on current events. In addition, he is tested on his knowledge of national and world history, geography and politics, and must show that he understands the meaning of important modern scientific terms. Those who pass this rigorous examination, then have interviews with *Asahi* executives in further screening. After the successful applicants have jumped these difficult hurdles and have taken physical examinations, they become apprentice journalists on *Asahi*'s staff.[8] And they begin a fierce competition to get anything into the paper at all. Space is limited in *Asahi* where seldom more than eighteen pages appear in the morning, and twelve in the evening. Many of the staff members actually "live" in the *Asahi* building. In the Tokyo plant, for instance, there is a dorm in which at least five hundred men sleep every night so as to be available in case extra help is needed.[9]

Journalists are usually poorly paid in Japan, although *Asahi* pays better than most and provides bonuses, prizes, and other special rewards to its journalists. Most journalists, however, write for magazines and book publishers so that their income compares well with other liberal professions in Japan.[10]

Asahi was founded in January, 1879, by Ryuhei Murayama and Noboru Kimura who formed a partnership to begin the paper in Osaka. Kimura withdrew from the management shortly after the first issue, and the next year Murayama was joined by Riichi Ueno, and they and their descendants have largely directed the paper until the present time. *Asahi*, like all Japanese papers, had to be licensed in those days.

Asahi's application for permission to publish stated its objectives in the following words which were quite courageous for that authoritarian age when the Tokugawas, a militaristic dynasty, were in power:

> The newspaper will be edited for easy reading, even by children, with illustrations and other devices . . . for the guidance of the common people, both men and women, young and old, in order to teach them social justice.[11]

Japanese papers at the time were little more than political sheets serving some leader or some cause; they were all extremely biased. *Asahi*, from its beginning, strove to be something different, to hold itself apart from factionalism, and to appeal to all thinking people who could read.[12] Murayama and his new partner, Ueno, worked well together; it is said that they were almost as brothers, and complemented one another. Murayama, enterprising and ebullient, was the "idea man," while Ueno, steadfast and prudent, added a strength and stability to the partnership.[13] In 1888 *Asahi* bought a small Tokyo paper and converted it into the *Tokyo Asahi Shimbun*, which for many years was to be subordinated to the main edition in Osaka, but which was ultimately to be the main edition and the *Asahi* headquarters paper.[14]

In 1900 came the Boxer Rebellion in China, and *Asahi*'s correspondent, Keitaro Murai, was the only Japanese newsman among the foreign group besieged in Peking for two months. His stories written after his release were translated and read throughout the world.[15] By the turn of the century the circulation of the Osaka and Tokyo editions together was more than 150,000, with the Osaka *Asahi* still by far the larger. In 1904 *Asahi* sent 26 reporters to the battlefronts in Manchuria to cover the Russo-Japanese War. This largely established *Asahi* as a paper which provided full and detailed news coverage and gave the paper an opportunity to make use of improved communication techniques.[16]

Although *Asahi* was usually on the side of moderation, it earned a name for attacking the Government in the early 1900's. In the second decade of the present century, its reporters, and even Murayama himself, were beaten up by right-wing extremists. It courageously opposed the remnants of feudalism and often its views offended traditionalists still in power. At a time when Japan was in a ferment of change under the impact of foreign ideas, *Asahi* persistently tried to present the best and most provocative ideas in a form easily understandable to the ordinary reader. It was clearly the most notable liberal voice among the Japanese daily newspapers.

During the period between 1918 and the beginning of World War II the history of *Asahi* was dominated by a ceaseless fight against governmental and militarist efforts to limit freedom of expression.[17] But depression hit Japan in the 1930's and the pressure of militarism grew rapidly. In 1935, three years before its surrender to the militarists who had seized power, the newspaper company had established another edition of *Asahi*, on the southern island of Kyushu. Murayama died in 1933 at the age of 83 and his interest in *Asahi* passed to his adopted son and son-in-law, Nagataka Murayama, who had joined *Asahi* in 1920. He and his wife still wield much influence on the newspaper. In 1936, young military extremists revolted in Tokyo and one of their first targets was *Asahi*, the people's champion for freedom and moderation.[18]

It was this same year, 1936, that the University of Missouri School of Journalism awarded one of its Honor Medals for distinguished journalistic achievement to *Asahi*. The citation, accepted for the newspaper by Toshishige Yabe of its New York office, read in part:

> To the *Asahi* of Tokio, Japan: For the cultural influence of the 'Asahi Prize'; for honoring contributors to intellectual development; for fostering constitutional government and public welfare in Japan; for an unusual emphasis upon reliable political news; for intelligibly and authoritatively reporting economic news . . . for its ably conducted foreign news service from America; for extending its liberal, clear-visioned reporting and interpretation of world news beyond the boundaries of its own nation in a way which contributes significantly both to an understanding of the Orient by the Occident and to an enlightened restraint upon the part of its immediate circulation in interpreting fast-moving events in a time of critical flux.[19]

In 1937 the war in China began and the government of Japan maintained a tight grip on newspaper policy through a device that has since become familiar: the control of newsprint. The militarists tried to force the papers to publish only official handouts and, although this did not succeed, the government eventually enforced the joint distribution of all newspapers, thus ending the free competition for circulation which had begun with the Japanese press itself in the previous century. Freedom of the press ended abruptly with the coming of World War II, or at least with Japan's entry into it.

During the war newsprint was controlled and carefully rationed. Censorship was extreme and every effort was made to turn the press into a single spokesman for the government. Even so, some editorial opinion remained free—but not much. In 1943, at the height of the war, *Asahi* still had the courage to rebuke the Prime Minister, General Hideki Tojo. The writer, Seigo Nakano, was arrested and later committed hara-kiri. During the war *Asahi* reporters and photographers covered the war, many of them suffering and dying with the soldiers and sailors.[20] In spite of a few rather mildly critical pieces, *Asahi* had offered little editorial opposition to the Japanese militarists during the war, and it was only in the closing days of the Occupation after the war that a spirit of liberalism was released. *Asahi* became dominated by very left-wing elements which harassed the weak postoccupation governments (in power from 1948). The newspaper led the press attacks on Prime Minister Nobusuke Kishi, who said on resigning: "Violence is not only that of pistols and fists; that of the pen is more dangerous."[21]

In a way, one "dark age" of Japanese journalism was substituted for another "dark age" with the defeat of Japan in World War II. *Asahi* ended the war with a depleted staff, a lack of supplies, and a run-down plant. *Asahi* was even suspended for a time by General Douglas MacArthur for printing propagandistic headlines and inflammatory news and editorial comment. The paper was extremely outspoken, and took delight in scoffing at atrocities attributed by Americans to Japanese troops; it also accused the United States of breaking international law in using the A-bombs on Hiroshima and Nagasaki. It took every opportunity to "react" against the American occupation forces.[22]

When the Occupation ended, *Asahi*'s liberal, even radical, editorial writers became even more extreme. Enjoying unprecedented freedom, they set about harrying a succession of weak governments, to champion democracy with vigorous attacks on the evils of militarism and nationalism. The paper even became known for a time as the "red *Asahi*" with its attacks on Kishi, the Prime Minister who had pushed the ratification of the United States Security Treaty through the Diet. Street demonstrations, not opposed by *Asahi*, got out of hand and the paper gave wide coverage to the violence.[23] Soon startled by the influence of press coverage and editorializing, *Asahi* with other newspapers published a joint statement to the effect that enough was enough. Ever since, *Asahi* has withdrawn into its old moderation and prudence, to the point of losing its bark and much of its bite.[24] This whole immediate postoccupation period, and especially that part of it during the attacks on Kishi, is probably the blackest spot in *Asahi*'s history and is one which it would like to forget.[25]

Asahi is still antimilitarist and its coverage of the United States' war in Vietnam usually evidences its strong "peace" feelings. In 1965 the United States State Department charged that *Asahi* (and *Mainichi*) was dominated by Communists after the paper had carried a series of articles criticizing the American presence in Vietnam and especially of repeated bombing of civilian targets.[26] The following excerpt from an editorial in the *Asahi Evening News* depicts *Asahi*'s attitude toward the war in Vietnam in 1965:

> The gravity of the conflict in Vietnam lies in the fact that it is neither a localized war fought between local forces nor a war fought by proxy, but a war involving a big power, which is taking direct part in the fighting with its vast resources in military power.
>
> We appeal generally to the good sense of the world and believe that the fighting should be quickly ended by the force of world opinion.
>
> The Johnson policy of retaliation against North Vietnam

> and his posture of placing the entire blame on the country and seeking its surrender gives us the impression that the Asian policy of the Democratic party, which ostensibly made a new start by revising the diplomacy of the Republican party, is assuming an even more inflexible stand than that of the Republicans.[27]

Asahi is a well-edited and systematic newspaper. Its readers can predict where certain types of material will be found. At least the reader can know in what order the various features will come throughout the paper. On the front page (the back page in Western papers) is found mainly national news, largely political, and occasionally important foreign stories. On page 2 is the editorial (sometimes two), international news and commentary, and foreign features. On the next page or two come features, profiles of persons in the news, contributed essays, columns and letters from readers (such letters are not addressed to the editor; rather they are considered as contributions). Next comes a page or two of economic news and commentary, both foreign and domestic. This economic section is followed by a page or two of book reviews, criticism of plays, movies, and radio-television programs. From one to two pages of sports follow, including national and foreign columns of commentary. Then come police news, human interest items, cartoons, and obituaries of prominent national and international persons. The last section of the paper is given to local news and views, including weather forecasts, local obituaries, items about meetings, and notes from readers about a variety of subjects related to the local community.[28]

Asahi is noted for its many sponsored projects in such fields as exploration and science, aviation, art, music, and photography, amateur sports, and the broad and limitless area of public health, charity, and welfare. One of its first projects was the sponsorship of Antarctic explorations beginning in 1911 and running through 1962. In 1911 *Asahi* sponsored the first airplane flight ever made in Japan. For a time the paper was actually in the airline business, but it has ever had a strong private air fleet. Today it has more than a dozen of the most modern aircraft, including three helicopters. *Asahi* has brought to Japan a wide selection of the finest Western artists, dramatists, musicians, and lecturers, and has sponsored in Japan a number of competitions for writers and photographers.[29]

Asahi publishes, in addition to its Japanese language dailies, the following: *Asahi Evening News* (an English daily) *Shukan Asahi* (similar to *Time* or *Newsweek* of the United States or *Der Spiegel* of West Germany), *Asahi Graph* (similar to *Life* of the United States or *Paris Match* of France), *Asahi Journal* (intellectual weekly review), *Asahi Sports* (sports newsweekly), *Shogakusei Asahi Shimbun* (a weekly for schoolchildren), *Nogyo Asahi* (agricultural monthly), *Kagaku Asahi* (scientific monthly), *Fujin Asahi* (women's interest monthly), *Asahi Camera* (photo art monthly), *Asahi Nenkan* (yearbook), *Shonen Asahi*

Nenkan (children's yearbook), *Japan Quarterly* (in English), *This is Japan* (yearbook in English), and many books.[30]

The *Asahi Shimbun*'s five buildings are all first-class modern newspaper plants. The main Tokyo building has been expanded several times and is now three times as large as the original building completed in 1927. It is now a large, eight-story triangular structure near the Sukiyabashi intersection in the center of downtown Tokyo. This building houses the Far East headquarters of several world-famous foreign news services as well as *Asahi*'s own newspaper enterprises. The *Asahi* building in Osaka, the old head office, is being replaced by another ultramodern plant which will supplement the *Asahi* complex at Kakanoshima, Kita-ku. The other three *Asahi* newspaper plants are the new Tokyo Shibaura printing plant (opened in 1964), the complete newspaper plant in Seibu, and a smaller one at Sapporo. Of course, the newspaper has many smaller facilities and even owns large, modern buildings throughout the country which are not used in publishing.

Biggest stockholder in *Asahi* today is Nagataka Murayama, the founder's son-in-law and adopted son, and Ofuji Murayama, daughter of the founder. The present Murayamas have tried many times since 1960 to interfere in the matters of the paper, mostly without success. Actually the control of the paper is vested in a board of directors drawn from *Asahi*'s ranks, and the Murayamas were trying to meddle to a far greater extent than the directors felt they should. In 1964 five directors threatened to resign, but the Osaka District Court directed the Murayamas and the directors to work out a peaceful settlement. The directors stayed and the Murayamas promised to keep out of editorial matters.[31] However, some observers say that the Murayamas are continuing behind the scenes to snipe at certain editors and stockholders of the company.

Asahi has grown rapidly since World War II and is continuing to grow. In many ways it is a strange kind of elite newspaper which has managed to adapt many Western techniques to its Oriental character. It is one of the few newspapers of the world which is both the *largest circulation* daily of its nation and at the same time is the *leading quality* daily. Like many other elite newspapers of the world, but probably more than most, it has passed through trying times—dark periods where it almost died of authoritarian strangulation or choked itself to death with its own excessive exercise of freedom. But it has come through its periods of trial and finds itself today a liberal, though moderate, quality daily which might well serve as an example for aspiring newspapers everywhere wishing large circulations and, at the same time, international respect which comes from an emphasis on quality—both in content and in production.

It is perhaps fitting that this book should end with *Asahi*, for this leading daily of Asia is also a leading daily of the Western world. It has managed to bridge the gap between cultures, to moderate its views, to adapt to new ideas, in short, to change and become an international newspaper without giving up its special character. Liberal but not radical, appealing to a mass audience but not flippant and sensational, peaceful but not unrealistic, hopeful but not naive, *Asahi Shimbun* typifies the best among the elite press of the world. It has a world concern without shedding a pride in its nation; it recognizes the importance of intelligent, serious dialogue without forsaking the interests of the reader desiring "popular" news and features; it constantly seeks to pull up its readers and not bring down its journalism to meet them; it is vitally interested in what is going on everywhere in the world and wants its readers to be also. Typifying all elite newspapers, especially those quality dailies published in libertarian nations, *Asahi* is a rational paper endeavoring to make the whole world one large community of reason.

Notes

Chapter 1

[1] *Journal of the Institute of Journalists*, London, 50:492 (July-August, 1962), p. 89.

[2] Lecture, April, 1961, at School of Journalism, University of Iowa, Iowa City.

[3] Quoted in Robert U. Brown, "Shop Talk at Thirty," *Editor & Publisher* (April 30, 1960), p. 112.

[4] William Stephenson, "The Ludenic Theory of Newsreading," *Journalism Quarterly*, 41:3 (Summer, 1964), pp. 367–374, Compare, Stephenson, *The Play Theory of Mass Communication* (Chicago, University of Chicago Press, 1967), pp. 147–159. Dr. Stephenson, a psychologist on the University of Missouri journalism faculty, has described a "play" theory of newsreading that is basically "communication pleasure," enjoyable, and calling for no action. Many persons, however, Stephenson points out, play at newsreading very seriously. There is "an air of mystery and ritual" about newsreading, Stephenson says. "It is deeply absorbing, almost trancelike."

[5] In *The Press in Perspective*, ed. by Ralph D. Casey (Baton Rouge, Louisiana State University Press, 1963), p. 35.

[6] *Ibid.*, p. 44.

[7] In *Propaganda and International Relations*, ed. by Urban G. Whitaker (San Francisco, Howard Chandler, 1960), p. 126.

[8] Casey, *op. cit.*, p. 106.

[9] H. H. Hayman in *Journal of the Institute of Journalists*, London, 51:501 (September, October, 1963), p. 103.

[10] Materials sent the writer by Dr. Fred Luchsinger, foreign editor of the *Neue Zürcher Zeitung*, August 6, 1965.

[11] Casey, *op. cit.*, p. 35.

[12] Helen Hill Miller, "The Best Newspaper in Europe," *Esquire* (February, 1962), p. 72.

[13] *A Free and Responsible Press* (Chicago, University of Chicago Press, 1947), p. 20. There were four other standards for the press given by this group headed by Robert Hutchins, and they will be discussed later in this book. Britain's Royal Commission on the Press expected much the same of the press. Compare, "The Standard by Which the Press Should Be Judged," in *Reader in Public Opinion and Communication*, ed. by

Bernard Berelson and Morris Janowitz (Glencoe, Ill., The Free Press, 1953), pp. 489–496.

[14] Such criticism is provided in numerous journal and magazine articles and in such recent books as A. J. Liebling's *The Press* (New York, Ballantine Books, 1961), Bernard C. Cohen's *The Press and Foreign Policy* (Princeton, Princeton University Press, 1963), and Felix Greene's *A Curtain of Ignorance* (New York, Doubleday, 1964).

[15] "The Press, Atlantic Union and World Peace," *Montana Journalism Review* (Spring, 1962), p. 9.

Chapter 2

[1] Ithiel de Sola Pool, *The "Prestige Papers": A Survey of Their Editorials* (Palo Alto, Stanford University Press, 1952), p. 1.

[2] Wilbur Schramm, *One Day in the World's Press* (Palo Alto, Stanford University Press, 1959), p. 5.

[3] Unfortunately, there is an abysmal ignorance about the international press among American journalism students and practicing journalists. Although the situation is improving, it is still safe to say that the average American student and journalist knows less about the press of other countries than do their counterparts in other major nations. This writer, in fifteen years of teaching journalism, has never had more than three students in any one class who could even name, much less comment on, as many as ten newspapers published outside the United States.

[4] Schramm, *op. cit.*, p. 4.

[5] Robert W. Desmond, *The Press and World Affairs* (New York, Appleton-Century-Crofts, 1937), p. 375.

Chapter 3

[1] Heinz-Dietrich Fischer in his *Die grossen Zeitungen* (Munich, Deutscher Taschenbuch Verlag, 1966) says that "Weltpresse" has long been used in Germany for these serious supranational newspapers which have reputations and circulations beyond the national borders. He makes the point that although such newspapers are generally called "Weltblätter," they often are referred to as "Qualitätszeitungen," "Prestige-Zeitungen," "grossen Zeitungen," and are contrasted to the "populäre Presse" or the "Massenpresse," known also in Britain as the "popular" and "mass" press. *Die grossen Zeitungen*, pp. 12–22 *passim.*

[2] Alberto Gainza Paz, making the presentation of the 1965 World Press Achievement Award of the American Newspaper Publishers Association Foundation to the editor of the small provincial *Yeni Adana* of Adana, Turkey (New York City, April 21, 1965).

[3] Jean Daniel, "Camus as Journalist," *New Republic* (June 13, 1964), p. 19.

[4] *Ibid.* The American, Leo Rosten, agrees with Camus, and says that too much of what appears in the press is "dreadful tripe; inane in content; banal in style; muddy in reasoning; mawkish in statement, and offensive to men of learning and refinement." Leo Rosten, "The Intellectual and the Mass Media," *Daedalus* (Spring, 1960), p. 27.

[5] Daniel, *loc. cit.*

[6] *Ibid.*, p. 21.

[7] Roy E. Larsen (Chairman of the Executive Committee of Time, Inc.) in a lecture, "Communication and Education," at Boston University, 1960.

[8] Andrew Sharf, *The British Press and Jews Under Nazi Rule* (London, Oxford University Press, 1964).

[9] "Rating the American Newspaper," *Saturday Review* (May 13, 1961), p. 62.

[10] "La Grandeza de *Excélsior*," *Excélsior*, Mexico City (August 28, 1964).

[11] *Ibid.*

[12] Walter O'Hearn, "Canada's Dailies are Provincial—With a World Outlook," *IPI Report*, Zurich, 10:12 (April, 1962), p. 6.

[13] *The Press in Perspective*, ed. by Ralph Casey (Baton Rouge, Louisiana State University Press, 1963), p. 44.

[14] "What Americans Can Learn from the Foreign Press" (Seventeenth annual lecture sponsored by the American Newspaper Guild and the Minnesota School of Journalism, Minneapolis, October 24, 1963).

[15] Casey, *op. cit.*, p. 33.

[16] Felix Greene, *A Curtain of Ignorance: How the American Public Has Been Misinformed about China* (New York, Doubleday, 1964), pp. 321–323 *passim.* Compare, A. T. Steele, *The American People and China* (New York, McGraw-Hill, 1966), pp. 141–169.

[17] "Vietnam Witness," *Newsweek* (April 11, 1966), p. 98.

[18] Wilbur Schramm, *One Day in the World's Press* (Palo Alto, Stanford University Press, 1959).

[19] *Ibid.*, p. 5.

[20] *Ibid.*, p. 137.

[21] *Ibid.*

[22] "Rating the American Newspaper," *Saturday Review* (May 13, 1961), pp. 59–62.

[23] John C. Merrill, "U.S. Panel Names World's Ten 'Quality' Dailies," *Journalism Quarterly*, 41:4 (Autumn, 1964), pp. 568–572. Compare, Merrill's "What Are the World's Best Dailies?" *Gazette*, Leiden, 10:3 (1964), pp. 259–260, and "Los 20 Mejores Diarios del Mundo," *La Prensa*, Buenos Aires (August 22, 1964); Heinz-Dietrich Fischer, *op. cit.*, pp. 17–18, 293–295.

[24] John C. Merrill, "International 'Elite Press' Survey, 1965." (Sponsored in part by the Research Council, University of Missouri, Columbia.)

Chapter 4

[1] D. H. Radler, *El Gringo: The Yankee Image in Latin America* (New York, Chilton, 1962), p. 8.

[2] *Ibid.*

[3] *Ibid.*

[4] *Ibid.*, pp. 8–9.

[5] John Tebbel, "How the British View Their Press," *Saturday Review* (December 8, 1962), p. 68.

[6] Letter from Dr. Robert Desmond to writer, July 27, 1964.

[7] Probably the best-known younger American scholars in international journalism today are John B. Adams (North Carolina), Marvin Alisky (Arizona State), Floyd Arpan (Indiana), Carter Bryan (Maryland), Alex Edelstein (Washington), Mary Gardner (Michigan State), Theodore Kruglak (Southern California), James W. Markham (Iowa), John McNelly (Wisconsin), John Merrill (Missouri), William Porter (Michigan), Wilbur Schramm (Stanford), Harry Skornia (Illinois), Quintus Wilson (West Virginia), and Frederick T. C. Yu (Columbia).

[8] Jacques Kayser, *One Week's News: Comparative Study of 17 Major Dailies for a Seven-Day Period* (Paris, UNESCO, 1953).

[9] Wilbur Schramm, *One Day in the World's Press: Fourteen Great Newspapers on a Day of Crisis* (Palo Alto, Stanford University Press, 1959).

[10] Mimeographed release by E. L. Bernays (26 East 64th St., New York) on February 13, 1961.

[11] John Tebbel, "Rating the American Newspaper," *Saturday Review* (May 13, 1961), pp. 60–61. Other U.S. papers listed most frequently, after the top ten, were the Atlanta *Constitution, Minneapolis Tribune, Kansas City Star, Los Angeles Times, Des Moines Register, Denver Post, Washington Star, Minneapolis Star, San Francisco Chronicle, Toledo Blade, Miami Herald, Chicago Sun-Times, St. Louis Globe-Democrat, Detroit Free Press,* and *Buffalo News.*

[12] John C. Merrill, "Foreign News Media," *Modern Journalism* (New York, Pitman Publishing Corp., 1962), Chap. 11, pp. 214–231. See especially Table 11:1, "Leading Foreign 'Quality' or 'Prestige' Daily Newspapers."

[13] "Amerikanische Professoren über die 'besten Zeitungen'," *Neue Zürcher Zeitung,* Zurich (November 11, 1963).

[14] John C. Merrill, "U.S. Panel Names World's Ten Leading 'Quality' Dailies," *Journalism Quarterly* (Autumn, 1964), p. 570.

[15] John C. Merrill, "International 'Elite Press' Survey, 1965" (University of Missouri Study).

[16] Questionnaires were sent to editors in the United States, West Germany, Britain, Japan, Switzerland, Italy, Mexico, Denmark, Australia, and India.

[17] Steen Albrectsen and Niels Holst, *Avisen og Ungdommen* (Arhus, Kanniki Trysk, 1965), pp. 57–58.

[18] The known examples of the "popular" press, and the ones having the largest circulations are Japan's *Yomiuri* (circ. about 3 million), West Germany's *Bild* (circ. about 4.5 million), France's *France-Soir* (circ. 1.5 million), Britain's *Daily Mirror* (circ. 5 million), and *Daily Express* (circ. 4.5 million), and the United States' New York *Daily News* (circ. 2 million).

Chapter 5

[1] John C. Merrill, "The Press and Social Responsibility" *Freedom of Information Center Publication,* No. 001, University of Missouri (March, 1965).

[2] The Monarchist *ABC* and the Catholic *Ya,* for example, often carry outspoken criticisms of municipal officials and are taken seriously in Spanish ministerial circles. *ABC, Ya,* and *La Vanguardia* (Barcelona) have circulations of about 100,000 each, but the total daily circulation of the country is not much more than 600,000—about one copy of a paper to every 50 Spaniards.

[3] Most elite papers of the world are small—under 300,000 daily circulations. The largest are found in the U.S.S.R., Red China, and Japan where *Pravda, People's Daily,* and *Asahi* have circulations exceeding two million. A few other elite dailies, like *The New York Times* and Italy's *Corriere della Sera,* have circulations of more than 500,000.

[4] Leo Rosten, "The Intellectual and the Mass Media," *Daedalus* (Spring, 1960), pp. 333–346.

[5] In most parts of Africa the problems of establishing some sort of stable government while various factions are vying for political power hamper the development of any type of viable press, much less an elite press. Aside from political unrest, other problems face newspapers of the new African states: financial instability, unskilled journalists, a multiplicity of lan-

guages, high illiteracy, unsettled political direction, and a widespread absence of native national leadership.

6 Tertius Myburgh, "The South African Press: Hope in an Unhappy Land," *Nieman Reports,* 20:1 (March, 1966), p. 6.

7 *Ibid.,* p. 4.

8 "Newspapers of the World—IX," London *Times* (March 10, 1965).

9 "Israel's Serious Press," *Service Documentaire F.I.J.*, Brussels (May, 1965).

10 *Ibid.*

11 Brazil, with its Portuguese-language press sitting like an island in a sea of Spanish, has developed an extremely vigorous and qualitative press—especially in its two largest cities, Rio and São Paulo. Several dailies are outstanding, with *O Estado de São Paulo* and *O Globo* of Rio undoubtedly the best.

12 Quincy Howe, "What Americans Can Learn From the Foreign Press" (Lecture in Minneapolis, Minn., October 24, 1963).

13 *Ibid.*

Chapter 6

ABC

1 *Editor & Publisher International Yearbook, 1966;* Kenneth Olson, *The History Makers* (Baton Rouge; Louisiana State University Press, 1966), p. 276; Compare, "Prensa Española," *L'Echo de la Presse et de la Publicité* (June 19, 1967), pp. 28–29.

2 This edition's director in 1966 was Joaquín Carlos López Lozano, one of Spain's most distinguished journalists.

3 Nicolás González Ruiz, *El Periodismo: Teoría y Práctica* (Barcelona; Editorial Noguer, S.A., 1953), opposite p. 352.

4 Antonio Espina, *El Cuarto Poder: Cien Años de Periodismo Español* (Madrid; Agilar, 1960), pp. 266–267.

5 The weekly airmail edition for foreigners, starting in the spring of 1950, has the bulk of its circulation in Latin America; however, its dispersal throughout the world—especially in university libraries—is very widespread.

6 Olson, *op. cit.*, p. 283.

7 Letter and typed material from Julián Cortés-Cavanillas (Secretary General of *ABC* editorial staff) to author, July 2, 1966. In 1966 the foreign correspondents of *ABC* were Alfonso Barra (Bonn), Pedro Massa Pérez (Buenos Aires), Antonio de Obregón (Lisbon), Claudio y Mercedes (London), Salvador Jiménez (Paris), José Salas y Guirior (Rome), Luis Calvo Andaluz (Saigon), Samuel Cohen Garzón (Tangiers), and José María Massip (Washington). The last-named, Massip, writes daily *cronicas*, or daily summaries, of the State of the Union from Washington, which have long been one of the best features of the Spanish press. (See Robert E. G. Harris, *Spain's Move Toward Freedom of the Press,* offset typescript, UCLA Department of Journalism, 1966.)

8 Espina, *op. cit.*, p. 296; Cortés-Cavanillas material.

9 Torcuato Luca de Tena was born in Seville in 1861. The son of an industrialist, he studied law and traveled widely through Europe, developing a love for journalism as he observed the great progress in the graphic arts in Germany and France. He brought back to Spain the idea of an illustrated magazine from Berlin, and launched *Blanco y Negro* in May,

1891. It was an immediate success. Then in 1903 he began *ABC* as an experiment in tabloid journalism of a serious nature; it, too, caught on at once. King Alfonso XIII honored him with the title of "Marqués de Luca de Tena" on January 23, 1929. (Espina, *op. cit.*, p. 264 and Cortés-Cavanillas material.)

[10] Cortés-Cavanillas material. For early history of *ABC* and its first two editors, see Arturo Mori, *La Prensa Española de Nuestro Tiempo* (Mexico, Ediciones Mensaje, 1943), pp. 61–64.

[11] "Prensa Española, S.A." today publishes, in addition to *ABC* and *Blanco y Negro*, a foreign air edition of *ABC*, which is a weekly.

[12] Cortés-Cavanillas material. The writer is grateful for much historical material, as well as current descriptive data, furnished by Michael Perceval from his radio script "The Madrid A.B.C." prepared as part of a series on great newspapers of the world by "Radio Liberty," Munich, July 27, 1964.

Aftenposten

[1] Olson, *op. cit.*, p. 79; *Editor & Publisher International Year Book*, 1966.

[2] *Bergens Tidende* of Bergen, however, is probably the second best-known Norwegian paper among international readers.

[3] Much of the statistical information and some other material in this profile was furnished the author by Einar Ostgaard of Haslum, Norway (June, 1966). Most other information comes from *Aftenposten* itself and from the author's study of copies of the paper during 1966 and 1967.

[4] Statistical information from *Aftenposten*, July 28, 1966 ("Statistisk Avdeling" of January 27, 1966).

[5] *Ibid.*

[6] Ostgaard, *loc. cit.*

[7] Olson, *op. cit.*, p. 72. Compare, Olav Brunvand, "The Underground Press in Norway," *Gazette*, Leiden, 9:2 (1963), pp. 125–132.

[8] Richard B. Eide, *Norway's Press, 1940–1945 During the Occupation*, (Stillwater, Oklahoma A&M College, 1948). Compare articles dealing with this bleak period of *Aftenposten*'s history in *Journalism Quarterly*, 18:1 (March, 1941), pp. 64–65, and 24:4 (December, 1947), pp. 343–347.

[9] Ostgaard, *loc. cit.*

[10] *Ibid.*

[11] S. Fiorentini, "Serious, Well Written and Reliable," *World Press News and Advertisers' Review*, London (August 27, 1965) p. 25.

Dagens Nyheter

[1] Ian Rodger, "The Swedish Press in the Eyes of a British Journalist," *IPI Report*, Zurich (June, 1964), p. 3.

[2] Thomas Harris, "Something for Everybody in Sweden's 'Dagens Nyheter'," *IPI Report*, Zurich (February, 1959), p. 7. Compare, Frederic Fleisher, "The Swedish Press Subsidy Plan and the Collapse of Stockholms–Tidningen," *Gazette*, Leiden, 12:2/3 (1966), p. 186.

[3] Wilbur Schramm, *One Day in the World's Press* (Palo Alto, Stanford University Press, 1959), pp. 57–58.

[4] Harris, *op. cit.*, p. 6.

[5] Anders Yngve Pers, *The Swedish Press* (Stockholm, The Institute, 1963), pp. 25–26.

6 See Ake Thulstrup, "German Pressure on the Swedish Press During the Second World War," *Gazette*, Leiden, 9:2 (1963), pp. 115–122.

7 Pers, *loc. cit.*

8 Rodger, *loc. cit.*

9 *Ibid.*

Le Figaro

1 Jacques Derogy and Serge Richard, "The Revolt of the Fourth Estate," *Atlas* (September, 1965), pp. 151–153. Many circulation figures can be found for *Le Figaro*, ranging from 390,000 to 525,000; the 400,000 figure seems a good compromise. Derogy and Richard call *Le Figaro* the most prosperous of Parisian dailies and say that readership of other French papers is declining because the press has "failed to adapt itself to a changing situation." What the public wants today, they say, is less "hot" news and more detailed reports and background material.

2 *Figaro* was the *Barber of Seville*, put on the stage by Beaumarchais and to music by Mozart.

3 Pierre de Bacourt and John W. Cunliffe, *French of Today* (New York, Macmillan, 1927), p. 27.

4 "Fools and Opposition," *Time* (June 5, 1950), pp. 70–74.

5 Eugène Tavernier, *Du Journalisme* (Paris, H. Oudin, 1902), p. 199.

6 *Ibid.*, p. 237.

7 *Ibid.*, p. 302. Compare, René Pucheu, "Dans la Lumiere du Figaro," *Presse-Actualité*, Paris (February, 1967), pp. 6–17.

8 Pierre Lazereff, *Deadline* (New York, Random House, 1942), p. 42.

9 Robert W. Desmond, *The Press and World Affairs* (New York, Appleton-Century-Crofts, 1937), p. 217.

10 From a speech given by Nicolas Chatelain at the University of Missouri School of Journalism, April 30, 1954, on accepting an Honor Medal for Distinguished Service in Journalism in behalf of *Le Figaro*, which he represented as Washington correspondent.

11 When *Le Figaro* began publication again in 1944, Mme. Yvonne Cotnareanu, owner and former wife of the late François Coty, was virtually ignored; Brisson seemingly had full power and government support. Through an intricate series of court decisions Brisson managed to hold out against Mme. Cotnareanu's attempts to oust him. In July, 1950 Mme. Cotnareanu sold half her stock to a pro-Brisson group headed by Jean Prouvost.

12 J. Alvarez del Vayo, "Who's Who in the French Press," *The Nation* (June 22, 1946), pp. 745–747.

13 E. Putnam, "Press in Europe," *New Republic* (November 3, 1947), p. 35.

14 Theodore H. White, *The Reporter* (November 7, 1950), p. 28.

15 Jean Genêt, "Letter from Paris," *New Yorker* (October 4, 1958), p. 108.

16 John Hohenberg, *Foreign Correspondence* (New York, Columbia University Press, 1964), p. 445. Compare, "The Reassurance of St. Figaro," *Time* (November 25, 1966), pp. 95–96: "In addition to eleven foreign bureaus, it keeps some half dozen correspondents on the road in search of background stories, any one of which may fill a full page."

17 Olson, *op. cit.*, p. 193.

18 Louis Gabriel-Robinet is a distinguished journalist who served under Pierre Brisson as *Le Figaro*'s editor-in-chief. He is the author of several books on French journalism, and gives insights into the philosophy and character of *Le Figaro* in his autobiographical *Je suis Journaliste* (Paris, Éditions du Conquistador, 1961).

The Scotsman

[1] "Honor Awards for Distinguished Service in Journalism, 1963," *University of Missouri Bulletin*, No. 157 (January 6, 1964), p. 20.

[2] Material sent in letter to the author by Alastair M. Dunnett, editor of *The Scotsman*, June 21, 1965.

[3] *The Observer* is Britain's oldest, and probably best, Sunday paper, founded in 1791 by W. S. Bourne. Along with the *Sunday Times* and the *Sunday Telegraph*, it forms the quality Sunday press of Britain. Until 1942 it was avowedly Conservative; then it became politically Independent. Usually considered *The Observer's* finest hours was the period 1908–1942 when it was edited by J. L. Garvin under whom the circulation rose from 20,000 to 240,000. The contemporary *Observer* owes much of its universality to Garvin although it has departed from his politics. Today the paper is considered liberal with a small "l," and is aimed at the younger, better-off, better-educated segments of the community. It probably has more influence abroad than at home. Its liberalism is manifested in its editorial position that the United States should recognize Red China and that Red China should be a member of the United Nations. The paper has seventy-five foreign correspondents, and its reputation mainly rests, as always, on its coverage of foreign affairs and the arts. (Letter and completed questionnaire from J. Brunner, assistant manager of *The Observer*, August 10, 1965.)

[4] Dunnett material.

[5] *Ibid.*

[6] *Ibid.*

[7] *Ibid.*

[8] *Ibid.*

[9] Harold Herd, *The March of Journalism* (London, Allen & Unwin, 1952), p. 167. It should be noted, however, that although *The Scotsman* had flourished during and immediately after World War II, its fortunes declined slowly until, by 1953, it had a bank overdraft and was losing heavily each year. It was at this point that Roy Thomson bought the paper and instilled new financial life into it. (See Russell Braddon, "Croesus in a Crumpled Suit," *The Sunday Times*, London, October 10, 1965, p. 46.)

[10] Russell Braddon, *Roy Thomson of Fleet Street* (New York, Walker and Company, 1965), p. 225.

[11] *Ibid.*, p. 236. Compare, Francis Williams, "Roy Thomson Invades America," *Harper's* (February, 1962), pp. 70–77, and John Tebbel, "The Amazing Communications World of Roy Thomson," *Saturday Review* (October 9, 1965), p. 67.

La Stampa

[1] Kenneth E. Olson, *op. cit.*, p. 252; *Editor & Publisher International Yearbook*, 1966.

[2] Frank Brutto, "In Italy: The Word is Complicated," *Montana Journalism Review* (Spring, 1962), p. 11; "Newspapers of the World—XIV," London *Times* (March 30, 1965).

[3] "Newspapers of the World—XIV."

[4] The period of *La Stampa* in Mussolini's early days is discussed (from a Fascist standpoint) in Adolf Dresler, *Geschichte der italienschen Presse* (Berlin, Oldenbourg, 1938), Pt. 3, pp. 48, 118.

[5] "Newspapers of the World—XIV."
[6] Interview with Dr. Paolo Bonaiuti in Milan, Italy, July 23, 1966.
[7] For a good discussion of this special and varied page of serious essays and other assorted articles of quality, see Chap. 16, "La Terza Paginâ," in Sam Carcano, *Il Giornalismo* (Milan, Casa Editrice Dr. Francesco Vallarde, 1956), pp. 205–211.
[8] "Newspapers of the World—XIV."
[9] *Ibid.*; interview with Dr. Giovanni Pini (USIS) in Milan, Italy, July 24, 1966.

Svenska Dagbladet

[1] Pers, *op. cit.*, pp. 27–28.
[2] *Svenska Dagbladet*'s plant moved in 1962 from the traditional newspaper district of Klara. The new fourteen-story structure at Marieburg in central Stockholm is larger than is needed today but provides ample space for expansion. The paper has two 275-ton rotary presses, each capable of printing over 50,000 copies an hour.
[3] "Newspapers of the World—XIII," London *Times* (March 23, 1965).
[4] Pers, *loc. cit.*
[5] Letter and completed questionnaire from Allan Hernelius, chief editor, May 14, 1966.
[6] Pers, *loc. cit.*
[7] Hernelius Letter/Questionnaire.
[8] *Ibid.*

The Yorkshire Post

[1] Mildred A. Gibb and Frank Beckwith, *The Yorkshire Post: Two Centuries* (Leeds, The Yorkshire Conservative Newspaper Co., Ltd., 1954), p. 3.
[2] Harold Herd, *The March of Journalism* (London, Allen & Unwin, 1952), p. 183.
[3] Gibb and Beckwith, *op. cit.*, p. 34.
[4] *Ibid.*, p. 44.
[5] *Ibid.*, p. 54; Information supplied by Denis B. Wylie, publicity manager of *The Yorkshire Post.*
[6] Wylie information.
[7] Gibb and Beckwith, *op. cit.*, p. 88.
[8] *Ibid.*, p. 95; Wylie information.
[9] H. R. Pratt Boorman, *Newspaper Society: 125 Years of Progress* (Maidstone, Kent Messenger, 1961), pp. 149–150.

Chapter 7

Borba

[1] "Newspapers of the World—XXII," London *Times* (April 22, 1965).
[2] Interview with Sergije Lukac, Belgrade editor, April 12, 1965, at the University of Missouri School of Journalism.
[3] "Newspapers of the World—XXII"; Lukac interview.
[4] Kenneth E. Olson, *The History Makers* (Baton Rouge, Louisiana State University Press, 1966), pp. 426–428.

[5] Since 1956, Yugoslav papers have been owned by what is called "society"—not the same as "the State." Each paper is operated by its employees who share in its profits. This has had the effect of freeing the press from financial and administrative control by the State, and has brought a greater degree of independence and a greater reliance on Western journalistic procedures.

[6] "Newspapers of the World—XXII."

[7] John C. Merrill, Carter Bryan, and Marvin Alisky, *The Foreign Press* (Baton Rouge, Louisiana State University Press, 1964), pp. 126–127.

[8] *Editor & Publisher International Yearbook, 1966.*

[9] Lukac interview, April 12, 1965.

Ha'aretz

[1] Aviv Akrony, cultural attaché of Israeli Consulate (Chicago) in interview with author in Columbia, Mo., April 22, 1966; see also entire issue of *Gazette*, Leiden, 7:1 (1961) given over to Israeli press.

[2] "Newspapers of the World—XVIII," London *Times* (April 7, 1965), p. 11.

[3] *Ibid.*

[4] *Ibid.*; Akrony interview.

[5] Moshe Ron, "Press and Journalists in Israel," *I.F.J. Information,* Brussels (January–June, 1965), p. 2.

[6] "Newspapers of the World—XVIII."

[7] *Ibid.*

[8] The 23–27 dailies of Israel (number varies with each source) are centered in Tel Aviv (Jerusalem has a daily) and all are nationals. Only about half of them are in Hebrew; others are in a dozen languages, ranging from English to Yiddish, from Arabic to German, and from Hungarian to Polish. There is even a Bulgarian daily. Most are subsidized by the political parties, ranging from *Hamodia* (ultraorthodox) to *Kol Haam* (Communist). The three in the best financial situation are the political independents: *Ha'aretz, Ma'ariv,* and *Yediot Ahronot.* Although many of the dailies are political, they try to be quality also; there are no sensational "yellow" papers among them. (Dan Pines, "The Press of Israel," *IPI Report*, Zurich [May, 1961], p. 1).

Harry Golden, "The Israeli Press," *Publisher's Auxiliary* (June 20, 1964), p. 4.

Helsingin Sanomat

[1] "Newspapers of the World—XIX," London *Times* (April 13, 1965), p. 11.

[2] Gayle Waldrop, "Eljas Erkko, Publisher, and Source of News," *Editor & Publisher* (November 10, 1956), p. 76. Compare, E. A. Berg, "The Development of the Press in Finland," *Gazette,* 9:2 (1963), pp. 101–107.

[3] "Newspapers of the World—XIX."

[4] *Ibid.*

[5] A. E. Petersen, Jr., "Kekkonen and the Finnish Press," *Montana Journalism Review*, No. 5 (1962), p. 18.

[6] Waldrop, *loc. cit.*

[7] *Ibid.*

[8] "Newspapers of the World—XIX."

Izvestia

1 "Newspapers of the World—II," London *Times* (February 24, 1965).

2 Leo Gruliow, "After Khrushchev," *IPI Report,* Zurich (December, 1964), p. 2; "Revisionism in Russia," *Time* (July 30, 1965), p. 32; Olson, *op. cit.,* p. 322.

3 Michael Milenkovitch, *The View from Red Square* (New York, Hobbs, Dorman & Co., 1966), p. 10. Compare, J. C. Merrill, C. Bryan and M. Alisky, *The Foreign Press* (Baton Rouge, Louisiana State University Press, 1964), p. 111.

4 "Newspapers of the World—II."

5 Antony Buzek in his *How the Communist Press Works* (New York, Frederick A. Praeger, 1964), pp. 176–177, points out that news reporting is improving and, especially as it relates to foreign countries, the Soviet press generally is printing much more straight or "hard" news (*e.g.,* news of American space achievements). Compare, E. I. Bugaev, "Press Policy Since Khrushchev, The Role of a Growing Press," *Sovetskaya Pechat,* No. 5 (1965) in *The Soviet Press* (Spring, 1966), p. 11.

6 "Newspapers of the World—II." Compare, Buzek, pp. 223–224, and "The Soviet Press . . . a fresh view by three U.S. newspapermen," *The Quill* (October, 1966), p. 18.

7 Much care is given to aesthetics of page layout and typography in *Izvestia* and most Soviet newspapers. The pages are planned carefully, often twenty-four hours ahead, and there are seldom changes made to accommodate last-minute news. *Izvestia* has no large newsroom as is common in United States papers; each writer has a separate glass-walled office done in modern decor.

Pravda

1 "For a Businesslike Tone in Our Press," *Pravda* editorial (June 27, 1965), p. 1 in *Current Digest of the Soviet Press,* 17:30 (August 18, 1965), pp. 34–35.

2 Antony Buzek, *How the Communist Press Works,* p. 215.

3 *Ibid.,* pp. 215–216.

4 "U.S. Newsman Draws Portrait of Pravda," *Editor & Publisher* (November 12, 1960), p. 38.

5 "The Voice of Pravda: Russia's Popular Party Paper Turns Fifty," *National Observer* (May 13, 1962), p. 9.

6 Michael M. Milenkovitch, *op. cit.,* pp. 7–14; Olson, *op. cit.,* p. 322; Buzek, *op. cit.,* p. 216; Bugaev, *op. cit.,* p. 11; *The Quill* (October, 1966), p. 17.

7 Heinz-Dietrich Fischer, *Die grossen Zeitungen* (Munich, Deutscher Taschenbuch Verlag, 1966), pp. 175–176. Compare, Pavel Satyukov, "Pravda's Golden Jubilee," *USSR* (May, 1962).

8 Wilbur Schramm, *One Day in the World's Press* (Palo Alto, Stanford University Press, 1952), p. 7. Compare, Jacques Kayser, *One Week's News* (Paris, UNESCO, 1953), pp. 39–40, and W. Phillips Davison, *International Political Communication* (New York, Praeger, 1965), p. 109.

9 Victor Zorza, "End of a Liberal Pravda Editor," *The Guardian,* London (September 22, 1965), p. 11.

10 *Ibid.;* Olson, *op. cit.,* p. 330.

11 "U.S. Newsman Draws Portrait of Pravda," p. 38.

[12] "Russians Upgrade Regional Newspapers," *Editor & Publisher* (July 9, 1966), p. 32.
[13] *Ibid.* Compare, "Revisions in Russia," *Time* (July 30, 1965), p. 32.
[14] L. Karpisky, "Pravda" in *Current Digest of the Soviet Press*, 17:21 (June 16, 1965), pp. 26–27.

Die Presse

[1] Adam Wandruszka, *Geschichte Einer Zeitung* (Vienna, Neue Wiener Presse Druck-und Verlagsgesellshaft m.b.h., 1958), pp. 11–12.
[2] *Ibid.*, p. 54.
[3] Olson, *op. cit.*, pp. 200–201; Wandruszka, *op. cit.*, p. 64.
[4] Wandruszka, *op. cit.*, p. 79.
[5] *Ibid.*, p. 111.
[6] *Ibid.*, "Das Feuilleton," pp. 123–136.
[7] Fischer, *op. cit.*, p. 97.
[8] *Ibid.*, pp. 98–99.
[9] *Editor & Publisher International Year Book, 1966.* Compare, Olson, *op. cit.*, p. 213.

Chapter 8

The (Baltimore) Sun

[1] Completed questionnaire and letter from Paul A. Banker, managing editor of *The Sun*, dated October 18, 1966. Also, a random-copy analysis of the paper by the writer from November, 1966 through August, 1967.
[2] "Sun Shine," *Time* (May 6, 1963), p. 88.
[3] *Ibid.*
[4] "The Top U.S. Dailies," *Time* (January 10, 1964), p. 58.
[5] Based on randomly studied issues of the paper, November, 1966 through August, 1967.
[6] Banker Questionnaire and Letter, October 18, 1966.
[7] *The Baltimore Sunpapers* (a thirty-one-page booklet published by the Sunpapers, no date, containing historical sketch and policy description) sent the writer in October, 1966. Most of the historical data is from this booklet.
[8] *Ibid.*, p. 11.
[9] Banker Questionnaire and Letter.

The Christian Science Monitor

[1] Mimeographed material sent the writer by *The Monitor*, March 1, 1965.
[2] *The World in Focus* (booklet about *The Monitor* published by the Christian Science Publishing Co., 1965).
[3] Erwin Canham on "Today" Show, NBC-Television, April 19, 1966.
[4] Completed questionnaire from Courtney R. Sheldon, managing editor of *The Monitor*, dated September 29, 1966.
[5] *Ibid.*
[6] Quoted in *The World in Focus.*

[7] Analysis of copies of *The Monitor* from November, 1966 through January, 1967.

[8] *The World in Focus.*

[9] *The Christian Science Monitor*, March 1, 1965. Compare, Edmund C. Arnold, "A New Look for The Christian Science Monitor," *The Quill* (May, 1965), pp. 12–15.

St. Louis Post-Dispatch

[1] Pulitzer had begun his journalistic career in St. Louis in 1868 as a reporter for the old *Westliche Post*, a German-language paper. As his English improved, he was elected to the Missouri House of Representatives (1869), and acquired an interest in the *Westliche Post* in 1871. Two years later he sold his interest in the paper and bought another bankrupt German-language paper (*Staats-Zeitung*). He sold its Associated Press franchise and its mechanical equipment for enough to buy the *Dispatch* in 1878. After his time in St. Louis, he bought the *New York World* from Jay Gould in 1883 and moved to New York; it was actually there with the *World* that he made his most notable mark on American journalism. (There are several excellent biographies of Joseph Pulitzer; see the Bibliography at the end of this book.)

[2] *The Story of the St. Louis Post-Dispatch*, 7th ed. (St. Louis, Pulitzer Publishing Co., 1962), p. 6.

[3] Completed questionnaire and letter from Frank Leeming, public affairs director of the *Post-Dispatch*, September 2, 1965; interviews in St. Louis, November and December, 1966.

[4] *The Story of the St. Louis Post-Dispatch*, p. 58.

[5] Leeming Questionnaire.

[6] "Dr. King's Move into Viet Nam," Max Freedman column, *Post-Dispatch* (August 19, 1965).

[7] Editorial in *Post-Dispatch* (August 20, 1965).

[8] Leeming Questionnaire.

[9] *The Story of the St. Louis Post-Dispatch*, pp. 7–11.

[10] Leeming Questionnaire.

[11] From printed brochure "Career Opportunities in the Newspaper Industry" sent writer by Public Affairs Department of the *Post-Dispatch* (January, 1967).

[12] *The Story of the St. Louis Post-Dispatch*, p. 56.

[13] *Ibid.*

[14] *Ibid.*, p. 55.

[15] *Ibid.*, p. 57.

[16] *Ibid.*, p. 12.

The Globe and Mail

[1] Completed questionnaire and letter from James L. Cooper, editor-in-chief of *The Globe and Mail*, dated September 30, 1966.

[2] Letter from R. J. Doyle, editor of *The Globe and Mail*, dated November 30, 1964.

[3] *Globe and Mail* historical and informational material (undated) sent the writer in December, 1966; most of the historical data here is from this material.

[4] "Industrialist's Bid Wins Toronto Globe," *Editor & Publisher* (February 19, 1955), p. 8.

[5] *Ibid.*

[6] Stuart Keate, "How Good are the Newspapers of Canada?" *Nieman Reports,* 20:3 (September, 1966), pp. 28–32.

[7] *Ibid.*

[8] Cooper Questionnaire, September 30, 1966.

[9] "Your Daily Newspaper" (special section on Canadian press), *The Gazette* of Montreal (September 15, 1966), p. 39.

[10] Cooper Questionnaire.

Winnipeg Free Press

[1] Bruce Hutchinson, "Canada's Gadfly: The Winnipeg Free Press," *Harper's Magazine* (April, 1963).

[2] Letter to the writer from Shane MacKay, executive editor of *Free Press,* dated September 29, 1966.

[3] Hutchinson, *loc. cit.*

[4] MacKay Letter.

[5] Hutchinson, *loc cit.*

[6] Although most critics have nothing but praise for Dafoe's editorials, there have been dissenting voices. Grattan O'Leary, a Canadian journalist who was very familiar with the work of Dafoe, wrote in 1966: "I thought some of Dafoe's editorials during the election of 1917 were irresponsible, lacked measure and perspective. At the same time, I must add this: I think the two finest pieces of journalism I have ever read in my day were the last two pages of Dafoe's 'Laurier' and his obituary tribute to his friend, Harry Sifton." ("A Century of Journalism" in *The Gazette,* Montreal, September 15, 1966—a special section on Canadian journalism.)

[7] "Newspapers of the World—XX," London *Times* (April 14, 1965).

[8] Malone is publisher and vice president of the Winnipeg Free Press Company Ltd. President is John Sifton, grandson of Sir Clifford Sifton who was owner of the *Free Press* when Dafoe was first editor.

[9] MacKay Letter.

[10] Hutchinson, *loc. cit.*

[11] MacKay Letter.

[12] *Ibid.*

O Estado de S. Paulo

[1] Completed questionnaire from José M. Homem de Montes, assistant to the Director of *O Estado,* dated November 9, 1966.

[2] *O Globo* of Rio, with 200,000 circulation daily, was founded in 1925. An independent conservative evening paper, it has played a large part in the social and political life of Brazil. *O Globo* is the paper which absorbs the highest percentage of young journalists from Brazil's schools of journalism—at the National University and the Catholic University, both in Rio. The paper has seven foreign correspondents—in California, Buenos Aires, Lisbon, London, Paris. *O Globo,* of all Brazilian papers, is probably best known for its crusading spirit and it believes itself to be the country's best paper, listing *O Estado de São Paulo* as second best. (Completed questionnaire from Walter Ramos Poyares, public relations director of *O Globo* and letter from Roberto Marinho, editor, dated September 16, 1965.)

[3] "Best in Brazil," *Newsweek* (February 3, 1964), p. 75. Compare, Homem de Montes Questionnaire.

[4] Content analysis of *O Estado* (randomly selected issues) during November and December, 1966, and January, 1967.

[5] Antonio L. O. Figueiredo, columnist for Diarios Associados with headquarters in São Paulo, in an interview with the writer in Columbia, Mo., November 10, 1966.

[6] Jacques Kayser, *One Week's News* (Paris, UNESCO, 1953), p. 47.

[7] James W. Markham, "Foreign News in the United States and the South American Press," *Public Opinion Quarterly,* Vol. 25 (Summer, 1961), p. 254.

[8] Homem de Montes Questionnaire.

[9] Kayser, *loc. cit.*

[10] Homem de Montes Questionnaire.

[11] "Best in Brazil."

[12] *Editor & Publisher* (November 5, 1966), p. 60.

[13] "Best in Brazil."

[14] Homem de Montes Questionnaire.

Chapter 9

The Age

[1] *The Australian* was established in Canberra, the capital, in July, 1964, the first new daily in twenty years. While the paper is made up in Canberra, matrices are flown to Sydney and Melbourne. In October, 1966, the paper's circulation was some 70,000 and by the end of the year it was still growing. It is a modern paper, using computerized typesetting techniques. It is trying to build up an outstanding network of correspondents all over Australia. Although it faces many problems, it seems to have become rather firmly established at the beginning of 1967.

[2] Henry Mayer, *The Press in Australia* (Melbourne, Melbourne University Press, 1964), p. 221.

[3] Promotion booklet sent the writer by *The Age,* October, 1966.

[4] Franklin C. Banner, *A Study of the Australian Press* (Pennsylvania State College, 1950), p. 10.

[5] "Newspapers of the World—XII," London *Times* (March 19, 1965).

[6] *Ibid.*

[7] Letter and Questionnaire from Graham Perkin, assistant editor, October 10, 1966.

[8] Mayer, *loc. cit.*, has written that Melbourne's *Herald* (along with *The Age*) would be read by the reader "who chose by quality only." In a letter to the writer from the *Herald's* editor, Dudley E. Giles (August 31, 1965), it was learned that the *Herald,* founded 1840, had a circulation of about 500,000 and, as the only PM paper in Melbourne, aimed at all classes of readers. The paper had twenty-four foreign correspondents—five in London, three in New York, and one in each of these cities: Jakarta, Tokyo, Singapore, Hong Kong, Toronto, Johannesburg, New Delhi, Auckland, Rabaul, Paris, Athens, Moscow, Vienna, Bonn, The Hague, and Brussels.

[9] Perkin Questionnaire.

[10] Mayer, *loc. cit.*

[11] Perkin Questionnaire.

[12] *Ibid.*

[13] Mayer, *loc. cit.*

[14] "Newspapers of the World—XII."

[15] Perkin Questionnaire.

[16] Promotion booklet from *The Age*.
[17] Perkin Questionnaire; also, W. Sprague Holden, *Australia Goes to Press* (Detroit, Wayne State Unversity Press, 1961), pp. 131–132.
[18] "Newspapers of the World—XII."

Al Ahram

[1] "Newspapers of the World—IX," London *Times* (March 10, 1965).
[2] Edward R. Sheehan, "The Birth Pangs of Arab Socialism," *Harper's* (February, 1962), p. 91.
[3] "Monopoly in Cairo," *Time* (June 6, 1960), p. 84.
[4] Richard H. Nolte, "Arab Nationalism and the Cold War," *The Yale Review* (September, 1959), p. 10.
[5] Wilbur Schramm, *One Day in the World's Press* (Palo Alto, Stanford University Press, 1952), p. 81.
[6] "Newspapers of the World—IX"; Schramm, *loc. cit.*
[7] "Newspapers of the World—IX."
[8] *Atlas Magazine* (June, 1965), p. 326.
[9] *Atlas Magazine* (August, 1966), p. 7.

Die Burger

[1] For a good discussion of these two basic types of South African papers, see Adam Clymer, "The Divided Press of South Africa," *Nieman Reports* (July, 1960).
[2] Tertius Myburgh, "The South African Press: Hope in an Unhappy Land," *Nieman Reports* (March, 1966), p. 4.
[3] The *Rand Daily Mail* of Johannesburg, with a circulation of some 115,000, won the 1966 World Press Achievement Award. The English-language morning paper was honored for the broad scope of its news coverage and outstanding public service in pressing for improved living conditions, freedom of expression and social justice for all citizens. (*ANPA Newspaper Information Service Newsletter,* February 28, 1966.)
[4] See Morris Broughton, *Press and Politics of South Africa* (Capetown, Purnell & Sons Ltd., 1961) for a good discussion of press-government relationships and for a good understanding of the daily operations of South African newspapers in general.
[5] "Newspapers of the World—XI," London *Times* (March 16, 1965); also completed questionnaire from P. J. Cillié, editor of *Die Burger,* sent the writer November 23, 1966.
[6] Saturday circulations are larger for all these papers; they contain weekend magazines and popular features. No Sunday papers are published.
[7] Louis M. Lyons, "Observations on the African Press," *Unitarian Universalist Register-Leader* (May, 1963), p. 12.
[8] Louis M. Lyons, "Press Notes from Africa," *Nieman Reports* (July–October, 1962), p. 22.
[9] Cillié Questionnaire, *op. cit.,* p. 1.
[10] *Ibid.,* p. 2.
[11] From a lecture, "The conditions for a free, vigorous and responsible press in South Africa" (given August 1, 1966 at the University of Cape Town) and mailed to the writer by W. J. Wepener, chief news editor of *Die Burger,* October 5, 1966.

The Hindu

[1] The two dailies, the *Times of India* and *The Statesman,* are certainly to be included with *The Hindu* as the "Big Three" elite papers of India. The *Times of India* was founded in 1861 by Robert Knight who was to become one of the very great editors of the country. Under Knight's direction the Bombay paper established great traditions of serious, responsible journalism and was known throughout Asia for its general excellence. Knight sold his shares in the paper in 1875 and moved to Calcutta where he founded *The Statesman.* A forceful campaigner for Indian freedom, Knight was one of the best-loved of all Indian editors. *The Statesman* (formed by a merger of the *Friend of India* and the *Indian Statesman*) grew rapidly and gained a loyal following among national leaders and intellectuals. In 1931 the paper began publishing in New Delhi as well as in Calcutta, and has since become well-established as one of the two (with *The Hindu*) most independent and articulate newspapers of India. The strongest parts of *The Statesman* appear to be its outstanding financial pages and its vigorous editorials, while the main strength of the *Times of India* is undoubtedly its wide range and thorough coverage of national and world news.

[2] "Newspapers of the World—VI," London *Times* (March 3, 1965).

[3] Nadig Krishna Murthy, *Indian Journalism* (Mysore, "Prasaranga" of University of Mysore, 1966), p. 173.

[4] "Newspapers of the World—VI."

[5] A. E. Charlton, "The English Language Newspapers," in *Journalism in Modern India,* ed. by Roland E. Wolseley (New York, Asia Publishing House, 1964), Chap. 1, p. 9.

[6] Murthy, *op. cit.,* p. 175.

[7] "Newspapers of the World—VI."

[8] Murthy, *op. cit.,* p. 176.

[9] *Ibid.*

[10] *Ibid.,* p. 178.

[11] "Newspapers of the World—VI."

[12] The paper has been specifically compared to *The Guardian* by British press critic Francis Williams; see *New Statesman* of London (August 16, 1958), p. 87.

Jen-min Jih-pao

[1] The newspaper's name is often transcribed phonetically into English from the Chinese as *Renmin Ribao,* an alternate form of *Jen-min Jih-pao* which is more common.

[2] Ian Stewart, "The Paper That Spreads the Cult of Mao," *The New York Times Magazine* (December 18, 1966), p. 27.

[3] "The Voice of Red China," *Time* (June 23, 1958), p. 77.

[4] Stewart, *loc. cit.*

[5] Frederick T. C. Yu, *Mass Persuasion in Communist China* (New York, Praeger, 1964), pp. 96, 111.

[6] "Newspapers of the World—VIII," London *Times* (March 5, 1965).

[7] Hideo Ono, *A Brief History of Domestic and Foreign Newspapers* (Tokyo, Nihon Shimbun Kyokai, 1961), p. 144.

[8] Robert Guillain, 600 *Million Chinese* (New York, Phillips, 1957), p. 148.

[9] L. La Dany, "Mainland China Non-Newspapers," *IPI Report* (July, 1966), p. 9.
[10] "Newspapers of the World—VIII."
[11] *Peking Review* (February 26, 1965), p. 11. For a good study of the paper's anti-U.S. stance, see Alex S. Edelstein and Alan Ping-lin Liu, "Anti-Americanism in Red China's *People's Daily:* A Functional Analysis," *Journalism Quarterly,* 30:2 (February, 1963). Compare, Stewart, *op. cit.,* pp. 27, 65–66, 73, 75–76, 78.
[12] *People's Daily* (November 10, 1965).
[13] *People's Daily* (December 30, 1965).
[14] Stewart, *op. cit.*, p. 27; La Dany, *loc. cit.*; Yu, *op cit.*, p. 164.
[15] Ono, *loc. cit.* Compare, Ono, *Overview of the World Press* (Taipei, 1956), p. 146; Yu, *op cit.*, p. 162.
[16] "Newspapers of the World—VIII."

The Sydney Morning Herald

[1] W. Sprague Holden, *Australia Goes to Press* (Detroit, Wayne State University Press, 1961), p. 236.
[2] *Ibid.*, pp. 52, 55.
[3] Henry Mayer, *The Press of Australia* (Melbourne, Lansdowne Press, 1964), p. 221. Compare, "Newspapers of the World—XVII," London *Times* (April 6, 1965).
[4] "Newspapers of the World—XVII."
[5] *A Century of Journalism: The Sydney Morning Herald and Its Record of Australian Life, 1831–1931* (Sydney, 1931), p. 761.
[6] John Fairfax Ltd. is a holding company, organized in 1956, which publishes *The Sydney Morning Herald.*
[7] In spite of the paper's Conservative inclinations, it has supported the Labour Party in several instances since World War II.
[8] "Newspapers of the World—XVII."

Chapter 10

The Guardian

[1] T. S. Matthews, *The Sugar Pill: An Essay on Newspapers* (London, Victor Gollancz, Ltd., 1958), p. 125.
[2] Completed questionnaire and letter from Rex Hearn, promotion manager of *The Guardian,* dated November 2, 1965.
[3] Karl E. Mayer, "The English Press: Nasty, Obsolete, the Best in the World," *Esquire* (July, 1966), p. 56.
[4] Matthews, *op. cit.,* p. 140.
[5] *Ibid.,* p. 30.
[6] Hearn Questionnaire.
[7] "For Distinguished Work in Journalism," Missouri's Honor Awards for 1931, *University of Missouri Bulletin,* 22:32 (August 1, 1931), pp. 7–8.
[8] Hearn letter to writer, November 2, 1965.
[9] Matthews, *op. cit.*, p. 138.
[10] *Ibid.*, p. 140.
[11] *Ibid.*, p. 29.

[12] Henry Fairlie, "Anglo-American Differences," *Encounter,* 26:6 (June, 1966), p. 83.

[13] This feeling that *The Guardian* had "dropped in quality" was manifest to the writer in numerous interviews and conversations in Europe during the summer of 1966—in interviews conducted in Britain, Holland, Belgium, West Germany, Switzerland, and Italy.

[14] Meyer, *op. cit.,* p. 126.

[15] Jim A. Hart, "Foreign News in U.S. and English Daily Papers: A Comparison," *Journalism Quarterly,* 43:3 (Autumn, 1966), p. 444.

[16] *The Story of the Guardian* (London, *The Guardian,* 1964), p. 5.

[17] William H. Mills, *The Manchester Guardian: A Century of History* (London, Chatto and Windus, 1921), pp. 4–8.

[18] *The Story of the Guardian,* pp. 1–2.

[19] *Ibid.,* p. 2. Compare, Mills, *loc. cit.*

[20] Matthews, *op. cit.,* p. 92.

[21] Mills, *op. cit.,* pp. 105–107; Matthews, *op. cit.,* p. 92.

[22] Matthews, *op. cit.,* p. 93.

[23] *Ibid.*

[24] J. L. Hammond, *C. P. Scott of the Manchester Guardian* (New York, Harcourt, Brace & World, 1934), p. 33.

[25] D. Hudson, *British Journalists and Newspapers* (London, Collins, 1945), p. 45.

[26] Frederick Muller, *C. P. Scott, 1846–1932* (London, F. Muller Ltd., 1946), p. 78.

[27] Matthews, *op. cit.,* p. 100.

[28] *Ibid.,* p. 107.

[29] *Ibid.,* p. 109.

[30] Meyer, *op. cit.,* p. 126.

[31] *The Story of the Guardian,* p. 6.

[32] *Ibid.*

[33] *Ibid.*

[34] Hearn Questionnaire.

The Times

[35] *IPI Report,* Zurich, 15:2 (June, 1966), p. 60. Compare, "The Old Lady's New Face," *Time* (May 13, 1966), p. 77.

[36] "Thomson Takes The Times," *Time* (October 7, 1966), p. 61. Compare, "Thomson Acquires Times of London," *Editor & Publisher* (October 8, 1966), p. 11.

[36a] Haley left the paper in 1967 to become editor of *The Encyclopaedia Britannica* in New York.

[37] "Lord Thomson Köper Times," *Pressens Tidning,* Stockholm, 47:19 (October 15, 1966), pp. 1, 10.

[38] "Missouri's Honor Awards—1933," *University of Missouri Bulletin,* 34:25 (September 1, 1933), p. 10.

[39] H. F. Ellis, "The Times and Punch," *Holiday* (April, 1958), pp. 28, 32.

[40] John Hohenberg, *Foreign Correspondence* (New York, Columbia University Press, 1964), p. 62.

[41] "The New Thunderer," *Time* (May 8, 1964), p. 49.

[42] Kurt von Stutterheim, *The Press in England* (London, Allen & Unwin Ltd., 1934), pp. 66–67.

[43] "The Thunderer," *The Spectator,* London (July 10, 1959), p. 23.

[44] Maurice Fabre, *A History of Communications* (New York, Hawthorn Books, 1963), p. 63.

[45] Robert W. Desmond, *The Press and World Affairs* (New York, Appleton-Century-Crofts, 1937), p. 19; Fabre, *loc. cit.*

[46] A good summary of Russell's coverage of the Crimean War is given in Hohenberg, *op. cit.*, pp. 44–56.

[47] Stutterheim, *op. cit.*, p. 68.

[48] *Ibid.*, p. 125.

[49] Fairlie, *op. cit.*, p. 82.

[50] Hart, *op. cit.*, p. 444; Peter B. Warr and Chris Knapper, "A Content Analysis of the English National Daily Press," *Gazette*, Leiden, 11:2/3 (1965), pp. 139–146.

[51] Magnus Turnstile, "After Haley?" *New Statesman* (May 14, 1965), p. 753.

[52] London *Times* (November 30, 1965).

[53] Completed questionnaire and letter from Sir William J. Haley, editor of *The Times*, dated May 3, 1965.

[54] "The New Thunderer," *Time* (May 8, 1964), p. 49.

[55] *The Press in Perspective*, ed. by Ralph D. Casey (Baton Rouge, Louisiana State University Press, 1963), p. 37.

[56] Fairlie, *op. cit.*, pp. 77–78.

[57] Analysis of *The Times* by writer during 1966 and 1967.

[58] Meyer, *op. cit.*, p. 128.

[59] *Ibid.*

[60] *Ibid.*, p. 129.

[61] H. L. Hopkin, "Why Thomson Decided It Had To Be The Times," *World's Press News and Advertisers' Review*, London (October 7, 1966), p. 3.

[62] Desmond Fisher, "The Times of London Faces Modern World Under New Leadership," *St. Louis Review* (July 28, 1967). Compare, "Newspapers," *Time* (August 11, 1967), pp. 34–35.

[63] Fisher, *loc. cit.*

Chapter 11

Berlingske Tidende

[1] Letter and materials from Dr. Vincent Naeser dated August 11, 1966. (Hereafter: Naeser letter, August 11, 1966.)

[2] "The Great Dane," *Time* (January 4, 1963), p. 29.

[3] Completed questionnaire from Terkel M. Terkelsen dated August 11, 1966. (Hereafter: Terkelsen Questionnaire.)

[4] "Newspapers of the World—XXI," London *Times* (April 20, 1965). Compare, Kenneth Olson, *The History Makers* (Baton Rouge, Louisiana State University Press, 1966), p. 63.

[5] Letter from Terkel Terkelsen dated August 10, 1965.

[6] Terkelsen Questionnaire. Compare, Svend Thorsen, *Newspapers in Denmark* (Copenhagen, Det Danske Selskab, 1953), p. 105.

[7] Terkelsen Questionnaire.

[8] Olson, *loc. cit.*

[9] "Newspapers of the World—XXI."

[10] Terkelsen Questionnaire.

[11] *Ibid.*

[12] *Ibid.*

[13] *Berlingske Tidende* material sent the writer, especially a promotional booklet called *The Story of an Old Newspaper* (1963); much of the historical data about the newspaper are taken from this booklet.
[14] Thorsen, *op. cit.*, p. 13.
[15] *Ibid.*, p. 72.
[16] *Ibid.*, pp. 164–165.
[17] Olson, *op. cit.*, p. 58.
[18] "The Great Dane," *op. cit.*, p. 29.
[19] *Honor Awards for Distinguished Service in Journalism, University of Missouri Bulletin*, 63:2 (January 15, 1962), pp. 13–14.
[20] Naeser Letter, August 11, 1966.
[21] Information furnished the writer by Terkel M. Terkelsen dated August 9, 1966. The masthead of *Berlingske Tidende* in copies during December, 1966, listed Terkelsen as the Chief Political Editor. Svend Aage Lund was listed the Administrative Chief Editor. Two other Chief Editors were listed: Aage Deleuran and Niels Nørlund. The "Responsible Editor" was listed as Axel Moos.
[22] "The Press on the Press," *IPI Report* (November, 1965), p. 7.

Chapter 12

LE MONDE

[1] *Le Monde*'s circulation is right at 300,000. Often its sales will increase by at least another 100,000 on days of big news.
[2] Abel Chatelain, *Le Monde et ses lecteurs* (Paris, Armand Colin, 1962), pp. 28–29.
[3] Herbert R. Lottman, "The Newspaper de Gaulle Has to Read," *Harper's* (January, 1967), p. 63.
[4] Letter to the author from Hubert Beuve-Méry, directing editor of *Le Monde*, with completed questionnaire, dated September 23, 1965. (Hereafter referred to as Beuve-Méry Letter or as Beuve-Méry Questionnaire.)
[5] Beuve-Méry Questionnaire.
[6] Helen Hill Miller, "The Best Newspaper in Europe," *Esquire* (February, 1962), p. 72.
[7] Lottman, *loc. cit.*
[8] Maurice Herr, "Readers 'Melting Away' from Political Press of France," *IPI Report* (May, 1962), pp. 3–4.
[9] Beuve-Méry Letter.
[10] "Newspapers of the World—I," London *Times* (February 23, 1965).
[11] Miller, *op. cit.*, p. 70.
[12] Lottman, *op. cit.*, p. 64.
[13] *Le Monde* (December 19, 1944), p. 1 (translation by Christo Cameris).
[14] "Newspapers of the World—I."
[15] Miller, *op. cit.*, p. 140.
[16] Beuve-Méry Letter.
[17] Joseph Kraft, "The World of Le Monde," *The Reporter* (March 31, 1960), p. 46.
[18] Jean-André Fauchet, "Devant la tombe de Pierre Brisson," *L'Echo de la Presse* (January 15, 1965), p. 12.
[19] Beuve-Méry Letter and Questionnaire.
[20] *Ibid.*

[21] Content analysis of randomly selected issues of *Le Monde* during 1966 and 1967.

[22] "Presse et Publicité," *L'Echo de la Presse* (January 5, 1965), p. 4. Compare, "Newspapers of the World—I."

[23] Abdus Salam Khurshid, "I.P.I. Asian Conference," *Gazette*, 4:1 (1958), p. 120.

[24] Beuve-Méry Letter.

[25] Miller, *op. cit.*, p. 140.

[26] Kraft, *loc. cit.*

[27] Lottman, *op. cit.*, p. 64.

[28] Beuve-Méry Letter.

[29] Raymond Manevy, *L'Evolution des Formules de Presentation de la Presse Quotidienne* (Paris, Editions Estienne, 1956), p. 37.

[30] Chatelain, *op. cit.*, p. 24. Compare, "Dis moi ce que tu lis," *Esprit*, Paris (March, 1959), pp. 480–482.

[31] Miller, *op. cit.*, p. 139.

[32] "Journaux et Journalistes," *L'Echo de la Presse* (February 15, 1965), p. 7.

[33] J. A. Faucher, "Portrait du journaliste idéal," *L'Echo de la Presse* (September 15, 1964), p. 7.

[34] René de Livois, *Histoire de la Presse Française* (Paris, Les Temps de la Presse, 1965), Vol. 2, p. 564.

[35] Chatelain, *op. cit.*, p. 223.

[36] *Manchester Guardian* (November 9, 1956).

[37] *L'Express*, Paris (April 13, 1956).

Chapter 13

Frankfurter Allgemeine

[1] Founders of the *Frankfurter Allgemeine* were Franz Böhn, Alex Haffner, Max Schmid, Friedrich Sieburg, and Erich Welter. Editorial policy, which has marked the *FAZ* from the start, was set by these founders. Of these five men, only Prof. Dr. Erich Welter (he teaches at University of Mainz) is still one of the publishers. On April 22, 1959, the founders, in order to further separate the operation of the paper from the administrative arm of the corporation, established the *Frankfurter Allgemeine Zeitung*, G.m.b.H. Since then the paper has been an extension of the parent corporation (*Fazit-Stiftung*) and is operated on a nonprofit basis.

[2] *FAZ: The Face of a German Newspaper* (a thirty-eight-page book in English published by the *FAZ*, n.d.), p. 6.

[3] Georg Bitter, *Zur Typologie des Deutschen Zeitungswesens in der Bundesrepublik Deutschland* (Munich, Eduard Pohl & Co., 1951), p. 68.

[4] *Ibid.*, p. 69.

[5] *Ibid.*, p. 68.

[6] *Ibid.*, p. 69.

[7] Analysis of *FAZ*, July and August, 1967.

[8] *Ibid.*

[9] Completed questionnaire from Prof. Dr. Erich Welter, *FAZ* editor, August 20, 1965.

[10] *Sie Redigieren und Schreiben Die Frankfurter Allgemeine* (*FAZ*, 1964), pp. 80–81.

[11] *FAZ: The Face of a German Newspaper*, p. 8.

[12] Welter Questionnaire.

13 *Sie Redigieren . . .*, p. 83; Welter Questionnaire.
14 "Frankfurter Allgemeine Zeitung für Deutschland" (twenty-page booklet in German) sent the writer by *FAZ* in July, 1967, pp. 4–5.
15 Welter Questionnaire.
16 Many sources refer to *FAZ* as "conservative"; *e.g.*, Kenneth Olson, *The History Makers* (Baton Rouge, Louisiana State University Press, 1966), p. 132; "Concentration in the Federal Republic," *The Economist*, May 22, 1965, p. 19; *Atlas* (New York) regularly describes it as conservative.
17 Welter Questionnaire.
18 Letter from Robert H. Garey, advertising director for Life International Editions (London), dated June 25, 1962.
19 *Ibid.*
20 Letter from Jürgen Tern, *FAZ* editor, October 29, 1964.
21 *Ibid.*

Die Welt

22 Questionnaire (completed by W. Joachim Freyburg, *Die Welt*, Hamburg), sent the writer with letter, dated November 3, 1965.
23 Albert Lubisch, "Wie es begann" in *Die Ersten Jahre* (Beitrage zur Geschichte des Verlagshaus Die Welt, Hamburg, 1962), pp. 11–14.
24 Claus-Dieter Nagel, "Zeitungmachen in Berlin" in *Die Ersten Jahre*, pp. 194–200.
25 Speech ("Das Verlagshaus Die Welt und seine Zeitungen") by W. Joachim Greyburg in Hamburg, January, 1965, p. 10. (Typescript sent writer in late 1966).
26 See "I've Got a Sixth Sense," *Newsweek* (April 11, 1966), for a good brief profile of Axel Springer.
27 London *Times* (September 18, 1953), p. 6.
28 Hanno Hardt, "Dangers of Press Concentration in Germany," *Grassroots Editor* (January–February, 1967), p. 16.
29 Freyburg speech, pp. 8–9.
30 Typed information from W. J. Freyburg, dated July 12, 1966.
31 *Ibid.*
32 John Tebbel, "West Germany's Publishing Powerhouse," *Saturday Review* (January 14, 1967), p. 125.
33 Freyburg Questionnaire.
34 *The Economist*, London (May 22, 1965), p. 19.
35 "Newspapers of the World—XVI," London *Times* (April 2, 1965).
36 Freyburg Questionnaire.
37 Analysis of issues of *Die Welt* by writer, 1966–1967.
38 *Welt am Sonntag* must compete as a weekly with *Die Zeit* (Time) of Hamburg, undoubtedly West Germany's most influential weekly newspaper.
39 Freyburg speech, p. 14. Compare, *Verlagshaus Die Welt*, No. 68 (May 16, 1966), p. 9.
40 Freyburg speech, p. 11.
41 For information on the life and achievements of Hans Zehrer, see "Von Hans Zehrer zu H.F.G. Starke" (including a ten-page profile called "Hans Zehrer": June 2, 1899–August 23, 1966) in *Verlagshaus Die Welt*, No. 72 (September 27, 1966).
42 "Wechsel in der Chefredaktion Der Welt" in *Verlagshaus Die Welt*, No. 69 (June 20, 1966).
43 Tebbel, *op. cit.*, p. 126.
44 *Newsweek* (April 11, 1966), p. 103.

[45] See *Berlin Kochstrasse,* ed. by Hans von Wallenberg (Berlin, Verlag Ullstein, 1966) for a history in words and pictures of the famous newspaper quarter and of the men—like the Ullsteins, Mosse, Scherl, and now Springer—who have made it great. This book gives a good look at the new Springer building on the Kochstrasse, tells how it came to be there, and gives Springer's philosophy of journalism.

[46] Interview with Axel C. Springer, Columbia, Mo., May 4, 1967.

[47] Advertisement in *The New York Times* (Sunday, November 27, 1966).

[48] *Ibid.*

[49] "Auflagezahlen im 1. Quartal 1967," *Verlagshaus Die Welt,* No. 2 (April/May, 1967), p. 2.

[50] Many tributes poured in to *Die Welt* for its honor; special congratulations were received from many West German leaders, including President Heinrich Lubke, Chancellor Kurt-Georg Kiesinger, and Foreign Minister Willy Brandt.

[51] "Zeitung des Jahres," *Verlagshaus Die Welt,* No. 2 (April/May, 1967), pp. 1–2.

Chapter 14

NEUE ZÜRCHER ZEITUNG

[1] Dr. Luchsinger became editor in chief on January 1, 1968.

[1a] Letter to the author from Dr. Fred Luchsinger, *NZZ* foreign editor, dated July 26, 1965. Hereafter called Luchsinger Letter.

[2] Norbert Muhlen, "PRESS—An Encyclopedia With Three Deadlines a Day," *The Reporter* (July 23, 1959), pp. 38–39.

[3] John C. Merrill, "U.S. Panel Names World's Ten Leading 'Quality' Dailies," *Journalism Quarterly,* 41:4 (Autumn, 1964), pp. 568–572. Compare, Merrill, "What are the World's Best Dailies?" *Gazette,* Holland, 10:3 (1964), pp. 259–260.

[4] Reuters story datelined Syracuse, N.Y., November 8, in *The Guardian,* Manchester (November 9, 1963); also a story in *Neue Zürcher Zeitung* (November 11, 1963).

[5] "Newspapers of the World—X," *The Times,* London (March 12, 1965).

[5a] Bretscher became a *NZZ* board member on January 1, 1968 and was succeeded by Dr. Luchsinger.

[6] Material sent the author by *Neue Zürcher Zeitung* (August, 1965). (Hereafter called *NZZ* Material, August, 1965).

[7] Bernard Berenson, *Rumour and Reflection 1941–1944* (London, Constable, 1952), p. 295.

[8] Luchsinger Letter.

[9] *Ibid.* Compare, J. C. Merrill, "*NZZ*: the World's Best Newspaper?" *The Quill* (February, 1967).

[10] *Time* (February 7, 1955).

[11] William Guttmann, "A Famous Swiss Newspaper," *IPI Report* (June, 1959), p. 8.

[12] "Newspapers of the World—X."

[13] Questionnaire completed by Dr. Luchsinger, and mailed to the author, July 26, 1965. (Hereafter called Luchsinger Questionnaire.)

[14] Indicative of the fact that there is no "line" found in the paper is the refreshing discovery that the *NZZ's* correspondents frequently take stands on its pages quite different from those advocated by the editors.

15 "Newspapers of the World—X."
16 Luchsinger Questionnaire.
17 Luchsinger Letter.
18 Luchsinger Questionnaire.
19 *NZZ* Material, August, 1965. Compare, J. C. Merrill, "NZZ: die beste Zeitung der Welt?" Zurich, *NZZ* (May, 1967).
20 A good discussion of the *NZZ* foreign correspondents and world coverage is "Auf Vorposten—Augen und Ohren der Leser in Aller Welt" by Dr. Urs Schwarz in *1780–1955 Neue Zürcher Zeitung*, Zurich (1955), special 175th anniversary booklet, pp. 20–21.
21 Guttmann, *loc. cit.*
22 *NZZ* Material, August, 1965.
23 *Ibid.*
24 Luchsinger Questionnaire.
25 Luchsinger Letter.
26 *Ibid.*
27 *The Flow of the News* (Zurich, International Press Institute, 1953), pp. 249–250.
28 Actually it is "Sheet 2" by the *NZZ's* style; the paper does not number each page, only each "sheet" or *Blatt.*
29 *NZZ* Material, August, 1965.
30 For a good survey of this early period of *NZZ's* history, see Chap. 1 of Elizabeth Wiskermann, *A Great Swiss Newspaper* (London, Oxford University Press, 1959). Compare, Leo Weisz, *Die Redaktoren der Neuen Zürcher Zeitung bis zur Gründung des Bundesstaates, 1780–1848* (Zurich, Verlag *NZZ*, 1961).
31 Extremely useful to the person interested in a survey of the historical highlights of the paper as well as its inner workings is the beautifully illustrated and printed book, *NZZ: Blick in das Getriebe der Zeitung* (Zurich, *NZZ*, 1960).
32 The best source on this important period of the *NZZ's history* (dealing with Dr. Felber and his successor, Eugen Escher) is Leo Wiesz, *Die Neue Zürcher Zeitung in Kampfe der Liberalen mit den Radikalen, 1849–1872* (Zurich, Verlag *NZZ*, 1962).
33 *Time* (February 7, 1955).
34 *Ibid.*
35 Muhlen, *op. cit.*
36 For a good commentary on this phase of the *NZZ's* story, see Fred Luchsinger's article, "Im Schatten des Totalitarismus" in the special book, *1780–1955 Neue Zürcher Zeitung,* Zurich (1955), pp. 6–10.
37 *NZZ* Material, August, 1965.
38 Muhlen, *op. cit.*
39 Guttmann, *op. cit.*
40 *NZZ* Material, August, 1965. Compare, Merrill, "NZZ: die beste Zeitung der Welt?" Zurich, *NZZ* (May, 1967), p. 8.

Chapter 15

CORRIERE DELLA SERA

1 Irving R. Levine, *Main Street, Italy* (New York, Doubleday, 1963), p. 350.
2 Most of the material in this profile was obtained by the author in conversations and interviews with members of the *Corriere della Sera* staff in

Milan during the last two weeks in June, 1966. Certain other information was furnished by mail by Alfio Colussi of the paper's advertising and public relations staff, during 1966 and early 1967; it will be referred to subsequently as Colussi Material.

[3] Colussi Material.

[4] Interview with Alfio Colussi in Milan, June 27, 1966.

[5] *Ibid.*

[6] Interview with Alfio Russo, Editor of the *Corriere,* in Milan, June 25, 1966.

[7] See Chap. 16 ("La Terza Pagina") in Sam Carcano, *Il Giornalismo* (Milan, Case Editrice Dr. Francesco Vallardi, 1956), for a good discussion of the "third page" and the importance of the "elzeviro."

[8] Interview with Paulo Bonaiuti of the *Corriere*'s advertising staff, in Milan, June 28, 1966.

[9] Colussi Material.

[10] Adolf Dresler, *Geschichte der italienischen Presse* (Munich, Verlag Oldenbourg, 1933), Vol. 2, p. 136.

[11] *Corriere d'Informazione* was started immediately after World War II and was the first evening paper in Italy to attempt to mix serious general news with the popular journalism typical of the PM press.

[12] Francesco Fattorello, "A Short Survey of the Italian Press," *Gazette,* Leiden, 11:1 (1965), p. 6.

[13] Ignazio Weiss, *Il Potere di Carta: Il Giornalismo Ieri e Oggi* (Turin, Editrice Torinese, 1965), p. 424.

[14] Jacques Kayser, *One Week's News* (Paris, UNESCO, 1953), p. 37.

[15] Weiss, *loc. cit.*

[16] *Prestigio,* Milan (March 5, 1962), p. 3, and Russo Interview, June 25, 1966.

[17] Russo Interview, June 25, 1966.

[18] Stagno, a native of Taranto, is a leading press figure in Italy, having been an official in the Italian Federation of Newspaper Publishers, and director of the national news agency, ASNA.

[19] Russo Interview, June 25, 1966.

[20] *Ibid.*

[21] *Ibid.*

[22] Frank Brutto, "In Italy: The Word is Complicated," *Journalism Review,* School of Journalism, Montana State University, No. 5 (1962), p. 11.

[23] *Service Documentaire F.I.J.*, Brussels, 9:21 (May 21, 1966), p. 10.

[24] Russo Interview, June 25, 1966.

L'Osservatore Romano

[25] Levine, *op. cit.*, p. 360.

[26] Weiss, *op. cit.*, p. 107.

[27] *Newsweek* (July 10, 1961), p. 41.

[28] *America* (July 27, 1961), p. 541.

[29] The circulation of the *Osservatore Romano* is a matter for conjecture. Writers give figures ranging from 60,000 to as high as 400,000. Even the yearbook of *Editor & Publisher* (New York) seems to have problems: for some four or five years the circulation was given as an unchanging 200,000, but for 1963 the figure mysteriously dropped to 70,000 where it has remained since.

[30] Andrea Lazzarini in the centennial edition of *L'Osservatore Romano* (July 1, 1961), p. 7. Compare, Lazzarini, "The True Story and the Origin of 'L'Osservatore Romano'," *Catholic Press Annual* (1962), p. 12.

[31] "Newspapers of the World—VII," London *Times* (March 4, 1965).

[32] Lazzarini, centennial edition.
[33] *Ibid.*
[34] George Seldes, *The Vatican: Yesterday, Today, Tomorrow* (New York, Harper & Row, 1934), p. 242.
[35] *Ibid.*
[36] J. J. Casserly, "Voice of the Vatican," *Ave Maria* (February 22, 1958), p. 24.
[37] "Newspapers of the World—VII."
[38] Denis Gwynn, *The Vatican and the War in Europe* (London, Burns Oates & Washbourne, Ltd., 1940), p. 204.
[39] *Time* (April 18, 1960), p. 98.
[40] "Newspapers of the World—VII."
[41] Don Sharkey, *White Smoke Over the Vatican* (Milwaukee, Bureau Publishing Co., 1943), p. 105.
[42] *Catholic Digest* (January, 1961), pp. 48–50. This is a condensation of an article by Barrett McGurn, "The Vatican's Newspaper" in the *Holy Name Journal.*
[43] Levine, *op. cit.*, p. 360.
[44] *Newsweek* (July 10, 1961), p. 41.
[45] Levine, *op. cit.*, p. 362.
[46] *Catholic Digest, loc. cit.*
[47] *Time* (April 18, 1960), p. 96.
[48] G. B. Montini, "The Difficulties of L'Osservatore Romano," *L'Osservatore Romano,* centennial edition (July 1, 1961), p. 11.
[49] Analysis of the content of selected issues of the *Osservatore Romano,* 1966.
[50] *L'Osservatore Romano,* centennial edition (July 1, 1961), p. 57.
[51] *Ibid.*, p. 64.

Chapter 16

EXCÉLSIOR

[1] Marvin Alisky, in a letter to the writer (October 7, 1966), says that *Excélsior* is technically considered a "co-op," but it is not really that since only the top or key employees own it and run its board of directors.
[2] Interview with Rodrigo de Llano in Mexico City, August, 1960.
[3] *Ibid.*
[4] Erling H. Erlandson, "The Press of Mexico: Past, Present and Future," *Journalism Quarterly* (Spring, 1964), p. 233.
[5] Bruce Underwood, "A Survey of Contemporary Newspapers of Mexico" (unpublished Ph.D. dissertation, University of Missouri, 1965), pp. 335–339. Compare, Ronald H. Chilcote, "The Press in Latin America, Spain, and Portugal" in *Hispanic American Report* (Stanford University, August, 1963) which called *Excélsior* during this period "conservative, consistently pro-U.S." and "one of Latin America's best newspapers."
[6] Underwood, *loc. cit.*
[7] Miguel Valasco Valdés, *Historia del Periodismo Mexicano* (Mexico, Manuel Porrua, 1955), p. 199.
[8] *Ibid.*, p. 200.
[9] Interview with Rafael Martínez Fuentes, Mexico City public relations counsel and correspondent for several dailies in northern Mexico, in Mexico City, July, 1960.
[10] Alisky Letter, October 7, 1966.

[11] John C. Merrill, "The Image of the United States Presented by Ten Mexican Daily Newspapers" (unpublished Ph.D. dissertation, University of Iowa, February, 1962).

[12] John C. Merrill, *A Handbook of the Foreign Press* (Baton Rouge, Louisiana State University Press, 1959), pp. 285–289.

[13] *Ibid.*

[14] Alisky Letter, October 7, 1966.

[15] Underwood, *loc. cit.*

[16] Letter and questionnaire from Manuel Becerra Acosta, director general of *Excélsior,* dated August 18, 1965.

[17] *Ibid.*

[18] *Ibid.*

[19] *Ibid.*

La Prensa

[20] Octavio de la Suarée, *Socioperiodismo* (Havana, Cultural, 1948), p. 371.

[21] Donald B. Easum, " 'La Prensa' and Freedom of the Press in Argentina," *Journalism Quarterly* (Spring, 1951), p. 427.

[22] Editors of *La Prensa, Defense of Freedom* (New York, The John Day Co., 1952), pp. 15–16.

[23] "Newspapers of the World—V," London *Times* (March 2, 1965).

[24] *Ibid.*

[25] Alberto Prando, *A Century and a Half of Journalism in Argentina* (University of Texas, 1961), p. 6.

[26] *The Quill* (February 1957), p. 12.

[27] Prando, *op. cit.*, p. 9. Compare, *Defense of Freedom,* pp. 36–37.

[28] *Education and Journalism in the Struggle for Freedom: An Address by Dr. Alberto Gainza Paz* (Evanston, Ill., Northwestern University, 1951), pp. 19–20.

[29] *Ibid.*, p. 21. Compare, J. C. Merrill, *A Handbook of the Foreign Press,* pp. 299–301.

[30] Merrill, *Handbook,* p. 300.

[31] Letter to the author from Dr. Alberto Gainza Paz, dated June 27, 1965.

[32] *Ibid.*

[33] Completed questionnaire sent author by Dr. Gainza Paz, with letter of June 27, 1965.

[34] Paul R. Hoopes, "Content Analysis of News in Three Argentine Dailies," *Journalism Quarterly* (Autumn, 1966), pp. 536–537.

[35] *Ibid.*, p. 537.

[36] Mary A. Gardner, "The Argentine Press Since Perón," *Journalism Quarterly* (Summer, 1960), p. 429.

[37] Wayne Wolfe, "Images of the United States in the Latin American Press," *Journalism Quarterly* (Winter, 1964), p. 82.

[38] Robert U. Brown, "Shop Talk at Thirty," *Editor & Publisher* (November 17, 1962), p. 74.

Chapter 17

Los Angeles Times

[1] Frank Riley, "The Changing Direction of the 'Times'," *Los Angeles Magazine* (June, 1966), p. 29.

[2] Otis Chandler, "The Role of the Metropolitan Daily in Today's Changing Environment," *Journalism Educator* (Fall, 1964), p. 94. Compare, "A publishing giant takes a long step," *Business Week* (March 14, 1964), pp. 72–78.

[3] Booklet, "The Los Angeles Times" (1966), sent writer in 1967, by the *Los Angeles Times,* p. 2. Compare, "How to Build an Empire," *Newsweek* (January 2, 1967), p. 41.

[4] "The Los Angeles Times" (1966 booklet), pp. 9–12.

[5] T. E. Kruglak, "World-Wide View," *IPI Report* (February, 1967), p. 11.

[6] Mitchell Gordon, "A Family Empire," *The Wall Street Journal* (October 13, 1965), p. 1.

[7] *The Economist,* London (May 22, 1965), p. 12.

[8] *Ibid.*

[9] "Making News Two Ways," *Frontier* (June, 1966), p. 23.

[10] *Editor & Publisher* (October 8, 1966), p. 28.

[11] Letter from Ted Weegar, *Times* assistant managing editor, July 19, 1966.

[12] Material from *Times* (June, 1967).

[13] Weegar Letter, July 19, 1966.

[14] Data sent writer by *Times* in August, 1967.

[15] *Ibid.* Compare, Frank P. Haven, "L.A. Times—A 'How' Story of Journalism," *The Quill* (October, 1965), p. 36.

[16] Kruglak, *loc. cit.*

[17] Chandler, *op. cit.*, p. 94.

[18] Gordon, *loc. cit.*

[19] Peter Bart, "The New Look at the 'Times'," *Saturday Review* (June 12, 1965), p. 71.

[20] *Ibid.*

[21] Historical data on the *Los Angeles Times* from material sent writer by newspaper in late 1967 and from standard journalism histories.

[22] Data sent writer by *Times* in August, 1967.

[23] Analysis of copies of the *Los Angeles Times* (October, 1966–August, 1967).

[24] "The Los Angeles Times" (1966 booklet), p. 26.

The New York Times

[25] John Tebbel, "National Newspapers," *Saturday Review* (November 11, 1961), pp. 69–70.

[26] "Circulation Gains Cut New York Times Profits," *Editor & Publisher* (July 29, 1967), p. 36.

[27] "The New York Times, Alas," *Esquire* (April, 1963), p. 55.

[28] John Hohenberg, *Foreign Correspondence: The Great Reporters and Their Times* (New York, Columbia University Press, 1964). Hohenberg in this book (p. 442) says *The Times* has the "best foreign service in the world."

[29] *Ibid.*, p. 267.

[30] See *The Working Press: Special to the New York Times,* ed. by Ruth Adler (New York, G. P. Putnam's Sons, 1966) for essays dealing with international coverage by many of the paper's leading foreign correspondents.

[31] John Lofton, "The Press Manages the News," *The Progressive* (June, 1963), p. 18.

[32] A. T. Steele, *The American People and China* (New York, McGraw-Hill, 1966), p. 143.

[33] *Ibid.*, p. 157.

[34] Hohenberg, *op. cit.*, p. 447.

[35] David Halberstam, *The Making of a Quagmire* (New York, Random House, 1964), p. 35.

[36] George Lichtheim, "Reflections on The New York Times," *Commentary* (September, 1965), p. 33.

[37] *Ibid.*

[38] "The New York Times, Alas," *loc. cit.*

[39] *Ibid.*, p. 56.

[40] *Editor & Publisher* (May 29, 1965), p. 8.

[41] See Hohenberg, *op. cit.;* Bernard C. Cohen, *The Press and Foreign Policy* (Princeton, Princeton University Press, 1963), pp. 134–140; James Reston, *The Artillery of the Press: Its Influence on American Foreign Policy* (New York, Harper & Row, 1966); Francis E. Rourke, *Secrecy & Publicity: Dilemmas of Democracy* (Baltimore, Johns Hopkins Press, 1966); William L. Rivers, *The Opinionmakers* (Boston, Beacon Press, 1965). These and many other books deal with the influence of *The Times* on political decision-makers.

[42] Roger Kahn, "The House of Adolph Ochs," *The Saturday Evening Post* (October 9, 1965), p. 38.

[43] Jake Highton, "The New York Times: I'm Grateful," *The Quill* (April, 1966), p. 17.

[44] "Newspapers of the World—III," London *Times* (February 25, 1965).

[45] Frank S. Adams, "The Times' Editorial 'We'," *The Masthead,* Washington (Spring, 1966), p. 20.

[46] Kahn, *op. cit.* provides an especially good concise history of *The New York Times*; basic journalism histories such as F. L. Mott, *American Journalism, 1690–1960* (New York, Macmillan, 1962) and Edwin Emery, *The Press and America: An Interpretative History of Journalism* (Englewood Cliffs, N.J., Prentice-Hall, 1962) are also good; without a doubt the best books dealing with the *Times* exclusively are these: Elmer Davis, *History of The New York Times 1851–1921* (New York, *The New York Times,* 1921); Gerald W. Johnson, *An Honorable Titan: A Biographical Study of Adolph S. Ochs* (New York, Harper & Row, 1946); Meyer Berger, *The Story of The New York Times, 1851–1951* (New York, Simon and Schuster, 1951).

[47] Frank Luther Mott, *American Journalism,* p. 280.

[48] *Ibid.*

[49] Kahn, *op. cit.*, p. 47.

[50] *Ibid.*

[51] A long article—nearly thirty pages—in late 1966 (Gay Talese, "The Kingdoms, The Powers, And The Glories of The New York Times," *Esquire,* November, 1966, p. 91 ff.) does an excellent job of describing the complexities of *The Times* and the personalities of many of its leading journalists, especially executives Clifton Daniel, Turner Catledge, James Reston, Theodore Bernstein, John Oakes, Harrison Salisbury, and A. M. Rosenthal.

Chapter 18

ASAHI

[1] *Asahi* means "morning sun" or "dawn sun" and *Shimbun* means "newspaper."

[2] Questionnaire received from *Asahi* on July 15, 1966.

[3] "Newspapers of the World—IV," London *Times* (February 26, 1965).
[4] *Ibid.*
[5] Masaaki Kasagi, "The Accomplishments of the Japanese Newspaper Industry," *The Journalist's World,* Brussels, 3:3 (1965), p. 9.
[6] Questionnaire, *op. cit.*
[7] "It Gives Us Light," *Newsweek* (July 6, 1964), p. 44.
[8] Hisashi Maeda, "A National Newspaper in Japan," *Nieman Reports* (April, 1956), pp. 9–10.
[9] "Newspapers of the World—IV."
[10] Kisaburo Kawabe, *The Press and Politics in Japan* (Chicago, University of Chicago Press, 1921), pp. 117–118; interview with Yoshihide Yada, Columbia, Mo., November 27, 1966.
[11] *The Asahi Story* (Tokyo, Asahi Shimbun, 1965), p. 13.
[12] Hideo Ono, *Naigai Shimbunshi* (Tokyo, Nihon Shimbun Kyokai, 1961), pp. 60–61.
[13] *The Asahi Story,* p. 19.
[14] Masanori Ito, "History of the Japanese Press" in *The Japanese Press—Past and Present* (Tokyo, Nihon Shimbun Kyokai, 1949), p. 6. Compare, Ono, *op. cit.,* p. 173.
[15] *The Asahi Story,* p. 17.
[16] Ito, *op. cit.,* p. 7.
[17] *Asahi Shimbun: The Foremost Newspaper in Japan* (Tokyo, Asahi, 1966), p. 13.
[18] *The Asahi Story,* p. 13.
[19] "Missouri Honor Awards for 1936," Columbia, Mo., *University of Missouri Bulletin,* 37:19 (July 1, 1936), p. 7.
[20] *The Asahi Story,* p. 29.
[21] "Japan's Big Dailies," *Economist,* London (May 22, 1965), p. 15.
[22] Lafe F. Allen, "Effect of Allied Occupation on the Press of Japan," *Journalism Quarterly,* 24:4 (December, 1947), pp. 323–331.
[23] Ono, *op. cit.,* pp. 189–191.
[24] "Newspapers of the World—IV."
[25] For a good study of the *Asahi's* part in the anti-Kishi demonstrations, see E. P. Whittemore, *The Press in Japan Today . . . A Case Study* (Columbia, University of South Carolina Press, 1961).
[26] Albert Axelbank, "Japan—the Two Reischauers," *New Republic* (November 13, 1965), p. 11.
[27] "A Japanese View of Viet Nam," *St. Louis Post-Dispatch* (April 13, 1965), p. 2B.
[28] Content analysis of *Asahi,* November, 1966 through January, 1967; translation help from Yoshihide Yada, graduate student in journalism (University of Missouri), from Tokyo.
[29] *The Asahi Story,* pp. 54–59.
[30] Hisashi Maeda, "A National Newspaper in Japan," *Nieman Reports* (April, 1956), p. 9.
[31] "The Founder's Daughter," *Time* (July 3, 1964), pp. 60–61. Compare, "It Gives Us Light," *op. cit.*, p. 44.

Bibliography

I. Articles

Adams, Frank S., "The Times' Editorial 'We'," *The Masthead* (Spring, 1966).

Adzhubei, Alexei I., "Journalism is a Calling," *Sovetskaya Pechat*, Moscow, No. 12 (December, 1959).

"The Age: Newspapers of the World—XII," *The Times*, London (March 19, 1965).

"Al Ahram: Newspapers of the World—IX," *The Times*, London (March 10, 1965).

Allen, Lafe F., "Effect of Allied Occupation on the Press of Japan," *Journalism Quarterly* (December, 1947).

"Amerikanische Professoren über die 'besten Zeitungen'," *Neue Zürcher Zeitung*, Zurich (November 11, 1963).

Arnold, Edmund C., "A New Look for the Christian Science Monitor," *The Quill* (May, 1965).

"Asahi Shimbun: Newspapers of the World—IV," *The Times*, London (February 26, 1965).

Axelbank, Albert, "Japan—the Two Reischauers," *New Republic* (November 13, 1965).

Bart, Peter, "The New Look at the 'Times'," *Saturday Review* (June 12, 1965), about *Los Angeles Times.*

Béguin, Pierre, "The Press in Switzerland," *Gazette*, Leiden, 13:2 (1967).

Berg, E. A., "The Development of the Press in Finland," *Gazette*, Leiden, 9:2 (1963).

"Berlingske Tidende: Newspapers of the World—XXI," *The Times*, London (April 20, 1965).

"Best in Brazil," *Newsweek*, February 3, 1964 (about *O Estado de S. Paulo*).

"Borba: Newspapers of the World—XXII," *The Times*, London (April 22, 1965).

Brandt, Joseph A., "Testing Time for West German Press," *Journalism Quarterly* (Spring, 1957).

Brutto, Frank, "In Italy: The Word is Complicated," *Montana Journalism Review* (Spring, 1962).

Bugaev, E. I., "Press Policy Since Khrushchev: The Role of a Growing Press," *Sovetskaya Pechat*, Moscow, No. 5 (1965).

"Die Burger: Newspapers of the World—XI," *The Times*, London (March 16, 1965).

Casserly, J. J., "Voice of the Vatican," *Ave Maria* (February 22, 1958), about *Osservatore Romano.*

Cattani, Alfred, "The Neue Zürcher Zeitung," *Gazette,* Leiden, 13:2 (1967).

Chandler, Otis, "The Role of the Metropolitan Daily in Today's Changing Environment," *Journalism Educator* (Fall, 1964).

Clymer, Adam, "The Divided Press of South Africa," *Nieman Reports* (July, 1960).

"Concentration in the Federal Republic," *The Economist,* London (May 22, 1965).

Daniel, Jean, "Camus as Journalist," *New Republic* (June 13, 1964).

Del Vayo, J. Alvarez, "Who's Who in the French Press," *The Nation* (June 22, 1946).

Derogy, Jacques, and Richard, Serge, "The Revolt of the Fourth Estate," *Atlas* (September, 1965).

Easum, Donald B., " 'La Prensa' and Freedom of the Press in Argentina," *Journalism Quarterly* (Spring, 1951).

Edelstein, Alex S., and Ping-lin Liu, Alan, "Anti-Americanism in Red China's *People's Daily:* A Functional Analysis," *Journalism Quarterly* (Spring, 1963).

Ellis, H. F., "The Times and Punch," *Holiday* (April, 1958).

Erlandson, Erling H., "The Press of Mexico: Past, Present and Future," *Journalism Quarterly* (Spring, 1964).

Fairlie, Henry, "Anglo-American Differences," *Encounter,* London (June, 1966).

Fattorello, Francesco, "A Short Historical Survey of the Italian Press," *Gazette,* Leiden, 11:1 (1965).

Faucher, J. A., "Portrait du journaliste idéal," *L'Echo de la Presse,* Paris (September 15, 1964).

———, "Devant la tombe de Pierre Brisson," *L'Echo de la Presse,* Paris (January 15, 1965).

Fiorentini, S., "Serious, Well Written and Reliable," *World's Press News and Advertisers' Review,* London (August 27, 1965).

Fisher, Desmond, "The Times of London Faces Modern World Under New Leadership," *St. Louis Review* (July 28, 1967).

Fischer, Heinz-Dietrich, "Das Zentralorgan der chinesischen Kommunisten," *Neue Zürcher Zeitung* (June 15, 1963).

Fischer, Henry, "Great Papers of Continental Europe," *Bookman* (January, 1900).

"Fleet Street Rush," *Time* (March 31, 1967).

Freyburg, W. Joachim, "Das Image einer Tageszeitung," *Der Volkswirt,* Frankfurt am Main (November, 1965).

Gardner, Mary, "The Argentine Press Since Perón," *Journalism Quarterly* (Summer, 1960).

Golden, Harry, "The Israeli Press," *Publisher's Auxiliary* (June 20, 1964).

Gordey, Michel, "What You Can Read in Russia," *Harper's Magazine* (April, 1952).

Gordon, Mitchell, "A Family Empire," *The Wall Street Journal* (October 13, 1965), about *Los Angeles Times.*

Govindarajan, S. A., "Reporting for the Big Dailies," *Gazette,* Leiden, 12:4 (1966).

"The Great Dane," *Time* (January 4, 1963), about *Berlingske Tidende.*

Gruliow, Leo, "After Khrushchev," *IPI Report,* Zurich (December, 1964).

Guttmann, William, "A Famous Swiss Newspaper," *IPI Report,* Zurich (June, 1959), about *Neue Zürcher Zeitung.*

"Ha'aretz: Newspapers of the World—XVIII," *The Times,* London (April 7, 1965).

Hardt, Hanno, "Dangers of Press Concentration in Germany," *Grassroots Editor* (January–February, 1967).

Harris, Thomas, "Something for Everybody in Sweden's 'Dagens Nyheter'," *IPI Report,* Zurich (February, 1959).

Hart, Jim A., "Foreign News in U.S. and English Daily Papers: A Comparison," *Journalism Quarterly* (Autumn, 1966).

Haven, Frank P., "L.A. Times—A 'How' Story of Journalism," *The Quill* (October, 1965).

"Helsingin Sanomat: Newspapers of the World—XIX," *The Times,* London (April 13, 1965).

Herr, Maurice, "Readers 'Melting Away' from Political Press of France," *IPI Report* (May, 1962).

Highton, Jake, "The New York Times: I'm Grateful," *The Quill* (April, 1966).

Hills, Lee, "The Press in Russia—In Contrast to Ours," *The Quill* (October, 1962).

"The Hindu: Newspapers of the World—VI," *The Times,* London (March 3, 1965).

Hirsch, Felix E., "How Free is the German Press?" *Current History* (April, 1963).

Hoopes, Paul R., "Content Analysis of News in Three Argentine Dailies," *Journalism Quarterly* (Autumn, 1966).

Hopkin, H. L., "Why Thomson Decided It Had to Be The Times," *World's Press News and Advertisers' Review,* London (October 7, 1966).

"How to Build an Empire," *Newsweek* (January 2, 1967), about *Los Angeles Times.*

Hutchinson, Bruce, "Canada's Gadfly: The Winnipeg Free Press," *Harper's Magazine* (April, 1963).

"If 'Le Monde' can do it . . .," *World's Press News and Advertisers' Review,* London (December 16, 1966).

"Industrialist's Bid Wins Toronto Globe," *Editor & Publisher* (February 19, 1955).

"Israel's Serious Press," *Service Documentaire F.I.J.,* Brussels (May, 1965).

"It Gives Us Light," *Newsweek* (July 6, 1964), about *Asahi.*

"I've Got a Sixth Sense," *Newsweek* (April 11, 1966), about Axel Springer.

"Izvestia: Newspapers of the World—II," *The Times,* London (February 24, 1965).

"Japan's Big Dailies," *Economist,* London (May 22, 1965).

"Jen-min Jih-pao: Newspapers of the World—VIII," *The Times,* London (March 5, 1965).

Jones, Nancy C., "U.S. News in the Soviet Press," *Journalism Quarterly* (Winter, 1966).

"Journaux et Journalistes," *L'Echo de la Presse* (February 15, 1965).

Kahn, Roger, "The House of Adolph Ochs," *The Saturday Evening Post* (October 9, 1965).

Karpisky, L., "Pravda," *Current Digest of the Soviet Press,* 17:21 (June 16, 1965).

Kasagi, Masaaki, "The Accomplishments of the Japanese Newspaper Industry," *The Journalist's World,* Brussels, 3:3 (1965).

Keate, Stuart, "How Good are the Newspapers of Canada?" *Nieman Reports* (September, 1966).

Kerr, Walter B., "The House of Pravda," *Saturday Review* (December 9, 1967).

Kraft, Joseph, "The World of Le Monde," *The Reporter* (March 31, 1960).
Kruglak, T. E., "World-Wide View," *IPI Report* (February, 1967), about *Los Angeles Times.*
La Dany, L., "Mainland China Non-Newspapers," *IPI Report* (July, 1966).
Leibovitz, Pinhas, "The Press in Israel," *FIEJ-Bulletin,* Paris (April, 1967).
Lichtheim, George, "Reflections on the New York Times," *Commentary* (September, 1965).
Lofton, John, "The Press Manages the News," *The Progressive* (June, 1963).
"Lord Thomson Köper Times," *Pressens Tidning,* Stockholm, 47:19 (October 15, 1966).
Lottman, Herbert R., "The Newspaper de Gaulle Has to Read," *Harper's Magazine* (January, 1967), about *Le Monde.*
Lueth, Erich, "Die Zeitungsstadt Hamburg," *Zeitungsverlag und Zeitschriftenverlag,* Bad Godesberg (September, 1967).
Lyons, Louis M., "Observations on the African Press," *Unitarian Universalist Register-Leader* (May, 1963).
———, "Press Notes from Africa," *Nieman Reports* (July–October, 1962).
McCormack, Buren H., and others, "The Soviet Press," *The Quill* (October, 1966).
Macdonald, Dwight, "The New York Times, Alas," *Esquire* (April, 1963).
Maeda, Hisashi, "A National Newspaper in Japan," *Nieman Reports* (April, 1956), about *Asahi Shimbun.*
Markham, James W., "Foreign News in the United States and the South American Press," *Public Opinion Quarterly* (Summer, 1961).
Merrill, John C., "Che cosa s'intende per 'stampa di qualità'," *Prestigio,* Milan, 5:2 (September, 1966).
———, "Das Zeitungssterben in Amerika," *Neue Zürcher Zeitung* (June 13, 1967).
———, "Die 'soziale Verantwortlichkeit' der Presse: Diskussionen in Amerika," *Neue Zürcher Zeitung* (August 13, 1967).
———, "La Prensa de Calidad: Un Problema de Semántica y de Contexto," *Revista Española de Documentación,* Madrid, No. 7 (October–December, 1966).
———, "Los 20 Mejores Diarios del Mundo," *La Prensa,* Buenos Aires (August 22, 1964).
———, "NZZ: the World's Best Newspaper?" *The Quill* (February, 1967).
———, "The Press and Social Responsibility," University of Missouri, FOI Center Publication No. 001 (March, 1965).
———, "Today's Journalism Might be Tomorrow's Literature," *The Quill* (October, 1964).
———, "U.S. Panel Names World's Ten 'Quality' Dailies," *Journalism Quarterly* (Autumn, 1964).
———, "What are the World's Best Dailies?" *Gazette,* Leiden, 10:3 (1964).
———, "Who Can—or Should—Evaluate the Press?" *Gazette,* Leiden, 12:2/3 (1966).
Miller, Helen Hill, "The Best Newspaper in Europe?" *Esquire* (February, 1962), about *Le Monde.*
"Le Monde: Newspapers of the World—I," *The Times,* London (February 23, 1965).
"Le Monde's World," *Newsweek* (December 11, 1967).
Montini, G. B., "The Difficulties of L'Osservatore Romano," *L'Osservatore Romano,* centennial edition (July 1, 1961).
Muhlen, Norbert, "Press—An Encyclopedia With Three Deadlines a Day," *The Reporter* (July 23, 1959), about the *Neue Zürcher Zeitung.*

Myburgh, Tertius, "The South African Press: Hope in an Unhappy Land," *Nieman Reports* (March, 1966).
"Neue Zürcher Zeitung: Newspapers of the World—X," *The Times,* London (March 12, 1965).
"The New Thunderer," *Time* (May 8, 1964), about the London *Times.*
Nolte, Richard N., "Arab Nationalism and the Cold War," *The Yale Review* (September, 1959).
"The New York Times: Newspapers of the World—III," *The Times,* London (February 25, 1965).
Nussberger, Ulrich, "Die schweizerische Tagespresse," *Vertrieb,* Flensburg, 18:442 (September, 1967).
O'Hearn, Walter, "Canada's Dailies are Provincial—With a World Outlook," *IPI Report,* Zurich (April, 1962).
O'Leary, Grattan, "A Century of Journalism," *The Gazette,* Montreal (September 15, 1966).
"The Old Lady's New Face," *Time* (May 13, 1966), about the London *Times.*
"L'Osservatore Romano: Newspapers of the World—VII," *The Times,* London (March 4, 1965).
Pastor, Gena, "La Grandeza de EXCÉLSIOR," *Excélsior,* Mexico City (August 28, 1964).
Peterson, A. E., Jr., "Kekkonen and the Finnish Press," *Montana Journalism Review,* No. 5 (1962).
Pines, Dan, "The Press of Israel," *IPI Report,* Zurich (May, 1961).
Pratt, Baden M., "The Australian Down Under," *Grassroots Editor* (July–August, 1967).
"Pravda Raps N.Y. Times Articles," *Editor & Publisher* (October 28, 1967).
"La Prensa: Newspapers of the World—V," *The Times,* London (March 2, 1965).
"The Press, Atlantic Union and World Peace," *Montana Journalism Review* (Spring, 1962).
"La Presse de Prestige," *L'Echo de la Presse et de la Publicité,* Paris (January 25, 1963).
"The Professional View" (a series of short articles on *The New York Times, Le Monde,* and *Berlingske Tidende*), *Forum 5,* Brussels, No. 57 (December, 1965).
Purvis, Hoyt, "London Times Swings Into New Prominence," *Editor & Publisher* (October 21, 1967).
Putnam, E., "Press in Europe," *New Republic* (November 3, 1947).
Raskin, A. H., "What's Wrong With American Newspapers?" *The New York Times Magazine* (June 11, 1967).
"Rating the American Newspaper," *Saturday Review,* May 13, 1961.
Riley, Frank, "The Changing Direction of the 'Times,'" *Los Angeles Magazine* (June, 1966).
Rivers, William L., "California's Press," *Saturday Review* (September 23, 1967).
Robertson, Deane, "Russian Magazine Reviews the Press," *Editor & Publisher* (October 28, 1967).
Rodger, Ian, "The Swedish Press in the Eyes of a British Journalist," *IPI Report,* Zurich (June, 1964).
Ron, Moshe, "Press and Journalists in Israel," *I.F.J. Information,* Brussels (January–June, 1965).
Rosten, Leo, "The Intellectual and the Mass Media," *Daedalus* (Spring, 1960).
"Russians Upgrade Regional Newspapers," *Editor & Publisher* (July 9, 1966).

Satyukov, Pavel, "Pravda's Golden Jubilee," *USSR* (May, 1962).
Schulte, Henry F., "The Press in Spain," *The Journalist's World,* 4:2 (1966).
Sheehan, Edward R., "The Birth Pangs of Arab Socialism," *Harper's Magazine* (February, 1962).
"La Stampa: Newspapers of the World—XIV," *The Times,* London (March 30, 1965).
Stephenson, William, "The Ludenic Theory of Newsreading," *Journalism Quarterly* (Summer, 1964).
Stewart, Ian, "The Paper That Spreads the Cult of Mao," *The New York Times Magazine* (December 18, 1966), about the *People's Daily.*
Stock, Ernest, "The Press of Israel: Its Growth and Freedom," *Journalism Quarterly* (Fall, 1954).
"Svenska Dagbladet: Newspapers of the World—XIII," *The Times,* London (March 23, 1965).
"Sydney Morning Herald: Newspapers of the World—XVII," *The Times,* London (April 6, 1965).
Talese, Gay, "The Kingdoms, The Powers, And The Glories of The New York Times," *Esquire* (November, 1966).
Taormine, Philippe, "La Presse Italienne," *Presse-Actualité,* Paris, No. 35 (June–July–August, 1967).
Tebbel, John, "How the British View Their Press," *Saturday Review* (December 8, 1962).
———, "Rating the American Newspapers," *Saturday Review* (May 13, 1961).
———, "West Germany's Publishing Powerhouse," *Saturday Review* (January 14, 1967).
"Thomson Acquires Times of London," *Editor & Publisher* (October 8, 1966).
"Thomson Takes The Times," *Time* (October 7, 1966).
Thulstrup, Ake, "German Pressure on Swedish Press During Second World War," *Gazette,* Leiden, 9:2 (1963).
"The Thunderer," *The Spectator,* London (July 10, 1959), about the London *Times.*
Tolkunov, Lev V., "Izvestia's 50th Anniversary," *The Soviet Press,* 5:3 (Spring, 1967).
Tsuchiya, K., "News Reporters as Professionals," *Shimbun-Kenkyu,* No. 6 (1966).
Turnstile, Magnus, "After Haley?" *New Statesman,* London (May 14, 1965), about London *Times.*
"U.S. Newsman Draws Portrait of Pravda," *Editor & Publisher* (November 12, 1960).
Victor, Walter, "German Press Must Start from Scratch," *The Quill* (November–December, 1945).
"The Voice of Pravda: Russia's Popular Party Paper Turns Fifty," *National Observer* (May 13, 1962).
"The Voice of Red China," *Time* (June 23, 1958), about *People's Daily.*
Waldrop, Gayle, "Eljas Erkko, Publisher, and Source of News," *Editor & Publisher* (November 10, 1956).
Wallech, Walter, "Le Monde—De Gaulle's Daily Paper," *The Listener* (September 14, 1967).
Warr, Peter B., and Knapper, Chris, "A Content Analysis of National Daily Press," *Gazette,* Leiden, 11:2/3 (1965).
"Die Welt: Newspapers of the World—XVI," *The Times,* London (April 2, 1965).
Williams, J. Emlyn, "Journalism in Germany 1933," *Journalism Quarterly* (December, 1933).

"Winnipeg Free Press: Newspapers of the World—XX," *The Times,* London (April 14, 1965).
Wolfe, Wayne, "Images of the United States in the Latin American Press," *Journalism Quarterly* (Winter, 1964).
Zorza, Victor, "End of a Liberal Pravda Editor," *The Guardian,* London (September 22, 1965).

II. Books

Adler, Ruth, ed., *The Working Press: Special to the New York Times,* New York, G. P. Putnam's Sons, 1966.
Ainslie, Rosalynde, *The Press in Africa: Communications Past and Present,* London, Gallancz, 1966.
Albrectsen, Steen, and Holst, Niels, *Avisen og Ungdommen,* Arhus, Kanniki Trysk, 1965.
Anderson, Martin, *Avisen i Dag, Copenhagen,* Erichsen, 1947.
Asahi Shimbun: The Foremost Newspaper in Japan, Tokyo, Asahi, 1966.
The Asahi Story, Tokyo, Asahi Shimbun, 1965.
Bacourt, Pierre de, and Cunliffe, John W., *French of Today,* New York, Macmillan, 1927.
Banner, Franklin C., *A Study of the Australian Press,* Pennsylvania State College, 1950.
Barns, Margarita, *The Indian Press: A History of the Growth of Public Opinion in India,* London, Allen & Unwin, 1940.
Beltrán, Oscar R., *Historia del periodismo argentino,* Buenos Aires: Sopena, 1943.
Berelson, Bernard, and Janowitz, Morris, eds., *Reader in Public Opinion and Communication,* Glencoe, Ill., The Free Press, 1953.
Berenson, Bernard, *Rumour and Reflection 1941–1944,* London, Constable, 1952.
Berger, Meyer, *The Story of The New York Times, 1851–1951,* New York, Simon and Schuster, 1951.
Berlin Kochstrasse, Berlin, Verlag Ullstein, 1966.
Bitter, Georg, *Zur Typologie des Deutschen Zeitungswesens in der Bundesrepublik Deutschland,* Munich, Eduard Pohl, 1951.
Böddeker, Günter, 20 *Millionen täglich: Wer oder was beherrscht die deutsche Presse,* Oldenburg and Hamburg, Gerhard Stalling Verlag, 1967.
Boorman, H. R. Pratt, *Newspaper Society: 125 Years of Progress,* Maidstone, Kent Messenger, 1961.
Bowman, William D., *The Story of "The Times,"* London, Routledge, 1931.
Braddon, Russell, *Roy Thomson of Fleet Street,* New York, Walker and Co., 1965.
Bradley, Duane, *The Newspaper—Its Place in a Democracy,* Princeton, N.J., Van Nostrand, 1965.
Brodzky, Vivian, ed., *Fleet Street: The Inside Story of Journalism,* London, Macdonald, 1966.
Broughton, Morris, *Press and Politics of South Africa,* Capetown, Purnell & Sons Ltd., 1961.
Burnham, Edward F. L. (Lord), *Peterborough Court: The Story of the Daily Telegraph,* London, Cassell and Co. Ltd., 1955.
Buzek, Antony, *How the Communist Press Works,* New York, Praeger, 1964.
Canham, Erwin D., *Commitment to Freedom,* New York, Houghton Mifflin, 1958 (about *The Christian Science Monitor*).

Carcano, Sam, *Il Giornalismo,* Milan, Casa Editrice Dr. Vallarde, 1956.

Casey, Ralph D., ed., *The Press in Perspective,* Baton Rouge, Louisiana State University Press, 1963.

Cavling, Ole, *Journalistik,* Copenhagen, Gyldendal, 1928.

Chatelain, Abel, *Le Monde et ses lecteurs,* Paris, Armand Colin, 1962.

Cohen, Bernard C., *The Press and Foreign Policy,* Princeton, N.J., Princeton University Press, 1963.

Commission on Freedom of the Press, *A Free and Responsible Press,* Chicago, University of Chicago Press, 1947.

Cutten, T. E. G., *A History of the Press in South Africa,* London, Central News Agency, 1936.

Davis, Elmer, *History of The New York Times 1851–1921,* New York, *The New York Times,* 1921.

Davison, W. Phillips, *International Political Communication,* New York, Praeger, 1965.

De Jessen, Franz, *Two Hundred Years "Berlingske Tidende,"* Copenhagen, Det Berlingske Bogtrykkeri, 1948.

De Livois, René, *Histoire de la Presse Française,* 2 Vols., Paris, Les Temps de la Presse, 1965.

Desmond, Robert W., *The Press and World Affairs,* New York, Appleton-Century-Crofts, 1937.

Die Ersten Jahre: Erinnerungen aus den Anfängen eines Zeitunghauses, Hamburg, Die Welt, 1962.

Doob, Leonard, *Communication in Africa,* New Haven, Yale University Press, 1961.

Dresler, Adolf, *Geschichte der italienischen Presse*, Berlin, Oldenbourg, 1938.

Editor & Publisher International Yearbook, New York, 1966 and 1967.

Emery, Edwin, *The Press and America: An Interpretive History of Journalism,* Englewood Cliffs, N.J., Prentice-Hall, 1962.

Espina, Antonio, *El Cuarto Poder: Cien Años de Periodismo Español,* Madrid, Agilar, 1960.

Fabre, Maurice, *A History of Communications,* New York, Hawthorn Books, 1963.

The Face of a German Newspaper, Frankfurt, Frankfurter Allgemeine Zeitung, n.d.

Farrell, R. Barry, ed., *Approaches to Comparative and International Politics,* Evanston, Northwestern University Press, 1966.

Fischer, Heinz-Dietrich, *Die grossen Zeitungen: Porträts der Weltpresse,* Munich, Deutscher Taschenbuch Verlag, 1966.

Flach, Karl-Hermann, *Macht und Elend der Presse,* Mainz, v. Hase & Koehler Verlag, 1967.

The Flow of the News, Zurich, IPI, 1953.

Gabriel-Robinet, Louis, *Je suis Journaliste,* Paris, Editions du Conquistador, 1961.

Ghose, H. P., *The Newspaper in India,* Calcutta, University of Calcutta, 1952.

Gibb, Mildred A., and Beckwith, Frank, *The Yorkshire Post: Two Centuries,* Leeds, The Yorkshire Conservative Newspaper Co., Ltd., 1954.

Gollin, Alfred M., *The Observer and J. L. Garvin, 1908–1914: A Study in a Great Editorship,* London, Oxford University Press, 1960.

González Ruiz, Nicolás, *El Periodismo: Teoría y Práctica,* Barcelona, Editorial Noguer, S.A., 1953.

Greene, Felix, *A Curtain of Ignorance,* New York, Doubleday, 1964.

Groth, Otto, *Die unerkennte Kulturmacht,* Berlin, Verlag Walter de Gruyter, 1960.

Gwynn, Denis, *The Vatican and the War in Europe,* London, Burns Oates & Washbourne, Ltd., 1940.

Halberstam, David, *Making of a Quagmire,* New York, Random House, 1965.

Hammond, J. L., *C. P. Scott of the Manchester Guardian,* New York, Harcourt, Brace & World, 1934.

Harris, Robert, *A Report from Spain—The Press in an Authoritarian State,* Department of Journalism, Los Angeles, University of California, 1964.

———, *Spain's Move Toward Freedom of the Press—The Reappearance of Public Dissent,* Department of Journalism, University of California, Los Angeles, 1966.

Hartmann, Frederick H., *The Swiss Press and Foreign Affairs in World War II*, Gainesville, University of Florida, 1960.

Herd, Harold, *The March of Journalism*, London, Allen & Unwin, 1952.

History of the London Times, 1785–1948, London, The Times; New York, Macmillan, 1935–1948, 4 Vols.

Hohenberg, John, *Foreign Correspondence,* New York, Columbia University Press, 1964.

Holden, W. Sprague, *Australia Goes to Press,* Detroit, Wayne State University Press, 1961.

Hornby, Robert, *The Press in Modern Society,* London, Frederick Muller Ltd., 1965.

Houn, Franklin W., *To Change a Nation: Propaganda and Indoctrination in Communist China,* New York, The Free Press, 1961.

Hudson, D., *British Journalists and Newspapers,* London, Collins, 1945.

Inkeles, Alex, *Public Opinion in Soviet Russia: A Study of Mass Persuasion,* Cambridge, Harvard University Press, 1950.

Johnson, Gerald W., *An Honorable Titan: A Biographical Study of Adolph S. Ochs,* New York, Harper & Row, 1946.

Kawabe, Kisaburo, *The Press and Politics in Japan,* Chicago, University of Chicago Press, 1921.

Kayser, Jacques, *One Week's News: Comparative Study of 17 Major Dailies for a Seven-Day Period,* Paris, UNESCO, 1953.

———, *Le Quotidien Français,* Paris, Librairie Armand Colin, 1963.

Kesterton, W. H., *A History of Journalism in Canada,* Toronto, McClelland and Stewart Ltd., 1967.

Knipping, Franz, *Jeder vierte zahlt an Axel Cäsar: Das Abenteuer des Hauses Springer,* Berlin, Rütten & Loening, 1963.

Lazereff, Pierre, *Deadline,* New York, Random House, 1942.

Lee, Win-yi, *The Press in China,* Hong Kong, International Studies Group, 1964.

Leithäuser, Joachim G., *Journalisten zwischen zwei Welten: die Nachkriegsjahre der Berliner Presse,* Berlin, Colloquium Verlag, 1960.

Levine, Irving R., *Main Street, Italy,* New York, Doubleday, 1963.

Liebling, A. J., *The Press,* New York, Ballantine Books, 1961.

Livois, René de, *Histoire de la Presse Française,* Paris, Les Temps de la Presse, 1965.

Luca de Tena y Brunet, Torcuato, *La Prensa Ante las Masas,* Madrid, Anteneo, 1951.

Manevy, Raymond, *L'Evolution des Formules de Presentation de la Presse Quotidienne,* Paris, Editions Estienne, 1956.

Markham, James W., *Voices of the Red Giants,* Ames, Iowa State University Press, 1967.

Matthews, T. S., *The Sugar Pill: An Essay on Newspapers,* London, Victor Gollancz, Ltd., 1958.

Mayer, Henry, *The Press in Australia,* Melbourne, Melbourne University Press, 1964.

Mendelssohn, Peter de, *Zeitungsstadt Berlin: Menschen und Mächte in der deutschen Presse,* Berlin, Verlag Ullstein, 1959.

Merrill, John C., "Foreign News Media," *Modern Journalism,* Chap. 11, New York, Pitman Publishing Corp., 1962.

———, *Gringo: The American as Seen by Mexican Journalists,* Gainesville, University of Florida Press, 1963.

———, *A Handbook of the Foreign Press,* Baton Rouge, Louisiana State University Press, 1959.

———, "NZZ: die beste Zeitung der Welt?" in a pamphlet published by Neue Zürcher Zeitung, Zurich, 1967.

Merrill, John C., and others, *The Foreign Press,* Baton Rouge, Louisiana State University Press, 1964.

Milenkovitch, Michael, *The View from Red Square: A Critique of Cartoons from Pravda and Izvestia, 1947–1964,* New York, Hobbs, Dorman & Co., 1966.

Mills, William Haslam, *The Manchester Guardian: A Century of History,* London, Chatto and Windus, 1921.

Mott, Frank L., *American Journalism 1690–1960,* New York, Macmillan, 1962.

Muller, Frederick, *C. P. Scott, 1846–1932,* London, F. Muller Ltd., 1946.

Murthy, Nadig Krishna, *Indian Journalism,* Mysore, "Prasaranga" of the University of Mysore, 1966.

Natarajan, S., *A History of the Press of India,* New York, Asia Publishing House, 1962.

NZZ: Blick in das Getriebe der Zeitung, Zurich, Neue Zürcher Zeitung, 1960.

Olson, Kenneth E., *The History Makers: The Press of Europe from Its Beginnings Through 1965,* Baton Rouge, Louisiana State University Press, 1966.

Ono, Hideo, *A Brief History of Domestic and Foreign Newspapers,* Tokyo, Nihon Shimbun Kyokai, 1961.

———, *Naigai Shimbunshi,* Tokyo, Nihon Kyokai, 1961.

Østgaard, Einar, *Nyheter Til Salgs,* Oslo, H. Aschehoug & Co., 1967.

Pers, Anders Yngve, *The Swedish Press,* Stockholm, The Institute, 1966.

Pool, Ithiel de, *The "Prestige Papers": A Survey of Their Editorials,* Palo Alto, Stanford University Press, 1952.

Prando, Alberto, *A Century and a Half of Journalism in Argentina,* Austin, University of Texas, 1961.

La Prensa, editors of, *Defense of Freedom,* New York, The John Day Co., 1952.

Pross, Harry, ed., *Deutsche Presse seit 1945,* Berne and Munich, Scherz Verlag, 1965.

Radler, D. H., *El Gringo: The Yankee Image in Latin America,* New York, Chilton Company, 1962.

Rammelkamp, Julian S., *Pulitzer's Post-Dispatch 1878–1883,* Princeton, N.J., Princeton University Press, 1967.

Reston, James, *The Artillery of the Press: Its Influence on American Foreign Policy,* New York, Harper & Row, 1966.

Rivers, William L., *The Opinionmakers,* Boston, Beacon Press, 1965.

Rourke, Francis E., *Secrecy & Publicity: Dilemmas of Democracy,* Baltimore, Johns Hopkins University Press, 1966.

Ruiz de Luque, Francisco J., *Un argentino ilustre: José C. Paz,* Buenos Aires, Aguamarina, 1942.

Schramm, Wilbur, *One Day in the World's Press,* Palo Alto, Stanford University Press, 1959.

Seldes, George, *The Vatican: Yesterday, Today, Tomorrow,* New York, Harper & Row, 1934.

Sharf, Andrew, *The British Press and Jews Under Nazi Rule,* London, Oxford University Press, 1964.

Sharkey, Don, *White Smoke Over the Vatican,* Milwaukee, Bureau Publishing Co., 1943.

Sie Redigieren und Schreiben Die Frankfurter Allgemeine, Frankfurt, FAZ, 1964.

Steed, Henry Wickham, *The Fifth Arm,* London, Constable, 1940.

Steele, A. T., *The American People and China,* New York, McGraw-Hill, 1966.

Story of the Guardian, London, The Guardian, 1964.

Story of an Old Newspaper, Copenhagen, Berlingske Tidende, 1963.

Story of the St. Louis Post-Dispatch, St. Louis, Pulitzer Publishing Co., 7th ed., 1962.

Stutterheim, Kurt von, *The Press in England,* London, Allen & Unwin Ltd., 1934.

Suarée, Octavio de la, *Socioperiodismo,* Havana, Cultural, 1948.

Szulc, Tad, *Latin America,* New York, Atheneum, 1966.

Tang, Peter S. H., *Communist China Today,* Washington, Research Institute of the Sino-Soviet Bloc, 1961.

Tavernier, Eugene, *Du Journalisme,* Paris, H. Oudin, 1902.

Taylor, H. A., *The British Press: A Critical Survey,* London, Arthur Barker Ltd., 1961.

Thorsen, Svend, *Den Danske Dagspresse,* Copenhagen, Udgivet af det Danske Selskab, 1953.

———, *Newspapers in Denmark,* Copenhagen, Det Danske Selskab, 1953.

Valdés, Miguel V., *Historia del Periodismo Mexicano,* Mexico, Manuel Porrua, 1955

Walter, Gerard, *Paris Under the Occupation,* New York, The Orion Press, 1960.

Wandruszka, Adam, *Geschichte Einer Zeitung,* Vienna, Neue Wiener Presse Druck-und Verlagsgesellshaft, 1958.

Weiss, Ignazio, *Il Potere di Carta: Il Giornalismo Ieri e Oggi,* Turin, Editrice Torinese, 1965.

Weisz, Leo, *Die Neue Zürcher Zeitung in Kampfe der Liberalen mit den Radikalen, 1849–1872,* Zurich, Verlag NZZ, 1962.

Wettstein, Oscar, *Die schweizerische Presse: Ihre rechtlichen, moralischen und sozialen Verhältnisse,* Zurich, J. Leemann, 1902.

Whittemore, E. P., *The Press in Japan Today . . . A Case Study,* Columbia, University of South Carolina Press, 1961.

Williams, Francis, *Dangerous Estate: The Anatomy of Newspapers,* London, Longmans, Green & Co., 1959.

Williams, Raymond, *Communications,* London, Chatto & Windus, 1966.

Windlesham, Lord, *Communication and Political Power,* London, Jonathan Cape, 1966.

Wiskermann, Elizabeth, *A Great Swiss Newspaper,* London, Oxford University Press, 1959 (about the *Neue Zürcher Zeitung*).

Wolseley, Roland E., ed., *Journalism in Modern India,* New York, Asia Publishing House, 1964.

The World in Focus, Boston, Christian Science Monitor Publishing Co., 1965.

Yu, Frederick T. C., *Mass Persuasion in Communist China,* New York, Praeger, 1964.

Zveteremich, Pietro, *Stampa e Giornalismo nell'URSS*, Rome, Italia URSS Editrice, 1953.

III. Unpublished Materials and Interviews

Akrony, Aviv (Chicago). Interview in Columbia, Mo. (April 22, 1966) about Israeli press.

Alisky, Marvin. Letter to the writer about *Excélsior* of Mexico (Tempe, Arizona, October 7, 1966).

Banker, Paul A. Letter to the writer with materials about the Baltimore *Sun* (Baltimore, October 18, 1966).

Barth, Heinz (Washington). Interview in Columbia, Mo. (May 4, 1967) about *Die Welt.*

Becerra Acosta, Manuel. Letter to the writer with materials about *Excélsior* (Mexico City, August 18, 1965).

Beuve-Méry, Hubert. Letter to the writer with materials about *Le Monde* (Paris, September 23, 1965).

Bonaiuti, Paolo. Interviews in Milan, Italy (July 23–28, 1966) about *Corriere della Sera.*

Botha, W. M. Letter to the writer with materials about *Die Burger* of South Africa (Washington, D.C., November 1, 1967).

Bretscher, Willy. Letter to the writer about the *Neue Zürcher Zeitung* (Zurich, April 28, 1967).

Brunner, J. Letter to the writer with materials about *The Observer* (London, August 10, 1965).

Cameris, Christo C. "Le Monde: A Search for Quality and Independence" (M.A. thesis, University of Missouri, 1966).

Canham, Erwin (Boston). Interview with Hugh Downs on NBC's "Today" Show (April 19, 1966) about *The Christian Science Monitor.*

Castro Arenas, Mario (Lima, Peru). Interview in Columbia, Mo. (September 15, 1966) about daily newspapers of South America.

Chang, Yong. Letter to the writer about Japanese and Chinese newspapers (Seoul, Korea, July 4, 1967).

Chatelain, Nicolas. Speech about *Le Figaro* at the University of Missouri (April 30, 1954).

Colussi, Alfio. Interviews in Milan, Italy (June, 1966) about *Corriere della Sera.*

———. Letters to the writer with materials about *Corriere della Sera* (Milan, October 25; December 19, 1966; May 2, 1967).

Cooper, James L. Letter to the writer with materials about *The Globe and Mail* (Toronto, September 30, 1966).

Cortés-Cavanillas, Julián. Letter to the writer with materials about *ABC* (Madrid, July 2, 1966).

Cramer, Ernst J. (Berlin and Hamburg). Interviews in Columbia, Mo. (May 3 and November 27, 1967) about *Die Welt.*

De Boinville, David. Letter to the writer about *The Times* and *The Guardian* (Washington, D.C., October 11, 1967).

De Llano, Rodrigo (Mexico City). Interviews in Mexico City (August, 1960) about *Excélsior.*

Dørsjøe, Jon (Oslo). Interview in Columbia, Mo. (September 17, 1964) about Norwegian daily newspapers.

Dunnett, Alastair M. Letter to the writer with materials about *The Scotsman* (Edinburgh, June 21, 1965).

Figueiredo, Antonio (São Paulo). Interview in Columbia, Mo. (November 10, 1966) about *O Globo* of Rio and *O Estado de S. Paulo.*

Fischer, Heinz-Dietrich. Letters to the writer about West German press (Münster, November 7, 1965; January 11, 1966; February 3 and May 18, 1967).

Fogler, Edward N. (La Paz, Bolivia). Interviews in La Paz (February and March, 1967) about Latin American press.

Freyburg, W. Joachim. "Das Verlagshaus Die Welt und seine Zeitungen" (Speech in Hamburg, January, 1965).

———. Letters to the writer with materials about *Die Welt* (Hamburg, November 3, 1965; July 12, 1966; January 30, April 11, May 25, June 9, and July 7, 1967).

Fujii, Akio (Tokyo). Interviews in Columbia, Mo. (November and December, 1967) about Japanese daily press.

Gainza Paz, Dr. Alberto. Letter to the writer with materials about *La Prensa* (Buenos Aires, June 27, 1965).

Gaspar Revesz, Jorge (Caracas). Interview in Columbia, Mo. (October 16, 1967) about leading Latin American dailies.

Gossin, Dr. Albert (Berne). Interview in Columbia, Mo. (October 14, 1964) about Swiss dailies.

Habib, Mohamed. Letter to the writer about *Al Ahram* (Washington, D.C., November 3, 1966).

Haley, Sir William J. Letter to the writer and materials about *The Times* (London, May 3, 1965).

Hamilton, Ian. Letter to the writer about *The Sydney Morning Herald* and the Melbourne *Age* (New York, October 24, 1967).

Hansen, Preben. Letters to the writer about *Berlingske Tidende* (Washington, D.C., November 4, 1966 and October 13, 1967).

Hearn, Rex. Letter to the writer with materials about *The Guardian* (London, November 2, 1965).

Hernelius, Allan. Letter to the writer with materials about *Svenska Dagbladet* (Stockholm, May 14, 1966).

Homem de Montes, José M. Letter to the writer with materials on *O Estado de S. Paulo* (São Paulo, November 9, 1966).

Howe, Quincy. "What Americans Can Learn from the Foreign Press" (Lecture in Minneapolis, Minn., October 24, 1964).

Larsen, Roy E. "Communication and Education" (Lecture at Boston University, 1960).

Leeming, Frank. Letter to the writer with materials about *St. Louis Post-Dispatch* (St. Louis, September 2, 1965).

Le Floch, Loik (graduate student from France at University of Missouri). Interviews during 1967–1968 at Columbia, Mo. about *Le Monde* and *Le Figaro.*

Luchsinger, Dr. Fred. Letters to the writer with materials about the *Neue Zürcher Zeitung* (Zurich, July 26 and August 6, 1965).

Lukac, Sergije (Belgrade). Interview in Columbia, Mo. (April 12, 1965) about Yugoslav daily press.

MacKay, Shane. Letter to the writer with materials about the *Winnipeg Free Press* (Winnipeg, September 29, 1966).

Marinho, Roberto. Letter to the writer with materials about *O Globo* (Rio de Janeiro, September 16, 1965).

Merrill, John C. "The Image of the United States Presented by Ten Mexican Daily Newspapers" (Ph.D. dissertation, University of Iowa, 1962).

———. "International Elite Press Survey, 1965" (Sponsored in part by Research Council, University of Missouri).

Möller, Gunhild. Letter to the writer about *Dagens Nyheter* and *Svenska Dagbladet* (Washington, D.C., October 12, 1967).

Mori, Roland. Letter to the writer about Swiss daily newspapers (Berne, June 17, 1967).

Naeser, Dr. Vincent. Letters to the writer with materials about *Berlingske Tidende* (Copenhagen, May 25 and August 11, 1966).

Okkonen, Antero (Turku, Finland). Interview in Columbia, Mo. (February 29, 1965) about Finnish daily newspapers.

Opas, Pauli. Letter to the writer about *Helsingin Sanomat* of Finland (Washington, D.C., October 13, 1967).

Østgaard, Einar. Letters to the writer with materials about Norwegian newspapers (Haslum, June 8 and November 2, 1966).

Perceval, Michael. Letter to the writer with materials about *ABC* and other Spanish dailies (Madrid, July 27, 1966).

Perkin, Graham. Letter to the writer with materials about *The Age* (Melbourne, October 10, 1966).

Pini, Giovanni. Interview in Milan, Italy (July 24, 1966) about Italian daily newspapers.

Raimondi, Luigi. Letter to the writer about *Osservatore Romano* (Washington, D.C., October 13, 1967).

Rowley, Allen. Letter to the writer with materials about the *Yorkshire Post* (Leeds, October 20, 1967).

Russo, Alfio. Interview in Milan, Italy (June 25, 1966) about *Corriere della Sera.*

Sapieha, Nicholas (graduate student, University of Missouri). Interviews during 1967–68 in Columbia, Mo. about the quality dailies of Europe, especially those in the French language.

Schoup, Henri (Brussels). Interviews in Columbia, Mo. (October 16–30, 1967) about quality dailies of Europe.

Schulmeister, Dr. Otto. Letter to the writer about *Die Presse* (Vienna, November 16, 1967).

Sheldon, Courtney R. Letter to the writer with materials about *The Christian Science Monitor* (Boston, September 29, 1966).

Springer, Axel C. (Berlin). Interview in Columbia, Mo. (May 4, 1967) about *Die Welt.*

Starke, H. F. G. Letter to the writer about *Die Welt* (Hamburg, November 8, 1966).

Terkelsen, Terkel M. Letters to the writer with materials about *Berlingske Tidende* (Copenhagen, August 10, 1965, and March 1, 1967).

Tern, Jürgen. Letter to the writer with materials about the *Frankfurter Allgemeine* (Frankfurt, October 29, 1964).

Uchikawa, Yushimi (Tokyo). Interview in Columbia, Mo. (September 19, 1967) about *Asahi Shimbun.*

Underwood, Bruce. "A Survey of Contemporary Newspapers of Mexico" (Ph.D. dissertation, University of Missouri, 1965).

Weegar, Ted. Letters to the writer with materials about *Los Angeles Times* (Los Angeles, July 19, 1966, and April 10, 1967).

Welter, Dr. Erich. Letter to the writer with materials about *Frankfurter Allgemeine* (Frankfurt, August 20, 1965).

Wepener, W. J. Letter to the writer with materials about *Die Burger* (Cape Town, October 5, 1966).

Wylie, Denis B. Letter to the writer with materials about the *Yorkshire Post* (Leeds, September 16, 1965).

Yada, Yoshihide. Letter to the writer with materials about *Asahi Shimbun* (Tokyo, August 3, 1967).

Závala W., Guillermo (La Paz). Interviews in La Paz, Bolivia (February–March, 1967) about Latin American daily press.

Index